FIVE AFRICAN STATES

Responses to Diversity

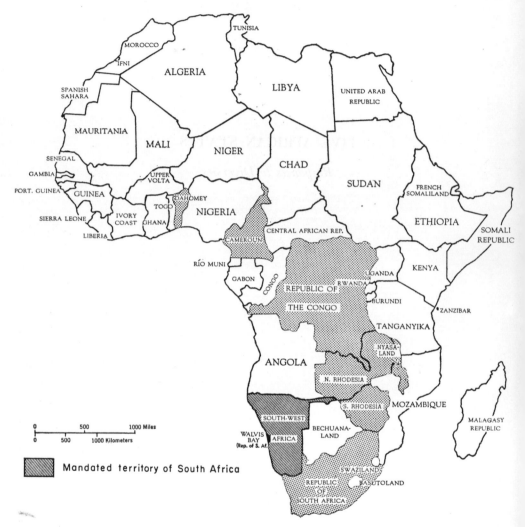

Africa. (Adapted from a Department of State map of November 1, 1962.)

Five African States

RESPONSES TO DIVERSITY

THE CONGO * DAHOMEY
THE CAMEROUN FEDERAL REPUBLIC
THE RHODESIAS AND NYASALAND
SOUTH AFRICA

EDITED BY

GWENDOLEN M. CARTER

CONTRIBUTORS

Edouard Bustin, Virginia Thompson,
Victor T. Le Vine, Herbert J. Spiro,
Thomas Karis

Cornell University Press

ITHACA, NEW YORK

CORNELL UNIVERSITY PRESS

First published 1963

Library of Congress Catalog Card Number: 63-18867

PRINTED IN THE UNITED STATES OF AMERICA
BY VAIL-BALLOU PRESS, INC.

PREFACE

In the whole of Africa it would be difficult to find five states more varied in background and characteristics than those presented in this volume. Yet all five have one element in common: they are strained by counterpressures toward internal division and toward unity. To study these countries side by side is to gain insight into the effect of forces that are present in most, if not all, of the African countries and, indeed, are characteristic of developing states.

In three of these countries—the Congo (Léopoldville), Dahomey, and the Cameroun Federal Republic—great efforts are being made to achieve political and constitutional unity in the face of assertive regional and ethnic diversity. In the Rhodesias and Nyasaland, the unifying effects of historic connections, a contrived constitutional structure, and some impressive economic advance have proved less strong, at least temporarily, than the divisive pressures of African nationalism in the two northern territories and of white self-protective-ness in the southern unit. In contrast, South Africa, paradoxically, is deliberately widening the divisions between its white and nonwhite peoples, divisions which the country's advanced and well-integrated economic activity might otherwise overcome.

As in *African One-Party States* (1962), which dealt with Tunisia, Senegal, Guinea, the Ivory Coast, Liberia, and Tanganyika, the authors of this volume worked from a common outline provided by the editor. Naturally the major differences between a long-established state such as South Africa, with its mature administrative structure, and the

Congo, which is still feeling its way toward administrative cohesion, made it neither possible nor desirable exactly to align the sections within which the countries were treated. Despite the fact that the contributors did not meet together or see each other's sections, the finished products testify to their cooperative response to the discipline of the outline and to the critical suggestions of the editor. The Preface and the Introduction have been read by all the contributors but remain the responsibility of the editor.

The order in which the sections are placed is in some sense arbitrary but in general reflects a progression from the least to the most developed and from countries under African control to those under minority white control. The Cameroun Federal Republic and the territories making up the former Federation of Rhodesia and Nyasaland are placed side by side to aid comparisons.

Each of the five contributors of substantive material has undertaken extensive research work in the country about which he or she has written. The editor has personal knowledge of all five countries. All six persons concerned with this volume are teaching in the field of political science.

Edouard Bustin is lecturer in political science at the University of California, Los Angeles. He has served on the staffs of the Centre Interuniversitaire de Droit Comparé and the Centre de Formation Sociale in his native Belgium and at the State University of the Congo, Elisabethville. He is the author of *La decentralisation administrative et l'évolution des structures politiques en Afrique orientale britannique* (Liège: Faculté de Droit, 1958), as well as of numerous articles in periodicals and books.

Virginia Thompson is lecturer in the political science department at the University of California, Berkeley. She is the author, with her husband, Richard Adloff, of two basic books on the former French territories in Africa: *French West Africa* (Stanford University Press, 1958) and *The Emerging States of French Equatorial Africa* (Stanford University Press, 1960). Her most recent research trip to Africa was in the autumn of 1962.

Victor T. Le Vine is assistant professor of political science at Washington University, St. Louis, Missouri. He spent fifteen months in field research in the Cameroun and West Africa in 1959 and 1960–1961. He has written sections in *The Educated African* (New York: Praeger, 1962), edited by Helen Kitchen, and in the forthcoming volume, *Political Groups in Middle Africa,* edited by James Coleman and Carl Rosberg, as well as contributed to scholarly periodicals and served as book-review editor of the *American Political Science Review.* His book, *The Cameroun: From Mandate to Independence,* will be published by the University of California Press in the fall of 1963.

Herbert J. Spiro is associate professor of political science at Amherst College. He spent nine months in the Federation of Rhodesia and Nyasaland in 1960–1961 and returned in the summer of 1962. His publications include *Politics in Africa: Prospects South of the Sahara* (Englewood Cliffs: Prentice-Hall, 1962), *Government by Constitution: The Political Systems of Democracy* (New York: Random House, 1959), and "The German Political System" in *Patterns of Government,* edited by Samuel H. Beer and Adam B. Ulam (New York: Random House, 1962; earlier ed., 1958). He represents Amherst College on the Four-College Committee that directs the Asian-African Studies Program.

Thomas Karis is associate professor at the Baruch School of Business and Public Administration of the City College of New York. He spent two years on the staff of the American Embassy in Pretoria, South Africa, following extensive research on that country as a member of the intelligence and research branch of the Department of State. He has prepared for the Hoover Institution a guide to the material presented in the South African treason trial and published an article in the *Political Science Quarterly,* June 1961, entitled "The South African Treason Trial."

Gwendolen M. Carter is Sophia Smith Professor at Smith College, representative for her college on the Four-College Committee which directs the Asian-African Studies Program, and former president of the African Studies Association. She has made six field trips to different areas of Africa. Her publications include *The Politics of Inequality: South Africa since 1948* (New York: Praeger, 1958), *Independence for Africa* (Praeger, 1960), *Major Foreign Powers: The Governments of Great Britain, the Soviet Union, Germany, and France* (4th ed., New York: Harcourt, Brace and World, 1962; earlier eds., 1949, 1952, 1957), and *Government and Politics in the Twentieth Century* (Praeger, 1961)—the latter two written with John H. Herz. She is editor of *African One-Party States* (Cornell University Press, 1962) and co-editor with William O. Brown of *Transition in Africa: Studies in Political Adaptation* (Boston University Press, 1958).

The editor and contributors express their appreciation to the director and staff of Cornell University Press for their unfailing aid and support in the preparation of this book.

GWENDOLEN M. CARTER

Northampton, Massachusetts
March 1963

CONTENTS

        Manufacturing 65
        Power and Transportation 66
        Foreign Trade 68
      Social Structure 72
        Ethnic Diversity 72
        The Growth and Effect of Cities 76
        The Proletariat and Trade Unions 80
        The Effect of the Missions 82
        The Press 86
      The Political Process 87
        The Formal Structure 87
          The Fundamental Law 90
          National Institutions 93
          Provincial Institutions 96
          The Future of the Structure of Government . . . 97
        Political and Electoral Dynamics 99
          Political Parties 99
          The Political Elite 106
          The 1960 Election 109
          The Provincial Returns 111
        Local Government 114
      Contemporary Issues 117
        The Problem of National Unity 117
          The Background of Katanga Separatism . . . 119
          Crosscurrents in the Central Government . . . 125
          Further Course of Separatism 126
          Interaction between Congolese Centers . . . 127
          The Trend toward a Federal Association . . . 129
          Can Congo Cohesion Be Secured? 131
        Economic and Financial Problems 133
          The Dominant Position of the Companies . . . 133
          Postindependence Economic Strains 136
        Human Resources: Administration and Education . . 138
      External Relations 141
      Bibliography 144

III Dahomey, *by Virginia Thompson* 161

    Historical Background 161
      The Precolonial Period 161
      Colonial Rule 168
      The Nationalist Movement 173
    The Contemporary Setting 179
      Land and People 179
      The Economy: Resources and Potential Resources . . 181
      Social Structure 200

MAPS

FIVE AFRICAN STATES

Responses to Diversity

I

INTRODUCTION

By GWENDOLEN M. CARTER

Smith College

The driving forces in Africa today are African and, to a lesser degree, Pan-African nationalism. African nationalism demands that political power shall be under African control; Pan-African nationalism maintains that there is a particular bond between all Africans that transcends ethnic, regional, and even national boundaries. Thus, the political slogans of African nationalism are "one-man one-vote" and "national unity under African leadership" while those of Pan-Africanism are that "no African is truly free until all Africans live under governments of their own choice" and "Africa belongs to the Africans."

Yet it is still true that both within and between African states the forces of African and Pan-African nationalism are powered more by assertions of right and of destiny than by deep, inward feelings of kind. Major barriers to the realization of these aims lie within the ranks of the Africans themselves as well as in continued white minority control in the territories of Southern Africa. In Dahomey, for example, continuing tension between the north and the south is scarcely overlaid by the compulsive trend toward one-party rule. In the Cameroun Federal Republic, the historical separation between the British and French trust territories (formerly mandates) has been hardly less difficult to overbridge than have the persistent ethnic, religious, and regional separatisms within the former French Cameroun itself. Above all, the conflicts within the former Belgian Congo following its precipi-

1

tate plunge into independence reflect ethnic and regional rivalries which found their supreme example not only in Katanga separatism but also in the intense and bitter antagonism between rival ethnic groups within that province.

African nationalists sometimes claim that ethnic and regional antagonisms have been deliberately fostered by the colonial powers. They point to the fact that not only within the Congo itself but also in Ruanda-Urundi (the adjoining trust territory which despite its small size and population voted in 1962 to divide into two separate independent states, Rwanda and Burundi,) Belgian administrative policy tended to uphold the authority of one ethnic group over another, most noticeably in the latter territories that of the historically dominant Watutsi tribe over the more numerous Wahutu. In Dahomey, the commercial and dynamic south provided the most responsive and active administrators and politicians under the French administration, a fact which tended to accentuate the contrast with the more traditional, less developed north. In the French Cameroun, however, the numbers and solidarity of the Muslim north gave it a dominant influence both before and after independence which finds a counterpart in developments in its huge, adjoining neighbor of Nigeria. Both in Dahomey and Cameroun, splits among southern politicians paved the way for a northerner to come to power.

It seems, therefore, that it was at least as much local circumstance and the characteristics of ethnic or regional groups themselves as the design of the colonial power which determined the group whose influence was enhanced by the modernizing influence of metropolitan policies. It is true that approaching independence brought into the open and even accentuated long-smoldering ethnic rivalries in the Belgian Congo, Ruanda-Urundi, the French Congo, and Dahomey, but this is because the transfer of political power into local hands threatened to reinforce, or challenge, a long-established *de facto* dominance of one African group over another. In these situations, the tendency has been for numbers to be the decisive factor, with the concept of "one-man one-vote" operating in respect to the possession of political power by African groups in their struggle for control as it had done in accelerating the process of independence from metropolitan powers.

The chief administrative answer to regionalism is federalism. Through a federal division of powers, over-all unity can be combined with scope for diversity. The Congolese Republic increasingly tends toward this resolution of the counterdrives for separation and for unity that have imperiled not only its own peace and stability but also those of its African neighbors. Had the Congo been endowed from the first with a clearly demarcated federal division of authority and responsibility, it is possible that it might have avoided much or at least some of the strains and conflicts which have bedeviled its short history. Uganda is attempting through a modified federal structure to harmonize the separate interests of historic Buganda and, on a lesser plane, of its other treaty kingdoms with those of the country as a whole. Kenya seems embarked upon the same road. Of necessity, the Cameroun Republic chose the federal path when the plebiscite in the British Cameroons in 1961 unexpectedly enlarged the country. The outstanding example of federation is in Nigeria, which has one-sixth of the total population of Africa to organize within the boundaries of a single state.

Yet the future in Africa of federalism, or of other constitutional devices for dividing decision making, is far from assured either as a means of holding together diverse entities or of reinforcing historic or regional differences in the face of centralizing pressures. The Mali Federation of Senegal and Soudan was sharply and bitterly severed in mid-1960 when the two partners proved too far apart in outlook and in aims to work together. In contrast, Ghana quickly disposed of the formal regional divisions which its ruling party, the CPP (Convention People's Party), had accepted reluctantly as a necessary condition of independence but which ran counter to its national and centralizing objectives. More surprisingly, Eritrea ended its federal relationship with Ethiopia in 1962 by voting for full incorporation within that state. Both types of development in their own way reflect the strength of pressures toward administrative and, if possible, political unity under a single direction and the difficulties of achieving such unity except through the pervasive influence, or even coercion, of a mass (often single) political party under a popular and politically shrewd leader like Nkrumah, Senghor, or Ahidjo or a traditional and forceful figure like Emperor Haile Selassie.

Still more difficult to maintain than a federation between African-led units is a federation in which a dominant, though minority, white resident group controls at least one unit (for example, Southern Rhodesia), particularly if that control extends, or threatens to extend, over the federal structure as a whole. The sharp spur provided by such a situation to the rise or growth of African nationalism has been

demonstrated not only by the persistent African opposition to the
Federation of Rhodesia and Nyasaland but also by the adamant refusal of African leaders in Uganda and Tanganyika to accept an East
African Federation so long as Kenyan policies were molded by predominant white resident influence.

The East African Federation of the future (if indeed it comes into
existence) will link African-controlled territories. Such a federation
and Kenya itself may well be nonracial in the sense that the remaining
white residents of the latter country accept an African-determined
concept of national development and of land tenure to the same degree as have the non-African residents of Tanganyika and of the
West African independent states and that they are accepted in turn
by the African majority because of their skills and material contributions to national development. But the acceptance of such a situation
seems closely related to the number of white residents in a particular
territory and their proportion of the total population. The number and
proportion of white residents in Kenya were always far smaller than
those in Southern Rhodesia, not to mention South Africa. Moreover,
both numbers and proportion are being reduced by a steady stream
of white emigration from Kenya. As a result in that country (and so
far elsewhere in Africa) nonracialism seems possible only when there
is African control of public policies and when the relatively small proportion of white residents are willing to accept the fact that they have
no particular role within the community except as individuals.

In view of their numbers, history, and cohesion, the white population of South Africa could hardly be expected to accept such a type
of nonracialism, and it would be difficult, though not impossible, to
envisage such a transition in Southern Rhodesia. The alternatives are
continued white domination, which is fiercely though so far ineffec-
tively opposed by African nationalists, and multiracialism, which
would involve a distinctive position for the minority group, somewhat comparable to that possessed by French-speaking Quebec within
Canada. Such a position is best protected by a federal division of
powers. But the situation is particularly sensitive when the minority
within the federation is also a minority within its own unit (as it was in
Southern Rhodesia though it is not in Quebec) and when its previous
dominance is being challenged on grounds of equity as well as numbers. Under such circumstances, as developments in Southern Rhodesia
have demonstrated, the gradual lessening of discriminatory practices
in landholding and education are an inadequate substitute for African

political advance in demonstrating the good faith of the dominant minority group and in paving the way for genuine working together in terms of mutual needs and legitimate aspirations. From the other side, the electoral success of the Rhodesian Front in December 1962 suggests that, at least for the foreseeable future, the white minority in Southern Rhodesia is determined not to share political power.

Is then the response to white-African diversity inevitably the dominance of the one or the other? The Afrikaner nationalist in South Africa maintains this to be the case. Despite the fact that the labor of all South Africa's people is increasingly intermixed in its economic processes, its dominant white minority (with relatively few exceptions) rejects both multiracialism and nonracialism as goals for the country's complex racial situation. Even the defeat of a modest proposal for white representation in the Transkei (scheduled to be the first Bantustan) is hailed by official sources which, presumably, feel that a modicum of multiracialism in what is supposed to be an African-controlled territory would constitute a dangerous precedent for the reinsertion of the token representation of Africans eliminated in 1960 from the all-white legislature in Cape Town.

But can white minorities retain their dominance in the face of local African majorities and the southward pressures of Pan-Africanism? The virtual monopoly of local power in the hands of white South Africans and, to a lesser degree, of Southern Rhodesians and the buttressing of their geographical positions by the Portuguese territories provide more enforced stability than the casual observer would anticipate. The opportunities afforded Africans by expanding economies are far from negligible in diverting attention from political objectives. Less effective, however, is even the most generous paternalism which, as the Belgian Congo demonstrated so clearly, arouses bitterness rather than gratitude once the African, or other nonwhite, ceases to accept its basic assumption of his inferior status in the community at large. In addition, it has yet to be proved that more than a small number of locally dominant Africans will be satisfied by the opportunities offered within the Transkeian Bantustan.

The current emphasis on the evolution of Bantustans provides a new dimension, however, in the South African scene. Where previously the integrating pressures of economic development were countered through legislative and administrative restrictions or prohibitions on personal, social, and/or political contacts between white and nonwhite, the South African government has now embarked formally on a more subtle and potentially more far-reaching means of encouraging the racial separation which is the core of its policy. In evaluating its potentialities for satisfying African aspirations, it is important to remember that the South African executive and legislature retain overriding powers, even over the Transkeian constitution, and that nationally minded African leaders oppose the Bantustan program not only because they do not believe that the government will permit genuine African self-government but also because they bitterly resent the fragmentation of South African territory. Nonetheless, a process has been started which may develop its own dynamic force. If so, it might split the country to a degree not intended by its sponsors.

Behind the paradox of deliberately developing new territorial units within what is economically the best integrated of African countries lies the basic paradox of the South African situation: the insistence by whites in the country whose Africans have most fully accepted Western values that the latter are a different kind of people, with different values and aims, and that their separate development is, therefore, in their own best interest. Paradoxical too in the light of this view is the fact that the system of government established for the new Bantustan unit follows so nearly the pattern of the Western-type institutions which imperial powers, in particular the British, have used in developing their colonies toward independence.

The South African Bantustan program raises many more questions than it answers. Will its African leaders be satisfied with the limitations on local powers and on the proportion of elected representatives in their assembly or will they follow the pattern of colonial territories in demanding the removal of these restrictions? If the Transkeian leaders accept the limited boundaries of their territory, will their separatism be attacked as fiercely by other Africans as was that of Tshombe? If so, will this division between Africans in South Africa, when added to others reflected in the rivalry between African nationalist organizations, notably the ANC (African National Congress) and PAC (Pan-Africanist Congress), blunt the force of African nationalism to the advantage of continued white control? Or might an enlargement of the Bantustan program and ensuing geographical consolidation of whites as well as nonwhites provide a basis for a genuine multiracial federation in which all the units would be predominantly white or African or Colored or Asian, with each sufficiently small so that no one unit clearly predominated over the others? Even in South Africa the responses to diversity are still not sure.

Throughout the continent of Africa, and beyond it, the demands of African and Pan-African nationalism are shaping thinking and action. Local African leaders in Southern Rhodesia might well have responded more warmly to the lessening of discriminatory restrictions had they not been pressed by events and by other African leaders to make more far-reaching demands. The Congo could not have been reunified, even to the degree it has been, without the forceful intervention of the United Nations operating through multinational forces. Moreover, the moral and legal channels of influence of the United Nations are being used increasingly by the African-Asian bloc to exert pressure on both Southern Rhodesia and South Africa to extend political rights to their majority nonwhites. These are, and will continue to be, factors in determining the evolution of individual African countries as well as of groupings and alignments within the continent. The force of ideas which are rooted in equity or, like nationalism, are commonly accepted remains a major power in the affairs of men.

Nonetheless, the claims of diversity are far from dormant. As primary attention turns from the drive for independence (which so strongly and widely determined the course of events in Africa from 1957 to 1962) to coping with the problems of independent states, the divisions between and within territories are highlighted once again. Thus, in the next period of Africa's history, the responses to diversity may well be the dominant theme.

II

THE CONGO

By EDOUARD BUSTIN

University of California at Los Angeles

Historical Background

For the second time in the twentieth century, the Congo has force-fully erupted into the Western world's consciousness, once again con-juring up a reflection of the barbaric violence and *hubris* which, to generations of casual observers, has passed for the essence of every-thing African. Quite obviously, the fact that this huge section of Central Africa was one of the last areas where the delightful fancy of ancient map makers could freely "place elephants instead of towns" seems to account at least in part for the aura of enigmatic weirdness which still clings to the name Congo. The seventy-five years of Belgian rule propagated new stereotypes, superseding the "heart of darkness" with a veneer of unromantic, businesslike efficiency and spreading images of orderly tenements, bearded missionaries, and copper smel-ters. Today's clichés once again refer to "savagery," "irrationality," and "immaturity," but none of these easy characterizations manage to cap-ture the intricate realities of the new republic. We cannot hope to circumscribe them within the scope of this essay, but we can at least point out some of the component elements of the modern Congo, without losing sight of the essentially transitional character of the present political scene.

The Congo is situated in the midst of Africa, straddling the Equator and covering most of the Congo Basin, as well as the full, 2,735-mile-

9

long course of the Congo River itself. However, the degree of logical unity which this geographical statement seems to imply is appreciably diluted by very real diversities in climate, landscape, and population. Tropical climate prevails over most of the country, but there are notable exceptions in such areas as southeastern Katanga and eastern Kivu, with the important consequence that European settlement has been made possible in these regions. Differences in landscape and vegetation are less obvious and probably less relevant: both the equatorial forest and the various types of savannah and bush which border it to the north and south transcend ethnic or physical boundaries and lend basic similitude to most, if not all, forms of precolonial subsistence economy.

Ethnic and linguistic cleavages have often been stressed—and perhaps overstressed—by what is usually termed "expert opinion," but to date no satisfactory study has yet been made of the social and political significance of such divisions. Nor, for that matter, has any acceptable definition of a "tribe" or "tribal group" emerged from years of research on the subject. Political behavior and voting patterns have offered few, if any, definite clues, as will be brought out later. Certain ethnic or linguistic ties have proved much deeper than had been expected, while others unaccountably dissolved into bitter feuds; in other cases still, party allegiance managed to transcend some extremely real barriers—as that between Bantu and non-Bantu groups.

Finally, the size of the Congo (next to the Sudan, the largest state in Africa) is also worth mentioning at this early stage. Merely to state that the country extends as far as from Helsinki to Istanbul on a north-south axis and from Odessa to Paris along an east-west line is misleading. On the one hand, the paucity of land and river communications seems to increase the relative size of the country; on the other hand, ecological and cultural identities offer a much more coherent picture than in a comparable area in Europe because of the common problems faced by Africans in their simple daily tasks. All in all, the dimensions of the country do not seem to have added much to its many problems, except in such purely material terms as the impeding of military action against secessionist regions or the thwarting of the late Patrice Lumumba's attempted flight from Léopoldville to Stanleyville. Indeed, intertribal frictions and exacerbated parochialism, which rank among the major problems of the new republic, usually operate at a much lower level and are frequently more bitter on the provincial than on the national scene. Close neighbors make the best hereditary foes. Although they have been more widely heralded, the problems that the Congo faces in this respect are not essentially different from those which have been experienced by Dahomey, the former French Congo, Cameroun, Nigeria, and other new African states.

PRECOLONIAL HISTORY

To what extent has the development of the modern Congo been conditioned by the precolonial history of its people? The most probable answer is: comparatively little. Modern analysts are, of course, sorely handicapped by the lack of reliable sources. The only written documents are of European (mainly Portuguese) origin, and these cover only the fringes of the present territory of the Republic. Autochthonous chronicles are oral and can be remarkably comprehensive (as in the case of the Bakuba people, who have retained the memory of their 124 successive kings from the fifth century A.D. to our day), but they leave numerous unexplained gaps and can seldom be fully corroborated. Nor have they yet been fully tapped or coordinated.

According to the most widely accepted conjectures, the Bantu peoples may have reached the Congo Basin (though not necessarily their present habitat) sometime during the first millennium of the Christian era. Why they came or where they came from is far from clear: perhaps the most satisfactory explanation is that which links these migrations with the increasing desiccation of the Sahara and Sahel. Most Bantu traditions concur in naming the pygmy hunters and food gatherers as the original occupants of the areas into which they moved, but they provide no information as to what form of social organization (if any) these Pygmies had evolved. The Bantu migrants (though perhaps not the earliest ones) were the carriers of metallurgy and of some notable agricultural skills, but it was only after centuries of ceaseless roaming and milling around by dozens of tribes that sedentary civilizations began to flourish in various areas of the Congo Basin. Indeed, certain meandering groups were still pursuing their intricate itineraries (the maze of which is often recorded by oral tradition) when the Europeans extended their control over the interior. Moreover, from the last decades of the seventeenth century new, non-Bantu groups had begun to infiltrate the northern fringes of the Basin, a fact which accounts for the complex ethnic and linguistic patterns of the northern districts of the modern Congo.

Although there are few clues concerning the process through which new forms of political organization developed among Bantu societies, two facts seem to be reasonably certain: on the one hand, the devolution of authority continued to follow patterns which had been established generations earlier, in the days of wandering, but on the other hand, the adoption of a sedentary mode of life acted as a catalytic factor in the crystallization and increasing concentration of power. The whole process is a familiar one, and each continent provides us with scores of similar examples.

The Kingdom of Kongo

The kingdom of Kongo first gained European renown shortly after the discovery of the mouth of the Congo River by Diego Cão in 1482, but it had apparently been founded some two hundred years earlier. When the Portuguese (who had cautiously been inching their way to the south along the African coast since 1270) first came in formal contact with King Nzinga a Nkuwu in 1484, the latter submitted what amounted to a request for technical assistance and allowed young noblemen of his court to be taken to Lisbon, where they were duly baptized and taught Portuguese. Although Nzinga himself half-heartedly embraced the Catholic faith in 1491, Christianity gained a firm foothold only after the converted son of the old King, Don Alfonso, had prevailed over his heathen brother in the struggle for succession. Don Alfonso's reign marks the height of an idyllic but short period in the relationship between Portugal and Africa: churches were built, European craftsmen, traders, and missionaries arrived in numbers, and ambassadors were dispatched to the court of Lisbon as well as to the Holy See. Indeed, Don Alfonso's own son, Henrique, was made a bishop in 1518 while the King of Portugal created a score of African dukes and earls. Most characteristic of this blissful interlude was the fact that the King of Kongo dealt on equal terms with Portugal and was awarded full recognition in Rome.

Yet from the very first years of his reign Alfonso had cause to detect the un-Christian ways of some Portuguese—particularly those of the freebooting traders of the island of São Tomé who cheated him on repeated occasions and even attempted to assassinate him when he tried to debar them from any further commerce with his kingdom in 1540. When asked for assistance in putting an end to these practices, the King of Portugal remained evasive, and although a Portuguese force did help one of Alfonso's successors in repulsing the marauding Jaga in 1570, the relations with Lisbon never regained their erstwhile friendliness. Slave trading had long ago replaced evangelization as the chief manifestation of European presence. It has been estimated that during the sixteenth century some 700,000 slaves were exported from the Congo alone—a figure that later was to increase to 150,000 in one year during the first half of the nineteenth century. Besides, Portuguese might was on the wane as the kingdom was absorbed by Spain from 1580 to 1640 and their African trading empire fell prey to various newcomers, chief among whom were the Dutch Protestants, who had lately rebelled against Portugal's new master, King Philip II.

The King of Kongo sought the alliance of the Dutch and sent ambassadors to Amsterdam, just as his predecessors had dispatched envoys to Lisbon. But when the pendulum swung back and the Portuguese finally evicted the Dutch, Kongo was no longer regarded as a friendly state, and in the conflict which developed soon afterward over the control of certain more or less imaginary mines, a Portuguese force from Luanda crushed the Congolese armies at Mpila in 1665. Thereafter the kingdom declined sharply: the flow of trade had shifted toward Luanda, rival pretenders feuded for the throne, and Christianity was gradually engulfed by traditional rites.[1] By the late eighteenth century Kongo had practically disintegrated, and its territory was eventually partitioned among Portugal, France, and the Congo Free State at the Berlin Conference of 1885.

Yet the lasting memories of the kingdom of Kongo have had interesting repercussions on the rise of nationalism under Belgian colonial rule. First, it left the populations of the Lower Congo region with a definite sense of their common affinities which transcended local particularisms, a fact which was recognized by the colonial occupants as they tended to treat the Bakongo people as a single unit. The ancient kingdom also offered an excellent focus for the type of cultural revivalism that has been a familiar component of so many other brands of African nationalism, although this form of historical chauvinism was not widely emulated in other parts of the Congo.

[1] In a report written some twelve years before the battle at Mpila, Capuchin missionaries mention that "No village is without its witch doctor, sorcerer, necromancer or conjuror" but also that "the worst obstacle to the diffusion of faith in this realm comes from the Portuguese priests who are few, unlearned and undignified. They give a most regrettable example to the populations, being often addicted to immorality and practicing concubinage. . . . They exact excessive fees for sacraments [and] never instruct their parishioners, either from negligence or ignorance" (from the Vatican Archives).

ABAKO (Alliance des Bakongo), the first Congolese political party, was founded in 1950 as a cultural, ethnic association of the Bakongo people, and it shortly concocted a fully rigged mythology which included the "restoration" of the kingdom by a reunion of its Belgian, French, and Portuguese segments. The real significance of this movement, however, derives from the fact that its first natural arena was the capital city of Léopoldville, where the Bakongo, who had been rubbing elbows with immigrants from the rest of the country, asserted their dubious claims over the area, thus coming into conflict with practically all other elements of the population. Later, when demands for Bakongo autonomy were bolstered by a campaign of civil disobedience, it was once again their proximity to Léopoldville which made the administration so anxious to secure their cooperation, and this, in turn, was probably an instrumental factor in speeding up the process of political emancipation. Thus, it matters comparatively little to what extent the memories of the Kingdom of Kongo may be founded upon myths, since they have undoubtedly generated and conditioned important manifestations of contemporary political behavior.

Other African Kingdoms

Other precolonial polities did not produce such obvious political descent. Some, like the kingdom of the Bakuba, remained mostly aloof from the main currents of nationalism; others, like the Luba state, were more or less artificially revived as a combined result of ethnic tensions and the personal ambitions of certain politicians. Others still have produced political leadership: thus, the ruling families of the Balunda and Bayeke have provided a sizable portion of the governing clique of Katanga.

The kingdom of the Bakuba (or Bushongo), located between the Kasai and Sankuru rivers, is best known for the outstanding quality of its art and for the elaborate minuteness of its oral traditions. When these chronicles were recited for the first time to a European explorer, they had recorded the reigns of no less than 120 successive kings and could be dated in Western terms by their reference to such universal memorabilia as solar eclipses. Yet, surprisingly in view of their cultural homogeneity and distinctiveness, the Bakuba did not organize a tribal faction but instead joined other ethnic groups of western Kasai in their common resentment against the enterprising Baluba.

The Baluba states seem to result from the intrusion of at least two successive waves of invaders from the northeast into the Lualaba (Upper Congo) area. The first Luba kingdom was apparently founded during the fifteenth century by a Songye dynasty. Local traditions record the name of one Kongolo Mkulu (or Kongolo Mwana) who was killed by the son of his own sister after having unsuccessfully attempted to murder him; what this tale possibly indicates is the replacement of the first dynasty by that of Ilunga Mbili around the sixteenth century. The Luba empire probably reached its apogee toward the end of the eighteenth century, under Kumwimba Ngombe, when it covered a territory stretching from Lakes Tanganyika and Moero to the Bushimaie River (a left-bank tributary of the Sankuru) and from Maniema to the present border of Northern Rhodesia, but its organization must always have remained rather loose.

What type of relationship existed between the Luba and Lunda spheres of influence is not particularly clear. The Balunda had settled to the southwest of the Baluba, and a number of indications suggest that they may have had a common origin. Lunda traditions themselves confirm this to a certain extent. They record the birth of a loose confederacy presided over by a senior chief, Mwata Mwaku, in the second half of the sixteenth century. Mwaku (or perhaps his successor) is said to have disinherited his two sons in favor of his daughter, Lueji, who married Ilunga Tshibinda, the son (or grandson) of Ilunga Mbili, founder of the second Luba dynasty. Whether this relation is the face-saving account of how the Balunda fell under the sway of the Luba empire is difficult to ascertain. The same chronicle, however, records how Lueji's dispossessed brothers left the country to found their own principalities to the west and south. The first brother, Tshinguli, made contacts with the Portuguese Governor of Angola during the early third of the seventeenth century, while the second one, Tshiniama, launched a state which indirectly gave birth to the Tshokwe stock (later to be the destroyers of the Lunda kingdom).

The Lunda state appears to have reached its peak around the mid-seventeenth century, when it controlled the upper course of the Kasai and Zambezi rivers, possibly stretching as far west as Kwango and as far east as Lake Moero. The eighteenth and early nineteenth centuries are remembered as periods of dynastic struggles—which may well reflect the growing ascendancy of the Luba empire—while in 1885, the Tshokwe overran the kingdom and were repulsed only in 1898. Yet, although the Lunda dominions had noticeably shrunk by the time the Belgians first entered the area, the Mwata Yamvo (king) wields considerable influence to this day, a fact to which the singular political career of his son-in-law, Moïse Tshombe, undoubtedly bears witness.[2]

Among the Mwata Yamvo's tributaries, those who wore the title of Kazembe are worth a mention, if only because one of them received in 1806 the visit of two mulatto traders, or *pombeiros,* Pedro João Batista and Anastacio José, who casually recorded in their diary (published only in 1843) that "green stones are found in the earth named catanga," thus revealing the existence of copper deposits.[3]

The last—and ephemeral—principality to be founded in the southeastern part of the modern Congo was that of Msiri, which lasted no more than a generation but left a significant aftermath. The descendant of a family of small chieftains from Unyamwezi (in present-day Tanganyika) who had for a number of years led caravans for Arab traders, Msiri came to Katanga as a youth and settled there with a group of musket-carrying followers. He attracted the favors of local chiefs by acting as their enforcer, was rewarded with wives belonging to the ruling families of the land, and finally wrested the succession from the lawful heirs, setting up his capital at Bunkeya, on the upper reaches of the Lufira River. By 1870, his domains stood squarely between those of the Mwata Yamvo and those of the Kazembe and he had extended his control into Luba territory as far north as Manono. His capital was the center of an active trade in ivory, salt, copper, iron, and slaves, and he kept an army of some 10,000 men among whom only the descendants of his followers (locally known as the Bayeke, or "hunters") carried firearms. Needless to say, such a predatory regime had to rely heavily upon the most brutal forms of intimidation. It also proved exceedingly fragile, and after Misiri was shot down by a Belgian lieutenant in 1891, his empire quickly shrank to the size of a small cluster of villages centered upon Bunkeya, especially since the Belgian authorities had little interest in preserving its integrity. Yet memories of Misiri have remained vivid to this day, and his descendants still carry a considerable degree of prestige, as shown by the fact that they occupied such vital posts in the secessionist government of Katanga as those of Minister of the Interior,

[2] The late Mwata Yamvo, Ditende Yawa Nawezi III, was chosen as senator for Katanga in June 1960, but he fully endorsed the secession and sat on the Katanga "Grand Council," the very influential House of Chiefs. His son, Chief Bako Ditende, is a member of the Katanga Provincial Assembly, which became the lower house of the secessionist state.

[3] A. Verbeken and M. Walraet, *La première traversée du Katanga en 1806* (Brussels: Institut Royal Colonial Belge, 1953), p. 75.

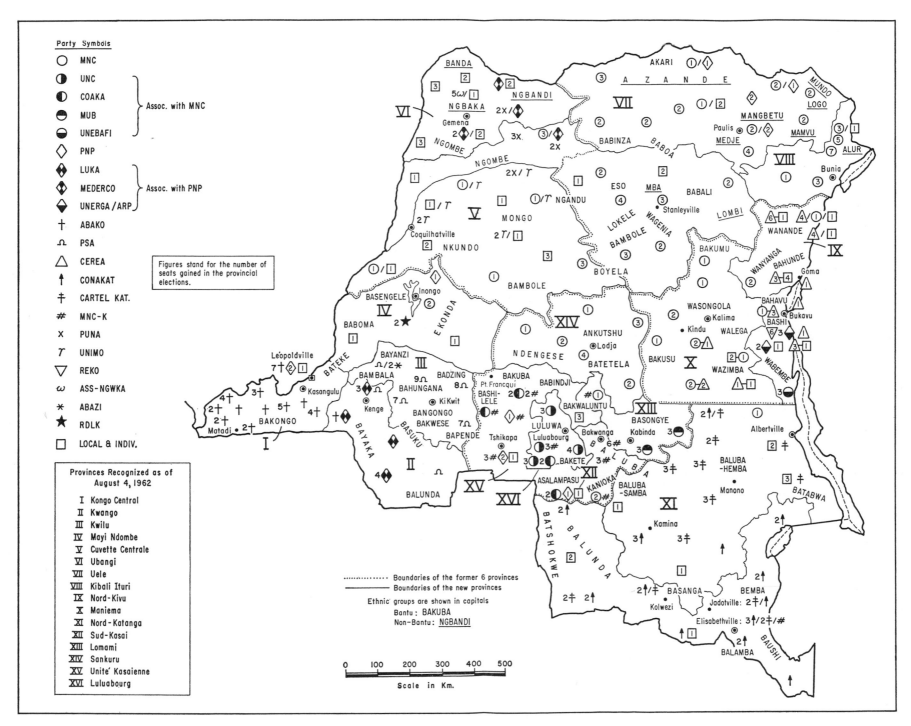

Map 1. Ethnic and political map of the Congo.

president of the Assembly, representative to the Common Market, etc.

In the northeastern section of the modern Congo, Sudanese tribes had been spreading among Bantu groups since the beginnings of the eighteenth century. The result of this infiltration was a number of small principalities in which Sudanese elements were more or less diluted by their Bantu environment. Thus, Bantu influences were much more apparent in the relatively sophisticated state founded by the Mangbetu conquering clan to the south of the Uele River than they were among the so-called "sultanates" of the warlike Azande. In any case, the process of state formation was still clearly in its incipient stage in this area; pressure from the north (especially from the slave raiders based in Khartoum) as well as the Zande custom of partitioning a principality among the sons of a deceased chief had prevented the emergence of any far-ranging or centralized authority when the Belgians advanced toward the Nile.

What emerges from this necessarily brief sketch of precolonial history is a fragmented pattern which leaves out important portions of the present Congolese territory, especially the whole central watershed commonly known to Belgian geographers as the *cuvette*. There is an obvious temptation for the casual observer to conclude that the Congo, never having known political unity before the Belgians' arrival, was ripe for its present dissensions. Yet much the same premise would apply to practically all the new African states, most of which have succeeded fairly well in weathering the centrifugal pulls of their component parts. Moreover, as previously noted, some of the severest tribal clashes in recent years have occurred between closely related groups —indeed, mainly between those that can look back to a common cultural heritage and stock of historical tradition. Such is the case with the tensions between the Baluba-Shankadi and Baluba-Hemba, which seem to reflect the corrosive strifes of the past century, or with those between Lunda and Tshokwe.

Admittedly, none of these Congolese polities can compare with the great West African empires of Ghana, Mali, or Songhai (although the artistic achievements of the Bakuba are a match for those of Benin), nor have they shown the pageantry of such central African states as Buganda, Bunyoro, or Rwanda. Yet because these kingdoms have been in existence until a comparatively recent date—some of them until the advent of the white man and even, in a diminutive form, throughout the colonial period—they retain a measure of significance on the contemporary scene. The role played by the ancient kingdom of Kongo in the political mythology of ABAKO is probably unique, but in other areas historically rooted antagonisms or feuds between royal clans vying for power were sometimes translated in terms of political affiliations.

How lasting and how deep these modern sequels of precolonial history may be is impossible to appraise with any degree of precision. It is worth remembering, however, that many of the present tensions have more recent causes. Economic competition between the Baluba and other ethnic groups in Kasai, for example, led the latter to coalesce in an anti-Luba front which was led by Patrice Lumumba's MNC (Mouvement National Congolais) and which gained control of the provincial assembly, thus precipitating the secession of southern Kasai. In the same way, the belief that too many of the well-paid jobs offered by the Union Minière and other companies operating in Katanga somehow seemed to be occupied by immigrants from Kasai (most of them Baluba) has been partly responsible for the xenophobic ring in the 1959 CONAKAT (Confédération des Associations du Katanga) platform, a fact which led in turn to the momentous *rapprochement* between some of the Katangese Baluba and those who had migrated from Kasai. Other such examples are not hard to come by—not surprisingly if we bear in mind that some 23 per cent of the total population have left their traditional environment to seek employment or at least a different way of life in the townships and tenements. But this has not merely engendered new frictions; it has also brought forth new forms of contact between peoples of different origins, from intermarriage to the foundation of professional, social, political, or alumni associations on a nontribal basis. All fashions of nationalist ideology, whether moderate or radical, were bred in the urban milieu. As a matter of fact, even ethnocentric parties were usually founded by urbanized Africans, a fact which suggests that the weight of historical factors cannot be properly estimated when abstracted from their contemporary context.

THE COMING OF THE WEST

Central Africa never was an absolute terra incognita to the Western European and Mediterranean nations in the same sense that the American continent and Australia were before their respective discoveries. The circumnavigation of Africa said to have been conducted under the reign of Pharaoh Necho (sixth century B.C.), the particulars given by Herodotus and Aristotle on the subject of Pygmies,[4] the details of Ptolemy's map concerning the headwaters of the Nile and the "Mountains of the Moon," and even the efflorescent medieval legends concerning the kingdom of "Prester John" are proof that at least a trickle of trade and information kept on reaching the Mediterranean and, thence, Western Europe. But none of this was, of course, comparable to the incessant stream of communications between the Maghreb and the empires of western Sudan or between the Asian and the African coasts of the Indian Ocean.

Explorations

Thus, the discovery of the mouth of the Congo by Diego Cão in 1482 truly marks the beginning of a new era for this portion of central Africa, if only because during the following three centuries all explorations of the interior were conducted by ascending the course of the Zaïre (as the Congo was then known). Most of these expeditions were stopped by the succession of rapids which later required the construction of a railway link between Matadi and Léopoldville, but a few traders and missionaries [5] extended their journeys as far east as the Kwango and as far north as the present location of Léopoldville. All the same, these various attempts indirectly proved that, contrary to most initial assumptions, land routes provided a better access to the heart of the continent, and it was not until the 1870's that Lieutenant Cameron and Henry Morton Stanley demonstrated—the former in theory and the latter in practice—that following the course of the Congo River could indeed be a realistic itinerary for penetrating the interior.

In the meantime, the Portuguese, controlling settlements on both the Atlantic and the Indian Ocean coasts of Africa, had formed the idea of linking their possessions by an overland route. The results were two ill-concerted expeditions, one starting from Mozambique and the other from Angola, with notions of meeting somewhere midway. The Mozambique expedition, under Dr. Francisco de Lacerda,

[4] One of them, incidentally, is depicted on a monument of the early Egyptian dynasties where he is identified as "Akka," a name worn to this day by a group of Pygmies in the Uele districts of modern Congo.

[5] Most of the traders were Portuguese and most of the missionaries were Capuchins, but in each group there were a few Belgians, such as Pierre Van den Broecke, who traveled through the Lower Congo region in 1609, or Father Adrian Willems, who compiled the first Latin-Kikongo-Spanish lexicon and was stoned to death in 1652 for smashing idols with characteristic zeal.

reached a point just south of Lake Moero, where Lacerda died in 1798. The eastward attempt from Angola was not undertaken until 1802, when the manager of an inland post on the upper Kwango, spurred by the Governor's orders, finally dispatched two of his *pombeiros,* the above-mentioned Pedro João Batista and Anastacio José, to try to reach the Zambezi. As noted earlier, they crossed the Lunda empire in the process and wound up at the court of the Kazembe, whom they found in possession of Lacerda's equipment and where they met a surviving member of his expedition. All together, they finally proceeded to Tete, an important Portuguese post on the middle Zambezi, thus achieving in practice, if not technically, the first crossing of the continent in 1811. Batista, for his part, was rewarded with the command of a patrol of scouts intended to keep a more or less permanent link between the settlements of Angola and Mozambique, but the results of this venture seem to have been tenuous and it was not until 1856 that David Livingstone again crossed Africa from west to east, from Luanda to Quilimane, keeping all the while to the south of the modern Congo.

Expeditions became more frequent after 1850—Livingstone, Burton and Speke, Baker, Schweinfurth, Cameron, and others—but as the area extending to the west of the great lakes increasingly fell under the shadow of the Arab slave trade, what they reported was frequently desolation and wretchedness. The Arabs—or, more commonly, the Swahili-speaking half-breeds of the eastern coast—had begun conducting their own caravans into the hinterland around 1820, primarily in search of ivory but with undisguised interest in such windfall profits as those to be derived from slave running. By 1840, they were extending their activities as far west as Lake Tanganyika, where they founded Ujiji, and within the following twenty years, they were carrying their incursions deep into the eastern part of the Congo from their new base at Yangwe on the Lualaba (that is, the upper Congo). Livingstone, Cameron, and Stanley reluctantly had to deal with them for safe-conducts or escorts, and when the Congo Free State was founded, nearly one-third of the area over which it theoretically extended its jurisdiction was in the hands of the slavers. Thus, it happened that from 1887 to 1890 the most powerful of the traders, Hamed bin Muhammed el-Murjebi (better known as Tippo Tip), was made Governor of a huge province of King Leopold's new empire, and after this incongruous situation had been abolished, it took another five years before Arab power was definitely curbed.

Stanley's arrival at Boma in 1877, almost exactly a thousand days after having left Zanzibar, received wide and immediate publicity, as it provided the key to a problem that had puzzled geographers and explorers for nearly four centuries. But none was more interested than the hardheaded, aggressive, lusty Leopold, second King of the Belgians, honorary president of the newly formed International African Association, and a firm believer in the imperial vocation of his country. Colonial expansion had long been a preoccupation of Leopold's own father, ever since Belgium had lost access to the Dutch possessions as a result of its divorce from Holland in 1830, but it reached obsessive heights with the heir apparent. While still a young man traveling through Greece and the Near East, Leopold had a stone from the Parthenon mailed to the Belgian Prime Minister, with the inscription *Il faut à la Belgique une colonie,* a heavy memorandum containing an equally heavy insinuation. Various plans were laid in the early years of Leopold's reign: Ethiopia, Mozambique, the Philippines, and China were successively considered from the viewpoint of their suitability for Belgian penetration. What Leopold seemed to have in mind at the time was the purchase of existing establishments—possibly through some chartered company to be used as a false front—but in August 1875, in a note to one of his ministers, he wrote: "For the moment, neither the Spaniards, nor the Portuguese, nor the Dutch are disposed to sell. I intend discreetly to gather some information as to whether anything might be done in Africa." [6]

A first step in this direction was the convening in Brussels, at Leopold's initiative, of an international geographic conference in September 1876. From this conference emerged the International African Association, with the declared aims of abolishing the slave trade and "opening up" Africa to international commerce. Expeditions were to be organized on a national basis, and by 1884 the Belgian section of the association had already set up five of them. In the meantime, however, Stanley had successfully completed his journey through Africa, and this had immediately started the King's thoughts in a fresh direction.[7] His emissaries managed to approach Stanley on his way back from Zanzibar but failed to lure him to Brussels, and it was only after

[6] Father A. Roeykens, *Les débuts de l'oeuvre africaine de Léopold II, 1876–1879* (Brussels: Académie Royale des Sciences Coloniales, 1955), p. 95. Unless mentioned otherwise, all translations from texts originally in French are the author's.

[7] This was particularly since one of his many schemes—the establishment of a Belgian protectorate over Transvaal—had just been foiled by British annexation of that small republic (April 12, 1877).

having been cold-shouldered in London that he finally accepted Leopold's overtures.

Having secured the services of Stanley, the King proceeded at once to set up another organization (this time under his more direct control), the Comité d'Etudes du Haut-Congo (Committee for the Study of the Upper Congo), with the participation of businessmen and a pronounced economic flavor. Activities were briskly pushed ahead: within four years, a road bypassing the lower Congo rapids had been opened, some thirty posts had been established, and—more important in view of future developments—treaties amounting to *de facto* protectorate agreements had been signed with scores of local chieftains, in accordance with Leopold's secret instructions to aim at "the foundation of a free State [which is] necessary to legalize our venture, to give it a true existence and to ensure its duration." [8]

The "Scramble" for Central Africa

Meanwhile, however, the committee had been reorganized—partly for financial reasons—and replaced by the International Congo Association over which the King exercised an even tighter control. Further confusion was skillfully spread by the use of the International African Association's lone gold star on a flag of blue throughout the entire expedition. Yet, by that time, every European power having interests or ambitions in central Africa was thoroughly alarmed, or at least watchfully awake. Britain moved first and, in an effort to contain Leopold's mushrooming Congo Association, recognized Portugal's rights over a coastal strip which extended from 5°12'S. to 8°S. lat., thus including the mouth of the Congo. Owing to the widespread opposition of mercantile and missionary circles at home and to vigorous protests from France and Germany, however, the proposed treaty eventually had to be shelved, but in the meantime Leopold had advanced his pawns in two simultaneous master strokes. On April 22, 1884, he secured the recognition by the United States of the International Congo Association as a territorial power, and on the following day he procured France's benevolent neutrality by granting it a right of preemption in the event of the association's alienating its territory. Both moves are typical of the methods employed by Leopold's diplomacy: U.S. recognition was obtained by a judicious mixture of humanitarian cajoling and business talk conducted by H. S. Sanford,

---

[8] Quoted in Roeykens, *Les débuts de l'oeuvre africaine,* p. 397. The date of this document (which was not written by Leopold himself) is Aug. 1879.

a former American ambassador to Brussels who had become the King's business associate,[9] while the granting of a right of preemption to France illustrates Leopold's skill in stressing his innocuousness, a combination which has apparently not been entirely forgotten.

It remained for Germany to take a decisive final step by summoning fourteen powers, plus the International Congo Association, to a conference in Berlin. The initial objects were the introduction of the freedom of navigation on two major African waterways—the Congo and the Niger—as well as the questions of free trade and the abolition of slavery throughout central Africa, but it was evident from the start that the vital core of the discussions would be the settlement of rival claims and the establishment of some form of imperial equilibrium over most of the African continent. Germany had of course excellent reasons to wish for a general settlement of claims. A late comer on the African scene, it had acquired its first interests on the continent (at Lüderitz Bay) a few months earlier and had, in quick succession, proclaimed protectorates over parts of South-West Africa (April 24, 1884), the Togoland coast (July 5, 1884), and the Cameroons coast (July 12, 1884). As a matter of fact, while the Berlin Conference was in progress, Karl Peters, the chief advocate of the German colonial movement, was busily signing treaties with native chiefs of the East African coast so that, nine days before the conference ended, Germany could sew the last patch of its African empire by declaring a protectorate over the whole coast of modern Tanganyika.

It was Leopold's luck in what has adequately been described as the "scramble for Africa" that his ambitions were viewed as a lesser evil by the major powers of the day, but this lone trump he most dexterously exploited. Formal German recognition was secured one week before the conference opened, and from then on it was a relatively easy task to win over the more reluctant members of the conference, Britain, Portugal, and Turkey. In little more than three months, the conference introduced a number of striking innovations in the field of international law: the establishment of an economic regime based upon an international agreement over a vast portion of the African continent, the adoption of delusively simple rules governing the acquisition of new territories in Africa, and, not least among them,

[9] Sanford later played a crucial role at the Berlin Conference, where he overshadowed the official U.S. delegate, the ambassador in Berlin, John A. Kasson. For a brief account, see Colin Legum, *Congo Disaster* (Baltimore: Penguin, 1961), pp. 19, 21–24.

the recognition of a private commercial corporation as a sovereign state, which was invited to sign the final Act of the conference (February 25, 1885).

Throughout these negotiations, it will be noted, Belgium had played a wholly insignificant role, although it was represented (separately from the International Congo Association, of course) at the Berlin Conference. In a sense, the lack of any Belgian governmental involvement indirectly helped King Leopold's endeavor by reassuring the major powers, but there was nothing tactical in this abstention. Although Belgium was at the time going through a period of unprecedented economic development, there was little interest for the type of venture that Leopold had been peddling since the first years of his reign. Indeed, like their counterparts in Manchester, most Belgian businessmen were believers in the virtues of economic, not political, imperialism——in other words, they were proselytes of neocolonialism long before the word had been coined. Thus, while "realistic" Belgian firms were investing in such safe areas as Russia, China, and Latin America, there was little enthusiasm about the prospect of underwriting the costs of the King's imperial dreams. But there was also little opposition to the establishment of the Free State and to Leopold's acquisition of a new crown: only two dissenting votes, one in the House and one in the Senate, were cast against the approval of the "purely personal union" between the two states in April 1885.

It should be mentioned at this stage that the Belgian parliament of the day was a decidedly oligarchical and conservative body; full and equal suffrage (of men) was not inaugurated until 1919, and the Belgian Labor Party (Parti Ouvrier Belge—later renamed Parti Socialiste Belge) was founded only a short time after the vote mentioned above took place. This should not suggest that there was any significant measure of popular opposition to the proposed measure but, rather, a vast unconcern that remained prevalent until 1960. In this respect, the misgivings felt by a large section of the Belgian bourgeoisie about the possibility of African embroilments may be considered as fairly representative of whatever public opinion there was at the time. In fact, such misgivings were later to be reflected in the constitutional amendment which accompanied the annexation of the Congo by Belgium in 1908 and which specified that both territories were to remain financially separate.

The Congo Free State

The Congo Free State began its existence in early May 1885, but the solemn proclamation of its accession to full international sovereignty was not made until July 19. From the start, the new state was faced with serious financial and organizational problems. Henry Morton Stanley had clearly understood that the whole Congo Basin might remain worthless if it was not linked to the Atlantic coast by a railroad which could bypass the 187-mile-long stretch of rapids beginning just above Matadi. Indeed, the construction of such a link had been a central objective of the Comité d'Etudes du Haut-Congo, and detailed surveys of the proposed itinerary were started only a few days after the official birth of the Free State. Capital was not forthcoming, however, and it was not until July 31, 1889, that a company was formed for the purpose of building such a railway. Two days later, Leopold drew up a will in which he stated his decision "to bequeath and transmit unto Belgium, after [his] death, all [his] sovereign rights over the Congo Free State." The suggestion that there may have been more than a fortuitous connection between these two events is supported by the fact that the royal testament was not publicized until the following year, when it played a decisive part in persuading the Belgian parliament to approve a loan of 25,000,000 francs to the Free State. Meanwhile, the Berlin Act had been revised, at Leopold's request, in order to make it possible for the Free State to levy import duties, provided, of course, that they should be applied without any sort of discrimination. This amendment to the Free State's charter was signed on July 2, 1890. The following day, the Belgian government consented to the above-mentioned loan of 25,000,000 francs, without interest but with a number of apparently restrictive clauses: the Free State was not allowed to contract further loans without the assent of the Belgian government; Belgium was to receive any form of economic, commercial, and financial information it desired and was empowered to annex the Free State within ten years, in case of default. The loan was approved on July 25, 1890, and the record suggests that the King's testament and also the permission for the Free State to raise import duties were instrumental as additional securities. In actual fact, however, none of the clauses of the loan was ever respected.

There is strong reason to believe that the determination on the part of Belgian financial circles to treat the Free State purely as a business proposition is partly responsible for Leopold's decision to turn the Congo into a profitable venture within the shortest possible time.

By the end of 1890, a new policy aiming at short-term returns had been framed, and by 1891, the King's agents were in the process of establishing a state monopoly of ivory and rubber. Protests against these undisguised violations of the freedom of commerce which had been guaranteed by the Act of Berlin led to the adoption in 1892 of a compromise system by which private companies were granted un-fettered access to a specified portion of the Free State while the rest was reserved for exploitation by the state or by its concessionaires. In the meantime, Katanga, which had been increasingly threatened by the British South Africa Company under Cecil Rhodes, was hastily occupied by the newly formed Compagnie du Katanga (1891). Im-portant administrative and political powers were delegated to its emis-saries, who acted in close liaison with the Free State's own expedition (Le Marinel), thus inaugurating the collaboration between private and governmental agencies which was to remain the chief character-istic of Katanga's economic regime.

But while the southeast was being secured at no great expense, the new economic policy and its corollary—the attempt to wrest the ivory trade from the Arabs—led to the breakdown of the snug *modus vivendi* which had developed between the Free State and the so-called "Arab zone." [10] Initial skirmishes soon escalated into a costly, full-scale war. The first large shipments of ivory and rubber were auctioned off in Antwerp, and a new, short-term loan of 5,000,000 francs had to be secured from a private bank in November 1892 (with-out the required approval of the Belgian government, which threat-ened annexation when it learned about the deal). Further complica-tions arose when a mutiny broke out among the native Batetela contingents of the armed forces in 1895.[11] By that time, however, the

[10] See Father R. Ceulemans, *La question arabe et le Congo, 1883–1892* (Brus-sels: Académie Royale des Sciences Coloniales, 1958). According to this author, "the Arab policy of the Free State was conducted primarily to advance its political and economic interests. Such was also the case, after 1885, with the other powers which were guided by their interests more than by humanitarian sentiments. The Arab question being viewed from this angle, it would be more proper to speak of campaigns of conquest rather than of antislavery campaigns" (pp. 362–363).

[11] The circumstances of this mutiny are too complex to be reported here, but they are related to the activities of Ngongo Lutete who had carried the Arab influence west of the Lomami River for his former master Tippo Tip, then had been supplanted, and had gone over to the side of the Free State, thus sparking the conflict between the Belgians and the Arabs. The Batetela mutiny was hardly

Arab threat had been virtually eliminated and the campaign had evolved into a deliberate bid for territorial expansion into the Bahr-el-Ghazal area.

This was by no means a new or improvised project: ever since the Anglo-Egyptian forces had been driven out of the Sudan by the Mahdists (Khartoum fell while the Berlin Conference was in progress), the whole region of the middle Nile had been a tempting vacuum as well as a potential pawn that could force the British to share their control of Egypt and the Suez Canal. The famous relief expedition headed by Stanley to "rescue" Eduard Schnitzer (better known as Emin Pasha), the German Governor of the southernmost province of Sudan, in 1888–1889, was a first attempt to secure an outlet to the Nile for the Free State,[12] but the operations—which, incidentally, were conducted with the help of Tippo Tip, the main Arab trader—were inconclusive and even ended in partial disaster. The second attempt was better prepared; preliminary spadework had been accomplished by the conclusion of the so-called MacKinnon treaty between the Free State and the Imperial British East Africa Company on May 24, 1890. In return for a strip of territory between Lake Edward and Lake Tanganyika (an important link to bypass the German sphere of influence if the all-British Cape-to-Cairo route was ever to materialize), Leopold was awarded the western bank of the Nile as far north as Lado. A Belgian expedition reached the Nile at Wadelai (in modern Uganda) in October 1892 and proceeded to occupy the area, but the British government, which never had officially recognized the agreement, showed increasing reluctance to endorse it until, out of alarm at the French advance (itself prompted by the Belgian progression), it leased to Leopold the left bank of the Nile as far north as Fashoda and west to 25°E. long. (May 12, 1894). Violent protests by France and Germany forced the abandonment of the deal within three months of its conclusion, and Leopold had to give up his claim to the portion of the lease north of the parallel 5°30′N. lat. Yet he continued to wager on the incompatibility of the French and British claims to the Sudan

---

a native uprising and was remembered chiefly because it was the only serious incident of its kind, but (superficial) memories of the rebellion were revived with some emotional flurry by the white population when Lumumba—himself an Otetela—began attracting widespread attention.

[12] In fact, Leopold II had tried to hire the services of General Gordon as early as 1880 and managed to secure them briefly in Jan. 1884. Gordon was the first to suggest expansion into the Bahr-el-Ghazal, but, although his project was studied at the time, it was not put into practice.

as well as upon his own demonstrated ability to play the major powers off against each other, and it was not until the British had unmistakably asserted their determination to regain the Sudan (during the Fashoda incident, in the autumn of 1898) that he resigned himself to retaining only the lifelong lease over the Lado enclave as the sole result of his Nilotic ambitions.

These prolonged and costly ventures had proved to be a severe drain for the state treasury, and the exploitative policies were accordingly tightened. Within months of the opening of hostilities against the Arabs, a new system of taxation in kind and labor was introduced. The collection of ivory and rubber was enforced with renewed harshness by the agents of the state and of its various concessionaires. A system of premiums encouraged them to procure these goods at the lowest possible price and provided the incentive which sent them scouring the bush in search of more produce. The exportation of rubber grew from 82 (metric) tons in 1891 to 1,662 tons in 1897 and to some 6,000 tons in 1901. Native uprisings (like those of the Bambuja in 1899) had to be forcibly suppressed.

Protests against the new economic policy had begun to trickle out as early as 1891 (chiefly from British missionaries and traders); the Aborigines Protection Society registered a formal complaint in 1893 and in 1897 inspired a parliamentary motion which was defeated, however, in the British House of Commons. By the turn of the twentieth century, the wave of protest had considerably swollen. The Belgian parliament was still very far from considering the possibility of even a mild censure, but it nevertheless experienced a slight shock when Leopold let it be known that he was not prepared to relinquish the Congo as the ten-year term set for the repayment of the 1890 loan came to a close. As the King tenaciously stalled all subsequent attempts to deprive him of his sovereignty over the Free State, it became increasingly clear that the Congo had ceased to be an unprofitable venture. It also became equally obvious that Leopold intended not only to retain the Congo until his death if possible but also to derive some lasting advantages from his venture for himself and his successors. For this purpose, he had turned the extensive Crown Lands over to a foundation, the existence of which was officially disclosed in 1902.[13] He also added to his previous will a codicil which

[13] A substantial portion of the funds accumulated by this foundation, it should be noted, was spent to subsidize various projects of public interest.

made it mandatory for Belgium to respect such foundations. The reactions of the Belgian parliament and government were distinctly unfavorable, and the amount of wrangling and quibbling which pervaded the last stage in the annexation of the Congo added a bitter
and undignified legacy to Belgium's African empire.

In the meantime, however, other factors had made the annexation
seemingly inevitable. These developments are well known, especially
in the English-speaking world, and there is little need to elaborate on
them. By 1903, agitation against conditions in the Congo had reached
vast proportions. The House of Commons unanimously passed a cen-
sorious resolution in which it sternly reminded the Free State of its
international commitments. The movement soon spread to Germany
and the United States and received new momentum with the publication, in December, of an excoriating report by the British consul at
Boma, Robert Casement. The Congo Reform Association, created in
Liverpool in February 1904, became famous through the vitriolic writings of its secretary and chief pamphleteer, E. D. Morel.[14] The mounting tide of international reprobation nettled Belgian chauvinism but
eventually led to some uncomfortable soul searching, and the King
himself resolved to hold an official inquiry in July 1904. The findings
of the three-man commission, which spent four and one-half months
in the Free State, were coated in layers of precautionary language
and sedative laudation, but they nevertheless confirmed the existence
of widespread abuses and made suggestions for possible reforms. There
was little immediate change, however, and the King devoted large
sums in lobbying and public relations activities in various countries
(including the United States). Nonetheless, a leaf had irrevocably
turned. In 1906, the Belgian parliament opened the procedure of annexation, which was finally voted on September 9, 1908, after months
of stiff bargaining.

Evaluation of Leopold II

Leopold II died in 1909, but this uncommon personality has never
been fully evaluated or elucidated. Between them, vehement critics
and official eulogists have distorted the image beyond recognition. The
stereotype of Leopold's "greatness," as contrasted with the "pettiness"

[14] *King Leopold's Rule in Africa* (London: Heinemann, 1904), *Great Britain
and the Congo* (London: Smith, Elder & Co., 1906), *Red Rubber* (London:
T. F. Unwin, 1906), etc.

of the Belgian people and parliamentarians, has been widely spread both in Belgium and in the Congo,[15] while the much-publicized German cartoon which depicted a cannibalistic Leopold was a typical contribution to the formation of a counterlegend. To be sure, there is abundant proof of the King's rapaciousness. Yet to consider Leopold as being exclusively motivated by greed would be to overlook important aspects of his personality. The fact that he seldom lost sight of his private interests does not necessarily rule out the sincerity of some of his early humanitarian pronouncements. Such a conjunction was entirely in keeping with the infectious mythology of the times, and nineteenth-century Belgium itself, it should be remembered, was notorious for the unrelieved destitution of its industrial proletariat. In addition, such grandiose dreams as those which implied expanding the Free State as far north as Egypt and as far south as Lake Nyasa and the Zambezi suggest that the King had a capacity for political scheming which exceeded that of a tightfisted businessman. Leopold's ability to spend munificently on some extravagant projects and the multifarious inventiveness of his financial dealings also combine to outline the exceptional figure of a man who could have been a tycoon or a *condottiere* in a different place or time but whose lust for power was constrained by his position as a constitutional monarch. The contradictions between the philanthropic phrasing of the Berlin Act and the realities of the Free State were justly denounced, but such hypocrisy was amply shared by a society which allowed nine-year-old boys to work in collieries: in this society, Leopold could have been a highly respected entrepreneur had he not been a King.

BELGIAN COLONIAL POLICY

The legacy of the Free State was a heavy one for any nation to assume, all the more so for Belgium which had little inclination and even less experience for imperial tasks. Thus, much of the existing apparatus was retained after 1908, and, while the most blatant abuses of the Free State were gradually corrected (the labor tax was abolished on May 2, 1910, and the Congo Reform Association closed shop

[15] "We should also like to mention the Belgian politicians of the 1875–1878 period who espoused the African cause. They alone are lacking. The reason: the incorrigible, petty partisan spirit which rendered them incapable of lifting themselves to those heights where alone are hatched the great ideas that make great nations" (Father A. Roeykens, *Léopold II et l'Afrique, 1855–1880: Essai de synthèse et de mise au point* [Brussels: Académie Royale des Sciences Coloniales, 1957], p. 316).

in 1913), the administrative process was not basically interfered with.[16] The prevailing circumspection toward African entanglements was reflected in the so-called Charte Coloniale (properly, the statute of October 18, 1908), the first article of which reads, "The Belgian Congo shall be a legal entity distinct from Belgium. It shall be governed by its own particular laws. The assets and liabilities of Belgium and the colony shall remain separate," or in the (amended) Section 1 of the Belgian constitution, which specified that any troops seconded to the defense of the Congo would have to be recruited exclusively by voluntary enlistments.

Having grown accustomed during twenty-three years to seeing the Congo governed by royal decree, the Belgian parliament made no effort to assert its control over the newly acquired colony. It was usually content to accept the yearly report it was entitled to receive under Section 37 of the Charte and to vote the budget without much caviling. Indeed, its most significant legislative contributions to the government of the Congo were the 1908 Charte (with its subsequent

[16] Additional examples might include the fact that the Free State flag continued to be flown alongside the Belgian tricolor or that the anthem *Vers l'avenir* (composed in 1905 to celebrate the 75th anniversary of Belgian independence as well as the 20th anniversary of the Free State) remained in general use. Indeed, both the anthem (pending the adoption of an official one) and the flag (with the minimal addition of six small golden stars) continued in existence after independence, a fact which the late Patrice Lumumba was said to resent. Yet Lumumba himself had been permeated by the Free State mythology at one stage in his career. In 1956, as he contemplated the various possible forms of a "Belgo-Congolese community" (then the official ultimate of Belgian policy), he wrote: "The last formula which could meet general consensus . . . would be the restoration of the former regime of the Congo Free State, which existed before Congo was annexed by Belgium in 1908. This would mean internal self-government. This autonomous republic or Congo Free State would form a federation with Belgium. It would be placed under the authority of a Belgian High Commissioner" (*Le Congo, terre d'avenir, est-il menacé?* [Brussels: Office de Publicité, 1961]).

Another interesting sequel will be found in the following excerpt from the platform of a minor, moderate party, the Parti Travailliste Congolais (created in 1959): "According to the [Berlin] Act, Congo did not belong to Belgium during the period from 1885 to 1908. It was a truly independent state, since most of the functionaries at the time were foreigners, such as Norwegians, Swedes, Danes, Italians, Germans, etc. When she took us in charge, Belgium made a big, and above all, a serious psychological mistake by summarily annexing us to her nation, not as an associated state . . . but simply as a colony . . . [thus] depriving us of the benefits of our independence, suspended by the uncourteous act of annexation, which reduces us to the status of a colonial country and even waives the idea of considering us as a protected state" (quoted by M. C. C. De Backer, *Notes pour servir à l'étude des "groupements politiques" a Léopoldville* [Léopoldville: Inforcongo, 1959], III, 11).

amendments) and the sequence of statutes which engineered the transition to independence in 1959–1960.[17]

Thus, the bulk of legislation was enacted by way of *décrets,* formally signed by the King but in fact (according to Belgian constitutional practice) submitted and countersigned by a member of the cabinet (usually, but not always, the Minister for Colonies). Emergency legislation (*ordonnances législatives*) could be passed by the Governor-General in Léopoldville, and the practice became fairly frequent. The legal framework was completed by executive orders and regulations which could be decreed by the King (*arrêtés royaux*)—subject to the usual countersignature—by the Minister for Colonies (*arrêtés ministériels,* an unusual occurrence), or by the Governor-General, vice-governors, and provincial governors (*ordonnances*), each within his prescribed sphere of competence.

Under these circumstances, the boundary between legislative and executive norms was in fact a tenuous one, even though it remained fairly clear in theory. The chief corollaries of this difference were the existence of a hierarchy in the binding force of these various measures, the possibility for the Belgian Conseil d'Etat to nullify certain administrative acts, and the requirement for the King to consult (but not to heed) a body of elder statesmen, the Conseil Colonial, before enacting his legislative *décrets.*

Thus, the Congo developed largely without the forum of national politics and was literally regarded as a sort of preserve which should remain immune from the virus of partisan strife. By and large, the Socialist opposition concurred in this tacit agreement, and, even after it had entered governing coalitions (that is, after World War I), it left colonial responsibilities in the conservative hands of Catholic or Liberal ministers. The only exception was the meteoric tenure of Lodewijck Craeybeckx, who held the post for a period of eighteen days in the ill-fated, all-Socialist Spaak cabinet of March 1946. Indeed, if there ever was anything like a Belgian "policy" for the Congo, this custom of insulating the colony from the rough-and-tumble of parliamentary politics was one of its main tenets.

Paternalism: Merits and Liabilities

Belgian objectives in Africa were never clearly defined; neither is there any likelihood that they ever were clearly conceived by govern-

[17] Another parliamentary prerogative of potential significance (which, in fact, was seldom used) was the supervision of certain important land grants and concessions (Sec. 15 of the Charte Coloniale).

ing circles until the early 1950's. "The Belgians are reluctant to define their colonial policy," said Colonial (later Foreign) Minister Pierre Wigny in 1951. "They are proud of their first achievements and are sure of the rectitude of their intentions." Presumably, the Congo was meant to remain under Belgian tutelage "as long as a substantial portion of the African community proves incapable of exercising political control over its own affairs." In the words of Governor Ryckmans, who coined the catchword of Belgian colonial rule, *Dominer pour servir*, "Domination is a fact. So it must be with service—and increasingly so, until our Task is performed and domination has become useless." [18] Just how long this curiously Marxist-sounding process might take was never considered a proper subject for speculation. Governor Ryckmans' farewell address, delivered at the end of 1946, loftily suggested: "If I were to leave you a last message, I would tell you that the function of the State is to make and to safeguard man's happiness, that a country's prosperity is the prosperity of the mass of its inhabitants and that Belgium shall have completed her colonial task when our natives live happily under the shadow of our flag."

Nor was this a mere paternalistic bromide. Between 1950 and 1958, the annual rate of growth of the gross national product was 5.7 per cent, and the portion contributed by African commercial activities rose from 6.5 per cent in 1950 to 19.3 per cent in 1956. African consumption increased by 76.1 per cent between 1950 and 1957. During the same period, the mortality rate fell from 13.5 to 8.3 per thousand in Léopoldville and from 25.2 to 17.8 per thousand in eight selected rural areas where a population of nearly 870,000 had been under close medical supervision. Whereas less than 80,000 babies had been born in maternity wards in 1950, there were 223,424 births (46.5 per cent of the registered total) under proper care in 1957. Over 3,000 medical units with a total staff of nearly 8,400 persons treated 2,876,164 persons during 1958.

Paternalism was indeed another staple of Belgium's rule in Africa. It blandly assumed that political rights could be safely denied as long as social and economic needs were met, and, to a large extent, it succeeded in keeping the Congolese sufficiently interested in their material advance so that they were not overly preoccupied with their political progress. This colonial version of the "full dinner pail" was the result of convergent trends on the part of the administration, the missions,

[18] P. Ryckmans, *Dominer pour servir* (Brussels: Ed. Universelle), preface to the 1948 edition.

and the business world in response to concurrent but frequently over-lapping motivating factors: the desire to wipe off memories of the Free State, the spirit of charity, or a well-understood form of self-interest.

In its highest breed, paternalism could be an admirable form of solicitude for the welfare of the African; in its coarser versions, it could be insupportably overbearing.[19] In either case, its bedrock was the unquestioned postulate of the essential superiority of European values, a self-confident assertion which, as usual, was most complacently put forward by those least entitled to do so but which also produced among three successive generations of Africans a considerable number of

> those who do not console themselves for being made not in the image of God but of the devil,
> those who consider that being a Negro is like being a second-class official: waiting for better and with the possibility of rising higher, . .
> those who say to Europe: See, I know like you how to make courtesies, how to present my respects, in short, I am no different from you; pay no attention to my black skin, it is the sun that has burned me.[20]

[19] In a little handbook written for the use of the *évolués* which was still commonly on sale in 1960, a former Belgian official wrote: "Up to now, you have been the auxiliaries of the European ruling class. You have performed the menial tasks which were entrusted to you as best you could [*tant bien que mal*]. You have adjusted to them more or less successfully. You have developed—unconsciously in most cases—a routine which sometimes led you to believe that you had come to replace the European wheel when it momentarily failed. Thus was hatched a conceit which was often immoderate and all the more naïve since you had not realized that you were performing your activity in the absence of any responsibility. You worked like perfectly oiled and tuned machines that can turn for hours without any supervision. . . . You often complain, rightly or wrongly, about the Europeans' lack of considerateness toward you. You have reached a point where you attach a prejorative connotation to the word *évolué* and you demand that this word . . . be stricken from common usage. Yours is an understandable concern. For you have discovered that this label compelled you to behave in a way which, in most cases, was above your capabilities. You had thought, naïvely, that wearing fine clothes or using sophisticated language would suffice to force consideration from those whose education has been shaped and molded by twenty centuries of civilization. . . . Be more realistic in the future. Make a conscientious and complete inventory of your assets and liabilities. Turn inward. Try to improve. And cast away this conceit which brings out smiles. Turn away from this category of fools imbued with arrogant fatuity. Leave them to stagnate in their mediocrity. When the European perceives that you are making real efforts to improve and to lift yourself up toward him, without any cockiness or vanity, then he will lean to you with even greater solicitude to make your ascent easier" (J. M. Domont, *Elite noire* [3d ed.; Brussels: Office de Publicité, 1957], pp. 131–134).

[20] Aimé Césaire, *Poignards de soleil.*

Yet paternalism had its own built-in limitations, both in theory and in practice. As early as 1947, a Catholic scholar had warned against its sterilizing effects:

If tomorrow all the squalid huts that remain in the workers' quarters could be removed, water and electricity laid on, family allowances and social insurance extended, and wages and living standards raised, the European companies would have done their duty, but the industrialized native would be very little happier. The object of paternalist policy is to make him someone who is assisted, insured and pensioned, instead of making him a free man; the person is sacrificed to the individual. Each native is provided with his standardized house, mass-produced furniture, pre-determined scale of food, his free time regulated to the last detail and without a trace of imagination; on top of which, to stop him making an unwise use of his money, a part of his wages is replaced by payment in kind. Man is turned into a sort of vegetable. . . . But at all times, men have found freedom in misery preferable to a comfortable slavery. . . . We must remember that liberty which has once been taken away is difficult to give back. . . . The object which we seek, after all, is the native's own happiness, and a man can only receive his true happiness at his own hands.[21]

But perhaps the most real shortcoming of paternalism was that its application implied a measure of social communication between whites and blacks, which was often lacking. Patrice Lumumba testifies to this:

When the boss or the European makes contacts with the Africans, all he sees is smiling faces, without knowing that those faces sometimes hide sorrows or anxiety. Only with reluctance will he disclose this anxiety to the European, for fear of being branded as a revolutionary or a ringleader and finally losing his sympathy. To keep his job and to retain the appreciation he enjoyed, each employee, each worker, will conceal his dissatisfaction, his anxieties, his problems, in order not to make the least move which might irritate his employer and cause his "downfall." [22]

Racial Differentiations

Thus, the success of paternalism was narrowly linked to the achievement of a smooth adjustment in the fields of race relations, a fact which was realized at a comparatively early date by a few persons in the highest ranks of colonial bureaucracy. Pointing out that Belgians had

[21] G. Malengreau in *La Revue Nouvelle*, V, no. 2 (Feb. 1947), 101. The translation is that of Ruth Slade in *The Belgian Congo: Some Recent Changes* (London: Oxford for Institute of Race Relations, 1960), p. 5.

[22] Lumumba, *Le Congo*, p. 198. The original French text is not perfectly clear: thus, the passage "the appreciation he enjoyed" should normally be translated as "his own self-esteem" (*l'estime qu'on a pour soi*), but the context seems to indicate that Lumumba mistakenly used *soi* for *lui*.

no deep-rooted notions of racial superiority (which is probably true) did not alter what Governor Pétillon termed "the indifference of many Europeans for all that concerns native thought and life." Although racial discrimination was not institutionalized, differential treatment on the grounds of race was provided for in a vast number of statutes and regulations, some of them (like the ban on alcoholic beverages, which was a consequence of the Berlin Act) ostensibly in the interest of the Africans, others (like the restrictions upon the circulation of Africans after dark) in the interest of Europeans, and others still (like the various limitations placed upon the sale and ownership of land) in the mutual interest of both groups. More important differences existed in the administration of justice, where an almost wholly distinct apparatus meted out justice to Africans (as in other colonial territories, its main characteristic was the possibility for administrative officials with insufficient legal qualifications—and no independence—to impose criminal penalties, including death, upon the Africans); in the field of penal law, which provided that certain offences (for example, "disrespect") could be committed only by natives; or in matters of prison administration, where the treatment applied to Africans included corporal punishments as a disciplinary measure.[23] Ordinances provided for separate housing of Africans and Europeans, and, although no functions were legally barred to Africans, legislation regarding employment, social benefits, retirement, and salaries was twofold: the Africans worked under a *contrat de travail* and the Europeans under a *contrat d'emploi*.[24]

Certain forms of racial segregation (in such matters as sexual relations or the accommodation of Africans in hotels, restaurants, and cafés) never had any legal basis, but, by and large, they were practiced just as effectively.

Beginning with the immediate postwar years, the colonial authorities started—in a somewhat irresolute fashion—to ease some of the more rigid aspects of racial differentiation. Well-meaning officials, like Governor-General Jungers, publicly wished to see racial discrimination

[23] As a matter of fact, in order to avoid the problems generated by the "proper" jailing of Europeans, the colonial authorities tended to make wide use of their powers of expulsion—which could sometimes mean imprisonment in the metropole.
[24] The euphemism was borrowed from Belgian legislation where it had, however, wholly different implications: roughly speaking, the *contrat d'emploi* applied to clerical work and the *contrat de travail* to manual labor. Although there was some initial justification for the introduction of this difference in the Congo, it soon ceased to be relevant, since an African performing clerical duties still remained subjected to the *contrat de travail*.

erased from men's minds, adding: "When the present evolution reaches its full development, [social] hierarchy must be based solely on differences of competence, of efficiency and of education."

A timid first step was the adoption of a more liberal status for "civilized Africans," a procedure which had nominally been on the books since 1892 and the revival of which had been advocated in 1938 by the Commission Permanente pour la Protection des Indigènes (Standing Commission for the Protection of Natives).[25] In 1948, the *carte du mérite civique* was introduced for "the best of our wards," as the Governor-General phrased it. By 1952, however, following the report of a commission appointed in 1949, a fresh status was introduced for "civilized Africans"—*immatriculation. Immatriculation* and the *carte du mérite civique* were supposed to supplement each other: *immatriculation* (which afforded exemption from most regulations applying to Africans) was reserved for those who could convince a commission of their "ability to enjoy the rights and fulfill the duties provided by statutory law," while the *carte* was meant for those who had "not quite succeeded" in becoming completely Europeanized or who preferred to retain parts of their traditional status.

By 1952, also, these cautious reforms had been given for the first time a political context: the "Belgo-Congolese community," which was to remain the official objective of Belgian policy until 1958, made its formal appearance in the last days of Governor Jungers' incumbency, then was taken up and amplified by his successor, Governor-General Pétillon. Originally, the very notion of this Belgo-Congolese community was largely cluttered up with ambiguities and wishful thinking—its main substance being apparently the improvement of human relations between whites and blacks—but, gradually, it assumed a number of hazy political implications which were rather loftily summed up by King Baudouin after his return from Africa in 1955:

The time will . . . come—the date cannot yet be determined—to give our African territories a status which will guarantee, for the happiness of all, the continuing existence of a true Belgo-Congolese community, and which will assure to each, white or black, his proper share in the country's government, according to his own qualities and capacity. Before we achieve this high ideal, Gentlemen, much remains to be done.

[25] The Standing Commisison was meant to "watch over . . . the protection of natives and the improvement of their moral and material conditions of existence" (Charte Coloniale, Sec. 6). It was also supposed to meet "at least once a year"; in fact, it met only eight times between 1908 and 1947.

Much, indeed, remained to be done if—in the words of an American observer—paternalism ever was to be replaced by "fraternalism." [26] Some legal barriers between Europeans and African *évolués* (in such matters as transportation or the sale of alcoholic beverages and beer) had been removed, but others remained in existence until late 1959. The enforcement of equality was another problem. A handful of whites were fined or even expelled (in literal accordance with Pétillon's invitation to those who did not like the new policy to "go pack their bags") for resisting integration or for their offensive behavior, but the authorities discovered that racial discrimination often could not be legislated out of existence. Various recreational facilities (for example, bars or swimming pools) were turned by their owners into private clubs, and forbidding prices—combined with subtle but distinct coolness—further discouraged the Africans. This question of prices was in fact part of a much wider problem, the equalization of pay between Africans and Europeans performing the same functions. African demands of "equal pay for equal work" were consistently and bitterly resisted by European civil servants' unions like the AFAC (Association des Fonctionnaires et Agents de la Colonie), and even after the principle had been adopted (with amendments leaving the Europeans still ahead), some circles of the colonial bureaucracy kept on deploring openly "the inconsequent granting to people inflated by a rudiment of civilization of material advantages out of proportion with the progression of their formation and of their normal needs." [27]

In the light of these circumstances, such mild opiates as *immatriculation* or *mérite civique* were bound to appear strikingly inadequate. Indeed, by the time the "Belgo-Congolese community" had acquired its first truly political overtones, the failure of both procedures was already becoming obvious. Only a trickle of Africans had been integrated: at the end of 1955, there were 884 persons holding a *carte du mérite civique* and 116 family heads had received *immatriculation* [28]

[26] J. H. Huizinga, in the *Reporter*, May 1958. The expression was suggested by Governor Pétillon's reflection—in July 1956—that the Congolese would soon be calling the whites "Brother" instead of "Father."

[27] Letter addressed by the section of AFAC in the province of Kivu to the Minister for Belgian Congo and Ruanda-Urundi, June 13, 1959, reproduced in *Congo 1959* (Brussels: Centre de Recherche et d'Information Socio-Politiques, 1960), p. 32.

[28] *Rapport sur l'administration du Congo belge pendant l'anné 1955* (Brussels, 1956). By the end of 1958, these numbers were, respectively, 1,557 and 217 (*Rapport* for 1958).

—an even poorer record than that which the Portuguese had attained with the *assimilados.*

More serious and significant was the fact that African interest in such forms of promotion had sharply declined. The reasons for this situation were many. While most Congolese did not quibble about the fact that Westernization was taken as the sole criterion of "civilization," quite a few of them resented the elaborate inquiries into their homes and families as a needless form of badgering. Others objected to the establishment of castes, which they felt would weaken the sense of African solidarity among the educated. But perhaps the most pertinent criticism was that semiassimilation brought few of the advantages and most of the disagreements linked with European status. In the candid and pungent words of a group of *évolués:* "Immatriculation is a trick for suckers [*un attrape-nigaud*], an item of Belgian propaganda in the U.N. We are sorry we applied for it because it did not bring us any advantage. Europeans and other Africans scoff at us. The only change is that we must now pay higher fines and taxes." The ultimate blow was the refusal of most Congolese priests and university students to apply for registration as *immatriculés*. To some narrow-minded whites, the breakdown of *immatriculation* was taken as proof that the Africans had the sense to "keep in their place"; to more discerning observers, however, it meant that further political advance would have to involve the whole population.

Administrative Organization

Belgian administrative policy was largely determined by reasons of convenience and economy. Administrative subdivisions were summarily carved out and frequently redrawn until 1933, when a fairly permanent pattern was established with the division of the territory into six provinces, subdivided in turn into 16 districts. Minor revisions took place, the provinces changed names, and the number of districts was increased to 24, but the structure remained essentially unchanged until independence. Provincial boundaries were largely artificial.

As early as 1891, the Free State had found it convenient to rely upon a sort of chartered company to secure a prompt occupation of Katanga, and this company had accordingly received a substantial delegation of sovereignty as well as a one-third share in the appropriation of a huge portion of territory. In 1900, the company agreed to turn over its share to a jointly administered entity, the Comité

Spécial du Katanga, which was to exercise a monopoly over all land transactions within an area estimated at 112,500,000 acres.[29] Katanga thus continued to be administered as a sort of state within the state for a number of years. When Belgium reorganized the administrative structure in 1910, following the annexation of the Free State, the Comité Spécial formally turned over its administrative privileges to the new colonial authorities, but Belgium soon reconfirmed them by placing Katanga under the direction of a Vice-Governor-General who was to be appointed by the Comité Spécial. Other vice-governors (entrusted with the same legislative powers as those of the Governor-General) were commissioned between 1913 and 1919 in the three other regions of the colony (Eastern Congo, Equator, and Congo-Kasai), but although they enjoyed proconsular powers, they were exclusively civil servants and did not possess the exceptional status of their colleague in Katanga. It was not until the centralizing reforms of 1933 that the situation was fully normalized—not without some acrimonious grumbling on the part of the white population of Katanga who had come to regard the region as being somewhat apart from the rest of the colony.[30] The significance of this state of things hardly needs to be emphasized, and it has rightly been considered the deepest root of Katangese separatism.

In 1914, advisory councils were inaugurated to assist the Governor-General and the vice-governors, and the system was continued after the 1933 reorganization, although the new provincial commissioners (later renamed provincial governors) did not have nearly as much power as the former vice-governors. Most important of these councils (even though merely consultative) was the Conseil de Gouvernement, auxiliary to the Governor-General. By 1947, this body had acquired an "unofficial" [31] majority, and by 1951, its eight members representing African interests were actually Africans. The Conseil de Gouvernement momentarily gained fresh importance in 1959, when it was designed by the Belgian government to become the nucleus of the future House of Representatives (while the Conseil Colonial was to become the

[29] See *Le Comité Spécial du Katanga* (Brussels: C.S.K., 1950).

[30] See the scathing article published in Katanga's chief newspaper, *L'Essor du Congo,* on July 3, 1933 (reproduced in J. Sépulchre, *Propos sur le Congo politique de demain—Autonomie et fédéralisme* (Elisabethville: L'Essor du Congo, 1958), pp. 61–67.

[31] "Unofficial" is a British colonial usage describing persons who are not officials when these persons serve on a governmental body (e.g., the Legislative or Executive Councils of the British colonial system).

future Senate), but subsequent developments disposed otherwise.

The basic unit of the Belgian administrative grid was the *territoire,* which came nearest to following ethnic boundaries. Yet there was a considerable amount of fluctuation in the number and size of *territories* —mainly for reasons of economy. Thus, the administrative remodeling of 1933 reduced the number of *territoires* (then 205) by nearly one-half. One major consequence of the reform was to double the size of most *territoires* (thus making them more difficult to administer as well as seriously understaffed); another was that the intermediate rank of district commissioner (*commissaire de district*), which used to be the pivotal relay in the administrative network—as it was in the British territories—gradually lost much of its importance to its immediate superior and inferior, the newly created provincial governors and the *administrateurs de territoire.*

Indirect versus Direct Rule

The administration of African affairs in the Belgian Congo tended to follow an empirical, matter-of-fact course between indirect rule and direct interference with the traditional forms of authority. The weight of official pronouncements and policy statements is clearly in favor of letting "the chiefs and subchiefs exercise their authority to the extent and in the manner prescribed by native custom, inasmuch as it is not contrary to universal notions of public order or to the statutory provisions intended to substitute other rules for the principles of native custom." [32] In practice, however, local authorities "seldom missed an opportunity to apply direct administration every time the ambiguity of the legislative text permitted it." [33] Indeed, the conflict was as old as the Free State, whose sovereignty was often based upon protectorate-type treaties but whose agents frequently treated the chiefs in a high-handed fashion. Another problem faced by the early administrators was the state of disruption of many autochthonous societies. After 1908, the Belgian authorities reaffirmed (particularly in 1910 and again in 1920) that the African populations should be, as much as possible, administered by their "lawful rulers." The most outspoken advocate of this policy was Minister Louis Franck, whose statements bear a striking resemblance to those made five years later by Sir Donald Cameron during his incumbency as Governor of Tanganyika.

[32] *Décret* of May 2, 1910, Sec. 17.
[33] G. Malengreau, "La politique coloniale de la Belgique," in *Principles and Methods of Colonial Administration* (London: Butterworths Scientific Publications, 1950), p. 43.

The accession of primitive populations to a higher and better status, Franck said in 1920, will be possible only if, instead of importing our conceptions, our principles, our institutions into Africa in ready-made formulas, we patiently endeavor to develop the native civilization on its own substratum, according to its mores and tendencies, and in its own language. . . . There is no fruitful colonial policy without this respect for race and environment.[34]

In both territories, the applicability of indirect rule was severely challenged by ethnic fragmentation and the administration's efficiency requirements. In both territories also, these circumstances led to the appointment of "artificial" chiefs and to the grouping of small units into larger, more manageable zones, or *secteurs,* as they were called in the Congo.

Between 1910 and 1920, hundreds of chiefs and subchiefs had been formally recognized, and the number of *chefferies* (a piece of Belgian administrative jargon designating a chief's bailiwick) had accordingly swollen from 1,068 in 1909 to 6,095 in 1917. But the problems involved in the delineation of boundaries or in the discovery of the "true" traditional authorities often exceeded the administrators' patience, with the result that (as one author put it)

some of the chiefs have been 'invested' out of complacency, lassitude or for immediate practicality, in spite of the fact that they lacked all qualifications. . . . *Chefferies* have been fragmented in violation of tradition. Groups of natives have been constituted in *chefferies* and erroneously considered as separate entities.[35]

Louis Franck himself had encouraged the creation of *secteurs* to stem the proliferation of small native units, many of which had no more than 100 to 300 taxpayers, but there still were nearly 5,000 *chefferies* and *sous-chefferies* by 1930, when the Congo began to feel the full impact of the depression.

The same motives of economy which brought about the 1933 reorganization of the administrative superstructure led to a drastic overhaul of the native administration system. By a decree of December 5, 1933, the *secteurs* were given a formal status, and the amalgamation of all undersized units proceeded with steamroller thoroughness: by

[34] Quoted in V. Vermeulen, *Déficiences et dangers de notre politique indigène* (Brussels: Impr. I.M.A., 1953), pp. 19–20.

[35] G. Van der Kerken, "Notre politique indigène au Congo belge," in *Congo,* July 1929. Similar views had already been expressed by the same author in the Dec. 1924 issue of *Congo,* as well as in his *Les sociétés bantoues du Congo belge et les problèmes de la politique indigène* (Brussels: Bruylant, 1920).

1938, a total of 340 *secteurs* had been created and the number of *chefferies* had declined to 1,212; twenty years later, there were 523 *secteurs* and only 343 *chefferies*. To the shattering effect of this wholesale juggling of native jurisdictions should be added the well-established practice of appointing and dismissing chiefs, a prerogative which did not spare those who had a clear traditional status, although they were usually treated with greater caution. A passage from the 1949 report to the Belgian parliament illustrates the extent of this practice in certain areas: "Among the 230 chiefs of native units in the [Equator] Province, 84 are considered really good; the others are rated as average or mediocre. Nineteen chiefs were dismissed during the year 1949."

The fact that most of these chiefs were illiterate was not by any means the only reason for their poor administrative records; rather, it seems that the magnitude and complexity of the tasks they had to face tended to overshadow their traditional functions and to reduce them to the lackluster status of second-class officials.

Carrying out various types of public works, implementing sanitation measures, enforcing the compulsory cultivation of certain cash crops, recruiting men for the Force Publique (or, in the early years, laborers), supervising the application of decrees and ordinances, arresting wrong-doers—these were some of the functions the chiefs were supposed to discharge.[36] Indeed, the colonial authorities not only burdened the chiefs with administrative responsibilities without much reference to their traditional status or to the customary channeling of their authority but also expected them to secure a broad measure of popular consensus for their prescripts. One result of this situation was that a sizable number of chiefs (especially the minor chiefs) felt no particular solidarity with the colonial regime. Their subordinate status and lack of stability in office precluded many of them from substantiating the high hopes of the 1904 commission of inquiry which had looked forward to the emergence of "an extremely useful class, interested in the preservation of an order of things which would uphold their prestige and authority." Another factor in the gradual decay of many native polities

[36] In the same sense, the native treasuries were depleted by the cost of maintaining some 60,000 miles of roads. In 1949, the provincial governors insisted that the "excessive burden" which this maintenance involved was "detrimental to the normal equipment of the communities and to social accomplishments." Yet in 1958 roadworks absorbed over 34 per cent of the expenditures supported by native treasuries (as compared with 7.2 per cent for sanitation and 1.83 per cent for education).

during the colonial period was, of course, the eroding effect of the economic development of the Congo and of its constant demands for African manpower. In 1957, 23.13 per cent of the total population was living outside the scope of the traditional native units, which means that rural communities were deprived of nearly 40 per cent of their adult male population.

Yet quite a few of the chiefs had managed to preserve a substantial degree of their former influence. Indeed, owing to the interethnic tensions which developed in the urban areas, particularly after the first municipal elections, a handful of them were able to retain a measure of ascendancy over their urbanized tribesmen. This was especially true of those traditional rulers who could claim loyalty as symbols of the national unity of their people (for example, the Mwata Yamvo of the Balunda or the Kiamfu of the Bayaka), but the political options of those chiefs frequently responded to local circumstances rather than to any nationwide pattern. Indeed, the only political formation which tried to bank upon the prestige of chiefs in the national elections, the Parti National du Progrès or PNP, met with comparative failure. This point will be taken up again at a later stage.

The transition from a system based upon "native administration" to a policy aimed at developing local government institutions—a characteristic feature of the postwar evolution in all British African territories—was echoed in the Belgian Congo by a series of reforms dated 1957. These reforms (of which more will be said later) were a timid first step toward the democratization of the native authority system but were also intended to provide a common basis for the future development of similar local government units—the communes—in both rural and urban areas. The implementation of this blueprint was still in its incipient stages, particularly in rural areas, when the Congo reached its independence but nevertheless deserves a mention if only because it afforded the Congolese their first experience with the ballot box and triggered many of the conflicts that later were to develop into national issues.

RISE OF NATIONALISM AND ACHIEVEMENT OF INDEPENDENCE

The emergence of an independent Republic of the Congo was so sudden and, in many ways, so unexpected that it left most observers dumfounded. Even the members of the second All-African People's Conference, Colin Legum reports, remained for a moment in stunned silence before they broke into cheers when they learned that the Congo

would become a fully sovereign nation within five months. In the confusion that followed this unprecedented decision, it became increasingly difficult to distinguish myth from fact. When Patrice Lumumba
stated in his avenging speech on Independence Day that "no Congolese
worthy of this name shall ever be able to forget that it was through
struggle that [independence] was conquered—a daily, ardent and
idealistic struggle, in which we spared neither our efforts, nor our
privations, nor our sufferings, nor our blood," he was clearly thinking
in terms of future national legends (although later events tragically
proved that he was in fact only anticipating). Conversely, the asper-
sive and pointless variations on the theme "Who killed Cock Robin?"
in the Belgian press and among Belgian politicians seem to imply that
the Congolese never would have developed an impatience of colonial
rule had they not been prompted by the injection of Belgian party
politics on the African scene, a highly dubious assumption, to put it
mildly. Yet the fact remains that, in a culminating touch of their traditional paternalism, the Belgian authorities left the Congolese little initiative in the achievement of their own emancipation. No Africans
were associated with the drafting of the successive blueprints of Belgian policy, and even the much-heralded Round Table conference of
January–February 1960 was deprived of most of its relevance when
it became clear that Belgium had already admitted the principle of
immediate independence as the negotiations opened.

The temptation is strong, as one looks in retrospect at the process
of Congolese emancipation, to reach as far back as possible for the
roots of contemporary nationalism. Various analysts have traced recent
developments to such antecedents as, *inter alia,* the Belgian surrender
in 1940, the appearance of messianic movements in the Lower Congo
in the 1920's, or the policies of the Congo Free State, and although
none of these inferences can be ruled out (the significance of the
messianic movements as a form of protonationalism, for example, is
clearly beyond doubt), to determine the filiation of such episodes is
a ticklish speculation.

Contrary to the assumptions of Belgian authorities (who liked to
describe it as an "oasis of peace"), the Congo never was insulated
from the rest of Africa. Most of the forces that helped shape modern
nationalism throughout the continent were present in the Congo, often
quite acutely so, and the various forms through which they operated
were no different from those that can be witnessed in other African
territories. Under a system which allowed few outlets, self-assertion

took oblique approaches. Messianic or revivalist movements were among those. It matters comparatively little whether such movements (Kimbangism, Kitawala, the Ba-apostolo, etc.) were xenophobic and subversive—as missionaries and officials claimed they were—or whether they were basically apolitical, as long as they are recognized as a form of protest. Spontaneous associations, or, if these tended to be curbed, the warping of authorized organizations, were another significant phenomenon. The importance of this factor is further enhanced if it is remembered that in recent years some 23 per cent of the population was living outside its traditional milieu (this percentage rises to 34 and 27 per cent, respectively, in the provinces of Katanga and Léopoldville) or that, in 1956, nearly 39 per cent of the adult male population of the Congo was working for wages.

Local Associations

One of these early associations was the APIC (Association du Personnel Indigène de la Colonie), a white-collar union which was instrumental in bringing about the equalization of African and European salaries and from whose ranks a number of politicians emerged. Another was the UNISCO (Union des Intérêts Sociaux Congolais), a study group chiefly made up of schoolteachers; this was the stage from which Joseph Kasavubu first delivered his ideas on the theme: the Congo for the Congolese and Lower Congo for the Bakongo. The UNISCO (which had no direct political offspring) was linked with yet another type of organization which was popular throughout Africa [37] but particularly so in the Belgian Congo: the alumni groups or, as Thomas Hodgkin dubbed them, the Old Boys' Associations. Such associations as ADAPES (Association des Anciens Elèves des Pères de Scheut), ASSANEF (Association des Anciens Elèves des Ecoles des Frères Chrétiennes), UNELMA (Union des Anciens Elèves des Frères Maristes), etc., were sponsored by various Catholic missionary groups, but, for lack of other outlets, they played a central role in the socialization of Congolese *évolués*, especially since they were organized on a nontribal basis. An impressive fraction of the new political class (including Kasavubu, Bolikango, Bomboko, and many others) belonged at one time or another to groups of this type. Those educated Congolese who did not belong to such organizations—along with quite a few who did—also gathered in one or more of a galaxy of *cercles*,

[37] For example, in French Africa, the Amicale Gilbert Veillard, the Association des Anciens Elèves du Lycée Terrasson de Fougères, the Association des Anciens Elèves de l'Ecole William-Ponty, etc.

amicales, clubs, debating groups, etc. Most of these groups had social, cultural, or recreational purposes, but the true sociological function they performed was to provide a convenient niche for the *évolués* within a system that had, as yet, found no suitable place for them.

Labor unions developed comparatively late: at the end of 1954, there were only 7,500 unionized Africans out of a total labor force of 1,146,000. Ethnic associations, however, were more flourishing. Much in the same way as the immigrant communities in the large American cities (and with somewhat similar political consequences), immigrant groups in the larger urban centers, such as Léopoldville or Elisabethville, strove to organize their own mutual assistance societies, funeral chests, and cultural leagues. The power of attraction of such circles on all newcomers from the rural districts was usually irresistible. Because they appealed to a much wider mass of people than the alumni groups or the debating circles of the *évolués,* the ethnic associations were much better geared for political action when elections were introduced for the first time in 1957, especially since these elections were held on the basis of a very extensive franchise. The very success of ethnic associations like ABAKO [38] in Léopoldville or those formed by the immigrants from Kasai in Elisabethville and Jadotville prompted similar organizations which had not yet assumed a clear political orientation to do so without delay, either alone or in alliance with each other. Thus, the Liboke lya Bangala (which grouped Lingala-speaking natives of the Middle Congo region under the chairmanship of Jean Bolikango) took the initiative of gathering all non-Bakongo groups of the capital into a sort of common front, the Interfédérale des Groupes Ethniques,[39] while in Katanga, the Confédération des Associations Tribales du Katanga (better known as CONAKAT) took a more militant aspect, although it did not formally organize itself as a political party until July 1959.

African interest groups such as the ACMAF (Association des Classes Moyennes Africaines), which had been founded in 1954, played no significant role. One reason was their association with official circles

[38] ABAKO had been founded in 1950 as a cultural organization (as indicated by its original title, Association des Bakongo pour l'Unification, la Conservation et l'Expansion de la langue Kikongo) and had published its first political manifesto in 1956. In the first municipal election, it polled 62 per cent of the vote but captured 133 seats out of 170 and swept eight mayors out of ten into office.

[39] This included (besides the Bangala group) the Fédération Kwango-Kwiloise, Fédération du Kasai, Fédération des Basonge, Fédération des Bateke, Fedequalac (a Mongo group), Fédération des Batetela, and Fédération du Kivu-Maniema.

and settlers' groups; another was that the emergence of a Congolese middle class was still in its embryonic stage.

Factors of Political Change

While the Congolese were carefully experimenting with their organized strength, the Belgians were gradually attempting to integrate their few postwar reforms within the more or less undefined framework of a "Belgo-Congolese community." In 1954, however, political developments in the metropole introduced a series of new factors on the African scene. A Socialist-Liberal coalition replaced the Catholic government and soon embarked upon a new educational policy which had the effect of reviving a dormant, century-old, domestic quarrel over the status of confessional schools. As an offshoot of this policy, the new Liberal Minister of Colonies, Auguste Buisseret,[40] decided to expand the almost nonexistent network of "lay" (that is, nonconfessional) schools throughout the Congo, thus challenging the *de facto* monopoly of education which the missions had been enjoying since the first days of the Free State. As the controversy raged, both sides produced their African "witnesses," and the Congolese found themselves courted and encouraged to express their views, an entirely novel situation. The result for the Africans was a definite increase in educational and political opportunities.

A number of analysts have described these developments as a breakdown of Belgian solidarity, a disintegration of the ruling "trinity" of government, church, and business, on whose understanding colonial stability had been resting. Yet many indications show that the Catholic Church had for some time been reconsidering its traditional links with secular authorities. For many years, the priesthood had been the only access to higher education and a limited measure of social recognition for the Congolese. Now, with its broader perspective of the African scene and a view toward its long-term interests, it was quietly africanizing its higher ranks and taking a hard look at Belgian colonial policy. Thus, in a sense, Buisseret's nettling measures provided the spur (or the excuse) to start the Church toward a gradual disengagement. Groups of Catholic progressives started the ball rolling. As early as October 1954, A. A. J. Van Bilsen, a young Catholic lecturer at the

[40] To avoid possible confusion, it should be pointed out here that the Belgian Liberal Party (now called the Parti de la Liberté et du Progrès) is a small, right-of-center party with a tradition of anticlericalism. Buisserest, a veteran politician, has never, by any means, been a radical. Of late, he has shown considerable regard for Tshombe's secessionist regime.

Antwerp Colonial Institute, advanced the notion of a timetable for the political emancipation of the Congo. Late in 1955, he published a more systematic version of this plan (in Flemish) in the relatively obscure monthly review of the Flemish Christian labor movement, and in early 1956, a French translation gave the "thirty-year plan" (as it was known) a nationwide notoriety.[41]

The thirty-year plan (which was considered brazenly improper by many colonial circles) was in fact bolder than its title suggested since it proposed that the Congo be granted full internal self-government within ten years, after which such "reserved powers" as those dealing with finance, currency, foreign relations, etc., would be gradually transferred to the Congolese authorities. Obviously, the duration of such a transitional period (in theory, twenty years) could easily be curtailed according to future developments. Indeed, only two years later, Van Bilsen himself acknowledged that a thirty-year timetable had become too long and psychologically unworkable. Even under its original form, however, the thirty-year plan had immediate repercussions. The Belgian Socialist Party (which had not given the Congo much thought since the annexation of the Free State) convened a special congress on the subject in June–July 1956. Simultaneously (and certainly by no mere coincidence), a group of Congolese intellectuals associated with the Catholic-sponsored publication *Conscience Africaine* issued a relatively tame manifesto which nevertheless considered independence as the ultimate goal, expressed serious misgivings about the notion of a "Belgo-Congolese community," and suggested Van Bilsen's plan as an appropriate timetable.[42] The ABAKO, which had been taking a markedly political orientation since Joseph Kasavubu had become its chairman one year earlier, soon reacted to the manifesto, both because its authors were not Bakongo and because ABAKO considered the document partly inspired by European circles. The result was a pungent address by Kasavubu to the general assembly of the association in

[41] A. A. J. Van Bilsen, "Un plan de trente ans pour l'émancipation politique de l'Afrique belge," in *Les Dossiers de l'Action Sociale Catholique*, no. 2, Feb. 1956. It was also reprinted in Van Bilsen's *Vers l'indépendance du Congo et du Ruanda-Urundi* [Kraainem, Belgium, 1958?]. The original Flemish version appeared in *De gids op maatschapelijk gebied*, Dec. 1955. An early formulation of Van Bilsen's views will be found in his "Pour une politique coloniale de mouvement," in *La Revue Nouvelle*, Nov. 1954.

[42] *Conscience Africaine*, special issue, July–Aug. 1956. The text of this manifesto has been reproduced in many publications, notably in the special issue of *Chronique de Politique Etrangère* ("*La Crise Congolaise*"), Brussels (Institut Royal des Relations Internationales), vol. XIII, nos. 4–6 (July–Nov. 1960).

August 1956. The future President of the Republic criticized the *Conscience Africaine* group for "wanting to govern but scorning the means by which a country is ruled" and concluded: "Since the time has come, better grant us our emancipation today than delay it for another thirty years."

Finally, during that same crucial summer of 1956, an assembly of the thirty-seven Catholic bishops of the Congo and Ruanda-Urundi produced a declaration which, despite its emollient formulation, stated clearly:

All inhabitants of a country . . . have the right to take part in the administration of public affairs. . . . The autochthons are under the obligation to become conscious of the complexity of their responsibilities and to render themselves able to assume them. It does not behove the Church to pronounce upon the modalities of a people's emancipation. It considers it legitimate as long as it is accomplished within the respect of mutual rights and of charity.[43]

Clearly, the Congo had now entered an era of political change.

The Belgian political parties did not fail to recognize this fact and proceeded at once to sponsor cognate groups in the major cities. The Liberal Party, advancing in the wake of Buisseret's popularity, appeared for a moment to be gaining considerable ground; one of its chief agents in Stanleyville, incidentally, was Patrice Lumumba. But none of the metropolitan parties was really equipped to cater to the needs of Congolese nationalism, and the influence of such circles always remained limited. The Belgian labor unions were more successful, both in their organizing work and in the extent of their indirect political influence. Yet, as is the case with the offshoots of metropolitan parties, the final impact of such influence is nearly impossible to estimate. Personalities who have at one time belonged to the same organizations have often followed entirely divergent careers and their political ideas have frequently taken opposite orientations, facts which tend to confirm that such "imported" organizations and ideologies have usually been considered by the Congolese as springboards from which to make a start or as schools for the acquisition of political skills.

By the end of 1956, Belgian governmental circles had gradually come to realize the necessity of bolstering up their slightly nebulous plans with a certain number of immediate, tangible political reforms. Yet a variety of adverse factors soon crippled the government's ability

[43] *Revue du Clergé Africain*, XI, no. 5 (Sept. 1956), 449–458.

and willingness to define any long-term policy. The perspective of approaching elections was one of these; the protracted tension between the government and the colonial administration—both in Brussels and in Africa—was another. A third and perhaps more potent factor was the serious deterioration of the economic situation in the Congo through 1956 and 1957. The price of copper had steadily declined from $1.12 per kilogram at the end of February 1956 to $.50½ at the end of December 1957. The favorable balance of trade had shrunk from $134,430,000 in 1956 to $47,760,000 in 1957; and the balance of payments, which had already slumped from a $17,100,000 credit in 1955 to a $5,880,000 drain in 1956, now plummeted down to the unprecedented deficit of $129,640,000 for 1957. The repatriation of investment returns and European salaries for 1957 amounted to a net leakage of nearly $100,000,000, and the gap in the balance of payments had to be stopped by taking $146,540,000 from the colony's reserves.[44] Thus, there was an understandable—if somewhat unjustified—fear on the part of the government that the announcement, or even the contemplation, of sweeping political measures might further shake the confidence of the business world in the Congo's economic future.

Finally, the only significant reform of 1957 was the introduction of a timid measure of local government in the rural areas and of a slightly bolder version of this plan in the three major cities of Léopoldville, Elisabethville, and Jadotville.[45] The inauguration of a system of elected borough councils in these three cities, although not a major reform in itself, gave the urbanized Congolese their first taste of the polls. As brought out before, they resulted in a clear victory for the best-organized groups: the Bakongo in Léopoldville and the (mainly Baluba) immigrants from Kasai in Elisabethville and Jadotville. But, in Léopoldville at least, the significance of the elections clearly exceeded the scope of municipal politics.

In his inaugural address of April 20, 1958, Joseph Kasavubu (who had been elected mayor of Dendale, one of Léopoldville's thirteen boroughs) delivered a perceptive indictment of Belgian policies:

[44] See *La situation économique du Congo belge et du Ruanda-Urundi en 1957* (Brussels: Ministère des Colonies, 1958).

[45] See the later section, "Local Government." The decree organizing municipal institutions was signed on March 26, 1957. The decree itself did not specify which urban centers were to be granted city status. At the time of the first municipal elections, only the three cities mentioned above had been recognized. The other four provincial capitals (Stanleyville, Luluabourg, Coquilhatville, and Bukavu) did not gain municipal status until 1958.

The establishment of democracy will be achieved only inasmuch as we shall secure autonomy—even if only internal. Democracy is not established where officials are appointed alongside the people's elected representatives to check the democratic process. Democracy is not established since, looking at the police, we see no Congolese captains. Similarly, within the militia, we know of no Congolese officer, nor of any Congolese director in the medical service. And what of the direction and supervision of education? There is no democracy as long as the vote is not generalized. Thus, the first step is not yet accomplished. We demand general elections and internal self-government.[46]

Within two months of this speech, new elections were taking place in Belgium and the Socialist-Liberal coalition was replaced by a Catholic-Liberal cabinet which immediately announced in its governmental program its intention "to settle clearly the political future of the Congo . . . in an atmosphere of mutual confidence between whites and blacks." Although his party still participated in the new coalition, Buisseret was shelved and replaced in his ministerial post by Governor-General Pétillon, with whom he had frequently been at loggerheads. The first political act of the new minister was to alter the name of his department from Ministère des Colonies to Ministère du Congo Belge et du Ruanda-Urundi (a lengthy title which administrative lingo soon reduced to "Minicoru"). His second major decision was to appoint in August 1958 a parliamentary study group for the purpose of preparing recommendations which could be used in the framing of a new policy.

As he was taking these steps, however, important developments were occurring in neighboring French Africa. General de Gaulle was launching his new *communauté* and, gambling on the Africans' unwillingness to forfeit French assistance as well as on his own personal prestige, he was boldly offering a choice between continued partnership with France and complete independence. On August 24, speaking at Brazzaville—directly across the Congo River from Léopoldville—he confidently assured the cheering crowds that "anybody who wishes independence may take it at once: the metropole will not oppose it." Two days later, a group of sixteen Congolese led by Patrice Lumumba submitted to the new minister a memorandum which criticized the government's failure to include a single African in the study group and made reservations concerning the validity of its findings. This motion was the first document of its kind to include representatives of all major ethnic groups of Léopoldville (including Bakongo) among

[46] Quoted in De Backer, *Notes,* I, 24.

its signatories and was the product of an alliance which, in a number
of ways, prefigured the birth of the country's first nationwide political
party, the Mouvement National Congolais (or MNC), some six weeks
later.[47]

Another factor which indirectly helped in bringing together a number of Congolese *évolués* was the Brussels World Fair of May–October
1958, which a number of them attended in various capacities. Contacts
were established, and discussions took place but little eventually resulted from these meetings, partly because of the relative tameness
of many of the participants (who had often been selected for their
"reliability") and partly also because of the variety of backgrounds
from which they came. The founding of the MNC before the fair had
closed stole this little group's thunder, and it was not until February
1959 that they finally launched the moderate, short-lived MPNC
(Mouvement pour le Progrès National Congolais).

As the year 1958 drew to a close, there was growing restlessness in
Léopoldville, both among the masses who were beginning to feel the
pinch of the recession and among the members of the teeming political
upper crust who were growing impatient with what they considered
Belgium's delaying tactics. The study group which had been appointed
in August did not leave Belgium until October, and before it had
completed its task, a cabinet reshuffle in Brussels had ousted Pétillon
and replaced him by Maurice Van Hemelrijck, whose only visible credentials were his successful negotiation of a truce in the protracted
quarrel over education. The Congolese took a dim view of this replacement until it turned out that Van Hemelrijck was in fact more liberal-
minded than his predecessor. By the time he was demoted ten months
later, he had acquired considerable popularity among the Africans.

The final version of the study group's report was not completed until
Christmas Eve, and discussions between cabinet members concerning
the exact wording of the projected governmental declaration continued
hotly until the very last day before it was finally publicized. Minister
Van Hemelrijck had been harnessed with a "drafting committee" of
four cabinet members, and the tug of war between the progressive and
conservative wings of the cabinet went on as tensions mounted in
Léopoldville. When the riots sparked by the banning of an ABAKO

[47] The name of Mouvement National Congolais had actually been used for the
first time at the end of 1956 by the group of educated Africans associated with
the publication of the *Conscience Africaine* manifesto. See *Conscience Africaine*,
Nov. 1956.

meeting broke out,[48] they provided new fuel for the argument over the inclusion of a reference to full independence. The crucial word (which the King had in any case already used in his prerecorded speech) was finally inserted into a slightly ambiguous context and both declarations (the King's and the government's) were broadcasted on January 13, 1959, but much of the psychological benefit which the Belgian authorities had hoped to reap from the announcement of their new policy was lost in the aftermath of the disturbances.[49]

The new policy formulated in the governmental declaration was primarily a broad outline of the proposed stages of political emancipation, and it bore a striking resemblance to the gradual process followed by Great Britain in its African territories: the introduction of the elective principle at the local government level, the injection of indirectly elected majorities in a three-tiered system of councils, the use of existing advisory bodies as nuclei of the future national parliament, and the gradual extension of the assemblies' sphere of competence. These measures were to be coupled with a development of rights and liberties, a program of africanization of the civil service, a boosted-up educational effort, and other reforms in such fields as land tenure, the judiciary, and labor. However (as the MNC was quick to point out), the declaration provided no precise timetable beyond the very first stages of this process, namely, the election of local government councils and the formation of provincial councils, which were scheduled respectively for December 1959 and March 1960. Yet the governmental declaration was given a reasonable (if sometimes qualified) welcome by European and African circles. The only exception on the African side was the ABAKO, which flatly rejected the whole plan and demanded instead the immediate creation of a separate Bakongo state. Finally, after Van Hemelrijck had gone to great lengths to placate the ABAKO leaders (Kasavubu and others who had been arrested after the riots were flown to Belgium for conversations, and charges against them were dropped), the party reluctantly watered down its uncom-

[48] Official casualty figures for the disturbances are 49 African deaths, 49 Europeans and 330 Africans wounded. The report of the official commission of inquiry threw little light on the actual causes of the riots. The effect of a rally held on Dec. 28 by Lumumba, Diomi, and Ngalula (all three had just returned from the first All-African People's Conference in Accra) and attended by some 7,000 persons has sometimes been played up in view of Lumumba's subsequent role, but substantial evidence is lacking. Nor is there any conclusive indication of the existence of a predetermined "plot."

[49] Contrary to normal constitutional practice, the King's speech was made public before the Belgian parliament had registered its formal approval of the new policy.

promising opposition into a demand for a federal system, but soon afterward reverted to its original positions. Within a few months, the Bakongo districts had quietly but irretrievably lapsed beyond the administration's control as a result of a generalized attitude of noncooperation on the part of the population. Although these developments were not particularly threatening, they took place sufficiently near Léopoldville to persuade a number of Belgian officials—and, in turn, the metropolitan authorities—that it might be wise to accelerate the process of political emancipation.[50]

The Background of Independence

Meanwhile, one of the first effects of the new policy had been a sudden mushrooming of political parties. Within a few months, over two dozen of them sprang up, half of them in Léopoldville. In the ensuing bid for recognition and leadership of the nationalist movement, each group increasingly strove to outdistance its competitors by intensifying its claims or by emphasizing its specific appeal to certain regional or ethnic groups. Federalism (in a variety of different brands) became a live issue. Demands for the establishment of a provisional government were another recurrent theme. In April 1959, the MNC and other related groups convened at Luluabourg suggested the date of January 1961; in June, the MNC and seven other groups (including one labor union) were urging the establishment of a provisional government by March 1960 and of a fully responsible government by January 1961.

On the whole, the older parties held their ground well and retained the head start they had over the newer formations. The clumsily conspicuous support which the Belgian administration tried to extend to those groups which it considered "moderate" proved to be a smothering embrace, and the various attempts made by such groups to coalesce met with indifferent success. Their most auspicious assemblage, the Parti National du Progrès (PNP), launched in November 1959, remained a rather loose affair which fared poorly in the first national elections. But for all parties, old or new, internal disruption remained a permanent threat. The MNC was the first to suffer a severe split when a group led by Ileo, Adoula, Ngalula, and others grew resentful of Patrice Lumumba's surging influence and reorganized their own version of the party (later to be known as the MNC-Kalonji) in July 1959.

[50] The chief documents concerning this episode were two reports by Vice-Governor Schoeller and a report by the Chief Secretary, Stenmans, written in July–August 1959. See *Congo 1959*, pp. 108–120.

As it turned out, while this breakaway group could reckon on a number of esteemed and brilliant individuals, the organization remained firmly in Lumumba's hands, but it took him some six months to reassert his hegemony. Later, internal dissensions also developed within some of the regional or ethnic parties such as CONAKAT, ABAKO, and CEREA (the major party of eastern Kivu).

But friction and controversy were by no means limited to the Congolese political scene. A disgruntled and confused administration was increasingly foundering in a morass of querulous irresolution. A severe rift had developed between Van Hemelrijck and the ineffectual Governor-General, Cornelis. Nor was it a secret that there was mounting hostility toward the minister within the Belgian cabinet itself. During the summer of 1959, Van Hemelrijck had become convinced (by a personal tour of inspection and by reports from senior officials) that it was imperative to define a precise timetable of Belgian policy and to speed up the process of emancipation. He also believed that it was both feasible and advisable to bring a provisional Congolese executive into being by 1960. His views met with considerable resistance in two cabinet meetings held at the end of August, but when the Prime Minister sent one of his personal aides to the Congo in order to check the validity of his colleague's intelligence without even consulting him,[51] Van Hemelrijck turned in his resignation and was replaced by one of the founding fathers of the Christian Socialist Party, Auguste De Schrijver, who had acted as chairman of the 1958 parliamentary study group. But Van Hemelrijck had made his point: the cabinet now was reconciled to the principle of accelerated independence and the new minister's first declaration specified that there would be a Congolese executive (under the Governor-General's chairmanship) within a year and that complete independence might be reached at the end of the first legislature (which could be interpreted as meaning 1964).

Thus, by mid-September 1959, it appeared that Belgium had clarified the situation and regained the initiative. The only weak point about Belgium's new stand was that it had been determined without any consultation of the Congolese nationalists, who could therefore level their sharpest criticism at the new policy in blissful irresponsibility. The Belgian authorities had been aware of the dangers of their

[51] This aide was Count Harold d'Aspremont-Lynden, who was closely associated with the King's entourage and who later supervised Belgium's "technical assistance" to secessionist Katanga, first as an official envoy, then as Minister of African Affairs.

position for some time, but they were reluctant to let the unrestrained questioning of their program degenerate into a demagogic free-for-all. Another quandary was how to determine what the French call *interlocuteurs valables* in the absence of either elected representatives or a monolithic nationalist front. By November, however, the Belgian government had come to accept the perspective of a comprehensive political conference (dubbed the Round Table) and apparently considered that the forthcoming local government elections (to be held in December) could provide a reasonable basis for weighing the importance of the various Congolese delegations. Even the boycott of these elections by some of the major parties (ABAKO, Parti Solidaire Africain, and MNC) did not deflect the course of its policy, and on December 15, 1959, De Schrijver informed the Belgian House of Representatives that the Round Table conference would be held in mid-January and that independence would be "an accomplished fact" by 1960. This far-reaching statement was rather inconspicuously wedged between the more detailed comments which dealt with the organization of the conference, but it nevertheless revealed the government's intention to give up its gradualist approach and to embark upon an unprecedented gamble.

The Round Table conference opened in an outwardly auspicious climate, but under the calm surface lay a complex medley of misgivings and apprehensions. The situation was indeed an ambiguous one: the African leaders, who had practically been swept ahead of their own positions by Belgium's quick succession of retreats, now feared to be outmaneuvered and blindfolded.[52] The Socialist opposition could hardly disapprove the policy of decolonization adopted by what was basically a conservative coalition, and Belgian opinion was completely nonplused by the swift reversal of a number of ingrained shibboleths. Within one month, the conference laid the foundations of the Congo's future political regime [53] which later was formulated (with a few significant changes) in the so-called *loi fondamentale* of May 19, 1960.

The members of the conference left Brussels in a unison of good will and benign agreement to return to the preparation of a cutthroat election in the Congo. Many parts of the country were now in a welter of feverish anticipation and rampant aggressivity: in Kasai, tribal con-

[52] Patrice Lumumba, for one, retained his suspicions even after the conference—which helps to explain the violence of his reactions to Belgian military intervention in July 1960.

[53] The institutions of the Congolese Republic will be examined in later pages.

flicts between Lulua and Baluba had resulted in the migration of some 35,000 Baluba and in the imposition of a state of emergency; serious incidents were taking place in Maniema (the western portion of Kivu); tension was mounting between the Mongo and the Ngombe in Coquilhatville; clashes between the Lunda and the Tshokwe had occurred in Elisabethville, and the CONAKAT party was toying with plans for a secession. In this state of increasing confusion, little attention was paid to the second Round Table conference, which dealt with economic problems and took place at the height of the electoral campaign (April 26 to May 16). Yet this conference, which few of the major leaders managed (or cared) to attend, revealed the full extent of the Congo's economic predicament: a public debt whose annual charge had reached 18.3 times its 1950 level, a budget that could be balanced only with the help of a $54,000,000 subvention from Belgium, a depleted treasury ($1,780,000), and a total indebtedness (consolidated plus floating debt) of over $900,000,000.

The general and provincial elections held at the end of May resulted in a clear (if not sweeping) victory for Lumumba's MNC: with its regional allies, it won 41 seats out of 137 in the House of Representatives and was substantially represented in four provincial assemblies out of six, controlling two of the six provincial governments. The MNC's success was all the more significant since it was the only party to operate on a nationwide basis, even though it had failed to take root in the two most particularistic regions of the country, Lower Congo and southern Katanga. Its nearest competitor, the "moderate" cartel known as PNP, won only 15 seats. The other results confirmed the regional or ethnocentric character of most Congolese parties.

The victory of the MNC induced a number of fence sitters to jump on Lumumba's bandwagon, and last-minute efforts to improvise an anti-Lumumbist coalition misfired. On June 23, one week before the date set for independence, Patrice Lumumba became the Congo's first Prime Minister, and the following day, Joseph Kasavubu was elected President of the new republic. Finally, on June 30, 1960, Congolese independence was decreed by a joint declaration of both governments and ratified by King Baudouin. Within less than two weeks, the Force Publique (army) had mutinied against its white officers, Belgian troops had intervened in contradiction to the newly signed treaty of cooperation, Katanga had declared its "independence," and the Congo was sinking into a gigantic debacle.

The Contemporary Setting

LAND AND PEOPLE

The Congo covers 905,062 square miles, making it 77 times the size of Belgium or nearly equivalent to the combined areas of the states of California, Nevada, Utah, Arizona, New Mexico, Texas, and Oklahoma. It is inhabited by a population estimated in 1962 at 14,700,000 people. The distribution of the African population (as of 1959) and the relative area of the six provinces into which the Congo was subdivided at the time of its independence are summarized in Table 1.

Table 1. Population and area, 1959

	African population		Area		
	Number	%	Sq. miles	%	Pop. density
Léopoldville	3,301,140	23.8	138,862	15.34	23.77
Equator	1,836,588	13.2	155,258	17.15	11.83
Eastern	2,506,398	18.1	194,299	21.47	12.90
Kivu	2,329,262	16.8	100,029	11.06	23.29
Katanga	1,709,659	12.3	191,878	21.20	8.91
Kasai	2,181,424	15.8	124,734	13.78	17.49
Congo	13,864,471	100.0	905,062 *	100.00	15.32

* The discrepancies in the totals are caused by the rounding off of figures.
Source: *La situation économique du Congo belge et du Ruanda-Urundi en 1959* (Brussels: Ministère des Affaires Africaines, 1960).

The population density shows greater variations than these figures may suggest. The highest degree of concentration is met in peripheral districts like the easternmost fringes of the Kivu and Eastern provinces or the westernmost tip of the Lower Congo region, while an under-populated belt stretches from the confluence of the Congo and Kwa (=Kasai) rivers to the upper reaches of the Aruwimi-Ituri and from Stanleyville to the southernmost parts of Katanga (Upper Katanga, with the exception of Elisabethville, has a population density of only 5.17 inhabitants per square mile). This means that two-thirds of the country's rural population are concentrated in less than one-fourth of the total area. The Congolese population is a fast-growing one: the birth rate has been estimated with reasonable accuracy at 43 per thousand, and the number of inhabitants is expected to double within twenty-five years. The population is also a young one: between 1955 and 1957, children under 14 years of age accounted for some 40 per cent of the total population, while only 15 per cent were over 45.

It is presently impossible to give accurate figures concerning the non-African population. In 1959, there were 115,157 whites (including 89,736 Belgians) and 1,469 Asians in the Congo. This nonnative population was unevenly distributed throughout the territory, as is shown in the following figures for the white population in 1959:

Léopoldville	29.9%
Katanga	28.7%
Eastern	15.5%
Kivu	12.4%
Kasai	7.6%
Equator	5.9%

In 1958, the active members of this nonnative community were mostly in the employment of business firms (43.7 per cent); only 20.7 per cent of them were self-employed, as farmers, stockbreeders, traders, contractors, etc. Government officials and employees accounted for 20.2 per cent of the active nonnative population and missionaries for 15.4 per cent.

The aftermath of independence has caused a marked decline in the non-African population, but the pattern has been an uneven one: certain areas, such as Kivu and the Eastern Province, have been sharply depleted whereas others, such as southern Katanga and the city of Léopoldville, have been less seriously affected. Another interesting feature of these recent movements has been that the Portuguese, Italian, and Greek communities (which together represented 10.9 per cent of the nonnative population in 1959) have decreased noticeably less than the Belgian group, owing apparently to the limited prospects which they could expect to find in their respective countries and to the fact that most of them were self-employed, small businessmen catering to the African population and unable to liquidate their assets.

THE ECONOMY

The Belgians have been justifiably proud of their economic achievements in the Congo and have sometimes contended that their tardiness in the sphere of political development was more than compensated by their remarkable accomplishments in the social and economic fields.

Mining

The country's resources (particularly its mineral resources) are abundant and more diversified than those of most of its African neighbors. Mineral production accounts for 55 to 60 per cent of the total value of exports, and Katanga normally contributes some three-quarters of this value. Copper is, of course, the chief item of mineral production, although the slump in the price of this commodity on the world market had reduced its relative share in the nation's economy at the time of independence. The output of copper represents approximately 9 per cent of the world production. The Congo also produces 53 per cent of the world's cobalt and 61 per cent of its industrial diamonds,[54] as well as substantial quantities of manganese ore, cassiterite (native tin dioxide), gold, zinc, uranium, tungsten, germanium, cadmium, columbo-tantalite, etc. The respective value of the major mineral exports is summarized in Table 2. For purposes of comparison, a list of the mineral exports of the Katanga "state" during the first half of 1961 has been included.

Table 2. Major mineral exports

	1956	1957	1958	1959	1961: first half (Katanga only)
	$000,000				
Copper	$219.60	$149.70	$108.03	$159.70	$90.92
Diamonds	26.91	30.74	33.61	34.49	—
Cassiterite and tin	28.94	30.72	19.17	20.93	.64
Gold	12.86	12.72	11.61	11.13	—
Cobalt	38.90	29.26	23.51	28.72	13.42
Manganese ore	7.81	8.79	8.91	6.75	3.84
Zinc & Zinc ore	13.44	15.08	10.62	11.94	7.24
Tungsten ore	3.43	1.79	1.70	1.54	—
Columbo-tantalite	2.17	.74	1.25	.83	.06
(Total value of mineral exports)	($358.12)	($288.04)	($227.36)	($280.46)	($121.14) *

* The total value of Katangese exports for 1961 was $251,119,948.

[54] Lately, the diamond mining industry of Kasai has been almost entirely disrupted by the massive smuggling of diamonds due to the breakdown of organized authority.

By its very nature, the mining industry has been (and remains) the exclusive concern of heavily concentrated non-African interest groups.[55] Chief of these is, of course, the well-known Union Minière du Haut-Katanga (UMHK) which, through its various subsidiaries (Sogelec, Sogechim, Sogefor, Métalkat, etc.), is involved in a variety of activities ranging from flour mills to shipyards, from coal to chemicals, and from forestry to the production of electrical power. The Union Minière itself is partly controlled by Belgium's largest financial group, the Société Générale de Belgique, and by the Tanganyika Concessions, Ltd., which is in turn linked with the multifarious interests commonly associated with the name of Harry F. Oppenheimer, the South African financier and industrialist (for example, Anglo-American Corporation of South Africa, De Beers Consolidated Mines, Ltd., Rhodesian Anglo-American, British South Africa Co.). Other important concerns are the diamond-mining Forminière—in whose bailiwick was founded "King" Albert Kalonji's secessionist "Mining State"—the Géomines, the Symétain (tin and allied metals), the Société des Mines d'Or de Kilo-Moto (gold), and the Société Minière des Grands Lacs (tin and allied metals, gold).

Agriculture

Congolese agriculture remains unevenly and incompletely developed: the sparseness of the population and the drain on rural manpower owing to the rapid growth of the mining industries are among the primary factors of this situation. Forests cover more than half the country's total area and contributed $8,600,000 worth of timber and allied products toward Congolese exports in 1959. Not counting fallow land, only 11,200 square miles (less than 1.25 per cent of the total area) is being cultivated, while land under productive cultivation was estimated in 1958 at 10,637 square miles. The productive average farmed by Africans and Europeans, as well as the respective acreage allotted to food crops and cash crops, is summarized in Table 3.[56]

As Table 3 shows, more than nine-tenths of the European farm land was devoted to cash crops; in fact, even the small acreage under food

[55] The Republic nominally fell heir to a sizable share of these interests, belonging formerly to the colonial government, but the actual transfer has been held up by Belgo-Congolese litigation and by the Katanga secession.

[56] The reliability and accuracy of the figure from which Table 3 has been compiled being sometimes questionable, it should be considered to describe an approximate pattern. For a critical appraisal of the validity of agricultural statistics, see P. Gourou, *La densité de la population rurale au Congo belge* (Brussels: Académie Royale des Sciences Coloniales, 1955), pp. 121–122.

crops was largely (81 per cent) assigned to the production of fruit and market vegetables. Moreover, four-tenths of the total acreage allotted to cash crops was farmed by Europeans. Indeed, although the African-owned cash-crop areas had increased by more than half between 1940 and 1958, the relative share owned by Europeans of the total acreage under cash crops was higher in 1958 than it had been at the

Table 3. Productive acreage, 1958 (in thousands of acres, with percentage of the total amount)

	African farm land	European farm land	Total
Food crops	4,933 (72.5%)	72 (1.1%)	5,005 (73.6%)
Cash crops	1,080 (15.8%)	723 (10.6%)	1,803 (26.4%)
Total	6,013 (88.3%)	795 (11.7%)	6,808 (100.0%)

beginning of World War II. This trend was further stressed by the respective values of African- and European-produced cash crops. While the value of cash crops produced on African farm land increased approximately at the same ratio as the acreage from which it was grown, the share of European production in the total value of cash crops expanded from less than half in 1940 to more than 63 per cent in 1958,—a fact which underlined the widening gap between European and African productivity. The respective value of food crops and cash crops grown by African and European farmers is summarized in Table 4, which offers an interesting comparison with the figures relating to the acreages on which these crops were grown (see Table 3).

Table 4. Food and cash crops, 1958 (in thousands of dollars)

	Grown by Africans	Grown by Europeans	Total
Food crops	$52,214 (30.2%)	$2,724 (1.6%)	$54,938 (31.8%)
Cash crops	43,146 (24.9%)	75,038 (43.3%)	118,184 (68.2%)
Total	$95,360 (55.1%)	$77,762 (44.9%)	$173,122 (100.0%)

The staple items in the Congolese production of food crops are cassava, plaintain bananas, peanuts, corn, rice paddy, peas and beans, and tubers. Chief on the cash-crop list are coffee, rubber (both almost wholly grown on European plantations), palm products, and cotton seed (both chiefly grown by African producers). Minor items include

cocoa and tea (European) and various fibers (African). A summary
of the agricultural production of 1958 will be found in Table 5.

Table 5. Agricultural production, 1958

| | Over-all production | | Commercialized production | | | |
| | (in 000 of short tons) | | Tonnage (in 000) | | Value (in $000) | |
	African	European	African	European	African	European
Cash crops						
Coffee	8.5	50.9	8.4	50.9	$4,380	$43,656
Rubber	3.9	37.4	3.9	37.4	2,120	21,928
Palm products	n.a.	338.3	69.3	338.3	14,860	2,824
Cotton seed	157.1	.1	157.1	.1	17,480	—
Cocoa	—	5.3	—	5.3	6	2,900
Tea	—	2.8	—	2.8	—	2,014
Fibers	14.9 *	.2 †	14.9	.2	3,080	52
Food crops						
Cassava	8,320.5	13.7	1,672.1	—	33,500	200
Plantain ba- nanas	1,955.6	1.4	439.6	—	5,280	32
Peanuts	186.0	.1	50.5	—	4,160	6
Corn	350.2	2.8	124.8	2.8	3,480	100
Rice (paddy)	191.1	—	121.3	—	3,200	—
Peas and beans	75.4	—	26.4	—	1,320	—
Tubers	366.9	2.1	34.3	.4	474	60

* Urena and punga (jutelike fibers).   † Sisal.   *n.a.:* not available.

Stock raising is fairly well developed. European breeders concentrated mainly on the raising of cattle (46 per cent out of a total of just
over 1,000,000 heads), while the Africans hold a virtual monopoly
over the herding of sheep and goats and raised some 85 per cent of
all pigs. As in other parts of central Africa and for the same reasons,
the use of animal labor in agriculture is virtually unknown, except
(on a limited scale) on European plantations.

Fishing yielded some 162,600 tons of fish in 1959, but the Congo
still had to import 31,777 tons of fish during that same year.

European agriculture has suffered more from postindependence developments than has any other type of European activity. There were
1,899 European farmers in the Congo at the end of 1958 (more than
two-thirds of them in the Eastern Province and Kivu), but today a

majority of these plantations either have been abandoned or are operating at a much-reduced capacity. There is, however, no reliable estimate of the present extent of this situation.

African agriculture has also suffered from the indirect effects of recent political developments, especially in those areas which have been affected by interethnic warfare. Thus, the sudden influx of Baluba refugees into southeastern Kasai, where they had to wait for new, hastily planted crops to grow, has caused an unprecedented famine in this area. Similar situations have occurred, on a lesser scale, in parts of northern Katanga and Kivu, and food from other parts of the country has seldom been forthcoming. Indeed, the price of the basic commodities of the African diet has shot up in all marketing centers as a combined result of the decline in the volume of production and of crippled communications. Although this situation may seem paradoxical in a country where little more than 1 per cent of the land area is being tilled, it reflects a situation already noted in 1957 by a Belgian economist, namely, that traditional African agriculture had reached a point of diminishing returns and that tillable land had actually become scarce in certain densely populated areas.[57]

Manufacturing

Congolese manufacturing industries are essentially linked with the processing and primary transformation of local resources, both mineral and agricultural. Lumberyards and sawmills, oil refineries, coffee hulleries, cotton ginneries, and plants for the curing of fish, the steeping of fibers, the tanning of hides, or the processing of rubber, cocoa, tea, tobacco, etc. together account for some two-thirds of the total number of industrial establishments. On a more advanced level of processing, soap factories, breweries, textile, rope and sacking factories, and shoe and leather goods factories cover a substantial portion of the needs of local consumers.[58] The production of cement, while not meet-

[57] Fernand Bézy, *Problèmes structurels de l'économie congolaise* (Louvain and Paris: Institut de Recherches Economique et Sociales, 1957), pp. 51–57. Although the over-all population density in 1954 was only 13 inhabitants per square mile, the average density of the agricultural population reached 1,058 inhabitants per square mile of cultivated land. To remedy this situation, the Belgian authorities had fostered projects of community development (*paysannats*) which, however, were still at an early stage at the time of independence.

[58] The Congo provides more than 90 per cent of locally consumed beer, soap, and cigarettes (although the last item, being produced in Katanga, has lately been in short supply), up to 80 per cent of sacks and cement, up to 60 per cent of paint and shoes, and up to 50 per cent of cotton fabrics and blankets.

ing all the country's needs, had reached 433,385 tons in 1958, and such items as cement tiles and concrete pipes were being turned out in growing numbers. The mining industry has developed, or sponsored as a side line, the production of certain chemicals which can be derived cheaply from its main output or of some relatively uncomplex metal articles. There is also a sizable production of various forms of containers (from tanks and vats to cans and bottles). Thus—as is the case with most countries whose chief economic asset is the production of raw materials—the main contribution of Congolese manufacturing industries to the nation's economy takes the form of "added value." In 1958, this "added value" was estimated at approximately $100,000,000, a fivefold expansion of the 1946 level.

Postindependence developments have in a sense proved a boon for Congolese manufacturing industries. Owing to the rapid deterioration of the trade balance, the country has had to rely increasingly on its own production of manufactured articles. For example, during the first nine months of 1961, industrial production in the Léopoldville and Lower Congo area (which accounted for approximately half the country's capacity in 1957) was 2.4 per cent higher than in 1959. Food industries were up 32.5 per cent, chemicals up 29 per cent, clothing and hosiery up 9 per cent. Slightly lower than the 1959 level were shoe and textile factories (—5.2 per cent) and metallic products (—5 per cent). The only sector suffering a sharp decline was construction, which was down to 44.2 per cent of its 1959 capacity.[59]

Power and Transportation

The development of the Congo's energy resources has been closely associated—as has so much else—with the growth and modernization of the mining industries. Major consumers like the Union Minière (which treats an increasing portion of its production by electrolytic methods) have provided for their own needs either in the form of coal [60] or, in recent years, by the building of giant hydroelectric power stations (at the Bia, Delcommune, and Le Marinel dams on the Lufira and Lualaba rivers). Thus, in 1958, 80 per cent of the country's hydroelectric capacity was located in Katanga and originated from plants whose average capacity (60,000 kilowatts) was twelve times that of the plants located in the other provinces.

[59] "La situation économique du Congo en 1961," in *Etudes Congolaises*, vol. II, no. 2 (1962).

[60] The Luena collieries, north of Elisabethville, were captured and held by Katangese troops at the cost of some severe fighting.

In a country that has to import every gallon of petroleum it consumes (489,938 tons in 1959, representing a total cost of $25,400,000 and accounting for 18 per cent of the power supply) and possesses only mediocre coal, hydroelectric power obviously represents the key to industrial development. On paper, the Congo controls half of Africa's share of potential hydroelectric resources or, in other terms, 13 per cent of the world total. Most of these reserves are concentrated 25 miles above the estuary port of Matadi at Inga, on the Congo River. There, within a span of 15 miles, the river discharges a massive flow of energy which, if harnessed, could yield at least 25,000,000 kw., that is, three and a half times the capacity of all power plants operating in the country in 1958. Surveys which have been conducted since 1954 have indicated that this giant project would have to be developed by gradual stages, the initial installation being designed for a power capacity of 200,000 or 300,000 kw. A related problem would be to find uses for this vast quantity of energy. Some bauxite deposits found in the Lower Congo have naturally evoked the possibility of developing a large aluminum industry, but enthusiastic planners, envisioning the birth of an "African Ruhr," also contemplate the creation of a whole array of industries in such fields as chemicals and fertilizers, ferrous alloys, wood pulp, cement, and so on. Unfortunately, the Inga project competes for investment with such other schemes as the Konkoure and Volta River dams in Guinea and Ghana or, closer to home, with the neighboring Kouilou project in the republic of Congo-Brazzaville, and wily President Fulbert Youlou found it profitable in more ways than one to encourage the "cause" of secessionist Katanga.

The Congolese transportation network has been built on the basis of an impeccably sound rationale: maximum development at a minimum cost. Full advantage has been taken of the navigable waterways wherever they existed, and railroads were primarily built to supplement them. The best examples of this policy are the 228-mile line bypassing the Lower Congo rapids between Matadi and Léopoldville and the 78-mile stretch that avoids the Stanley Falls between Stanleyville and Ponthierville. Thus, the longest uninterrupted railway lines are to be found in the portions of the territory which lie higher than 1,500 feet and particularly in Katanga which, in addition, is the only region to be directly connected with neighboring territories. Katanga is accessible from such points as Lobito, Beira, Lourenço Marques, and all major centers in the Rhodesias and South Africa. Indeed, the exportation of Katanga mining products by way of Lobito makes more economic sense than conveying them by the rail-water-rail link to Matadi, a route which the Belgian authorities had tried to render more attractive by the granting of rebates. The same fact applies to eastern Kivu, whose normal outlet is the Kigoma–Dar-es-Salaam line across Tanganyika. In 1959, 26.17 per cent of the total volume of exports and imports was conveyed through non-Congolese ports.

Most of the Congo railroads were built during the first forty years of Belgian penetration; 88 per cent of the present-day rail network was already built twenty-five years ago, and the tendency in recent years has been to replace minor rail links by road transports. On the whole, the network of surface transportation was designed to meet export requirements, not those of interregional communication, a situation which is emphasized by the fact that densely populated areas are not the best served. The conveyance of passengers represents only a minimal portion of the railroad companies' business, and the ratio of passenger miles to the total length of rail lines is only one twenty-fifth of what it is in Belgium. The development of roads has long been considered the most sensible way to increase the flexibility of the transportation network, and road building loomed large in the ten-year plan prepared in 1948 for the period 1950–1959. Unfortunately, only 17 per cent of the projected new all-weather roads have actually been built, and the network, though extensive, remains incomplete, especially between west and east.

The 1958 situation in terms of transportation can be summarized as follows:

Railroads	3,214 miles	
Navigable waterways	9,965 miles	
Rivers		9,009 miles
Lakes		956 miles
Roads	90,235 miles	
Main roads		20,995 miles
Local roads		58,291 miles
Private roads		10,949 miles
Airlines	20,816 miles	

Foreign Trade

The Congolese economy has been oriented for many years toward exports, and roughly one-half of the gross domestic produce is normally channeled toward foreign markets. Although it exports almost exclusively raw materials, the Congo has been less dependent than most developing territories upon the international prices of one or two commodities. For example, whereas cocoa, timber, and diamonds together accounted for 87 per cent of Ghana's exports in 1956, the three major items on the Congo's export list (copper, vegetable oils, and coffee) represented only 57 per cent of its sales abroad. A comparison between the average imports and exports of the three-year period 1936–1938 and those of 1956–1958 indicates the rates of growth given in Table 6.

Table 6. Rates of growth in imports and exports

	Volume		Value	
	1936–1938	1956–1958	1936–1938	1956–1958
Exports	100	291	100	1,188
Imports	100	525	100	1,964

In spite of the sharp decline of world prices after 1956, the Congo retained a favorable trade balance, as indicated in Table 7, but only at the cost of a drastic reduction of imports.

Table 7. Trade balance, 1956–1959 (in millions of dollars)

	Exports and reexports	Imports	Balance	Movement of trade
1956	$547.6	$413.2	+$134.4	$960.8
1957	485.9	438.2	+ 47.7	924.1
1958	415.7	359.7	+ 56.–	775.4
1959	500.1	307.9	+ 192.2	808.–

The structure of Congolese foreign trade is analyzed in Table 8. For purposes of comparison, figures for the first year of independence have been given alongside the figures for 1957 and 1958. To appreciate the parallel between figures for 1958–1959 and 1960–1961, it should be borne in mind that the last half of 1960 saw the secession of Katanga and southern Kasai and that the first half of 1961 saw the virtual economic secession of Kivu and the Eastern Province. As a final corrective, it should be added that the exports of Katanga between the time of its secession and the end of the first year of Congolese independence have been estimated at 11,073,000,000 francs.

The chief items on the export list in 1958 were, in decreasing order: copper (25.95 per cent), coffee (13.7 per cent), palm products (13.6

Table 8. Foreign trade (in millions of Congolese francs)

	1957	1958	July 1, 1960, to June 30, 1961 *
Imports			
Edible goods	2,613.0 (12.3%)	2,296.1 (12.8%)	2,149 (46.2%)
Nonedible goods	10,916.1 (51.3%)	8,434.1 (46.9%)	1,815 (39.1%)
Equipment and tools	7,486.5 (35.1%)	6,580.4 (36.6%) }	681 (14.7%)
Other	282.4 (1.3%)	675.4 (3.7%) }	
Total imports	21,298.0 (100.0%)	17,986.0 (100.0%)	4,645 (100.0%)
Exports			
Mineral products	14,402 (60.1%)	11,210 (54.5%)	1,136 (16.4%)
Vegetable and animal products	9,492 (39.6%)	8,850 (43. %)	5,716 (82.5%)
Industrial and sundry	64 (.3%)	521 (2.5%)	76 (1.1%)
Total exports	23,958 (100.0%)	20,581 (100.0%)	6,928 (100.0%)

* Figures for 1960–1961 are from "La situation économique du Congo en 1961," in *Etudes Congolaises,* vol. II, no. 2 (1962).

per cent), diamonds (7.2 per cent), cotton (5.2 per cent), rubber (4.1 per cent), cassiterite (3.4 per cent), zinc and zinc ore (3.2 per cent), and gold (2.8 per cent).

The orientation of Congolese foreign trade is outlined in Table 9. As the table indicates, the share of Belgium in the Congo's foreign trade was much less monopolistic than was that of France, for example, in the exports and imports of its overseas territories (61 and 68 per cent respectively). Moreover, the Congolese market represented a comparatively small portion (6 to 8 per cent) of Belgium's exports and an equally diminutive share of its imports (6 per cent), whereas in 1955, France sold 36 per cent of its exports and bought 27 per cent of its imports from its overseas territories. But the real economic significance of the Congo for Belgium lay elsewhere: in 1957, 365 colonial business firms, representing a total paid-up capital of $1,594,-000,000, together netted a profit of $180,000,000 and paid their stockholders a total of $120,000,000 in dividends. Although the trade balance remained favorable after 1956, the balance of payments rapidly deteriorated from a $17,100,000 surplus in 1955 to a staggering deficit

Table 9. Direction of foreign trade (in per cent of total exports and imports)

	Exports *			Imports †		
	1957	1958	1959	1957	1958	1959
Common Market and Ass.	(68.1)	(68.0)	(65.9)	(55.5)	(57.4)	(55.2)
Belgium and Luxembourg	49.3	48.2	44.4	35.0	36.0	31.1
France	6.1	5.3	5.8	3.2	3.5	4.1
West Germany	4.8	5.8	5.3	9.0	9.0	10.0
Italy	4.3	5.8	7.5	3.2	3.8	4.0
The Netherlands	2.9	1.9	2.4	4.7	5.1	6.0
French overseas terr.	.7	1.0	.5	.4	n	n
Sterling zone	(10.6)	(13.6)	(11.9)	(13.5)	(13.0)	(15.3)
United Kingdom	7.7	9.9	8.5	7.5	8.0	8.7
South Africa	1.1	1.4	1.4	3.3	2.7	3.4
Fed. of Rhodesia and Nyasaland	.7	.8	.8	1.4	1.0	1.5
India	1.0	.8	.7	.1	n	n
East Africa	.1	.7	.5	1.2	1.3	1.7
United States	13.5	14.5	10.9	18.0	15.0	12.9
Canada	n	n	n	.3	.5	.8
Others	7.8	3.9	12.3	12.7	14.1	15.8

* Export figures are based upon customs statistics and do not account for further reexportations. Thus, a large portion of Congolese exports to Belgium and the United Kingdom (diamonds) are later redirected toward other markets after having received proper treatment.

† As an illustration of the changing patterns of Congolese foreign trade, imports for the first half of 1962 originated from the following countries (in per cent): Belgium and Luxembourg, 26.36; other European Economic Community countries, 15; United Kingdom, 6.5; United States, 24.6 (communicated by the Federation of Belgium Industries).

n: not available, negligible, or not listed separately in governmental statistics.

of $149,600,000 in 1957. A massive influx of government capital ($120,-400,000 versus $11,400,000 in 1957) reduced the deficit to $5,900,000 in 1958; but subsequent political developments were not designed to stanch the flight of capital, and by the end of 1959, the balance of payments had relapsed to a deficit of $109,200,000. Reserves in gold, currencies, and bonds dwindled from $262,400,000 at the end of 1956 to some $80,000,000 at the time of independence and the first turmoil quickly reduced them to less than half this amount, after which international payments were virtually suspended for a few months.[61]

As a final commentary, let it be added that the gross domestic

[61] On January 1, 1961, reserves amounted to 3,789,000,000 Congolese francs. By the end of November, they had declined to 1,429,000,000 Congolese francs.

product was roughly estimated at some $1,200,000,000 a year at the time of independence. Measured at fixed prices and weighed by a consideration of the demographic increase, it shows a rate of growth of 2.4 per cent. In 1957, industry (including mining and building) accounted for 36 per cent of this product, while 25 per cent originated from agriculture, forestry, and fishing and 39 per cent from "services." Yet this remarkable expansion had not yet lifted the Congo from the ranks of the underprivileged nations. Between 1950 and 1958, the per capita income had risen from $50 to $70, but the share of the nonnative economy in the production of the national income was a heavy one (an average 48 per cent between 1950 and 1958), so that the Africans had in fact a per capita income of $23 in 1950 and $41 in 1958, roughly 2 per cent of the U.S. per capita income. Moreover, since most factors of economic growth were in the hands of non-Africans—and heavily dependent upon non-African investments—it was clear that the achievement of economic emancipation would be far later than the date of political independence.

SOCIAL STRUCTURE

"Tribalism" is probably the most overworked open-sesame used in probing the Congolese situation. Yet no one can seriously ignore the incidence of ethnic factors on recent political developments, even though these factors may require substantial qualifications.

Ethnic Diversity

Ethnographers currently distinguish at least 200 different groups within the boundaries of the Republic. While the linguists confirm this pluralism by labeling as many as 700 local dialects, they suggest, however, that these dialects may be classified in a number of broad groups which substantially reduce the complexity of the tribal pattern. It should also be noted that the six largest ethnic groups together account for some 30 per cent of the population, although only some of these have exhibited complete political solidarity.

In view of the intricacy of the linguistic contexture, the role played by the more or less debased or artificial languages that serve as vehicles of communication between the various groups deserves special notice. *Kingwana,* a local form of Kiswahili which spread with the "Arab" trade in the nineteenth century, is widely used and understood in the three eastern provinces (Eastern, Kivu, and Katanga) and has been seeping into Kasai. *Lingala,* which is derived from a group of dialects used by riverain tribes of the Middle Congo (particularly the Bobangi), has spread throughout the western portion of the Congo except in to the Lower Congo, Kwango, and Kasai. Its diffusion, which has even repulsed Kingwana from the Uele region (in the northern part of the Eastern Province) and challenged it in Stanleyville, was greatly enhanced by its deliberate use as a common vehicle within the Congolese militia, the Force Publique. In Léopoldville, where it collided with Kikongo, Lingala served as a medium in the political *rapprochement* of all non-Bakongo elements.[62] *Kikongo*—or rather a noninflected "kitchen Kikongo"—was used by government agents and Catholic missionaries in the Lower Congo and in the Kwango regions. *Kituba,* a pidgin form of Tshiluba (the language of the Kasai Baluba), was locally used in Kasai but never gained the same acceptance as Lingala or Kingwana. Finally, all educated Congolese accepted French as a superior type of lingua franca endowed with considerable prestige value and a high degree of flexibility and sophistication. French was the required medium of most political discussions of the Congolese elite, if only because it alone could provide the adequate terminology, and it remains the official language of parliamentary debate and government business.

The political implications of tribal divisions are difficult to assess, partly because of our limited knowledge of the snarled roots of most of the present tangles. Tanganyika, which offers a tribal diversity comparable to that of the Congo, has evolved into an orderly one-party state, and, within the Republic itself, the Eastern Province, an area of considerable ethnic complexity, returned a quasi-monolithic vote in favor of the country's only supratribal party, the MNC, a phenomenon which suggests that beyond a certain degree of ethnic fragmentation, tribal particularism may lose a good deal of its virulence.

Beyond the almost innate tendency for any group to resent and distrust its neighbors, certain more specific patterns of hostility have emerged in various parts of the Congo. One has been for smaller groups to react against the hegemony of larger groups: such was the case in Kasai, where those who did not belong to one of the two major tribes, the Baluba (whose vehicle was the MNC-Kalonji) and the Lulua (who had their own party, the Union Nationale Congolaise, later allied with Lumumba's MNC), tended to rally behind the Coali-

[62] Although the name "Bangala" should normally be reserved for the Lingala-speaking populations, the Bakongo of Léopoldville lump all non-Bakongo under this collective name.

tion Kasaienne, or COAKA, which consequently reaped most of the votes of the Bakete, Babindji, Balualua, Basalampasu, Bapende, and Bashilele. Another trend appears in the resentment felt against immigrant and squatter groups. This is, of course, partly linked with the phenomenon of urbanization, but in Kasai, it is also associated with the construction of the rail link between Katanga and Port-Francqui (at the boundary between the provinces of Kasai and Léopoldville). The Baluba, who were quicker to grasp the economic opportunities offered by the opening of the railroad, spread northwestward across the territories of the Bena-Lulua, Bakete, Bakuba, Bashilele, etc., and as they were to discover later, antagonized practically all of them. In time, Patrice Lumumba's MNC succeeded in capitalizing on anti-Luba sentiment in Kasai (incidentally settling an old score with the Luba leader, Albert Kalonji, who had taken the lead of the MNC's secessionist wing) and formed a provincial government in coalition with the Union Nationale Congolaise (UNC), the COAKA, the MUB (Mouvement de l'Unité Basonge), and other minor formations. In Katanga, as noted earlier, the CONAKAT originated from similar resentment against the immigrants from Kasai (most, but not all, of them Baluba) who seemed to hold an unduly large share of the well-paid jobs offered by the Union Minière and other companies.

In Léopoldville province, ABAKO naturally attracted the support of the Bakongo and their allied groups (Bayombe, Basundi), while the Bayaka of Kwango have rallied behind the LUKA (Union Kwangolaise pour l'Indépendance et la Liberté). But the strongest party in the province, the Parti Solidaire Africain, or PSA (to which Antoine Gizenga belongs), is more regional than tribal in character and enjoys the undiversified support of all local groups (Bambala, Bahungana, Bangongo, Bakewese, Bapende), with the sole exception of the Bayanzi, who belong to a different linguistic group and who organized their own party, ABAZI (Alliance des Bayanzi). Again, in the Equator Province, the strongest political group, PUNA (Parti de l'Unité Nationale), owing in part to the fact that most of its leading members were associated with a movement (ASSORECO) appealing to all immigrants from the Middle Congo in the city of Léopoldville, has attracted supporters on a regional rather than purely ethnic basis.[63] The same applies to CEREA (Centre de Regroupement Africain), the dominant party of Kivu.

[63] See D. Biebuyck and M. Douglas, *Congo Tribes and Parties* (London: Royal Anthropological Institute, 1961), p. 36.

Yet no party, whatever its ideology, could afford to ignore the reality of tribal sentiment. The best example is that of the MNC itself which had a genuinely national platform but was also endorsed by an important aggregate of tribes, the Ankutshu-Anamongo (to which Patrice Lumumba belonged). In their first congress, held in the small central town of Lodja, March 9–12, 1960, they "entrusted the defense of their interests to the MNC." This congress, which recognized "the dominant position held by the MNC in the region of the Ankutshu-Anamongo," illustrates the permeation of the whole Mongo language area by the MNC. The only other party launched among the Mongo, the UNIMO (Union Mongo), was a late comer on the political scene (1960) and attracted only marginal loyalty among the Mongo and Nkundo of the Equator Province. The full significance of this penetration comes from the fact that tribes belonging to the Mongo family are found in all provinces except Katanga, a fact which has led some observers to conclude that "if the provincial boundaries had been drawn in such a way as to include the Ba-Mongo within a single province, MNC-Lumumba might never have emerged as a national party." [64]

On the whole, however, regional rather than purely tribal particularism seems to have been the keynote of Congolese political life. The parochial behavior of Congolese voters can largely be accounted for by their unfamiliarity with the issues at stake. To a great majority of them, the problems of independence—let alone the debates on federal versus unitary government or on the dual executive—were hopelessly puzzling. Thus the natural inclination of the newly enfranchised Congolese was to rely upon men whom they felt they could trust to represent them adequately, one of "their own kind" whenever possible.[65] Indeed, such patterns of voting behavior are common in the oldest and most sophisticated democracies; nor is there anything inherently wrong with this as long as it is matched by a capacity to transcend sectional motivations in favor of national interest—which is precisely what has been lacking among the new Congolese political class.

[64] *Ibid.*, p. 25. This assumption is partly invalidated, however, by the fact that elections were held on the basis of strict proportional representation. The MNC still would have been the largest single party in the House, although its position in the various provincial governments (and in the Senate) would have been much weaker.

[65] This tendency may have been enhanced by the fact that the Congolese people's only previous experience with the polls had been at the local government level.

Ethnic particularism has been most common and most turbulent among the largest groups. When it involves hundreds of thousands of persons, however, the dividing line between "tribalism" and nationalism—or national chauvinism—becomes a fine one. The Bakongo, for instance, with a population of over 1,200,000 and large sections of their people living in the neighboring territories of Angola and Congo-Brazzaville, can advance some reasonable claims to nationhood. It is worth mentioning, incidentally, that the ABAKO, which was the first party to develop separatist tendencies, was also the first to demand immediate independence. ABAKO's logical link between the two demands was that, if the rest of the country was not ready for emancipation, the Bakongo—who felt they were—should not be forced to mark time. This is virtually the antithesis of the CONAKAT'S brand of separatism.

An interesting side effect of the resurgence of interethnic frictions has been the more or less artificial revival in a number of regions of traditional (or even, in some cases, pseudo-traditional) institutions. Thus, in order to express their solidarity in their conflict with the Kasai Baluba, 115 Lulua chiefs and headmen decided to elect a Mwanangana (paramount chief) in August 1959, but, significantly, this was accompanied by the formation of an ethnocentric party, the Union des Paysans et Ruraux Progressistes. The Baluba themselves, after having launched their own secessionist South Kasai "state," gave themselves a Mulopwe (king) in the person of Albert Kalonji, who thereupon embarked upon a quasi-psychopathic resuscitation of tribal ritual. Similarly, in the northernmost districts of the Republic, the Azande have desultorily indulged in the project of "restoring" a Zande empire resting upon somewhat doubtful historical precedents.

The Growth and Effect of Cities

As in other parts of Africa, the Congolese cities have had upon the social structure the dual effect aptly summarized by Thomas Hodgkin: "Seen from one standpoint, they lead to a degradation of African civilisation and ethic; seen from another, they contain the germs of a new, more interesting and diversified, civilisation, with possibilities of greater liberty." [66] Unlike West Africa, the Congo had no pre-European urban communities, and its towns literally sprang up from the ground. Whether they owed their origin to commercial, industrial, or adminis-

[66] *Nationalism in Colonial Africa* (New York: New York University Press, 1957), p. 63.

trative factors—or to a combination of all three—Congolese towns
have had one common quality, the rapidity of their growth. No city
in central Africa has expanded so quickly as Léopoldville, whose
African population grew from 26,622 in 1935 to 367,979 in 1958. Other
towns have also shown a remarkable, if not quite as impressive, rate
of development, as will be seen from the following figures (or estimates) of the population of five Congolese cities in recent years:

	1935	1940	1946	1951	1955	1958
Léopoldville	26,622	46,884	110,280	221,757	332,230	367,979
Elisabethville	22,858	26,789	65,397	95,559	131,184	168,775
Stanleyville		15,500	22,000	35,000	60,742	74,936
Matadi	7,500	9,000	18,000	42,500	69,945	57,392
Luluabourg			10,000	20,000	47,049	56,432

In 1958, there were fifteen towns with a population of over 20,000
inhabitants, and 8.7 per cent of the total population lived in communities with an African population of over 10,000. These 1,178,865 persons, however, represented only a fraction of the more than 3,000,-
000 Africans who had left their traditional environment—a fact
which suggests that there were degrees in the process of urbanization. The full effect of this process was felt only by those Africans
who were immersed in the larger centers: these offered the widest
variety of new contacts and experiences; these were more thoroughly
exposed to European influences; these were hardest hit by the economic recession and the subsequent unemployment which affected
every seventh family in 1958; [67] these were the breeding ground of
virtually every political party in the country. Socialization followed a
unique process in urban environments, and the phenomenon of association acquired new dimensions. In fact, the very notion of ethnic
(or subethnic) associations as we currently know them is a direct
product of the urban milieu.[68]

Political groups (many of which, as previously noted, had more or
less direct links with earlier, nonpolitical, associations) had their deepest roots in the towns and an almost wholly urban leadership. Elisabethville and Jadotville bred the CONAKAT and its rival, the Cartel
Katangais, and Bukavu had the CEREA, but Léopoldville was the

[67] Compiled from statistics of registered unemployment in eight major cities. One
method of computation suggests that 12.8 per cent of the African population of
these communities was affected; another method gives a figure of 13.7 per cent.
At any rate, the actual number of unemployed persons was evidently much higher.
[68] See above, p. 47.

center from which most political formations took their start—even those which later failed to gain a footing in the city or in its adjacent areas. Indeed, it is a characteristic feature of the Congolese political scene that many parties which first appeared in Léopoldville were later transplanted to flourish in their founders' respective bailiwicks, whether or not these parties originally had a regional or tribal bias. Such was the case with the PSA, which grew its roots in the districts of Kwilu and Kwango; with the PUNA, which developed out of the conjunction of ASSORECO (an association of immigrants from the Middle Congo in Léopoldville) and of the FEDUNEQ (Fédération du Nord de l'Equateur, a local formation of the Ngombe in the Equator Province); with the MNC-Kalonji (originally conceived as a national party but later gradually reduced to the size of an exclusively ethnic party for the Kasai Baluba); and even for Patrice Lumumba's MNC, which never held more than a narrow beachhead in Léopoldville.

Another notable effect of the development of urban communities was the increased differentiation of embryonic social classes. The birth of an African entrepreneurial class is attested by the fact that 21,683 African business firms were operating in 1958, more than two-thirds of them in the two provinces of Léopoldville and Katanga. Most of these small businessmen—craftsmen of various descriptions, traders and shopkeepers, bar owners, jobbers, building or transport contractors, and so on—ran their firm singlehanded and with a minimal outlay of capital. With a few exceptions, their economic backbone was brittle and their credit almost nonexistent. Moreover, as they catered almost exclusively to a population whose purchasing power was precarious, they were particularly vulnerable to phases of economic contraction and, just as they had been mushrooming in the affluent years, many were wiped out when the African population felt the full impact of the recession. Yet, marginal as its existence might be, an African bourgeoisie was definitely in the making during the last decade of Belgian colonial rule.

Starting in 1954 (largely as a result of the impetus provided by Colonial Minister Buisseret, whose own Liberal Party appeals mainly to the Belgian middle class), a number of these small businessmen organized the Association des Classes Moyennes Africaines (ACMAF) with the intent to promote the economic interests of its members. The first issue it raised was one which all African entrepreneurs had had to face throughout the continent: credit. Few banks were willing to take the risk—or the administrative bother—to extend credit to Congolese businessmen who usually lacked adequate collateral. In response to their demands, the statutes of the Société de Crédit au Colonat et à l'Industrie (a public organization granting credit to "colons" and small businessmen) were amended so that it could extend its benefits to Africans; yet, in 1956, Africans were accorded only twenty-seven loans amounting together to a mere 1.1 per cent of the $10,-600,000 advanced by this organization during that year.

Shortly after the foundation of ACMAF, settlers' associations began patronizing African entrepreneurial groups—a fact which resulted in some material and organizational assistance but also in a measure of disrepute for these groups. Some of the connections established in this contest, however, had interesting sequels: thus, Moïse Tshombe (himself the owner of a chain of business establishments) was serving a term as president of the Katanga branch of ACMAF when the CONAKAT—of which he was elected chairman—was launched as a political party by the conjunction of an earlier ethnic association and a European settlers' group, the Union Katangaise. Another member of ACMAF having gained some national prominence is the association's former president, Victor Nendaka, onetime vice-president of the MNC, then (April 1960) leader of a dissident faction, who failed to be elected to public office but who nevertheless became (in spite of an earlier police record) the notorious head of the Internal Security Service after the fall of Patrice Lumumba.

The emergence of an African middle class was not limited to urban communities and, during the last decade of their rule, the colonial authorities attempted, with limited success, to encourage the development of a class of Congolese planters. As brought out earlier, however, the share of Africans in the production of cash crops has remained limited.[69] Accordingly, no equivalent of the social layer constituted by the cocoa farmers in Ghana or in the Ivory Coast has emerged in the Congo. Nor has any organization comparable to the Ivory Coast's Syndicat Agricole Africain crystallized, although there was recurrent protest against the arbitrary determination of prices by the joint action of oligopolistic companies and official marketing boards: the production of cotton, for instance, which had been compulsorily introduced

[69] The share of independent African producers (mainly rural) in the total value of the gross monetary national product was estimated in 1954 at 10.6 per cent and had been declining over the previous years (*Bulletin de la Banque Centrale du Congo Belge et du Ruanda-Urundi*, quoted in Bézy, *Problèmes structurels*).

into the territory, was practically in the hands of the Compagnie Cotonnière Congolaise (COTONCO) and of the Comité de Gestion de la Caisse de Réserve (COGERCO).

The Proletariat and Trade Unions

By far the most significant social phenomenon in recent years has been the growth of an African proletariat. From 292,000 in 1925, the Congolese labor force had increased to 1,183,000 in 1955, and its incidence on the country's manpower resources had grown from 13.6 to 38.9 per cent over the same period, a higher proportion than that which was registered in any other sub-Saharan territory with the exception of South Africa and the Rhodesias. Accordingly, wages accounted for 69 per cent of the monetary income of the country's African population in 1954. Moreover, over half of the labor force employed by private firms worked in some 200 large enterprises using a manpower of 500 or more. Yet, despite circumstances normally conducive to the development of organized labor, only 60 unions existed in that same year of 1954, with a total membership barely exceeding 7,500.

This situation was due in part to the statutory limitations imposed upon the formation of labor unions. Unions of European employees had been organized as early as 1920, but their initial militancy was soon curbed by big business groups. As a matter of fact, it was the breaking of a strike of white railroad engineers which led for the first time to the training of African locomotive operators (a feature often hailed in later years as a proof of Belgian enlightenment). In any event, these European unions, like their counterparts in Southern Africa, were strongly opposed to the enrollment of African members. The right of Africans to unionize was not conceded until 1946 and, even then, with such restrictions (for example, the colonial authorities' right of access to all meetings and records of the unions) as to make it virtually impossible for organizations to develop freely. Strikes remained illegal until 1959.

Another factor inhibiting unions was the policy of many large firms of stabilizing their African manpower by encouraging the settlement of whole families or the importation of spouses (quite the opposite of the policy long practiced on the neighboring Copperbelt) and by providing their employees with adequate housing. Thus, after World War II, the Union Minière (the most notable promoter of this policy as well as the largest employer) was able to limit its yearly recruitment to no more than 3 per cent of its labor force, and by 1952, more than half of its employees had been with the firm for at least ten years.

The first unions which appeared in 1946 were sponsored by the Belgian Christian Democratic labor federation, the Confédération des Syndicats Chrétiens (CSC), and by 1954, 50 of the 60 unions in existence were affiliated with its Congolese branch, the CSCC. On the other hand, the Association du Personnel Indigène de la Colonie (APIC), the organization of African public employees which was also founded in 1946, had some superficial ties with the Belgian Liberal Party (some of its leading members, like Pinzi or Lumumba, were associated with Liberal *amicales*) but managed on the whole to remain unattached to any metropolitan group. Socialist unions, sponsored by the Fédération Générale du Travail de Belgique (FGTB), did not appear until after the advent of the Socialist-Liberal coalition government in the metropole. Their emergence, which Catholic unions tended to regard as an intrusion, touched off a considerable degree of emulation, resulting in a notable growth of organized labor after 1956.[70]

As independence drew near, all labor organizations (except APIC, which had always been wholly Congolese) hastened to africanize their cadres. In April 1960, within four days of each other, the CSCC and the FGTBC changed their names respectively to Union des Travailleurs Congolais (UTC) and Fédération Générale du Travail du Kongo (FGTK). The former became affiliated with the International Confederation of Christian Trade Unions as an autonomous movement, while the latter joined the International Confederation of Free Trade Unions. In the meantime, however, two new labor federations had been created. One, the Union Nationale des Travailleurs Congolais (UNTC, founded April 3, 1959), had a distinctly radical flavor, and many of its leading members were subsequently associated with the Gizenga "government in exile" at Stanleyville. The other, the Syndicat National des Travailleurs Congolais (SNTC, founded December 31, 1959), was directly sponsored by the ICFTU (and possibly by the American labor movement). After independence, the SNTC tried to foster an integration of all forces of labor and, although the UTC and the UNTC not surprisingly refused to join, the FGTK and the APIC (now renamed Association des Patriotes Indépendants du Congo) agreed to participate in the formation of a Confédération des Syndicats Libres du Congo (CSLC, founded April 10, 1961), which

[70] By the end of 1959, the CSCC claimed a membership of 55,682.

affiliated with the ICFTU. Later, however, the FGTK began to have second thoughts and withdrew from the CSLC in February 1962, although both organizations are still concurrently recognized by the ICFTU.[71]

Congolese labor unions, which had major social issues to fight for, played a comparatively minor part on the political scene before independence, although a few of its leaders made a political career (the most notable is, of course, the present Prime Minister, Cyrille Adoula, who was the secretary-general of FGTK). The more radical wing of the FGTK also sponsored a small political formation, the Action Socialiste, from which a minor party, the Parti du Peuple, was later derived.[72]

Since independence, the role of labor has been more complex and, in the political vacuum created by the breakdown of organized authority, some of its actions have tended to assume political dimensions. Thus, the UTC-led march of unemployed workers upon the parliament building, in mid-August 1960, was presumably part of the anti-Lumumbist campaign which culminated with the Prime Minister's dismissal. Similarly, the understandable bitterness generated by the spectacle of graft and profiteering in public circles may have been channeled by the UTC toward political agitation during the spring of 1962, and the charges to this effect by Adoula and by the Minister of the Interior, Kamitatu, were probably not completely unfounded. It seems unlikely, however, that the labor movement can seriously undermine the position of the legal government if the latter succeeds in restoring its authority and in securing national reunification.

The Effect of the Missions

Perhaps one of the most lasting forms of acculturation generated by the European presence in the Congo will have been that which accompanied the penetration of Christianity, and particularly of Roman Catholicism. Although the Berlin Act implied that equal treatment should be extended to all Christian missions, the Free State gave special encouragement to Catholic agencies and especially, in view of the early influence of French orders such as the Pères Blancs, to

[71] This is contrary to the ICFTU's normal practice of recognizing only one affiliated organization per territory, and it has evinced some bitterness from the Belgian Socialist labor circles which fostered the FGTK.

[72] The influence wielded by the Parti du Peuple, however, was somewhat larger than its electoral record might suggest, owing chiefly to the quality of its printed vehicle, *Emancipation*, one of the most articulate newspapers edited by Congolese.

Belgian missionary congregations, notably the Missions de Scheut. A concordat signed with the Vatican in 1906 entrenched the preponderance of Catholic missions, and after assuming power in the Congo, the Belgian authorities virtually confirmed this situation by restricting the grant of subsidies to "national" missions. It was not until 1948 that these differentiations were finally removed.

The growth of Christianity (under every denomination) has been impressive, although there is, of course, no way of ascertaining how deeply it may be rooted. The number of Catholic converts increased sevenfold between 1930 and the time of independence, while the Protestant community expanded nearly six times over the same period. By 1958, nearly 40 per cent of the population was supposedly Christian, as will be seen from Table 10.

Table 10. Penetration of Christianity *

	Catholic	Protestant	Total
Number of mission stations	669	297	966
Non-African personnel	5,904	1,653	7,557
African personnel	1,536 †	1,195	2,731
African cathechizers	25,566	14,728	40,294
Christian population	4,546,160	825,625	5,371,785

* The figures are those advanced by the churches themselves and are quoted in the *Rapport* for 1958.
† This includes 366 African priests.

But the impact of Christianity did not remain wholly contained by the missions' sedate teachings. As elsewhere in Africa, messianic movements and "native" separatist churches appeared on various occasions in different parts of the territory. Whether or not they had—as seems likely—some of their roots in pre-European beliefs, they are certainly "in the main to be regarded as contact and reaction phenomena arising from the shock constituted by the meeting between two cultures." [73] Some of these movements (like that which centered around the female seer Maria Nkoi, better known as "Marie aux Léopards," among the Nkundo of the Equatorial region in 1915) had virtually nothing to do with Christianity, but most of them revolved, consciously or unconsciously, around the belief that the teachings of Christ could be meaningful for Africa only if they were directly revealed to one of its sons.

[73] Efraim Andersson, *Messianic Popular Movements in the Lower-Congo* (Upsala: Almqvist & Wiksells, 1958), p. 258.

Among the earliest and most successful movements of this kind was the one which developed in the Lower Congo from the healing and preaching practiced during the year 1921 by Simon Kimbangu. Although Kimbangu himself was soon arrested [74] and eventually died in prison at Elisabethville in 1950, the movement did not disappear, and even tried to chasten itself by attempting to eliminate some of the most emotional forms of worship—such as trances and quaking—which had gradually perverted it. On Christmas Eve, 1959, the Belgian authorities finally lifted their ban on "Kimbangism," and the church is now legally organized under the somewhat lengthy name of Eglise de Jésus-Christ sur la Terre par le Prophète Simon Kimbangu. Although its early conceptions of the millennium implied the departure of the whites,[75] the Kimbangist movement was content to wait for God to take care of this detail, and it does not seem to have taken, as such, any significant part in the struggle for political emancipation. Yet it doubtlessly sustained among many Bakongo a spirit of passive resistance to the colonial authorities which later proved to be, as mentioned earlier, one of the most effective weapons used by the ABAKO. Nor is Kimbangism unrelated to the emergence of a Bakongo national sentiment; indeed, a common belief associated with movement (although it never was expressed by the prophet himself) was that Kimbangu would "ascend the ancient throne of Kongo." The fact that Kimbangu's eldest son, Charles Kisolokele, a member of ABAKO, has been one of the very few political figures to have retained ministerial office uninterruptedly from the day of independence until July 1962 may be interpreted as an attempt to propitiate an important special interest group.[76] The present Finance Minister, Senator Bamba, is also a prominent member of the Kimbangist church.

Other nativistic cults spread into southeastern Congo via the Rhodesias. Such was the case of the Watch Tower movement (Jehovah's Witnesses), born in America and first introduced into Katanga in 1926 by "Mwana Leza" (son of God), a native of Nyasaland residing in Northern Rhodesia. However, Kitawala ("Ki-" is a Bantu prefix and

[74] He was sentenced to death but, despite demands from the local settlers that he be hanged, he was not executed.

[75] An interesting hymn of the early Kimbangist period ran: "The land, aye, the land shall change. In sooth,/ The apostles of this idea shall rise / On the day appointed by the Lord. / Let everyone relinquish his raiment of mourning / And take instead the white raiment of joy! / Hope! the whites shall go away presently / This is the last tax we pay!"

[76] The "pope" of the Kimbangist church, however, is Simon Kimbangu's third son, Joseph Diangienda.

"-tawala" is an African rendition of "tower") did not really take root in Katanga until 1930, but it soon extended northward throughout the eastern portion of the territory. The deportation of some Kitawala members in northern Maniema in the late thirties also seems to have been responsible for the spread of the movement in the northeast, notably among the Bakumu where a rather serious rebellion, led by one Bushiri known as "Jesus' deputy" (Muluomozi wa Yezu) and by his assistant Hallelujah, occurred in 1944. In recent years, the South African Apostolic Church has also seeped into Katanga, where it is commonly known under the name of Ba-apostolo.[77]

Despite the inroads made by such para-Christian movements, the established churches have undoubtedly exercised and retained a vivid influence in the Congo. Perhaps the chief implement of this permeation has been the virtual monopoly held by religious agencies in the field of education. The Congo has acquired notoriety for its lack of university-trained elites, but its rate of elementary schooling was among the highest in Africa (56 per cent of the school-age population in 1959). In fact, however, this last figure requires some additional qualifications. The first two grades account for 64 per cent of the total elementary school population, and 12,408 of the country's 15,971 primary schools offer only these two grades. More important still is the fact that half of the children leave school forever after having attended only these two years. The school population rapidly thins out in the successive grades, so that in 1960 only 9 per cent of those who had entered school six years earlier finally completed the entire elementary school program.

This process is intensified at the secondary school level, which was attended in 1959 by 37,388 students (some 4,000 of whom were non-Africans), that is, 2.2 per cent of the elementary school population.[78] Higher education in the Congo itself was being extended to 1,445 students (including some 350 non-Africans) on the eve of independence. The two Congolese universities at Léopoldville and Elisabethville were attended by 420 African students, but an even greater num-

[77] The Muslim population was estimated in 1958 at 115,500, located in various centers along the Lualaba (Upper Congo) between Stanleyville and the northern border of Katanga. Eighty-three per cent of it was concentrated in the two southernmost *territoires* of the Maniema district.

[78] Besides the secondary school cycle, there are also some postelementary schools which lead nowhere and are now in the process of being gradually suppressed. The figures are from *Où en est l'enseignement au Congo?* quoted by B. Verhaegen in *Etudes Congolaises*, vol. III, no. 6 (June–July 1962).

ber of Congolese were being trained for priesthood in Catholic
seminaries. Indeed, the latter form of training had for many years
been the Africans' only access to higher education, and it is therefore hardly surprising that many of the present political leaders—
including notably Kasavubu, Gizenga, Kamitatu (the former president
of the Léopoldville provincial government, later the Minister of the
Interior), and Munongo (Katanga's Interior Minister, often nicknamed
the "strong man" of the Tshombe regime)—have studied for various
lengths of time in these seminaries. The enrollment at the different
levels of education in the year 1959 is summarized in Table 11.

Table 11. School enrollment

	Catholic	Protestant	Government	Companies	Total
Elementary schools	1,262,648	312,570	57,204	11,625	1,644,047
Postelementary (terminal)	18,268	2,561	1,951		22,780
Secondary schools	27,000	2,200	7,300		36,500
Higher education *					1,445

* Breakdown not available.

THE PRESS

The lack of a coherent and dynamic African press has been one of
the most characteristic features (and one of the severest shortcomings) of Congolese nationalism. In 1959, the country's nine daily newspapers (all of them in French) were financially and editorially in the
hands of Europeans and were published in the main centers of white
population (two in Léopoldville, two in Stanleyville, one in Bukavu,
and four in Katanga). Today, Léopoldville's only remaining daily, the
Courrier d'Afrique, is staffed by Africans, but it retains close connections (financial and otherwise) with the Belgian Christian-Democratic
labor movement which launched it and, despite some professions of
faith to the contrary, it has frequently tended to be strangely com-
placent toward the Katangese secession. During the summer of 1962,
the government attempted (with little success) to launch a rival daily,
Le Progrès. In Elisabethville, on the other hand, the major daily,
L'Essor du Katanga (formerly known as *L'Essor du Congo* and so
renamed after the secession), stands extremely close to the Tshombe
regime and may be considered its semiofficial mouthpiece.

Since independence the African political press has been multifarious in its tendencies, exuberant in numbers, but limited in circulation, irregular in frequency, generally short-lived, and rather heavily weighted in a conservative direction. The list in Table 12, while not complete, includes the most notable political periodicals which are, or have been, published in the Republic (excluding Katanga).

The Political Process

THE FORMAL STRUCTURE

The Congolese constitution has the usual quality of not having drawn up by the Congolese themselves. Indeed, there is as yet no constitution in the purely formal sense of this word but, in its place, a transitional instrument voted by the Belgian parliament, the *loi fondamentale* of May 19, 1960. True, this constitutional statute was largely based upon the recommendations of the Round Table conference of January–February 1960, in which Congolese delegates took a leading part, but the text finally voted by the Belgian legislature did not exactly duplicate the resolutions of the conference and, besides, the mandate of these delegates (who were selected by the Belgian authorities) was not derived from any valid consultation of the Congolese people.

Since no general election had yet been held when the Belgian authorities decided to hold negotiations with Congolese representatives concerning the timetable and modalities of the colony's political emancipation, the most logical criterion for selecting these representatives seemed to be the local government elections which were to take place in December 1959. This assumption, however, was extremely dubious, first because a number of parties, notably ABAKO, PSA, and ABAZI, had announced their intention to boycott these elections for various reasons [79] and also because such a procedure would have amounted to a complete distortion of the significance and issues of a local government election. A compromise solution was eventually adopted, and the 45 Congolese delegates fell into four groups. The traditional chiefs had 11 seats; the moderate, administration-supported PNP, which had not fared badly at the polls, received 11 seats; the cartel of federalist parties based in Léopoldville (ABAKO–PSA–MNC Kalonji–Parti du Peuple–ABAZI–FGC), which had boycotted the elections, was also awarded 11 seats; and the remaining parties (eight in

[79] The absention was observed almost unanimously in the two Bakongo districts and in the district of Kwilu.

Table 12. The political press *

	Political affiliation	Frequency	Circulation	Began publication	Ceased publication
Notre Kongo	ABAKO	F	3,000	1959	x
Kongo Dieto (Kikongo version)	ABAKO	F	?	1959	x
Kongo Dia Ngunga	ABAKO-Nzeza Landu	I	?	1953	1960
Kongo Dia Ntotila (successor)	ABAKO-Nzeza Landu	I	?	1960	1961
Fédération Congolaise (successor)	RAFECO †	I	2,000	1961	x
Le (Démocrate) Kongolais	ABAKO	M	2,000	1961	x
Muisi-Kongo (Kikongo version)	ABAKO	M	?	1962	x
L'Echo du Bas-Congo	ABAKO	M	3,000	1961	x
Vigilance	ABAKO Youth Movt.	I	?	1960	1960
Présence Congolaise ‡	Indep.-MNC-K	W	3,000	1956	x
La Voix du Peuple	MNC-K	F	?	1959	1962
Liberté	PNP		?	1959	1960
Le Vrai Visage	PNP-Eastern Prov.	W	?	1962	x
La Nation Congolaise	PUNA		?	1960	1960
Actualités Africaines	Indep. pro-Mobutu	W	?	1960	x
La Relève	RNJC §	I	500	1962	1962
Bantous	Indep.	F	?	1961	1961
Afrique Réelle	Pro-Adoula	F	?	1962	1962
Solidarité Africaine	PSA	F	3,000	1959	1961
Dignité Nouvelle	CEREA-Bisukiro		?	1961	x
La Vérité	CEREA-Kashamura	I	3,000	1960	1962

Emancipation	Indep. socialist	W	3,000	1959	x
Indépendance	MNC	W	?	1959	1960
Uhuru (Swahili version)	MNC	W	?	1960	x
Le Matin	MNC	F	2,000	1961	1962
La Semaine	MNC	W	2,000	1961	1962
Congo ||	Indep.-MNC	W/D	?	1957/9	1960
Notre Droit	UTC (labor union)	F	?	?	x
Le Travailleur Kongolais	CSLC (labor union)	F	?	1961	x
Le Combat	APIC (labor union)	F	?	?	x

* The list is from "La press à Léopoldville" in *Etudes Congolaises*, vol. III, no. 5 (May 1962). All these periodicals except two (*Uhuru* and *Dignité Nouvelle*) are published in Léopoldville. An "x" in the last column indicates that the periodical was still being published in June 1962. Frequency of publication is indicated as follows: D = Daily; W = Weekly; F = Fortnightly; M = Monthly; I = Irregular. These designations do not necessarily mean, however, that the periodical in question has followed its publication schedule regularly. Circulation figures are those advanced by the publications themselves.

† RAFECO (Rassemblement Fédéral Congolais) is a dissidence from ABAKO launched in May 1961 by Edmond Nzezalandu, the founder of ABAKO. *Kongo Dia Ngunga* and its successor were written in the dialect of the Bantandu (a Bakongo subgroup), while *Kongo Dieto* is chiefly written in the Manianga dialect.

‡ Originally a weekly supplement to the *Courrier d'Afrique*. It became autonomous in 1958, under the editorship of José Ngalula, who was Prime Minister, then Vice-President in the "state" of South Kasai until July 1961 but subsequently broke away from Kalonji.

§ Rassemblement National de la Jeunesse Congolaise.

|| *Congo* appeared first in 1957 and was suspended during that same year by the Belgian authorities. It reappeared in November 1959 and continued as a weekly. After independence, it supported Lumumba's government and briefly became a daily but was suppressed after Lumumba fell from power.

all) shared 12 seats.[80] As it turned out, however, this allocation of seats had relatively little importance, since during the negotiations all delegations agreed to form a united front (which was only partially effective) and since one of the very first rules of procedure adopted by the conference specified that resolutions would be voted upon by each of the eleven delegations acting as a whole and casting a single ballot.

The final resolutions of the conference were of two kinds. A first group dealt with the transferring of sovereignty to the new state: it named the date of independence, provided for some African participation in the colonial executive during the transitional period, and guaranteed that Belgium would retain no "reserve powers" in the future republic—a point which was underlined by a specific recommendation that a Belgo-Congolese treaty of friendship and assistance should be signed only after independence had been achieved.[81] A second group of resolutions was devoted to the political institutions and to the internal organization of the future state. In this field, however, while virtual unanimity was reached on a number of matters or principles (for example, the establishment of a bicameral legislature, with a House of Representatives based upon direct and proportional representation of the people and a Senate in which each of the six provinces would be equally represented; the restriction of the franchise to males of Congolese descent aged 21 or more; the endowment with constituent powers of the first congress, acting jointly; the insertion of a section on rights and liberties in the future constitution), no firm agreement was arrived at on such vital questions as the allocation of competence between the central and provincial governments, the possibility of creating new provinces after independence (although there was a fairly widespread agreement that they could not be created before), the internal organization of the provinces, or the extent of representation to be granted to the traditional chiefs in the central and provincial institutions.

The Fundamental Law

The resolutions of the Round Table conference found their way into the bill which was submitted to the Belgian parliament and

[80] MNC-Lumumba, 3; CONAKAT and ARP, 2 each; Cartel Katangais, CEREA, PUNA, UNIMO, and Union Congolaise, 1 each. In the May 1960 elections to the House of Representatives, these parties together gained 80 seats out of 137. The PNP and the chiefs had 24.

[81] Resolutions no. I, IV, V (partly), XII, and XIII.

which finally became the *loi fondamentale.* Yet quite a few of the
problems on which the conference had failed to reach a general agreement were left unsolved by the interim constitution. Thus, Section 107
offered a choice between a direct and an indirect procedure in the
election of the members of the provincial legislatures; similarly, it
was left for the senators themselves to decide whether they wanted
to enlarge the Senate by co-opting additional members and whether
there should be six or twelve of these supernumary Solons (Section
87); again, the transitional provincial executive councils were given
the task of resolving whether the number of traditional chiefs and
"notables" to be co-opted by the provincial assemblies should be 10
or 15 per cent of the assembly's membership. Nor was the thorny
dispute between the advocates of a federal state and those who favored a unitary form of government untangled. The Republic was to
have a federal type of Senate (the senators being selected by the
provincial assemblies and each province being awarded equal representation). The cabinet was to include at least one minister from
each province, and an independent jurisdiction was to arbitrate conflicts between the national and provincial governments concerning
their respective competence. On the other hand, the central government was to be represented in each province by a state commissioner
(appointed with the Senate's approval and after consultation with the
president of the provincial government) whose normal function was to
supervise the agencies of the national government operating in the
province but who could also, under certain circumstances, adjourn
the provincial assembly for a maximum period of one month, convene an extraordinary session, dissolve the legislature upon the provincial government's request, or even supplant the provincial authorities altogether when these refused to perform some of their statutory
functions.[82]

The respective spheres of competence of the national and provincial
governments were not wholly demarcated. Sections 219 and 220
enunciated the matters which fell respectively within the exclusive
jurisdiction of the national and of the provincial authorities,[83] but
mutual transfers of competence were possible (Sections 210 and 211).

[82] Secs. 134, 135, 138, 139, and 180 through 184.
[83] The provincial sphere of competence notably covered education (with the
exception of higher education), the granting of mining concessions (within the
rules of a national policy), local roads, railroads, and public works, the exploitation of hydroelectric resources designed to cover provincial needs, and the establishment of a provincial police force.

Furthermore, both the national parliament and the provincial assemblies could freely legislate upon those matters which were not enumerated in the list of their exclusive powers. In other words, such matters were subject to the concurrent jurisdiction of the central and provincial authorities, with the sole restriction that provincial statutes (*édits*) had to yield precedence to national legislation (Section 209).

The *loi fondamentale* did introduce a number of provisions, however, which either departed from the Round Table's resolutions or dealt with matters that had not been touched upon by the conference. In general, these innovations tended to slant the interim constitution along a federalist and conservative bias and to buttress the powers of the President of the Republic, whose status was normally comparable to that of a French President under the Third Republic or to that of a desacralized constitutional monarch. Thus, Section 100 took up the suggestion made by a minority of Congolese delegates at the Round Table conference that, after having been voted by the constituent congress, the future constitution should be approved by the provincial assemblies, a decidedly federalistic feature. Section 87 (1) specified that the fourteen senators to be elected from each province should include at least three traditional chiefs, a point which had been hotly contested during the conference and which had divided the delegates almost evenly.[84]

The powers conferred upon the President of the Republic pertained, however, to a different order of problems. Unfamiliar as it may be to an American audience, the notion of a dual executive, it should be remembered, is an essential component of most Western European political systems, where it has been a product of the transition from absolute monarchy to a modern parliamentary regime. The *loi fondamentale* mirrored this constitutional philosophy by providing for a politically immune head of state—the President of the Republic—along with a responsible cabinet ("government" in the European terminology) headed by a Prime Minister. The powers of the President of the Republic (for example, to appoint and dismiss the Prime Minister and the members of the cabinet, to pronounce the dissolution of the legislative bodies, to head the armed forces, to make appointments in the senior ranks of the civil service, or to commission officers, etc.) were modeled after those of Belgium's constitutional King,

[84] Six delegations (out of eleven) supported the solution which was to be cast in Sec. 87 (1). The general elections, however, gave these six groups only one-third of the popular vote.

and—as is the case in Belgium—they could not be exercised without a
ministerial countersign intended to safeguard the President's lack of
political responsibility (Section 20). In the European parliamentary
democracies, however, a subtle but effective tradition governs the relationship between the chief of state and the head of the cabinet (whatever their respective titles may be). Thus, the chief of state's function
is normally regarded as nonpartisan, and any attempt on his part to
use his powers, even though they may be formally spelled out as
personal prerogatives, in contradiction to a policy defined by the
cabinet and endorsed by the legislature would almost invariably be
considered as a violation—or at least as a serious distortion—of constitutional usage. No such built-in system of checks and balances was
injected into the *loi fondamentale* although it is not unreasonable to
surmise that the Belgian lawmakers, when they patterned Congolese
institutions after those of their own country, expected them to operate
along similar lines. Thus, when a conflict arose between President
Kasavubu and Prime Minister Lumumba, the former felt empowered
to resolve the deadlock in a manner which would have been considered unacceptable in a parliamentary democracy, that is, by dismissing the Premier and six members of his cabinet, although Patrice
Lumumba still appeared to enjoy the support of the Congolese parliament.[85]

National Institutions

The Congolese institutions, as contained in the *loi fondamentale,*
may be schematized as follows. The people (or at least the adult
male population, since woman suffrage has not been introduced) elect
directly the members of the House of Representatives as well as those
of their respective provincial assemblies. The basis of representation
for the House are the twenty-four administrative districts into which
the country is divided, the only exceptions being Léopoldville, which
constitutes an autonomous electoral circumscription, and the two
Katangese cities of Elisabethville and Jadotville, which are lumped
together to form another one. Each of these twenty-six electoral districts returned a number of representatives equivalent to as many
times 100,000 inhabitants as the population of that district contains
(with an additional representative for each remainder larger than
50,000). This system provides an almost perfect proportional repre-

[85] Two days after Lumumba's demotion, the House "nullified" it by a vote of
60 to 19 (out of 137 members) and the Senate followed suit by a vote of 41 to 2
with 6 members abstaining (out of a total membership of 84).

sentation, as will be seen from the comparison in Table 13 between the number of seats to be filled from each province and the population figures as of December 31, 1959.

Table 13. Apportionment of seats in the House of Representatives

	No. of seats	Pop. (Dec. 31, 1959)
Léopoldville	33	3,189,286
Equator	18	1,801,632
Eastern	25	2,473,633
Kivu	23	2,261,822
Katanga	16	1,654,176
Kasai	22	2,158,633
Total	137	13,539,182

The membership of the provincial assemblies depends upon the province's population: 60 if the population is less than two million; 70 if it is between two and two and one-half million; 80 if it stands between two and one-half and three million; and 90 if it is above three million. Thus, as the above figures indicate, the provincial assembly of Léopoldville has 90 members, those of the Eastern Province, Kivu, and Kasai each have 70, and those of the Equator Province and Katanga have 60. Within each province, the seats are allotted between the various *territoires* on a proportional basis. The elected councilors co-opt additional members (10 or 15 per cent of the assembly's original membership) from the traditional authorities of the province.

Being thus enlarged, each provincial assembly then proceeds to select 14 senators after having decided how many of these would be chosen among the traditional chiefs (the minimum number being three). The 84 indirectly elected senators may in turn decide to co-opt a maximum of 12 additional members, provided that they are selected in equal numbers from each province (which means that the number of additional senators could only be 6 or 12). The process of co-optation takes place in a plenary session of the Senate, but each senator may vote only for the man (or men) to be added to the delegation from his province.[86]

Both the Senate and the House elect their presidents,[87] vice-presi-

[86] The first Senate has not used this prerogative.

[87] The first president of the House of Representatives was Joseph Kasongo (MNC), while the first president of the Senate was Joseph Ileo (MNC-Kalonji but elected to represent UNIMO). At the end of 1962, the presidents of the House

dents, secretaries, etc. The president of the Senate, however, has no deliberative vote (Section 95). The Senate and the House hold their session simultaneously and have identical legislative capacity, with no procedure to resolve a deadlock, which means that a bill may shuttle back and forth endlessly between the two chambers without the possibility for a joint conference committee to iron out differences. Bills may be initiated by members of either house or by the government (that is, formally, by the President but with ministerial countersign); once adopted by parliament, they must be sanctioned and promulgated by the President of the Republic (Section 28). Here, again, is a provision borrowed from the Belgian constitution (with equivalents in other parliamentary systems) which has worked smoothly in its European context but which, in the absence of a lubricating tradition of noninterference on the part of the head of state, may be conducive to serious frictions, since it literally implies that the President holds an absolute veto over all legislation.

Aside from its legislative function, the Congolese parliament (in conformity with the nature of parliamentary government) exercises political control over the Premier and his cabinet. Although the President formally appoints all ministers, no cabinet may wield executive authority until it has been invested by an absolute majority vote in both chambers. Conversely, no cabinet may continue in power after a successful motion of nonconfidence carried either by an absolute majority in each of the two houses or by a two-thirds majority of those present in either of the two (Sections 42 and 43). An individual minister may also be censured according to a similar procedure, which, however, does not entail the collective resignation of the cabinet.[88]

The House and the Senate meet in a joint session to choose the President of the Republic. Since it was intended to be no more than a transitional instrument, the *loi fondamentale* did not specify the length of the President's term of office, nor did it concern itself with the question of a second term. Indeed, a literal interpretation of the text suggests that, under the present system, a renewal of the Congolese parliament (as a result of dissolution, for instance) would normally imply a new presidential election. Incidentally, the "basic law" relied upon the future constitution to determine the date of the first

and Senate were respectively Bertin Mwamba (elected on a CONAKAT list but rallied to the Cartel opposition of North Katanga) and Isaac Kalonji (Cartel Katangais).

[88] Through 1962, parliament exercised only individual censure.

general elections to be held after independence and merely specified that the first legislature should not serve for more than four years or for less than three.

Provincial Institutions

The provincial assemblies, with their quota of traditional chiefs, are qualified to legislate upon all matters not exclusively attributed to the national authorities or already regulated by nationwide statutes. They also choose the president and members of the provincial governments. The provincial president is elected separately by an absolute majority of all members present. The members of the government (ten in number [89]) are selected by a different procedure: a single ballot is cast and each councilor votes for one man only, the members being chosen according to the number of votes they have received, no matter how few (Section 123). The system was intended to ensure a rough form of proportional representation in the formation of the provincial executives, since any political group holding at least one-tenth of the seats in the provincial assembly could hope (with proper voting discipline) to secure one post in the provincial government. This procedure, however, did not work as smoothly as had been expected. In several provinces, the councilors' appraisal of the situation was influenced by the notions of majority versus minority (which, incidentally, were those upon which the formation of the national government revolved), and various groups (the ABAKO in the province of Léopoldville, the MNC-Kalonji in Kasai, the Cartel Katangais in Katanga, the UNIMO in Equator) assumed—or were cast in—the role of a parliamentary opposition, which was not consonant with the system governing the election of the provincial governments. Thus, for various reasons, the ABAKO, the MNC-Kalonji, and the Cartel Katangais in their respective provinces walked out of the provincial assemblies as the provincial governments were being formed.[90] In the

[89] According to the *loi fondamentale* (Sec. 163), the number of provincial ministers may be anything from five to ten, but all provinces have adopted the maximal solution; Léopoldville province has even elected a provincial vice-president for whom there is no provision in the interim constitution.

[90] These tactics were adopted by ABAKO and the Cartel because the *loi fondamentale* originally required a two-thirds quorum for the co-optation of additional councilors (chiefs) and for the election of the provincial government. Both parties, having more than one-third of the seats in the provincial assembly (which was not the case of the MNC-K), thus were in a position to block these procedures. Those provisions were soon corrected, however, by a hastily voted amendment passed by the Belgian parliament, and the boycott was deprived of its value as an instrument of pressure.

provinces of Léopoldville and Kasai, however, the other parties agreed to leave three ministerial posts vacant for their disgruntled opponents when and if they decided to rejoin their colleagues (three seats is exactly what the MNC-K could expect to gain since it held exactly 21 seats out of 70; ABAKO, with 36.6 per cent of the seats in the provincial assembly could hope for four seats, which is what it finally got). But in Katanga, the CONAKAT and its allies showed no such courtesy toward the Cartel, and they elected a virtually homogeneous provincial government (9 CONAKAT, 1 MNC-K); this was, in a sense, the first formal step toward secession.

The Future of the Structure of Government

Although it still remains the basis of Congolese political institutions, the *loi fondamentale* never possessed the compelling authority of a true constitution which, in fact, it was not intended to be. Its transitional character, the fact that it was voted by the Belgian, not by the Congolese, parliament, and, finally, the very nature of its provisions, which were merely statutory and not entrenched like those of most constitutions and could therefore be altered by a simple act of parliament—all these factors helped corrode the prestige of the *loi fondamentale*. Some of its provisions, notably those instituting a Constitutional Court (Sections 226 through 237), have never been applied. Others have been ignored, like those which specify that, until the constitution has been voted, the parliament must remain in session during at least one hundred days each year or the second paragraph of Section 44, which rules that a cabinet continues to hold interim power until its successor has been invested.[91] Finally, the *loi fondamentale* has been amended by the Congolese legislature: notably, Section 7 stating that the Republic "is constituted by six provinces" has been amended by a law of March 9, 1962, which adds that a law may create other provinces (this is precisely what was done in 1962).[92]

How much of the *loi fondamentale* will eventually survive in the final version of the future constitution drafted for the Congolese government by an international team of jurists is a point for speculation.

[91] However, the Congolese parliament, meeting under UN protection during the summer of 1961, indirectly confirmed this rule when it passed a resolution specifying that the new Adoula government would be the legal successor of the Lumumba cabinet, thus denying constitutional existence to the two volatile cabinets headed by Joseph Ileo and to the improvised "College of General Commissioners"—none of which had ever received (or solicited) parliamentary investiture.

[92] The creation of these new provinces will be discussed in the section dealing with "The Problem of National Unity."

The national parliament is likely to be preserved under its present
bicameral form, although the Senate's membership and recruitment
will inevitably have to be adjusted to the situation created by the
partitioning of the six original provinces. The provincial institutions
may retain some of their existing features; a recent ordinance (June 1,
1962) has ruled that the legislatures of the new provinces would include those provincial councilors who were returned from the electoral
circumscriptions included within the boundaries of each new province,
but this cannot be more than a stopgap measure. Another moot point
of considerable moment is whether or not to retain the dual executive
introduced by the *loi fondamentale*. The example of the new independent states of Africa, all but one of which (Cameroun) have concentrated the functions of the head of state and those of head of the
government in the hands of one and the same person, point toward
the adoption of a presidential regime (which Lumumba already wanted
to introduce in 1960), but a question of personalities might impede the
emergence of this solution.

The United Nations, whose dead-center neutrality between the legal
and the self-appointed authorities of the country had so often assisted
the latter in the past, endorsed in mid-1962 the draft of a constitutional
project sponsored by the Adoula government. Secretary General Thant
let it be known that the acceptance of this blueprint by Katanga might
have to be secured by appropriate forms of pressure, diplomatic and
economic. The final draft of this project,[93] now awaiting ratification
by the national parliament, provides for a decidedly federalistic structure within which all powers not attributed exclusively to the federal
government or to the concurrent competence of federal and provincial
authorities are held by the provinces (Sections 40–42). Fiscal resources
are also to be reapportioned between the central and the provincial
governments in order to leave the local authorities with a noticeably
larger quota of such resources than was the case under the Belgian
regime (Section 178): indeed, such a sharing might result in making
the provincial authorities at Elisabethville more affluent than the central government and in institutionalizing—at least in part—their economic stranglehold over the whole republic. Katanga's surrender to
the UN troops, myth-shattering as it was, may not have fully exorcized
the demon of secession but, when all is said and done, its resuscitation

[93] The drafting group was headed by T. Olawale Elias, Chief Justice of Nigeria.
For an (abridged) version of the project and of the accompanying report, see
Etudes Congolaises, vol. III, no. 10 (Dec. 1962).

depends primarily (as was the case in the summer of 1960) on whether
or not an effective central government sits in Léopoldville, rather than
upon the rancor of nostalgic white circles in the Copper Province.

POLITICAL AND ELECTORAL DYNAMICS

Never in the history of African emancipation has the concept of
"political party" been used by so many with as little justification as in
the Congo during the years 1959 and 1960. The announcement by the
Belgian government of its new policy line in January 1959 unleashed
a proliferation of organizations which soon assumed bewildering proportions. Since many of these improvised groups exhibited a definite
propensity to split within a few weeks of their foundation, this rash
of self-styled "parties" continued to spread on a near-geometric ratio
until some hundred and fifty were in more or less theoretical existence
and the Léopoldville daily, *Courrier d'Afrique*, was forced to announce
that it had to give up publishing their manifestoes and counterprocla-
mations. Ethnic fragmentation was of course partly responsible for
this quick-fire multiplication of parties, but the main stimulus was
almost certainly the sudden relaxation of the colonial authorities' repressive attitude toward such formations, combined with the equally
sudden perspective of a political vacuum. However, virtually none of
the parties created out of sheer, unsophisticated opportunism managed
to gain a firm footing unless it was able to preempt the clientele of an
existing ethnic association. On the whole, at least three-quarters of the
popular votes went to organizations which could trace their origins,
directly or indirectly, prior to 1959.

Political Parties

No safe criteria exist to categorize the various Congolese political
parties, and few of them can be made to fit under any satisfying label.
Ideological characterizations are particularly hazardous while even the
indication of such broad trends as "progressive," "moderate," or "conservative" are largely irrelevant. Perhaps the least unsuitable method
of clearing a path through the dense growth of exuberant formations
is to take into account the nature of the appeal exercised by the various
organizations as well as the range of their territorial penetration. In
this perspective, the parties may be roughly raked up in four major
groups: ethnic, regional, interethnic, and national movements.

Parties explicitly or implicitly centered upon ethnic loyalties are by
far the most numerous and, in a majority of cases, the most deeply
rooted, but they are also the most sharply limited in scope as well as

in their prospects of future development. Their appeal is wholesale
and generally unencumbered by any doctrinal pretensions, although
it may rely heavily upon an apparel of historical or legendary reminis-
cences. By their very nature, they are normally all-inclusive and es-
chew any type of relationship or identification (whether in terms of
class consciousness or of occupational or educational background)
which might detract from the sense of ethnic community. Thus, even
though such organizations may demonstrate considerable drive in their
propagandizing or in the collection of funds,[94] the notion of membership is frequently taken for granted and, unless two formations are
competing within a given group or subgroup,[95] there is relatively little
insistence on the act of joining and on the voluntary aspect of association.

The ABAKO is the best known and probably the strongest of all such
parties, although Bakongo nationalism in itself is already the product
of a regional integration between various tribal groups (such as the
Bayombe, the Manianga, the Bandibu, the Bantandu—and the Bakongo
sensu stricto) whose dialects can be widely different.[96] Also in Léopoldville province, the Bayaka and the Bayanzi left the regional Fédération
Kwango-Kwiloise (itself affiliated with the interethnic Interfédérale)
and set up their own parties: the Bayaka, who felt that the political
arm of the Fédération Kwango-Kwiloise, the PSA, was too closely
associated with the party of their traditional Bakongo foes, founded
the LUKA (Union Kwangolaise pour l'Indépendance et la Liberté)
with the encouragement of the Kiamfu (Paramount Chief) Panzu
Fumunkulu and the active participation of members of his family and
entourage while the Bayanzi set up the Alliance des Bayanzi (ABAZI).
In the Equator Province, the UNIMO appealed (with partial success)
to the Mongo, the Association des Ngwaka to the Ngwaka (or
Ngbaka), and the MEDERCO (Mouvement pour l'Evolution et le
Développement de l'Economie Rurale du Congo), in spite of its sweep-
ingly general title, was virtually limited to the Ngbandi. In Kivu, the

[94] It has been estimated that ABAKO had sold as many as 800,000 contributory
cards at an average $1 apiece in the Bakongo areas, which have a total population
of approximately 1,200,000 (*Courrier Africain*, April 22, 1960).

[95] Thus, the Mongo had a choice between the UNIMO (Union Mongo) and the
Union des Mongo-Nkundu, while the Basonge were courted by a Mouvement de
l'Unité Basonge, a Parti de l'Unité Basonge, and a Fédération des Basonge, operating in different locations.

[96] For example, the dialect spoken by President Kasavubu, who is a native of
Mayombe, is not easily understood by the Bantandu who constitute by far the
largest Bakongo subgroup in Léopoldville.

UNERGA (Union des Warega, or Union des Enfants de Lega) was clearly designed to win the allegiance of the Walega—which it did only to a certain extent—while the Union des Babembe de Fizi (UNEBAFI), which allied itself with the MNC, was directed at the Babembe (or Wabembe), a tribe living near the southern tip of Lake Tanganyika. In Katanga, the majority of the local Baluba (as opposed to the Luba immigrants from Kasai) organized the BALUBAKAT, which took part in the foundation of the regional and intertribal CONAKAT but left in November 1959, partly because of CONAKAT's mounting hostility toward the Kasai Baluba.[97] Another ethnic organization, the ATCAR (Association des Tshokwe du Congo, de l'Angola et de la Rhodésie)—which, in spite of its pantribal tag, was restricted to the Katanga Tshokwe—also kept aloof from the CONAKAT, because it regarded it as being dominated by the Tshokwe's traditional antagonists, the Balunda. In Kasai, the bitter climax reached by ethnic dissensions led the various tribal movements to seek tactical alliances: the Mouvement Solidaire Muluba virtually swamped the Kasai branch of the MNC-Kalonji, while Lumumba's own MNC attracted the support of the Mouvement Politique des Kanioka, of the Mouvement de l'Unité Basonge, and of the Lulua party, the Union Nationale Congolaise (UNC). The UNC itself, which had been hatched in the nest of the Kasai branch of an early but ill-fated national party, the Union Congolaise, was in fact the end product of a concentration process involving the Lulua's ethnic organization, the Association des Lulua-Frères, and its political vehicle, the Union des Paysans et Ruraux Progressistes.

Regional parties have usually been the offspring of urban associations. Indeed, the very notion of a "region" (rather than that of a tribal area) as a focus for political loyalty was in itself a characteristic product of the urban centers, where immigrants who came from the same general area and who were not numerous enough to form recognizable ethnic communities were commonly lumped together (both in terms of housing and in terms of their everyday identification by their neighbors) as being "the people from upstream" (*les gens du haut*), "the people from Kasai," "the people from Kwilu," etc. Linguistic kinship helped cement these links, which, in associational terms, frequently took the

[97] The Kasai Baluba follow matrilineal patterns of descent and speak Tshiluba while the Katanga Baluba follow a patrilineal system and speak a different dialect (Kiluba), but they still have enough in common to feel a certain degree of solidarity with each other.

form of "confederations" of ethnic organizations. Thus, in Léopoldville, the so-called "Bangala" had organized the Liboke lya Bangala
(whose political arm was the Front de l'Unité Bangala), while, on a
slightly higher level, the "people from upstream" congregated within
the ASSORECO. Natives of the Kwango and Kwilu districts formed
the above-mentioned Fédération Kwango-Kwiloise, those from Kivu
were associated in a Fédération du Kivu-Maniema, and the immigrants
from Kasai had their Fédération du Kasai, which had its counterpart
in Elisabethville under the title of FEDEKA. The CONAKAT itself
(as its name indicates) was originally a regional confederation of tribal
associations purporting to gather the "authentic" Katangese, and particularly the tribes of Upper Katanga; among its component organizations were the FETRIKAT (Fédération des Tribus du Haut-Katanga)
and the GASSOMEL (Groupement des Associations Mutuelles de
l'Empire Lunda). In this context, it is worth mentioning that neither
of the two major ethnic groups of Katanga, the Lunda and the Katanga
Baluba, can claim Elisabethville as being part of its traditional territory.

These regional associations fought the first municipal elections which
in turn led to new coalitions: thus, as will be recalled, all non-Bakongo
groups in Léopoldville combined into a loose alliance named the Interfédérale des Groupes Ethniques. But more important was the fact that
quite a few of the regional federations were transplanted (or simply
spread) into the Congolese hinterland as the prospect of a general
election drew near: for example, the Fédération Kwango-Kwiloise gave
birth to the Parti Solidaire Africain (PSA) and the ASSORECO to the
PUNA. In Kivu, the Centre de Regroupement Africain (CEREA),
which had been founded in 1958 at Bukavu, extended its action to the
whole of northern Kivu and (with less success) to southern Kivu and
Maniema, while the CONAKAT, having absorbed a small European
party (Achille Gavage's Union Katangaise), spread among the Balunda, Balamba, Batabwa, Bayeke, Babemba, Basanga, and Baushi as
well as among a fraction of the Katanga Baluba. However, these
regional parties were particularly vulnerable to the divisive effects of
tribal demagoguery or simply to the repercussions of ethnic clashes.
The PSA was weakened by the withdrawal of the Bayaka and the
Bayanzi; the PUNA failed to enlist the full support of the Ngbandi and
Ngbaka, although the members of these tribes living in Léopoldville
normally affiliated with the ASSORECO; the rural Bashi of Kivu not
only shunned the CEREA, although some of their urbanized fellow
tribesmen had taken part in its foundation, but were even divided

among themselves as a result of the different political affiliations of their two major chiefs; [98] the CONAKAT was deserted by the Tshokwe and by the Katanga Baluba, while the regional association of the Kasai immigrants in Katanga, the FEDEKA, suffered from the consequences of the tribal clashes in its home districts and lost its Lulua members to the CONAKAT. In Kasai, meanwhile, the Lulua had allied themselves with Lumumba's MNC for exactly the same reasons.

Interethnic parties differ from regional parties in that they cannot be functionally associated with one given area. Whereas the regional parties claim authority over a whole section of territory, or over the natives of this section who have been transplanted into a foreign environment, the interethnic organizations usually proceed from mere tactical convenience and represent alliances which frequently rest upon a community of antipathies rather than upon positive affinities. Thus, in spite of more or less adroit rationalizations supplied after its birth, the loosely jointed, ubiquitous cartel known as the PNP (Parti National du Progrès) had few factors of cohesion beyond a very subdued brand of nationalism, an unconnected chain of isolated strongholds, the more or less conspicuous support of the administration (which led its adversaries to nickname it "Penepene na Mondele"—"closest to the white man"), and a thick vein of what Nnamdi Azikiwe once dubbed "hat-in-hand-Uncle-Tomism." The PNP enlisted the support of a number of ethnic parties such as the LUKA, the UNERGA, or the MEDERCO, each of which retained enough autonomy, however, to follow its own course of policy before, during, and after the elections of 1960. The Cartel Katangais, a regional alliance formed between the BALUBAKAT, FEDEKA, and ATCAR, had certain ethnic affinities, especially after FEDEKA had been deserted by the Lulua. In Kasai, finally, the Coalition Kasaienne (COAKA) was also primarily the product of a tactical league between the small tribes, united by their common resentment of the larger ethnic groups, particularly the Baluba. Later, however, the COAKA leaders attempted to provide their party with a geographical *Lebensraum* by sponsoring the birth of the curiously gerrymandered Etat de l'Unité Kasaienne, which was proclaimed just in time to gain recognition at the Coquilhatville conference of April–May 1961.

[98] The reigning dynasty of the Ngweshe *chefferie* sponsored a minor party known as RECO (Ressortissants de l'Est du Congo), while the "Mwami" of Kabare (although he was the son-in-law of the Ngweshe queen mother) favored the PNP. In Oct. 1961, the two conflicting *chefferies* were set up as separate *territoires*.

Truly national parties have been an uncommon article on the Congolese scene, especially when a party's claims to a national audience are compared with its actual achievements: Léopoldville bred at least a dozen self-styled "national" parties which never expanded farther than the city limits. Nor is it possible to rely upon the lofty professions of faith included in virtually every party program. Even those movements which practiced what they preached frequently failed to live up to their original ambitions. An example of this is the Union Congolaise, founded at Elisabethville by a Belgian Christian-Democratic barrister on the eve of the first municipal elections (December 1957) and therefore, after ABAKO, the oldest political movement in the Congo.[99] Unlike the above-named Union Katangaise (a settlers' party which did not cooperate with the Africans until July 1959), the Union Congolaise was from the start a genuinely multiracial party, whose founder was often reviled by local whites as a "nigger-lover." It took a firm stand in favor of a unitary form of government and was a cosponsor (with the MNC, which had not yet split) of the first congress of political parties held in the country, the Luluabourg congress of April 7–12, 1959, which warned against the dangers of possible "balkanization." The Union Congolaise opened branches at Luluabourg, Stanleyville, and Bukavu but lacked the stamina and leadership which characterized Lumumba's party and rapidly lost ground. By the end of 1959, it was virtually out of the political race and gained only one seat in the Katanga provincial assembly. Its various branches followed the trend of local politics without any coordination: the Luluabourg cell became a front for Lulua chauvinism, its most influential members at Bukavu joined the UNERGA (itself linked with the PNP), while its section at Stanleyville adhered outright to the PNP. Even at Elisabethville, its African president (and only elected representative) forsook the party line and eventually rallied to the Katangese secession.

Most of the would-be national parties simply faded away. The Parti du Peuple, the only formation with a coherent doctrinal program, discovered (as similar parties had in other parts of Africa) that its socialist ideology was not attuned to the tenor of Congolese nationalism: it gained only one seat in the provincial assembly of Kasai though for reasons which had little to do with the nature of its official platform. Other parties degenerated willingly or unwillingly into *de facto* tribalism. Such was the case, as already noted, with the dissident wing of

---

[99] The first party to gain *legal* recognition, however, was the Action Socialiste (Dec. 1957), later reorganized as the Parti du Peuple.

the MNC which fell under the sway of the chiliastic leader of the Kasai Baluba, Albert Kalonji, and failed to take root anywhere but among this particular group.[100]

Thus, Patrice Lumumba's MNC was (and still remains) the only party combining a genuine national creed with a country-wide audience, and there is little doubt that only the unanticipated abridgment of the transition to independence (and consequently of the nationalist struggle under its most stimulative form) kept it from mobilizing an even greater proportion of the Congolese people. Yet the MNC itself exhibits some of the characteristics of other types of parties. Its electoral success was chiefly confined to a wide but recognizable region, it did not spurn the advantage it could derive from tribal loyalties, and it occasionally relied upon interethnic alliances of a purely tactical nature in order to penetrate new areas of potential interest. But even though it may have meant many things to many people, the MNC was unmistakably nationalist in its dialectics as well as in the policy which it tried to steer during its brief term in power, and no other party can match what it has accomplished in propagating a sense of national unity among the people of the Congo.

The Congolese political parties may of course be categorized according to various other criteria, but few of the tentative yardsticks which have been suggested are completely satisfactory. The distinction between "unitarists" (that is, those which favored a unitary form of government, such as the MNC, the CEREA, the PNP, the PUNA, the Union Congolaise) and the "federalists" (ABAKO, CONAKAT, MNC-Kalonji, Parti du Peuple, ABAZI, etc.) provides some interesting insights but leaves out a variety of important nuances and thus conveys the impression that there was a clear-cut dividing line between the two gospels, whereas in fact, owing to shifting positions, fence sitting, and conceptual fuzziness, there was a complete array of positions ranging in rainbowlike gradualness—even within a given party—from complete centralization to separatism, with a median majority favoring substantial decentralization. Parties like the PSA or BALUBAKAT, which had originally favored a federal form of government, drifted toward the

[100] Albert Kalonji's political career is an example of the ideological confusion which marked the beginnings of Congolese nationalism. Kalonji was, from the first, a champion of Luba chauvinism and gained national stature largely because of the colonial administration's clumsy handling of the Lulua-Baluba dispute. He had attended the Brussels World Fair in 1958 and joined nationalist circles there, but he did not attain national fame until he had been imprisoned for stirring up racial hatred in Kasai (Aug. 1959).

MNC's more centralizing views as a reaction against what they considered the excessive particularism of ABAKO and CONAKAT, while others followed a reverse itinerary. Finally, when the centrifugal trend seemed to be prevailing in the spring of 1961, many theretofore uncommitted factions espoused the new orientation out of a form of conviction that often seemed to be copiously interlarded with political opportunism.

Other types of classification are even less adequate, as they usually tend to draw upon irrelevant idiosyncrasies or to invoke notions which are wholly extraneous to most Congolese parties: such oppositions as those between "conservatives" and "progressives" or between "moderates" and "radicals" frequently transcend party lines and show elusive validity when applied to different sets of issues. The same can be said with even greater pertinence of the division between "left" and "right."

THE POLITICAL ELITE

The emergence of a Congolese political class has been deeply affected by the unusual circumstances which have surrounded the achievement of national independence. The abrupt change of Belgian attitudes from repressiveness to permissiveness snuffed out militancy and self-reliance while encouraging verbal audacities and irresponsible exuberance. Furthermore, just as it throttled the maturation of a pan-Congolese nationalist movement, the brevity of the emancipation process curbed the development of a genuine political elite by placing a premium on any kind of status, achieved or inherited. A similar phenomenon has of course been observed in other colonial societies, where education, wealth, or traditional influence have commonly proved to be convenient launching pads for aspiring politicians, but nowhere has the weight of a value system inherited from the colonial period been so apparent as in the Congo. The new political class was hastily recruited by a population which had had only a limited African elite to look up to, and it was just as hastily promoted or, rather, sucked up by the sudden vacuum created by Belgium's deliberate disengagement. Thus, any sort of ascendancy, whether it was due to education, to rank in a traditional society, to leadership in any type of group activity (unionism, friendly societies, social clubs, sports) or even to recognition by the colonial authorities (for example, membership in one of the numerous advisory bodies petted by the administration—*conseils de territoire, conseils de province*, etc.—or elevation to the status of native judge or of native solicitor—*représentant legal*—in an urban community), offered an opening for a political career. Former students of the *grands séminaires,* civil servants and minor officials, clerks and *commis,* medical assistants and male nurses, teachers and agricultural assistants constituted the overwhelming majority of the members of the central and provincial legislatures. Native chiefs were also well represented, though according to a peculiar pattern: while the *chefs de secteur,* who usually owed their status to the administration but who also frequently bore the brunt of its displeasure, did not hesitate to seek popular election—occasionally on a nationalist ticket—to bolster up their position, the traditional rulers of a homogeneous ethnic group either waited to be singled out by co-optation (as members of the provincial assemblies or as "customary senators"), or they pushed members of their families or entourages onto a political pedestal.[101]

A student of the Congolese political scene has compiled the data in Table 14 which sketches out the occupational and age patterns of the legislative chambers as they stood in 1960.[102] As this table shows, two-thirds of the members of the House of Representatives and nearly 60 per cent of the senators (whose minimum age was 30) were under 40 years of age, which denotes a young legislature, even when accounting for the fact that an African is usually considered "old" once he is in his late forties. The large number of legislators who have been employed by public agencies is also worth noting, as well as the dis-

[101] In this way the Mwata Yamvo of the Lunda, the Nyimi of the Bashilele, the Mwanangana of the Lulua, the Mwami of the Bashi at Kabare, chief Bantu of the Mundo, chief Tshisenge of the Tshokwe, chief Kabongo of the Baluba at Manono, etc., became senators, while Regent Lwanwa of the Bashi of Ngweshe, chief Kasongo Nyembo of the Baluba at Kamina, chief Londri of the Bahema, etc., were elected to the provincial assemblies. Notable members of chiefly families were Kavunzu-Delunda (president of the Léopoldville provincial assembly and nephew of the Kiamfu of the Bayaka), Mombele (provincial deputy elected on a RDLK ticket and son of the Paramount of the Bateke), Mopipi (national deputy and son of the chief of the Walega at Shabunda), Kabare (member of the Kivu provincial assembly and son of the Mwami of Kabare), Yumbu (national deputy for the PSA and son of chief Nganbunda of the Bambunda), Wafwana (national deputy and brother of the Mwanangana of the Lulua), Kibwe (minister of the Katanga "state" and grandson of two chiefs of the Batabwa), Bako Ditende (provincial deputy for CONAKAT and son of the Mwata Yamvo of the Lunda), Munongo (minister of the "state" of Katanga and half brother of chief Mwenda-Munongo of the Bayeke), and many others.

[102] René Lemarchand, "The Rise of Congolese Nationalisms: An Enquiry into the Origins and Development of Congolese Political Groups" (unpublished doctoral thesis).

Table 14. Ages and occupations of the members of the
Congolese parliament

	House of Representatives	Senate
AGE		
25–29	24	—
30–39	68	50
40–49	36	22
50–59	5	7
60 and over	0	1
Unknown	4	4
OCCUPATION		
1. *Public sector*	(66)	(31)
Civil servants *	20	11
Professional civil servants †	17	6
"Commis"	19	9
Teachers	10	5
2. *Private sector*	(34)	(16)
Lawyers	0	1
Commerçants	14	3
Accountants	4	6
Farmers	5	0
Clerks	7	2
Other ‡	4	4
3. *Native authorities & local govt.*	(22)	(30)
Customary chiefs	3	14
"Chefs de secteur"	12	13
"Bourgmestres"	5	0
Other §	2	3
4. Unknown	(15)	(7)

* Includes *commis principaux, commis-chefs, rédacteurs,* and *agents de la quatrième categorie.*
† Includes medical assistants, *infirmiers,* and agronomists.
‡ Includes journalists, technicians, artisans, etc.
§ Includes territorial and provincial councilors.

parity between the numbers of traditional chiefs in the House and in the Senate (the heavy representation of chiefs of all types in the Senate is of course an institutional phenomenon). A consideration of these data on a party basis suggests that the three major parties which supported Lumumba's coalition government (MNC, PSA, and CEREA) tended to have younger congressmen than the other groups, although the CONAKAT had also a "young" representation in the central legislature (perhaps because its most prominent members ran for the provincial assembly). These same parties (along with the Cartel Katangais and ABAKO) also included among their representatives in the House a larger than average number of public servants.

THE 1960 ELECTION

The electoral campaign opened officially on May 11, 1960, and lasted two weeks. Inevitably, however, the four months which followed the convening of the Round Table conference were in fact one long period of campaigning and organizational build-up. Thus, Patrice Lumumba, who had been selected with five other Congolese leaders to sit on the interim executive council presided over by the Governor-General,[103] farsightedly chose to resign upon the first legitimate pretext in order to strengthen his party's position. The whole campaign was marred by a considerable degree of confusion and violence. Owing to last-minute splits and squabbles over formal party endorsement of a single slate of candidates, party labels were frequently invoked by two or three rival candidates in a same district. Individual candidates and "local interest" groups added a final touch to this disconcerting jumble. Serious disorders occurred in Kasai (where the Lulua-Baluba dispute had never really subsided), in Maniema, in the Upper Lomami district of Katanga, and in various parts of the Eastern Province, notably Ituri.

According to the Belgian practice which normally tends to favor middle-of-the-road groups, voting was made compulsory, although the Belgian authorities well knew that they were no longer in a position to enforce such an injunction (or, for that matter, to prevent intimidation and to secure complete secrecy of the vote). Voters numbering 2,773,595—that is, some three-quarters of the total electorate—eventually turned out, and the voting participation, which fell to 60 per cent in some remote constituencies of the Equator Province, rose to 97 per cent in Léopoldville and to 91 per cent in Elisabethville and Jadotville. The electoral results confirmed the virtual monopoly of some of the ethnic and regional parties like ABAKO, PSA, and CEREA, as well as the anticipated defeat of the isolated candidates who were handi-

---

[103] This executive college (*conseil exécutif général*) had been set up in accordance with a recommendation of the Round Table conference. It included six Congolese members (one from each province) and had certain collegiate powers of decision under the Governor-General's ultimate responsibility.

capped by the electoral system. It also revealed that, as had been suspected for some time, the MNC-Kalonji was no longer a national party but merely a Baluba political machine: the only seats it won were reaped in the Luba districts of Kasai, and its non-Luba members (such as Adoula and Ileo) had to be rescued *in extremis* by indirect election to the Senate (Adoula being endorsed by PUNA and Ileo by UNIMO). The only major surprises were the magnitude of the MNC's success and the virtual debacle suffered by the PNP. (The electoral returns for the House are summarized by province in Table 15.

Some of the political leaders scored important personal victories, reflected in the number of preferential votes which they received in

Table 15. 1960 General election: House of Representaitves

	LEO.	EQUAT.	EAST.	KIVU	KAT.	KASAI	Total
MNC	1	2	21	5		4	33
MNC "cartels"							
(UNEBAFI, Unité							
Basonge, etc.)				1		2	3
MNC alliances							
UNC						3	3
COAKA						2	2
PNP	1 *	3	3			3	10
PNP alliances							
LUKA	3						3
UNERGA					1		1
MEDERCO		1					1
PSA	13						13
ABAKO	12						12
CEREA				10			10
MNC-Kalonji						8	8
CONAKAT					8		8
Cartel Katangais					7		7
PUNA		7					7
RECO				4			4
UNIMO		1					1
ABAZI	1						1
RDLK †	1						1
Local groups		4		1			5
Individuals	1		1	1	1		4
Total	33	18	25	23	16	22	137

* Won by a "common front" of the LUKA, PNP, PUNA, UNIBAT (a Bateke association), and a dissident wing of ABAKO, in the city of Léopoldville.
† Rassemblement Démocratique du Lac, Kwango et Kwilu.

their home constituencies. Patrice Lumumba netted 84,602 votes; Kalonji had 78,076, Kamitatu 60,511, Bolikango 53,121, and Gizenga 52,442; but certain parties (like ABAKO) discouraged such manifestations of a personality cult.

The Provincial Returns

The returns of the provincial vote are in many ways more illuminating than those of the general elections, not only because they reveal a more detailed pattern (coming from smaller constituencies) but also because they are indicative of some of the local conflicts that sometimes weighed heavily on the national situation.

In Léopoldville province, a regional bloc (PSA) controlled more than three-quarters of the seats in the districts of Kwilu and Kwango and emerged as the largest provincial group. It was faced by the slightly smaller but ethnically more homogeneous ABAKO. Between these two groups (neither of which was strong enough to control the provincial assembly singlehanded), a galaxy of smaller local or ethnic factions, most of which had little sympathy for the Bakongo, held a precarious balance of power. The only unusual feature was the presence of two MNC councilors returned by one of the few *territoires* that fell within the Mongo language area. The president of the provincial government was accordingly a member of the PSA (Cléophas Kamitatu), but after the ABAKO had sulked for a while and threatened to set up its own Kongo "state," the deadlock between the two major groups was resolved (at least temporarily) by appointing a member of ABAKO as provincial vice-president.

In the Equator Province, the situation was characterized by the large number of seats occupied by local groups and individual candidates (over one-third). The Mongo-speaking tribes were almost evenly divided between UNIMO and MNC, while the proportion of seats gained by PUNA was only half of what it was in the general election. The PNP was badly split, its national president, Paul Bolya, having rallied to the cause of UNIMO, while its provincial councilors (virtually all of them elected by the Ngbandi and Ngbaka in the northern part of the province) tended at first to support PUNA. Thus, the MNC was able to act as an arbitrator and secured three seats out of ten in the provincial government.

A similar situation prevailed in Kasai, where the MNC, entrenched in the Sankuru district and controlling nearly one-fourth of the seats, threw its weight between the Luba bloc (21 seats out of 70) and the three major non-Luba factions (UNC, COAKA, and MUB: 23 seats in all) and led the governmental coalition—the principal differences with Equator being, of course, the substantially stronger position of the MNC (one-quarter of the seats instead of one-sixth) and the existence of a fairly coherent, preestablished entente between the MNC and the three non-Luba groups. With the exception of one single councilor allegedly representing the Parti du Peuple, all other minor formations agreed to join the MNC-led bloc, leaving the Baluba in almost total isolation.

In Kivu, although it held exactly the same number of seats as in Kasai and appeared to be controlling Maniema just as it controlled the adjacent Sankuru district, the MNC was faced with a well-organized regional party, the CEREA. Despite internal dissensions between its radical and moderate wings, the CEREA (which had taken a dim view of the MNC's rapid expansion in the province) managed to retain its predominance by enlisting the support of various local groups, and the MNC was confined to a secondary role in the provincial government, receiving only two ministerial posts out of ten. This local tension between the MNC and the CEREA was partly allayed, however, by their coalition on the national scene and by their general affinities.

It was in the Eastern Province that the MNC scored its most resounding victory, virtually burying the PNP under a landslide of 58 seats to 6. The PNP and the few chiefs who had insisted on running on a separate ticket held their own only among certain non-Bantu groups (Azande, Mayogo, Medje, the Mangbetu cluster). Although one ministerial post was awarded to a PNP councilor, the MNC was obviously in complete control of the provincial government.

Katanga was the only province where both the MNC and the PNP failed to secure any significant beachhead (only one MNC councilor was elected in one of the northernmost *territoires* and none from the PNP). CONAKAT and the Cartel Katangais shared four-fifths of the seats almost evenly, and it was only by a margin of 7 votes out of more than 22,000 that CONAKAT nosed ahead of the Cartel in Elisabethville, thus emerging with 25 seats against its opponent's 23. However, the CONAKAT managed to buttress its flimsy advantage by attracting the support of most councilors elected on individual or "local" tickets and even succeeded (with Albert Kalonji's assistance) in prying loose a couple of Cartel councilors. How the Cartel's boycott of the provincial assembly was stymied by a stopgap amendment of the *loi fondamentale* and how CONAKAT set the formal prologue for secession by excluding its rival from the provincial government has already been recorded.[104] The hopes for a redress which the Cartel nourished in view of its alliance with the MNC at the national level were of course promptly quashed after the secession had become a *fait accompli*.

The results of the provincial elections are provided in Table 16.

Table 16. Provincial election returns, 1960

	LEO.	EQUAT.	EAST.	KIVU	KAT.	KASAI
MNC	2	10	58	14	1	16
MNC "cartels"						
with UNEBAFI				3		
with COAKA						2
with UNC						1
COAKA						5
UNC						10
MNC-MUB alliance						6
PNP	1		6			4
PNP alliances						
MEDERCO		5				
Assoc. Mbwaka		5				
UNERGA-ARP *				5		
LUKA	9					
Front commun (LUKA, PUNA, etc.)	2					
PUNA and associates		11				
UNIMO		8				
ABAKO	33					
ABAZI	2					
RDLK	2					
PSA	35					
Cartel PSA–MNC-Kalonji	1					
MNC-Kalonji					1	21
CEREA				30		
RECO				6		
CONAKAT					25	
Cartel Katangais					23	
Local groups	3	8	2	7	5	5
Individuals		13	4	5	5	
Total	90	60	70	70	60	70

* Alliance Rurale Progressiste.

[104] See above, pp. 96–97.

LOCAL GOVERNMENT

Although the semiofficial policy of indirect rule had never been wholeheartedly applied by the colonial administration, it was not until the last years of Belgian dominion that any serious attempt was made to introduce a certain measure of popular participation into the conduct of local affairs, other than through customary channels. The same reasons of administrative expediency which induced the conservation of the most manageable traditional units as well as the more or less artificial reshuffling of undersized *chefferies* also accounted for the colonial bureaucracy's tendency to resort to methods of direct administration when new and complex problems had to be faced and solved at the village level. The native authorities therefore acquired little familiarity with problems of modern administration, while (unlike what happened in the British territories after 1950) no systematic effort was made to appeal to the educated elements of the population in order to supplement the chiefs' failing capacities.

Yet, as early as 1928, some Catholic circles (possibly influenced by the missions' belief that traditional structures were an obstacle to evangelization) had advocated the introduction of a system of *communes* modeled after the Belgian local government units.[105] It was not until 1957, however, that a timid reform of the native authority system was introduced. Under the 1957 decree, local councils were to be created in every *chefferie, secteur,* or *centre extra-coutumier.* Such councils were to include, however, all chiefs, subchiefs, and "notables" stipulated by custom, together with an unspecified number of members having no traditional status. The latter were not elected in the proper sense but rather appointed by the district commissioner, upon the native authorities' recommendation and after the people had been "consulted." How this "consultation" was to be held was not spelled out in the decree; a formal electoral process was not ruled out but, for reasons of flexibility, it was not prescribed either. In fact, no elections were held anywhere, except in neighboring Rwanda-Burundi, where the elections involved not only an administrative reorganization but also a political reappraisal.

Similar chariness prevailed when it came to the selection of those

[105] See the views of Mgr. J. de Hemptinne (later Archbishop of Elisabethville) in "La politique indigène du gouvernement belge" in *Congo,* Oct. 1928, pp. 359–373.

chiefs who governed nontraditional units and who had been appointed directly in the past by the colonial authorities (that is, the *chefs de secteurs* and the *chefs de centres*): the same noncommittal reference to the "possibility of a prior popular consultation" left the door open for subsequent democratization while entailing little immediate change. Furthermore, the administrative powers of the chiefs remained largely unimpaired: the councils were to perform exclusively consultative functions, the only corrective being that a chief's decision not to abide by his council's formal advice had to be supported by explicit reasons, which the councilors could challenge by appealing to the district commissioner. A permanent committee of the council assisted the chief in discharging his administrative duties, but it exercised delegated powers only and the African local government personnel (which was to include at least a secretary, a treasurer, a police commissioner, and a local force) were to be appointed under the chief's sole authority.

A somewhat more liberal dose of local democracy was instilled in the administration of urban affairs, if only to satisfy perennial demands of the white population. The problem posed by the multiracial character of the urban communities was solved by subdividing them into boroughs: residential segregation (which retained its legal basis until February 1959) ensured that each borough (*commune*) would remain uniracial. Thus, although it was not formally required by the decree, an electoral process based on a common roll of voters could be introduced with a minimum of tension. Each *commune* elected its council, which in turn selected its mayor (*bourgmestre*), subject to administrative approval. Coordination of urban affairs was assured by an indirectly elected *conseil de ville*, presided over by a sort of supermayor, the *premier bourgmestre*, who was in fact a colonial civil servant having the rank of district commissioner.

In 1957, however, only three cities—Léopoldville, Elisabethville, and Jadotville—were brought under this new regime. As a result, the value of local government institutions as a means of political training was seriously diluted by the tardiness and the pusillanimity of the 1957 reforms. Yet, despite the administration's precautionary measures (for example, the prohibition for parapolitical groups to give formal sponsorship to the candidates), the 1957 municipal elections tended to assume political dimensions, at least in Léopoldville and under ABAKO's stimulus. The suggestion that this phenomenon was simply a form of tactical subrogation is confirmed by the fact that local government politics lost their polarizing effect as soon as nationalist forces were allowed to develop on a wider basis.

In December 1959, new municipal elections were coupled with the introduction of voting procedures in the rural areas at the *territoire* level. The object of these measures was, originally, the establishment of a first tier of councils which, in accordance with the policy formulated in January 1959, was intended to act as an electoral college in the selection of provincial assemblies. But, by the end of 1959, it had become obvious, both to the African leaders and to the Belgian authorities, that this form of cautious gradualism would have to be discarded in favor of more sweeping advances. This was confirmed by the announcement of the Round Table conference and the disclosure of the Belgian government's new policy of short-term independence.

The local government elections of December 1959 had therefore lost much of their significance even before they had actually taken place, and they consequently attracted little real interest. Only one-half of the potential electorate turned up at the polls, and nearly three-quarters of the vote went to individual candidates or to local and tribal interest groups. A negative success was scored by the political parties which had recommended abstention in the Léopoldville province (ABAKO, PSA, etc.): less than 82,000 persons took part in the polls, as against 650,000 in the subsequent general election. The only party that made a deliberate bid—the PNP—reaped 60 per cent of the "political" suffrage (that is, less than one-sixth of the total), but, as the general election was later to show, it had virtually exhausted its vote-getting capacity and the absolute number of votes it received in May 1960 was not substantially larger than what it had been in December 1959, although the electoral turnout increased by 50 per cent in the general election.

In short, democratic local government largely remains a superficial novelty in the Republic. The inconsistent product of belated innovations, it has been an instrument rather than a deliberate and autonomous goal. Modern local government has not yet taken a firm root, particularly in rural areas, and much of the colonial framework continues to exist, both in the letter and in the spirit of the existing institutions. The colonial regime's legacy of centralized control and direct administration remains virtually unimpaired and has been tempered only by the inability of central and provincial authorities to enforce their will in the rural hinterland. The determination of whether to retain such a system or to place, in the future, greater faith in grass-roots democracy will be one of the many important choices to be made by a restored government.

Contemporary Issues

THE PROBLEM OF NATIONAL UNITY

Except in the *loi fondamentale,* whose Section 6 grandly assumed that "the Congo constitutes, within its present frontiers, an indivisible and democratic State," Congolese unity was by no means a self-evident proposition when the Republic achieved full international sovereignty on June 30, 1960. Neither, however, had centrifugal trends attained irreparable decisiveness, and no *ex post facto* rationalization can conclusively demonstrate the inevitability of the postindependence disintegration of the Congolese Republic. Then as now, anarchy rather than ingrained separatism has been the fundamental issue on which the future of the Republic revolves. Even Katanga's proclaimed "independence" sprang more from the skillful exploitation of a political vacuum than from any form of "national" consciousness, propaganda notwithstanding.[106]

Most of the members of the new political class gained their first intimate contact with the realities of power and with the complexity of the colonial administrative machinery within the few days preceding independence: is it any wonder that they seldom had sufficient authority and decisiveness to deal with anything resembling an emergency situation? Like a hastily caulked ship launched before its time, the young republic was virtually at the mercy of a sudden gale, or even of a mere gust that might only have rocked a more seasoned crew.

Within forty-eight hours of the achievement of independence, the new government's control over the state apparatus was put to its first test when disgruntled Bangala and Baluba elements angrily demonstrated against the exclusion of their respective "great men" (Bolikango and Kalonji) from any form of executive responsibility. Two days later, the Congolese militia loudly demanded accelerated africanization. The government announced a reorganization of the army, but the Belgian general commanding the Force Publique immediately sent the Prime Minister a contumelious ultimatum and crudely blustered to his troops

---

[106] In the midst of many apparently conflicting statements, Katanga's official doctrine had always been that it was ready to retain some form of association with other provinces—though preferably on its own terms. This position indirectly and ingenuously confirmed the view that Katangese intransigency always contained a good deal of hard salesmanship.

that independence would not entail any change for them.[107] Within hours, the soldiers were leaving their barracks, and mutiny was loose in the Lower Congo. Improvised measures (including mass promotion and the dismissal of the Belgian commander) failed to appease the insurgents and panic spread to Léopoldville, both among the white population which frantically tried to flee or to arm itself and among the soldiers of the Congolese garrison who responded to the wildest rumors [108] and searched civilians for their weapons.

A similar pattern prevailed in Katanga, where two outbursts in the northern part of the province sparked off the chain reaction of mutual suspicion, panic, and hysteria in Elisabethville (July 9–10). A new dimension was added to the crisis when provincial President Tshombe called for Belgian military intervention: less than eight hours after a mutiny had broken out in Elisabethville, Belgian shock troops (which had been reinforced by fresh arrivals the previous days) went into action despite last-minute efforts by the Belgian ambassador to hold back the whole operation. The ambassador well knew that such an intervention was blatantly illegal and would result in a serious deterioration of Belgo-Congolese relations. The official position of the Belgian government, while less clear, showed similar circumspection and wisely side-stepped the legal issues while stressing the humanitarian imperatives which, it contended, had made intervention inevitable.[109]

In Elisabethville, meanwhile, Belgian officers were not so discreet. One day after the arrival of Belgian troops, President Tshombe declared the independence of Katanga and the Belgian commander set about the task of organizing the new "state." Commander Weber also

[107] To drive the point home, the general even chalked on a blackboard, "Before independence = after independence"—a disastrous statement in the eyes of a force in which no African had been allowed to rise above the rank of sergeant.

[108] One of these rumors concerned the alleged arrival of "Russians," whom the mutinous soldiers immediately sought out—not to welcome them (as many plot-prone correspondents instantly concluded, in accordance with their personal stereotypes) but to destroy them (in accordance with the militia's own conditioned reflexes). The incident is illustrative of the climate of irrational fear which pervaded this whole period.

[109] Tshombe tried to force the hand of the Belgian government by announcing his intention to request military assistance from Rhodesia. A cabinet meeting in Brussels attempted to wring legal sanction from Lumumba by warning him that if the Congolese government did not request Belgian military assistance, troops would intervene on their own initiative, but before this ultimatum had been conveyed to the Congolese Premier, the Elisabethville mutiny had erupted and military intervention was a *fait accompli.*

announced that he had "proofs" of a deliberate subversion in which
the Soviet Embassy had taken part (a charge which was never sub-
stantiated), and after Minister Munongo had personally prevented the
President of the Republic and the Prime Minister from landing at
the Elisabethville airport, he warmly congratulated him for "having
safeguarded order in Katanga." Shortly afterward, the head of the
Chiefs of Staffs' Committee, General Cumont, placed all Belgian troops
stationed in Katanga "at Mr. Tshombe's disposal."

In the meantime, the Congolese government had immediately reacted against Belgian military interventions at Elisabethville and
Matadi [110] by approaching the Assistant Secretary General of the
United Nations, Dr. Ralph Bunche, and then by requesting the assistance of UN troops (July 12). Within the next forty-eight hours, frantic
appeals for support were also dispatched to the United States, Ghana,
and the Soviet Union, and diplomatic relations with Belgium had been
severed. By July 16, the first UN contingents were landing at Léopoldville.

The Background of Katanga Separatism

No satisfactory evidence has ever been produced regarding the
existence of either a Belgian or a Congolese plot connected with the
Force Publique mutiny. There is, on the other hand, abundant proof
of premeditation in the process which led to the Katangese secession.
Separatism, as mentioned earlier, was by no means a novel feature
in the mining province, although it had always been an exclusively
white attitude associated with the quasi-folkloric *esprit de clocher*
which seems to be an essential component of the Belgian national character. The administrative reorganization of 1933 which had brought
Katanga in line with the rest of the colony had been fiercely criticized
in some European circles.[111] The vital role played by Katanga as a
supplier of strategic raw materials during World War II had further
helped to fan their regional pride. The vicinity of the Rhodesias and
the nebulous phraseology associated with the notion of a "Capricorn

[110] The unduly harsh Belgian intervention at Matadi (July 10) was not caused
by the desire to protect human lives (only ten Europeans remained in the city)
but was openly intended to control the country's major seaport. The news of
this incident was spread by the Force Publique's short-wave communication network and provoked several new outbursts. It also irretrievably compromised the
painfully extracted agreement by which Premier Lumumba had come to accept
the possibility of local Belgian interventions (July 11). The announcement of
Katanga's secession put a virtual end to such transactions.
[111] See above, p. 40.

federation" also exerted a measure of influence on the resident white community.

Katangese "colons" formed nearly 40 per cent of the membership of the largest and most dynamic of the settlers' organizations, the FEDACOL (Fédération des Associations de Colons du Congo Belge et du Ruanda-Urundi), whose Katanga affiliate (UCOL-Katanga) repeatedly pressed for a restoration of provincial autonomy. The FEDACOL, which kept on demanding a parity of representation for Europeans and Africans long after the January 1959 policy reappraisal, had been active in trying to enlist the support of the incipient African bourgeoisie, and, although it met with no appreciable success, this tendency was later reflected in the various attempts to set up Eurafrican political associations, the most notable of these being the CONAKAT.[112] In December 1959, a first, half-baked, secessionist plot, purporting to take advantage of King Baudouin's presence in Elisabethville to proclaim an autonomous "dominion" linked with Belgium under the Crown, was easily foiled by the colonial authorities, but similar views (assorted with covert threats of secession) were developed by the CONAKAT delegates at the Round Table conference of January–February 1960. The "Belgo-Congolese community," as originally presented by those delegates, would have consisted of a "federation" of autonomous states linked individually with Belgium.

Shortly after the end of the Round Table conference, the Prime Minister of the Central African Federation, Sir Roy Welensky, was approached by unknown envoys concerning the feasibility of some form of union between Katanga and the Federation. On this occasion, hostile reactions in the Congo were so strong that the CONAKAT felt compelled to issue a formal disclaimer denying any participation in such negotiations and suggesting that the whole incident might have been a trial balloon launched by Sir Roy himself. Yet in the tense week during which the Cartel Katangais attempted to buttress its complaints by boycotting the Provincial Assembly, a leading CONAKAT councilor, Jean-Baptiste Kibwe (later to become the Vice-President and Finance Minister of Katanga), lost his temper and violently declared that, if its opponents persisted in their obstructionary tactics, the CONAKAT would proceed to form a government of its own and immediately enter into a compact with Rhodesia "openly, this time, not underhand." [113] At that time, a tentative "constitution" had already

[112] On the FEDACOL see *CRISP-Courrier Hebdomadaire,* 1959, no. 25.
[113] Session of June 12, 1960, of the Katanga Provincial Assembly, quoted in *Congo 1960,* p. 248.

been drafted by a group of Europeans, and within less than two weeks it was discovered that the CONAKAT-led provincial government had appointed a (white) "ambassador," whose mission was to secure diplomatic recognition from Belgium and the United States (and subsequently from Great Britain and Portugal) for an "independent" state of Katanga to be proclaimed a few hours ahead of the transfer of sovereignty to the Congolese Republic (June 25–27).[114] This last-minute machination was also thwarted by the Belgian authorities, but, as later developments were to demonstrate, the CONAKAT leaders did not give up their designs.

The mutiny of the Force Publique was primarily a convenient pretext to fulfill a long-established plan, but it goes without saying that the partial breakdown of law and order which accompanied the mutiny was an additional boon to the secessionists. Not only did it relieve them from the menace of coercive action on the part of the central government, but the abuses perpetrated by the insurgents against European civilians indirectly engendered sympathy for Katanga in the traumatized Belgian public. The fact that this emotional impulse seemed to many small shareholders to coincide—at least superficially—with the preservation of their interests only served to make the Katangese "cause" appear worthier. A skillful press also helped to exacerbate public opinion and to raise it to a pitch of indignant self-pity and clamorous jingoism.

Of course, Congolese independence must be respected [wrote a leading conservative daily]. But not any kind of independence! Not independence in anarchy! Not independence under the lead of the present Léopoldville government whose incapability is blatant and several members of which have behaved like primitive and imbecile savages, like vulgar scoundrels, or like creatures of communism. . . . It will be necessary . . . to install an energetic and intelligent military governor or resident by the side of the Congolese government, to ensure that the maintenance of law and order continues. . . . Of course, this military governor will have to be maintained as long as necessary. . . . We must secure from the Congolese Parliament a reshuffling of the Léopoldville government through the elimination of certain men who have demonstrated their incapability or their anarchical tendencies. . . . It may be objected that Belgian troops are not numerous enough in this immense territory. But it is Belgium's task to reinforce them. And when number is lacking, there is always one method to maintain order, namely, to be merciless against anyone who makes a move and who commits

[114] *La province du Katanga et l'Indépendance congolaise (République du Congo —Documents du Ministère des Affaires Etrangères No. 1)* (Léopoldville, n.d.), pp. 17–19.

execution or murder. The Congo was conquered with rifles. It would be strange indeed if a modern army could not maintain itself with jet planes and cannon! [115]

Belgian political circles largely reflected the country's emotional attitudes. The national chairman of the Belgian Liberal Party (a partner in the governing coalition) wished "that the State of Katanga become truly a State recognized by all governments and also by the Belgian government," while the Catholic Premier stated that "it would be inconceivable for the UN to intervene for or against the independence of Katanga" and dispatched one of his personal aides to Elisabethville to organize Belgian "technical assistance" to Katanga. The Socialist opposition followed a cautiously wavering line. The veteran Socialist Senator Rolin gave unofficial expression to the party's uncomfortable fence sitting when he declared:

There is no doubt that the situation is better in Katanga than in most other regions, and I willingly add that if, in order to attain this result, it was indispensable for Mr. Tshombe to break all ties subordinating him to the central government of Léopoldville, I personally could not blame him. But [he went on to add] if Belgium were the first to recognize Katanga's independence, we would find ourselves for the first time in an embarrassing situation, since this decision would inevitably be used to qualify in retrospect certain imprudent declarations lately issued by Belgian officers in Elisabethville as so many acts of collaboration and complicity. . . . On the other hand, it is quite obvious that the lack of recognition does not preclude us from continuing to extend to the provincial government of Katanga—as to any other provincial government—the technical assistance which we have been proffering up till now, or from maintaining all the personnel that is prepared to remain there.[116]

Indeed, although it was issued by an opposition leader, this statement neatly sums up the position finally adopted by the Belgian government. Belgian public servants stationed in Katanga were ordered under serious penalties to stand by their assigned posts, and the Belgian military commander was empowered to conscript all male Belgian civilians between 20 and 45. Recognition continued to be withheld, but a Katangese delegation took part in important economic and financial negotiations with Belgium, while the Belgian Foreign Minister briefed the head of the Belgian technical assistance mission in Elisa-

[115] *La Libre Belgique,* July 12, 1960.
[116] July 19, 1960, quoted in *Congo 1960,* p. 736.

bethville on the advisability "to encourage the rallying of other Congolese provinces around Katanga—discreetly of course." [117]

Tshombe had repeatedly asserted that a number of political leaders from other provinces had expressed their intention of joining forces with Katanga in the formation of a "Congolese confederation" (a CONAKAT leitmotiv of long standing), and the Belgian press had delightedly announced the possible emergence of an assemblage that would gather Kasai, Kivu, Rwanda, and Burundi around the "Katangese core." As a matter of fact, as the Belgian Foreign Minister was cabling his above-mentioned instructions, the Baluba of Kasai were reviving their plans for a "Luba province," which was eventually proclaimed on August 8, 1960. There was, however, some uncertainty as to the exact degree of sovereignty claimed by the new "Mining State," housed in the Bakwanga premises of the Forminière diamond-mining company: while a letter addressed to Dag Hammarskjöld insisted on the wish to retain close links with the rest of the Congo, Albert Kalonji, speaking at Elisabethville, clearly referred to the new state's "independence." Moreover, although there is no indication of coordination between the two movements, it is worth noting that as secession was being proclaimed in Southern Kasai, a similar but abortive attempt was made by the PUNA leaders in the Equator Province. Also at the same date, members of the ABAKO youth movement staged a demonstration in Léopoldville in favor of Bakongo autonomy.

Meanwhile, in Léopoldville, Patrice Lumumba was understandably alarmed by the rapid disintegration of the Republic and thoroughly exasperated with the United Nations for failing to accomplish the primary task which they had specifically been asked to perform, namely, to preserve the Congo's territorial integrity. An extensive visit to the United States and Canada failed to produce any significant result. Convinced of the need to curb the secessionist movements before massive external assistance had turned them into impregnable strongholds, the Prime Minister decided to act against the weaker of the two secessionist "states," Southern Kasai. During the night of August 26–27, a small contingent of the "Congolese National Army" (the new official designation of the former Force Publique) moved into Bakwanga without meeting any significant resistance.[118] The Belgian forces quar-

[117] July 19, 1960, quoted in *Congo 1960*, pp. 744–745.

[118] Two years later (Oct. 2, 1962), the Adoula government had to reenact virtually the same action against Bakwanga, thus belatedly ratifying the late Premier's last political initiative.

tered at Kamina (the military base situated halfway between the two secessionist capitals of Elisabethville and Bakwanga) wisely declined to intervene to defend Albert Kalonji's still shaky regime, and within the next few days, the central government's troops were impressing their authority on the Baluba tribesmen with callous rigor. Katanga's position now appeared to be seriously threatened: in the BALUBAKAT stronghold of northern Katanga, the smoldering opposition to the Tshombe regime was rapidly assuming the dimensions of an organized guerrilla war, thus opening the way to a possible offensive from Kivu, while the collapse of the improvised buffer of Southern Kasai brought the national army within reach of the province's western frontier.

Although every contingent of the Force Publique that had been quartered in Katanga at the time of independence had been carefully screened and purged of all elements believed to be loyal to the central government, the building of a reliable Katangese force was still in its preliminary stage and many vital positions across the potential invasion routes were manned chiefly by white volunteers. These meager defenses were considerably reinforced, however, by Belgian troops and equipment serving officially in various capacities. Despite the Security Council's unambiguous injunctions, Belgium had availed itself of every possible loophole to delay the withdrawal of its best combat units from Katanga [119] and had allowed a substantial number of men to enlist in the Katangese forces under the veil of some tenuous legal fictions. Yet, by the end of August, most Belgian troops were in the process of leaving the province and the UN forces had taken control of the base at Kamina. But the appointment of the head of the Belgian mission of technical assistance in Katanga to the post of Minister of African Affairs was an unmistakable indication of the Belgian cabinet's deliberate intention to give more overt assistance to the secessionist regime. Thus, on September 7, nine tons of Belgian arms were unloaded at the Elisabethville airport, much to the embarrassment of the Belgian Foreign Minister who had been trying for weeks to impress upon world opinion the image of his government's candid innocuousness.[120]

[119] See Secretary General Hammarskjöld's note of protest to the Belgian government, Aug. 30, 1960. On Sept. 10, the Brussels correspondent of a London daily revealed that some 500 members of the Belgian forces (89 from the former Force Publique, 70 members of the metropolitan *gendarmerie,* and 326 "volunteers") were serving in Katanga.

[120] One of Moïse Tshombe's Belgian advisers bluntly declared on this particular occasion that this delivery was part of a continuous airlift that had been taking place for several days between Belgium and Katanga.

Crosscurrents in the Central Government

But Katanga's most effective relief was eventually supplied from Léopoldville where, on September 5, President Kasavubu yielded to weeks of persistent pressure and dismissed Premier Lumumba and six members of his cabinet. Tshombe reacted at once by advancing the suggestion of an "anti-Lumumbist league," but the Congolese parliament stood behind the deposed Premier and propped him up by two unequivocal votes of confidence (September 7–8). The UN forces irresolutely tried to intervene for the sake of neutrality by decreeing the closure of the Léopoldville radio station as well as of all airfields (a ban which did not prevent President Kasavubu from broadcasting his appeals from Brazzaville or Katanga from receiving Belgian arms and flying its military aircraft). Meanwhile, Senator Ileo, Kasavubu's choice for the Premier's office, had begun to realize that his chances of securing the national parliament's investiture for his tentative cabinet were extremely slight. On September 14, President Kasavubu parried the presumable disavowal of his protégé by adjourning the Congolese congress for a period of one month (it did not, in fact, convene again until July 1961).

Later that same day, however, in an unexpected development, the Chief of Staff of the national army, the freshly appointed Colonel Mobutu, announced his decision to "neutralize" all legal institutions until the end of the year and to rule through an improvised junta of university students and graduates. To many observers, Mobutu's putsch appeared to be a classical example of the military's disgusted reaction toward the politicians' bedlam. Yet virtually none of the usual postulates of a military coup were present at the time in the ranks of the Congolese army. No Sandhurst or Saint-Cyr had imbued the newly promoted Congolese officers with any form of mystique or caste consciousness. Mobutu himself (though advised by an authoritarian officer of the UN forces, Moroccan General Kettani) was no Rais—and no Ibrahim Abboud either—but simply a one-time army paymaster, neophyte newsman, and occasional police informer whose swift new career with the army had been that of a Lumumbist political commissar.

Although Colonel Mobutu's *coup d'état* had originally been aimed at both President and Premier, it took less than two weeks for Kasavubu to become reconciled with the insurgent officer and to appropriate the latter's suggestion of a ruling clique of graduates by giving it the valuable endorsement of his formal sanction. Ostensible anti-communism provided a convenient packaging for the convergent interests of the various groups that had backed the President and the colonel—either separately or simultaneously. Four days after the putsch, a cease-fire was negotiated and the advanced elements of the Congolese troops which had already entered Katanga were flown back by the UN. The Katangese *gendarmerie* was, however, left free to resume its attacks on the anti-Tshombe rebels of northern Katanga. By the end of September, President Kasavubu felt sufficiently assured to suggest the convening of a "round table" of national reconciliation.

Yet the Congo had never seemed farther away from peace and unity. By November, five different governments were claiming authority over the whole or parts of the Republic. Two of them (Ileo's phantom cabinet and Mobutu's amateurish "College of General Commissioners") were operating from Léopoldville though increasingly under a *de facto* UN guardianship, while President Kasavubu, carried by the sole virtue of his recognizable status as by a sort of life buoy, was managing to keep politically afloat in spite of his questionable behavior in the events which led to the assassination of Patrice Lumumba.

Further Course of Separatism

The rump of the Lumumba cabinet, led by Vice-Premier Gizenga, had retreated to the nationalist strongholds of Eastern Congo and, from its redoubt in Stanleyville, was actively striving to extend its control over Kivu and northern Kasai, while giving sporadic support to the northern Katanga rebels. Unlike the Tshombe and Kalonji regimes, however, the Stanleyville government never demanded separation from the Republic but, on the contrary, persistently claimed to be the sole legitimate authority in the Congo, a pretension which received diplomatic endorsement but little material assistance from a score of foreign governments.[121]

Conversely, the country's third focal point, Elisabethville (with its quasi-satellite based on Bakwanga) secured no formal recognition but a considerable measure of diplomatic connivance and material aid from the colonial nations of Europe and from the white-dominated governments of Southern Africa. For several months, a recruiting office functioned openly in Brussels. After August 1961, however, most Belgian

[121] The Casablanca group of African nations, Yugoslavia, Iraq, Cuba, and members of the Sino-Soviet bloc (concerning the alleged "communism" of Lumumbist and Gizengist circles, see Senator Humphrey's remarks in the *Congressional Record*, vol. CVII, pp. 20607–20613, Sept. 21, 1961).

"advisers" and mercenaries were ousted by the UN, a move which indirectly enhanced the influence of other foreign groups over the Katangese ruling circles. The vast resources derived from the exportation of mineral products were applied to the building of an expensive administrative and military machine as well as to establishing a far-reaching network of public relations and lobbying. Soldiers of fortune were recruited—on an average salary of $20 a day—from South Africa, the Rhodesias, Kenya, Algeria, and, of course, Belgium. The Katangese "cause," which had from the outset meant many things to many people, increasingly came to be associated with various shades of privateers and extreme right-wing activists, some of them apparently operating in a dual capacity. But, in spite of its considerable resources, the Tshombe regime was unable to eliminate the northern Katanga rebellion and had to limit its action to the control of a few key centers and to the conduct of retaliatory raids.

Interaction between Congolese Centers

Even though they were separated by deep-seated feelings of mutual antagonism, the three rival capitals maintained a ramshackle relationship interspersed by spasmodic fits of aggressiveness and mutual denunciation. Since Elisabethville and Stanleyville were hardly on speaking terms, Léopoldville acted as a sort of centerpiece in subsequent negotiations, vacillating between the two extreme poles according to a fairly uncomplicated balance-of-power pattern. No sooner had the Lumumbist government in exile entrenched itself in Stanleyville than the Léopoldville authorities sought a *rapprochement* with Katanga. Meetings between Kasavubu, Ileo, Tshombe, Kalonji, and others took place in Brazzaville under President Fulbert Youlou's sponsorship during December 1960 but led to no immediate agreement; both sides concurred on the need for further conversations but each went on to summon two separate "round tables" at different times and places.

Meanwhile, in Léopoldville, those who wished for a policy of national reconciliation rather than for the organization of a mere anti-Lumumbist league were voicing increasingly loud protests against Mobutu's illegal rule and demanding that representatives of the nationalist bloc (including Lumumba himself) be invited to any future political conference. The new Kennedy administration's alleged inclination toward such a scheme combined with reports of the restiveness of Lumumba's military jailers precipitated the cold-blooded design to have the deposed Premier murdered by proxy.[122] Lumumba's transfer to Elisabethville wrecked all chances of a nationwide reconciliation but failed to secure Katangese participation in the Léopoldville "round table" (January 25–February 15, 1961) which ended inconclusively after the fabricated version of the former Prime Minister's death had been officially disclosed by the Katanga government.

Guilt by association prodded Léopoldville circles to accept Katangese terms for further negotiations: three weeks later, delegates met in the capital of the Malagasy Republic, Tananarive, and endorsed Tshombe's blueprint for a confederacy of autonomous governments, the virtual invalidation of the national parliament, and a military axis between Léopoldville, Elisabethville, and Bakwanga (March 8–12, 1961). Concurrently, the Léopoldville authorities (the "College of General Commissioners" had now officially stepped down but Mobutu's praetorian guard still retained its blatant prominence on the political scene) had been exhibiting an increasing aggressiveness toward UN efforts to contain the Congolese army. The resolution of February 21, 1961, which a shocked Security Council adopted after the death of Patrice Lumumba, called for the evacuation of "all Belgian and other foreign military and para-military personnel and political advisers not under the UN Command, and mercenaries" and empowered the UN troops to use force "if necessary, in the last resort." This was a direct threat to those who had colluded in the murder of the former Premier and of other Lumumbist congressmen.[123] Both Tshombe and Ileo angrily denounced the resolution and threatened in strangely similar terms to use force against the UN. Within a week of the Security Council meeting, the tripartite military axis, later to be confirmed at Tananarive, had been compounded. Only three days later, violence erupted in the Lower Congo area between Mobutu's troops and UN contingents; by March 5, a greatly outnumbered Sudanese battalion

[122] The Catholic weekly *Présence Congolaise* had insinuated on Jan. 14, 1961, that Lumumba should be transferred to Elisabethville "for his own personal safety." The actual transfer was supervised by a Congolese undergraduate from the University of Louvain, part-time member of the "College of General Commissioners" and later minister of Kalonji's secessionist "kingdom." Only the presence of a UN detachment at the Bakwanga airport prevented him from delivering Lumumba into the hands of Albert Kalonji. On Feb. 9, however, Kalonji received his own contingent of six Lumumbist prisoners, who were subsequently put to death with hideous refinement. Kalonji was later sentenced to thirty months in prison for these and other crimes, but escaped from jail soon afterward.

[123] Doc. S/4741. On Feb. 1, 1961, Tshombe told the Secretary General of the UN that Lumumba's transfer was due to a request originating with President Kasavubu. It is significant to note that one of the very first actions of the Tananarive conferees was to demand the nullification of this resolution.

of the UN force was forced to evacuate the major seaport of Matadi, a serious blow to the organization's prestige in the Congo.

The Tananarive conference marked the height of Katanga's influence over the Congolese scene as well as the maximum strength of centrifugal strains; it also marked the extreme point of a tide which began to recede almost as soon as the talks were over. The obvious elation displayed by the Katangese press (as well as by some of the Belgian circles which had originally backed the secession) appeared especially ominous to those who had entertained persistent misgivings about the wisdom of the *rapprochement* with Elisabethville. Even those who had favored a federal structure for the Republic were now apprehensive about the amplitude of the "balkanization" process contemplated at Tananarive. Moreover, the fact that Katanga showed no particular alacrity to tender the economic assistance which it had repeatedly promised to its "Congolese brethren," coupled with the disquieting revival of military operations against the northern Katanga "rebels," reinforced the belief that the Tshombe regime was not prepared to recognize for its Luba opponents the principle of regional self-determination it championed for itself and that it was also determined to retain as long as possible the weapons of economic blackmail.[124]

The Trend toward a Federal Association

The turning of the tide was stressed by two significant developments. One was the initiation of genuine negotiations with the Stanleyville government which had been plagued by economic difficulties (unlike Katanga, Northeastern Congo had no easy access to the outside world and had been fairly effectively blockaded) and by political unrest in Kivu. Some irresolute feelers soon revealed the existence of an incipient rift in the Lumumbist stronghold between a moderate wing—chiefly represented by General Lundula's army—and the more radical MNC youth movement. The second major factor was President Kasavubu's gradual reconciliation with the United Nations. The increasingly evident resolve of American policy makers to encourage a political neutralization of the Congolese army in favor of the establishment of a government of national union quite possibly played a decisive role in the achievement of the agreement of April 17, which

[124] Moïse Tshombe himself lent credit to such judgments by the ambiguity of some of his public statements, e.g., "The Tananarive conference has achieved a dual result: on the one hand, it vindicates the independence of Katanga; on the other hand, it safeguards the former Belgian Congo's territorial integrity" (March 18, 1961, quoted in *Congo 1961*, p. 45).

urged "that all foreign personnel . . . who have not been recruited or recalled under the authority of the President be removed from the Congo." The agreement went on to suggest that, within "the sovereign rights of the Republic and the constitutional powers which he holds," the President "re-examine the appointment of foreign civilian, military and para-military personnel made under his authority." [125] Léopoldville's loyal adherence to this agreement was further secured by the promise of the urgently needed financial assistance which Katanga had failed to deliver. The final agreement on this point was significantly suspended, however, until the termination of the second round of negotiations between the Congolese political leaders at Coquilhatville.

Thus, a subtle but unmistakable change in the political climate had taken place by the time the Coquilhatville conference (April 23–May 30, 1961) convened. In the absence of a delegation from Stanleyville, Moïse Tshombe tried to recapture the initiative and to revive the "spirit of Tananarive" by bluntly demanding the repudiation of the agreement passed with the United Nations. When this gambit failed, Tshombe abruptly walked out of the conference but was prevented by the army from leaving Coquilhatville. He was then arrested and later transferred to Léopoldville, but was eventually released, after having spent two months in mild confinement, in return for pledges which he promptly repudiated after his return to Katanga. Meanwhile, the Coquilhatville conferees had resolved that the Congo should be converted into a federal republic with a maximum of twenty-three member states and that a federal constitution should be drafted by a governmental commission with UN assistance.

This constitutional draft was not completed until October 15, 1962. The proposed "provinces" or "states" of the federation are as follows. From the former Léopoldville province: *Kongo central* (Lower Congo), *Mayi Ndombe* (lit., "Black Water," the African name for Lake Leopold II), *Kwango,* and *Kwilu* (the state of Northern Kwilu, sponsored by the ABAZI at Coquilhatville, has not been retained); from the former Kasai province: *Sud-Kasai, Etat de l'Unité Kasaienne* (also known as *Kasai Occidental*), *Luluabourg, Sankuru,* and *Lomani* (claiming encroachments into southwestern Maniema and northwestern Katanga); from the former Equator Province: *Cuvette centrale* (also known as *Etat Mongo*), *Ubangi,* and *Congo-Ubangi;* from the former Eastern Province: *Ueles, Kibali-Ituri,* and *Congo oriental* (in fact, the rump of the

---

[125] Doc. S/4807/Ann. 1. The agreement was opposed by Ileo, whose cabinet it entirely ignored and who from that moment on held even less authority than previously.

Eastern Province, with Stanleyville); from Kivu: *Maniema, Nord-Kivu,* and *Sud-Kivu;* from Katanga: *Lualaba* and *Sud-Katanga* (that is, the zone controlled by the Tshombe regime).

The twenty-one resolutions of the conference formed by themselves a fairly detailed sketch of what the future constitution should be. What they outlined was a rather loose federation which was only slightly more centralized than the confederacy planned at Tananarive. In a sense, however, the two most significant decisions reached at Coquilhatville—namely, the endorsement of the agreement passed with the UN on April 17 and the general consensus to reopen the Congolese parliament—were arrived at outside the formal deliberative process of the conference.

The two months following the conference were almost entirely filled by the negotiations which eventually led to the meeting of the national parliament on July 22–23, 1961. Since the reanimation of the elected assemblies (where the Lumumbist bloc had held a majority) had been the chief demand of the Stanleyville regime, a reconciliation on these premises was fairly easy to attain. The "Nationalist Bloc" agreed to send its delegates to the reopening of parliament, although Antoine Gizenga diffidently remained in Stanleyville. Katanga, on the other hand, now found itself increasingly isolated, although it knew that, if it came to the worst, it now had a capacity to resist (with its army heavily equipped and staffed and the opposition jailed, killed, or isolated in "refugee camps") which it had lacked at the time of the secession. Although the strength of the Lumumbist bloc had apparently not been seriously impaired by months of intrigue and intimidation, Ileo and Gizenga's claims to legitimacy were equally dismissed by parliament, which then proceeded to approve Cyrille Adoula's cabinet of national union by a near-unanimous vote as the sole legal successor to the first central government of the Congo.[126]

Can Congo Cohesion Be Secured?

Yet, in spite of this apparently extensive support, the foundations of Adoula's power remain exceedingly fragile, as indeed they have been from the outset. While Katanga continued to defy the new central government, the Eastern Province maintained a diffident aloof-

[126] The Adoula government was invested by a vote of 121 out of 122 in the House of Representatives and by a unanimous vote of the 70 members present in the Senate. Sixteen of the 26 ministers had been members of the Lumumbist coalition in June 1960, and 13 had held responsible posts in the Lumumba government. Seven had been members of the Gizenga government and 7 of the Ileo government. Besides the 26 ministers, there were also 15 secretaries of state (9 of them belonging to the Lumumbist bloc of 1960).

ness that sometimes seemed to contradict the endorsement which its representatives had officially granted to the new cabinet, not to mention Gizenga's vice-premiership in the Adoula government. Clearly, Premier Adoula's firmness toward Katanga was to be the touchstone of continued Lumumbist support. The UN military operations in Katanga, clumsy and unfinished as they were, sustained the loyalty of nationalist circles and even elicited their partial endorsement of the swift liquidation of the last sequels of the Gizenga regime in Stanleyville. Even when Gizenga was interned and his post offered to Moïse Tshome, at least a fraction of the nationalist bloc was willing for the sake of national reconciliation to countenance this breach in the Adoula government's policy of balanced retribution against both extremes. After Katanga had once again repudiated the pledges made by Tshombe during his conversations with the Premier at Kitona, there was a distinct malaise, however, between the radical and moderate wings of the national government.

Another source of friction within the governing coalition was the important role retained by the military and by some of the appointees held over from the Mobutu era. Thus, the MNC Minister of the Interior, Christophe Gbenye, tried in vain to oust the strongly tainted chief of the internal security service, Victor Nendaka, but was himself eventually "kicked upstairs" into an innocuous vice-premiership (and later arrested) without having been able to establish his control of the state police.

After nearly a year, however, the permanent threat of a radical outflanking had somewhat receded: the spoils of office, the lures of foreign assignments, the fresh perspectives opened by the creation of new states, as well as a sort of postclonic lassitude had mollified nationalist ardor and produced a certain erosion of the Lumumbist bloc of 1960, particularly among the ethnic parties, such as the MUB, the UNC, and the BALUBAKAT, which had formed tactical alliances with the MNC. Thus, in July 1962, a cabinet reshuffle resulted in the elimination of virtually every member of the government who had held ministerial office in Stanleyville under Antoine Gizenga. Although Premier Adoula in this manner deliberately whittled down his parliamentary basis of support, the new opposition has so far been too disjoined to destroy the precarious stability of the Congolese government,[127] but if this shift toward the center was intended, as has been

[127] The Adoula cabinet has been defeated in the House of Representatives on one occasion but chose not to consider this vote as expressing censure.

surmised, to appease the Katangese secessionists, it has failed to produce the desired short-term effect while jeopardizing the internal cohesion of the Republic. Adoula's fragile power rests almost exclusively upon his capacity to restore national unity—an achievement which he is, by international consensus, virtually disabled to accomplish otherwise than through negotiation or vicarious pressure. Whether the Congolese Premier eventually succeeds in walking this tightrope depends a great deal upon factors over which he has little or no control; hence, the importance for those who have to realize that the ineluctable alternative is a return of anarchy to central Africa.

ECONOMIC AND FINANCIAL PROBLEMS

The Dominant Position of the Companies

From the early days of the Free State when Leopold II (himself no mean businessman) was seeking the support of Belgian financial circles to extend his hold over the remotest provinces of his new African domain, the links between governmental authorities and the business world have been uncommonly close. Most of the major financial groups acquired their initial foothold in the Congo in return for their participation in the construction of urgently needed railway links: thus, the building of the Chemin de Fer des Cataractes, which connected the interior to the Atlantic coast, was undertaken by a concern dominated by one of Leopold's early aides and collaborator, Albert Thys, whose Banque d'Outremer was later absorbed (1928) by Belgium's most powerful banking establishment, the Société Générale de Belgique. The Société Générale itself did not enter the scene until 1906, when it became associated with the opening of the Chemin de Fer du Bas-Congo au Katanga (BCK), the exploitation of diamond fields along the projected route (Forminière), and the formation of the Union Minière. A third group, that of the Empain interests, took care of the construction of a link between the upper course of the Congo and Lake Tanganyika through the Compagnie des Chemins de Fer du Congo Supérieur aux Grands Lacs Africains (CFL, founded in 1902) and was also rewarded with mining privileges which were handed over to a subsidiary, the Compagnie Minière des Grand Lacs.

With the exception of the Lambert bank, an early associate of Leopold and Albert Thys, whose banking arm in Africa is the Socobanque,[128] other Belgian financial groups (Banque de Bruxelles,

[128] However, two foreign banks, the French Banque Nationale pour le Commerce et l'Industrie and the Bank of America, each hold a 20 per cent interest in the

Nagelmackers, Allard, Solvay) acquired their major colonial interests after the Congo had been annexed by Belgium. Having gained control of the Banque d'Outremer, however, the Société Générale has long been the overwhelmingly dominant force on the Congolese scene through its chief holding company, the CCCI (Compagnie du Congo pour le Commerce et l'Industrie, originally created by Thys), whose involvements extend from mining to canning and from cotton to cement. Several Belgian corporations controlled by the Société Générale have also opened their own African subsidiaries in a variety of fields. All together, it has been estimated that at the time of independence some 70 per cent of the Congo's economy fell directly or indirectly within the scope of the Société Générale.

Yet, because King Leopold intended to preserve his economic ascendancy, the Free State had retained a substantial share in all major concerns, whether they were chartered companies or private corporations. Thus, the chartered Compagnie du Katanga, formed in 1891 to secure the occupation of the southeastern part of the territory, joined with the Free State in the foundation of the Comité Spécial du Katanga which took over the development of the whole area and subsequently became a major partner in the launching of the Union Minière. The original interest-sharing agreement between the Free State and the Compagnie du Katanga (in which, incidentally, the Free State held a 10 per cent interest, later increased to 12 per cent) provided for the division of the entire 215,000 square-mile area into a checkered pattern of some 4,600 lots, with the freehold of every third lot being assigned to the chartered company. This solution soon proved to be unworkable, and the two partners resorted to a system of joint ownership, for which purpose the Comité Spécial du Katanga was created in 1900. The share of the Free State in the CSK was two-thirds and that of the Compagnie du Katanga was one-third.

Similarly, in return for the handsome privileges granted to the Chemin de Fer des Grands Lacs, the Free State retained a portion of the votes (25 per cent) and of the profits (47.4 per cent) of that corporation, although it was kept out of the CFL's profitable mining subsidiary, the Minière des Grands Lacs. The Free State also acquired

---

Socobanque. Other important non-Belgian interests are those of Unilever (palm oil, rubber, and cocoa), the Rockefeller group (which holds an undetermined share in the Union Minière through the Tanganyika Concessions, Ltd., a dominant share in a textile concern, etc.), the Ryan-Guggenheim group (a quarter share in the Forminière), and the French Banque de Paris et des Pays-Bas.

a dominant share (50 per cent, later expanded to 55.6 per cent) in the Forminière, which was created to exploit the deposits held by the Minière du Bécéka, itself the mining branch of the BCK railroad company.

Much the same course was maintained after Belgium had taken over the Free State and, in 1928, notably, the colonial government took part with several financial groups (Société Générale, Empain, Allard) in the founding of a development corporation, the Comité National du Kivu, which came to exercise virtually the same kind of monopoly over all types of real-estate operations as the Comité Spécial du Katanga in its respective area. The colonial government also had substantial interests (ranging from 2 to 98 per cent of the capital) in a variety of firms with such diverse activities as the production and sale of electricity, all types of mines and plantations, land, sea, and air transport, real estate, fisheries, etc.—not to mention the direct exploitation of the Kilo-Moto gold fields (65 per cent of the Congo's gold output) and the operation of the Société de Crédit au Colonat et à l'Industrie, the OTRACO (a nonmonopolistic transport agency), and the REGIDESO (a corporation specializing in the supply of water and power).[129]

Although the colonial authorities were thus in a position to play an active part in the management and in the supervision of private concerns which frequently owed their flourishing condition to the prerogatives they had derived from their association with the state, it was, as a rule, extremely uncommon for the agents of the public sector to interfere in any way with the operations of such companies. Even in those corporations where it held a majority position (for example, the CSK or the Forminière), the colonial government was always content to leave board presidencies and managerial positions to representatives of private interest groups.[130] Indeed, over the years, government and business evolved a smooth and implicit *modus vivendi* by virtue of which many colonial civil servants of senior rank acquired well-remunerated directorates in one or several colonial firms —usually, but not always, after an early retirement. Similarly (al-

[129] The total value of the Congo's portfolio of securities was assessed at between $640,000,000 and $760,000,000 as of Jan. 1, 1960. The revenue derived from these securities during the year 1959 approached $24,000,000. A list of the Congo's holdings will be found in *Etudes Congolaises*, III, no. 5 (May 1962), 104–109.

[130] In the case of the Forminière, the presidency of the board was traditionally assumed by a representative of the Société Générale, although this group's interests in the company had dwindled from 25 per cent in 1906 to 5 per cent in 1959.

though in a slightly different perspective), several members of the political class—including notably leading members of the House and Senate committees on colonial affairs, as well as most ministers of colonies—sat on the boards of various Congolese syndicates.

While no Congolese political party had opened advocated nationalization, the possibility that independence (and the correlative transfer of the colonial government's interests to the future republic) might disturb this suave relationship caused some serious apprehensions among Belgian official and business circles. Thus, by two decrees passed during the last month of Belgian sovereignty, the two chartered companies in which the colonial government held a majority interest (Comité Spécial du Katanga and Comité National du Kivu) were dissolved and their assets divided among shareholders. In contrast, the charter of the Compagnie des Chemins de Fer des Grands Lacs, in which the government controlled only 25 per cent of the vote, was renewed for another thirty years. The dissolution of the CSK was particularly momentous, since it had owned some 55 per cent of the voting stock of the Union Minière: through its two-to-one ascendancy within the CSK, the Congolese government would have been able to control that powerful mining concern by strictly legal means; after the dissolution, however, the share of the Republic was reduced to a less ominous 40 per cent. Although this operation met, at the time, with little if any hostility on the part of ill-informed nationalist circles,[131] it can be considered as illustrative of the mistrust which continues to pervade the relations between Belgium and its former colony, as well as of the gap that separates political emancipation from economic autonomy.

Postindependence Economic Strains

If the prospect of independence had caused some alarm in the world of business, subsequent developments did not improve the economic situation of the Republic. The disruption of Congolese unity and the abrupt detachment of the two prosperous areas of Katanga and South Kasai, followed in the last months of 1960 by the increasing estrangement of the Eastern Province and Kivu, led to the virtual partition of the country into four economic zones. This situation was partially reflected in the diverting of the flow of trade away from traditional channels: thus, the movement of goods at the country's major

---

[131] Indeed, the measure could even be construed as being consonant with the impatience expressed by some nationalist leaders toward the chartered companies, as they operated under Belgian rule.

seaport, Matadi, fell under 60 per cent of its normal pre-1960 volume, in spite of the additional traffic brought by the presence of UN contingents.

On the whole, however, the productive capacity of the Congolese economy remained remarkably stable despite political fluctuations. Total exports from the former Belgian colony during 1961 have been estimated at some 20,000,000,000 francs, that is, only 25 per cent less than the comparable figure for 1959 (a year which, owing to the uncertainty of the political future, had seen an abnormal swell of exports). But, satisfactory as they may appear, these results must be judged in the light of the fact that at least one-tenth of all exports (notably those of diamonds and gold) followed more or less clandestine routes and brought no profit to the central government, while Katanga alone accounted for more than 11,000,000,000 of these 20,000,-000,000 francs. Thus, the most drastic decline was suffered by those areas which remained loyal to the Léopoldville regime.

In terms of public finance, the secession of Katanga entailed a loss of approximately one-half of the receipts of the central authorities. Even in those provinces which continued to pay nominal allegiance to Léopoldville, the proceeds from taxation and other forms of revenue, when they were collected at all, dwindled appreciably below their preindependence level. At the same time, public expenditure authorized by these same provincial governments and ascribed by them to the national account frequently went on unchecked.

The structural pattern of public disbursements incurred by the central authorities has also been substantially modified by the headlong increase of emoluments paid to all classes of government personnel. Not surprisingly, the most impressive raise has been that which was granted to the army: 450 per cent. Members of the political class have also boosted their own salaries by an average 380 per cent, while the pay of schoolteachers, civil servants, and other government employees was raised, respectively, by 96, 93, and 115 per cent (but only one year after independence).[132]

On the other hand, public investments have been slashed mercilessly and the payment of interest on the public debt has been almost

---

[132] During the first year of independence, the salaries of the last three categories had been raised only by 18, 12 and 30 per cent respectively. The amazing raise enjoyed by the army accounted for 58 per cent of the additional expenditure incurred for salaries by the central government between June 30, 1960, and May 30, 1961. The army and the police received 25.3 per cent of the sums paid by the national government to its personnel during 1961.

wholly discontinued. As a matter of fact, the Republic went without a formal budget throughout 1961 while the deficit of expenditures over receipts mounted to 8,800,000,000 francs (that is, approximately one-seventh of the estimated gross national product at the time of independence). For the first quarter of 1962, the income of the central government added up to a mere 1,612,000,000 francs while expenditures (including 2,464,000,000 francs in subsidies to the provincial authorities) reached a figure of 5,117,000,000 francs.[133] Advances for a total of 3,195,000,000 francs from the Conseil Monétaire (which acts as the nation's agency for the issuing of currency) have helped to fill the alarming gap but have of course not solved the country's medium- or long-term problems—not to mention the permanent threat such measures represent for the already precarious stability of the Congolese currency. Although for various reasons inflation has not assumed the wildfire character that had been feared, it mounted irresistibly throughout 1962 and the slightest convulsion might suffice to unleash an irretrievable process of deterioration. Indeed, one of the benefits to be derived from the return of Katanga to the Congolese fold—apart from its financial implications, which, in any case, would not provide an automatic solution to the Republic's economic plight—lies in the restoration of badly needed international confidence in the country's future. No measure of financial or monetary surgery can be performed in the absence of a reasonably stable governmental authority; nor were the occasional and parsimonious charities offered by Katanga an adequate substitute for economic reunification.

HUMAN RESOURCES: ADMINISTRATION AND EDUCATION

The financial difficulties faced by the Congolese Republic are directly linked to its administrative problems. Not only does the Léopoldville government continue to maintain a ponderous administrative superstructure inherited from the colonial period to rule a truncated territory, but it does so with a noticeably larger and more expensive personnel. Whereas in 1960, the colonial administration employed 190,000 persons and spent 6,300,000,000 francs in salaries (including 2,500,000,000 for its 10,000 European employees), the Congolese government devoted at least nine-tenths of its expenditures for 1962 to the

---

[133] Revised budgetary estimates for 1962 reckon on receipts of little more than 4,000,000,000 francs with expenditures probably reaching over 19,000,000,000. The proceeds yielded by the commercialization of foodstuffs donated by various foreign countries (notably the United States), although normally earmarked for development programs, may help to reduce the gap to 10,000,000,000 francs.

remuneration of its political and administrative personnel, the ranks
of which have swelled to some 205,000 persons. The most substantial
addition to the governmental payrolls comes from the army, which
now receives some 3,000,000,000 francs a year (that is, approximately
one-fifth of all salaries), with effectives of over 35,000—not including
the Katangese troops!—as compared with 24,000 for the whole colony
prior to independence. Much the same comment applies to the police:
from less than 9,000 in 1960, it has increased its numbers by some
1,200 units and received an estimated 800,000,000 francs in 1962. The
African educational staff (to which must be added approximately one-
half of the 2,500 "technicians" dispatched by the Belgian government)
has increased from 36,000 to 42,000 and draws salaries for a total
amount of over 4,200,000,000 francs. The number of civil servants and
government workers (including those in the service of local government authorities) has not substantially increased, at least as long as
Katanga's own cadres are not taken into account. In 1960, the 12,000
African members of the colonial civil service (*agents sous statut*) who
were paid on the same basic salary scale as Europeans received emoluments to a total amount of 1,400,000,000 francs; two years later, this
amount had increased by some 50 per cent for a comparable number
of employees—a change which chiefly represents a mere consequence
of rapid promotions due to an accelerated process of africanization.

But the chief problem posed by the Congolese civil service—at
least for the immediate future—is not so much that of its budgetary
onus. The number of Belgian technicians employed by the Léopoldville
government has stabilized at approximately one-fourth of its 1959
level and, owing to the fact that Belgium supports a share of their
salaries, the strain on the Congolese budget is not excessive. The UN
has also contributed a small international contingent of experts (most
of them engaged in the fields of public health and communications).
The cause for alarm remains, however, in the unvarnished fact that
there is a continued shortage of qualified African personnel in the
highest ranks of the national administration. At the beginning of 1962,
only 361 Congolese had reached senior rank in the civil service and
the judiciary.[134] Moreover, many of these high-ranking Congolese
officials continue to rely to a considerable extent on the expertise of

[134] Much the same siutation prevails in the educational services, where only 12
Congolese were reported as having attained senior posts in 1962. On the other
hand, owing largely to their role on the political scene, the army and the police
have been widely africanized: there were 700 Congolese army officers, police
chiefs, and inspectors in early 1962—i.e., more than under the colonial regime.

foreign advisers, which means that duplication of functions is far from uncommon despite the over-all reduction in the top echelons of the Congolese bureaucracy. The effects of this procedure on the efficiency of governmental operations need hardly be enlarged upon and, to be sure, the present situation must be regarded as purely transitional. But normalization appears unlikely in the immediate future, and the prospect for the multiplication of several autonomous "state" bureaucracies, no matter what its political merits may be, hardly seems to make managerial sense in a country which has barely enough competent personnel to staff its centralized services.

The answer to the Congo's shortage of qualified cadres lies in a stepped-up educational effort—and to state this is merely to record the obvious. There is, unfortunately, no easy way out of this sort of deficiency. The Congo's record in the field of elementary education may be regarded as reasonably satisfactory, as already noted, but the secondary school system remains far from adequate, especially when viewed in terms of its value as an introduction to higher education and not simply as a dead-end complement to primary schooling. In 1962, no more than 200 students graduated from secondary school with sufficient credentials to gain outright admission to the university level. Hence, the importance of such institutions as the Ecole Nationale de Droit et d'Administration, founded in 1960, which opens its doors to—*inter alia*—civil servants who have not received the complete secondary training that would make them eligible for admission to the regular university programs leading to a formal academic degree.[135] Since 1961, however, Catholic Lovanium University at Léopoldville has eased its entrance requirements for students enrolling in special three-year programs which are known as *graduats* and in 1962 included the following fields: pharmacy, agronomy, economics, social science and community development, and business administration. In a different field, a new teachers college (Institut Pédagogique National) opened in December 1961 and is undertaking with UNESCO assistance the training of sorely needed teachers for the lower half of the secondary school system (a rough equivalent of the American junior high school).

All these efforts converge toward a similar aim—to fill the present

---

[135] Initial entrance requirements were four years of postelementary schooling, later increased to six, except for government employees having been in public service for at least two years. The enrollment for the first year included 46 per cent of civil servants, that for the second year 34 per cent.

gap between tomorrow's university-trained elites and those who have had to assume vital responsibilities in one of the most tormented periods of the country's history. Even if a minimum of continuity is assured, however, it will inevitably be some years before a truly stable and homogeneous administration emerges or, correlatively, before the nation's administrative structure is coherent enough to form the backbone of the governmental apparatus and to withstand periods of political stress.

In a contiguous order of problems, the temptation undoubtedly exists for the national administration to ensure efficiency by relying indiscriminately on the time-honored, coercive methods of the colonial *raj*. Beyond the short-term problems of africanization, the Congo (or, for that matter, any other African state) must sooner or later face the fact that the machinery of democratic government may be more cumbersome than that of authoritarian rule and resolve whether it wants to accept or reject the prospect of a bureaucratic tyranny dominating an alienated people.

External Relations

Ever since it achieved its independence, the Congo has been an *object* rather than a *subject* in the field of international relations. Whatever attitudes may have been assumed and whatever links may have been formed by the new republic have usually reflected internal strains and conflicts rather than any discernible stand on specific world- or continent-wide issues. Indeed, the Congo's foreign relations have followed not one but several simultaneous, conflicting patterns.

Patrice Lumumba's government program published on July 23, 1960, contained a fairly articulate passage on foreign policy:

The Congo shall practice a policy of absolute neutrality. It shall not adhere to any bloc. . . . The Congo is prepared to pass agreements or conventions with any country in the world as long as they do not entail an alienation of national sovereignty. . . . The Republic of Congo affirms its solidarity with other African countries. It shall avail itself of every opportunity to become associated with any effort toward *rapprochement* and collaboration among all nations on the continent. The Congo shall do this while preserving its own individuality. . . . Without impairing the Republic's doctrine of positive neutralism, the government shall turn toward those foreign countries which are able to offer possibilities for the recruitment of technicians and the supply of capital. Within the framework of an independent Congo, the government intends to pursue its relationship with Belgium on the basis of equality. In conformity with the good relations we wish to entertain with the Belgians, we shall turn to them in the first place in order to solve our immense technical, administrative, financial, military, and educational problems.[136]

Yet, before this document had been released, the Congo had virtually severed its diplomatic relations with Belgium [137] and had become a focal point of international tensions the control of which was entirely beyond the command of its government.

Just as it marked the beginning of a process of political and economic disintegration, the secession of Katanga precipitated the emergence of strongly antithetical orientations in the rival capitals of Léopoldville, Elisabethville, and (later) Stanleyville. By providing the Soviet Union with what seemed to be an unfailing opportunity to advance pawns on the African continent and to act as the champion of Congolese unity, the breakaway province and its backers unpremeditatedly—but unquestionably—injected the cold war into central Africa. From that moment, few attitudes or pronouncements of the Congolese leaders have been unencumbered by extraneous factors of polarization. Thus, Mobutu's decision to expel Soviet and other Communist-bloc missions from Léopoldville in September 1960 was motivated not so much by considerations of internal security or ideological commitment as by a desire to preempt unconditional support from the West for his military putsch, in conformity with a fairly hackneyed process. Similarly, the overt or covert endorsements received by the Stanleyville authorities (from the Communist bloc, the "Casablanca powers," etc.) or by the Katanga regime (from South Africa, the Federation of Rhodesia and Nyasaland, Portugal, the Congo-Brazzaville) did not reflect the interests, much less the ideological aspirations, of the populations administered by these two governments.

The investiture of the Adoula government (which was recognized by East and West alike) has sometimes been interpreted as an African version of disengagement and the governmental declaration presented by the new Premier appeared to recognize that the safest and most sensible policy course for a country which had had the ill fortune to become a pawn in the East-West feud was one of painstaking neutrality.[138] Thus, Congolese foreign policy has come full circle and sev-

---

[136] Cited in *Congo 1960*, pp. 574–575.

[137] They were resumed on Nov. 27, 1961.

[138] This was a conclusion already reached, in a different setting, at the Berlin Conference of 1885.

eral parts of Premier Adoula's 1961 program are strongly reminiscent of Patrice Lumumba's earlier options, notably when he underlined his government's intention "to defend our independence against any outside interference through a policy of nonalignment" and "to extend its moral and material support to all African movements of national liberation." [139] The latter pledge has taken the form of offering a refuge and some material facilities to certain groups of guerrilla fighters from Angola. On the African scene, the Congo studiously sought to retain an uncommitted position between the so-called "Casablanca" and "Monrovia" groups. Since cutting itself from its Lumumbist wing, however, the Adoula government has steered increasingly closer to the French-speaking, generally pro-Western nations of the Union of African and Malagasy States, but, as a sort of counterpart, it has also become affiliated with the Pan-African Freedom Movement of East, Central, and Southern Africa (PAFMECSA). The Republic has also sought association with the European Economic Community.

Although the Congo may have been momentarily extricated from the cold war, this could hardly be considered as an end in itself by Western policy makers, let alone by the Congolese people themselves. Indeed, even this purely negative result will remain problematical as long as the Republic has not been irrevocably reunified. While the reintegration of Katanga may admittedly not prove a panacea for every one of the Congo's ailments, the secession of this affluent province has affected virtually all aspects of its present problems. Until this issue has been solved successfully (an achievement requiring more than the formal surrender of Katanga), the Congo will remain an area of precarious stability, a permanent invitation to the maneuvering skills of the major nations.

Yet, momentous as it seemed over two and a half years, the question of reunification represents only a preface to the true problems of an independent, developing nation. It is yet too early to discern whether the Congo (or, for that matter, the other newly independent nations of Africa) will be able to ward off the plights of economic stagnation, political "caudillismo," and social ossification which have afflicted many Latin American nations long after their emancipation

---

[139] *Compte-rendu analytique* (*Chambre*), Aug. 2, 1961. One month after his investiture, Premier Adoula attended the Belgrade conference of nonaligned nations.

from Europe. The struggle for national independence has yet to be won. But the Congo has not forfeited all prospects of playing a major role on the African scene. Its economic chances remain virtually intact. And to believe in the Republic's future is not merely an act of simple faith.

BIBLIOGRAPHY

OFFICIAL PUBLICATIONS

Government documents concerning the Congo have been issued by the three successive regimes under which the country has lived since 1885. The Berlin Act of Feb. 26, 1885, and other international conventions relating to the existence of the Free State are collected in A. De Busschere, *Code des traités et arrangements internationaux intéressant la Belgique—Extrait contenant les actes relatifs à l'Etat indépendant du Congo* (Bruxelles, 1896). The Berlin Act and the conference itself have also been studied by E. S. Crowe in *The Berlin West African Conference, 1884–1885* (London: Longmans, 1942). The acts of the Congo Free State can be found in the *Recueil usuel de législation de l'Etat indépendant du Congo* (Bruxelles, 1905) and also, partly, in O. Louwers and P. Grenade, *Codes et lois du Congo belge* (Bruxelles: Weissenbruch, 1923). Another valuable document of the Free State period, the report of the 1906 parliamentary commission of inquiry, has been published in English in an abridged version by George W. MacAlpine, *Abstract of the Report of the Commission of Enquiry into the Administration of the Congo Free State* (London: Clarke, 1906).[1]

The basic document of the Belgian colonial period (1908–1960), the *Loi du 18 octobre 1908 sur le gouvernement du Congo belge* (usually referred to as the *Charte Coloniale*), can be found not only in the *Moniteur Belge* of that year but also (along with major *décrets, arrêtés,* and *ordonnances*) in P. Piron and J. Devos, *Codes et lois du Congo belge* (8th ed.; Léopoldville: Ed. Codes et Lois, 1959). Several treaties have been devoted to the public law and government of the Belgian Congo. The earliest and most comprehensive is M. Halewijck de Heusch, *La Charte Coloniale* (4 vols.; Bruxelles: Weissenbruch, 1910). A more recent but occasionally inaccurate study is that of J. P. Paulus, *Droit public du Congo belge*

[1] The following abbreviations have been used in this bibliography: ARSC, Académie Royale des Sciences Coloniales (Brussels); CEDESA, Centre de Documentation Economique et Sociale Africaine; CRISP, Centre de Recherche et d'Information Socio-politique; IAI, International African Institute; IALI, Inter-African Labour Institute; IRCB, Institut Royal Colonial Belge (Brussels); IRES, Institut de Recherches Economiques et Sociales (Louvain and Léopoldville); IRR, Institute of Race Relations (London); IRRI, Institut Royal des Relations Internationales; and Solvay, Institut de Sociologie Solvay at the Université Libre de Bruxelles.

(Bruxelles: Solvay, 1959). The best-documented and most authoritative modern commentary is offered by T. Heyse in his *Congo belge et Ruanda-Urundi—Notes de droit public et commentaire de la Charte Coloniale* (2 vols.; Bruxelles: Van Campenhout, 1955–1957). The unfrequent interventions of the metropolitan parliament in colonial affairs are recorded in the *Annales Parlementaires* and *Compte-Rendu Analytique* of the House of Representatives and Senate. Draft legislation and reports are reproduced in the *Documents Parlementaires* (House or Senate, respectively); this is true for the report of the commission appointed to inquire into the Léopoldville disturbances of Jan. 1959. The yearly *Rapports sur l'administration générale du Congo belge* (which corresponded to the British "Colonial Reports" and had a comparable value as collections of factual data and statistical information) were also circulated as parliamentary documents.

The official gazettes of the Belgian colonial government were the *Bulletin Officiel* and the *Bulletin Administratif*, which merged in 1960 under the title of *Moniteur Congolais*. Among the miscellaneous publications of an official character put out by the colonial administration, those which concerned the Congolese economy were particularly noteworthy: the *Bulletin Mensuel des Statistiques Générales du Congo Belge et du Ruanda-Urundi* and the *Bulletin Mensuel du Commerce Extérieur du Congo Belge et du Ruanda-Urundi* as well as the yearly reports entitled *La situation économique du Congo belge et du Ruanda-Urundi* (all three of which began appearing in 1950) provide valuable data but little economic analysis. The situation in terms of public finance was appraised by the *Bulletin de la Banque Centrale du Congo Belge et du Ruanda-Urundi* as well by this institution's yearly *Rapports*. The Governor-General's address at the opening session of the Conseil de Gouvernement was chiefly a lofty appraisal of the over-all situation during the preceding year but sometimes contained cautious pronouncements on future policies; those speeches (*Discours du Gouverneur Général à la séance d'ouverture du Conseil de Gouvernment*), accompanied by a selection of assorted statistics, were normally published annually, beginning in 1932. The colonial information service (INFORCONGO) performed its public relations task by disseminating countless roseate accounts; one of its publications, however (*The Belgian Congo*, 2 vols., 1960), deserves notice as a useful compendium of generally accurate facts and figures.

The transitional period which saw the emergence of an independent Congolese Republic has produced a complex mass of official and semiofficial documents, to which have been added, since July 1960, a copious sheaf of international records. A path has fortunately been cleared through this dense growth by two Belgian research institutions, the Centre de Recherche et d'Information Socio-politiques and the Institut Royal des Relations Internationales. The first of these two institutions publishes yearly surveys of the

Congolese scene which combine penetrating analysis with an extremely wide selection of relevant documents; no one can hope to acquire a full knowledge of the Congo crisis without resorting to these volumes: *Congo 1959* (1960); J. Gérard-Libois and Benoît Verhaegen, *Congo 1960* (3 vols.; 1961); and Benoît Verhaegen, *Congo 1961* (1962)—all Bruxelles. The IRRI, on the other hand, has been more preoccupied with the publication of documents which it considers relevant to the presentation of Belgium's case. It has devoted five issues of its bimonthly review, *Chronique de Politique Etrangère* (Bruxelles), to the presentation of 209 such documents, gathered in two volumes: *La crise congolaise—1er janvier 1959–15 août 1960* (*Chron. Pol. Etrangère*, vol. XIII, nos. 4–6, July–Nov. 1960) and *Evolution de la crise congolaise de septembre 1960 à avril 1961* (*ibid.*, vol. XIV, nos. 5–6, Sept.–Nov. 1961).

Both CRISP and IRRI, in their respective collections, have published the resolutions of the political and economic Round Table conferences convened in 1960, as well as the text of the Congo's provisional constitution, the *loi fondamentale*. The official sources for these documents remain, however, the Belgian *Documents Parlementaires* and official gazette (*Moniteur Belge*), together with congressional records. The only available commentary on the *loi fondamentale* is offered by F. Perin in his *Les institutions politiques du Congo indépendant* (Bruxelles: CRISP, 1960).

The official publications of the Republic of the Congo have followed a fairly irregular schedule. The debates of the national parliament (House and Senate) are recorded in a *Compte-Rendu Analytique,* and the few laws it has voted are published—with the government's executive decrees—in the *Moniteur Congolais*. The central government has put out a few occasional documents of a political character, such as the Foreign Ministry's white paper, *La province du Katanga et l'indépendance congolaise* (Léopoldville-Kalina, n.d.), which presents the Léopoldville authorities' version of the Katanga secession. A few government agencies have kept on publishing statistical data, and the Monetary Council, which handles the Republic's public finances, began publishing its *Bulletin Mensuel du Conseil Monétaire–Institut d'Emission* in Dec. 1961.

The Congo has also found itself the unwilling subject of numerous reports, memoranda, and pronouncements issued by foreign governments and international agencies. The debates and resolutions of the Security Council and the General Assembly of the United Nations, as well as the several reports submitted to and by the Secretary General, constitute obvious source material for the study of the Congolese crisis and have been published through the usual channels. The various documents released by the services of the United Nations Operation in the Congo have not, however, received the same public diffusion, and the general availability of such valuable items as the successive *Progress Reports on UN Civilian Operations in the Congo* remains comparatively limited. U.S. policy statements regarding the Congo will normally be found in the *U.S. Department of State Bulletin*. The Bureau of Intelligence and Research of the State Department has also issued a *Chronology of Significant Events in the Congo, January 1959–December 21, 1961* (Washington, D.C., GPO, 1961), and the Department of the Army has sponsored the preparation by the Foreign Areas Studies Division, Special Operations Research Office of the American University, of an *Area Handbook for the Republic of the Congo (Léopoldville)* (Washington, D.C.: GPO, 1962).

NEWSPAPERS AND PERIODICALS

Mention has been made of the limited role played by the press in the political development of the Congo, and a census of the Congolese press will be found on pp. 88–89. Although they usually maintained permanent correspondents in the Congo and gave news from the colony a fairly extensive coverage, Belgian newspapers were not notable for the perceptiveness of their reporting of African affairs prior to 1958. The most substantial fare offered by such dailies as *La Libre Belgique* (Catholic conservative), *Le Soir* (Independent conservative), and *Le Peuple* (Socialist) or by the weekly *Pourquoi Pas?* was in the form of serialized reporting by senior journalists or free-lance writers. Several of these occasional surveys were subsequently published in book form, but few, if any, commend themselves to the student or scholar. One of the most penetrating of such reports is F. Demany's *Le bal noir et blanc* (Bruxelles: Ed. Labor, 1955), which suffers, however, from the author's partisan involvement in the then burning conflict between church and state.

Since Jan. 1959 the reporting of Congolese affairs in the Belgian press has been abundant, though frequently biased and tinged with emotional overtones. Among the specialized periodicals concerning themselves with Congolese problems, the foremost is undoubtedly *Zaïre*. Other valuable publications are *Problèms Sociaux Congolais* (formerly known as *Bulletin du Centre d'Etude des Problèmes Sociaux Indigènes*), *Problèmes d'Afrique Centrale*, and the review of the major white settlers' organization, *Eurafrica*. Social and political issues are given primary emphasis in such younger periodicals as CRISP's *Courrier Africain*, *Etudes Congolaises*, and *Remarques Congolaises*. A subsidiary of the weekly mimeographed newsletter *Courrier Hebdomadaire* (which began publication in Jan. 1959 and devoted substantial space to Congolese affairs), the *Courrier Africain* publishes meaningful political, social, and economic documents, together with case studies and periodical surveys of the Congolese scene. A good portion of this material is subsequently reprinted by CRISP in its yearbooks (see above). The *Courrier Africain*, which formerly followed an approximately weekly schedule (45 issues in 1961), has now become an occasional publication and has been largely superseded by *Etudes Congolaises* (10 issues a year). A joint publication of CRISP and of the Institut Politique Congolais, *Etudes Congolaises* prints much the same type of documents and studies as the *Courrier Africain,* with the addition of a valuable chronology of political developments in the Congo, a review of the Congolese press, and periodical surveys of the economic situation. *Remarques Congolaises,* on the other hand, is a well-documented but much more "committed" publication which has adopted a number of clear-cut positions and defends them in militant language.

COLONIAL AND PRECOLONIAL HISTORY

No single work has seriously attempted to deal with all the precolonial societies of the Congo basin. For an inventory of ethnic groups, see the partly outdated work of J. Maes and O. Boone, *Les peuplades du Congo belge* (Bruxelles: Impr. Vᵛᵉ Monnom, 1935, with map), to be completed by O. Boone's "Carte ethnographique du Congo belge et du Ruanda-Urundi," in *Zaïre,* vol. VIII, no. 5 (1954), and by her more detailed *Carte ethnique du Congo: Quart Sud-Est* (Annales du Músée Royal de l'Afrique Centrale, Série in 8ᵛᵒ, Sciences humaines, no. 37; Tervuren, 1961) which covers Katanga.

Linguistic groups have been primarily studied by missionaries. Two of them have produced slightly conflicting surveys of the complex linguistic patterns of the Congo: G. Van Bulck, *Les recherches linguistiques au Congo belge* (Bruxelles: IRCB, 1948, with map), and G. Hulstaert, *Carte linguistique du Congo belge* (Bruxelles: IRCB, 1950, with map). Both works, together with the subsequent controversy between the two authors, have been published in the collections of the Institut Royal Colonial Belge (today Académie Royale des Sciences d'Outre-Mer), whose *Mémoires* ("Section des sciences morales et politiques") are an abundant and usually valuable source of documentation in the fields of anthropology, history, law, and sociology.

General studies dealing with convergent aspects of traditional societies are few. Father P. Tempels' bold and partly biased effort to probe the foundations of the Negro-African *Weltanschauung* in his famous *Bantu Philosophy* (Paris: Ed. de Présence Africaine, 1959) is one of those. Aspects of social organization are appraised in a brief but valuable study by Alan Merriam, "The Concept of Culture Clusters Applied to the Belgian Congo," in the *Southwestern Journal of Anthropology,* vol. XV (1959). Traditional legal systems are examined with great perceptiveness by A. Sohier in his *Traité élémentaire de droit coutumier du Congo belge* (2d ed.; Bruxelles: Larcier, 1954).

Most studies, however, are in the form of monographs. Thus, on the Bakongo: J. Van Wing, *Etudes Bakongo: Sociologie, religion et magie* (2d ed.; Bruges: Desclée de Brouwer, 1959); Karl Laman, *The Kongo* (2 vols.;

Upsala: Studia Ethnographica Upsaliensia, 1953–1957); J. Cuvelier, *L'ancien royaume de Kongo* (Bruges: Desclée de Brouwer, 1946). On the Bayaka: M. Planquaert, *Les Jaga et les Bayaka du Kwango* (Bruxelles: IRCB, 1932); E. Torday and T. A. Joyce, "Notes on the Ethnography of the Bayaka," in the *Journal of the Anthropological Society,* vol. XXXVI (1906); H. Bailleul, "Les Bayaka: Aperçu de l'évolution économique et politique de leur pays jusqu'en 1958," in *Zaïre,* vol. XIII, no. 8 (1959). On the Baluba: E. Verhulpen, *Baluba et Balubaïsés du Katanga* (Antwerp: Ed. l'Avenir Belge, 1936); W. F. P. Burton, *Luba Religion and Magic in Custom and Belief* (Tervuren: Musée Royal du Congo Belge, 1961); E. P. R. Van Caeneghem, *La notion de Dieu chez les BaLuba du Kasai* (Bruxelles: ARSC, 1956). On the Bakuba: J. Vansina, *Les tribus Ba-Kuba et les peuplades apparentées* (London: IAI, 1954), and several articles by the same author (e.g., in *Zaïre,* vols. X and XI [1956–1957]). On the Lele: Mary Douglas, "The Lele of Kasai," in Daryll Forde, ed., *African Worlds* (London: Oxford, 1954), and other articles by the same author (in *Zaïre,* vol. IX, no. 4, and vol. XIII, no. 4; *Africa,* vol. XXII, no. 1). On the Lunda: D. Biebuyck, "Fondements de l'organisation politique des Lunda du Mwaantayaav," in *Zaïre,* Oct. 1957. On the Ankutshu-Atetela: Luc de Heusch, "Autorité et prestige dans la société Tetela," in *Zaïre,* vol. VII, no. 10 (1954), and his "Valeur, monnaie et structuration sociale chez les Nkutshu," in *Revue de l'Institut de Sociologie Solvay,* vol. XXVIII, no. 1 (1955). On various groups of northeastern Congo: H. Van Geluwe, *Les Bira et les peuplades limitrophes* (1957), *Mamvu-Mangutu et Balese-Mvuba* (1957), and *Les Bali et les peuplades apparentées* (1960)—all London: IAI. On the Azande: P. T. W. Baxter and A. Butt, *The Azande and Related Peoples of the Anglo-Egyptian Sudan and Belgian Congo* (London: IAI, 1953). On various groups of northern Congo: H. Burssens, *Les peuplades de l'entre Congo-Ubangi* (London: IAI, 1958). On the Ngombe: Alvin W. Wolfe, *In the Ngombe Tradition* (Evanston, Ill.: Northwestern Univ. Press, 1961) and "The Dynamics of the Ngombe Segmentary System," in W. R. Bascom and M. J. Herskovits, eds., *Continuity and Change in African Cultures* (Chicago: Univ. of Chicago Press, 1959). On the Mongo: G. van der Kerken, *L'ethnie Mongo* (Bruxelles: IRCB, 1944).

The coming of the West and the foundation of the Free State have been recounted in a number of works, most of them colored by their authors' involvement in the events they relate or in the controversies raised by King Leopold's policies. One of the chief actors of this period, H. M. Stanley, has left us valuable recollections of some of the events which led to the Berlin conference in his *The Congo and the Founding of Its Free State* (2 vols.; New York: Harper & Bros., 1885). Leopold's role in the creation of his African empire has been the object of several well-documented and favorably inclined studies by Father A. Roeykens, e.g., his *Léopold II et l'Afrique,*

1855–1880 (Bruxelles: ARSC, 1957). The Berlin conference and the circumstances which surrounded it form the subject of Crowe's *The Berlin West African Conference* (see above) and A. Berriedale Keith's *The Belgian Congo and the Berlin Act* (Oxford: Clarendon, 1919). P. Van Zuylen's more recent *L'échiquier congolais* (Bruxelles: Dessart, 1959) offers a Belgian view of the diplomatic maneuvering which surrounded the Congo from the early days until World War II.

The Free State regime was the object of equally passionate attacks and vindications long after it ceased to exist. The bitter denunciations of E. D. Morel—*King Leopold's Rule in Africa* (London: Heinemann, 1904), *The Economic Aspect of the Congo Problem* (Liverpool, 1907), *Red Rubber* (London: T. F. Unwin, 1906), etc.—as well as the more sober assaults of H. R. Fox Bourne—*Civilisation in Congoland* (London: P. S. King & Son, 1903)—are generally well known in the English-speaking world. An interesting and articulate expression of the criticism leveled against the King in certain Belgian circles can be found in A. Wauters, *Histoire politique du Congo belge* (Bruxelles: Van Fleteren, 1910). Raymond L. Buell's classic, *The Native Problem in Africa* (2 vols.; New York: Macmillan, 1928), offers a more dispassionate and pertinent appraisal of this early period, while some recent studies—e.g., Father R. Ceulemans, *La question arabe et le Congo, 1883–1892* (Bruxelles: ARSC, 1958)—shed a more scholarly light on certain aspects of Leopold's policies. By far the most balanced and comprehensive work on the Free State, however, is Ruth M. Slade's *King Leopold's Congo: Aspects of the Development of Race Relations in the Congo Independent State* (London: Oxford for IRR, 1962), which includes a substantial bibliography. Several works have also been devoted to limited aspects of the early colonial period: R. J. Cornet's *Katanga* (2d ed.; Bruxelles: L. Cuypers, 1944) deals with the penetration of the Southeast, while *La Force Publique, de sa naissance à 1914* (Bruxelles: IRCB, 1952) is an official but well-documented account of the foundation of the Congo's colonial militia. The process by which the Free State was taken over by Belgium has been studied by A. Stenmans in *La reprise du Congo par la Belgique* (Bruxelles: Ed. Techniques & Scientifiques, 1949).

THE CONTEMPORARY SETTING

The administrative structure created by Belgium in Africa was stabilized in 1933 and remained virtually unchanged for a quarter of a century. This structure has been described by several authors, but whereas postwar discussions of the administrative system usually paid at least lip service to the advisability of some future change, studies prepared in the late 1930's, such as M. Halewijck's "Organisation politique et administrative du Congo belge" in *Organisation des colonies* (Bruxelles: Institut Colonial International, 1936), were blissfully free of these subsequent doubts. The official policy of the Belgian authorities has occasionally been expounded in the bland and somewhat elusive statements of colonial ministers—e.g., P. Wigny, "Methods of Government in the Belgian Congo," in *African Affairs*, vol. L, no. 201 (1951), or A. Buisseret, "Trois voies parallèles d'une politique belge au Congo," in *Synthèses*, June 1956—but the best-formulated rationalizations of colonial rule will be found in P. Ryckmans, *Dominer pour servir* (Bruxelles: DeWit, 1931; rev. ed., Ed. Universelle, 1948) and *Etapes et jalons* (Bruxelles: Larcier, 1946). Belgian methods of "native administration" are treated by A. Gille, "La politique indigène du Congo belge et du Ruanda-Urundi," in vol. III of the *Encyclopédie du Congo belge* (Bruxelles: Bieleveld, 1953), and by J. Sourdillat, *Les chefferies au Congo belge* (Paris: Domat, 1940). More recent studies include A. Marzorati, "Political Organization and Evolution of African Society in the Belgian Congo," in *African Affairs*, vol. LIII, April 1954; G. Malengreau, "Organization of Native Administration in the Belgian Congo," in the *Journal of African Administration*, vol. VIII, no. 2 (1956); G. Brausch, "Origines de la politique indigène belge en Afrique," in *Revue de l'Institut de Sociologie Solvay*, 1955, no. 3, and "Le paternalisme: Une doctrine belge de politique indigène," *ibid.*, 1957, no. 2. Criticism of the native administration system was voiced as early as 1920 by G. Van der Kerken in his *Les sociétés bantoues du Congo belge et les problèmes de la politique indigène* (Bruxelles: Bruylant, 1920). This criticism was echoed after the war in V. Vermeulen's cogent but rather limited *Déficiences et dangers de notre politique indigène* (Bruxelles: Impr. I.M.A., 1953). The administrative problems created by urbanization were studied in their early stage by G. Baumer's *Les centres indigènes extra-coutumiers au Congo* (Paris: Domat, 1939), while the introduction of municipal local government has been adequately summed up by C. A. G. Wallis, "The Administration of Towns in the Belgian Congo," in *Journal of African Administration*, vol. X, no. 2 (1958). No real evaluation of Belgian administrative methods is available as yet. G. Brausch's *Belgian Administration in the Congo* (London: Oxford for IRR, 1961), which comes closest to providing such an assessment, is biased by the author's ties with policy-making circles during the controversial Buisseret administration.

Lord Hailey's *An African Survey* (rev. ed.; London: Oxford, 1957) is remarkably informative but seldom ventures beyond the bounds of a factual depiction. In a different vein the succinct passages devoted to Belgian policy in Thomas Hodgkin's brilliant *Nationalism in Tropical Africa* (New York: New York Univ. Press, 1957) contain several terse and perceptive judgments.

A general description of the Congolese economy will be found in J. Lefébvre's manageable but already somewhat outdated survey, *Structures économiques du Congo belge et du Ruanda-Urundi* (Bruxelles: Ed. Treurenberg, 1955). However, a much more illuminating representation of the country's problems will be derived from F. Bézy's *Problèmes structurels de l'économie congolaise* (Louvain: IRES, 1957), which contains a highly pertinent criticism of the Belgian administration's economic planning. This work should be supplemented with Bézy's own "Principes pour l'orientation du développement économique au Congo," in *Zaïre*, vol. XIII, no. 1 (1959). The Colonial Ministry's official yearbooks entitled *La situation économique du Congo belge et du Ruanda-Urundi* (the last one, relating to 1959, appeared in 1960) have already been mentioned as a reliable source of figures and data. A brief, deliberately optimistic survey of the Congolese economy was published in 1960 by the Federation of Congolese Enterprises (Fédération des Entreprises Congolaises) under the title *The Congolese Economy on the Eve of Independence* (Bruxelles?, 1960). A hostile but invaluable survey of financial concentration in the Belgian Congo has been compiled by two Marxist authors, P. Joye and R. Lewin, in *Les trusts au Congo* (Bruxelles: Société Populaire d'Editions, 1961), which in fact completes P. Joye's earlier work *Les trusts en Belgique* (Bruxelles: Soc. Populaire d'Editions, 1956; 3d ed., rev., 1961). Understandably, there is no "capitalistic" counterpart to this sort of work. Company literature does exist, however, and at least one corporation, the giant mining concern Union Minière, has been the subject of a recent monograph by a sympathetic Belgian journalist, Charles d'Ydewalle, *L'Union Minière du Haut-Katanga* (Paris: Plon, 1960). The mining industry as a whole has been studied by F. Bézy in his brief *Changements de structure et conjoncture de l'industrie minière au Congo, 1938–1960* (Léopoldville: IRES, 1961). A wealth of raw factual information will be found in *The Mining Yearbook* (London: The Financial Times, 1961), while a brief article by Alvin Wolfe, "The 'Team' Rules Mining in Southern Africa," in *Toward Freedom*, Jan. 1962, provides a nutshell description of interlocking directorates among the mining companies of South Africa, the Rhodesias, and the Congo.

The problems of Congolese agriculture have been approached by G. Peeters in his article "L'agriculture congolaise et ses problèmes de structure" (*Zaïre*, vol. XII, no. 5 [1958]). (See also his earlier "Problèmes d'économie agraire congolaise" in *Zaïre*, vol. XI, no. 4 [1957].) The efforts made by the Belgian authorities to develop a profit-conscious peasantry were appraised in their early stage by G. Malengreau, *Vers un paysannat indigène: Les lotissements agricoles au Congo belge* (Bruxelles: IRCB, 1949). A more recent assessment has been attempted in a symposium sponsored by the Solvay Institute of Sociology of Brussels University: *Vers la promotion de l'économie indigène* (Bruxelles: Solvay, 1956), which also deals with other forms of economic activity by Africans.

The present situation of the Congolese economy is too fluid to have been the object of more than limited description; some of it, however—and notably the *Notes et Documents* put out by the Institut de Recherches Economiques et Sociales at Lovanium University—is of a high caliber. Studies of the Republic's foreign trade (by F. Herman and by L. Baeck and C. François), financial and monetary problems (by H. Leclercq), manufacturing industries (by F. Bézy and J. L. Lacroix), and retail prices (by G. Boddez and B. Ryelandt) have appeared in this collection since 1960. Also noteworthy are F. Herman's occasional studies of the economic and financial situation of the Congo in *Etudes Congolaises* (nos. 1, 2, and 4 of 1961 and 2, 3, and 8 of 1962). Good summaries of the Congo's economic predicament may be found (in English) in the ECA's *Economic Bulletin for Africa.*

Perhaps the most significant effects of economic change in the Congo have been the birth of a large African labor force and the correlative phenomenon of urbanization. Both developments have been closely studied by Belgian observers. The problems involved in the training of a modern, efficient African labor force have been scrutinized in two works by A. Doucy and P. Feldheim, *Problèmes du travail et politique sociale au Congo belge* (Bruxelles: Librairie Encyclopédique, 1952) and *Travailleurs indigènes et productivité du travail au Congo belge* (Bruxelles: Solvay, 1958). R. Poupart's *Facteurs de productivité de la main d'oeuvre autochtone à Elisabethville* (Bruxelles: Solvay, 1962) deals with similar matters on a limited scene. Data relating to the problems of labor in the Congo can also be derived from the Inter-African Labour Institute's survey, *The Human Factors of Productivity in Africa* (Bamako: IALI, 1956; 2d ed., London, 1960). P. F. Bouvier's "Some Aspects of Labour Migration in the Belgian Congo," in the *Bulletin of the IALI*, vol. VI, no. 6 (1959), sheds some light on a phenomenon which connects industrialization with urbanization. See also, in the same *Bulletin* (vol. VII, no. 2 [1960]), a study entitled "Urban Employment in Africa South of the Sahara—Unemployment in the Belgian Congo." The American reader may also find it convenient to refer to a compilation prepared by the Division of Foreign Labor Conditions of the Bureau of Labor Statistics, *Foreign Labor Information: Labor in the Belgian Congo* (Washington, D.C.: GPO, 1959).

A comprehensive background study of the development of a labor movement in the Congo is provided by R. Poupart, *Première esquisse de l'évolution du syndicalisme au Congo* (Bruxelles: Solvay, 1960). A shorter and earlier study (J. Rijckbost, "La liberté syndicale et la grève en droit congolais," in *Zaïre*, vol. XIII, no. 3 [1959]) deals more specifically with the legal restrictions placed upon the freedom to unionize, while recent developments have been covered in a serial published by the *Courrier Africain* under the title, "Syndicalisme congolais, 1959–1962" (nos. 2–5 of 1962). Such periodicals as *Etudes Congolaises* and *Remarques Congolaises* also print fairly regular chronicles of the current activity of the labor unions.

Urbanization in Africa has been approached mainly through case studies of isolated cities and townships. Attempts to coordinate research have produced such results as the well-known *Aspects sociaux de l'industrialisation et de l'urbanisation en Afrique au sud du Sahara* (Paris: UNESCO, 1956), edited by D. Forde. Equally noteworthy, in a slightly different line, is Father J. Denis' singlehanded effort at synthesis, *Le phénomène urbain en Afrique centrale* (Bruxelles: ARSC, 1958), which dwells heavily on the Congo and carries an extensive bibliography. Monographs are more frequent. Thus, on Léopoldville: J. Denis, "Léopoldville: Etude de géographie urbaine et sociale" (*Zaïre*, X, no. 6 [1956]); L. Baeck, "Léopoldville, phénomène urbain africain" (*ibid.*); P. Raymaekers, "Le squatting à Léopoldville" (*Bulletin of the IALI*, vol. VIII, no. 4 [1961]); L. Baeck, "An Expenditure Study of the Congolese *Evolués* of Léopoldville, Belgian Congo," in A. Southall, ed. *Social Change in Modern Africa* (London: Oxford, 1961). On Elisabethville: F. Grévisse, *Le centre extra-coutumier d'Elisabethville* (Bruxelles: IRCB, 1951); P. Caprasse, *Leaders africains en milieu urbain* (Elisabethville: CEPSI, 1959); and, in general, all publications of the Centre d'Etudes des Problèmes Sociaux Congolais (formerly known as CEPSI), as well as several of the papers in *Congrés Scientifique d'Elisabethville*, vol. VI (Elisabethville, 1950). On Stanleyville: V. Pons, "Social Effects of Urbanization in Stanleyville, Belgian Congo," in Forde, ed., *Aspects sociaux* (see above). On Coquilhatville: F. De Thier, *Le centre extra-coutumier de Coquilhatville* (Bruxelles: Solvay, 1956).

Another factor of change, religion, has been abundantly studied by religious agencies themselves, and there is a considerable amount of what might be called "professional literature" on the subject. Ruth M. Slade's work on the *English-speaking Missions in the Congo Independent State* (Bruxelles: ARSC, 1958) deserves special notice for its scholarly qualities. The problems faced by the Christian churches in a changing African society have been appraised from a Catholic viewpoint by Marie-Joseph Lory, *Face à l'avenir: L'Eglise au Congo belge et au Ruanda-Urundi* (Paris and Tournai: Casterman, 1958), and from a Protestant angle by Henry F. Drake, *Some Contemporary Problems Confronting the Protestant Church in the Belgian Congo* (New York: Union Theological Seminary, 1960). Postindependence developments are summed up by R. Roelandt, "The Situation of the Church in the Congo," in *African Ecclesiastical Review*, vol. III, no. 3 (1961), and by Robert G. Nelson, *Congo Crisis and Christian Missions* (St. Louis, Mo.: Bethany Press, 1961).

Although they testify to the impact of Christianity, African messianic and revivalistic movements pertain to a wholly different order of problems. The most notable of such movements in the Congo, Kimbangism, has been the object of two major studies: Efraim Andersson, *Messianic Popular Movements in the Lower Congo* (Uppsala: Almqvist & Wiksells, 1958), and P. Raymaekers, "L'église de Jésus-Christ sur la terre par le prophète Simon Kimbangu," in *Zaïre*, vol. VIII, no. 6 (1954). See also G. Balandier, "Messianismes et nationalismes en Afrique noire," in *Cahiers Internationaux de*

Sociologie, vol. XIV (1953), and J. Comhaire, "Secret Societies and Prophetic Movements in the Belgian Congo," in *Africa,* vol. XXV, Jan. 1955.

THE POLITICAL SCENE

The absence of any significant political life in the Congo until the mid-1950's is reflected in the paucity of the literature relating to political change. Such comparatively "early" discussions of the problem as *L'évolution politique du Congo belge* (Bruxelles: Solvay, 1953) were chiefly concerned with sociological phenomena and with the feasibility of experimentation *in vitro.* In a bolder vein of speculation are the writings of A. A. J. Van Bilsen, best known for his "thirty-year plan." These have been collected by their author under the title *Vers l'indépendance du Congo belge et du Ruanda-Urundi* (Kraainem, Belgium?, 1958). From two entirely different quarters, the scrutiny of Basil Davidson (*The African Awakening* [London: Cape, 1955]) and the cautiously provocative views of Patrice Lumumba (*Le Congo, terre d'avenir, est-il menacé?* [Bruxelles: Office de publicité, 1961]; translated under the title *Congo, My Country* [London: Pall Mall Press, 1962]) provide additional dimensions to the study of this period. For the views of the European community in Katanga, see J. Sépulchre, *Propos sur le Congo politique de demain: Autonomie et fédéralisme* (Elisabethville: L'Essor du Congo, 1958), and also A. Rubbens, "La confusion politique au Katanga," in *La Revue Nouvelle* (Brussels), Oct. 1958. A brief but highly valuable summary of trends relating to political evolution will be found in A. Doucy's "Mouvement des idées relatives à l'avenir politique du Congo belge," a background paper prepared for the Dec. 1958 colloquium sponsored by the Institut Belge de Science Politique and published, along with the rest of the transactions, under the title *L'avenir politique du Congo belge* (Bruxelles: Librairie Encyclopédique, 1959). The Jan. 1959 riots were reported upon not only by a parliamentary commission of inquiry (see above) but also by two free-lance writers, J. Marres and P. de Vos, in their *L'équinoxe de janvier—Les émeutes de Léopoldville* (Bruxelles: Ed. Euraforient, 1959), which, however, never rises much above the level of passable journalism. The reforms of 1959–1960 are best approached through the various publications of CRISP (see above), but a good account in English of this period can be found in Ruth M. Slade, *The Belgian Congo* (London: Oxford for IRR, 1960; 2d ed., with an additional chapter by Marjory Taylor, London, 1961). The political Round Table conference of Jan.–Feb. 1960 has been studied by G. H. Dumont, *La Table Ronde belgo-congolaise* (Paris: Ed. Universitaires, 1961), and the events leading to the formation of the Lumumba government have been presented by the Belgian cabinet member who presided over those negotiations in a self-exonerating but highly interesting document: W. Ganshof van der Meersch, *Congo, mai-juin 1960* (Bruxelles, 1961).

Several works have already been devoted to the Congo crisis, most of them of purely transitory interest. Exception should be made, however, for Colin Legum's *Congo Disaster* (Hammondsworth, U.K., and Baltimore, Md.: Penguin, 1961), which, although it may devote too much space and attention to the Free State era, shows remarkable understanding of the Congolese situation. Alan P. Merriam's *Congo: Background of Conflict* (Evanston, Ill., Northwestern Univ. Press, 1961) contains minor inaccuracies but is especially valuable for its description of the impact of political change on a rural environment. The most comprehensive work published so far is Michel Merlier's *Le Congo de la colonisation belge a l'indépendance* (Paris: Maspero, 1962), written from a Marxist angle and frequently acrimonious but notable for its interpretative analysis of Belgian economic policy in Africa. J. Chomé's *La crise congolaise* (Bruxelles: Remarques Congolaises, 1960) is a highly pungent account of the ten momentous days that elapsed between the proclamation of independence and the time of Belgian military intervention.

Subsequent developments can be followed through the CRISP yearbooks, *Congo 1960* and *Congo 1961* (see above), and through such publications as the *Courrier Africain* and *Etudes Congolaises* (e.g., in the latter, B. Verhaegen's "Histoire des Tables Rondes du Congo indépendant," 1961, nos. 2, 4, and 5). See also A. A. J. Van Bilsen, "Some Aspects of the Congo Problem," in *International Affairs*, Jan. 1962; Alan P. Merriam, "Congo's First Year of Independence," in *Current History*, Oct. 1961; and, for an official Belgian view, P. Wigny, "Belgium and the Congo," in *International Affairs*, July 1961.

The crucial issue of Katanga has given birth to an abundance of partisan (mostly pro-Katangese) literature of little real value. The assumption that some degree of objective truth can be extracted from a sort of arithmetical mean of extreme positions is disproved by the fact that the conflicting arguments over Katanga usually move on several different planes and seldom lend themselves to an abstract confrontation. The views of the Léopoldville government have been put forth in the afore-mentioned white paper *La province du Katanga et l'indépendance congolaise*. The most articulate case against Katanga is presented by a former UN official and Irish diplomat, Conor C. O'Brien, sometime UN representative in Elisabethville, in his *To Katanga and Back* (New York: Simon & Schuster, 1963), which, in spite of its partly self-apologetic purpose, offers some of the most perceptive insights on the problem and has the additional distinction of being the only book on the Congo crisis to possess literary qualities. An American journalist, Smith Hempstone, argues the Katangese case with more militancy than profundity in his *Rebels, Mercenaries and Dividends* (New York: Praeger, 1962), which nevertheless contains some vivid biographical sketches of Katangese leaders. A fairly typical Belgian view of Katanga is offered by P. Davister's *Katanga, enjeu du monde* (Bruxelles: Ed. Europe-Afrique,

1960); the author's original sympathy with the Tshombe regime grows noticeably more guarded, however, in his sequel, *Croisettes et casques bleus* (with P. Toussaint; Bruxelles: Ed. Europe-Afrique, 1962). Perhaps the most dispassionate approach is that of R. Lemarchand in his valuable article, "Katanga: The Limits of Self-determination," in the *American Political Science Review*, June 1962, which offers an excellent background of the secession.

The UN operations in the Congo have come under fire from various quarters since their inception. An early wave of criticism attacked the organization's insistence upon an untenable "neutrality" between the Congolese government and secessionist Katanga (e.g., J. Chomé's *Le gouvernement congolais et l'ONU: Un paradoxe tragique* [Bruxelles: Remarques Congolaises, 1961]), while later denunciations were chiefly induced by the actions directed against the Tshombe regime (see Hempstone and Davister and Toussaint, mentioned above, and also Ernest van den Haag, "The United Nations War in Katanga," in *National Review*, vol. XII, no. 12 [1962]).

A balanced appraisal of the UN's role in the Congo is offered by Stanley Hoffmann, "In Search of a Thread: The UN in the Congo Labyrinth," in *International Organization*, Spring 1962. Various aspects of the UN operation have been studied by E. M. Miller, "Legal Aspects of UN Action in the Congo," in *American Journal of International Law*, Jan. 1961; P. O'Donovan, "Precedent of the Congo," in *International Affairs*, April 1961; R. L. West, "The UN and the Congo Financial Crisis: Lessons of the First Year," in *International Organization*, 1961, no. 4.

Perhaps the most neglected area of the Congolese political scene so far is that which covers political socialization and its various factors. Political parties themselves have been rather inadequately studied. INFORCONGO sponsored the publication, in 1959, of a useful compilation of platforms and manifestoes (M. C. C. De Backer, *Notes pour servir à l'étude des "groupments politiques" à Léopoldville* [3 vols.; Léopoldville, mimeo.]), which, however, covered only the capital and was not continued. A brief survey of the various parties at the time of the first general election will be found in R. Lemarchand, "Party Politics in the Belgian Congo," in *West Africa*, May 21, 28, June 4, 1960. To date, the only work devoted exclusively to one party is CRISP's *ABAKO 1950–1960* (Bruxelles: CRISP, 1962) which is primarily a collection of documents. The ethnic background of Congolese politics has been approached in a brief but valuable booklet by D. Biebuyck and M. Douglas, *Congo Tribes and Parties* (London: Royal Anthropological Institute, 1961), while the complex admixture of ethnocentrism and historical chauvinism which fueled the ABAKO has been studied in "Problèmes du Bas-Congo" (*Courrier Africain*, 1960, nos. 7 and 8) and in R. Lemarchand's "The Bases of Nationalism among the BaKongo," in *Africa*, Oct.

1961. The most widely publicized ethnic conflict, that between the Baluba and the Lulua, has been studied by J. Chomé in *Le drame de Luluabourg* (Bruxelles: Remarques Congolaises, 1960) and by a Congolese author, Mabika Kalanda, in *Baluba et Lulua: Une ethnie à la recherche d'un nouvel équilibre* (Bruxelles: Remarques Congolaises, 1960).

On one of the most elusive aspects of political dynamics, the role of individual personalities, little material is available as yet. Besides Patrice Lumumba, the only political figure to have received biographical treatment is General Mobutu, in F. Monheim's rather hagiographic *Mobutu, l'homme seul* (Bruxelles: Ed. Actuelles, 1961). The late Prime Minister has been the subject of many controversial writings. His biography by P. de Vos, *Vie et mort de Lumumba* (Paris: Calmann-Lévy, 1961), is more carefully documented than might appear on the surface, but it suffers from the fact that the author's cursory, matter-of-fact style does not always make it possible to distinguish between recorded fact, reconstructed fact, and stopgap speculation. J. Van Lierde's "Patrice Lumumba, Leader and Friend: A Testimony," in *Présence Africaine*, vol. IX, no. 37 (1961), is a sympathetic recollection by one of the few close friends that Lumumba had in Belgium. S. Michel's *Uhuru Lumumba* (Paris: Julliard, 1963) was written by one of the Prime Minister's cabinet aides. The question of Lumumba's Communist connections has been heatedly argued in two polemical pamphlets: P. Houart, *La pénétration communiste au Congo* (Bruxelles: Centre de Documentation Internationale, 1960), and its pro-Lumumba rebuttal by J. Chomé, *M. Lumumba et le communisme* (Bruxelles: Remarques Congolaises, 1960). Although not pretending to set the record straight between the two contenders, A. Wauters, ed., *Le monde communiste et la crise du Congo* (Bruxelles: Solvay, 1961), offers a more dispassionate, if somewhat superficial, view of the Communist bloc's interest in the Congo. See also the introduction written by Colin Legum for the English version of Lumumba's work, *Congo, My Country* (see above).

A collection of short biographical notices of Congolese politicians, labor leaders, and others will be found in Vol. III of CRISP's *Congo 1960*. P. Artigue's *Qui sont les leaders congolais?* (2d ed.; Bruxelles: Ed. Europe-Afrique, 1961) is more extensive but frequently biased.

BIBLIOGRAPHIES

Bibliographical data on the Congo have been collected chiefly by T. Heyse in several studies: *Bibliographie du Congo belge et du Ruanda-Urundi (Politique générale, politique indigène, etc., 1939–1950)* (Bruxelles: Van Campenhout, 1951); "Bibliographie juridique du Congo belge et du Ruanda Urundi, 1939–1951," in *Belgique coloniale et commerce international*, Feb. 1949–July 1952 (for legal sources); *Bibliographie des problèmes fonciers et du régime des terres (Afrique, Congo belge, Ruanda-*

Urundi) (Bruxelles: CEDESA, 1960) for the problems of land tenure. A recently created institution, CEDESA prepares valuable bibliographical indexes dealing with specific social and economic problems of Africa south of the Sahara (e.g., the condition of women), thus covering the Congo. Postwar sources are catalogued and classified according to the decimal system, in the bibliographical section ("Bibliographie courante–Literatuuropgave") of the periodical *Zaïre*. For colonial history, see M. Huisman, "Essai de bibliographie pratique d'histoire coloniale," in the periodical *Congo*, 1932, nos. 1–3. A geographically limited but masterly study is M. Walraet's *Bibliographie du Katanga* (Bruxelles: ARSC, 1958). Recent developments (up to the time of independence) are covered in R. Lemarchand, "Selective Bibliographical Survey for the Study of Politics in the Former Belgian Congo," in the *American Political Science Review*, June 1960. For current sources, *Etudes Congolaises* has published a special issue (vol. IV, March 1963) containing a very extensive bibliography on Congolese government and politics between 1959 and 1962.

III

DAHOMEY

By VIRGINIA THOMPSON
University of California at Berkeley

Historical Background

THE PRECOLONIAL PERIOD

Like other newly independent countries of the West African coast, the Republic of Dahomey owes its present frontiers not to geographical or ethnic unity but to the nineteenth-century rivalry in Africa of European powers. Eventually it was France which brought together under a single administration the independent kingdoms of the north and of the south then existing in Dahomey. But their divergent and individualistic populations have never fused into a single people, and the centrifugal forces of regionalism remain so strong as to make the creation of a national unified state in Dahomey exceptionally difficult.

In the north, some prehistoric remains suggest that this part of Dahomey was inhabited at least as early as was Europe. No comparable discoveries have as yet been made in the south. This may be due, however, to the dense vegetation which has hampered research, for the soil there is more completely covered than in the hilly savannah regions of the north. As elsewhere in West Africa, Dahomey possesses no written documents or monuments that might cast light on its remote past. Oral traditions, dating only from the end of the fourteenth century, dwell almost wholly on the migrations, alliances, and rivalries that led to the establishment of small kingdoms, mainly those of Allada, Abomey, Porto Novo, Ouidah, and Nikki.

According to these traditions, the history of the north was dominated by the kingdom of Nikki. At the outset, early in the fifteenth
century, its Bariba prince was a vassal of Boussa, a part of present-
day Nigeria. His successors became virtually independent, founding
principalities among neighboring peoples at Kouandé and Kandi,
which, in turn, later cast off the suzerainty of Nikki. Warfare seems
to have been the main occupation of the Nikki princes, who raided
not only in the north but as far south as Savé and even into Togo.
These raids provided a rich harvest of slaves, whose sale swelled the
Nikki treasury or whose labor produced crops from the land belonging
to its kings. Surprisingly, the rulers of Nikki came to an amicable alliance with nearby Peul (Fulani) tribes, which agreed to guard the
royal herds, and this arrangement has lasted to this day. Warrior-
princes, Peul herders, and slave farmers were the main human elements of this uneasy kingdom. Reigns were short and violent, for the
practice of choosing sovereigns from various branches of the royal
family meant that there were always many candidates for the throne.
The present Paramount Chief of Nikki is the thirty-seventh in the
Bariba dynastic line.

Fortunately, the history of the southern kingdoms is better known,
for they have had a more profound influence on the evolution of
Dahomey. Tradition assigns a common origin to the kingdoms of
Allada, Abomey, Ouidah (Juda or Ouéda), and Porto Novo. Some of
the Adja, a tribe related to the Ewe, left their home on the west bank
of the Mono River in the twelfth or thirteenth century and established
themselves in a small village known variously as Togouda, Ardres, or
Allada. This kingdom reached its apogee in the sixteenth century. But
it was still important enough in the late seventeenth century to exchange ambassadors with the court of Louis XIV and to maintain at
least a nominal suzerainty over the other Adja kingdoms. At its height
Allada was rivaled only by the kingdoms of Benin and Oyo along the
Slave Coast. Even after Allada was conquered by Abomey in 1724
and its kings reduced to the status of religious chiefs (fetishers), it
was still so great a religious capital that even the Abomey sovereigns
were not allowed to set foot inside it.

In the early seventeenth century, the three sons of King Kokpon of
Allada disputed the succession to this throne. One of them kept the
kingdom of his father, another went about 50 miles to the north where
his descendants became the kings of Abomey, and the third after long
wandering carved out for himself a domain in the region now known

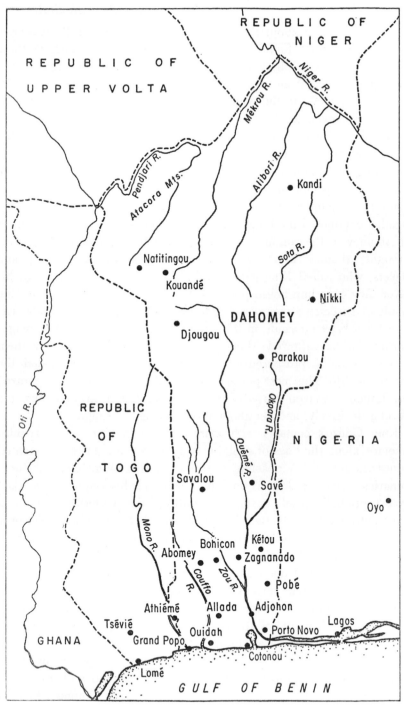

Map 2. Dahomey.

as Porto Novo. At about the same time, or perhaps a little earlier, a fourth Adja prince founded the kingdom of Ouidah. Each of these kingdoms evolved differently, but gradually Abomey emerged as the most powerful and aggressive among them and eventually gave its name—Danhomé—to the whole territory.

Until the seventeenth century the region of Abomey was inhabited by small groups of Yoruba or Nago, but they soon came under the control of the Adja prince from Allada. His son, Ouedgandja, was the first King of Abomey, and it was he who began construction of the royal palace which in recent years has been a museum containing many fine examples of Dahomeyan art. His successors, notably King Agadja, conquered the kingdom of Allada and expanded the frontiers of Abomey to the coastal region, including the port of Ouidah. This brought Abomey into close contact with European traders and slavers, who called King Agadja the "Black Alexander." To gain his favor they gave him lavish presents. But it was the sale of slaves, the result of successive conquests, that brought wealth to Abomey. Except for a brief interlude in the mid-eighteenth century, when neighboring Yoruba captured Abomey and forced its kings to pay them tribute, Abomey prospered—particularly after Guézo ascended the throne in 1818. This most powerful of all Abomey monarchs organized the famous Amazon corps of women, succeeded in defeating the Yoruba decisively, and set about reorganizing his kingdom.

King Guézo's contacts with Europeans enabled him to organize Abomey along the lines of contemporary European states. He created ministries under his absolute authority and appointed royal functionaries in clearly defined domains. Although his reign was marked by exceptionally cruel practices, including human sacrifice, he was a great patron of the arts, for which Dahomey became famous. Not only was Guézo an outstanding organizer but he was also a statesman who was able to adapt himself to changing circumstances. Abolition of the slave trade in 1830 dealt a severe blow to the main source of his wealth. On the advice of enlightened counselors, however, and with the aid of European traders he found a remunerative substitute in the produce of oil palms. In the 1830's the French trading firm of Régis Victor and Cyprien Fabre started the palm-oil industry in Dahomey. It was an agent of the former company who arranged the treaty of friendship and commerce that Guézo signed with France in 1851, whereby the French were ceded a foothold at Cotonou. In 1857 another French trading post was set up at Grand Popo. Guézo died the following year, but he left a great legacy to Dahomey in the form of vast oil-palm groves which are still the basis of such prosperity as the country has today. It was during the reign of his less talented son, Gléglé, that Dahomey's troubles with the European powers began, which were to culminate in the dismemberment of the kingdom of Abomey and the French conquest of the entire country.

The first Europeans who came to Dahomey, as elsewhere along the West African coast, were slavers. Beginning in the sixteenth century this trade attracted Portuguese, Norwegian, Dutch, and French traders who competed with each other to acquire a monopoly of this commerce. In 1666 the French East India Company set up trading posts at Savi (not to be confused with Savé) and at Ouidah, where its agents also built a fort in 1671. After a few years the French lost their early advantage for the English and Portuguese also built forts at Ouidah in the first decades of the eighteenth century. The Portuguese enclave remained under the sovereignty of Lisbon until it was taken over by the Republic of Dahomey in the summer of 1961. The construction of these forts, as well as the opportunities for trading that were offered by the presence of Europeans, attracted many Dahomeyans to settle nearby. The greater security provided by the forts was an added inducement, for in 1727 the kings of Abomey were extending their conquests to include Savi and Ouidah. Nonetheless, the King of Ouidah and most of its inhabitants were driven out, and after vain efforts to return they finally settled in the curious lake villages of Ahémé.

The King of Abomey closed the French trading post at Savi but permitted that of Ouidah to continue functioning, though he imposed severe restrictions and levied tolls on its European commerce. During the French Revolution the French fort at Ouidah was evacuated, and for the next half century French influence and trade markedly declined, while the fortunes of the Portuguese rose correspondingly. In 1810 the King of Abomey entrusted the administration of Ouidah to a Brazilian Portuguese, Francisco da Souza, to whom he was personally indebted. It was under da Souza's regency, from 1810 to 1841, that Ouidah knew a prosperity it has never since equaled. During this period Ouidah was the greatest slave port of the Benin coast, and great fortunes were made there from the sale of slaves for work on the plantations of Cuba, Brazil, and the Antilles. Da Souza's successors were not men of his caliber, and with the abolition of the slave trade the fortunes of both the Portuguese and Ouidah declined. Until the wharf at Cotonou was built in 1908, however, Ouidah was the sole port of Dahomey and it was used by ocean shipping until 1934.

It was not at Ouidah but at Porto Novo that the events took place which were to determine Dahomey's subsequent history. The successors of the Adja prince who founded the kingdom of Porto Novo engaged in fratricidal struggles and their reigns were usually short, but they succeeded in modeling their realm after that of Allada from which they had derived. Frequently and usually successfully they fought their cousins of Abomey; as often but unsuccessfully they tried to conquer the nearby Yoruba kingdom of Badagri (Nigeria). To this eastern part of Dahomey, Europeans came later than to Ouidah. It was not until 1752 that the first Portuguese set foot in Porto Novo and made a treaty with the local King. The French did not arrive till the nineteenth century when the Régis company established a post there, and, as in the west, its agents came to play an important political role. The opportunities to do so arose because of continuing struggles for power, within which Anglo-French rivalry was basic and the conflict between the kings of Porto Novo and Abomey chronic and secondary.

After Great Britain annexed the island of Lagos in 1861, its local representatives had persistent friction with King Sodji of Porto Novo, who had commonly secured his slaves from that area. In April 1861 the British bombarded Porto Novo, and as a result the King turned to the French for support. Two years later he signed a treaty under which Porto Novo became a French protectorate. Once again an agent of the Régis company played the role of intermediary. A few months later the French Admiral Didelot made an agreement with the British in Lagos which demarcated their countries' respective zones of influence. But the death of Sodji in 1864 revived Anglo-French rivalry, for his successor, King Mikpon, refused to be bound by Sodji's treaty. With Mikpon's permission, British warships twice anchored off Porto Novo, and in 1872 the King informed the French consul that his realm was no longer a protectorate of France.

Two years later the pendulum swung back once more in favor of France, when King Mikpon was succeeded by pro-French King Toffa. Twice, in 1882 and 1883, Toffa acknowledged Porto Novo's status as a French protectorate. The British refused to accept this decision and proceeded to occupy three villages which completely encircled Porto Novo. By this time the local potentates had ceased to play a major role, for the European powers had taken matters directly into their own hands. In July 1885 the Germans raised their flag over a region nominally dependent on Grand Popo, but two years later they agreed on a new frontier which settled their differences with France over Togo's eastern boundary. In September 1885 the Portuguese also ran up their flag over Ouidah and Cotonou but soon withdrew their claims, and those two regions were left temporarily in Dahomeyan hands. These developments were not unrelated to the appointment of the energetic Victor Ballot as *commandant supérieur* of the French Establishments on the Gulf of Benin. By the end of 1887 France and Britain finally agreed on Dahomey's eastern frontier, and the French were left in full command of the zone from Agoué to Porto Novo.

While the inter-European rivalries were being ironed out, relations between Porto Novo and Abomey were becoming worse than usual. Disagreement over the ownership of some prisoners of war, complicated by the not disinterested machinations of some of King Toffa's ministers and emissaries, led to a declaration of war by Abomey on Porto Novo in March 1889. Toffa's troops were defeated, but Glélé's army stopped short of capturing Porto Novo. Soon afterward, Glélé was succeeded by his more bellicose son, Béhanzin, who proceeded to levy heavier duties on French trade and then, though without success, to attack the French post at Cotonou in February 1890. An agreement was reached between him and the French the following October, but it proved to be only a truce. A year later Béhanzin again unsuccessfully attacked not only the French protectorate of Porto Novo but also, two months after, the post at Grand Popo.

After Ballot was named Lieutenant Governor of Dahomey in March 1892, the French took the offensive. Troops under Colonel Dodds captured Abomey after hard fighting, and Béhanzin was forced to agree to his country's becoming a protectorate of France. Almost at once, however, fighting broke out again, and this time Béhanzin's defeat led to his deportation to Algeria, where he eventually died. Following Béhanzin's exile, Dodds proceeded to reduce the area of Abomey by reconstituting the kingdom of Allada. It was also made a French protectorate and its chief given the same status as that of the kings of Abomey and Porto Novo. Nonetheless, it was found impossible to revive the temporal power of the old Allada kingdom, and when its chief died in 1909, he was not replaced. The kingdom of Porto Novo met a similar fate, for after the death of its King in 1913, no successor higher than a Paramount Chief was named as its nominal head. As to Abomey itself, Dodds elevated Agoli, a brother of Béhanzin, to the throne. He was promised an annual pension of 10,000 francs in return for his acceptance of French-protectorate status and his promise to suppress the slave traffic and human sacrifice. Although Agoli's kingdom had been considerably reduced by its separation from Allada, he was still obliged to maintain his court and followers. Consequently he made trouble when all of the promised pension was not paid. The French, accusing him of maladministration, deported him in 1900 to Gabon, from which he was later allowed to return and to live at Savé. Abomey was then divided into nine cantons, each placed under a chief responsible to the French Resident.

Gradually Dahomey acquired an administrative, geographic, and economic coherence. Even before Abomey was dismembered, Governor Ballot had sent a series of missions to central and northern Dahomey to persuade the local chiefs to accept a French protectorate. It took eight years (from 1892 to 1900) before the whole country was covered by a network of such treaties. With the demarcation in 1899 of its northern frontier, the boundaries of Dahomey were established as they remain today. The construction of a railroad to the north was begun in 1900, and eight years later Cotonou was provided with a "wharf" (actually a pier) that permitted an expansion of the country's foreign trade. In 1902 Dahomey was given the status of a colony. Two years later it became one of the eight territories of the newly founded Federation of French West Africa.

COLONIAL RULE

When originally constituted as a colony, Dahomey was divided into 15 *cercles,* of which 11 were in the south and 4 in the north. Porto Novo was made its capital though the administration of justice was located at Cotonou, which was also the country's commercial capital. Each *cercle* was headed by a French commandant and divided into cantons administered by chiefs appointed by the French Governor. Cantons were composed of groups of villages, each under a chief chosen by the villagers and remunerated by a share of the taxes that he collected for the central government. About 150 cantons in all were created for a total of some 3,600 villages. In the 1920's each large administrative unit was given an advisory Council of Notables, whose members were named by the Governor upon recommendation of the *commandant de cercle* who presided over their meetings. The Governor, responsible to the Governor-General at Dakar, was assisted by a secretary-general and a council composed of French officials, appointed French citizens, and Dahomeyan subjects. The French citizens were nominated by the Chambers of Commerce while the Dahomeyans were chosen by a college composed of African civil servants, chiefs, and selected merchants, war veterans, and landowners. This council, like those of the Notables at a lower level, had only advisory functions, but it, too, had the right to be consulted on certain subjects. Later, the creation of mixed communes at Porto Novo, Cotonou, and Ouidah, under appointed mayors and councils, gave some southern Dahomeyans a limited experience in municipal administration.

The administrative structure in Dahomey was the same as that of all other French West African colonies except Senegal. Dahomey differed from the others, however, in several respects: the survival of more traditional chiefs in the south, the regional differences that continued to differentiate the Abomey area from that of Porto Novo, and the sharper cleavage between the northern and southern parts of the country. In Abomey and, to a lesser degree, in Porto Novo, canton chiefs were appointed from among members of the old royal families. In addition to their salaries as chiefs, a handful of the most important of them received meager pensions from the French government in recognition of its protectorate obligations. But it was mainly the voluntary contribution of services and tribute from their erstwhile subjects that enabled the descendants of former kings to meet the expenditures that tradition still required of them. Their continued authority—albeit considerably reduced—perpetuated the long-standing differences between the eastern and western areas of the south. To this day, a strong regionalism pervades both Abomey and Porto Novo, and this has been clearly reflected in the political developments of the post-World War II period.

While the heritage of the past has perpetuated regional differences in the south, these differences are less marked than the cleavage which still separates all the southern portion of the country from the north. Like other early Europeans along the west African coast, the French who came to Dahomey did not penetrate into the hinterland for many years, convinced as they were that the "real" Dahomey ended at Abomey. Even after the railroad reached Parakou, their viewpoint changed little, the more so because it was shared by many southern Dahomeyans. North and south Dahomey knew virtually nothing about each other, having never developed either political or economic ties. The north was particularly isolated for, after the French put an end to the chronic warfare in that region, its tribes lived on their ancestral lands without mutual contact. Except for the paramount chiefs of

Nikki, Parakou, Kandi, and Djougou, whose subjects still obeyed their orders, there were no chiefs whose authority extended beyond the individual village boundaries, and outsiders were placed in charge of almost all the newly created cantons in the north. Gradually the growth of communications and trade drew the north and south closer together economically, but it did little to diminish their sense of separateness and especially the disdain felt by the southerners for their less developed "compatriots" in the north. To this day the teachers, doctors, and officials sent from southern Dahomey to northern posts feel that they have been exiled to a primitive, alien land. Conversely, the northerners resent the fact that the more educated, talented, and aggressive southerners have received the lion's share of development funds and believe that the whole country has been run by and for the benefit of the south. The regionalism of Abomey (and by extension Cotonou) and Porto Novo reflects a kind of corporate jealousy between equals, each proud of its own distinctive culture and progress. The regionalism of the north has been characterized, however, by withdrawal on the part of a mosaic of peoples with few bonds between them except a collective sense of inferiority vis-à-vis the south.

During the forty-six years that Dahomey was governed as a colony, the French did little, except in economic matters, to weld together the north and the south. In fact, Dahomey's governors periodically proposed a separate administration for the *cercles* of Parakou, Natitingou, and Kandi that would give the north greater autonomy and enable more local men to serve as its officials. But nothing came of such proposals, for the authorities at Paris and Dakar preferred not to disturb the calm of the north, even though it was the calm born of stagnation. To be sure, the number and boundaries of *cercles* were changed from time to time, but this did not alter the uniform, overrigid form of the administration. Occasionally, the *commandants de cercle* would bewail the dearth in the north of suitable candidates for the office of chief in contrast to the abundance of them in the south. In justice it must be said that the northerners did little to promote the advancement of their own men. Many of their traditional chiefs refused to send their sons to French schools for training. It was only natural, therefore, for the French to appoint literate southerners to posts in the north, even though they lacked there the moral authority conferred by tradition. Moreover, it was not easy for the government to know who actually were the traditional authorities, for the rules governing chiefly succession not only were very complicated but differed from one tribe to another. In Djougou, for example, the chieftaincy rotated by tradition among members of three families, descendants of the original founder of the dynasty. Because the French occupation had cut sharply into the revenues traditionally accruing to the chiefly families, princes belonging to the two branches out of power had to work at the most humble occupations while awaiting their turn at occupying the throne. This created discontent though it was on a far more localized and smaller scale than in the south.

Such restiveness as existed openly in Dahomey during the colonial period was confined to the south, and consequently so were the few political reforms initiated by the administration. Southern Dahomey was mildly shaken by the troubles that swept over all the eastern part of French West Africa during World War I. In 1922 a revolt at Porto Novo was serious enough for the French to declare a state of siege in that capital. This outbreak stimulated the setting up of the advisory Notables councils that same year and the subsequent promotion in 1921 and 1925 of the three main southern towns to the status of mixed communes. No further reforms were made until the advent of Governor F. J. Reste, whose incumbency coincided with the beginning of the world depression. In 1930 he enlarged the powers and the pay of the surviving paramount chiefs and laid down rules covering promotion and a more generous salary scale for their lesser colleagues. The world depression forced the administration to economize to such an extent, however, that in the mid-1930's Dahomey even shared some of its high officials with neighboring Togo. As of 1941, the total allocations given to paramount and canton chiefs came to only 783,500 francs (plus bonuses totaling 200,000 francs), while the rebates to village chiefs amounted to a mere 582,000 francs.[1]

Being so poorly paid, the traditional chiefs inevitably increased the pressure on their erstwhile subjects for extralegal contributions in money and in kind. In the north there was no noticeable resentment of such pressures, but in the more evolved and individualistic south the young men increasingly opposed the traditional authority of the chiefs and their exactions. Not only did many of them escape to the coastal towns, but some went so far as openly to accuse the traditional chiefs, in the local press and law courts, of bribery and an illegal abuse of their powers. The old-time French administrators were inclined to be indulgent toward the chiefs, who were financially hard pressed and were exacting what to them were only their hereditary rights. But by

[1] H. Desanti, *Du Danhomé au Bénin-Niger* (Paris, 1945), p. 87.

the time World War II broke out, the *crise de la chefferie* had not been resolved, and the basis had been laid in the south for a conflict between the hereditary chiefs and the young French-educated intelligentsia.

In 1939, Dahomey was a land divided both economically and psychologically. No country-wide infrastructure linked the south to the north, for the railroad had not been extended beyond Parakou. Nor was there a road network to permit contact between the mutually isolated villages in the north which, virtually untouched by trade currents and a money economy, continued to live by subsistence agriculture. Even in the more advanced south, the population remained all too dependent on palm-oil and kernel exports. Almost all of Dahomey's foreign trade was compelled to utilize Cotonou's now obsolete "wharf," where loading and unloading was by means of small barges precariously crossing the maritime bar. The long delays for shipping that this involved increased the already heavy freight charges. Dahomey was a country poor in natural resources, whose administration was marked by instability at the top and a scarcity of officials in the lower echelons. In the 46 years that Dahomey was a colony, it had 18 governors; in the interwar period lack of funds necessitated a reduction in the number of *cercles* from 15 to 7.

World War II brought Dahomey further divisions and hardships. Its officials, and especially its army officers, were divided between pro-Vichy and pro-Free French sympathies. The proximity of British Nigeria made Dahomey vulnerable to Allied propaganda, and it also offered pro-Gaullist partisans, both French and African, an easy means of escape. To bring Dahomey into line with the Pétainist regime, Governor-General P. Boisson made a special trip from Dakar in July 1942. Touring the country, he urged an increase in agricultural production and also in its recruits for labor service in France and Germany. After military conscription had been instituted in 1921 in Dahomey, the French had never had difficulty in finding recruits among the warlike Bariba tribes in the north, especially from Atacora *cercle*. But the more peaceable southerners had been recalcitrant to the point where some of them fled to nearby British colonies, and the increased wartime demand accelerated their exodus to Nigeria and the Gold Coast. After French West Africa joined the Allies at the end of 1942, the pressure for military manpower slackened, but the demand for increased production of palm oil, cotton, and peanuts grew. In filling the quotas for such products the chiefs used a very heavy hand, and this naturally added to the backlog of resentment felt toward them by the younger *évolués* (those who are partly Europeanized). This widespread rejection of authority in the south created an atmosphere which was receptive to the big political changes that came to all French Negro Africa in 1946.

THE NATIONALIST MOVEMENT

Although the Dahomeyans were psychologically ripe for more freedom, their actual experience in the management of their own affairs was confined to the very limited numbers who had been members of the country's few advisory councils. This situation quickly changed. In the first postwar years Dahomey was called upon to send representatives to France's three parliamentary bodies and then to its own territorial assembly, for whose members it voted in two separate electoral colleges.

In 1945 Dahomey chose as its delegates to the Constituent Assembly at Paris a French priest, Father Aupiais, and his protégé, a young Porto Novo-born accountant, Sourou-Migan Apithy. Aupiais, a very popular missionary who had lived for many years in Dahomey, died within two months of his election, but Apithy went on to become the dominant political figure in his country for the next twelve years. The election of these two men illustrated the exceptionally strong political influence of the Catholic Church in southern Dahomey. In fact, so long as Dahomey sent deputies to the French Chamber, Apithy and another Catholic, Hubert Maga, were regularly returned. Other Catholic leaders who early reached and retained political prominence are Dr. Emile Zinsou, former Senator in Paris and later Dahomey's ambassador to France; Paul Hazoumé, a member of the French Union Assembly throughout its lifetime; and Louis-Ignacio Pinto, onetime Councilor of the French Republic and now Dahomey's ambassador to the United Nations. Indeed, it is hard to name a prominent political leader of Dahomey who is not a Catholic. Even Justin Ahomadegbé, member of the Abomey royal family, is at least nominally a Catholic convert.

The coastal region of Dahomey is probably the French African territory where the influence of Catholicism has been the strongest, and the close entente between the missionaries and the outstanding political leaders—most of whom attended mission schools—has been reflected not only politically but also in the large grants regularly made to Catholic schools by the Dahomey asssembly. Catholic influence is said to have caused Apithy to withdraw in 1948 from the Rassemblement Démocratique Africain (RDA), then Communist-dominated.

This common denominator of Catholicism united Dahomey's leaders in the first postwar years in successfully opposing infiltration by the RDA so long as it was affiliated with the French Communist Party, and it may also have been responsible for the absence of disorders during the early electoral campaigns.

Other factors contributing to the general conservatism and absence of party strife in that period were the slowness of the north to develop a political consciousness and organization and, above all, the small size of the African electorate. Initially, the African electoral college was confined to a few rather curiously defined categories composed of individuals whose identity could be clearly established and whose loyalty to the administration was reasonably sure. In 1947, a new group was added—those who could demonstrably read French or Arabic. But even with this addition, the electorate then numbered only 54,208, of whom soldiers and veterans formed 58 per cent.[2] Other sizable categories were those of functionaries and permanently employed wage earners (10 per cent), licensed merchants (10 per cent), holders of driving or hunting permits (9 per cent), and chiefs (6 per cent). Twelve of the 30-member assembly were elected by citizens of French civil status—metropolitan Frenchmen and the few Africans who had become naturalized French citizens—whereas the remaining 18 were chosen by the rest of the electorate. The latter group was far more numerous for it comprised the great bulk of Dahomeyans who, albeit French citizens in other respects, remained subject to African customary law in civil matters. The fact that in January 1947 the first group (or electoral college) had elected three African doctors who did not have French civil status is a testimonial to the absence of Franco-Dahomeyan political animosity at this time. Docility to the wishes of the administration seemed assured by the fact that, of the 18 assemblymen elected by the African electorate, 11 were civil servants. In practice, this was an assembly of apprentices, eager to learn the business of government, especially in its financial aspects. Rarely indeed was it enlivened by disputes over the budget or by acrimonious criticism of the government.

The assembly elected in March 1952 proved to be a very different body from its predecessor, both as to composition and temper. Its size as well as that of the electorate had now increased. By a law of May 21, 1951, the French Parliament had given the vote to three new categories of Africans—pensioners, the heads of families who paid the personal

[2] R. Grivot, *Réactions dahoméennes* (Paris, 1954), p. 77.

tax (*minimum fiscal*), and mothers of two children. This law suddenly brought the Dahomeyan electorate up to 334,435, thus enfranchising 22 per cent of the total population. Concurrently, the number of those elected by French citizens was increased to 18 and those by Africans without French civil status to 32. Although the proportion of function-aries to the total membership was about the same as before, the number of merchants—notably from Ouidah and Porto Novo—was larger, and for the first time a Paramount Chief (that of the Kandi Peul) was elected. The most noteworthy change, however, occurred in the Euro-pean component, now reduced to 5 members, while only 10 of all the outgoing assemblymen were reelected. Such a rejection of the previous membership was due in part to the inclusion of many new elements in the electorate. But even more responsible for so drastic a change was the vote passed by the preceding assembly on the eve of the election which had doubled the head tax in the south and tripled it in the north.

Almost at once the new assembly reflected this decisive indication of popular feeling by assuming a definitely harder attitude toward the administration. A clash was made almost inevitable by the appoint-ment in 1951 of a new Governor, C. H. Bonfils, who brought with him from Indochina an exceptionally conservative group of administrators. In December 1952, the assemblymen openly showed their resentment against the rather peremptory message sent them by Governor Bonfils asking that no changes be made in a budget that he had "compressed to the utmost." In April 1953, the secretary-general of the territory walked out of a session in which the assemblymen insisted on discuss-ing a matter that the administration claimed lay outside their com-petence. Nor was the 1952 assembly sparing in its criticism of the policy of the Paris and Dakar authorities, notably their economic neg-lect of Dahomey and their saddling of its budget with unnecessary and expensive officials.

From 1954, however, relations between the assembly and the local government improved, for the administration became more restrained. Obviously it was dealing with a remarkably intelligent and now politi-cally mature group of assemblymen, whose advice on policy matters was not only worth heeding but dangerous to ignore. The 1952 elec-tions had proved that the electorate, at least in the south, was follow-ing current events closely and would punish those regarded as too subservient to the administration. Then, too, the riots of April 1951 at Porto Novo, though not politically oriented, had shown how strongly the population there resented the brutality of the *gendarmerie,* for which the administration was held largely responsible. Not only was the evolution of adjacent Nigeria, and to a lesser extent that of Togo, providing a stimulus to Dahomeyans eager for more political and economic power, but by their proximity they served as a convenient refuge for the discontented.

Contributing to this political evolution was the development of political parties. Naturally parties proliferated in the south where, by the time legislative elections were held on June 17, 1951, there existed six, not counting the smaller ethnic associations. Of these the Union Progressiste Dahoméenne was easily the most popular and best organized. With the exception of the Rassemblement du Peuple Français (RPF), which was almost wholly composed of Europeans and which polled only 5,000 votes in the 1951 elections, the others were not genuine parties with definite programs but rather were cliques built around outstanding personalities, such as Apithy, Zinsou, Poisson, Pinto, and Quénum. The first positive expression of the northerners' political attitude was the recently formed Groupement Ethnique du Nord, led by a Parakou-born schoolteacher from Natitingou named Hubert Maga. Around this "party" crystallized the regional sentiments of the north, a fact that gave the Groupement significance, although at the outset its only definite contribution was its insistence on reducing the area of electoral circumscriptions to the level of the subdivision. The southern *évolués* bitterly opposed Maga's party as an expression of a regional separatism that might in time lead to a permanent schism.

By 1951, the number of deputies allotted to Dahomey in the French National Assembly had been increased from one to two, so that the southerners and northerners could henceforth each be represented at the Paris seat of government. In general, the number of supporters for each candidate was about equal and localized: virtually all the south voted for Apithy (about 53,000) and all the north for Maga (some 49,000). To be sure, only 44 per cent of the registered electorate exercised their franchise. The center and north curiously enough turned in both the highest (Djougou, 92 per cent, and Natitingou, 65 per cent) and the lowest percentages (Nikki, 12 per cent). The March 1952 vote for the territorial assembly confirmed the popularity of both Apithy and Maga, for in all the electoral circumscriptions except Abomey, their parties were victorious.

The legislative elections of January 2, 1956, seemed to mark no profound change in territorial politics. Apithy and Maga were duly reelected to the French Chamber: of the 10 candidates running for office, 6 came from the families of traditional chiefs. Yet under this seemingly placid surface, significant new trends could be discerned. A new radicalism was stirring in the south, where the currents flowing throughout the rest of French West Africa were making themselves strongly felt for the first time. Consequently the popularity of Apithy, who had allied himself in Paris with a conservative metropolitan party, ebbed even in the south. There he found himself opposed not only by two former followers, Zinsou and Hazoumé, who had joined the Indépendants d'Outre-Mer (IOM) in the French Parliament, but also by a young RDA militant, Alexandre Adandé. After a stiff contest Apithy won the election. He renamed his party the Parti Républicain du Dahomey (PRD), while Zinsou led a splinter group that retained the old Union Progressiste label. Later Zinsou and Apithy came together, and then parted again on the federalist issue, only to find themselves eventually both ministers in the same government of independent Dahomey. Much more important in the immediate future than the fluctuating opposition between Zinsou and Apithy was the rise of the Union Démocratique Dahoméenne (UDD), the territorial branch of the RDA, which posed the most serious threat in the late 1950's to Apithy's long-standing domination of the south.

It was not until 1954 that the local RDA, which had been dormant since 1948, showed signs of revival. Ironically enough, soon after the Ivory Coast leader, Félix Houphouët-Boigny, had transformed his RDA into a conservative pro-French movement, the UDD became the political spokesman of Cotonou's radical labor unions. Even more surprising was the fact that their leader, Justin Ahomadegbé, was a canton chief and a member of the Abomey royal family. Such inconsistencies could not be explained in terms of party labels or programs but only by the resurgence of regional feeling taking a modern political form. Apithy's stronghold was his native Porto Novo, the seat of Dahomey's government, whereas Ahomadegbé's center was Cotonou, of which the Abomey kings had been the traditional sovereigns. Abomey's power had long since vanished, and it was now Cotonou that had become not only the region's nerve center but the commercial capital of all Dahomey. Cotonou's population felt that its economic importance was not sufficiently recognized, and they resented their subordination to the decisions taken at Porto Novo. The basic issues involved were largely Dahomeyan, both personal and regional, but aggravated by wider ideological concepts. The very fact that the UDD was linked to so widespread a movement as the RDA and that the Union Progressiste leaders were members of a rival inter-African party, the IOM (later the Convention Africaine), inevitably meant that Dahomey could not continue to be impervious to the trends toward independence and unity that were beginning to be felt in all of West Africa.

The *loi cadre*, or Enabling Act, passed by the French Parliament on June 23, 1956, profoundly altered the relations between France and its African dependencies. By its provisions, the governments-general at Dakar and Brazzaville were suppressed, and each of France's black African territories was given internal autonomy and an embryonic form of parliamentary government. This law went far to meet the Africans' aspiration for a greater share in the management of their own affairs, but it also introduced a divisive element among them. A substantial body of African opinion, represented by the IOM–Convention Africaine and its leader L. S. Senghor, wanted to re-create in different form the federations of French West and Equatorial Africa and as such "primary federations" to organize their future relations with France. Félix Houphouët-Boigny, president of the dominant interterritorial RDA, was opposed to this view, but some of his principal followers favored primary federations because they would check the trend toward a "balkanization" of French-speaking Negro Africa. The primary-federation issue, which was essentially that of unity among France's Negro African territories, split the RDA. This rift was further widened when a new question arose—that of independence from France. This was posed on September 28, 1958, when the French overseas dependencies were asked to vote for or against the constitution of France's Fifth Republic. A vote in favor of that constitution meant adherence to the newly constituted Franco-African Community, a federation to be composed of autonomous states whose central organs, located in Paris, would control their common policy in regard to foreign affairs, currency, and defense. A negative vote meant that a territory opted for total independence, and at this time Guinea was the only country to choose a sovereign status.

Later other French-speaking African territories were to choose independence, but in the mid-1950's—the period in which the UDD was becoming a force in Dahomeyan politics—the main issue was African unity. In regard to the primary federation (and independence), the UDD followed Houphouët's lead. The northerners under Maga and a few southern leaders such as Zinsou supported the stand of the IOM, whereas Apithy blew hot and cold in this matter. But none of Dahomey's parties took a clear-cut stand in regard to federalism or any ideological concept, for each was almost wholly concerned to seize and retain power in a country where local considerations were paramount.

Thus unity, even on a territorial scale, was slower in coming to Dahomey than to any other French West African territory. The strength of the three major parties was evenly matched, and to all appearances permanently so, for each rested on a regional support of about the same numerical proportions. The Porto Novo region in general and the civil servants in particular supported Apithy; the north, with the temporary exception of some elements in Djougou, backed Maga; while the populations of Abomey and especially of Cotonou favored Justin Ahomadegbé. It was the individual leader alone who could rally a region's support, and parties changed their names and alliances frequently. So politically unstable was Dahomey during the period from May 1957 to December 1960 that it had six coalition cabinets made up of various party combinations which proved unable to consolidate any government's power. While each leader jockeyed for power, Dahomey's already mediocre economy further deteriorated. Eventually it became clear to even the most partisan Dahomeyan that his country must not only be united but seek new alliances in Africa and at the same time not sacrifice France's economic support.

The Contemporary Setting

LAND AND PEOPLE

Dahomey is the smallest country of former French West Africa, covering an area of 44,290 square miles. Thus it is about one-fifth the size of France. Its form is that of a narrow corridor, 415 miles long by 77 miles wide, squeezed in between Nigeria to the east and Togo to the west and bounded on the north by Upper Volta and Niger.

In the extreme south the coastal zone consists of a narrow sandbank, one to three miles wide, lying between the ocean with its maritime bar and a network of lagoons and swamps. The coast provides no natural harbor, but the chain of interconnecting lagoons affords two outlets to the sea at Cotonou and Grand Popo. North of the lagoons is the great Lama marsh, from which the land rises gently and evenly to a clay-based plateau called the *terre de barre*. This plateau, covered by savannah-type vegetation, is broken by isolated groups of hills some of which are over 1,500 feet high.

Upper Dahomey—the portion of the country lying north of 10°N. lat.

—consists in large part of a rather monotonous plateau, broken by the Atacora chain of low mountains and to the east by the Borgou hills. The Atacora, which lies in a northeast-southwest direction, has summits that reach as high as 2,500 feet. Around the Niger River there are dunes which give that part of the country a Saharan aspect, but upper Dahomey also has some fertile plains near the Borgou hills and around Kandi in the northeast.

The Mono is the most important river in lower Dahomey, being navigable for about one-third of its 217-mile length. Before flowing into the Gulf of Guinea at Grand Popo it forms Dahomey's boundary with Togo, where it rises. The Couffo River, 75 miles long and of secondary importance, drains the Abomey plateau and forms Lake Ahémé before debouching in the lagoon region. Of all Dahomey's rivers, the Ouémé is the longest and most useful, being navigable for nearly half of its 280-mile course. It rises in the Atacora mountains, receives on both banks numerous tributaries (of which the most sizable are the Okpara and Zou), and empties itself into Lake Noukoué near Porto Novo. Upper Dahomey, for the most part, is drained by tributaries of the Niger River—the Kokigorou, Alibori, and Makrou—but they tend to dry up except in the rainy season. Togo's main river, the Oti, has all its headwaters in adjacent French-speaking territory. One of them, the Pendjari, is in upper Dahomey, draining the western slope of the Atacora.

The climate of Dahomey is marked by continually warm temperatures, hovering around 80 degrees Fahrenheit, but the south is generally hotter and more humid than the north. The south has four seasons, the two dry ones alternating with the two wet ones, whereas upper Dahomey has only two seasons, of which the dry one becomes shorter as the northern boundary is approached.

As in other West African countries that lack clear-cut natural boundaries, Dahomey has a population made up of a variety of ethnic groups which is the result of many years of ceaseless migrations.[3] Of its 1,719,400 or so total inhabitants, 1,716,600 are Africans and the balance are Europeans or *assimilés*. This total represents an average density of 38.7 to the square mile, but the variations from one region to another are marked. In the coastal zone there are as many as 268 persons to the square mile, while in the northern *cercles* the density falls in some places as low as 10.

[3] For a description of the main ethnic groups, see p. 201.

THE ECONOMY: RESOURCES AND POTENTIAL RESOURCES

Dahomey is essentially and almost exclusively an agricultural country, of which the most important resources are its oleaginous products. Of these, oil palms supply Dahomey's basic exports of oil and kernels and also fats for the local diet. Additional oleaginous produce for indigenous consumption and export is furnished by coconut palms, the karite or shea tree, peanuts, and castor beans. Other export crops, which are of minor importance, include cotton, kapok, coffee, and tobacco. Of the country's food crops, only corn has been exported in the past; its millet, fonio, rice, tubers, beans, and citrus fruits are consumed wholly by the Dahomeyans. Dahomey's sparse forests cannot even supply the needs of the local market, its animal husbandry is of only mediocre significance, and fishing on a large scale is practiced only in the rivers and lagoons. There is no evidence as yet that Dahomey's soil contains minerals worth extracting, but traces of a few ores have been sufficiently promising to encourage further prospecting.

For over a century, the oil palm has been the basis of Dahomey's wealth, and its products account now for about three-fourths of the country's total exports in both tonnage and value. The oil-palm groves, made up of two species, cover about 1,550 square miles, mainly in the *terre de barre* region between Abomey and the coast. Only a little over half of these groves—for many of which the Abomey kings were responsible—are now exploited. Palm-kernel exports grew steadily from 48,000 tons in 1927 to a maximum of 75,000 in 1936, but since then they have declined irregularly and by 1961 had returned to the 1927 level. Even at this comparatively low point, kernels accounted for over 51 per cent of the tonnage of total exports and for nearly 38 per cent of their value. Palm-oil exports shrank steadily from 18,000 tons in 1927 to 13,000 in 1957. The following year they rose to 18,600 tons, only to sink once more in 1961 to some 11,000, accounting in that year for 11.7 per cent of the volume of all exports and for 14.6 per cent of their value. This decline has been due partly to stiff competition for markets from the oil-producing countries of Asia and Africa but more to increased local consumption. It has occurred despite strenuous official efforts to encourage further production and improve quality.

In the postwar period, the French development fund Fonds d'Investissements pour le Développement Economique et Social (FIDES) supplied the money required for building four oil mills, for planting areas with selected palms, and for improving transport in the producing regions. The French research Institut de Recherches pour les Huiles et les Oléagineux (IRHO) from its experimental station at Pobé has been supplying selected palms to increase industrial-type plantations, especially in the Adjohon region. The government has encouraged the replacement of obsolescent trees and penalized the cutting down of palms to make a local toddy called *sodibé*. In February 1959, the Dahomey cabinet drafted a law to encourage the creation of associations of oil-palm growers by subsidies from public funds and has declared all plantations of selected palms to be of "public utility." More time is required before increased production can result from these official efforts.

Of lesser though growing importance to Dahomey's economy is the coconut palm, of which there are at least eight large European-owned plantations. Coconut palms cover nearly 30,000 acres along the coast. Some of their output is consumed locally but most is exported in the form of copra—6,000 to 7,000 nuts giving one ton of copra—and a few tons of nuts. Because of the aging of Dahomey's palms, production has steadily decreased. To reverse this trend the government in 1954 launched "Opération Cocotier," which consisted mainly of distributing thousands of new plants to coastal farmers. In January 1959, special funds were earmarked for the rejuvenation of groves along the seaboard. Copra exports reached a peak of 2,200 tons in 1953 but since then have sunk to an average of 200 to 300 tons a year. In addition to this a considerable tonnage each year is smuggled into Togo, but naturally this does not enter into the official statistics.

An even smaller-scale oleaginous output of Dahomey is that of the karite or shea tree, which provides nuts and butter for local consumption and export. This tree grows throughout the savannah zone, north of a line running from Kétou to Abomey. The sharp fluctuations in its export show how irregular is its production. In 1952, Dahomey shipped out 2,000 tons of nuts and one ton of butter, and in 1958, 1,300 tons of nuts and 73 tons of butter. Exports of both nuts and butter rose to a total of 2,891 tons in 1961 but accounted for only 3 per cent of the total tonnage of exports and 1.6 per cent of their value.

It was not until World War I that castor-bean culture was introduced into Dahomey, and it has never been a great success there despite markedly favorable conditions. Exports declined steadily until 1955 when they became stabilized at around 500 tons of castor beans a year, and they come mainly from the regions of Savalou, Savé, Parakou, and Pobé. The price paid to growers is guaranteed, a market is assured in France, and yields have been doubled thanks to the research undertaken by the IRHO. Dahomey's Advisory Council on Agronomic Research is buying decorticating machinery, and it hopes to increase production to 5,000 tons a year.

Peanut culture is remunerative and undemanding, and in the south two crops can be harvested annually. Many parts of Dahomey are suited to the cultivation of this plant, including the littoral, the environs of Savalou and Parakou, and most of the north. The rainy-season crop is consumed locally because it is difficult to store, while that of the dry season is of better quality and suitable for export. Shipments of shelled nuts have been growing steadily, reaching 12,522 tons in 1961, when they supplied 13.4 per cent of the tonnage and 15.4 per cent of the value of all Dahomey's exports. Only the difficulty of marketing this crop abroad hampers its further expansion. The French market, which pays higher than world prices for Dahomey's peanuts, has allotted that country an annual quota of only 11,000 tons, and the local market has had to absorb the surplus at a much lower price.

Traditionally cotton and kapok have supplied Dahomeyans with oil and material for clothing and some household furnishings, and only in comparatively recent times have they been cultivated for export. For some years a great many varieties of cotton have been grown throughout Dahomey, but exports have shown little progress because of the low prices paid for them in the world market. Since World War II, two French organizations have been trying to remedy this situation. The Fonds de Soutien des Textiles d'Outre-Mer has now stabilized the price paid to producers, and the Compagnie Française pour le Développement des Fibres Textiles has been fighting plant diseases and developing selected seed for distribution to farmers. The Dahomeyan government is also anxious to encourage production and intends to create and finance cotton cooperatives. In May 1959, it divided Dahomey into two cotton zones, the more northerly of which was to grow only the Allen variety and the southerly one exclusively the Mono species. These efforts are still too recent to give any noticeable results. As of 1961, Dahomey exported only 1,330 tons of cotton fiber and seed, which accounted for but 1.4 per cent of the tonnage and 5.1 per cent of the value of its total exports. Kapok, Dahomey's other fiber plant, cannot be described as even promising, though it grows widely in the central and northern parts of the country. The means of transport in the producing regions are deficient, markets are few and distant, and the price paid too low to provide an incentive.

Production for some years has amounted to only about 200 tons, of which three-fourths were exported, but it now looks as if exports might disappear altogether.

Dahomey's two remaining industrial crops are coffee and tobacco, and though high hopes are held for cocoa, the country now produces only about 100 tons of it a year. Coffee, thought to have been introduced into Dahomey by the Portuguese, grows in all the regions suited to oil palms. The only variety cultivated for export is the Niaouli, named for the experimental station in the Allada subdivision which developed it. Because it is resistant to disease, both the French and Dahomeyan governments have encouraged cultivation of Niaouli, though it is not a variety popular with Western consumers. Exports, which amounted to 110 tons in 1931, grew to 989 tons in 1957 and then soared to 2,079 tons in 1961, at which time they formed 2.2 per cent of the tonnage and represented 7.7 per cent of the value of all Dahomey's exports. Dahomey's shipments of this commodity probably cannot be expected to exceed 2,000 tons, for the possibilities of increasing it are limited. Even the maintenance of production at its present level depends on continued price supports derived from rebates on export duties.

Tobacco, both for smoking and for snuff, has long been cultivated on small family plots in the north of Dahomey, but it has been grown as an industrial crop only since 1920. In 1942 the Socotab firm, a subsidary of the Job company, established itself at Savé and distributed seed developed in Corsica to the farmers of northern Dahomey. Its success was sufficient to encourage another tobacco company, the Sopa, to start a similar enterprise at Bohicon. By 1958 Dahomey was producing nearly 500 tons, or about half of all the industrial tobacco harvested in French-speaking West Africa, and it was selling a fourth of its output in foreign markets. Production may be expected to increase considerably if the proposal materializes to build a cigarette factory in Dahomey.

Of all Dahomey's food crops, corn deserves special mention because of the large place it occupied among the country's prewar exports and because more land is still devoted to corn than to any other food crop. Apart from the littoral and swampy areas, all lower Dahomey is suited to its cultivation, and it is the basic food of that region. As early as 1908 corn exports amounted to 20,000 tons, and they rose to a peak of 35,000 in 1938. All such exports went to France until the outbreak of World War II, when they were deflected to Senegal to replace the rice that had formerly been imported into that territory from Indo-china. Toward the end of the war Dahomey's corn was afflicted by a blight, called the "rust" disease, and by plagues of locusts. These developments along with the population's growth and corn's tendency to impoverish the soil, caused the government in 1946 to begin to forbid exports. Since then the Niaouli station has been working suc-cessfully to develop a disease-resistant variety, which it is distributing to farmers in the south. Dahomey now produces some 170,000 tons a year.

Millet and sorghum are food crops as important for the northern peoples as is corn for those in the south, and production averages some 60,000 tons annually. Rice, to the amount of about 1,000 tons a year, is grown in Djougou *cercle*, where all of it is consumed. About 2,000 tons of fonio is harvested in the Atacora region exclusively for the consumption of the people of that area. Of the tubers produced in Dahomey, manioc is by far the most important, and its production is estimated at around 830,000 tons annually. Since 1958, when the north suffered from famine, efforts have been made to promote its cultiva-tion there by distributing seed developed at the Niaouli station and at the Ina experimental farm. Among Dahomey's other food crops grown wholly for local consumption are yams (some 600,000 tons a year) and sweet potatoes (25,000 tons). Among the citrus fruits the most promising are oranges. The annual production of this fruit now comes to some 12,000 tons, of which about one-fourth are exported.

In southern Dahomey the intensive cultivation of food crops and palm trees long ago destroyed the great tropical forest. Only vestiges of it have survived in the scattered stands of mahogany, iroko, and *rônier* now found chiefly in the Lama swamp region. To the north of it grows the vegetation typical of savannah country, such as the karite and kapok trees which are of economic importance for their produce rather than for their wood. Although Dahomey's forests provide some firewood, charcoal, and a small amount of building material, the coun-try must import about 2,000 cubic meters of sawn timber a year from the Ivory Coast and Cameroun. After its creation in 1937, the Forest Service at first concentrated on preserving what remained of Dahomey's forest heritage, mainly for the protection of wild life but also of the soil from further degeneration. Since World War II, funds supplied by FIDES have enabled this service to increase the area of forest reserves, which now cover over 14 per cent of the total wooded regions, and also to embark on a reforestation program. The most promising species it has introduced into Dahomey is teak, which adapts itself well to local climatic and soil conditions. Further regeneration and expansion of the forest area are included in Dahomey's four-year plan, but it will take many years before the effects of such a program can be felt by the local population.

Animal husbandry is of only slight importance in contemporary Dahomey's economy, largely because of the presence of the tsetse fly in the south and the total lack of care of animals by their owners everywhere throughout the country. The southern animists rear pigs (about 190,000 head) and poultry, including chickens, ducks, and guinea fowl. Sheep and goats, to a total of some 600,000, are to be found throughout Dahomey, while the rearing of cattle (300,000) and horses (2,500) is restricted to the northern savannah zone. The Animal Husbandry Service has been combating epizootic diseases, weeding out undesirable breeding animals, and supervising the operations of the urban abattoirs. Grants from FIDES since the war have enabled this service to set up immunization centers at fourteen places, of which those of Cotonou and Parakou are the largest. To the Parakou center is attached the pilot stock-raising farm of Okpara, and Cotonou is the base of mobile units which inoculate distant herds. It is planned to build three modern abattoirs at Cotonou, Parakou, and Kandi in order to concentrate and facilitate the marketing of animals and meat. When completed, these abattoirs should remedy the present deficiencies in meat of the southern towns. There meat is now scarce, costly, and of poor quality, for the animals driven south on foot arrive in poor condition and the meat brought by plane from Niger is very expensive.

To a limited extent, the fish caught in Dahomeyan waters provide some of the proteins which are otherwise lacking in the local diet. The southern lagoons and rivers abound in fish, and the annual catch amounts to some 40,000 tons. Fishing in these waters employs over 100,000 persons, of whom about one-fourth earn their living exclusively from that occupation. Sea fishing, on the other hand, has until recent years been little practiced by Dahomeyans. The 10,000 or so tons caught off the coast of Dahomey have been fished almost exclusively by Ghanaians from Quittah. To encourage more Dahomeyans to take up sea fishing, a Center for Scientific Study and Techniques was created in 1958 and is now beginning to provide data on the currents and migration habits of fish in the Gulf of Benin.

Although adjacent Nigeria and Togo are working deposits of petroleum and phosphates respectively, Dahomey's sluggish economy has not yet been enlivened by the discovery of any significant mineral resources. Superficial prospecting, however, has uncovered traces of a variety of minerals. In the south, some signs of phosphate were found in 1951 in Mono *cercle,* as well as calcareous deposits; lignite has been discovered near Pobé; and in 1958 ilmenite was detected in the coastal sands. The hope of finding petroleum in the south induced three oil companies—French, Canadian, and American—to ask for prospecting permits in 1962. But the north appears to be richer, at least in regard to known mineral deposits. For many years gold has been panned at Perma, near Natitingou, where the Société Minière du Dahomey-Niger (SOMIDANI) has also been operating on a limited scale since before World War II. Iron has been found in the regions of Kandi and Mossey, but of a quality too poor to justify the cost of extraction and transport. The government is naturally eager to have the whole country thoroughly prospected in the hope that a basis may be found for the development of a mining industry. Fiscal concessions have recently been granted to foreign capitalists willing to invest locally in mining enterprises.

Dahomey possesses only a handful of industries and generates only a small amount of electricity. Its enterprises only process local agricultural materials, of which by far the most important are oleaginous produce. These include oil mills, karite-butter plants, and a few soap factories. The crushing of palm kernels dates back to the mid-nineteenth century, but it was not until the interwar period that the first slight attempt was made to mechanize this activity by using mobile, hand-operated presses.

After World War II, the FIDES directorate chose Dahomey as the center for creating a modern palm-oil industry because its vast palm groves were virtually the only source of cash income for the large and impoverished southern population. Beginning in 1950, four motor-powered oil mills were successively constructed at Avrankou, Gbada, Ahozon, and Bohicon, with funds supplied by FIDES and with the technical aid of the IRHO. But from the outset these mills ran into trouble. After the first two were built, there was difficulty in finding a private company willing to operate them under the guidance of the IRHO, both because of the conditions laid down by the local government and of Dahomey's high tax rates. Finally, in 1952, the Etablissements Fournier-Ferrier agreed to form with the government the Société des Huileries Modernes du Dahomey. (A third of its capital was open to Dahomeyan subscribers, but very few of these took advantage of the opportunity.) The mills found it hard to get regular supplies, however, because their mode of operation upset the traditional system whereby the women of the grove-owning families were entitled to the proceeds of the sale of kernels and also of shells, pulp, and fiber useful in their households. Moreover, there were difficulties in transporting and storing the oil to be shipped out of Cotonou. In addition, there were grave strikes at the Avrankou mill in the first months of 1958, which led eventually to the overthrow of the Apithy government. The net result of all these difficulties was that the mills failed to reach their joint capacity of about 13,000 tons of oil a year, though production in 1958 reached the record figure of 11,580 tons. Discouraged by such consistent adversity, the private companies withdrew, but a state-owned firm was set up in 1961 to operate the mills. The enthusiasm of Dahomey's leaders for mechanized palm-oil production continues unabated, and the government is now planning to build three more mills with a total initial capacity of 6,000 tons of oil.

On a much more modest scale but for some of the same reasons, two small plants producing karite butter in Parakou *cercle* failed to come up to their creators' expectations. These have stayed in operation, however, and in 1958 they managed between them to turn out 79 tons of butter. Of Dahomey's three soap factories, that of the Etablissements Peterson at Porto Novo is the most important. For the record it should be mentioned that there also exist in the south a factory producing shredded coconut, a plant treating dried tobacco, a branch of Air Liquide at Cotonou, a brewery in process of construction, and a company that makes soft drinks and ice. Scattered throughout the country are a host of very small enterprises which grind corn, saw wood, make bricks, and the like for purely local needs.

This stark picture is somewhat brightened by the industrial program of Dahomey's four-year plan and by the prospect of three new large-scale private industrial ventures. An international company called Serta has been formed within the framework of the European Economic Community, though French private capital predominates, which from its headquarters at Cotonou proposes nothing short of "industrializing Dahomey within the near future." There is also the possibility that Unilever will create a multipurpose enterprise in the country whose activities may range from building cheap housing to making fish flour. Finally, an agreement reached early in 1962 between the governments of Dahomey and Israel provides for the establishment of a company that is to build a chain of factories to produce a wide range of consumer goods for all the Entente countries. Sixty per cent of the capital is to be supplied from Dahomeyan public funds, while Israel will contribute the other 40 per cent as well as experts and equipment.

This rapid survey of Dahomey's resources makes it clear that a subsistence economy prevails in the north, that the exchanges between that area and the south are confined to the produce of agriculture, stock raising, and fishing, and that Dahomey's small exports originate almost wholly in the south.

For a short period, from 1910 to 1918, Dahomey enjoyed a favorable trade balance, but ever since then—except in 1924—its imports have exceeded its exports. This persistently unfavorable trade balance does not mean that Dahomey's exports have not been increasing as to both volume and value but reflects a chronic imbalance between its scale of living and its indigenous resources as currently developed. In general, Dahomey depends too much on agricultural exports, whose tonnage varies according to climatic conditions, and in particular on oleaginous shipments for which the price paid in world markets is unstable and usually low. Production costs are high, communications are inadequate and costly, and the increasing population now consumes a larger proportion of the commodities produced. Labor strife, political ferment, and uncertainty as to the Maga government's economic policy have also played a part in hampering production and foreign trade. Since 1961 it has become increasingly obvious that the administration intends to exercise a close control over the whole economy and to direct its development toward nationalistic goals. This policy does not simply reflect the general trend prevailing in the great majority of French-speaking African countries. It is also the outcome of distinctive conditions in Dahomey, where the economy is stagnating, smuggling and unemployment are rife, and resentment against the established European trading firms has long been building up.

Generalizations about Dahomey's internal economy must be made with the greatest caution, for the number of elements still unknown is appalling. No reliable figures are available for the rate of population growth, the real income and standard of living, or the capacity to produce and save money. The only fairly dependable statistics are those for the country's foreign trade, and even here the extent to which they are falsified by contraband trade is uncertain. All that can be said is that, despite a few encouraging signs such as the increase in peanut and fish exports and a shrinkage in the trade deficit, Dahomey's economy appears to be static if not actually going downhill.

The quantity and price paid for Dahomey's exports of palm kernels and oil continue to be the dominant factor in its trade situation, and political independence has not yet diminished its dependence upon the French market for the sale of oleaginous produce. In 1961 imports amounted to 157,577 tons and cost 6,274,000,000 CFA francs, compared with 191,938 tons costing 7,643,000,000 CFA francs in 1960. (The CFA —Colonies Françaises d'Afrique—franc was worth two metropolitan francs.) Exports also declined both in amount and value: in 1960 they came to 107,917 tons and brought in 4,513,000,000 CFA francs whereas in 1961 they amounted to 93,497 tons and were worth 3,578,000,000 CFA francs. Between those two years the fall in world prices for palm oil by 12 per cent and for kernels by 29 per cent led to a shrinkage in Dahomey's purchasing power and imports. In 1961 oleaginous produce accounted for 79 per cent of the tonnage and 69.5 per cent of the value of its total exports.

Throughout the years since World War II, the value of Dahomey's imports has annually exceeded that of its exports by 20 to 30 per cent. Since 1952, the franc zone, especially France, has been taking 80 to 90 per cent of Dahomey's exports and paying a guaranteed high price for the bulk of its oleaginous shipments. In return, Dahomey has purchased from 60 to 70 per cent of its imports in the franc zone, particularly in the French market. In fact, 1961 saw an increase in this trend, for Dahomey bought more and exported less to France than it had in the preceding year. Not only are the goods imported from France exceptionally expensive but Dahomey has recently been purchasing more consumer and fewer equipment goods than during the first postwar decade. Aside from cement and other building materials, imports consist mainly of textiles, foodstuffs, fuel, and motor vehicles.

The Dahomeyan government is naturally concerned about this deteriorating state of affairs, though at the same time pleased that it reflects improved local living standards. Because it was not firmly in the saddle until December 1960, the Maga administration could not begin taking action until the following year. In the domain of foreign trade, it has taken steps to control smuggling and also to enter customs unions with neighboring African states and, farther afield, to expand trade in every direction. With complete impartiality it has sent missions and, in some cases, entered into trade agreements with countries in the Western camp (Austria, France, Israel, Nationalist China, Switzerland, Turkey, the United States, and West Germany) and with those of the Eastern bloc (the USSR, its Eastern European satellites, and Red China), as well as with the United Arab Republic.

Dahomey's relations with its African neighbors have been a continuing preoccupation of its leaders. To only a minor extent have political considerations influenced their decisions to join the various groups promoted by Houphouët-Boigny, and it was certainly the prospect of financial aid from the rich Ivory Coast that prompted Dahomey to join the Council of the Entente. Of its three Entente partners, it is only Niger, however, with which Dahomey has trade relations of real significance. For some years before Dahomey became independent, the French government in an effort to save its reserves of sterling had been trying to deflect most of Niger's peanut exports away from the Nigerian railroad and the port of Lagos to Cotonou. This movement of peanuts by road from Niger to the railhead of the Dahomeyan tracks at Parakou was known as "Opération Hirondelle." Although it was only moderately successful, this operation has been continued by the Maga government, the railroad has been placed under the joint management of the two countries involved, and in the past two years periodic conferences have been held between the Finance ministers of Dahomey and Niger for the purpose of harmonizing their fiscal and tariff regimes. Landlocked Niger and northern Dahomey will be less isolated from external trade currents when the deepwater port is completed at Cotonou, and it seems certain that the ties between the two countries will be further strengthened if the railroad is prolonged from Parakou to Dosso in Niger.

The absence of customs barriers between Dahomey and Niger dates from the creation of the French West African Federation and was perpetuated by the formation of the Council of the Entente in 1959. In contrast, Togo's international status as a trust territory excluded it from the federal free trade zone, and a customs barrier separated it from Dahomey despite the active trade and close tribal relations existing between their respective populations. But because the boundary between them was artificial and because imported goods were much cheaper in Togo than in Dahomey, there was a good deal of smuggling of Togolese merchandise into Dahomey, which caused the latter's revenues heavy losses in duties and taxes. For many years the Dahomeyans have wanted to form a customs union with Togo, but the Togolese were indifferent and the whole issue was complicated by the question of locating a deepwater port on the Gulf of Benin that could jointly serve both countries.

With the accession of both countries to independence and the decision to build separate ports, the project of creating a customs union was revived by Dahomey. The Togo-Dahomey customs union might have materialized very soon, in fact, had it not been for Dahomey's adherence to the Entente customs union and the subordination of this matter in 1962 to Maga's ambition to promote a wider Benin union (see below, pp. 249–257). As the situation worked out, Dahomey first reached a customs agreement in July 1962 with Nigeria, with which it had wanted such an arrangement for much the same reason as with Togo. Close tribal relations and the lack of natural barriers between the Nigerian and Dahomeyan populations, as well as lower taxes in Nigeria, had led to so much smuggling of Nigerian goods into Dahomey that the contraband trade was believed to equal one-third of their legitimate commercial exchanges. No great increase in the export of Dahomey's products to neighboring countries is expected to result from such agreements, for the production of all three Benin states is too similar. By checking smuggling, by aligning its tariff more closely with that of Togo and of Nigeria, and by revising its laws in order to increase the penalties imposed on smugglers and corrupt customs officials, Dahomey hopes, however, to swell its revenues and also to bring down the local cost of living. Concurrently, the Maga government lightened or suppressed the import duties on seventeen consumer-goods items for an experimental period of six months, with the aim of reducing retail prices and increasing purchasing power in Dahomey.

Dahomey's present leaders have also shown their determination to control internal trading. On January 20, 1960, fixed prices were imposed for "articles of prime necessity" and a National Price Committee was set up, under the Minister of Commerce, whose members included representatives of trade and industry, agriculture, and consumers as well as officials. The complications involved in establishing an effective price-control system and in suppressing smuggling were doubtless responsible for the committee's lack of visible progress. More than two years were to elapse before further steps were taken. In February 1962 the government announced that henceforth all goods sold in Dahomeyan markets must bear tags on which was written not only the price but the amount of taxes and duties paid on each item. At the same time, all subprefects were assigned the duty of enforcing price controls in their respective circumscriptions pending the appointment of full-time price *controleurs.*

If the Maga administration had stopped short with customs agreements and an attempt at price controls, Dahomey's European merchants might have rested comparatively easy. But they were given cause for genuine alarm by the government's moves aimed directly at curtailing their activities. Behind these moves was a deep-seated and increasing resentment against the monopolies held by the entrenched European trading firms, a resentment clearly evident in the speeches by African deputies in Dahomey's territorial assembly between 1947 and 1958. It will be recalled that some of these trading firms had been founded in the time of Abomey's kings and had launched the palm-oil industry in that period. These and other European firms—most of them branches of big French and British companies operating throughout West Africa—not only kept a grip on the export of oil-palm products but acquired a virtual monopoly of the import trade as well. As these were the only remunerative branches of Dahomey's commerce, Dahomeyan merchants were left with only the crumbs of commerce, while Dahomeyan farmers felt that it was the European firms—not themselves—which were profiting from their toil.

As early as 1954 the territorial assembly passed a resolution asking that the farmers' interests be safeguarded by the establishment of a Chamber of Agriculture separate from the existing Chamber of Commerce, Industry, and Agriculture because the latter was dominated by Cotonou's European merchants. It was not until early 1961, however, that the first serious breach was made in the European trading stronghold. At that time, as already noted, the government took advantage of the withdrawal of the French firms that had been running two of the country's oil mills to set up a state company to operate them and market their output. Despite the dog-in-the-manger attitude of the former managing companies, the newborn Société Nationale des Huileries du Dahomey succeeded not only in increasing the mills' output but in setting up a sales agency in Paris. Heartened by this success, Paul Darboux, then Minister of Economic Affairs, urged Dahomeyan merchants to organize themselves and promised them government aid. By the end of 1961 they had duly formed a Syndicat des Commerçants Africains du Dahomey. As his move clearly foreshadowed a general reorganization of the internal trade, the representatives of the big European firms—principally the Société Commerciale de l'Ouest Africain (SCOA), the Compagnie Française de l'Afrique Occidentale (CFAO), John Holt, and Walkden et Cie.—asked Darboux for an explanation of official policy. Darboux and then Maga tried to reassure local big business that the government had no intention of nationalizing private foreign enterprises and that they could still freely transfer funds out of the country. In addition, the established European firms could still handle the wholesale trade, and they and other foreign investors would be welcome in the country if they adapted themselves to the new pattern of Dahomey's economy as laid down in the four-year plan. But it was also made clear that henceforth retail trade would be reserved to African merchants. In March 1962, the government at long last created a separate Chamber of Agriculture and reorganized the Chamber of Commerce. Jean Agier, the perennial French president of the Chamber, resigned and a Dahomeyan was elected in his place. While these measures have been not at all so drastic as those taken earlier in Guinea, they have been supplemented by similar moves in the banking and planning domains. At the same time, Dahomey's economy remains in the doldrums and its prospects are far from brilliant. If it were not for the probable enhancement of the country's trade through construction of the deepwater port at Cotonou, the European firms might well be pulling out.

Dahomey has had a financial as well as a trade deficit for so many years that it is hard to remember that until the world depression of the early 1930's it had been making fairly regular contributions to the federal budget of French West Africa. Thereafter, however, the country became so dependent on subsidies from the government-general at Dakar and from France that it was particularly hard hit by the breakup of the Federation in 1959 and the resulting end of rebates from the more prosperous French West African countries. The Ivory Coast, by creating a solidarity fund for Entente countries, came to the rescue after Dahomey joined that grouping in May 1959. Moreover, France has continued and even increased its financial contributions to Dahomey for both budget deficits and development projects. Since 1960, other Western countries have also proffered aid though on a limited scale. Because of its backlog of deficits, successive revisions of the basis of taxation, a stagnant economy, and new outlays since independence for defense and diplomatic missions, Dahomey's budget has grown steadily, however, and thus its dependence on outside financial aid.

Dahomey has recently been making a greater effort to meet its own expenditures, but with varying success. The 1958 budget amounted to 3,210,000,000 CFA francs for operating expenses and 325,000,000 for equipment, of which a large part had to come from its reserve fund. Of the operating expenses, 62 per cent went to pay personnel, including nearly 25 per cent to the education service and almost 16 per cent to the health services. This was the first Dahomeyan budget drawn up by the government council that was set up under the *loi cadre,* and it embodied a drastic change in the tax system that had been adopted at the end of 1957. The aim of this fiscal revision was to distribute the tax burden more equitably by increasing the revenue from indirect taxation to the point where it should approximate the amount derived from direct taxes. Contrary to its authors' intentions, the immediate result was a shrinkage in national revenues. Not only did taxes become harder than ever to collect, but the rise in customs duties encouraged fraud, corruption, and smuggling. In consequence, Dahomey sank even deeper into debt, and France had to bail it out to the amount of some 2,000,000,000 CFA francs.

In 1959 the Dahomeyan government, though beset by political and labor conflicts, made a greater effort than before to pull itself out of the financial morass. It set up circumscription budgets so that taxpayers would be associated directly with the management and utilization of their financial contributions, particularly in the fields of education and health. This did not affect the size of the state budget, however, which rose in 1960 to a total of 5,582,000,000 CFA francs, of which over 3,500,000,000 went for operating expenses. A mission had to be dispatched to Paris, and the French government agreed to contribute 1,700,000,000 CFA francs toward meeting Dahomey's deficit. This was a somewhat smaller contribution than before, but it by no means represented all of France's financial aid to Dahomey. Between 1948 and 1958 French public funds channeled through FIDES amounted to over 9,000,000,000 metropolitan francs, of which about 48 per cent had gone to improving the infrastructure, 22 per cent to the development of the rural economy, 29 per cent to social equipment, and the balance to detailed studies of various projects. Moreover, the Fonds d'Aide et de Coopération (FAC), which had been set up at the end of 1958 to replace FIDES, was financing the construction of Cotonou's deepwater port, the remodeling and enlargement of that city's hospital, and a host of smaller enterprises.

With the advent of greater political stability in December 1960, the Dahomeyan government was able to expand its revenues and compress its expenditures. It acquired enough authority to impose an austerity program that led to salary cuts of up to 30 per cent for ministers and deputies and of 10 per cent for civil servants. The economies thus effected went far to offset the new expenditures that resulted from Dahomey's accession to national sovereignty. Inevitably the budget continued to grow, totaling 6,338,000,000 CFA francs for 1961, but Dahomey's contribution from local resources also rose to 4,500,000,000 CFA francs. Although this was wholly an operating budget with nothing earmarked for development expenditures, it represented some progress in that the deficit was reduced. France's subsidy was correspondingly smaller, but Paris agreed to pay the salaries of a larger number of Dahomeyan officials and technical assistants.

The main stumbling block to any further compression of expenditures has been the 18,298 civil servants carried on the government payroll. The disproportionate size and pay of the civil service have been a grave problem for all the newly independent African states, but in Dahomey it was and still is particularly acute. Because of their superior education and intelligence and because of the sparsity of remunerative posts at home, Dahomeyans had long supplied a goodly percentage of the functionaries working throughout French Negro Africa. With the growth of nationalist sentiment, their presence was increasingly resented, as witness the anti-Dahomeyan riots in the Ivory Coast and Niger in 1958 and in 1960. Even in the countries where no such violence occurred, their leaders naturally preferred after independence to employ their own nationals. In consequence, Dahomeyans were dismissed and returned home only to find that their own government had no place for them. Far from being able to recruit more functionaries, Dahomey could barely pay those already in office. Indeed, the government would have been relieved to pare down the civil service, except that this would have aggravated the already serious unemployment problem and been both politically and economically dangerous. By cutting salaries and suppressing such privileges as free housing, travel bonuses, and the use of official cars, the government perhaps hoped not only to save money but also to induce some of its surplus civil servants voluntarily to retire. This proved a forlorn hope, however, for in the current state of Dahomey's economy there were no job openings that had advantages comparable to those still accruing to the civil service.

Since it was impolitic to cut down the civil service—the only category of government expenditures where economies might have been really effective—the Maga administration had no alternative but to raise money by squeezing out more national revenue and by soliciting capital investments from abroad. In August 1961 the assembly approved another revision of the fiscal system whereby taxes on business profits and the cost of merchants' licenses were raised, import duties on textiles and alcoholic beverages were reduced to stimulate trade and check smuggling, but no change in the head tax was made. These measures proved to be insufficient, and to balance the budget the assembly was forced four months later to tighten the screws still further. On December 31, 1961, it voted to raise the rates of some direct taxes, such as those on income, transportation, and hunting and woodcutting permits. Finally, the 1962 budget was balanced at 6,310,000,000 CFA francs, a total only slightly larger than that for the preceding year. To this budget Dahomey was able to contribute more than ever before —5,310,000,000 CFA francs—but this still left a sizable deficit, which was filled mainly by a French subsidy of 1,000,000,000 CFA francs, and the balance was supplied by the Entente's solidarity fund. Thus on the eve of launching Dahomey's four-year plan, the country was not able to meet even its recurrent expenditures, much less contribute to an ambitious program which would cost 30,000,000,000 CFA francs. Obviously new sources of investment, both public and private, must be tapped to finance it.

In September 1960, the government had created a Banque Dahoméenne de Développement for the purpose of mobilizing local savings, but little could be expected from so poor a population as that of Dahomey, whose per capita cash income even in the south did not exceed 45,000 to 80,000 CFA francs a year. The next step was to coax or pressure the local banks into investing generously in the official development projects and into granting more liberal credit terms to Dahomeyan borrowers. Of the four French banks which had agencies in Cotonou, the Crédit Lyonnais proved to be the most amenable. Prolonged negotiations resulted in the creation in January 1962 by the government and the Crédit Lyonnais of a state bank called the Société Dahoméenne de Banque, capitalized at 100,000,000 CFA francs. The government controlled 51 per cent of its stock and the Crédit Lyonnais 49 per cent. This state bank was to take over management of the funds for agricultural-credit operations formerly handled by the Banque du Bénin.

The years 1960 and 1961 saw a proliferation of both state companies and companies of mixed economy. In September 1960, a monopoly of the transport of all merchandise moving between Cotonou and Niamey was granted to the Organisation Commune Dahomey-Niger des Chemins de Fer et Transports. In July 1961, the Société Nationale du Développement Rural was set up, which initially was to supervise the cooperative movement and later take over all state projects financed by FAC funds. During the final months of that year several companies were formed: the Société des Huileries du Dahomey, the Société d'Hôtellerie du Dahomey, the Société Dahoméenne pour le Développement Economique (SDDE), and the Société de Développement de la République du Dahomey (SODERDA). The last-mentioned company was Dahomey's first venture in associating its own public funds (51 per cent) with private capital supplied by French, Swiss, and German stockholders (49 per cent). Between them, the SDDE and the SODERDA were to control trade between Dahomey and the Common Market countries and all large-scale development operations including urbanization projects, the extraction of ores, and the establishment of factories producing consumer goods for the local market.

The years 1960 and 1961 also saw a determined effort by the government to increase foreign investments in Dahomey. Its leaders warmly received foreign businessmen and officials and sent out many missions to all countries from which aid might be obtained. In the spring of 1961 Dahomey was promised a share of the $7,500,000 granted by the United States to the four Entente countries. In July, Maga made a special trip to Paris and other capitals in order to elicit additional long-term investments in his country. Switzerland, Israel, and Nationalist China proved responsive, but the aid they offered was chiefly in kind and in services. Finally, on the last day of December, the assembly passed a liberal Investment Code: fiscal stability for a twenty-five-year period as well as the free transfer of funds was guaranteed to investors in enterprises judged to be of "public utility."

What inspired this feverish activity, particularly at the end of 1961, was that the government had set January 1, 1962, as the date on which its four-year plan would enter into operation. Originally geared to a ten-year period and comprising many ambitious schemes, this plan was progressively revised both as to its time span and its specific projects. As approved by members of the Parti Dahoméen de l'Unité (PDU) congress in November 1960, the plan was to be inspired by a "dynamic socialism that would rationalize the systems of production and trade so as to assure an equitable division of wealth for the benefit

of the people who produce and suffer." [4] When it was shorn of its
Marxist rhetoric and cut down to size, the plan set as its objectives an
appreciable increase in the quantity and quality of agricultural production for both export and local consumption, the setting up of processing industries and a cement factory, and a few projects that would
produce enough revenue to enable Dahomey to balance its budget.
As befitted so thoroughly an agricultural country, half the funds invested under the plan were to go to the extension and rejuvenation of
oil and coconut palms in the south and of teak and mahogany forests
in the center and north, with lesser sums devoted to the development
of cotton, peanuts, castor beans, and tobacco as well as food crops.[5]
Ten per cent of the funds were allocated to the promotion of processing industries, notably oil mills, and the manufacture of cement. The
balance was to be devoted to certain health and education projects,
improvement of the means of communication, encouragement of the
cooperative movement, mineral prospecting, expansion of the fishing
industry, and the like.

To bring the plan within the realm of reality during its initial phase,
all but the most remunerative projects were temporarily shelved. Of
the investments required in its first year, estimated at 4,500,000,000
CFA francs, 1,000,000,000 were to be supplied by "human investment."
According to Maga's rather delicate explanation of this decision,[6] "human investment would replace the classical methods of financing."
The role in the total played by this form of investment would be increased in the years to come, in proportion as village councils could
be created to promote and supervise the collective cultivation of fields.
To assign so large a place to such "civic service" was a tacit admission
that investments from Dahomey's public funds, which were theoretically to constitute half the total 30,000,000,000 CFA francs required for
the whole four-year period, would for the most part not be forthcoming in the form of cash. But Dahomey's planners seem unduly
optimistic in believing that the remainder will be supplied by foreign
capital, in view of the fact that between 1948 and 1960 both public
and private investments in Dahomey totaled only 14,000,000,000 CFA
francs.[7]

Maga and his ministers have been indefatigably touring the coun-

[4] *Afrique*, Nov. 1961.

[5] For specific goals set by the plan see *Afrique Nouvelle*, May 31, 1961; *Marchés
Tropicaux*, Aug. 5, 19, Dec. 23, 1961; and *Afrique*, Nov. 1961.

[6] See *Afrique Nouvelle*, Jan. 17, Feb. 21, 1962.

[7] *Marchés Tropicaux*, Aug. 19, 1961.

try, trying to stir up enthusiasm for the plan's objectives and promising that uncultivated land would be distributed to those willing to work it. They have set a good example by accepting big salary cuts and other austerity measures. If they fail in carrying out the plan, it will not be from lack of trying. By word and by law the government has promised protection to private investors, has reserved a sizable sphere in the plan for their operations, and has reiterated its pledge not to leave the franc zone. Dahomey is already receiving a considerable amount of financial aid from FAC and Fonds Européens de Développement Outre-Mer (FEDOM) and lesser amounts from a number of countries besides France, but the prospect of any appreciable increase in foreign investments is not bright. Uncertainty is felt as to the stability of the Maga administration, and even more as to its economic policy should it survive. Local businessmen and foreign governments have looked with some apprehension upon nationalization of the oil mills and of retail trade, the creation of monopolies in charge of state- or government-controlled companies, successive tax increases of which the most recent occurred in February 1962, and the strength shown by the radical labor unions. Reportedly there exists in the PDU a left-wing element headed by Apithy, Tevoedjre, and the new Finance Minister, Bertin Borna, whose zeal to apply further socialist measures is held precariously in check by the more conservative Maga, Darboux, and Arouna Mama. There is no doubt that all of them fully intend to carry out the plan, but uncertainty exists as to the means that will be used for its implementation. To be sure, the steps thus far taken by the Dahomeyan government are far less drastic than those of more Marxist-oriented countries, and probably they would not frighten away capitalists were Dahomey not so poor a country and one whose mineral resources are not comparable to those of Guinea. If foreign investments actually materialize to the amount set for them in the plan, it will be because motives other than economic ones have become imperative.

SOCIAL STRUCTURE

As of 1957, Dahomey's population was estimated at 1,716,000, of whom about 2,800 were classified as Europeans. Of the latter group some 1,200 were employed in about equal proportions in the public and private sectors. A sampling taken in the summer of 1961 indicated that the total population had grown to somewhat over 2,000,000. If this accurately reflected the demographic situation, the rate of annual growth approximates 3 per cent, and by 1985 Dahomey will have a population of 4,300,000.

Towns with a population of over 15,000 in 1959 were headed by Cotonou, 1,300 of whose 62,000 or more inhabitants were non-Africans. Porto Novo, the capital, had then only 35,000, of whom 500 were not Africans; and Abomey, a population of 19,000 Africans and 70 non-Africans. Following these three cities in declining order of numerical importance came Kandi, Ouidah, Djougou, Savalou, Natitingou, Parakou, and Athiémé.

As in other African countries which lack natural frontiers, the population is a mosaic of many tribal groups. In every respect the most important among them are the Fon, who are related to the Ewe of Togo, number over 700,000, and live mainly in the regions of Cotonou, Ouidah, Abomey, and Savalou. After the French conquest, the Fon turned from warfare to farming, and in recent years their elite has entered the civil service, the liberal professions, and politics. Related to them are the Adja, a farming people over 220,000 strong, who live in Athiémé *cercle* on the banks of the Mono and Couffo rivers. Next in importance in lower Dahomey are the more than 160,000 Yoruba or Nago, whose ancestors migrated from Nigeria. Most of their descendants live in dense clusters along Dahomey's eastern frontier or in smaller groups either as farmers or traders in the *cercles* of Porto Novo, Ouidah, Abomey, and Savalou. Related to them are the approximately 15,000 Holli of the Pobé region. Other tribes also settled in the south are the 92,000 or so Aïzo, mainly in the Ouidah and Cotonou areas; the Pédah (12,000), who are fishermen living on the banks of Lake Ahémé; and the Pla (15,000) and the Mina (9,500), found in the region between Mono and Ouidah. In upper Dahomey the Bariba are the dominant tribe, and they number over 175,000 in the *cercles* of Parakou, Nikki, Kandi, Djougou, and Kouandé. They found it harder than did the Fon to give up warfare for farming, and their agricultural activities are largely confined to gathering the natural produce of kapok and karite trees. The second most important northern group are the 68,000 or so Peul, who are seminomadic herders living intermingled with the Bariba and Somba of Atacora. The Somba form the last major tribe of the north, who are farmers and hunters in the region between Atacora and Togo. Their total number is over 90,000, but they are broken up into four sizable groups.

Excepting the Somba of Natitingou, who live in scattered fortress-like family compounds, the great majority of Dahomeyans are villagers.

The basic cell of their social structure is the joint family, living under the authority of its paterfamilias. Dahomeyan customs, originally much the same as in other similar regions of West Africa, have been greatly modified by the French occupation.[8] The traditional collectivity is disintegrating with the emergence of the small family and the individual, and the tendency in the postwar years to organize trade unions and chiefs' associations is a by-product of a profound politico-economic evolution. The paterfamilias has lost almost all his authority except in the religious domain, and even there it has been lessened by numerous conversions to Christianity and Islam. However, the majority of Dahomeyans—well over 1,144,000—are still animists, whose fetishist cults are locally called *vodoun*. The vitality of such rites and ceremonies still provides the anthropologist with a rich field for study.

Christianity was brought to Dahomey by Catholic missionaries in the seventeenth century. Despite, or perhaps because of, persecution by the kings of Abomey and Porto Novo it took firm root in the south. There Christianity's spiritual center has been at Ouidah, where today the Catholic cathedral and the fetishist snake temple face each other across the town's main square. It was at Ouidah that the fathers of the Lyon missionary society found their first followers among former slaves returned from Brazil where they had been baptized. Nowadays the descendants of such liberated slaves (called *brésiliens*) form one of the most staunchly Catholic groups in lower Dahomey. After the French conquest, the Catholic missionaries were able to extend their work to the north, and it is now said that there is no town in the territory that has not a Catholic church or chapel. Catholics are estimated at nearly 240,000; African priests number only 44, but more than 300 Africans are now in training for the priesthood; and in 1960 the first Dahomeyan archbishop, Monseigneur Gantin, was installed as head of the country's Catholic Church.[9] As the most Christianized country in French-speaking West Africa, Dahomey has been profoundly influenced by its Catholic missionaries, especially by Monseigneur Steinmetz and Father Aupiais. In particular, the Catholic mission schools have left a strong imprint on the territory's present leaders. Among the French-speaking Negro African states, only Togo has a leadership comprising such a large proportion of mission-educated men.

Although Protestant mission activity in Dahomey dates from 1843,

[8] See A. Akindélé and C. Aguessy, *Dahomey* (Paris, 1955), p. 41.
[9] *Afrique Nouvelle,* Aug. 3, 1960; *Le Monde,* March 19, 1960.

when King Guézo of Abomey permitted a British Methodist to preach and open schools in his realm, Protestant influence and conversions cannot approach those of Catholicism. Dahomeyan Protestants number fewer than 20,000 throughout the country. In part this has probably been due to the French colonial administration's chronic distrust of missionaries of British and American nationality, and in part to the splits that have occurred among the Dahomeyan Protestants themselves. Like the Catholic missionaries, the Protestants first concentrated on the south (in this case, the Porto Novo region) and after a period of royal favor were subjected to persecution. After this persecution had ceased, the Protestant churches recovered their strength, only to be torn by dissension at the turn of the century. In 1901 a group of Dahomeyan Protestants of Porto Novo broke away to form their own church, which they called that of the Union des Natifs Africains. The subsequent division of the whole country into two ecclesiastical zones, one administered by British missionaries in the south and the other by American missionaries in the north, has both reinforced Dahomey's regional separatism and contributed to disunity among its Protestants. Further rifts in their community in the Porto Novo–Cotonou region have been caused by the flowering there of messianic cults, such as the Eledja Church, the Sacred Order of Cherubim and Seraphim, and the like, which admit the practice of polygamy.

Islam, the other great proselytizing religion of West Africa, has penetrated both upper and lower Dahomey. It was brought to the south in the eighteenth century by Yoruba immigrants from Nigeria, who were granted by the King of Porto Novo the right to serve as a Muslim unit in his army and to build mosques in his domain. After the abolition of the slave trade, some of the Portuguese who stayed on in lower Dahomey were converted to Islam and became the most active propagators of their new faith in the south. In upper Dahomey, Islam was introduced by the Haoussa from Niger, who failed to convert the Somba but who found zealous followers among the Bariba and Peul. Islam, like Protestantism, has put down roots throughout the country but in lower Dahomey has been subject to rifts and disunity. Over the seemingly minor issue of building a great mosque at Porto Novo, its Muslim community split on the eve of World War I into two groups, one led by Yoruba and the other by Portuguese. Until harmony was restored in 1925, the tension generated between the two groups was so great that at times it threatened to degenerate into civil war.[10] Today, Dahomey's 280,000 or so Muslims are to be found throughout the country in communities of varying size, of which the largest have Koranic schools where the rudiments of Arabic are taught. Their greatest concentration is in upper Dahomey, where Islam has certainly contributed to the strength of regional feeling. (Paradoxically, fetishism remains strongest in the most Christianized areas.) But the division is far from clear-cut, and there is a wide margin of error in such generalizations as those that refer to the "Muslim north" or to the "Christianized south."

If Dahomey now leads French-speaking West Africa in having 30 per cent of its school-age children attending school, this is largely due to the impetus given to education by the Catholic and, to a much lesser extent, the Protestant missions. (The British Methodist and American Assembly of God missions together teach a total of some 4,500 primary school children, compared with more than 46,000 students attending Catholic mission primary, secondary, and technical schools.) By 1900 the Fathers of the Lyon mission had opened forty schools in lower Dahomey. And it was not until the 1950's, when education made a big spurt in Dahomey, that the number of students attending state schools came to exceed those in mission schools. The missions' stronghold is primary education, particularly for girls, whereas the state has taken the lead at the secondary, technical, and university levels. To round out the picture of the educational role played by religious groups, mention should be made of the Muslim school at Porto Novo, named for the French Governor Léon Bourgine who, in the 1930's, was markedly sympathetic to the advancement of Muslim youth.

As of 1960, Dahomey had a total of 558 primary schools (of which 220 were run by the Christian missions), 1,984 instructors (992 of whom were employed by the missions), and 88,189 pupils (of whom 42,535 attended mission schools). Seven of Dahomey's 15 secondary schools belonged to Catholic missions, as did 97 of the 146 professors and 1,562 out of the 3,175 in the student body.[11] At the technical-education level, mission activity tapered off, being responsible for only 10 of the 35 professors and 162 of the 894 pupils in Dahomey's seven such institutions. In the domain of higher education, the missions play

[10] Akindélé and Aguessy, *Dahomey*, p. 48.
[11] "L'Afrique d'expression française," *Europe-France-Outremer*, March 1962, p. 98.

no role except as regards their theological seminaries at Ouidah (Catholic) and at Porto Novo (Protestant). Public funds, both French and Dahomeyan, are financing Dahomey's scholarship holders in the universities of France (218) and at Dakar (138). French teaching personnel, now working under contract with the Dahomeyan government, total 73, all but 7 of whom occupy the country's top academic posts.

Since World War II, France has supplied virtually all of Dahomey's high-ranking teaching and educational administrative personnel, and FIDES has provided a very large proportion of the funds used for new school buildings. Contributions from local resources, including subsidies to mission schools, have averaged between 21 and 24 per cent of the total budget revenues, but this does not match the FIDES grants. So great is the zeal of Dahomey's leaders for more educational facilities that they would gladly increase that percentage if the country's resources permitted. Obviously, Dahomey should spend more money on developing education in the north, where schools are scarce and where attendance is much smaller than in the south. Whereas from 30 to 63 per cent of school-age children are receiving formal instruction in the *cercles* of Porto Novo, Ouidah, and Cotonou, the corresponding figures for Kandi and Natitingou *cercles* are only 11 and 13 per cent respectively. This disparity is traceable to various causes: the general neglect of upper Dahomey; the resistance of its Muslim population to lay or Christian-mission education, especially for girls; the dispersion of its inhabitants; and the reluctance of teachers from the south to accept posts elsewhere than in lower Dahomey. In very recent years some progress has been made in respect to making state schools more accessible and more popular in the north by building there a few boarding schools and starting canteens in some others.

Because of the concentration of educational institutions in lower Dahomey, such student agitation as has occurred in the country has taken place in the south. The ferment generated by the new freedom that came with application of the *loi cadre* throughout French Negro Africa affected students in such widely dispersed centers as Rosso (Mauritania), Conakry (Guinea), Ouagadougou (Upper Volta), Libreville (Gabon), and also Porto Novo and Cotonou. In April 1958, students of the Lycée Victor Ballot launched a campaign against some of their professors who had dared to criticize them for their "pretensions and lack of humility." Oké Assogba, then Dahomeyan Minister of Education, sent all 400 members of the student body back to their parents for a ten-day cooling off period. This proved to be effective, and it was not until almost two years later, in February 1960, that another big school strike occurred. This time the strike was at the Technical College of Cotonou, where the strikers demanded the dismissal of two professors who, after failing some students, had them expelled. The government tried the same tactics as before, but this time the college was closed for eight months. Such manifestations were simply part of a widespread protest on the part of African youth against authority, particularly when it was exercised by Frenchmen. But the activities of Dahomeyan students in France had a more distinctively and radical political orientation. Two of the most brilliant agitators among them were brought into Maga's government in 1960. Bertin Borna, now Minister of Finance, had distinguished himself by his fiery oratory as a student spokesman when he attended the Parti du Regroupement Africain (PRA) congress at Cotonou in July 1958. And Albert Tevoedjre, later Secretary of State for Information, had been at one time editor in chief of *L'Etudiant Noir,* organ of the left-wing Fédération des Etudiants de l'Afrique Noire Française.

No sooner had Tevoedjre become active in Dahomeyan politics in the fall of 1960 than he applied himself to the task of propaganda with vigor and skill. He announced that a corps of official town criers would regularly keep the illiterate masses informed about current events and government activities. For the reading public, three newspapers would be printed: *L'Aube Nouvelle,* which he described as a national journal of opinion; *La Nation,* the PDU organ; and *La Depêche du Dahomey,* a fortnightly giving detailed news about the events of the day. The editorials that Tevoedjre wrote for *L'Aube Nouvelle* were outstanding, for he brought to his new task an unusually rich background of knowledge and experience. After studying at Toulouse, Fribourg, and Geneva, he had taught at the *lycées* of Cahors, Dakar, and Porto Novo. During his sojourn in Paris he had published two works, *L'Afrique révoltée* in 1958 and *Afrique debout* the next year, whose titles reflect the left-wing views of the circles he frequented. He attended various cultural congresses at Paris, Rome, and Tashkent, and, in addition to French, he acquired a knowledge of German, English, and Spanish. Despite such wide-ranging activities, he did not lose touch with the African scene. He helped to found the proindependence Mouvement Africain de Libération Nationale and the Ligue pour la Promotion Africaine and was head of the Syndicat National des Enseignants du Dahomey before becoming administrative secretary of the PDU in October 1960 at the age of thirty-one.

The energy with which Tevoedjre invaded Dahomey's very small-scale journalistic scene inevitably led to a conflict with the existing press, notably with the UDD organ, *Dahomey-Matin*. A law passed in February 1961 that restricted the freedom of the press enabled him to suspend *Dahomey-Matin* and then its successor, *Cotonou-Matin*, in mid-April. Not content with having disposed of his main competitors, Tevoedjre, in July 1961, got the cabinet to approve his project of creating an Agence Dahoméenne de Presse to be placed under his control. By the end of the year he had secured for this new agency the exclusive use of Agence France Presse's wire services. But a monopoly in the field of journalism was only one step in his self-imposed task of building up a national consciousness that would solidly back the PDU. One of his projects was to build a national museum that would bring together in one place all of Dahomey's art treasures. Another, and a more important one for his purposes, was to make more effective use of the radio. In the latter objective he was greatly aided in July 1961 by the gift from Société de la Radiodiffusion de la France d'Outre-Mer (SORAFOM) of a 30-kilowatt transmitter, which was over seven times as powerful as the one then in use by Radio Dahomey. In November 1961, Tevoedjre was named secretary-general of the Union Africaine et Malgache (UAM), thus opening up a vastly enlarged field for his talents. By this time mass media of communication in Dahomey were already firmly under the PDU government's control.

The Political Process

Ninety-seven per cent of the voters of Dahomey who went to the polls on September 28, 1958, accepted the constitution submitted by General de Gaulle. On the following December 4, its assembly, which had been elected by universal suffrage on March 31, 1957, transformed itself into a constituent body, proclaimed the Republic of Dahomey, and as such opted to become a member state of the Franco-African Community. That same month, Dahomey sent delegates to the federal congress convened at Bamako and agreed to join the proposed Mali Federation. Within a few weeks, however, Dahomey's Premier, S. M. Apithy, turned against the federation as it was constituted at Dakar, saying that he preferred a less rigid grouping of African states in which each would be accorded more autonomy. Despite the opposition of some federalists, this decision was accepted by the assembly, in which Apithy's PRD party held an absolute majority. On February 14, 1959, its members unanimously voted in favor of the constitution that he submitted to them.

Dahomey's 1959 constitution, like that of most other French-speaking African states at the time, was closely patterned after that of the Fifth French Republic. Consequently the chief executive, who was also head of state, had extensive powers, compared with which those of the legislative assembly were decidedly limited. In brief, Dahomey accepted a parliamentary regime but one in which the Prime Minister was clearly predominant. Nevertheless, the first legislative elections held under the constitution on April 2–3, 1959, led to the ousting of Apithy, and on May 21 he was replaced as Premier by Hubert Maga. Within a few days of his investiture, Maga brought Dahomey into the Council of the Entente.

At that time, membership in the Entente was tantamount to acceptance of the leadership of Houphouët-Boigny. Under his aegis Dahomey, along with the Ivory Coast, Niger, and Upper Volta, jointly came to an agreement with France which enabled Dahomey to declare its independence on August 1, 1960. On the following November 25, Dahomey accepted a new constitution that was almost identical with those of its Entente partners. Like them it acquired a presidential type of government, but with one distinguishing feature, in that it instituted the office of Vice-President.[12]

The President of the Dahomey Republic is elected for a five-year term by direct universal adult suffrage. At the same time and for the same period is elected a Vice-President who, in case of need, can replace the President either temporarily or permanently. The chief executive, who is also head of state, is the "incarnation of national unity." He is commander in chief of the armed forces, can negotiate treaties, and is empowered to issue regulations on certain subjects. If he asks the assembly to reconsider a bill, it must then be passed by two-thirds of the membership to become law. If he so wishes, he may submit measures to a popular referendum. Members of the unicameral legislature are elected on the same day, for the same period, and by the same electorate as the President and Vice-President. Its sixty members enjoy parliamentary immunity, vote the budget, and pass laws on matters enumerated in the constitution. Its powers are

[12] See D. G. Lavroff and G. Peiser, *Les constitutions africaines* (Paris, 1961), pp. 72–85.

inferior to those of the President and may even be suspended if the President is able to get the assembly's permission to rule by decree for a specified period. The constitution provides for the creation of a purely advisory Economic and Social Council and for the independence of the judiciary vis-à-vis both the executive and legislative branches. Its preamble contains an affirmation of Dahomey's belief in the Declaration of the Rights of Man and of the Citizen; Article 1 states that its official language is French and its motto "Fraternity, Justice, and Work"; and Article 2 proclaims that the secular republic is one and indivisible and rests upon the sovereignty of the people.

POLITICAL DYNAMICS

In view of the extent of the powers assigned to the chief executive, even under the February 14, 1959, constitution, it seems surprising that Apithy's government was so rapidly overthrown by the assembly elected only a few weeks after its promulgation. From the end of World War II until 1956, Apithy's political leadership went almost unchallenged in Dahomey. During those ten years he had been elected and reelected to the French National Assembly, to the presidency of the territorial assembly, and to the Grand Council of French West Africa. In fact, he had become such a fixture in the Dahomeyan political scene that his more unsophisticated followers confused the office of "deputy" with his name, Apithy. Largely through his eloquence and ability Apithy had been able to build up a very large and devoted following in the south, which was more remarkable because he had been out of the country for some years prior to his successful bid for election to the first French Constituent Assembly in 1945.

Apithy and His Regime

Born at Porto Novo in 1913, Apithy was first educated in local mission schools and then at Bordeaux and Paris, where he acquired degrees in political science and accountancy. Thereafter he worked for some time in Paris as an expert accountant. It was support from the Catholic missionaries in Dahomey that explained in large part his initial political success and probably also his quitting the RDA in September 1948. Subsequently, however, it was his own skill and personality that enabled him to retain power for so many years. He succeeded in playing a lone hand both in the National Assembly and in Dahomey. At Paris in 1948 he joined the IOM and then left it to align himself with a metropolitan party (Indépendants Paysans et Action

Sociale). In Africa, he kept Dahomey aloof from the big interterritorial political parties. This isolation enabled him long to remain the undisputed master in Dahomey.

But because Apithy represented no following outside his own country, he never played a prominent role in the wider French or West African political scenes. Although he distinguished himself as a speaker on African questions in the National Assembly and as *rapporteur* of its Overseas Commission, he was never given a French cabinet post as were such outstanding Negro leaders as Senghor, Houphouët-Boigny, and even Hubert Maga. And partly because he refused to associate himself closely with the movements working toward unity and independence that swept over French West Africa in the period following passage of the *loi cadre*, he lost his preeminence even in Dahomey.

It would be a mistake, however, now to write off Apithy as a political cipher in his own country. In Dahomey, where political power is so precariously balanced between north and south and where there are so many able candidates vying with each other for high office, Apithy has shown that his personality, long experience, and regional following are indispensable to the survival of successive governments. It was undoubtedly the need to appease Apithy that induced the authors of Dahomey's 1960 constitution to create the office of Vice-President for him. Although obviously an opportunist, Apithy is also an exceptionally able political strategist. Currently he has teamed up with the left-wing element in Maga's administration, and he may again rise to the top if the radicals succeed in seizing power.

It was the territorial assembly elections of March 31, 1957, that first clearly showed Apithy's star to be waning, though his PRD party won 43.3 per cent of the popular vote and 35 of the assembly's 60 seats. This moderate electoral success enabled Apithy to form Dahomey's first government council, taking over the Finance portfolio as well as the premiership. Most of his cabinet posts were given to PRD members—many of whom are still politically prominent—plus a few Independents. Sébastien Dassi was given the portfolio of Interior; Oké Assogba, that of Education; Paul Darboux, Social Affairs; Guillaume Fagbamigbé, Labor; L. I. Pinto, Trade and Industry; and Bio Tchane, Technical Instruction. The omissions, as well as this selection, were soon to affect the stability of Apithy's government. Neither Valentin Djibode Aplogan nor Pinto Madeira were included, and they soon were expelled from the PRD on the charge of party indiscipline. (It was a measure of the force of parochial sentiments in Dahomey that their expulsion was taken as a personal insult by the citizens of Ouidah whom they represented.) [13] Then the appointment of Fagbamigbé, for-mer head of Dahomey's Confédération Générale du Travail (CGT) unions, antagonized some of Cotonou's labor leaders, and this was also to contribute to the downfall of Apithy's first government.

If familiar faces were absent from the government council, this was also true of Dahomey's new assembly. The failure of Paul Hazoumé and Emile Zinsou to be elected looked like a defeat for the IOM–Convention Africaine (CA) forces in the south. Seemingly this was more than offset by the 6 seats from Natitingou *cercle* won by Hubert Maga, long-time member of the IOM and follower of Senghor. But at the same time 10 men were elected from the north who were not members of the Mouvement Démocratique Dahoméen (MDD) who called themselves independents. This situation could be interpreted either as a rejection of Senghor's federalist thesis or, more likely, as indicating that Maga as a person was no longer so widely accepted as the spokesman for the north. In any case, the fact that none of the Independents joined Apithy's PRD suggested that regional feeling among the northerners was still paramount.

To all outward appearances, the same could be said about Justin Ahomadegbé's UDD. It captured the seven seats allotted to Abomey *cercle*, of which he was the traditional chief. Because of the division of electoral circumscriptions, however, the composition of the assembly failed to reflect accurately the expressed will of the southern electorate. The small number of seats obtained by the UDD did not show that it had won 27 per cent of the popular vote or that its following had now overflowed the Abomey region to include a large percentage of Cotonou's working class. In the confusing welter of personal and regional loyalties, the position of the UDD seemed more clear-cut than that of the MDD, partly because the former was more closely integrated in the RDA than was the latter in the IOM-CA. In general, the 1957 elections indicated that interterritorial West African issues had begun to enter Dahomeyan politics but were still subordinated to purely local considerations. At any rate, it was certain that neither the RDA nor the IOM-CA would be able to gather strength in Dahomey until each was cast in a regional mold and under the leadership of a strong native son.

It had not been until 1954, more than three years after Houphouët

[13] Gil Dugué, *Vers les Etats-Unis d'Afrique* (Dakar, 1960), p. 81.

had transformed the RDA into a "respectable" conservative movement, that its territorial branch in Dahomey found the setting and the leadership it needed to emerge from the shadows into the political limelight. Its new-found leader was Justin Ahomadegbé, whose background bears a striking resemblance to that of his mentor, Houphouët. Both are wealthy traditional chiefs and graduates of Dakar's Medical School; both were for some years functionaries of the local French administration. But, unlike Houphouët, Ahomadegbé never served in a French cabinet, nor was he head of a vast political movement. His prestige derived from being the direct descendant of the powerful Abomey kings who had resisted the French conquest, his influence was confined to the region over which his ancestors had ruled, and he did not enter politics even on a territorial scale until he was elected to Dahomey's assembly in 1952. There he distinguished himself as a sharp critic of the local French administration, but he might have remained known simply as a firebrand from Abomey had he not subsequently allied himself with the trade union leaders of Cotonou. In the municipal elections of November 18, 1956, Ahomadegbé was chosen to be mayor of Abomey, and two of his lieutenants, Gilbert Kpakpo and Théodore Hessou, became respectively mayor and deputy mayor of Cotonou. The popular vote on March 31, 1957, confirmed the success of this alliance on the territorial level, and six months later Ahomadegbé's rise in the RDA hierarchy was marked by his nomination to its coordinating committee. But the independent and individualistic Dahomeyan leaders of the UDD were not pleased by the high price that they had to pay for integration in the RDA and for its support. The comparatively poor showing made by the Dahomey delegation at the RDA congress at Bamako in September 1957 was probably a reflection of this attitude.[14] Increasingly they resented interference by Houphouët's emissaries in their internal disputes and, above all, in their labor policy. This resentment was to become acute following the anti-Dahomeyan riots of October 1958 in the Ivory Coast, but even before then the local Union Générale des Travailleurs de l'Afrique Noire (UGTAN) unions were recalcitrant in their attitude toward the interterritorial RDA leadership. This was because Dahomey's economic situation was deteriorating, unemployment was growing in the south, and the UDD leaders saw that their best chance of overthrowing the PRD government lay in exploiting labor's grievances.

[14] André Blanchet, *L'itinéraire des partis africains depuis Bamako* (Paris, 1958), p. 23.

The Influence of Labor

In 1957 the active population of Dahomey was estimated to include 820,000 workers, of whom only 22,000 were wage earners.[15] This category was made up of about 2,000 agricultural laborers scattered throughout the south; 7,000 functionaries and manual workers of the administration, chiefly at Porto Novo; and some 13,000 craftsmen and industrial workers employed in Cotonou's factories and the country's four oil mills. This geographical concentration of Dahomey's wage earners at specific points in the south made it comparatively easy to organize them into unions. For the same reason, the UGTAN unions affiliated with the UDD were able by mid-1957 to bring organized labor largely under their control. However, the strength of the labor movement under the UDD aegis did not become apparent until January 1958. Then the UGTAN unions of Cotonou struck to show their solidarity with the workers at the Avrankou oil mill who had gone on strike two months before against the Société des Huileries Modernes du Dahomey (SHMD), the semiprivate company that managed two of the country's four oil mills.

On October 16, 1957, the Avrankou workers demanded a 20 per cent pay rise, but the French manager of the SHMD replied that he would not discuss the matter until December, when he planned to submit a collective agreement to all the millworkers. On November 9, he was asked for an immediate decision; when he failed to reply a strike was called by the Avrankou unions on November 20. The SIIMD management consulted the territorial labor inspector, and after he had pronounced the strike to be illegal, 125 of the striking workers were dismissed by the SHMD. The Apithy government then intervened and asked the SHMD to relent, and the company agreed to take back all but the strike ringleaders. This did not satisfy the UGTAN leadership, which on December 3 called for a general work stoppage in order to force the SHMD to take back all of the strikers. Not only did this fail to move the SHMD, but it incited all the employers affected to dismiss those of their workers who had participated in the sympathy strike.

At this point the territorial assembly entered the picture, and the whole question assumed a definitely political coloration. The attack led by the UDD members on the SHMD's management had distinctly antiwhite and anticapitalist overtones. Most of the assemblymen

[15] *Marchés Tropicaux,* Dec. 23, 1961.

showed little interest in the timing or the questionable legality of the strike but much concern for the "misery" of the strikers. In fact, the assembly unanimously passed a resolution supporting the unions' demand that all the strikers be immediately reemployed. Encouraged by this vote, the UGTAN called for a new solidarity strike on January 24, which rapidly degenerated into violence. Private homes and shops were pillaged and cars stoned, 2 persons were killed and 60 wounded, and troops had to be called in to restore order. On January 30 Premier Apithy broadcast an appeal for calm, condemned all agitators, and said that those responsible for the violence would be prosecuted. But the next day the UGTAN not only repeated its demand that all the strikers be reinstated at once but also insisted that the head of the SHMD be dismissed within forty-eight hours. If this ultimatum went unheeded, it was added, an unlimited strike would be called beginning February 4. Without waiting for such an eventuality, the Avrankou mill closed down on February 3 and the Apithy government resigned the same day.

Because of the general gravity of the situation, and especially because the SHMD's decision would adversely affect not only its nonstriking workers but also the 30,000 or so Dahomeyans who supplied the Avrankou mill with palm nuts, Governor Biros decided to take the situation in hand. He persuaded the UGTAN to call off the general strike slated for February 4 and the SHMD to reopen its plant and rehire all of its former workers on February 9. Thus, an immediate economic paralysis of the country was averted. But the chronic unemployment and underemployment situation was not resolved, and a sense of profound malaise persisted, particularly among the resident Europeans. In its trial of strength with both employers and the Apithy government, the UDD-UGTAN combine had won all along the line, and it had thereby been encouraged to create a truly revolutionary situation. This posed the crucial question as to whether or not Dahomey's next government would be strong and representative enough to impose its will.

Twelve days were to pass while Apithy negotiated futilely with Maga and Ahomadegbé. Because he still held an absolute majority in the assembly, he would not accept their proposal to form a government in which the three major parties had equal representation. On February 14 he constituted a cabinet composed of six PRD ministers, two Independents from the north, and two technicians of whom one— Jacques Plassard—was a Frenchman. The last-mentioned appointment was formally protested by the UDD on the ground that he was a foreigner, and in June the Dakar Federal Cour des Contentieux invalidated Plassard's nomination as Dahomey's Minister of Economic Affairs. Naturally this was regarded as a victory by the opposition, and the resident European community was hardly reassured by a broadcast made on June 14 by Paul Darboux, the new Minister of Labor, who blamed the selfishness of Dahomey's employers for the workers' recourse to the strike weapon.

But if the Apithy government saw eye to eye with the UDD in sympathizing with the Dahomey working classes vis-à-vis capitalistic European employers, it resented the UDD's use of organized labor to promote that party's political interests. Moreover, Apithy showed little skill or enterprise in his dealing with the Cotonou wage-earner groups. It was not until the eve of May Day 1958 that he released 28 of the 45 men held in Cotonou prison as responsible for the violence that had occurred on January 24. Three more weeks were to pass before he took steps to implement the recommendations made four months before by a semiofficial committee to raise wages and to promote collective labor agreements. These belated moves did not prevent a small-scale strike later in June and the growth of tension, not only between workers and employers but also between the government and the unions. Organized labor had been alienated by such measures as the PRD had taken to enforce law and order, and its leaders continued to regard the government as a supporter of the employer group, especially of the companies in which the territory was a shareholder.

Attempts at Political Unity

At the same time that Apithy was vainly and weakly trying to wean laborers away from the UDD, he made a more successful attempt to win back some of the defectors from his own party. Some had left solely because of personal quarrels, but those whose departure had more seriously weakened the PRD ranks were the outstanding Dahomeyans who differed from Apithy on broad policy issues: men like Emile Zinsou, Djibode Aplogan, and Michel Ahouamenou. They had deserted the PRD with their personal followers to form small parties dedicated to the principle that Dahomey must join the federalist movement that was then gaining strength especially at Dakar. Their defection made Apithy realize that so long as he kept Dahomey aloof from the prevailing trend toward African unity he could never make his party sufficiently strong and united to compete with the growing power of the UDD. To join the federalist camp was not too difficult for Apithy, because he had been outstanding in the National Assembly in his opposition to the balkanization of French Negro Africa. Such a move would also facilitate a *rapprochement* with Maga, who controlled a precious bloc of votes in the local assembly. Therefore late in March 1958 Apithy attended the second regroupment conference at Dakar, where he became a founder-member of the PRA which was formed at that time. Upon his return to Dahomey, Apithy succeeded in getting the PRD, Maga's party now called the Rassemblement Démocratique Dahoméen (RDD), and some independents to come together in a Parti Progressiste Dahoméen (PPD), which would be the territorial branch of the PRA.

In typical Dahomeyan fashion, no sooner had a "united party" been formed than dissension broke out in its ranks. Six small groups withdrew after the bigger parties refused their request for more seats on the executive committee. At the same time a split occurred among the northerners who had just joined the newborn PPD: the four assemblymen from Djougou—of whom the most important were Apithy's ministers Darboux and Bio Tchane—refused to accept Maga as their leader. Therefore they proceeded to form the Union des Indépendants du Dahomey which, though not a member of the PPD, agreed to collaborate with any government headed by Apithy. Maga had made the mistake of forming his loyal Natitingou followers into an Association des Frères de la Savane, and his election as president of the PPD-PRA on June 18 further alienated the Djougou group. To a limited extent these losses to the PPD were offset by the acquisition of some new members. These were a few young men who left the UDD because they were offended by a "patronizing" speech made at Cotonou by the RDA Soudanese leader, Haidara Mahamane. Within only a few weeks of its founding, the PPD's strength had so rapidly ebbed and flowed as a result of personal and regional antagonisms that it was impossible to appraise its exact strength.

It was on such shifting sands that Apithy had rapidly to build a new coalition government. The imminence of the PRA constituent congress, which was to be held at Cotonou the end of July, made at least a cabinet reshuffle imperative. Naturally he wanted to capitalize on such unity as he had managed to achieve through formation of the PPD, and the presence in the government of Zinsou (Economic Affairs), Pinto (Civil Service), and Adandé (Agriculture) was evidence of his success. He had trouble in persuading Maga and Bio Tchanc to enter the same cabinet, but eventually Maga accepted the Labor portfolio and Bio Tchane that of Finance. Inclusion of the two PRD stalwarts, Sébastien Dassi (Interior) and Oké Assogba (Education), gave the new government a degree of continuity.

On July 4, 1958, Apithy's coalition government was invested by the assembly by 41 votes in support to only 4 votes against and 6 abstentions. This was more than three weeks ahead of the date on which the Cotonou PRA congress was to open. At that conference, which called for immediate independence and African unity, no Dahomeyan —with the possible exception of the student leader, Bertin Borna— played an outstanding role. It was characteristic of the parochial nature of Dahomeyan politics that such vital questions as French-speaking Africa's future relations with France should arouse far less dissension among its representatives than their own *affaires de clocher* (small-town rivalries). Since all of Dahomey's leaders recognized the need for continued French aid, acceptance of de Gaulle's constitution was not made a local party issue, and both Apithy and Ahomadegbé appealed for an affirmative vote in the referendum of September 1958. To be sure, a small Parti Dahoméen de l'Indépendance was formed by two obscure PPD militants, who proclaimed their fidelity to the resolutions of the Cotonou PRA congress. But the small size of the negative vote cast—9,240—as compared with 418,963 affirmative votes showed that the vast majority of Dahomeyans favored joining the Franco-African Community. Real trouble was brewing over the federalism issue, which had not been resolved by the referendum, but this did not come to the fore until early in 1959. For the balance of 1958, Apithy had the political situation well enough in hand to be able to fend off a demand by the UDD for dissolution of the assembly and the holding of new elections. On December 3, Dahomey was proclaimed a republic and a member state of the new Community.

If Apithy, thanks to the unity created by formation of the PPD, had sufficient control at this time to maintain relative political calm, the same could not be said of his authority in the economic domain. Early in September, an interterritorial meeting of the UGTAN was held at Cotonou, at which it was decided to form the branch of that labor movement in Dahomey into the Union des Syndicats des Travailleurs du Dahomey. This decision alienated the Confédération Africaine des Travailleurs Croyants (CATC) unions which in Dahomey, as elsewhere in French West Africa, opposed the UGTAN's growing attempts

to monopolize and politicize the labor movement. This reaction was
certainly not unrelated to the last-minute cancellation by the CATC
of its order to participate in a series of strikes called by the UGTAN
unions in late October. Ostensibly these strikes were called to protest
the return to Dahomey of the unpopular French head of the CFAO,
the territory's most important trading firm. In all probability they
were called principally to back up the UDD's demand for dissolution
of the assembly and the holding of new elections. However, the outbreak of anti-Dahomeyan (and anti-Togolese) riots in Abidjan just at
this time and the return to Dahomey of thousands of refugees from the
Ivory Coast provided a diversion. Although the Ivoirian government
agreed to pay reparations and the salaries of Dahomeyans who had
been serving in its administration, in the long run this development
gravely aggravated Dahomey's unemployment problem. But it did
have the immediately beneficial effect of at least temporarily uniting
the Dahomeyan political parties and labor unions in a sense of collective grievance against the Ivory Coast. Moreover, the fact that the
master of the Ivory Coast was also the leader of the RDA further
weakened Houphouët's control over the territorial branch of that
movement in Dahomey, as well as over the local UGTAN unions.

On December 3, the eve of the proclamation of the Republic of
Dahomey and of its membership in the Community, the UGTAN
launched a general protest strike, which paralyzed Dahomey's foreign
trade, transport, and government services for three days. Despite an
official order forbidding public meetings, 500 persons gathered together at Cotonou on December 7 and threw into the lagoon a coffin
in which they had placed an effigy of Apithy.[16] At this point it seemed
so likely that the UDD's objective of overthrowing the government
would be achieved that Apithy hastily called a meeting of all party
leaders at which their differences were patched up. This was only a
truce, however, and the convening of a federalist congress at Bamako
a few days later was to provide the mutually unreconciled Dahomeyans
with a fresh bone of contention.

The Issue of Larger Groupings

It was quite logical for Apithy, as a long-time opponent of the balkanization of West Africa and as an outstanding member of the PRA,
to attend the Bamako congress and to agree there to Dahomey's membership in the future Mali Federation. Yet on January 31, 1959, Apithy

---

[16] *Ibid.*, Dec. 13, 1958.

handed in his resignation from the PRA and announced his strong opposition to Dahomey's participation in the proposed federation. In explaining this change of front, Apithy said that the overrigid structure of the new federation would not permit Dahomey to develop properly its own personality and its ties with its immediate neighbors. Obviously he had come to believe that Dahomey's interests would be better served by creating a union with Togo, Niger, and Nigeria than with distant Senegal and Soudan. (Moreover, Upper Volta, the fourth country that had signed the federation agreement at Bamako, was also showing signs of defection.)

While the foregoing reasons given by Apithy were valid enough, there were certainly others that motivated his sudden about-face. Reportedly he had received a pledge from France to build a deepwater port at Cotonou, as well as a promise of financial aid from Houphouët if he withheld Dahomey's adherence to the Mali Federation. On the domestic political front, Apithy must have weighed very carefully the pros and cons of such a decision. If he failed to join the proposed federation, he would alienate his prefederalist supporters, particularly Zinsou, Adandé, Pinto, and possibly Maga. On the other hand, such a move might effect a *rapprochement* with his most dangerous opponents, the UDD leaders, who on this issue echoed Houphouët's unalterable opposition to any primary federation. Furthermore, there was an element inside the PPD which also opposed Dahomey's joining the Mali Federation, and it was with this group that Apithy decided to re-form the PRD following his resignation from the PRA. For a short time it looked as if Apithy's gamble would succeed. His biggest trump card was France's pledge at long last to build the Cotonou port, which the whole country ardently desired and which assured him in particular of the support of the isolated north. Apparently the UDD was appeased by Apithy's turning against the federation and even more by his promise to hold elections soon for a new assembly. Even the profederalist ministers agreed to remain in his cabinet. On February 14 the assembly unanimously accepted the constitution he submitted to it, and the elections for the seventy members of the new legislature were scheduled for April 2.

Preelection Negotiations in 1959

During the weeks that intervened between the passage of the constitution and the holding of elections, all the parties' leaders were involved in complicated maneuverings. With a view to reaching some working agreement with Maga, Apithy made a special trip to take the political temperature of the north. Despite a few openly expressed regrets by profederalists and a few echoes of separatist sentiments there, Apithy found the north still more firmly under Maga's control than in 1958 and Maga more amenable to his advances. The two leaders discussed a revision of the electoral law and agreed that Maga's party (now renamed the Rassemblement Démocratique Dahoméen, or RDD) would present no candidates in the south and that Apithy's PRD would reciprocate by not contesting seats in the north. Since the profederalists of the former PPD decided to abstain during the electoral campaign, this left the PRD face to face with the UDD in the southern region. To obviate a dangerous struggle there, Apithy, in mid-March, tried to strike a bargain with the UDD leaders. If successful, Apithy's tactics would have made the elections a complete farce, but he found Justin Ahomadegbé a hard bargainer. Reportedly the UDD insisted on being allotted the same number of seats in the new assembly as the PRD and RDD together, and this Apithy refused to accept. In regard to European participation there was no conflict between them, for both parties included French candidates on their respective lists. Indeed, there was a striking absence of ideological differences between the various Dahomeyan parties contending the election.[17] Maga's RDD was frankly a regional group, and its members regarded Apithy's PRD simply as its counterpart in the south. Nor was there any ideological conflict between the UDD and the PRD since the federal issue had been resolved. The electoral struggle was confined to the south, and it revolved around the person of Apithy. The partisans of Apithy would automatically vote for the PRD, while his adversaries would vote just as automatically for the UDD because Ahomadegbé was Apithy's most determined opponent.

After Apithy had failed to come to terms with the UDD, he resorted to the classical method of trying to ensure his party's victory by a revision of the electoral circumscriptions. He also took the precaution of forbidding voters to attend campaign meetings in any circumscription other than their own. The net result of his over-all strategy was to make the southwestern circumscription of Mono, where eighteen seats were at stake, the focus of the UDD-PRD struggle.

[17] *Le Monde*, March 29–30, 1959.

Postelection Maneuvers

Thanks to elaborate security measures, including the presence of gendarmes sent in from Togo, election day passed off calmly. But when the results were made known, rioting broke out in which over 100 persons were injured. According to the figures given out by the government, the PRD had received 144,038 votes and won 37 seats in the assembly; the RDD, 62,132 votes and 22 seats; and the UDD, 162,179 votes and 11 seats. Thus, the UDD which had got the biggest popular vote obtained only 11 of the 70 seats at stake. Its leaders formally protested, particularly in regard to the frauds allegedly committed in Mono circumscription, and its militants seized several border posts and barricaded the roads to Lomé and Parakou. To maintain order, the French flew in troops from Niger. Apithy's three profederalist ministers resigned from the cabinet as a mark of their disapproval of his tactics. Maga, not wishing to become involved, prudently retired to the north.

Faced with a situation bordering on civil war, Apithy realized that he must make some concessions. Partly as a result of Houphouët's intervention, a compromise was reached with the UDD whereby that party and the PRD divided the 18 seats of Mono circumscription between them. This reduced Apithy's following in the assembly to 28 members. The UDD now had 20, and the RDD, with its 22 seats, was thus well placed to hold the balance of power between them. To ensure his retaining the premiership, Apithy was willing to let Ahomadegbé be elected as president of the assembly. But this did not satisfy the UDD high command which, despite further pleas from Houphouët's emissaries, was determined to oust Apithy as head of the government. Early in May, Houphouët again tried his hand at reconciling Dahomey's warring parties, for he wanted Dahomey to join his Council of the Entente. Thus, he invited them to send representatives to confer with him in Paris. Ahomadegbé resented the RDA leader's interference in what he considered to be a purely internal Dahomeyan conflict and wanted to maintain his freedom of maneuver. He did not accept the invitation, therefore, but in his place sent Kpakpo, mayor of Cotonou, and Albert Akindès, secretary of the UGTAN unions.[18] The upshot of these moves and countermoves was to fasten attention on Maga as a compromise Premier, whose candidacy was vigorously and ably promoted by Bertin Borna, now a rising

[18] Dugué, *Vers les Etats-Unis d'Afrique*, p. 237.

star in the RDD. But Maga played hard to get and waited to receive Apithy's reluctant consent before he agreed to accept the assembly's investiture. Yet when Maga constituted his cabinet, Apithy was disconcerted to find himself named only Minister of State without portfolio, while the post of Vice-Premier which he coveted was given to his lieutenant, Oké Assogba. Apithy did not forgive this affront, and it soon became evident that to regain power he would not stop at overthrowing the government of Maga.

Hubert Maga and His Administration

When Hubert Maga became Premier of Dahomey, he was still largely an unknown quantity in the country as a whole, although he had been in public life since 1947. Born into a peasant family at Parakou in 1916, Maga was educated at the Ponty normal school in Dakar and had become converted to Christianity. Posted to Natitingou as a schoolmaster, he served there from 1936 to 1946. In a region that sorely lacked trained leaders, he and his wife—who was a trained nurse and also a Christian—gained widespread influence. It was therefore not surprising that Maga founded the first political organization in the north and was elected to Dahomey's territorial assembly in 1947. Regularly reelected to that assembly and also to the Grand Council of French West Africa, Maga became a deputy in the French National Assembly in 1951 and again in 1956. There he joined the IOM but, unlike Apithy, remained faithful to Senghor's leadership, and for this he was rewarded by the post of Secretary of State in the Gaillard government from November 1957 to April 1958. From this it could be deduced that Maga was a federalist, but he never took a strong stand on this matter, and when he came to power it was not known whether his sympathies lay with the Mali Federation or with the Council of the Entente. This unwillingness to commit himself ideologically was to prove characteristic of Maga's administration. His position has often been compared with that of Ahmadou Ahidjo in Cameroun: both are northerners who rose to the top because the more advanced and talented southerners in their respective countries could not agree among themselves on any other candidate. Not being endowed with a magnetic personality or with a mass following, Maga had to rely on his natural prudence and his ability to keep his balance in the treacherous footing of Dahomey's turbulent politics.

It required all of Maga's skill as a practical politician to form a government that was sufficiently representative to be acceptable to the three main parties and also one that could cope with the deterioration of Dahomey's economy. During the debate on Maga's investiture, the UDD leader, Emile Poisson, predicted that before the year ended Dahomey's deficit would reach over 2,000,000,000 CFA francs. Capital investments were at a standstill, unemployment was growing with the return to Dahomey of thousands of its nationals from the Ivory Coast and other countries of French Negro Africa, and some politicians had even been urging their compatriots not to pay taxes. Labor was restless, and the UGTAN unions insisted on being consulted before Maga named his Minister of Labor. He acceded to their demand and appointed Paul Darboux to that post and also made Gilbert Kpakpo a Secretary of State. The key portfolio of Interior he reserved to an RDD follower, Arouna Mama, and transferred the previous PRD incumbent, Sébastien Dassi, to the lesser position of Minister of Agriculture. The other cabinet posts were judiciously distributed among the three major parties. Maga's policy declaration contained a number of harmless generalizations, but it also struck some prophetic warning notes. He proclaimed his intention of destroying tribalism and regionalism, revising the status of chiefs, encouraging investments from any and every source, freezing wages and prices, and enforcing austerity measures.

Maga's first months in office were taken up mainly by consideration of foreign relations questions: membership in the Entente, negotiations with the Ivory Coast regarding Dahomeyan victims of the October 1958 riots, getting a subsidy from France, and reaching a technical agreement in Paris for construction of Cotonou's port. On the home front there was evidence of intense political activity, but it did not take a violent turn. The orientation being given to the Mali Federation and the fact that sovereign status would soon be acquired by neighboring Togo, Cameroun, and Nigeria had their repercussions in Dahomey. Many new groups were formed, especially by young people, under the slogan of African independence and unity. The brilliant young Albert Tevoedjre (see pp. 206–207) with the Voltaic leader, Joseph Ki Zerbo, founded the proindependence Mouvement Africain de Libération Nationale (MLN); in July, a small Communist party was formed at Cotonou under the name of Parti de la Révolution du Bénin; and at Porto Novo the Union Générale des Etudiants du Dahomey urged Maga to leave the Entente and the Community and to fight for Dahomey's "freedom" and for African unity.

Apithy, with his customary opportunism and acute sense of timing, now jumped on the bandwagon. On September 2, he got the PRD national congress to pass a resolution demanding national independence by 1960 and the transformation of the Franco-African Community into a multinational confederation. He informed Maga that if he did not promise to organize a popular referendum on the independence issue, he would withdraw the PRD ministers from his government. A few days later Apithy joined with the old PPD-PRA federalists and the local branch of the MLN to form a Front de la Lutte pour l'Indépendance du Dahomey, to whose program the country's CATC unions promptly gave their support.

Maga's reaction was not slow in coming. On September 19 he dismissed Apithy from his cabinet and warned the other PRD ministers that a similar fate awaited them if they disagreed with him on so important a policy issue. His strong action, as well as second thoughts, caused many Dahomeyan leaders to waver and then finally to support him. The MLN, now suspicious of Apithy's motives, withdrew from the Front, and on October 3 the Front dissolved itself, "judging the moment inopportune to fight for independence." [19] But the PRD's announcement that it would hold a meeting at Cotonou on October 10 precipitated rioting between militants of the UDD and those of the erstwhile Front, in which 3 persons died and 22 were wounded. Maga first forbade and then permitted the meeting to be held, after he had assembled enough gendarmes at Cotonou to ensure the maintenance of order. He then issued a stern warning to all agitators and fomenters of future disorders.

It should be noted that once again an ideological issue—this time that of independence and African unity—served in Dahomey as a screen for a struggle that concerned purely local interests. Apithy was hoping that by riding the popular tide in West Africa he would be returned to power. Maga and some of his followers, though they wanted to remain at the helm, were mainly motivated by what they considered to be the safeguarding of Dahomey's best interests. Undoubtedly all of them favored independence and unity for their country in principle. But at this time they feared that any brusque change in their relations with France (and with the Entente) might jeopardize the construction of Cotonou's port, on which their hopes for Dahomey's economic future were pinned.

Frankly practical and self-interested as was Maga's policy, it was at least on the national level, and it represented a step above the

[19] *Afrique Nouvelle,* Oct. 9, 1959; *Le Monde,* Oct. 11, 1959.

purely personal and regional considerations that up to this point had almost completely dominated Dahomeyan politics. It was to take Maga another year and a half before he could achieve enough political stability to begin carrying out a program of national construction. Before Maga got the upper hand by a combination of shrewd moves and strong-arm methods, Dahomey was to pass through another prolonged period of politico-economic strife. Parties were formed and dissolved, alliances between leaders were made and reversed, the local administration and judicial system were reorganized, and the power was finally concentrated in one party at the expense of the democratic freedoms proclaimed in the country's constitution. In Dahomey, the *enfant terrible* of French-speaking Negro Africa, its exceptionally individualistic and able people have had to pay a very high price for nationhood, but the alternative, they now seem to realize, would be anarchy and misery.

Dissolution of his Front could not long discourage a man so tenacious and ambitious as Apithy, and he rightly judged that if its formation had been premature its stress on independence and African unity had evoked a warm response among many politically conscious Dahomeyans. He was not at all disconcerted that his alliance with Zinsou and the federalists now entailed his advocating that Dahomey join the Mali Federation, thus completely reversing the stand that he had taken less than a year before. Together the PRD and federalists commanded enough support to get a resolution passed by the assembly in December 1959 stating that Dahomey's membership in the Entente was not incompatible with its eventual membership in the Mali Federation.

This move had the effect of drawing Maga and Ahomadegbé closer together. Since September 1959 Maga had good reason to believe that Apithy had become his principal adversary, and it was not surprising that in his cabinet reshuffle of early January 1960 Maga took more UDD members into his government. In inter-African affairs the UDD remained loyal to Houphouët and the Entente. How unalterably opposed it was to the Mali Federation was shown by a dramatic incident that occurred in Dahomey later that month. Modibo Keita, a prime mover in the Mali Federation, visited Dahomey at the invitation of the local federalists, but when he was so ill-advised as to go to Ouidah, a UDD stronghold, his car was stoned by some of its militants. In retaliation, Modibo refused to attend a reception at Cotonou that was given him by Maga and left Dahomey in a huff.[20] Relations between Mali and Dahomey were hardly improved by the dismissal of over

[20] *Le Monde,* Jan. 8, 17, 1960.

2,000 Dahomeyans formerly employed by the government-general at Dakar, which inevitably swelled the number of Dahomey's unemployed elite. A few weeks later the Malian leaders strongly protested against a press law initiated by the Maga government which they alleged was directed against the local federalist organ, *L'Etendard.* With unusual violence Maga reacted against this "interference by Mali in Dahomey's internal affairs," and he added that the "mission of protest" that the Malians were planning to send to Porto Novo would not be welcome in his country.[21]

If the *rapprochements* between the PRD and the federalists, on the one hand, and between the RDD and the UDD, on the other, had remained restricted to their common reactions to events taking place elsewhere in West Africa, they might never have been more than informal and fluid. But the creation by Maga in January 1960 of new local government institutions, for which six general councils were to be elected on April 3, led to the hardening of political formations. Early in February the PRD voted to merge with the federalists in an organization to be called the Parti des Nationalistes du Dahomey (PND). Their opponents did not go so far as to merge, but Maga— whose party was again supreme in the north—gave his support to the UDD candidates who competed in all the southern circumscriptions against those put up by the PND. The results of this election showed no change in the basic regional pattern of Dahomeyan politics.[22] Of the 225 seats at stake, the PND won 84, the UDD 71, and the RDD 70. To avoid the perpetuation of this stalemate and to give the government a working majority in the assembly, Maga made moves in April 1960 to bring the RDD and the UDD close together. He supported Ahomadegbé's reelection as president of the assembly and voiced Dahomey's loyalty to the Entente more strongly than before.

Increasingly Maga was becoming directly involved in Entente politics, a development closely related to Houphouët's new policy of demanding independence from France for all the Entente states. Houphouët's strategy enabled Maga at one stroke to remain loyal to the Entente and draw closer to the UDD, and also to steal much of the PND's thunder. During the early summer of 1960 the movement toward internal unity rapidly gained strength, and when independence was declared on August 1, it looked as if the country at long last would be solidly united behind the Maga government. Indeed, for a few

[21] *Marchés Tropicaux,* March 12, 1960.
[22] See the article on Dahomey's regionalism in *Afrique Nouvelle,* March 2, 1960.

brief weeks in the autumn of the year all of Dahomey's parties—the UDD, RDD, PND, and MLN—joined in a Front d'Action Patriotique (FAP). In the glow of their new-found unity all the parties in the FAP even accepted a law making Dahomey into a single electoral circumscription, in which the list of candidates receiving a majority of the votes would fill all the seats in the new legislature.

It might reasonably be thought that the acquisition of political independence and admission to the United Nations were achievements of sufficient stature to ensure Maga's government of strong support from Dahomey's newly formed single party. But because developments in the domain of foreign relations and the realization of national unity did not yet appear to be of overriding importance to Dahomey's politicians, the FAP fell apart before the cement that bound it together had had enough time to harden. Although the antagonism between Maga and Apithy remained acute, it was from another quarter that the most disruptive forces were unleashed. The UDD, which in the two months prior to independence had been the most active and vocal party demanding internal political mergers and unity, now proceeded to try to take over the government. For this purpose it utilized and encouraged the agitation of radical student and labor leaders who, like their counterparts elsewhere in French-speaking West Africa, demanded that their country sever all ties with France and nationalize the economy.

Agitation by Student and Labor Leaders

In Dahomey, the student and labor leaders found a ready-made situation that gave special cogency to their demands. The early expansion of education in Dahomey had given that country a trained elite far in excess of its powers of absorption, and France had encouraged their employment in official and private posts throughout French Negro Africa. With the breakup of the governments-general in 1959 and the accession of their component territories to independence in 1960, many thousands of Dahomeyans lost their jobs and had perforce to return to their home country. As Dahomey's schools continued to graduate hundreds of students each year, the number of unemployed educated men grew to dangerous proportions. The numerical size of this elite was matched by the scope of its ambitions. A bon mot of many years' standing is that every Dahomeyan "intellectual" considers himself ministerial timber, so that the gap between his aspirations and his current plight in 1960 made him a particularly inflammable element. Because of Dahomey's stagnant economy, the elite's grievances on the economic level coincided with those of the country's many unemployed laborers. Together they represented a formidable source of malaise and agitation which the UDD was quick to exploit, though not openly at first.

When the first wave of student and labor strikes hit the country in September and early October 1960, the UDD took pains to dissociate itself from that movement of unrest. On October 15 it issued a communiqué which "denied rumors to the effect that its program had ever envisaged the expropriation or closing down of European enterprises in the country." [23] A few days later, in an interview granted to the Agence France Presse, Ahomadegbé showed more but not all of his hand. After analyzing the causes of Dahomey's present plight, he came out in favor of a strong one-party government. But he failed to mention that this single party should be none other than the UDD.

Experience has shown that neither a two-party nor a three-party system can lead Dahomey out of its present stagnation. Only a majority party that truly represents the nation can under the circumstances reach decisions that are acceptable to the bulk of the population. I refer to a truly majority party, and not an artificial coalition. What divides Dahomey's political leaders is much less questions of policy than their fear of not being called upon to share in the responsibilities of government. The only constructive formula in our eyes would be the union of all worth-while elements in a single party . . . and in this way no one will feel hurt. All important decisions, both in regard to allotting posts and to taking action, will be reached according to democratic procedures by the party's governing bodies—either the executive committee or the national council, according to circumstances—which are the emanation of all its basic organizations.[24]

Had Dahomeyan politicians accepted this formula as outlined by Ahomadegbé, they might have achieved a single-party system analogous to that of the PDCI (Parti Démocratique de la Côte d'Ivoire). But several developments in late September and early October ruined such a prospect. Maga brought into the RDD the Dahomeyan members of the MLN, among them the able and dynamic Albert Teveoedjre. This injected fresh blood and a political philosophy into a party that had heretofore lacked any doctrine and was only the expression of a vague regionalism. The RDD, thus reinforced, then sought admission to the RDA with the blessing of Houphouët. Immediately this brought it into sharp conflict with the UDD, which had—without ever having

---

[23] *Marchés Tropicaux*, Oct. 29, 1960.
[24] Broadcast from Radio Dakar, Oct. 19, 1960.

wholly accepted Houphouët's leadership—long regarded itself as the official Dahomeyan branch of that great movement.

Outraged at both Maga and Houphouët, the UDD leaders called a general strike at the end of October, and their representatives in the assembly moved a vote of censure against the government. They accused it of responsibility for the country's grave social unrest, through its failure to formulate a plan for genuine progress in general and to promote labor's welfare in particular. The strike proved highly effective, for the CATC unions supported the UGTAN unions that had called it. The towns of Cotonou and Porto Novo were paralyzed for two days, and the police had to use tear gas to keep the agitators under control. More than that, Maga felt that he had to call in the north to redress the balance in the south. According to André Blanchet:

One morning in November 1960, Cotonou—fief of the UDD—woke up to find itself occupied by a force as surprising as it was picturesque. Trucks had brought down from the north men clothed in animal skins and carrying bows and arrows, and they took up their stand in front of the ministers' residences. These warriors of another age remained at Cotonou for some days, walking the streets first as patrols and then as tourists. They had never before seen the sea, and they marveled at Cotonou's buildings which, though modest, were several stories high. Whether or not their presence was a decisive factor in breaking up the strike, Maga in any case gave the credit to his northern archers for his victory over the unions.[25]

Next, to quell the parliamentary opposition, Maga had to make an alliance with the PND. This proved to be easier than might be expected, for Apithy—in eclipse for the preceding half year—was eager to return to the front of the political stage, and the breakup of the Mali Federation in August 1960 left the PND federalists without any clear-cut objective. Together Maga and Apithy mustered enough votes in the assembly to reject the UDD's motion of censure, and the 5 UDD ministers were expelled from the government.[26] Maga then formed a new cabinet composed of 5 RDD members, in addition to himself, and 6 from the PND. On November 13 this alliance became formal when the RDD and PND merged to form the Parti Dahoméen de l'Unité (PDU), of which Maga was chosen head. Its announced platform included approval of Dahomey's joining the African solidarity movement, and specifically of its membership in the Entente; rational

[25] *Nice-Matin,* Feb. 2, 1961.
[26] These were Gavarry, Poisson, Lassisi, François Aplogan, and Kpakpo.

planning and austerity on the economic level; and a revision of the trade union movement's objectives and methods in the social domain.

The Election of December 1960

The assembly, in which Djibode Aplogan (PND) had now replaced Ahomadegbé as president, transformed itself into a constituent body and on November 25 adopted the Republic's new constitution (see pp. 208–209). Under its provisions elections were held on December 11 for the presidency, the vice-presidency, and a new legislature. Participation in this election was exceptionally high: 71 per cent of Dahomey's 971,012 registered voters went to the polls. The UDD received 31 per cent of the popular vote and the PDU 69 per cent. Under the recently passed electoral law, all 60 seats in the new assembly went to the PDU. Maga was elected President and Apithy Vice-President of the Republic.

On December 30 Maga announced the composition of his new government, of which he would be Premier and Apithy Vice-Premier. Most of the outstanding leaders of the RDD and PND were represented: Arouna Mama (RDD) was named Minister of the Interior; Assogba (PND), Foreign Affairs; Paul Darboux (RDD), Trade and Economic Affairs; Sébastien Dassi (PND), Agriculture and Cooperatives; Victorien Gbaguidi (PND), Public Works and Transport; Joseph Kekeh (PND), Justice; René Deroux (RDD), Health and Social Affairs; Michel Ahouamenou (PND), Education; and Alexandre Adandé (PND), Finance. Newcomers to ministerial responsibility were Bertin Borna, given the Labor and Civil Service portfolio, and Albert Tevoedjre, Secretary of State for Information. Thus, not one member of the UDD was represented in either the government or the legislature, a situation which left about one-third of the country's voters, mainly those in its commercial capital, without a voice in the management of public affairs. Maga was aware of the dangers of such a situation, especially in a party whose name proclaimed it to be one of unity, and of the ease with which the UDD-guided labor unions could paralyze the country's nerve center. Fortunately for him, the opposition to his government was concentrated in Cotonou, where 90 per cent of the population had voted for the UDD and where at this time some 15,000 to 20,000 of its over 80,000 residents were unemployed. Without officially transferring the capital from sleepy, bureaucratic Porto Novo, Maga took up his residence in Cotonou and began transferring his ministerial services there.

The End of the Union Démocratique Dahoméenne

The violence that marred the December elections, in which 3 had been killed and 18 wounded, did not subside after the results were made known, and Maga had fair warning that more trouble lay ahead. Already he was finding it difficult enough to work harmoniously with a prima donna like Apithy and to reconcile in one party those favorable with those hostile to Dahomey's membership in the Entente. But he knew his most urgent task was to eliminate the UDD opposition and to draw the fangs of the labor unions which were the basis of its strength. To do this he tried both persuasion and forceful methods. By getting the assembly on January 18, 1961, to pass his security bill despite the protests of the UGTAN and CATC unions, the government acquired the legal means to deal summarily with the opposition press and any persons it considered likely to foment disorder. At the same time, Maga tried to persuade members of the UDD to join his party, declaring that the PDU's doors were still open to all men of good will. But at this time the UDD leadership was little disposed to seize the olive branch that he proffered. It even went so far as to have printed in Togo for distribution in Dahomey a newspaper which reiterated in strong language the charge that the December 11 elections had been rigged and the UDD leaders slandered and persecuted by the Maga government.[27]

The showdown between the major opposing forces came late in March, when at a party congress at Allada the PDU secretary-general, Chabi Mama, announced that Houphouët had accepted the PDU as the RDA's sole territorial branch in Dahomey. This announcement paralleled the declaration made a month earlier that the Union Générale des Travailleurs du Dahomey, which had just then been formed through Maga's efforts, was the only authentic UGTAN movement in the country. Most of the UDD leaders now realized that the game was up and that they must join the PDU if they were to save their political skins. At a UDD party congress held early in April the hard uncompromising core of the UDD, led by Ahomadegbé and Hessou, refused to follow the majority lead. But the fact that theirs was a minority position enabled Maga to dissolve the UDD on April 11 (after having suspended its party organ, *Dahomey-Matin,* the day before) and to declare optimistically that the Dahomeyan nation had at last been born.

Ahomadegbé's stand at this time, and the path he subsequently fol-

[27] *Afrique Nouvelle,* Feb. 15, 1961.

lowed, compounded the errors in judgment made by the UDD high command over the preceding months. These grave mistakes included consistently underestimating Maga; letting him capture the loyalty of the dynamic, youthful leaders of the MLN; permitting him to set up a labor movement that competed with that of their party; and finally putting their faith in the support of Houphouët, whose advice they had many times rejected. In all probability Houphouët, the great conciliator, had not acted in a spirit of reprisal but, with characteristic realism, had judged Maga better able than Ahomadegbé to give Dahomey a strong and stable government. In any case, Ahomadegbé still refused to capitulate to Maga, and since he lacked the means to stage a South American–style *coup d'état*, he chose conspiratorial methods to overthrow his enemy.

On May 26, Tevoedjre announced the discovery of a plot to murder Maga and his ministers and the subsequent arrest of Ahomadegbé and Hessou and ten other ringleaders. Their trial by a special court did not take place till December 5, and the accused were allowed to obtain lawyers from France to defend them. A traditionally Dahomeyan atmosphere was created by the testimony of fetishist chiefs and sorcerers, who turned state's evidence. They swore that they had received money from the main defendants to protect the hirelings who had been charged with execution of the political murders. Ahomadegbé denied all the accusations brought against him, arguing cogently that he, "a man of science and a Christian," would never have given money to those claiming the power to make men "invisible and invulnerable." [28] Nevertheless, the court sentenced him to five years in prison, Hessou to forced labor, and the other defendants to terms of imprisonment ranging from one to ten years. In view of the gravity of the charges brought against them these were light sentences, and the government's leniency opened the way to eventual conciliation. After five years behind bars, Ahomadegbé would have ceased to be dangerous and might even be willing to use his undeniable talents for leadership in constructive activities. In the meantime, his "plot" enabled the government to wrest wider repressive powers from the legislature.

Action against Labor and Student Leaders

With his main political enemies either in prison or in the PDU, Maga was now free to turn to less dangerous rebels and agitators—

---

[28] *Ibid.*, Dec. 13, 1961.

organized labor and youth groups. Until the UDD began to use the trade unions for political purposes, Maga had done little for Dahomey's wage earners. He was fully preoccupied with keeping his political balance, and wage earners represented only 1 per cent of the total population. Moreover, he probably regarded them as a privileged category of workers, who were protected by advantageous labor laws and whose monetary income was at least fifteen times larger than that of the bulk of their compatriots.[29] Although the minimum wage had not been raised since 1958, it amounted to 35 CFA francs an hour for the highest-paid category. Among French West African countries, this rate was exceeded only in Senegal and the Ivory Coast, whose resources were far greater and where living costs had risen more rapidly than in Dahomey.[30]

Almost all of Dahomey's wage earners were organized into two federations, the UGTAN and the CATC, and both were concentrated in Cotonou. Since the UDD dominated that town, it was comparatively easy for its leaders to gain control of the unions and to promote strikes for political purposes. But when the UDD's power was broken in April 1961, Maga had little further trouble from organized labor. Five days after he dissolved the UDD, he also dissolved the UGTAN, which it had dominated. In short order, most of its component unions joined the Union Générale des Travailleurs du Dahomey, which he had set up two months before. Nor did Maga—unlike most West African premiers—have much trouble from the civil service, because the supply of trained persons in Dahomey far exceeded the demand. Both the white-collar and manual wage earners in Dahomey were aware that it was dangerous to engage in agitation for improved working conditions when there were so many candidates eager and qualified to replace them. Under the PDU's austerity program, Dahomey's civil servants took a 10 per cent cut in their salaries with barely a whimper. So long as they were not dismissed from their posts, the civil servants accepted a reduced standard of living, and despite the burden their payment represented for the budget, Maga did not cut down their number. Where Maga showed himself severe was toward those Dahomeyans who refused to leave the more highly paid French administrative cadres. In July 1961 he told those who refused to return and

[29] According to *Afrique Nouvelle*, Feb. 15, 1961, the average monthly cash income for all Dahomey was estimated at 800 to 1,000 CFA francs compared with 15,000 to 20,000 for wage earners.

[30] *Marchés Tropicaux*, April 1, 1961.

serve their country that they would lose their nationality and find closed to them employment in all the UAM nations.[31]

Student and youth groups were disposed of with as much dispatch as were the labor unions. In February 1960, the student strikers at Cotonou's technical college were sent home to their parents: for the next three years their ringleaders would not be admitted to any educational establishment in Dahomey or be employed in its public services. Maga scolded the students who, at their Parakou congress the following July on the eve of Dahomey's independence, demanded replacement of the Minister of Education and attacked the government's policy, but he did not reduce the amount of their scholarships. As was the case with recalcitrant functionaries, Maga's retaliatory measures were reserved for Dahomeyan students who, after receiving their training in France at government expense, refused to return to their country unless given the particular jobs they coveted. Like so many other present-day West African leaders, Maga has come to regard those who refuse to carry out his program as traitors to their country. To ensure the docility and services of the country's youth, Maga forced their two main organizations in the country, including various religious groups, to merge in a Union Nationale de la Jeunesse du Dahomey in December 1961. This new association further agreed not to affiliate itself with any analogous world organizations and to place itself unreservedly at the service of the PDU.[32]

Maga's Accomplishments

When Maga made his state visit to France in the fall of 1961, he had reason to look back with satisfaction on his accomplishments over the preceding two and a half years. He had come to power only because of the rivalry between the two southern parties, but he had managed to stay in power by playing their leaders off against each other. After trying alliances first with one and then with the other, he had asserted his leadership over both. To be sure, this had been accomplished by using undemocratic methods, but with a minimum of bloodshed. He had brought to heel the most ungovernable of all French-speaking West African territories, and through forging a one-party system had given it a relatively stable administration. In the process he had acquired a tried and fairly true all-African team of collaborators. His

[31] *Afrique Nouvelle*, Aug. 9, 1961.

[32] The Conseil de la Jeunesse du Dahomey had been affiliated with the World Assembly of Youth, and the Union de la Jeunesse du Dahomey with the World Federation of Democratic Youth.

cabinet of February 1962, as well as his ambassadorial appointments, represented merely a reshuffling of portfolios and assignments among his now-proved supporters. After thirty months in office, Maga had also managed to reorganize the local administration and judiciary. Even before all this had been accomplished, he had found time to deal with foreign affairs and to draw up a plan designed to revive and transform Dahomey's economy.

LOCAL ADMINISTRATION

During the first post-World War II decade, Dahomey was divided into ten *cercles,* each under a French commandant who was an administrator of the overseas cadre. Each *cercle* was composed of subdivisions placed in charge of lower-ranking French officials. In turn, the subdivisions were divided into some 150 cantons, administered by African chiefs responsible to the *cercle* commandant. These canton chiefs were appointed by the Governor upon recommendation of the *cercle* commandant. In some cases they were chosen according to tradition, but in others the Governor appointed men who were not indigenous to the area. As for Dahomey's 3,600-odd villages, the great majority of their headmen were selected according to custom, but in some areas—such as the Atacora, where the population lived in isolated one-family compounds—the French had had to create both villages and cantons. In each *cercle* there had been set up a Council of Notables during the interwar period, whose function was to advise the commandant on certain local matters. After World War II its membership was enlarged beyond the canton and village chiefs to include outstanding farmers, merchants, and artisans of the area. In the early 1950's, the administration was toying with the idea of having the Notables elected rather than appointed to such councils.[33]

Such was the classical pattern of French local government throughout West and Equatorial Africa, but it was somewhat complicated in Dahomey by the survival of a number of paramount chiefs. The most important of these were the descendants of the former kings of Porto Novo, Savé, and Nikki, whose antecedents gave them a politico-religious influence and prestige greater than that of the canton chiefs. While in the north their authority remained unquestioned, in the south they were the target of attacks on the part of the youthful intelligentsia. After World War II, a chiefs' association was formed for the collective defense of their prerogatives, but it failed to achieve the

[33] Grivot, *Réactions dahoméennes,* p. 77.

solidarity desired by its founders. This organization could not bridge the gap between the wholly traditional chiefs and the more modern, educated ones, between whom there were few interests in common and who were mutually jealous. When the association tried to increase its membership and its funds by admitting village chiefs, it became wholly ineffectual and foundered.

Unable to help themselves, the chiefs required support from the public authorities, and in 1948 the administration proposed a revision of their legal status. The division of feeling on the subject among Dahomey's elite was reflected in the assembly debates on this proposal. Although all acknowledged the need to improve the material position of the chieftaincy, the assemblymen could not even agree on the exact definition of a traditional chief. One of their number refused to accept as traditional chiefs the descendants of King Béhanzin of Abomey, while another insisted that the only traditional chiefs were those whose ancestors had ruled before the French conquest and were buried in their own compounds.[34] Finally, the assembly asked the administration to make the post of canton chief elective, but then its members disagreed as to whether those elected should serve for life or for a specific time period. In view of the assembly's lack of unanimity in regard to the chieftaincy, the local administration decided to let the matter ride pending the decision by the French Parliament on a bill then under consideration, which aimed at revising the status of all chiefs throughout its Negro African territories. The Dahomeyan government did declare itself in favor of respecting tradition, wherever possible, in the selection of chiefs, but it rejected any change in the existing regulations that would impose a rigid uniform system on the country. In June 1955, just one year before the *loi cadre* brought internal autonomy to Dahomey, Governor C. H. Bonfils made one minor change in the structure of the local administration. Without altering the electoral circumscriptions or the geographical boundaries, he proposed that all of Dahomey's subdivisions be raised to the rank of *cercles*. The announced objectives of this reform were to decentralize the administration, make local government more closely coincide with traditional authority, and enable more African officials to accede to posts of responsibility.

Also in the years preceding passage of the *loi cadre,* some slight progress was made in the domain of municipal administration. As early as 1921 Porto Novo and Cotonou had been made first-degree *com-*

[34] *Ibid.,* p. 101.

munes mixtes, as was Ouidah four years later. By the end of World War II they had moved up to the position of third-degree mixed communes, which meant that while they still had an appointed official as mayor they also had a municipal council elected by their towns-people voting as a single college. In 1948 the territorial assembly asked that Porto Novo, Cotonou, and Ouidah be promoted to the status of full communes, which would give those cities elected mayors and more financial autonomy, and that other towns be provided with the basis of self-governing institutions. Since the administration's yardstick in the matter was purely a financial one, the assembly debate on this question should have concentrated simply on the resources available to a given community. Because an element of choice was involved, however, it brought out all of the assemblymen's fiercely regional loyalties. Each one insisted that the headquarters of his own circumscription was fully qualified for promotion in the municipal hierarchy, and the debate grew heated. Finally, it was decided to raise only two to the status of *communes de moyen exercice* [35]—Parakou, capital of the north, and Abomey, the royal capital of the south. In 1955 the Municipal Reorganization Bill solved the problem at one stroke by promoting Porto Novo, Cotonou, Ouidah, Parakou, and Abomey to the status of full communes.

For some years after the *loi cadre* was applied to Dahomey, its leaders were too preoccupied with jockeying for power to make any further changes in the local government setup. In 1959 the government created some new *cercles*, but this development was short-lived. In January 1960, Maga divided the whole country into six regions or departments. Each was placed in charge of a prefect named by the central government, who was assisted by an elected council. The number of councilors varied according to the demographic importance of the region, and a total of 225 were elected on April 3, 1960 (see p. 226). Two years later, Maga gave the regional capitals an analogous regime. Parakou, Porto Novo, Cotonou, Abomey, and Ouidah were made urban circumscriptions and administered by a subprefect aided by an elected municipal council. To all appearances these moves increased Dahomey's local government institutions, and they provided a growing number of Dahomeyans with experience in the management of their own affairs. Yet the net result was much the same as in other French-speaking West African countries, which had already been mov-

[35] *Communes de moyen exercice* represented a halfway stage between full communes and third-degree mixed communes.

ing in the same direction. Through its appointed officials, the prefects and subprefects, the powers of the central government were actually increased under the guise of promoting a decentralization of authority. Much the same could be said about the village councils also created in 1962. Theoretically their purpose was to establish democracy at the village level, but in the eyes of the government their real function was to ensure that the whole population would be mobilized to carry out the four-year plan.

ROLE OF THE JUDICIARY

Before 1946, two separate judicial systems functioned in Dahomey, as elsewhere in French West Africa. Justice was rendered to French citizens by a court located at Cotonou, in which French law was applied by a professional magistrate. To African subjects, justice was dispensed by native courts of first and second instance which functioned in the main centers and over which presided French administrators, assisted by Dahomeyan assessors. After the French Parliament passed the law of April 30, 1946, all criminal cases were judged according to French law. Civil and commercial cases in the *cercles* of Cotonou, Ouidah, and Athiémé fell within the jurisdiction of Cotonou's court of first instance. Similar cases in other areas were judged by Justices of the Peace of Wide Jurisdiction, stationed at Parakou and Abomey. Throughout the country, courts of first and second instance applying customary law continued to function under either a French administrator or a Dahomeyan Notable appointed by the Governor. Appeals from the verdicts of these courts could be made first to the Cotonou Cour d'Homologation and then to the Chambre d'Annulation at Dakar.

In 1958 occurred the first of a series of changes that resulted from Dahomey's acquisition of autonomy and later of independence. These were more in the nature of modifications than of a basic transformation of the existing system.[36] That year a court of appeals was established at Cotonou, and the competence of Cotonou's court of first instance was widened to include all the central and northern *cercles*. The Republic of Dahomey's first constitution, that of February 14, 1959, laid down the principle that the judicial branch was to be independent of the legislature and executive. It also envisaged the establishment of a Court of State comprising administrative, constitutional, and auditing

---

[36] See G. Mangin, "L'Organisation Judiciaire des Etats d'Afrique et de Madagascar," *Revue Juridique et Politique d'Outre Mer*, Jan.–March 1962, pp. 86–87.

sections. A year after Dahomey became independent, further changes were made, and the courts of second instance were replaced by higher courts set up in each of the six new departments. On October 17, 1961, the assembly unanimously accepted the government's proposal to place at the summit of the judicial system a Supreme Court, comprising four Chambers, that would combine the functions which in France were performed by the Conseil d'Etat, the Cour de Cassation, and the Cour des Comptes. Except at the level of the Supreme Court, the existing two types of jurisdiction—modern and customary—were maintained.

In the constitution of November 25, 1960, the independence of the judiciary was confirmed. Moreover, the President and his ministers were made liable to trial for high treason before the Supreme Court if they were impeached by a two-thirds majority of the assembly. Yet in practice the special powers progressively granted to the government by the assembly have largely nullified the legislature's ability to control the executive. In addition, the assembly's self-abnegation has opened the way for the government to ignore the theoretical independence of the judicial branch. A significant case in point was the government's establishment in 1961 of a special court to try Ahomadegbé and others charged with plotting against the security of the state.

Contemporary Issues

The persistence of strong regional feeling has been the main cause of Dahomey's failure to achieve national unity. Regionalism has been largely responsible for the country's governmental instability and sterile competitions for leadership and in part also for its economic stagnation. Dahomey was slower than any other French-speaking West African territory except Mauritania to achieve a one-party government under a single leader, and even now it suffers from three basic weaknesses. These are the insecurity of its leadership, the lack of a strong party structure, and—most important of all—the indifference of the population at large to national issues in which they do not feel personally involved.

REGIONALISM

Hubert Maga worked his way to the top because the south was split between two mutually hostile regional parties. During the process he saw that Dahomey's so-called political parties were simply the crystallization of regional feeling around a handful of native sons. To avoid the chaos into which the rivalries between these regional parties were leading Dahomey, he realized that he must replace them with a single nationwide organization. Both because of his temperament and of his origin, it took Maga a year and a half to constitute the PDU. In so doing he had to subdue or eliminate his main competitors for the leadership of the government. His natural inclination and the insecurity of his position led him to use persuasion and strategy first and only as a last resort to employ forceful methods. Maga was no charismatic leader like Sékou Touré of Guinea, nor did he have behind him a solidly entrenched and well-organized party as did Modibo Keita of Soudan. Moreover, in the south, where lay the center of political power in Dahomey, he was still regarded as an outsider and a northerner. Even after he became Premier, his hold on the reins of government continued to be unsure. To remain firmly in the saddle he had to jail Ahomadegbé, his most uncompromising rival, and to take Apithy, his other major competitor, into the PDU and his government. This meant that the followers of the imprisoned Ahomadegbé were left without any political representation and that his own "united" party was liable to a split in its high command. To obviate the dangers inherent in such a situation, Maga had to bring under his control the regional and special interest groups that constituted the support of his rivals and thus discourage them from trying again to seize power.

Hence Maga has had to tackle the basic problems which in the first instance enabled Ahomadegbé and Apithy to threaten his rule. These were regional and personal rivalries, Dahomey's deteriorating economy, and—to a limited degree—ideological differences among the country's main leaders. He had to substitute a sense of nationhood for the existing loyalties to persons and places; in order to remedy the economic situation he had to make the country prosperous through external aid and through increased local production; and to reconcile ideological differences he had to evolve a domestic and foreign policy that would preseve Dahomey's "originality and personality" and at the same time not isolate it from the prevailing trends in West Africa.

Since a number of these problems were interrelated, he was able to work out an over-all policy that in most cases provided generally satisfactory compromise solutions. By bringing Tevoedjre and Bertin into his government, he cut the ground from under the feet of the opportunistic Apithy, who might have led a breakaway left-wing movement. Thanks to the collaboration of these capable young radicals, Maga was able to reorganize and unify the labor and youth movements and also bring under his control the press and radio media of mass communications. In foreign relations he was able to placate not only the left-wing but also the local federalists by participating in some of the interterritorial movements then gaining ground in West Africa. However, Maga was careful not to join the radical-nationalist Ghana-Guinea-Mali Union but to link up only with those groups likely to be of practical advantage to his country. Thus by remaining in the Entente and joining the UAM, he secured backing against the possible encroachments of his powerful neighbors and at the same time was assured of receiving aid from France and the Ivory Coast. By promoting a Benin union that would include Ghana, he hoped not only to win immediate trade advantages for Dahomey but also to please those of his followers who were partisans of Pan-African doctrines. (See pp. 253–255.)

THE UNEMPLOYED ELITE

Although the aid which Dahomey continued to receive from the Ivory Coast, and especially from France, permitted it to meet most of its running expenses, Maga needed more than such stopgap measures to make his country prosperous and economically independent. To solve the problem of mass misery and of the unemployed elite he had to develop a more positive and comprehensive program. Contrary to the situation in most other French Negro African countries, it has not been the lack of an elite in Dahomey but an overabundance of it which is a source of both political and economic weakness. Like all the other new Negro African nations, Dahomey's rural population is underemployed, and many of its young people have been drifting to the towns, where they cannot find jobs and where they live parasitically at the expense of their more fortunate relatives. But Dahomey's particular drama lies in the large number of its skilled unemployed and their concentration in Cotonou, the only town in the country of any economic importance. (Between 1953 and 1961, the population of Cotonou was estimated to have risen from 22,000 to nearly 82,000 persons.) Dahomey's stagnant economy has been unable to provide a livelihood for a population which is increasing—at least in the south —at the rate of 3 per cent a year and whose elite has recently and suddenly been numerically swelled by the return from abroad of thousands of civil servants and commercial employees. In the immediate future, the Maga government can expect that the construction of the port of Cotonou will absorb a large number of that town's unemployed laborers, but this will not help its jobless intellectuals. The latter represent not only an economic problem but a political and social one as well. There are simply not enough posts in the administration or in the private sector to go around, and many of the unemployed elite, especially those with degrees from French universities, either have unrealistic political ambitions or will accept only certain exceptionally well-paid positions. The elite, as well as the rural underemployed, form a largely unutilized manpower resource, as well as a restless and potentially revolutionary element in the population.

THE DRIVE FOR ECONOMIC DEVELOPMENT

The Four-Year Plan

To this problem and to many others, Maga thinks that he has found an answer, one that closely resembles the solutions which appeal to his fellow premiers in West Africa. This solution is the one-party government, which is to be the focus and promoter of national unity and the executor of its national development plan. This four-year plan, drawn up in 1961 by the Société d'Etudes et de Réalisations Economiques et Sociales, was inspired by what its authors term "dynamic socialism." Its principles reflect the thinking of Maga's left-wing collaborators, but its scope has been tailored to the meagerness of Dahomey's resources. The goals set by the plan and its cost, too, are appropriately modest. Its main stress is laid on raising rural living standards through regular and substantial increases in agricultural output and the local processing of its products. Throughout the country, unused arable land is to be cultivated and the yields of the areas already farmed are to be increased through the multiplication of cooperative societies using mechanized methods of production. To provide the framework and over-all supervision required, mixed companies have already been created for agricultural and industrial development, a state company has been formed for agricultural development, and the transformation has begun of the Sociétés de Prévoyance into Sociétés Mutuelles de Développement Rural. Technical assistance is to be provided by ORSTOM (Office de Recherche Scientifique et Technique d'Outre-Mer) and IRHO, working through the existing agricultural stations of Ina, Pobé, and Niaouli. It is noteworthy that this plan includes no new radical ventures but instead aims mainly at an increase in the production of vegetable oils and teak and in the means of communication in the producing areas. But it should not be concluded that the plan is exclusively agricultural in its orientation. It includes projects for the expansion and improvement of rural education, health, and housing and is being accompanied by an expansion of governmental controls over internal and external trading.

Most of the hard cash required to finance the four-year plan, estimated to cost some 30,000,000,000 CFA francs, will have to come from foreign sources, mainly FAC and FEDOM. Dahomey's own contribution is principally to take the form of "human investment." In the eyes of Dahomey's planners, this will combine the advantages of being economical, of checking the flow of rural youths to the towns, and of helping to solve urban unemployment. The main object of Maga's many recent tours of the country has been to whip up popular enthusiasm for the plan. At the same time laws have been drafted to compel widespread cooperation when and if it is not spontaneously forthcoming. Village councils are being installed throughout the country, their main purpose being to round up all available hands. In March 1962, a beginning was made in the distribution to the population of the Boppa region of all fallow arable lands and in the creation of collective farms in the Athiémé area. At about the same time a law was being drafted that would make work compulsory for all Dahomeyans within certain age limits and require a certain proportion of them to remain on the land.[37]

Special Projects

Comprehensive as it is, the four-year plan does not include three special projects that have been initiated outside of its framework. The oldest of these is the Mono River hydroelectric scheme, which Dahomey hopes to build jointly with Togo (see pp. 250–251). Another long-mooted project, also located in the south, is that of developing the Ouémé Valley, which covers an area of 620 square miles and has a population of some 85,000 persons. Most important of all is the construction of Cotonou's deepwater port, which is scheduled to be completed in 1964. If worked to capacity, this port will be able to handle some 400,000 tons of freight a year, and neither now nor in the foreseeable future can the foreign trade of Dahomey alone justify in economic terms the cost of its construction. Dahomey, of course, expects Niger to increase its use of Cotonou for the export of its peanuts and also hopes to attract to its port some of Upper Volta's foreign trade. But it was more because of political considerations than for such nebulous economic prospects that France finally decided to finance so costly a project. Thereby France undoubtedly hopes to reinforce the

---

[37] Radio Cotonou broadcast, March 13, 1962.

Maga government, strengthen its ties with the franc zone, and diminish the attraction exerted on Dahomeyans by Nigeria in general and by the port of Lagos in particular. To Dahomey itself, the port will bring certain benefits: for five years it will provide jobs for hundreds of laborers, and eventually reduce handling charges by an estimated 1,200 CFA francs on each imported ton of merchandise.

STRENGTHENING PARTY ORGANIZATION

In carrying out its four-year plan, the government is counting on the PDU to prod the population into cooperation, through a judicious mixture of persuasion and coercion. But the PDU did not begin to function as an organization until 1961—the year in which the four-year plan was drawn up—and it is gravely handicapped by so late a start. Its organization on a country-wide scale coincided with the government's efforts to bring all local government institutions and various labor and youth associations under its control. Inevitably, the central authority's hold on the country is still shaky. As Maga cannot give his full time to party organization, the task of reinforcing the PDU's structure has been entrusted to its hard-working secretary-general, Chabi Mama. In September 1961, Chabi Mama made a 2,500-mile tour of the country, during which he established contact with 136 party cells. The PDU, he reported, had been suffering from growing pains and his trip had promoted unity and dissipated misunderstandings. Said Chabi Mama:

We know from experience that getting organized is the only way for a young nation to become successful. So all the sons of this country must rally around the ideal of the PDU. An end must be put to excessive ambitions, hatred, envy, regionalism, racism, divisive action, and the personality cult. Henceforth Dahomey, through the PDU, must live with a single body and a single soul.[38]

Just how this is to be done in some spheres is not yet clear. One of the thorny questions which Chabi Mama did not resolve is that of the relationship between the provincial party agents and the officials heading the new administrative units. A government spokesman, addressing the congress of prefects and subprefects held on November 22, 1961, admitted that this was "one of the most difficult and pressing problems facing the party." [39] Another unresolved though comparatively minor difficulty has to do with the role to be played by the

[38] *Ibid.*, Sept. 26, 1961.   [39] *Ibid.*, Nov. 23, 1961.

traditional chiefs in the new setup. In the economic domain, another question that needs ironing out is that resulting from the complex ownership of palm groves in the south. This affects the whole land-tenure system and may hamper execution of the plan in a vital sector. Still another unresolved matter is revision of the educational system according to the government's intention of bringing the curriculum into line with the needs of the plan. Above all, special attention will have to be given to raising the economic and cultural level of the whole northern region to that of the south. These are only some aspects of the unfinished business that is urgently awaiting governmental decisions.

Time is on the side of Maga, but he will need plenty of it. Many years must elapse before his party structure can jell and an effective network of PDU cells cover the whole country. Yet when one looks at Maga's accomplishments during the short period in which he has been able to operate with a relatively free hand, one cannot but admire the patience, perseverance, and skill with which he has acted. Probably no other Dahomeyan leader could have resolved as satisfactorily the numerous and complicated problems he has encountered in his determination to bring unity to Dahomey. Indeed, his very effectiveness poses the question of his succession. Should Maga's career be cut short prematurely, Apithy's ambitions would doubtless again be unleashed and there would ensue a free-for-all among Dahomey's many candidates for the role of leader. At present Maga is not expendable, for only he seems capable of controlling the centrifugal tendencies which are still so conspicuous today in Dahomey.

External Relations

WITH OTHER AFRICAN STATES

None of Dahomey's leaders has been more than a shaky member of any alliance into which he has entered, either inside or outside the country—and for many of the same reasons. In every instance, they have felt compelled because of their own or their country's weakness to reach some kind of working agreement with others. Insomuch, however, as their motives have been neither ideological nor disinterested, they have felt equally free to cut their partners adrift when and if they no longer found them useful. By and large, inside Dahomey it has been personal ambition or the promotion of regional interests that has provided the driving force for their affiliations and disaffiliations.

In Dahomey's foreign relations it has been—at best—the desire to preserve the country's "personality" or to further its development and —at worst—a leader's aspiration for personal power that has made him draw Dahomey in and out of successive alliances. Among Dahomey's older top politicians, perhaps only Emile Zinsou has consistently acted from principle. A founder of the RDA in 1946, he left it as soon as he realized the extent to which it was being dominated by the French Communist Party. Then, after joining Senghor's IOM, he became and remained a dedicated federalist. Zinsou, however, has never been at the helm of Dahomeyan affairs, and it was first Apithy and then Maga who have determined the country's foreign policy.

The Entente

When Apithy withdrew from the RDA in 1948, he thought that he and Dahomey could go it alone politically. Because he regarded the IOM, which he joined that same year, as a purely parliamentary grouping, his viewpoint in that respect remained unchanged. A decade later, after he had become the head of Dahomey's first government council, the situation was profoundly altered by the creation of the Franco-African Community and by the rapid growth of sentiment in favor of federation throughout the former French West African territories. Even then, he failed to understand how strong were the forces working for African independence and unity, and he continued to act as if he and his country could, if they so chose, remain with impunity indefinitely aloof from the prevailing trends. He joined the Mali Federation in December 1958, primarily because he needed to placate the Dahomeyan federalists whose support was valuable to him vis-à-vis the UDD; he left it when he felt that membership in the Mali Federation might hamper his freedom of maneuver and that he could make a better bargain elsewhere. Again it was his fear of Ahomadegbé, head of the territorial branch of the RDA, which early in 1959 made him lend an ear to the blandishments of Houphouët. The leader of the RDA was anxious not only to make Dahomey forget the Abidjan riots of October 1958 (see p. 218) but also to persuade it to enter his new Council of the Entente.

Although each wanted Houphouët's support to further his party's interests, neither Apithy nor Ahomadegbé was willing, however, to pay the price for it in terms of loyally accepting Houphouët's leadership. On different occasions both men expressed their resentment of the "missions of conciliation," which Houphouët from time to time

sent to Dahomey and which they declared to be an unwarranted interference in the country's internal affairs. In the end it was neither
Apithy nor Ahomadegbé who received Houphouët's endorsement but
Maga, a longtime member of the IOM. Moreover, Maga won Houphouët's blessing just at the time he was engaged in a life-and-death
struggle with the UDD, which had been since 1954 the official territorial branch of the RDA. It was not because he so admired Houphouët or his ambitious projects that he asked membership for his
PDU in the RDA but, rather, because he needed to deprive Ahomadegbé of external support. If unabashed self-interest, in either personal,
regional, or—more recently—national terms, has been the mainspring
of Dahomey's foreign policy, Houphouët has shown himself to be
equally realistic. From the outset he had no illusions as to why Dahomey joined the Entente. He chose to sponsor Maga in preference
to his rivals because he believed that Maga was more likely than they
to give Dahomey the governmental stability it required. Small and
poor as Dahomey was and remains, its geographical location has made
it a desirable member of the various groups which Houphouët has
been forming throughout French-speaking Negro Africa.

Although Maga had been ignored in the negotiations which Houphouët had been conducting with Apithy in the weeks before the latter
fell from power, he accepted Houphouët's invitation to attend the first
meeting of the Entente premiers held at Abidjan only a few days after
Maga's investitutre by the Dahomeyan assembly. It was noteworthy
that when Maga was on the way to Abidjan, he made a point of stopping off at Lomé for talks with the Togolese Premier, Sylvanus Olympio. Moreover, at the Abidjan meeting Maga refused to make a firm
commitment about joining the Entente, so that he had time to weigh
the pros and cons involved. Maga felt no such personal loyalty to
Houphouët as did the staunchly RDA Premier of Niger, Diori Hamani,
nor did he need access to Abidjan's seaport, as did the Premier of
Upper Volta, Maurice Yaméogo. Indeed, he had a genuine grievance
against the Ivory Coast for its hostile treatment of the Dahomeyans
serving there. Of all the Entente countries, only Niger had close relations with Dahomey, but these had developed long before the Entente
was formed and presumably would continue even if Dahomey did not
join that group. Niger for some years had been using Cotonou port
for much of its foreign trade, and it still employed many Dahomeyans
in its administration. If Maga joined the Entente, he knew he would
alienate the Dahomeyan pro-Mali federalists who, though few in num-

ber, included some of the ablest men in the country. On the other hand, Dahomey desperately needed money. Its economy was in bad shape, and its budget deficit was growing as a result of the suppression of subsidies formerly allotted to Dahomey by the federal government at Dakar. What in the end really won Maga over to the Entente was Houphouët's decision to create a solidarity fund for it and his insistence on the apolitical nature of his objectives. The solidarity fund, to which each of the Entente members was to contribute one-tenth of its revenues, was in fact nothing other than a means whereby the rich Ivory Coast subsidized its poorer partners.

The solidarity fund was bait enough to lure Maga into the Entente in 1959, but as other sources of funds opened up to Dahomey after independence, it progressively lost some of its earlier importance. In fact, in the spring of 1961, Maga lost no time in making a trade agreement with Houphouët's archenemy, Nkrumah, after Upper Volta had shown that a better bargain could be struck with Ghana than with the Ivory Coast. However, by this time Dahomey had become a more reliable member of the Entente than at the outset, and for reasons that were political as well as economic. Some Bariba in the north had shown signs of preferring a union with the Niger Republic to remaining linked to the Fon in the south,[40] and certain outbreaks in Niamey had indicated that Dahomeyan functionaries were no longer so welcome as before in the administration of Niger. Maga still held a trump card in Niger's dependence on Cotonou port, which would surely grow with the big increase in its handling capacity, but in the meantime he took steps to strengthen communications between the two countries. The management of Cotonou port and of the Dahomeyan railroad was placed under the joint administration of Dahomey and Niger, and on September 30, 1960, this Organisation Commune was given a monopoly of the transport of goods in transit between them. Thus, there existed a ready-made organization that might greatly intensify its operations if Maga could persuade the French government to carry out the long-mooted prolongation of the railroad from Parakou to Dosso.

If Maga was finding the framework of the Entente increasingly useful as a means of cementing his ties with Niger, he was also utilizing it as a barricade against the encroachments of his neighbors on the Benin Gulf. Whenever Togo or Nigeria expressed any expansionist tendencies, Maga at once proclaimed his fervent attachment to the Entente. Moreover, he found the Entente's structure flexible enough

[40] *Le Monde*, Aug. 8, 1958.

to permit his making other agreements and alliances without forfeiting Houphouët's support. Because Houphouët has given Maga plenty of leeway, Maga has followed him dutifully into the UAM and the Monrovia group. Early in 1960 Maga even helped to smooth out difficulties that had arisen between Upper Volta and the Ivory Coast. After he assumed the rotating presidency of the Entente on January 24, 1962, Maga announced a policy which clearly showed his intention of making the Entente even more serviceable to Dahomeyan interests than in the past. Noteworthy among such proposals was one that would make Cotonou the "natural" port of Upper Volta as well as of Niger, and another would provide an outlet in the Entente states for Dahomey's surplus civil servants.[41]

So long as Houphouët's policy coincides in the main with what Maga believes to be Dahomey's best interests, he will probably not break away from the Ivoirian's leadership. By not opposing Maga's efforts to create a regional economic union with the Benin Gulf countries and by making Cotonou the headquarters of the UAM secretariat, Houphouët has shown a statesmanlike grasp of the Dahomeyan psychology. He is aware that Dahomey will always be a restless partner in any alliance because of its leaders' fear that if they adhere firmly to one group they may lose out on a better bargain elsewhere. Knowing that the Dahomeyans are too realistic, however, to aspire to a leadership role in West Africa, Houphouët seems quite willing to have them play an important part on a smaller, strictly localized stage.

The Benin Gulf Countries

Dahomey's attitude toward its neighbors of the Benin Gulf has been compounded of mixed and sometimes contradictory emotions. In this area, its leaders have consistently favored an economic union, mainly to check the contraband trade that flourishes between Cotonou and Lomé to the west and between Porto Novo and Lagos to the east. On the other hand, they have also ardently pressed for the construction of a deepwater port at Cotonou that would free Dahomey from its perennial dependence on Lagos for the inward and outward flow of heavy merchandise. Because Dahomey's trade alone would not justify the cost of constructing such a port at Cotonou, the Dahomeyans have tried to persuade the Togolese to agree to use it for their foreign commerce. As to political relations with both Nigeria and Togo, they have been as consistently colored by the emotions of fear and jealousy.

[41] See *Marchés Tropicaux*, Feb. 3, 1962.

The Dahomeyans have been envious of their neighbors' greater prosperity and more rapid progress toward self-government and at the same time frightened of their expansionist tendencies. In short, Dahomey has wanted Togo and Nigeria to accept closer economic ties that would be all to its own advantage but has rejected any extension of such ties into the political domain lest in the process Dahomey might lose its "personality" and freedom of action.

On the score of imperialistic ambitions, Dahomey obviously had less to fear from little Togo than from gigantic Nigeria. Yet in the early 1950's the Dahomeyans were resentful of the territorial aspirations voiced by some Togolese groups who reportedly claimed for their country the mouth of the Mono River.[42] Furthermore, the Dahomeyan leaders were sensitive in regard to the more rapid progress Togo was making toward autonomy because of its international status as a trust territory. During this period, too, there was keen competition between the two countries as to the location of the deepwater port which France planned to build on the Benin Gulf. According to the Dahomeyans, Cotonou was the only possible site, for naturally Lomé seemed out of the question to them, and they also turned down any compromise point midway between those two capitals. Not unnaturally, the Togolese equally rejected Cotonou, some hundred miles distant from Lomé. Nor did they have any interest in a customs union with Dahomey, because their freer tariff regime made imported goods less expensive in Togo and the production of the two countries was more competitive than complementary. Before Togo and Dahomey became independent, little progress had been made toward realizing closer relations between them. In 1957 a mixed Togolese-Dahomeyan commission was set up to study the coordination of their road systems and also the joint construction of a dam on the Mono River at Adjaralla. Again the latter project would mainly benefit Dahomey by providing water to irrigate 10,000 hectares of palm groves on the eastern side of the river, but it also promised definite advantages to Togo in that the dam could generate cheap electric current for both countries. As it turned out, however, the cost—estimated in 1957 at 700,000,000 to 800,000,000 CFA francs—prevented this project from materializing.

Early in 1959, France's pledge to finance construction of the deepwater port at Cotonou brought a new element into the picture. Obviously the Dahomeyans were elated by this decision, which would make

[42] Grivot, *Réactions dahoméennes*, p. 167.

them independent of Lagos port and at the same time make Niger's economy more dependent on Cotonou port. So confident were they that the Togolese would also have to use Cotonou for much of their foreign trade that the construction of a railroad between the two capitals began to seem a likely prospect to the Dahomeyan leaders. As the time drew near for Togo to declare its independence in April 1960, Maga became increasingly anxious to reach some agreement with Sylvanus Olympio. He had long favored a customs union with Togo, and because of Olympio's worsening relations with Nkrumah, Maga felt that the time had come when he could profitably press the matter. Houphouët encouraged Maga's initiative, probably in the hope that Togo might thereby be drawn into the Entente, and thus there was no opposition from that quarter. On the eve of Togo's independence, Maga said frankly, "Dahomey sees in an understanding with Togo the means for both countries to resist the territorial appetites of Ghana and Nigeria." [43]

Several meetings between the premiers of Togo and Dahomey during 1959 and 1960 were climaxed by Olympio's visit to Cotonou for Dahomey's independence celebrations. It looked as if at long last a customs agreement between the two countries was on the point of consummation, but it failed to materialize. Ostensibly Dahomey's membership in the Entente was the main stumbling block, for Togo had consistently refused to become involved in any French West African political formation. Moreover, Olympio, apprehensive as he was about Ghana's expansionist policy, could hardly have regarded Dahomey as a substantial bulwark against Nkrumah's ambitions. Then two developments in 1961 made a Togo-Dahomey customs union seem a still less likely eventuality. Maga's trip to Accra and the trade agreement he made with Nkrumah in June annoyed Olympio. He retaliated by refusing to let Togo provision the Dahomeyan border town of Agoué, which had always depended for its foodstuffs on imports from the Togolese side of the frontier. Nevertheless, Togo and Dahomey had so many common ties that they could not long remain estranged, and a compromise was reached at a meeting between their two premiers in October. Optimism regarding the establishment of closer relations in the future between the two countries was voiced in the communiqué issued after this meeting. But such an outlook among the Dahomeyans received a shattering blow when they learned of Togo's decision to

[43] Radio Brazzaville broadcast, April 6, 1960.

build its own deepwater port with German assistance. Some new formula had to be found to meet Dahomey's need for a wider free trade zone, and to this end Maga now turned to his eastern neighbor.

As far as transfrontier family ties and smuggling were concerned, the relations between Dahomey and Nigeria closely resembled those between Dahomey and Togo. However, the disparity between their respective areas, population, and economies gave their relationship a David-and-Goliath aspect. Nigeria's attraction for Dahomey lay in its prosperity and not in its political regime. Such official contacts as existed between them were excellent but not close, owing to the differences in their official languages and types of administration. With the accession of both countries to independence in 1960, the language barrier seemed to be the only obstacle to a *rapprochement*. Early in April of that year, however, the Dahomeyans were alarmed by the expression of expansionist ambitions on the part of some Nigerians. At that time a series of articles appeared in *Daily Service,* organ of Nigeria's Action Group, which favored the integration of Dahomey as a province of independent Nigeria and urged that the question be submitted to a popular referendum in Dahomey. This suggestion was taken up by the Yoruba in eastern Dahomey, who favored a reunion with their relatives across the border because they had long been excluded from administrative and commercial posts by the indigenous peoples of the Porto Novo region.[44]

At a press conference held later in April, Maga sternly rejected the demand for a referendum, asserting that Dahomey would enter no new political grouping and especially one that was not favorable to its interests. He added that Dahomey was not isolated, as the Nigerian journalist had claimed, but was a firm member of the Entente which he described as an instrument capable of defending Dahomey against the neoimperialism of its English-speaking neighbors.[45] His attitude toward Nigeria became still chillier when the Nigerian government broke off diplomatic relations with France because of the third French atomic explosion in the Sahara. With the departure of France's diplomatic mission from Lagos, the sizable Dahomeyan minority in Nigeria was left without official representation. Moreover, much of the equipment needed for building Cotonou's new port could not be unloaded at Lagos because of the Nigerians' refusal to handle cargo from French ships. This situation, as well as some minor clashes between

[44] For details, see *Afrique Nouvelle,* March 2, 1960.
[45] *Economist,* May 7, 1960.

Nigerians and Dahomeyans at Porto Novo in January 1961, led to the dispatch by Dahomey of a mission to Lagos and to its decision to open an embassy there. Nigeria proved receptive to Dahomey's move, and its Governor-General, Dr. Azikiwe, accepted an invitation to pay an official visit to Dahomey. Relations between the two countries continued to improve throughout 1961, especially after the Nigerian Parliament unanimously rejected a motion to strengthen the frontier between them. In approving this stand, Nigeria's Foreign Minister said: "We are brothers, and many Dahomeyans are of Nigerian origin." [46] The prospects that Dahomey could establish an economic union with Nigeria appeared at least as good as those of forming such a union with Togo, and this outlook encouraged Maga to envisage an even wider ensemble. In January 1962, the Lagos meeting of the Monrovia group, of which all three countries were members, provided him with the occasion to promote a more extensive Benin union.

The groundwork for such a union had been carefully laid during the year that preceded the Lagos conference. The project as it evolved came to include Ghana, although Nkrumah was a member of the Casablanca group and hostile to both the Entente and the UAM. Despite the difficulties involved, all of the Dahomeyan leaders were for once agreed on the desirability of establishing strong ties with Ghana, as well as with Togo and Nigeria. In particular, Apithy and Tevoedjre approved of Nkrumah's Pan-African thesis. Ideologically, Maga was less attracted to Nkrumah's doctrines than they were, but he had practical reasons for wanting an agreement with Ghana. Some 150,000 Dahomeyans lived in Ghana, where they worked on cocoa plantations or as transporters and traders.[47] Since many of them were small-scale merchants who shuttled between Accra and Cotonou, their operations were considerably hampered by the hostility between Ghana and Togo. If Dahomey could make a trade agreement with Ghana and then iron out the differences between Olympio and Nkrumah, it not only would improve its own foreign trade but might also pave the way for an economic union between the three countries.

As a first step toward this objective, good-will missions were exchanged between Dahomey and Ghana in February 1961; then in June, Maga went to Accra, where he negotiated a trade agreement with Nkrumah. Of itself this agreement effected little change in the

[46] Radio Cotonou broadcast, Nov. 22, 1961.
[47] *Afrique Nouvelle*, April 11, 1962.

respective policies of the two countries or in their commercial exchanges. It simply made official a trade current between them that had theretofore escaped all governmental controls. The situation in Angola and South-West Africa at this time provided the two leaders with the chance to express their common disapproval of colonialism without feeling compelled to back it up with strong action. (In the case of Dahomey, the Maga government a few weeks later broke off diplomatic relations with Lisbon and then with comic-opera fanfare took over the tiny Portuguese enclave at Ouidah.) Friendly relations between Ghana and Dahomey had been established, but not much more. It was possible, however, that with time the trade agreement might enhance the role of Dahomey as a transit country for Ghana's merchandise and also open up the Ghanaian market to Dahomey's fish and food exports.

The next forward step was not taken till the following December after Olympio had announced the discovery of a Ghanaian plot against his government. The subsequent closing of the frontier between Togo and Ghana adversely affected Dahomey's economy, but it provided Maga with a good chance to play the role of peacemaker between Nkrumah and Olympio. On December 20, *La Nation,* the PDU organ, ran a special issue devoted to extolling Dahomey's friendship with Ghana, in which Tevoedjre stressed the many goals which the countries had in common. Nine days later Maga flew to Lomé, presumably to pursue the conversations with Olympio regarding Dahomey-Togo cooperation which he had begun the preceding October. Apparently he found Olympio far more receptive than before to his proposal for a customs union and above all to one that would include Nigeria. Closing of the frontier with Ghana had seriously hurt Togo's trade, and Olympio's increasingly bad relations with Nkrumah made him now eager for the political as well as economic support of Nigeria.[48]

Encouraged by this favorable reception, Maga arranged to meet Nkrumah on January 18 at a place in northern Ghana near the Voltaic frontier. Later, when questioned about the gist of this interview, Maga would say only that he had met Nkrumah "to discuss with him matters concerning Dahomey and our relations with his country," [49] but there is little doubt that he sounded out Nkrumah regarding his projected economic union. Perhaps Maga made some headway, for in a speech two days later Nkrumah indicated that Ghana's policy toward its neighbors might be softening. Although he denied any renuncia-

[48] *West Africa,* Feb. 24, 1962.   [49] Radio Cotonou broadcast, Jan. 20, 1962.

tion of an all-African political union as his ultimate goal, he added that "no one seeks a revision of present boundaries unnecessarily." [50] Olympio must have felt this to be a hopeful sign, for at the Lagos conference he proposed the formation of a Benin union from which Ghana would not be excluded.

In interviews given a few days later, first at Cotonou and then at Lomé, Olympio expanded the proposal he had outlined at Lagos. In a union of the Benin countries he saw a concrete realization of the Monrovia group's principles as accepted at Lagos. "Given the very friendly relations existing between Dahomey, Togo, and Nigeria, we think that we can begin by giving an example [of a regional union] to other states by eliminating the tariff restrictions between us, which are not very important." [51] Nigeria had already begun to coordinate its system of communications with that of Dahomey. Elimination of smuggling, he admitted, might be more complex because Nigeria, on the one hand, and Dahomey and Togo, on the other, belonged to different monetary zones. Nevertheless, such difficulties should be overcome because "it is important for us to give a practical example of African unity on the regional scale." [52] Togo's role would be that of a link between the former British and the former French territories "because we have had experience with both systems and can therefore bring them closer together." He saw no reason why other countries, notably Niger and Ghana, should not join such a union. Niger's membership presented no problems; "as to Ghana, it is up to that country for it has broken off all economic relations with Togo."

Maga, who was present at the Cotonou interview, added his endorsement of the proposed Benin union and expressed the hope that it would include Ghana, "if the people of that country so wish." Going a step farther, Maga invited the foreign ministers of Togo and Ghana to meet in Dahomey with Oké Assogba to discuss plans for such a regional economic union. Tevoedjre and Apithy were particularly anxious for Ghana to be included in the proposed Benin union. With Ghana as a member, real progress would be made toward their ultimate goal, which was to bridge the gap between the Monrovia and Casablanca groups, with Dahomey cast in the role of conciliator. Both Ghana and Togo accepted the invitation, and their delegations met at Cotonou on February 6–7 in an atmosphere that was surprisingly cordial. So eager was Tevoedjre, however, for his project's success

[50] *West Africa*, Feb. 24, 1962.   [51] Radio Cotonou broadcast, Feb. 2, 1962.
[52] *Afrique Nouvelle*, Feb. 21, 1962.

that he announced prematurely over Radio Dahomey that the foreign ministers' meeting would soon be followed by one of the three heads of state. Plans for such a meeting were certainly discussed at Cotonou—but it did not take place. A minor difficulty was disagreement between the Ghanaian and Togolese delegations as to the site of the proposed meeting, and a short talk which Maga had with Nkrumah at the Accra airport a few days later apparently did not eliminate this hurdle. The major obstacle remained the unresolved differences between Ghana and Togo, specifically Olympio's conviction that Nkrumah was still scheming to swallow up his country. At a press conference at Washington on March 21, Olympio did not rule out cooperation in the economic and cultural fields but he added: "Togo cannot so soon forget the attempted coup of last December that was inspired by Ghana. . . . We strongly oppose any idea of integration between Ghana and Togo, and I think that Ghana spends most of its time interfering in the affairs of other countries throughout Africa." [53]

Although Dahomey was checkmated in its plan to bring both Ghana and Togo into the projected Benin union, it had greater though not immediate success with its eastern neighbor. In general, the Nigerian press reacted favorably to Olympio's proposal for an economic union with Togo and Dahomey. On the other hand, it was cool to the inclusion of Ghana, whose current attacks on Nigerian leaders were the subject of an official protest to Accra.[54] Sir Abubakar, the Nigerian Premier, was not enthusiastic even about a more limited Benin union. He thought that it might be a good idea in principle, but he did not want it to become "another Guinea-Ghana-Mali affair which exists only at Accra and not at Bamako." [55] Nevertheless, some progress was made toward reaching a closer understanding with Dahomey. By mid-February 1962, joint teams of surveyors were working to demarcate the boundary between the two countries, which in some places had not been clearly defined by the Anglo-French agreement of 1906. Moreover, on February 28, a Dahomeyan delegation went to Lagos to discuss terms for a customs union between the two countries.

An increase in Nigerian taxes the following April brought its tariff regime more in line with that of Dahomey, and this seemed to clear away the last obstacles to the proposed customs union. The actual signing of the agreement was delayed, however, until July 18 by one of those manifestations of national hypersensitivity that are characteristic of the new states of Asia and Africa. On April 15, an article in the

[53] Radio Lomé broadcast, March 22, 1962.
[54] Radio Lagos broadcast, Feb. 8, 12, 1962.   [55] *Ibid.*, Feb. 21, 1962.

Lagos newspaper, *Daily Express,* stated that an offer of aid made by Nigeria to the famine-stricken people of northern Dahomey had been resented by the Dahomeyan government as evidence of Nigeria's "overbearing ostentation." [56] According to this source, Dahomey's Undersecretary for Foreign Affairs had said indignantly that "Dahomey has no need for secondhand clothes or to beg for food from anyone." The authenticity of this statement was immediately denied by the Porto Novo government, which expressed gratitude to Sir Abubakar for his generous offer and dispatched Foreign Minister Zinsou to Lagos to smooth over Nigeria's ruffled feelings. Six weeks later a somewhat similar incident threatened to disrupt the friendship which Dahomey had been assiduously cultivating with Ghana. On June 1 the Maga government expressed shocked surprise concerning an article in the semiofficial *Ghanaian Times* on May 16, in which it was stated that Dahomey was receiving American arms and had entered into a military alliance with the United States.[57] When the Accra government failed to print the denial of this charge made by the local Dahomeyan chargé d'affaires, a spokesman of Dahomey's Foreign Ministry spoke acidly about Ghana's interference in the affairs of a sovereign state. At once Accra tried to make amends by naming an ambassador to Porto Novo—the first English-speaking envoy thus far accredited to Dahomey—and to all appearances the Dahomeyans have forgotten and forgiven the episode. But if the normally friendly relations between Dahomey and Nigeria and between Dahomey and Ghana could be so easily upset by trifling incidents, it was no wonder that the Benin union failed to materialize rapidly. Far more important than the stumbling block of Dahomey's easily wounded pride was the assassination of Sylvanus Olympio in January 1963. This event has drastically altered the political complexion of Togo and consequently of Togo's relations with its neighbors. Although the future political orientation of Togo is not yet clear, there is no doubt that the bases for a Benin union that would include both Togo and Ghana have been profoundly modified. Once again, Maga must accept—at the least—postponement of the realization of his plan for a four-nation union of the Benin Gulf countries.

Nonneighboring African States

Dahomey's relations with African countries other than its neighbors have generally remained within the framework of the policy determined by the UAM. Along with the majority of the Brazzaville bloc,

---

[56] *Afrique Nouvelle,* April 18, 1962.   [57] *Ibid.,* June 13, 1962.

Dahomey favored Algerian independence through direct negotiations between de Gaulle and the FLN (Front de Libération Nationale), opposed Portugal's suppression of the Angolan nationalists, supported the Adoula government against Tshombe, and sided with Tunisia against France in the dispute over Bizerte. General statements defining Dahomey's foreign policy were few and far between until July 31, 1961, when Maga in a speech to the assembly came out strongly in favor of African unity, good relations with all countries that respected Dahomey's sovereignty, and neutrality in the world power struggle. These were the views of Albert Tevoedjre, a recent comer to Maga's cabinet, and it was not by chance that their enunciation coincided with the sending of Dahomeyan missions to any and every country that might help it in carrying out the four-year plan.

Until Tevoedjre became a power in the Maga government, Dahomey had been conspicuous among West African countries for its lack of a political doctrine. Absorbed by the internal power struggle and concerned about the deterioration of the country's economy, Maga had joined the Entente and later the UAM almost wholly out of practical considerations. When Tevoedjre entered his government in November 1960, Maga acquired an able and aggressive theoretician, who proceeded to give the PDU a doctrine. Not only did this doctrine include a justification of Dahomey's existing membership in the Entente and the UAM and of its solicitation of aid from countries of the Eastern as well as of the Western bloc, but it also oriented Dahomey toward Pan-Africanism.

Beginning in the summer of 1961, Maga increasingly voiced Tevoedjre's thesis about the overriding need for African unity. Only by the coordination of national economic plans, defense systems, and foreign policy on an all-African scale, he suggested, could misery be abolished from the Dark Continent and its voice be heard in world councils. The only effective way of keeping Africa out of the cold war was to reconcile the Casablanca and the Monrovia groups, and Dahomey could make a modest start toward this goal by promoting a widely based union of the Benin countries. Until Olympio's assassination, it was Ghana's intransigence that had prevented realization of the union as conceived by Tevoedjre, but it has not been the only obstacle he has encountered in his larger project of African reconciliation. At home he is hampered by the temperament and parochial preoccupations of the Dahomeyan people, who are highly individualistic and little interested in the affairs of distant countries. The austerity of proletarian Guinea and Mali has no attraction for them, and they find it hard to get worked up about concepts that have no apparent bearing on their daily lives. It will be little short of a miracle if the present government can get their wholehearted support for the execution of a plan whose realization should be to their ultimate advantage but which entails sacrifices in the immediate future.

WITH NON-AFRICAN COUNTRIES

France is the only non-African country with which Dahomey has as yet developed relations of any real importance. On a limited scale Dahomey has been receiving aid in money and in kind from many sources since independence. Among the countries of the Western bloc, the European Economic Community, the United States, Israel, and Nationalist China have provided funds or technicians or both. As for the Eastern bloc, the USSR, Red China, and North Vietnam have sent more cordial messages and good-will missions than real assistance. It is still France, however, that pays Dahomey's bills, enables it to balance its budget, and is building the Cotonou port. Dahomeyans, therefore, no matter what their local political stripe, are vitally concerned that French aid should continue.

In the referendum of September 1958, of the Dahomeyans who voted 97 per cent chose to join the Franco-African Community. Moreover, there has never been any large group in the country that pressed fanatically for independence. To be sure, there were some youthful radicals who demanded that Dahomey become independent. But the outstanding leaders among them—Tevoedjre and Bertin—entered Maga's government and then cooperated in its policy of collaboration with France. When independence came to Dahomey, it was more as a by-product of its membership in the Entente than as the result of internal pressure. When the Ivory Coast declared that the Entente countries would leave the Community, the Maga government was so shocked that it censored the broadcast of that announcement.[58] In applying for admission to the United Nations, Dahomey gratefully accepted France's sponsorship. Since independence there have been some stirrings of nationalism, as witness the renaming of Dahomey's two *lycées* for Béhanzin and Toffa. Yet such isolated manifestations seem to be confined to regions of the south where Dahomeyan kingdoms formerly existed and to have little influence on the government's conduct of foreign affairs.

[58] André Blanchet, *Nice-Matin*, Feb. 2, 1961.

The cordiality long characteristic of Franco-Dahomeyan relations has been marred by no untoward incidents or even by divisive major issues. Africanization of the administrative cadres has posed no problem, for Dahomey has a plethora of qualified civil servants. Nor have Dahomey's current efforts to break the monopolies of the local French trading firms given rise to acrimonious disputes. Obviously Dahomey has no intention of leaving the franc zone or of requiring France to evacuate its few local military installations. Moreover, France has agreed to train and equip the new national army and to reserve places in its military academies for Dahomeyan cadets. Agreements of financial and technical assistance and cooperation were signed in April 1961. In addition, there is the construction of Cotonou's deepwater port—a truly royal gift that will cost the French treasury some 7,500,000,000 CFA francs. When Maga made his official visit to France in October 1961, the compliments he exchanged with General de Gaulle had the ring of genuine warmth and mutual appreciation. The French President saluted Dahomey as "France's friend and good companion for over 100 years." And in reply, Maga expressed his gratitude to *l'homme du 18 juin,* emancipator of the overseas territories, and leader of France, the country of freedom. . . . We do not feel like foreigners here but like members of one vast family." [59]

The fact that Dahomey's chronic dependence on France has never bred in its people an inferiority complex is a main cause of their prevalent good relations. Temperamentally, as well, the two peoples have so much in common that Dahomey has sometimes been called the Latin Quarter of West Africa. As André Blanchet has observed, the Dahomeyan elite is perfectly at ease in the company of whites and feels neither intellectually nor socially inferior to them.[60] Refreshingly realistic, they even make jokes about their poverty and with nonchalance blame this on everyone but themselves. If they are poor, they say without bitterness, it is because France encouraged Dahomey to concentrate on oil-palm exports, which fetch low prices in world markets. If their intelligentsia are without jobs, it is because France urged them to take up posts in other countries of its African empire. Without false shame, Maga has said, "we ask France for subsidies, and we hope that through the four-year plan we can become economically as well as politically independent." More forthrightly, Tevoedjre has stated that "France's aid is simply France's plain

[59] *Le Monde,* Oct. 26, 1961.
[60] *Nice-Matin,* Feb. 2, 1961.

duty." So long as Paris accepts the burden of the "duty," Dahomey will probably continue to express its "special friendship" for France.

BIBLIOGRAPHY

Books wholly devoted to Dahomey are few and far between even in French, and in English there exists only Herskovits' pre-World War II study of the Abomey kingdom. Valuable information about the kingdom of Abomey, albeit in the form of fiction, is also to be found in Paul Hazoumé's exceptionally well-written *Doguicimi*. More recently, a short book written by two Dahomeyan doctors, A. Akindélé and C. Aguessy, gives both historical and contemporary data on the country not to be found in analogous works, but it suffers from having been written with an eye to official approval. Two other volumes, also by Dahomeyan writers, should be read for an understanding of the contemporary political scene. These are Albert Tevoedjre's comprehensive tract, *L'Afrique révoltée,* and S. M. Apithy's collected speeches and reports entitled *Au service de mon pays.* For an able presentation of the viewpoint of French administrators with long experience in Dahomey, the volumes by H. Desanti and R. Grivot are recommended. A summary of Catholic mission work in Dahomey is given in G. Hardy's biography of Father Aupiais.

A fairly wide range of official documents and shorter studies provide the student with scattered data on a varitey of subjects. Scholars interested in historical and social monographs should consult the *Etudes Dahoméennes* published by the Cotonou branch of the Institut Français de l'Afrique Noire and accessible in the largest American libraries. Up-to-date, factual information about Dahomey's economy is contained in the pamphlet, *La République du Dahomey,* brought out by the Documentation Française center in Paris. A much-abridged condensation of this study has been printed by the French Embassy's Press and Information Service at New York under the title *The Republic of Dahomey.* By all odds the richest source of material on the reactions of the Dahomeyan elite to post-World War II developments is in the minutes of Dahomey's various territorial assemblies, but they are very hard to obtain even in Porto Novo.

Of the current local press, the two PDU organs, *L'Aube Nouvelle* and *La Nation,* shed interesting light on the Maga government's policies and intentions, but they have been published for only a very limited period. Other journals and periodicals containing short accounts of current events in Dahomey have been cited in the footnotes. Of these, *L'Afrique Nouvelle* is the most generous in its space allotment to Dahomey.

OFFICIAL PUBLICATIONS

Ambassade de France, Service de Presse et d'Information. *The Republic of Dahomey.* New York, Nov. 1960. 32 pp.

Bulletin Statisque du Dahomey. Porto Novo: Imprimerie du Gouvernment. Annual.

Documentation Française, La. *La République du Dahomey.* (Notes et Etudes Documentaires, no. 2620.) Paris, Dec. 31, 1959. 38 pp.

Gouvernement Général de l'A.O.F. *Le Dahomey.* Paris: Editions Maritimes et Coloniales, 1931.

Procès-verbaux de l'assemblée territoriale du Dahomey. Porto Novo: Imprimerie du Gouvernement, 1947–1958.

NEWSPAPERS AND PERIODICALS

L'Aube Novelle, Cotonou.
La Nation, Cotonou.

BOOKS

Akindélé, A., and C. Aguessy. *Dahomey.* Paris: Editions Maritimes et Coloniales, 1955. 121 pp.

Apithy, S. M. *Au service de mon pays.* (Supplement to the Sept. 1956 number of *Ouest Afrique.*) Montrouge, 1957. 263 pp.

Desanti, H. *Du Danhomé au Bénin-Niger.* Paris: Larose, 1945. 262 pp.

Dugué, Gil. *Vers les Etats-Unis d'Afrique.* Dakar: Editions Lettres Africaines, 1960.

Etudes dahoméennes. (Trimonthly, beginning in 1946.) Cotonou: Institut Français de l'Afrique Noire.

Grivot, R. *Réactions dahoméennes.* Paris: Berger-Levrault, 1954. 180 pp.

Hardy, Georges. *Le Révérend Père F. Aupiais.* Paris: Larose, 1949. 317 pp.

Hazoumé, P. *Doguicimi.* Paris: Larose, 1938. 510 pp.

Herskovits, M. J. *Dahomey—An Ancient West African Kingdom.* 2 vols. New York: J. J. Augustin, 1938. 752 pp.

Tevoedjre, A. *L'Afrique révoltée.* Paris: Présence Africaine, 1958. 155 pp.

ARTICLES

Aguessy, C. "Esclavage, colonisation et tradition au Dahomey Sud," *Présence Africaine,* Feb.–March 1956, pp. 58–67.

A.O.F. Magazine. *Le Dahomey.* Dakar, Sept. 1953.

Huchet, P. J. "La lente mais certaine évolution des Sombas du Dahomey," *Marchés Coloniaux,* May 7, 14, 21, 28, 1949.

Mangin, G. "L'Organisation Judiciaire des Etats d'Afrique et de Madagascar," *Revue Juridique et Politique d'Outre-Mer,* Jan.–March 1962, pp. 86–87, 112–115.

IV

THE CAMEROUN
FEDERAL REPUBLIC

By VICTOR T. LE VINE

Washington University, St. Louis

Historical Background

The Cameroun[1] is unique among African states in the remarkable variety of its historical experiences. Once a major portion of the infamous west African slave coast, it became a German protectorate; then, divided, it was transformed into two League of Nations mandates. Thereafter by further metamorphoses, it became two United Nations trust territories. Finally, with the passing of the trusteeships,

[1] A number of different spellings of "Cameroun" will be used in this essay to identify the components of the present federation at various stages of their political evolution. The spellings are those employed during those periods. "Cameroun," the French spelling, was used in what is now the East Cameroun during the periods of the French mandate and trusteeship and during the period of the Republic of Cameroun (January 1, 1960—October 1, 1961) and is still used in the French-speaking East Cameroun. "Cameroon" or "Cameroons," the anglicized version, was used to refer to the Cameroons under United Kingdom mandate and later trusteeship and is still used by the English-speaking inhabitants of the West Cameroun. "Southern Cameroons" was the southern administrative half of the former Cameroons under British trusteeship, the section which now corresponds to the West Cameroun. "Northern Cameroons" was the northern section of the British Cameroons, the part of the former trusteeship which, in February 1961, elected to merge with Nigeria. Finally, "Cameroun" will be used in this essay to refer *generally* to the territory, to the federation, or to either of its components.

there was brief independence for one part, and then unification of both in an independent federal republic.[2]

The Cameroun's experiment in federalism is not without its unusual aspects. It is the only union—thus far—of French- and English-speaking territories on the continent (not excepting the Ghana-Guinea-Mali union, which has not progressed beyond the rhetorical stage) and the first attempt to blend the political offspring of French, British, and United Nations tutelary experiences. Then too, it represents an attempt to provide the two parts of the federation, separated by forty years of administative, political, and economic development under different colonial regimes, with a viable formula for co-existence under the same constitutional roof. The only other African bilingual territorial merger, that of the Somalis, resulted in a unitary state.

Unique too is the fact that the Cameroun lies at important geographical and demographic crossroads; it divides the Niger and Congo River basins, but shares physical characteristics of both, and moreover is the ethnic shatter zone where cultures of both regions meet and mingle. Cameroun political development, then, can be understood only in the light of interaction between the complex physical and human facts of Cameroun experience.

THE PRECOLONIAL PERIOD

There is some question concerning the period in which the Cameroun is first noticed by recorded history. According to some interpretations of the celebrated periplus of the Carthaginian Hanno, who claimed to have sailed the coast of the "Lybic lands beyond the Pillars of Hercules," the farthest extent of his voyage is believed to have been the Bight of Biafra, where he and his crews beheld volcanic eruptions of Mount Cameroun and on the island of Fernando Po. However one reads Hanno, there is no question that insofar as recorded European history is concerned, the Portuguese were the first Europeans to reach the Cameroun coast, to visit the island of Fernando Po, and to sail into the estuary of what is now known as the Wouri River, near the site of modern Douala. The year was probably 1472,

[2] The field research on which this essay is based would not have been possible without the support of the Ford Foundation, whose Foreign Area Fellowship Program enabled the author to spend a year in the Camerouns. Grateful acknowledgement is made of that support and of the assistance and valuable counsel provided by Dr. James S. Coleman, director of the African Studies Center, University of California, Los Angeles.

Map 3. The Cameroun Federal Republic.

a date which also marks the occasion on which the Portuguese named
the river Rio dos Camaroes, or River of Prawns, after catching and
eating—and mistaking for prawns—a variety of crayfish found occasionally in the estuary.[3] The name stuck and subsequently was
generally applied to the entire coastal area between Mount Cameroun
and Río Muni (Spanish Guinea).

The early Portuguese visitors to the Rio dos Camaroes opened the
adjacent coastal areas to the slave trade, a commerce that had begun
to flourish after 1530, when the burgeoning plantations in the New
World found imported African labor increasingly necessary. For the
next three centuries the Cameroun coast was systematically exploited
for its human commodity, with Portuguese, Spanish, French, British,
American, and German traders competing for a share of the market.
In the process, the Spanish acquired Fernando Po, using it as one of
their main collection points for slaves taken along the Bight of Benin.
French, German, and British traders established semipermanent posts
along the coast, principally at the mouth of the Wouri, where the
indigenous Douala became useful middlemen in the traffic of slaves.

By the beginning of the nineteenth century European, and particularly British, sentiment had begun to turn against continuation of
the slave trade, a development which coincided with the establishment of British predominance in West African waters from Dakar to
the Gulf of Guinea. In 1827 Britain obtained permission from the
Spanish to occupy Fernando Po for the purpose of basing a squad-
ron to control the shipment of slaves from the Bights of Biafra and
Benin. By the 1830's and 1840's, the British had explored the interior
for some distance and, under the aegis of one of its itinerant consuls,
established a "court of equity" for the multinational trading community at Douala. Finally, in 1858, Alfred Saker, at the head of an
English Baptist mission community, established the first permanent
settlement, Victoria, at the foot of Mount Cameroun.

The extent of British influence along the Cameroun coast, at Douala,
and the Gulf of Guinea, coupled with repeated demands from various
Camerounian chiefdoms for British protection, made annexation of
the area by Britain seem a foregone conclusion. This conclusion was
not shared by either the French or the Germans. The French established a number of trading posts southward along the coast, in the

---

[3] See Joseph Bouchaud, *La coté du Cameroun dans l'histoire et la cartographie
dés origines à l'annexion allemande* (Yaoundé: IFAN, Centre au Cameroun, 1952),
for a full discussion of the precolonial period.

process signing treaties with a number of local chiefs. German commercial interests, long active in the Cameroun area, had by 1882 convinced Bismarck of the desirability of extending imperial protection to the Cameroun coast. Quietly, and under the unsuspecting nose of the Gladstone government, Bismarck in the spring of 1884 dispatched Gustav Nachtigal—explorer and lately German consul general in Tunis —to the Guinea coast, ostensibly to investigate the "state of German commerce" in the area. In the meantime, a dilatory British government, having finally become aware of the possibility that the Cameroun might fall into other, particularly French, hands, authorized their itinerant "floating Consul," Edward H. Hewett, to conclude treaties of annexation with the petty "kings" at Douala. Hewett, to his eternal chagrin, arrived in Douala a week too late. On July 12, 1884, Nachtigal, who had arrived the day before, signed a treaty with two of the Douala kings establishing the German protectorate.[4]

COLONIAL RULE

The Kamerun Protectorate

The German protectorate lasted thirty years. Under a succession of governors of varying abilities, the protectorate was extended by 1911 to the edge of Lake Tchad in the north and was almost doubled in size in that year following a deal with France in which substantial chunks of the then French Congo were ceded to Germany in return for the withdrawal of imperial interests in Morocco. Moreover, the German administration laid the foundation for the modern Cameroun's social overhead capital (that is, basic transportation, communication, irrigation, and power facilities): wharves and docks at Douala, Kribi, Campo, Tiko, and Victoria; rail lines north from Douala to Nkongsamba and west almost to Yaoundé, as well as the narrow-gauge Victoria Plantation railroad; a large number of bridges, roads, and paths; and well-constructed public and private buildings, many of which are still in use today. Furthermore, the plantation and development projects started by the Germans cannot be overlooked. In all, the French and British inherited in the Cameroun an established basis for further economic development, that is, a basic infrastructure and

[4] The circumstances surrounding the German annexation of the Cameroun and the nature of their protectorate over the territory are detailed in Harry Rudin's excellent study, *Germans in the Cameroons* (New Haven: Yale University Press, 1938), and in René Douala Manga Bell, "Contribution à l'histoire du Cameroun de 1884 à 1914," *L'Effort Camerounnais* (Yaoundé), nos. 210–223, Oct. 25, 1959— Jan. 24, 1960.

a productive plantation economy, both with considerable potential for further growth.

The Kamerun protectorate also left behind some less easily measurable legacies. By encouraging missionary and educational activity, the Germans consciously developed an indigenous Camerounian stratum capable of mediating between Europeans and the Africans of the hinterland. By introducing large numbers of Camerounians to the money economy, the Germans effectively laid the basis for urban life in the southern portions of the country and for the subsequent growth of an indigenous trading community. The Germans have often, and with some justice, been accused of using harsh methods to further their aims. Objective examination of the facts reveals that whatever can be said of some of their methods or motives, the Germans maintained a colonial administration in the Kamerun that compares favorably with any other in Africa at the time. In another context, however, the quality of German rule becomes irrelevant. For Camerounians of later periods, anxious to attack the French or British administrations for alleged wrongs of commission or omission, the brighter the German experience could be painted, the more useful it became as a political weapon. The "Kamerun" became, in this connection, an important touchstone for Camerounian nationalists, a potent and evocative symbol of a half-mythical "golden age" when the Cameroun was one and undivided.

The Mandates

World War I brought the Kamerun protectorate to an abrupt end. During 1914 and 1915, French, British, and Belgian troops, invading the Kamerun from several sides, gradually converged upon Yaoundé, the administrative capital, forcing the German forces south and into eventual internment in Spanish Guinea. Upon the departure of the Germans, the British and French created a short-lived condominium over the territory that ended in March 1916, when the victors agreed on a provisional partition of the territory. The *ad hoc* partition, in which the territories ceded to the Kamerun in 1911 were returned to France, divided the country into two unequal parts. The British accepted two noncontiguous portions in the west bordering Nigeria that amounted to about one-fifth of the territory's total area (after the return of the 1911 cessions). The French took the remainder. The partition was confirmed by the Versailles peace treaties, and in 1922, after some French hesitation (France wanted to convert the territory into a colony), the two Camerouns became League of Nations mandated territories under the respective administrations of France and Great Britain. The creation of the mandates marked the beginning of thirty-five years of separate administrative, economic, and political existence for the two Camerouns. It was not until 1947 that the question of reuniting them was again raised.

Except for German agitation in the southern section, life in the British Cameroons mandate was relatively uneventful during the interwar period. The territory, joined to Nigeria in an administrative union, was generally considered somewhat of a backwash in the mainstream of Nigerian development. The forces which were shaping the course of Nigerian and French Camerounian events had few echoes in the British Cameroons; both Africans and Europeans in the territory were more concerned with economic than political problems. In general, contacts between the two Camerouns fluctuated according to the tide of labor going from the French to the British mandate and with the scattered commercial relations maintained across the border. Contacts with Nigeria were similarly sparse, including seasonal labor coming in from eastern Nigeria and some commercial links overland with eastern Nigeria and by the way of the Cross River. By far the most important influence on the economic development of the British mandate was the group of German plantations in the Southern Cameroons, repurchased by most of their former owners after 1924. Within two years after their return, the Germans, comprising the largest European group in the territory, had begun to make their plantations pay. As a consequence of their activity, trade with Germany from 1925 to 1938 comprised the territory's principal source of revenue. With the rise of Hitler, German settler sentiment became increasingly pro-Nazi and militantly nationalist, to such an extent, in fact, that with the coming of World War II the German community in the British Cameroons might well have been termed a small fifth column. During the war, however, these Germans were repatriated and their plantations once again expropriated.

Finally, a word must be said about British policies in the Cameroons north of the Southern Cameroons plantation area. Here, indirect rule seems to have worked quite well. With the possible exception of the so-called Kirdi areas (see p. 291), the traditional chiefs in the Bamenda highlands and in the Muslim-dominated northern sections proved quite amenable to the administrative devolution envisaged by Lord Lugard.

Two keystones of French colonial policy dominated the administration of their Cameroun mandate: (1) the *politique de protectorat* as it developed in practice and (2) the economic policy of *mise en valeur*. The *politique de protectorat*—protectorate policy—was the consequence of a shift in French colonial policy from assimilation (complete integration of indigenous peoples into French political, social, and economic life) to one of association (slow development of the indigenous community toward eventual assimilation, with separation of European and African communities until assimilation was achieved). In practice, even though the system provided for some minimal participation of Africans in the making of policy, it tended to maintain the political and cultural gap between the French and the assimilated African on the one hand and the so-called *indigénes sujets* (subject natives) on the other. One of the primary props of the system was the legal separation of the two groups, a separation of which the *indigénat*—a comprehensive set of violations and penalties which local French administrators could invoke almost at will and without control—was the key. The *indigénat* applied wholly to members of the *indigénes sujets* group. The practical consequence of the system was to retard the political advancement of the latter group, an end openly espoused by the administration. As one French commissioner put it: "It was not, moreover, the wish of the local Administration that too rapid progress should be made; it wished to prevent any disturbance of the balance in the organization of the native tribes, which were still backward, and whose evolution should proceed steadily and reasonably." [5]

The policy of *mise en valeur* (development), first elaborated by Colonial Minister Albert Sarraut in 1923, called for an extensive local economic development as the basis of fruitful relations between the colonies and metropolitan France. Applied to the Cameroun, the policy resulted in a fivefold increase of the territory's total trade between 1922 and 1938, a successful weathering of the worst years of the depression, and a considerable enlargement of the social overhead (that is, infrastructure, education, and so on) and of the economy as a whole. Much of the success of the *mise en valeur* in the Cameroun was due, however, to a heavy tax burden and the use of conscript or *corvée* labor reinforced by the *indigénat* system. This use of forced labor aroused a great deal of indignation abroad. As a result of the

[5] Statement by Commissioner Marchand before the Permanent Mandates Commission, in *Minutes and Reports of the Fifteenth Session, 1929,* p. 131.

urging of the Permanent Mandates Commission of the League of Nations and the adverse publicity created by the situation, the French administration finally diminished its use of *corvée* labor in 1933, later abolishing it altogether in 1952.[6] During the latter years of the mandate, before the outbreak of World War II, the French also instituted a number of important political reforms. There is little question, however, that these reforms were motivated at least in part by the need to stimulate pro-French sympathies in the Cameroun and to counter the possibility that Germany's massive propaganda for the return of its former colonies might undermine African support for the administration. In all, although the mandate saw the Cameroun's economy developed significantly, it left as one of its less pleasant residues widespread ill will toward the French, an ill will that was translated into nationalist activity after the war.

The Trusteeship Period

In 1946, following the demise of the League of Nations, the two Cameroun mandates were converted into trust territories under the United Nation's trusteeship system. By accepting the new system, both Britain and France undertook to honor the political objectives stated in Article 76 of the United Nations Charter: "Progressive development towards self-government or independence." Insofar as France was concerned, the commitment represented a new departure, radical as compared to its former policies but wholly in line with the new colonial policies enunciated in the constitution of 1946 and spelled out in the legislation which flowed from it. For both Camerouns, then, the postwar era involved rapid political change culminating in the attainment of independence for the French Cameroun on January 1, 1960, followed by the merger of the Cameroun Republic with the former British Southern Cameroons in October 1961 and the creation of the Cameroun Federal Republic. A few of the more significant steps toward those goals may be recalled.

Under the system of classification developed in the French constitution of 1946, the French Cameroun became an "Associated State" within the French Union. Overriding control of the territory still remained in the hands of the French National Assembly, but the Cameroun now sent representatives to both houses of the French national parliament, as well as to the various organs of the French

[6] See Raymond Leslie Buell, *The Native Problem in Africa*, vol. II (New York: Macmillan, 1928), for one of the sharpest such condemnations of forced labor in the Cameroun.

Union. A representative assembly with limited, principally advisory powers was set up in the Cameroun, and elections to the new assembly were held under a dual electoral roll in which the African registry was restricted.

Significantly, the assembly had an African majority from the start, one destined for rapid growth. A new assembly elected in 1952 did not enjoy greater powers but had substantially more African seats due to an increase in the African rolls of nearly fifteen times the 1946 registration. Under the sweeping reforms of the 1956 *loi cadre*, a new Cameroun assembly was elected for the first time under a single roll embracing an electorate of 1,740,000 voters, a figure almost three times that of the total registration in 1952. The terms of the 1956–1957 reforms gave the Cameroun assembly and government almost complete internal control.

The first Cameroun government was formed in 1957 with André-Marie Mbida as the Premier. A ministerial crisis in February 1958 forced the resignation of Mbida, and Ahmadou Ahidjo became the new Premier. Ahidjo at once entered into negotiations with the French government for still greater autonomy and the setting of a date for complete independence. During 1959 the Cameroun enjoyed complete internal self-government, a prelude to the achievement of full independence on January 1, 1960. This recital, of course, gives only the skeletal outlines of the major steps toward independence; the flesh and blood of the story are provided by the rise and development of Camerounian nationalism, which will be discussed in the next section.

Events in the British Cameroons were somewhat more complex but can also be traced in broad strokes in anticipation of the next section. The terms of the trusteeship agreement for the British Cameroons permitted the continuation of the administrative union under whose terms the Southern Cameroons were administered from Enugu, the capital of Eastern Nigeria, and the Northern Cameroons from Kaduna, the administrative center of Northern Nigeria. When, in 1947 (under the "Richards Constitution") Nigeria became regionalized, the Southern Cameroons became a province of the Eastern Region. With the reforms of Nigeria's "MacPherson Constitution" (1951), the Southern Cameroons sent thirteen elected members to the Eastern House of Assembly, among them Dr. Emmanuel L. M. Endeley. In the meantime, political sentiment was growing for greater Southern Camerounian autonomy. In 1953, Dr. Endeley, then leader of the "Cameroons faction" in the Eastern House, won a domestic election on the issue of separation from Eastern Nigeria. The Nigerian "Lyttleton Constitution," promulgated in 1954, recognized the Southern Cameroon's wishes and made it a quasi-federal territory (in effect, giving it regional status) with its own House of Assembly and Executive Council. Further, the Southern Cameroons sent six representatives to the Nigerian House of Representatives in Lagos and was guaranteed one ministry. The Northern Cameroons, whose spokesmen had expressed no desire for separation from the Northern Region, were also given representation, but in the Northern Regional House of Assembly and House of Chiefs at Kaduna, plus a Minister for the Northern Cameroons and a Consultative Committee for Northern Cameroons Affairs.

The Southern Cameroons House of Assembly met for the first time in October 1954, and Dr. Endely was named Leader of Government Business. In 1957, after his electoral alliance had won a close election, Dr. Endeley was renamed Leader of Government Business, a title which he held until May 1958, when new constitutional arrangements came into force. Under the new system, the Southern Cameroons received ministerial government, and Dr. Endeley was named Premier. In January 1959, general elections in the Southern Cameroons resulted in the defeat of Dr. Endeley's coalition and a narrow victory for the party led by John N. Foncha, a schoolmaster from Bamenda, who had campaigned on a platform of unification of the two Cameroons. Foncha thus became Premier, succeeding Dr. Endeley.

In May of the same year, 1959, the United Nations General Assembly, at the end of a special "Cameroons Session," recommended that separate plebiscites be held in the Northern and Southern Cameroons to decide their political future. The one in the north was scheduled to take place that November, but the Assembly took no further action on a plebiscite for the Southern Cameroons, owing to unresolved differences between Foncha and Endeley over the date of the plebiscite and the questions to be put. By October, however, these two leaders had reached agreement on the outstanding issues, and the General Assembly, in December, set February 11, 1961, as the date for the plebiscite in the south and for a second plebiscite in the north. (The November plebiscite in the Northern Cameroons had resulted in a vote to defer decision on the political future of that part of the trusteeship.)

The question posed in both Northern and Southern Cameroons was whether to join Nigeria—which had become independent in

October 1960—or to unite with the Cameroun Republic. On February 11, 1961, polling took place without incident in the Southern Cameroons and resulted in an overwhelming vote for unification with the Cameroun Republic. In contrast, the voting in the Northern Cameroons on February 11 and 12 produced a sizable margin for joining Nigeria. The figures for the plebiscites [7] were as follows:

Southern Cameroons: For Cameroun Republic   235,571
For Nigeria   97,741

Northern Cameroons: For Cameroun Republic   97,659
For Nigeria   146,296

The unificationists' victory in the Southern Cameroons was even more substantial than that predicted by the most optimistic KNDP (Kamerun National Democratic Party) leaders. Some 83 per cent of those registered voted, and the "white box" (the unification alternative) received 48,637 more ballots than the "green [pro-Nigeria] box." Although Endeley vowed that he would continue to fight "to the end," and Mbile, deputy leader of the opposition Cameroons Peoples' National Convention, repeated his demands for a partition of the territory along ethnic lines, the decisiveness of the vote could not be challenged. "Reunification" had been achieved without bloodshed and in an unimpeachably democratic manner.

RISE AND CHARACTER OF THE NATIONALIST MOVEMENT

Cameroun nationalist sentiment developed first in the French Cameroun and then gradually found its way into the British Cameroons as it grew in strength and intensity. Two dominant themes in the growth of Camerounian nationalism can be traced in each part of the Cameroun: (1) in the French Cameroun, Cameroun nationalism per se and its outgrowth, the demand for the "reunification" of the two Camerouns (to use Cameroun nationalist terminology); (2) in the British Cameroons, first, Southern Cameroonian separatism (from Nigeria) and later, under the impetus of ideas and pressures from

[7] A full description of the plebiscites, including the breakdown in voting for all the Southern and Northern Cameroons electoral districts, is found in *Report of the United Nations Plebiscite Commissioner for the Cameroons under United Kingdom Administration, Plebiscites in the southern and northern parts of the Territory, on 11 and 12 February 1961,* UN Doc. A/4727 (New York, 1961), originally issued as UN Docs. T/1556/Appendix and T/1556/Appendix/Add. 1 and 2, dated 11 April 1961.

the east, a mounting pressure in that territory for "reunification" with the French Cameroun.

The French Cameroun

Although a number of political parties from metropolitan France established branches in the French Cameroun after 1946 and several purely indigenous political groups had already arisen by then, Cameroun nationalism dates from 1948. In that year the Union des Populations du Cameroun (UPC) was formed by Ruben Um Nyobé, a former government clerk active in the Cameroun's nascent trade union movement, Dr. Félix Moumié, a medical officer recently returned from his studies at Dakar, and several other trade unionists and government employees. The UPC represented a new turn in Cameroun politics as it was both a political party and an ideological innovator. As a party, it drew its initial strength from the leadership of the Cameroun's leftist trade unions and from among the more militant members of the older political groups. As an ideological innovator it was the creator and carrier of what was essentially a two-point nationalist program: the unification of the two Cameroons and rapid progress toward complete independence under the terms of the United Nations Charter. Within two months the UPC became the Cameroun branch of the Rassemblement Démocratique Africain (RDA) and had begun to attract support from influential "traditional" organizations such as Ngondo (Douala) and Kumsze (Bamiléké).[8] By the time the first United Nations Visiting Mission arrived in Douala in November 1949, the UPC had become by all odds the best-organized political party in the French Cameroun.

The next five years saw the formation of a large number of political parties and organizations, including Louis Aujoulat's Bloc Démocratique Camerounais (BDC, the lineal precursor of the present Parti des Démocrates Camerounais—PDC), Charles Okala's Union Sociale Camerounaise (USC, which became the present Parti Socialiste Camerounais), several traditional organizations converted into political parties by ambitious politicians, and a number of *partis de*

[8] Ngondo comprises the community councils which existed in the various Douala villages long before the twentieth century. The Ngondo mentioned here is the "traditional" council of Douala "notables," converted in the late 1940's into an organizational adjunct of the various political formations created by such leaders as Paul Soppo Priso. Similarly, *kumsze*, originally the generic designation of a type of adult age-grade society among the Bamiléké, became a single organization with political rather than traditional functions.

l'administration, often organized specifically to counter UPC activity in one area or another. During this period, the UPC became increasingly frustrated. It found the French administration hostile, the other parties preempting its nationalist program for their own use, and its candidates unable to win seats in the Cameroun assembly. Its only successes lay abroad, where repeated appearances by Um Nyobé and Moumié before United Nations organs served to propagandize the UPC's position and to make friends for it among anti-French or anti-colonial delegations at the UN.

Even though most Camerounian political parties by the beginning of 1955 had openly espoused both the goals of independence and re-unification (with varying qualifications), the UPC had failed to gather much support and decided to turn from verbal extremism to more violent action. During May of 1955, the UPC launched a series of riots, demonstrations, and attacks on property and persons in Douala and Yaoundé and throughout the southwestern part of the country, apparently hoping to ignite a nationwide insurrection. The attempt failed, having misfired in the north, and lost momentum in the south-west in the face of swift and harsh government countermeasures. The UPC and its affiliate organizations were banned in July, and soon thereafter its leaders fled into the British Cameroons to set up emergency headquarters at Kumba. In September, the UPC directorate split, one wing (Um Nyobé and Mayi-Matip) returning to continue the fight as maquis and the other (Moumié, Ouandié, Kingué) eventually (after 1957) taking refuge first in Khartoum, then in Cairo, and finally in Accra and Conakry.

Officially banned and its leaders either in exile or in the maquis, the UPC, paradoxically, dominated the political scene between 1955 and 1960 as it had never been able to do when it was legal and competed openly with its opponents. The continuing rebellion in-spired by the UPC—initially among the Bassa in the Sanaga-Mari-time, later spreading to the Bamiléké and other western areas and recurring with sporadic violence in the principal towns—plus the UPC's propaganda campaign waged from the halls of the UN and through the facilities provided by the United Arab Republic, Guinea, and Ghana, preoccupied both the French administration and the re-maining political parties. One of the consequences of this preoccupa-tion was the introduction of a third theme as an article of nationalist faith, that is, "reconciliation" by bringing the rebellion to an end through rescinding the ban on the UPC and including its leaders in the government. Significantly, the downfall of the coalition Mbida government in 1958 was due to the fact that Mbida used excessively harsh measures to combat the UPC—at least so it appeared to many Camerounian leaders—that he had not pursued "reconciliation" with sufficient vigor, and that he had not pressed for early independence from France. The new government headed by Ahmadou Ahidjo was formed through an alliance of the Union Camerounaise (UC) group in the assembly (composed primarily of Muslim Fulani from the north and controlling twenty-nine seats) and the Mouvement d'Action Nationale Camerounaise (MANC) formerly in opposition, which included such leaders as Paul Soppo Priso and Charles Assalé. MANC had a general outlook that was at once vigorously nationalist and actively reconciliationist. A small group of deputies (Paysans Indépendants), representing important indigenous agricultural interests in the western areas, completed the coalition.

Throughout 1958 sporadic violence broke out in the southwest, and not even the death of Um Nyobé in September 1958 brought an end to it. (It did end the Bassa revolt.) Throughout 1958, the external UPC, from Cairo, Conakry, and Accra, continued to stoke the fires of unrest in the countryside and in the principal towns to such an extent that substantial portions of the southwest became economically paralyzed. Moreover, the UPC kept up constant agitation at the United Nations and almost managed to convince that body that general elections—in which it expected to emerge victorious—should be held before independence was attained on January 1, 1960. With Guinean, Ghanaian, and Egyptian support, the UPC sought unsuccessfully to force itself into power by exploiting the unrest for which it had been largely responsible. It is interesting to observe that the only party which had the organization, the ideological dynamism, and the militant leadership to grow into an all-Cameroun movement dissipated its vitality by a premature attempt to seize power. The French Cameroun, then, attained independence not under the aegis of a national movement such as the Convention People's Party in Ghana or the Tanganyika National Union, but in the care of a loose coalition of regional and ethnic-based parties into whose hands power had been thrust almost by default.

British Cameroons

In the British Cameroons, nationalist sentiment developed only in the Southern Cameroons, where longer contact with modern ways and a relatively good educational system had developed considerable popular political sophistication. The observation holds true even in the face of minor political party activity in the Northern Cameroons during the November 1959 plebiscite campaign and thereafter up to the February 1961 plebiscite. The latter activity had limited aims quite obviously connected with the alternatives posed in the two plebiscites and cannot be said to represent anything like a continuing political tradition. In this context, the two threads of Cameroons nationalism, separatism and reunification, can be traced in outline in the Southern British Cameroons.

The first steps in the direction of a Cameroons nationalism were taken in 1940, with the formation of the Cameroons Youth League (CYL) in Lagos by P. M. Kalle and E. M. L. Endeley. Kalle, together with L. N. Namme and N. N. Mbile, participated in the founding of Dr. Azikiwe's National Council of Nigeria and the Cameroons (NCNC), and these men were at various times members of the party's national executive. In 1946 the Cameroons mandate was converted into UN trusteeship, and a year later, on the occasion of the first visiting mission, Dr. Endeley, now speaking for the Cameroons Federal Union (CFU), submitted a memorandum demanding a separate Cameroons region in Nigeria. The 1947 "Richards Constitution" failed to create a separate Cameroons region, and in late 1947 Dr. Endeley, this time connected with the NCNC, returned to the Cameroons with Mbile to assume the leadership of the Cameroons Development Corporation Workers' Union. The embers of separatism were kept glowing during 1948 and 1949 by the CYL (with NCNC backing) and the CFU. In 1948 the CFU added "unification" of the two Camerouns to its demand for Southern Cameroons autonomy. There was even a motion by the Cameroons provincial council in Victoria demanding a separate region. The year 1949 also saw the formation of the Cameroons National Federation (CNF) by Dr. Endeley, Mbile, S. T. Muna, and S. A. George. By 1951 the CNF had become the Kamerun National Congress (KNC) and Endeley its president. In 1951 also, two meetings in Kumba (Aug., Dec.) brought the UPC and Southern Cameroons nationalist groups together for the first time. Dr. Endeley led the Southern Cameroons' representatives to the Eastern Nigerian House of Assembly in 1951 and 1953, as well as the Cameroons' delegation to the constitutional conferences of 1953 and 1954. Still pursuing regional autonomy, Endeley and his delegation in 1953 won a virtual promise of regional separation if Endeley should win a general election at home on the issue of separation from Eastern Nigeria. In December of that same year the KNC won 12 of the 13 seats to the Eastern House (the other going to the Kamerun Peoples' Party—KPP—a splinter from the KNC), and the 1954 "Lyttleton Constitution" provided quasi-federal status for the Southern Cameroons. In October, the Southern Cameroons House of Assembly met for the first time and Dr. Endeley was named Leader of Government Business. The first objective had been reached. The Southern Cameroons had achieved separate status within the federation. Developments within the French Cameroun, however, soon began to change the complexion of Southern Cameroonian politics.

The Southern Cameroons' unificationist strand must begin not only with Endeley but more particularly with the person of Jabea K. Dibonge, a Douala from the French Cameroun residing in Buea (Southern Cameroun) and for many years a government clerk. In 1949 Dibonge organized the French Cameroons Welfare Association among the Douala residing in the Southern Cameroons. Dibonge was interested in strengthening Douala solidarity and, by implication, asserting old Douala claims for hegemony over the Cameroons. That same year the UPC, emboldened by the success of Ewe irredentist propaganda at the United Nations debates over Togo, launched a full-fledged campaign in the French Cameroun for unification, and the UPC leadership lost no time in securing Dibonge's cooperation. It was 1955, however, that saw unification emerge as a fully fledged nationalist goal in the Southern Cameroons. Two important events were responsible. First was the formation of the Kamerun National Democratic Party (KNDP), led by a Bamenda schoolteacher, John N. Foncha, with a program of complete secession from Nigeria and unification with the French Cameroun. Second was the appearance of the UPC directorate at Kumba following the party's abortive revolt in the French Cameroun.

The KNDP joined forces with the UPC, but by the time the UPC was banned in the Southern Cameroons and its leaders deported (1957), Foncha and his party had become disenchanted with the extremism of the UPC. Unification still remained, however, as one of the KNDP's primary programmatic goals. The UPC left a rump party in its wake, the One Kamerun Party (OK) headed by Ndeh Ntumazah. The March 1957 general elections in the Southern Cameroons resulted in a narrow loss for Foncha (KNDP, 6 seats; KNC-KPP alliance, 7 seats), and the KNDP—as well as the OK, with whom the

KNDP leadership declined to be identified—continued to agitate for reunification.

In 1958, Ahmadou Ahidjo, a partisan of unification, became Prime Minister of the Cameroun, and France announced that it was prepared to grant its trust territory its independence on January 1, 1960. Both events strengthened the hand of the unificationists in the Southern Cameroons. In January 1959, the KNDP won 14 seats in the enlarged House of Assembly, while the KNC-KPP took 12. The stage was now set for the 1959 dialogue, conducted both at home and in the UN, to decide the ultimate fate of the entire British trust territory.

At the spring 1959 "Cameroons Session" of the United Nations General Assembly, that body decided that separate plebiscites would be held in the two portions of the British trusteeship. Foncha and Endeley were unable to agree, however, on either the date of the plebiscite in the south or on the questions to be put. Endeley had now come full circle from advocating separation from Nigeria and eventual union with the French Cameroun to favoring integration with Nigeria as a regional component of the federation. He wanted an early plebiscite offering clearly stated alternatives. Foncha asked for immediate separation from Nigeria and—in somewhat of a retreat from his ardent unificationist position—an extension of the trusteeship until the political courses of the Southern Cameroons' two neighbors became clear. Thereafter, he urged two plebiscites to decide the territory's attachment.

Under pressure from a number of African states at the United Nations in the fall of 1959, Foncha finally agreed to an early plebiscite, to be held between September 1960 and April 1961, that would pose a clear choice between an independent Nigeria and the Cameroun Republic. Throughout 1960, Foncha met with Ahidjo to discuss the shape of a future union, but little came of the talks except the vague outlines of a loose federal union. His party, however, began to campaign vigorously for unification. Endeley, for his part, undertook to convince the electorate that its only rational choice lay with Nigeria, and he strove to magnify the point that union with the Cameroun Republic meant getting involved in the sanguinary troubles of that country. Foncha and his party played on local fears of Ibo domination (many Eastern Nigerians including some Ibo had already come to pose an economic threat to indigenous Southern Cameroonians) and the prospects of profitable union with ethnically related "brothers" (the relationship is rather limited, in fact). The plebiscite—February 11 in the south, February 11 and 12 in the north—unequivocally resolved the issue. The advocates of unification won resoundingly in the south, as already noted, but lost by a considerable margin in the north.

INDEPENDENCE AND UNIFICATION: REPUBLIC INTO FEDERATION

The results of the plebiscite in the Southern Cameroons were received with joy in the Republic, and Foncha became the hero of the hour. In contrast, the Republic took the results in the Northern Cameroons with ill grace. It claimed at the United Nations that Great Britain and Nigeria had exerted undue pressure on the northern electorate to the extent (for example) of bringing in 700 armed Nigerian policemen to coerce the voters into voting for Nigeria.[9] The importance of the complaint, it may be added here, was not that the Cameroun government thought that the plebiscite had been badly conducted but that it was genuinely disappointed at losing the Northern Cameroons as a potential reservoir of votes for the UC and as a strong counter in the bargaining with Foncha over the status of the Southern Cameroons in the new federation. Without the north, the Ahidjo government realized that Foncha's hand would be strengthened and that his demands for maximum local autonomy for his part of the federation would be difficult to deny. The Ahidjo government actively pursued its complaint until April 1961, when the UN ratified the plebiscite, and did not get down to the business of a full-scale consultation with its new partners on the shape of the new federation. Pressures for agreement only produced the text of a proposed federal constitution in July, after much foot dragging by the Republic.

On October 1, 1961, the two Camerouns were united and trusteeship over the British Southern Cameroons came officially to an end. The Northern Cameroons' trusteeship status had terminated on June 1, 1961, with the formal attachment of that portion of the territory to Nigeria. The Northern Cameroons became thenceforth the Sardauna Province of the Northern Region. Following the end of the trusteeship in the south, the former British Southern Cameroons became West Cameroun, and the Cameroun Republic was designated East Cameroun.

[9] Republic of Cameroun, Ministry of Foreign Affairs and Secretariat of State for Information, *Position of the Republic of the Cameroun following the plebiscite of the 11th and 12th February 1961 in the northern portion of the Territory of the Cameroon under the administration of the United Kingdom of Great Britain and Northern Ireland* (Yaoundé, March 1961): "It is impossible to talk of self-determination when voters go to the polls at bayonet point" (p. 17 and *passim*).

By July 1962, federal institutions had come into being. In the federal legislature of 50 seats, 10 were allocated to the West Cameroons, and the rest to the eastern state. Ahidjo became Federal President, and Foncha the Vice-President of the federation. Foncha also retained his post as Prime Minister of West Cameroun as a result of the KNDP's decisive victory in the West Cameroun general elections held in January 1962. In addition, a full team of federal ministers were named, with five major posts going to West Camerounians. Other developments included definite moves toward a one-party state in the East Cameroun, a tendency aided by the disintegration of the independent bloc in the Eastern Assembly and by the reduction of the Démocrates' and the UPC's legislative ranks. (For a fuller discussion of this trend, see below, pp. 320–324.) Finally, President Ahidjo announced the dissolution of the Eastern Assembly after its 1962 session and general elections to take place in the East Cameroun in January 1963.

The Contemporary Setting

GEOGRAPHY

The Cameroun is roughly 700 miles long, approximately the size of California, and resembles in shape an irregular triangle with its apex touching Lake Chad and its base resting approximately on the line of 2°N. lat. The Cameroun is bounded on the south by Spanish Guinea, Gabon, and the Republic of Congo (Brazzaville), to the east by Chad and the Central African Republic, and to the west by Nigeria. A part of the Cameroun triangle's western side is bounded by the Bight of Biafra, the easternmost reach of the Gulf of Guinea. The coastline is dominated by Mount Cameroun, 13,500 feet in elevation and the highest mountain in west Africa. Mount Cameroun, an occasionally active volcano, is the southernmost peak of an irregular chain of mountains and rocky hills along the western border extending north by northeast virtually to the edge of Lake Chad.

The Federal Republic can be roughly divided into five geographic zones on the basis of dominant topographic, climatic, and vegetative features:

(1) The western mountain region, containing, in sequence, Mount Cameroun, the Manengouba, Banbouto, and Mbam massifs (which include most of the Bamenda, Bamiléké, and Mambilla Highlands), comprises as well portions of the Atlantika Hills, and, north of the Benue River, some of the Mandara Hills.

(2) The coastal forest plain extends from 10 to 50 miles inland

to the edge of the plateau of the inland forest region. This coastal region is very hot and humid and in it may be found some of the wettest places on earth, particularly on the seaward slopes of Mount Cameroun, where annual rainfall of over 30 feet has been recorded at Debundcha.

(3) The inland forest plateau, dominated by the tropical rain forest, lies on the average some 1,500 to 2,000 feet above sea level and extends about 300 miles to the northernmost edge of the rain forest. Climatically it is less humid than the coast, but daytime temperatures are as hot.

(4) Running east-west, the Adamawa plateau region is in fact an extension of the mountain region. Average elevation is around 3,400 feet. The plateau region varies between 50 and 150 miles in width and tends to have a relatively pleasant climate. There is a fairly abrupt transition between the plateau and the northern savannahs.

(5) The northern savannah plain extends from the Adamawa plateau region to Lake Chad, with the principal vegetation either scrub or grass cover. Humidity decreases and temperatures increase as one moves north.

The main rivers of the Cameroun are the Wouri, near whose mouth Douala is located; the Sanaga; the Dja-Ngoko, flowing southwest into the Congo River; the Logone, draining into Lake Chad and comprising part of the northwestern frontier; and the Benue, the eastern extension of the Niger. Garoua on the Benue is accessible from Lagos for about six weeks during the rainy season (July 15–September 15), making it one of the most important ports of the Cameroun. Other ports are Douala, the country's principal seaport; Kribi, an important port during the German period but now in some decline; and Tiko and Victoria-Bota, both in the West Cameroon and that state's principal outlets to the sea.

THE ECONOMY

Resources and Potential Resources

An objective assessment of the Cameroun's natural resources cannot support much optimism that the Federal Republic will ever become significant as an economic power, even in west Africa. Its principal resources are those which will permit it to expand and exploit its agricultural sector. Its limited industry—with one important exception, the aluminum plant at Edéa—has been and undoubtedly will continue to be tied to agriculture.

Soils and climate in the southern parts of the East and West Cameroun encourage intensive cultivation of plantation crops such as cocoa, coffee, and bananas. These products, as a matter of fact, have long constituted the state's principal cash crops. An area of considerable present and potential growth has been the timber reserves of the tropical forest, an area estimated (in the East) to cover some 39,536,000 acres, of which, however, only some 4,942,000 are accessible under present conditions.

The main rivers are a source of potential hydroelectric power. But it is unlikely that, except for expansion of the existing facilities at Edéa and the development of a few hydroelectric stations to provide additional power for the towns, the growth of industry will ever be sufficient to warrant large-scale utilization of that potential.

Finally, a word must be said about minerals. Cassiterite and gold are mined in such small amounts as to be unimportant to the economy. An exceptionally large deposit of bauxite has been discovered on the Adamawa plateau, near Tibati. It is estimated at over 500,000,000 tons, with a 44 per cent assayed proportion of recoverable alumina. The deposit is too far, however, from the coast (approximately 500 miles from Edéa, where it would have to be processed) to be presently exploitable. Even when the deposit becomes accessible with the construction of the Douala-Chad railway—which is projected to pass near Tibati—it is doubtful if it would be economically worth while to bring the bauxite to Edéa in view of the fact that extensive bauxite deposits elsewhere in Africa (notably in Ghana and Guinea) lie near or on the Atlantic coast and are in consequence much more exploitable.

Organization of the Economy

Except in some areas, the economies of the two Camerouns, separate for over forty years, have not yet meshed to the extent that it is possible to speak except in the most general terms of an economy of the Federal Republic. As of July 1, 1962, only the most rudimentary common economic measures had been undertaken by the new federation. These included the introduction of the CFA franc as the common currency in both states, the promulgation of the first federal budget, and the taking of various steps to ease the flow of goods and trade between the states.

The economy of the Federal Republic is based almost entirely upon agriculture. The predominant pattern is subsistence farming, though a not inconsiderable portion of the agricultural sector is devoted to the production of exportable crops. Manioc, millet, cassava, and various tuberous vegetables are the principal crops produced almost exclusively for local consumption. Whereas palm oil produced in the East Cameroun is mainly consumed locally, that which is produced in the West Cameroun constitutes that state's fifth most valuable export crop. Peanuts and bananas, which are important items in the local diet, are also produced in both states in important quantities for export. During 1959, bananas were the most important export crop of the West Cameroun (followed by cocoa) and the fourth most important export crop in the East. The major exports of the East are cocoa and coffee, which between them accounted for over 70 per cent of that state's exports in 1960. The East Cameroun also exported wood, rubber, meat, and livestock in significant quantities; the West Cameroun has important exports of wood, rubber, and palm kernels.

In the East Cameroun, cocoa and bananas were, until recently, by far the dominant export crops. During the last decade, however, the production of bananas has declined for a number of reasons—among them, crop diseases and terrorist activity in the principal banana-growing areas—while cocoa output has increased. In the meantime, coffee production has increased prodigiously. The output of forest products has become the third most important export, and cotton now ranks as an important export commodity. Thus, the structure of the economy, though still remaining oriented toward agriculture, has in fact changed remarkably over the past several years. To a large extent, these increases in output were preceded by significant improvements in the transportation system, which opened up new areas for production on a large scale. Unlike the traditional money crops of cocoa and bananas, which are still largely in the hands of Africans who organize production as a family enterprise, the export crops, such as cotton and coffee, whose production is soaring, are now organized largely on a plantation basis. Many agricultural experts believe that it would be possible to achieve similar progress in the traditional crops such as cocoa if improved methods of cultivation, harvesting, and processing are used. Cocoa production now averages only 350 kilograms per hectare (1 hectare: 2.471 acres), but a few modern plantations are capable of producing up to and beyond 1,000 kilograms per hectare.

The export sector of the West Cameroun's economy is dominated by the plantations located mainly in the coastal Victoria division. The plantations, of which the most important are those run by the Cameroons Development Corporation (a statutory agency whose capital is held by the West Cameroons government and the Colonial Development and Welfare Agency in London), were originally started by the Germans following their alienation of about 250,000 acres of land. About 70,000 acres of this land throughout the territory are now under cultivation. Bananas are the principal plantation crop, and in 1958 the plantations produced roughly 63 per cent of the bananas exported by the Southern Cameroons. Rubber is the second most important crop grown on plantations and is expected eventually to replace bananas, which are gradually declining under the onslaught of almost uncontrollable diseases. Cocoa, the second most valuable export crop, is grown almost wholly on native farms. Other plantation crops are palm kernels, oil, and tea. However important the plantation sector is to the West Cameroun's export market, peasant agriculture still dominates the economic picture. Sample data taken in 1951 suggest that there were at that time some 500,000 acres in peasant cultivation as against 70,000 in the plantation areas. Further, as Kenneth Berrill warns, it is easy to overstress exported cash crops, and it should be recalled that about three-quarters of the output from native farms is consumed locally.[10]

Another aspect of the West Cameroun's economy that deserves mention is the remarkable growth and effectiveness of the cooperative producing and marketing system. Between 1952 and 1957, membership in cooperatives rose five times to 11,000, and the value of cooperative-grown produce expanded seventeen times to £3,000,000. During this period, the banana crop came to dominate the cooperative effort, with its sales worth over 60 per cent of the total receipts. As in the plantation sector, however, efforts are now being made to convince banana growers that slower-growing crops such as rubber offer them the most promising future. Table 17 gives an indication of the volume and value of the principal export commodities of the two Camerouns.

Insofar as the West Cameroun is concerned, manufacturing industry is only of slight importance at the present stage of the territory's development. The economy of the East Cameroun, although still basically preindustrial, contains a growing industrial sector. Its single important ornament is the aluminum-processing plant at Edéa, which in 1960 produced some 43,000 tons of raw aluminum. The plant, which has a capacity of 45,000 tons per annum, uses bauxites brought principally from France and only secondarily (though increasingly) from African sources. Other industries include two hydroelectric power

[10] Kenneth Berrill, *The Economy of the Southern Cameroons under United Kingdom Trusteeship* (Cambridge, Aug. 1960; mimeo.), p. 5.

Table 17. Exports from the two Camerouns (principal commodities)

West Cameroun (1960)			East Cameroun		
Commodity	Quantity	Value	Commodity	Quantity	Value
	(metric tons)	£ *		(long tons)	CFA frs.†
Cocoa	7,764	2,022,000	Cocoa (1960)	58,900	8,106,000,000
Bananas (fresh & dried)	68,534	2,625,000	Coffee "	30,510	4,579,000,000
Palm kernels	2,016	123,000	Cotton "	10,000	1,047,000,000
Palm oil	3,314	267,000	Timber "	127,000	929,000,000
Rubber	2,246	489,000	Bananas "	36,710	601,949,000
Timber (logs & milled	4,503 cu. ft.	1,279,000	Peanuts "	12,000	ca.400,000,000
			Rubber (1959)	3,956	650,055,000
			Palm kernels (1959)	22,568	893,029,000

* £1 = $2.80. † 490 CFA frs. = $1.00.

Sources: For West Cameroun, see *Report on the Cameroons under United Kingdom Administration,* 1959. For East Cameroun, see "Magistral bilan économique de M. Charles Assalé," *La Presse du Cameroun,* May 4–10, 1961, and *Cameroun, terre d'avenir* (Douala: Chambre de Commerce et d'Industrie du Cameroun, 1960), p. 64.

plants (the main one, at Edéa, with an output of 125,000 kilowatts, services the Edéa plant and the Douala area) and seven smaller thermal power plants; several cotton mills; four rice-shelling plants; a rubber latex plant; several plants extracting oils from peanuts, palm kernels, and the like; a cocoa-treatment plant; and a number of secondary industrial enterprises—most of them small—producing such items as aluminum utensils, soap, clothing, beer, shoes, and cigarettes.

Lines of External Trade

The fact that the two states of the new federation continue, as they did before unification, to trade principally with their former metropolitan powers makes it necessary to consider the foreign trade of the federation in terms of the trade of each section.

The West Cameroun's principal buyer of its bananas, rubber, and timber continues to be the United Kingdom, which takes almost 60 per cent of the exported production of those commodities. Only with respect to cocoa is the picture different; here the Netherlands are the state's principal customer. The import picture shows a more diversified market, but it, too, is dominated by the United Kingdom. In 1959 some 65 per cent of the territory's imports came from Great Britain, and the indications are that the pattern still continues. Other sellers to the West Cameroun include, in the order of their importance, the Netherlands, the United States, Germany, Japan, Italy, Belgium, and Luxembourg.

Similarly, the foreign trade of the East Cameroun continues to be dominated by the European Economic Community, particularly by France, which is the East Cameroun's principal market for its bananas, cotton, and coffee. In 1960, the Netherlands supplanted France as the East Cameroun's principal purchaser of cocoa and timber. Other important buyers within the EEC include West Germany, Italy, and Belgium. Outside the EEC the main trading partners are the United States and Switzerland. The USSR, once an important customer of Camerounian exports, is no longer so. The import market is dominated by France to a much greater extent than the export market; thus in 1959, of a total import value of 18,901,843,000 CFA francs ($77,150,-378), France was responsible for over 14,000,000,000 (ca.$57,000,000).

The data given here, it must be added, are derived from 1961 figures whenever these were available; from earlier years when more recent data were not obtainable.[11] In the light of the fact that, as far as is known, unification has not changed the two Camerouns' patterns of trade to any appreciable degree, the older figures were used because they continue to suggest the dominant patterns.

Dependence on Outside Economic Aid

Kenneth Berrill concluded in 1960, prior to the plebiscite in the British Cameroons, that whichever way that territory turned, it would still need an estimated £1,000,000 per annum to maintain its rate of economic growth.[12] The key fact for the West Cameroun is that its economy is far from being viable and that if it is to move forward sizable injections of development capital are needed. The United Kingdom, notably through its Colonial Welfare and Development Program, has been mainly responsible for providing these funds. With unification, the West Cameroun can still rely on substantial economic aid from Britain, but on a much more limited scale and within definite time limits. The United Kingdom gave the Southern Cameroons some $2,000,000 as a parting gift and extended Commonwealth preference for West Cameroun exports to September 1963. However, the West

[11] See Table 17 sources.
[12] Berrill, *The Economy of the Southern Cameroons*, p. 15.

Cameroun can still continue to rely on British markets for its primary export products. But although new development capital may still come from Great Britain, it is likely to be from private rather than public sources; the majority of the funds it needs will therefore have to come from its sister state and from public and private international sources. Already, for example, American aid is helping to pay for a part of the West Cameroun's road-building program, the UN is underwriting approximately $200,000 worth of development projects, and in 1962 U.S. Peace Corps volunteers were assigned to various primary and secondary schools in the territory.

French aid to the East Cameroun after it attained independence continued virtually on the same level as before. During 1960 and 1961 this was estimated to run close to $40,000,000, if such items as the salaries of French "technical counselors," French military aid, subsidies to Cameroun students in France, and the like are included as well as the more obvious forms of aid such as direct subventions from the French Treasury, loans, and grants. The conclusion is unavoidable that without massive foreign aid, particularly French aid, the Cameroun Federal Republic cannot continue its present rate of development. In this connection, it is interesting to note that the East Cameroun's twenty-year plan, prepared in 1959, estimated that 42 per cent of the financing of the plan, at least for the first five years (1961–1965), would have to come from "external sources." [13] Substantial international aid has already been granted the new federation. One example of this is the extension of the Dauala-Yaoundé railway northward, which was initially financed by a consortium of EEC, American, and French funding amounting to about $31,615,000.

SOCIAL STRUCTURE

Ethnic Divisions and Their Strength

The Cameroun Republic presents an unusually complex and fragmented ethnic picture. It has been estimated that there are over 136 identifiable linguistic groupings in the East Cameroun and about 100 vernaculars in the West Cameroun. Of the total population of about 4,100,000 (approximately 860,000 in the West; 3,225,000 in the East), only about 17,500 are non-African. On the basis of the taxonomy suggested by Murdock, with some modifications, a rough breakdown of

---

[13] Société Générale d'Etudes et de Planification (for the Ministry of the Plan, Republic of Cameroun), *Cameroun: Plan de développement économique et social*, vol. I, *Rapport général* (Paris and Yaoundé, 1960), pp. 37–40.

the principal ethnic groups can be made.[14] The figures given in
Table 18 are approximate, since no census has ever been conducted
in the East Cameroun, and the last census in the West Cameroun was
part of the 1953 Nigerian census. (The latest "official" figure for the
federation, reported in the UN *Monthly Bulletin of Statistics,* is for
December 1961: 4,907,000.)

Table 18. Principal ethnic divisions in the Cameroun
(approximate numbers)

Groups	West	East
Southern Nigerians	155,000	—
Northwestern and Coastal Bantu	24,000	267,000
Equatorial Bantu	—	773,000
Pygmy	—	6,500
Cameroun Highlanders	375,000	728,071
Plateau Nigerians	12,500	28,000
Eastern Nigritic	20,000	248,000
"Kirdi" (northern animist)	?	550,000
Islamized pagans	—	65,000
Chadic	15,000	55,000
Fulani	15,000	400,000
Non-Cameroun Africans	100,000	80,000

Among the Southern Nigerians, who are found mainly in the West
Cameroun, the aggressive and commercially adept Ibo, numbering
some 25,000, are the most important. The Ibo have tended increasingly
to dominate the petty commerce of the West Cameroun and are, as
a consequence, resented by many indigenous West Camerounians. A
measure of the importance of this fact is that the threat of Ibo domination was skillfully utilized by Premier Foncha and the KNDP as
an argument for unification with the Cameroun Republic during the
February 1961 plebiscite. Other southern Nigerians include Ibibio,
Ekoi, Anyang, Boki, Edo, Tiv, and Ijaw.

The Northwestern and Coastal Bantu comprise a group of important ethnic units including the Douala, presently about 45,000 strong

[14] George Peter Murdock, *Africa: Its People and Their Culture History* (New
York: McGraw-Hill, 1959), pp. 12 ff. See also *Report on the Cameroons under
United Kingdom Administration,* 1959; *Rapport annuel . . . sur l'administration
du Cameroun placé sous la tutelle de la France,* 1957, pp. 14–15; and *Etat du
Cameroun: Bulletin de la Statistique Générale, Supplément* (Feb. 1958), p. 47.

and the first Camerounians to be subject to Western influences, and the Bassa-Bakoko, a grouping of about 195,000 occupying the general area of the Sanaga River Valley. The Bassa, it will be recalled, were the first of the southern ethnic groups to participate in the political violence which began in 1955.

The most important numerical component of the Equatorial Bantu is the so-called Beti-Pahouin agglomerate, a widely dispersed grouping which includes the tribes inhabiting the Yaoundé area. The principal dialects of the agglomerate are Ewondo (460,000 speakers), Bulu (128,000), and Fang (48,000).

Pygmies, thought once to have been the original inhabitants of the southern forest area, are now dispersed in small villages and isolated in the equatorial forest of the southeast.

The largest ethnic grouping in the Cameroun is that of the Cameroun Highlanders, composed principally of the Bamiléké (about 700,000); the various related tribes of the Bamenda plateau, most of them of Tikar origin (about 300,000); and the Bamun (80,000). Most Bamiléké live in the five Bamiléké departments on the East-West border, but some 100,000 have emigrated to take up residence elsewhere in the two Camerouns. The largest number of Bamiléké emigrants are found in the towns of the East Cameroun. The various Tikar tribes are also known as "grassfielders," after the characteristic cover of the Bamenda Highlands, a name that is also often used by the Bamiléké. The Bamun are of particular interest because they represent a cultural development differing greatly from that found among the Bamiléké and Tikar. The Bamun were Islamized and have enjoyed unbroken dynastic monarchical rule through (they claim) forty-four descendants of their founder. The Bamun also boast a remarkable Sultan, Njoya, who at the turn of the twentieth century invented a written language and had a history of his people inscribed in it.

Plateau Nigerians, Eastern Nigritic tribes, and the so-called "Kirdi" are different agglomerates of what are essentially numerous small communities of animist peoples living in the western hills or, in the case of the Kirdi (*kirdi* is the Fulah term for "pagan"), both as hill dwellers and as nomads on the plains of the Logone. Most of these peoples are quite primitive, particularly the Kirdi, the majority of whom still reject clothing and tend to shy away from modernizing contacts.

The Islamized pagans and the Chadic peoples are found mainly near Lake Chad. The principal groups of the latter classification are the Shuwa (Choa) Arabs, the Kanuri, and the Hausa.

Finally, the Fulani, of which there are some 415,000 in the Cameroun, are mainly pastoralists and represent the dominant ethnic group in the north. Fulani emirates, lamidates (a chiefdom ruled by a lamido, or Fulani chief), and sultanates of the Cameroun north derive from the Fulani conquests of the Chad plain at the beginning of the nineteenth century. The principal towns of the Cameroun north, such as Maroua, Garoua, and Ngaoundéré, owe much of their importance to the fact that they are also capitals of chiefdoms.

Degree and Impact of Urbanization

The Cameroun's first contacts with the West were along the coast, and it was natural that the early coastal trading centers should have been the nuclei around which the Cameroun's first urban centers grew. The burgeoning coastal towns, as nexuses of the Western exchange economy, fostered the growth of trade and, in the process, created an elite based on nontraditional values (mechanical skill, education, money, and so on), and thereby speeded the breakdown of traditional social structures. The new townsmen could assert their independence from their traditional milieus and, in so doing, escape from the ancient hierarchies of status and birth. This dissociation completed the breakdown of the Douala political system and is well on its way to destroying that of the Yaoundé (Beti) group. In point of time, of course, Douala, as the site of the first European trading activity along the Cameroun coast, was the first Camerounian town to receive the full impact of the Westernization process, though Victoria, historically the first permanent European settlement, was founded as late as 1858. Yaoundé was not occupied by Europeans until after 1890, when the Germans opened a station there. Other trading stations, such as Edéa, Tiko, Kribi, and Nkongsamba, grew into towns only after the Germans had converted them into commercial centers or ports. Douala became, after 1884, the largest town in the Cameroun and remains so today. Table 19 gives the current estimated population of the principal Cameroun towns.

Two related sets of problems illustrate the continuing difficulties faced by the Cameroun's urban centers: (1) the relative sociodemographic and economic decline of the indigenous population of the towns in the face of the increasingly numerous immigrant populations and (2) the complex social and economic problems caused by the growing inability of the towns to absorb the influx. These are, of course, problems that are common to many urban centers in Africa; what makes them crucial in the Cameroun is that the situations they create have promoted recruitment to extremist political causes and thereby undermined attempts to solve them. Three Cameroun towns, Douala, Yaoundé, and Kumba, serve as useful examples.

Table 19. Principal Cameroun urban centers (estimated population, 1962)

West Cameroun		East Cameroun	
Tiko	15–20,000	Douala	130,000
Kumba	15,000	Yaoundé	59,000
Victoria-Bota	15,000	Nkongsamba	25,000
Mamfe	12,500	Foumban	18,000
Buea	5,000	Maroua	18,000
Bamenda	5,000	Garoua	15,400
		Dschang	15,000
		Ebolowa	15,000
		Ngaoundéré	15,000
		Bafoussam	8,600
		Sangmélima	7,500
		Eséka	6,600
		Batouri	6,000
		Edéa	6,000
		Mbalmayo	5,500
		Kribi	3,200

Douala is the Cameroun's largest town, its principal port, and its most important commercial center. Its urban social problems are also the most serious. One cause of this is the change in the ethnic composition of the town, a change due principally to the influx of workers from the north and east. In 1947, the town had a population of 51,077, and the Douala, the original inhabitants, comprised 22,927, or 46 per cent, of the total. The Bassa, Bamiléké, and Beti then represented respectively only 14.9, 16.3, and 16.3 per cent of the population. In 1955–1956, official census figures revealed that the pattern had changed considerably. The Douala had not increased to any measurable degree (they then numbered 23,073) but they now constituted only 20.4 per cent of a total population of almost 125,000. Moreover, other ethnic groups had increased in size, particularly the Bamiléké, who with almost 30,000 now constituted 26.2 per cent of the total. The immigrants, unfortunately for the Douala, were aggressive and commercially vigorous and by 1956 had come to dominate petty trading and retailing, transportation, and most of the unskilled labor fields. They had even made inroads into the so-called "learned trades" (government service, mission work, education), at the expense of the local Douala who had formerly dominated these fields. Incidental to the influx of unskilled labor into Douala have been the growth of unemployment and the attendant problems caused by the presence of a large idle group. Government censuses of the unemployed in 1960 estimated that about 25,000 unemployed lived in Douala. One authority has pointed out that if the estimates include those who have never held a job, and hence have never been counted as "unemployed" on the censuses, approximately—at a minimum—one-fourth of the population of Douala is composed of men without visible means of support.[15] The presence of this unemployed mass undoubtedly contributed to the recurrence of UPC extremism and violence in Douala and to the fact that the UPC still commands a considerable degree of loyalty within the immigrant community. The rapid growth of Douala, its large numbers of unemployed, and the prevalence of a good deal of ethnic tension among the *nouveaux arrivés* seems also to have contributed to the growth of prostitution and of widespread alcoholism in the town.

These problems are duplicated on a lesser scale in Yaoundé and Kumba. In Yaoundé, it is the Bamiléké again who represent the principal economic threat to the local Beti. Here, as in Douala, the Bamiléké have taken almost complete control of petty trading and transport. Moreover, again a sizable group of unemployed continue to be a source of tension and political unrest. In Kumba, it is not the Bamiléké who constitute the principal threat but immigrant Ibo and others from Eastern Nigeria, who are just as aggressive and enterprising as the Bamiléké across the eastern border. Exact figures are not available, but it has been estimated that almost one-third of Kumba's population is Eastern Nigerian in origin. The Ibo have taken over much of the petty trading and, like the Bamiléké, tend to gather local transportation into their own hands. The indigenous Camerounians in Kumba resent these developments, and their resentment provided a political field which

[15] George Chaffard, "Cameroun à la veille de l'indépendance," *Europe France Outremer*, no. 355 (June 1955), p. 65. The figures and analysis derive from Etat du Cameroun, Service de la Statistique Générale, *Résultats du recensement de la ville de Douala (1955–1956): Population autochtone* (Yaoundé, 1957).

both the KNDP, with its anti-Ibo propaganda, and the extremist OK could plough with ease. It is significant to note that the Kumba area is one of the OK's principal strongholds and to recall that Kumba town voted 5,349 to 719 (the Ibo, as non-Camerounians, could not vote) in favor of unification at the February 1961 plebiscite.

Socioethnic Problems

In the previous section the Bamiléké and the Ibo were described as the core of a wave of migration into the towns, a wave which posed important socioeconomic—and, in the final analysis, political—problems for the urban centers. At least one consequence of the influx has been a restructuring of the African social milieus that resulted in the newcomers' assuming leading, and often dominant, positions in the community. In another context, the Bamiléké and Ibo also exemplify the problems caused by large-scale extra-urban migration in both Camerouns.

The Bamiléké, found mainly in the five Bamiléké departments, number some 700,000, to which must be added another 100,000 who have taken up residence elsewhere in the East Cameroun, particularly in the larger towns. The wave of Bamiléké migration began and continues for a number of related reasons. The Bamiléké areas are over-populated (up to 800 per square mile in some localities) in respect to the land traditionally available within these areas. Moreover, undivided inheritance of rights and property restricts the number of claimants on the land and forces the younger siblings of the named heir off the land, either to found their own line or to seek their fortunes outside the traditional areas. Further, tradition endows Bamiléké chiefs with considerable power over the land, inasmuch as the chief, who is considered to hold the land in trust for the tribe, has the authority to allocate usufructuary rights—though never ownership in the Western sense. Still further, the chiefs have tended to resist change and modern technology and often abuse their powers, at least in the eyes of the younger Bamiléké. The net result of this situation has been, over the years, a growing wave of migration from the Bamiléké areas, principally southward in the direction of Douala and east toward Yaoundé.

The emigrants, highly energetic and opportunistic by nature, gradually took economic control of the Mungo region between the Bamiléké area and Douala and have come to dominate the Douala area itself. Mention has already been made of their influence elsewhere in the

Cameroun. An important by-product of the exodus has been the high level of politicization among the immigrants, a fact which has made them vocal opponents of government, of the old mores, and of the traditional Bamiléké chiefs and often willing recruits to the UPC maquis. When the Republic was created and large numbers of *maquisards* "returned to legality" following relegalization of the UPC, the government of Prime Minister Ahidjo secured the adherence of a group of Bamiléké deputies (most of them ex-UPC *maquisards*) and even made the group's leader, Pierre Kamdem-Ninyim—an important maquis chief—a Minister of State. The move was interpreted, with justification, as an attempt to placate the younger Bamiléké dissidents, both in the Bamiléké areas and in the principal towns. Kamdem-Ninyim was subsequently eased out of the cabinet, but only, apparently, when the government felt that the Bamiléké situation had become more manageable.

Much of the tension underlying Bamiléké unrest has not been directly faced, however, by the East Cameroun government. Some administrative devolution has taken place, and most guerrilla bands have been gradually decimated due to stringent government measures. But the basic problems concerning the use of Bamiléké land, the power of the chiefs, the progressive alienation of Bamiléké youth, and the frictions caused by Bamiléké emigration have yet to be fully confronted.

In the West Cameroun almost continuous migratory activity seems to be the rule. Kenneth Berrill summarizes the situation:

There is migration into the Bamenda Highlands by Northern Fulani seeking tse-tse-free grazing for their cattle; there are migrants from the over-populated villages of East Nigeria who come to provide labour both for plantations and peasant farms; there is migration within the Territory as Cameroonians move from the bush to the roads or from village to village in search of better land; and above all there is the now traditional migration from interior to coast of young men coming for a few years to work on the plantations and see something of a wider world.[16]

The process has produced a variety of tensions throughout the territory. Grasslanders on the northern fringes of the Bamenda plateau have been in almost constant friction with the herding Fulani. Inhabitants of the southern portions of the West Cameroun, particularly the Victoria division, are faced with Ibo-Ibibio economic pene-

---

[16] Berrill, *The Economy of the Southern Cameroons*, p. 2.

tration from the west and the presence of large numbers of grassfielders and Eastern Nigerians in the labor force of the plantations.
The importance of these tensions—with regard to the Ibo especially
—has already been noted in a previous section, but it is worth reiter-
ating that the presence of immigrant outsiders in the territory was
sufficiently threatening to be useful as political capital for two of the
three major West Camerounian parties (the Kamerun National Democratic Party and the Cameroons Peoples' National Convention).

Modern Social and Economic Groups

Almost all East Camerounian trade unions, with the exception of
a few local ones, play an important role in the political life of the
country. Wherever trade unionism is strong in the East Cameroun—
in the principal towns and in some plantations in the southwest—the
unions have no hesitation about endorsing candidates, actively campaigning on behalf of parties, and even occasionally presenting candidates of their own under independent or new party labels. But,
however important the labor organizations have been to the formation
of some parties or are to the current support of others, the influence
of the trade union movement is still small even though it was estimated that in 1959 26 per cent of the East Cameroun's salaried labor
force of about 135,000 had trade union connections. Moreover, what
trade unionism exists is in the southern areas; almost none is found
in the predominantly Muslim north.

Trade union activity is rather more significant in the West Cameroun: in 1959 some 14,880 of the salaried labor force of 37,828—
39.3 per cent—were connected with trade union organizations. The
two principal unions, the Cameroons Development Corporation Workers' Union and the Likomba Plantation Workers' Union, have organized workers in the largest plantation enterprises in the West
Cameroun. These two trade unions, unlike the largest unions in the
East, have not become appendages of any of the main political parties,
a fact largely due to their heterogeneous ethnic composition. In their
recent study the Ardeners and Warmington have shown that in January 1958, of a total of 17,742 CDC workers enumerated, 11,426 originated in various parts of the British Cameroons, 5,414 came from
Nigeria, 895 came from the French Cameroun, and 7 from other
African areas.[17] A similar ratio is found on the Likomba plantations

[17] Edwin Ardener, Shirley Ardener, and W. A. Warmington, *Plantation and Village in the Cameroons* (London: Oxford University Press for the Nigerian Institute
of Social and Economic Research, 1960), pp. 356–358.

of Elders & Pfyfe. All West Cameroun labor organizations have, since unification, cut formal ties with their Nigerian parent organizations. Even though the trade unions now tend to be apolitical, the CDCWU at least provided valuable training and no doubt furthered the political careers of such important politicians as Dr. E. M. L. Endeley, who was the first CDCWU president, and N. N. Mbile, who followed Endeley in that post.

As the French Cameroun became increasingly autonomous, the Cameroun branches of French trade unions (these branches were the first trade unions in the territory) became either independent or semiautonomous in relation to their parent organizations in France. This pattern of increasing disassociation continues today. In January 1957, the Union des Syndicats Autonomes Camerounais (USAC), formed in 1952, and the Confédération Générale de Travail Camerounaise (CGTC or CGTK), which had been created in 1956 as the Cameroun branch of the French Confédération Générale de Travail (CGT), participated with other trade union organizations from the more "militant" African countries (that is, Guinea, Ghana, and Mali) in the formation of the independent Union Générale des Travailleurs d'Afrique Noire (UGTAN). The USAC has now almost no international connections, but the CGTC and the Union Générale des Travailleurs du Cameroun (UGTC) continue to maintain their affiliations with both UGTAN and the Communist World Federation of Trade Unions (WFTU). The other labor unions maintain liaison with their international or French affiliates but enjoy a great deal of local autonomy. As noted previously, the labor unions were in the vanguard of Camerounian nationalism, and the UPC still has close connections with both the CGTC and the UGTC. Most of the other unions, including a variety of minor ones not noted in Table 20, give their political allegiance to the government or the ruling party, the Union Camerounaise.

Table 20 also gives an indication of the range of modern agricultural organizations found in the Federal Republic. In both states the cooperative movement has flourished and now organizes a significant number of the smaller plantations on both sides of the frontier. Many of these cooperatives are organized along ethnic lines, principally because of the convenience of dealing with people of the same background and because the plantations, more often than not, tend to be physically located within the traditional geographic boundaries of the tribe to which their owners belong. In the West Cameroun, most

Table 20. Principal modern social and economic groups in the Cameroun

Name and type (by function)	State	Affiliates	External connections	Approx. membership	Commentary
Labor unions					
Confédération Camerounaise des Syndicats Croyants (CCSC)	E	42	International Federation of Christian Trade Unions (IFCTU)	5,000	Formed 1948 as local of French Confederation of Christian Workers; in 1955 became independent
Union des Syndicats Autonomes Camerounaise (USAC)	E	55	None	10,000	Formed 1952, participated in formation of UGTAN
Confédération Africaine des Syndicats Libres-Force Ouvrière (CASL-FO)	E	99	International Confederation of Free Trade Unions (ICFTU)	5,000	Formed 1958, formerly territorial union of CGT-FO
Confédération Générale de Travail Camerounaise (CGTC)	E	197	World Federation of Trade Unions (WFTU), UGTAN, UPC (representation on UPC Executive Committee)	18,000	Formed 1956, formerly a local of French CGT; participated in formation of UGTAN; admitted to WFTU, 1957
Union Générale des Travailleurs du Cameroun (UGTC)	E	—	UGTAN, WFTU, UPC (representation on UPC Executive Committee)	no information	Branch of CGCT
Cameroons Development Corporation Workers' Union (CDCWU)	W	—	ICFTU	10,700 (1958)	Principally in Victoria and Kumba divisions; formerly affiliated with National Council of Trade Unions, Nigeria (NCTUN)
Likomba Plantation Workers' Union	W	—	ICFTU	900 (1958)	Principally in Victoria (Likomba and Tiko); formerly affiliated with NCTUN

Table 20. Principal modern social and economic groups in the Cameroun (*cont.*).

Name and type (by function)	State	Affiliates	External connections	Approx. membership	Commentary
Other West trade unions	W	11	—	5,000	Total trade union membership ca.14,880; total work force in 1959 = 37,828; 41% of work force unionized
Other East trade unions	E	31	—	4,000	Total work force (paid or salaried) in 1961 ca.145,000; 26% of work force unionized
Agricultural organizations					
Cooperative Union of Bakweri Farmers	W	14	Export handled through Cameroons Development Corp.	2,000	Organized by E. L. M. Endeley in 1951–1952 using tribal basis, principally a marketing org.
Other cooperatives in West (by type)	W	191 (total)	None	16,251	Capitalized at £489,919 with a turnover for 1959 of £3,091,573; many organized on tribal basis
Thrift and credit		6		183	
Thrift and loan		5		215	
Produce and marketing		165		ca.14,000	
Secondaries		15		470	
Action Paysanne	E	ca.200	Loosely allied with Union Camerounaise Party	2–5,000	Quasi-political organization, organized 1957 principally to protect interests of Bulu and Fang farmer groups; Gaston Medou, president, is deputy to Eastern Assembly; most important are 4 coffee-producing and marketing co-ops of Bamiléké (8,000) and Bamoun (3,000) planters

Cooperatives in East	E	ca.1,500	None	10–15,000	None
Consumers		5			
Secondaries		4			
Produce and marketing		65			
Workers		4			
Mutual credit		ca.1,300			
Employees		2			
Others					
Boy Scouts	W		International Boy Scouts	2,000	
Girl Scouts	W		International Girl Guides	325	
Union des Etudiants Kamerunais, National Union of Kamerun Students	E-W	59	Informal, with UPC	?	Most Cameroun students studying abroad
Boys' brigades	W	4	Cam.-Baptist Convention		

cooperatives profess to be nonpolitical and to have little to do with the main political parties. This is not entirely true. The Bakweri cooperatives, for one, are intimately linked to Dr. Endeley and the CPNC.

In the East Cameroun, the picture is less clear. Although figures are not available, it is reported that many cooperatives have working liaisons with political parties. A loose organization, the Union Bamiléké, that grouped Bamiléké peasants and planters and included some cooperatives, was organized in 1948 for solidary, security, and political reasons. The Union Bamiléké was "dissolved" in 1961, and its members formally committed themselves to support the Union Camerounaise. A similar grouping of Bulu and Fang farmers, the Action Paysanne, organized originally to advance the agricultural interests of its members, became a political party and in 1956 elected nine deputies to the French Cameroun Legislative Assembly. The president and co-founder of Action Paysanne, Gaston Medou, is currently a member of the Eastern Assembly but sits under the Union Camerounaise banner, indicating this organization's current support.

These and a large number of other organizations play various roles in Camerounian society. They may act as organizational bases for and spokesmen of economic and social interests. They often provide psychological reinforcement for individuals of the same ethnic, social, and economic status and/or occupational categories. Finally, as seen above, to gain their ends they not infrequently become actively engaged in politics or ally themselves with political parties. These organizations, according to the reasons for their existence, may perform any or all these roles; indeed, in the context of the Cameroun's changing internal situation, it is often difficult to categorize them in this way. A case in point is the Action Paysanne (see Table 20), which is at once an interest group (representing a well-defined sector of farmers and planters), a social organization (it sponsors local and regional meetings at which not only the business of the organization is discussed but the members may as well participate in dances, dinners, "socials," and the like), and an adjunct to a political party, the Union Camerounaise.

Organizations of the type discussed here are often described in terms of the extent to which they have and maintain ties with particular tribal or ethnic groups. It is rather difficult, in both Camerouns, to dissociate these bodies from tribal or ethnic connections, simply because many use ethnic identification as the submerged base on which organization, programs, and goals are built. The distinction between "tribal" and "nontribal" ties becomes easily blurred since an organization's tribal identification very often simply represents a convenient framework for organization and may facilitate communication within the group. The point is simply that (for example) although a group of Bamiléké planters may organize a producers' cooperative, their primary concern is agricultural production and the Bamiléké connection is a convenience rather than the reason for the organization. It makes more sense, then, to discuss these groups according to the interests they represent or the activity in which they engage and to consider tribal affiliation (if it exists) as a factor which becomes important only to the degree that the organization stresses it. This is not to deny that there are many groups which function as modern or traditional organs of specific ethnic groups. The latter, however, usually take on importance if they become or are active participants in the political arena. They are more appropriately discussed in the section "Political Dynamics" below (see pp. 315 ff.).

The groups categorized in Table 20 are therefore modern groups to which the question of tribal or ethnic identification either is irrelevant or, if such identification exists, is secondary to the purposes of the organizations.

Religion

In neither of the Cameroun states is there an offical religion. Since the beginning of colonial activity in the Cameroun, various Christian missions have been proselytizing in the territory. The result of their activities has been that roughly 27 per cent of the population in the West Cameroon and 35 per cent of that of the East Cameroun have been Christianized. Muslim influences have operated for centuries in the Cameroun north, but not until the beginning of the nineteenth century and the jihad of Osman Dan Fodio was much of the Camerounian reaches of the Chad plain and Adamawa plateau Islamized. Two consequences of Muslim activity in the north are that Christian mission work has been more or less limited to the area south of the Adamawa plateau and that the overwhelming number of Cameroun Christians are found in that region. It is estimated that there are about 600,000 Muslims in the East Cameroun, most of them residing north of the inland forest plateau. Proselytizing on the part of both Christian missionaries and Muslim teachers still goes on, much of it directed at the large numbers of animist peoples comprising about 45 per cent of the population in the East and about 65 per cent in the West Cameroun. Table 21 provides an estimated breakdown of confessional affiliation in the two states.

The Christian missions, among the first Westernizing influences in the Cameroun, have tended to dominate the educational effort in the two states and continue to provide a variety of medical and social services such as hospitals, leprosaria, dispensaries, maternity centers, orphanages, and the like. In the East Cameroun 17 of the 24 hospitals and 69 of the 395 infirmaries and dispensaries are operated by religious voluntary agencies. In the West Cameroun the voluntary agencies operate 2 of the 21 hospitals, all the maternity centers, and both leprosaria. In both Camerouns the social service institutions—hospitals, schools, and so on—that are run by the voluntary agencies operate under government supervision and benefit from partial public subsidy.

Table 21. Religious affiliation in the Cameroun (as estimated for 1959) *

	Catholic		Protestant		Muslims
	Adherents	Catechumens	Adherents	Catechumens	
East Cam.	677,629	93,522	ca.500,000	?	550,000
West Cam.	85,595	9,836	98,138	10,725	25,000
Totals	763,224	103,358	ca.598,138	10,725 (?)	575,000

* In 1960 it was estimated that there were about 600,000 animists in the West Cameroun and about 1,500,000 in the East Cameroun. The *Annuaire des Diocèses d'Expression Française* (Paris, 1961) gives the 1960 Catholic figures (for East Cameroun only) as 703,820 Catholics and 93,172 catechumens.

Education

Unification of the Camerouns has not yet markedly affected the educational systems of the two states. Ultimately all education [18] above the primary level is to come under federal control, but until the necessary groundwork is laid to reconcile a system based upon French matriculation and grading patterns with one based upon British models, the two states' educational structures will retain their preunification characteristics.

The West Cameroun's system is organized to provide a thirteen-year consecutive, highly articulated pattern: four years junior primary,

[18] For an expanded discussion of this subject, see Victor T. Le Vine and Henri M'Ballah, "[Education in the] Federal Republic of Cameroon," in Helen Kitchen, ed., *The Educated African* (New York: Praeger, 1962), pp. 519–532.

four years senior primary, and five years secondary. Because of the high selection standards for admission into secondary levels, most students do not progress beyond the primary grades. Those that enter secondary schools work toward the Cambridge School Certificate. Over 80 per cent of all primary pupils attend voluntary agency (missions and the like) schools; all the West Cameroun's secondary schools are run by voluntary agencies. The western state has no establishments of higher education, although students from the West Cameroun have had access to the University Colleges at Ibadan and Nsukka, Nigeria, and to the Nigerian Colleges of Arts, Science, and Technology at Ibadan, Enugu, and Zaria on an equal footing with students from Nigeria. Government scholars have also been attending universities in England, the United States, and Ghana. Most of these students have been financed by scholarships or grants provided by the Nigerian, British, or American governments. Currently, although financial assistance is still available to West Cameroun students studying abroad through official channels of these three countries, the Cameroun federal government and private foreign agencies have increasingly underwritten the cost involved. Finally, limited teacher education is available at both mission and government schools, but such training does not provide adequately for the total system since over 44 per cent of all teachers in the primary grades have had no training beyond Standard VI.

Primary education accounts for 96.8 per cent of the total enrollment in the East Cameroun's schools. The average primary course, patterned on French models, consists of two years of preparatory courses, two years of elementary courses, and two years of intermediate courses. Since January 1960, there has been a serious attempt to give the elementary history, geography, and civics courses an African and "national" orientation. There are two alternative programs of secondary schooling: a short self-contained course for ages 12 to 16, designed for those who do not plan to continue their studies, and a longer program for ages 12 to 19 leading to the baccalaureate. The East Cameroun has developed numerous and diversified facilities for technical training, and the number of schools offering teacher-training courses is constantly being expanded.

Table 22 gives the most recently available educational statistics for the two states.

In 1961, more than 1,000 East Camerounian students were enrolled in foreign secondary and technical school and universities, most of

Table 22. Schools and enrollments in the Cameroun Federal Republic

Type of school	Total enrolled	Government		Voluntary agency	
		Enrolled	Schools	Enrolled	Schools
West Cameroun					
Primary (1958)	60,904	10,414	71	50,490	433
Secondary (1962)	923	51	1	872	6
Teacher training (1962)	953	101	1	852	11
Vocational—technical (1962)	106	106	1	—	—
Higher and postsecondary enrolled abroad (1958)	63	—	—	—	—
East Cameroun					
Primary (1961)	330,393	102,000	728	228,983	2,013
Secondary (1962)	18,387	5,975	22	12,412	62
Vocational—technical (1962)	5,740	2,691	51	3,049	20
Teacher training (1958)	1,808	570	5	1,238	7
Higher (1962)					
a. Cam. Federal University	588	588	1	—	—
b. Cam. School of Administration	115	115	1	—	—

them—including 504 on scholarships—in French institutions of higher learning. It was reported that in 1961 four Cameroun students were in Czech schools, two in the USSR, one in Yugoslavia, two in Tunisia, and one in India. In 1961 a National Center for Advanced Study was opened in Yaoundé, which, in 1962, became the Cameroun Federal University. In addition to the university, higher training is provided by the National School of Public Administration, and the Institute of Camerounian Research at Yaoundé is available for advanced study and research in the physical and social sciences.

PRESS AND COMMUNICATIONS MEDIA

As is the case in many African states, the press is restrained, but not altogether controlled. This generalization usually applies, however, only to the East Cameroun. The number of newspapers varies from month to month, but five (four in the East, one in the West) can be said to be more or less permanent.

The Cameroun's only daily, *La Presse du Cameroun,* is published in Douala and has an almost completely eastern circulation. The *Presse* is editorially apolitical, is owned by the Paris-Soir chain (which also publishes dailies in Dakar, Abidjan, and elsewhere), and reports local and international news without comment. It is, however, supervised by the government, which approves political notices, letters to the editor, and announcements of a political nature. It steers clear of controversy and follows official guidance about matters the government wishes to play down or suppress.

The only other regular private newspaper is *L'Effort Camerounais,* published weekly by the Paulist Fathers in Yaoundé. *L'Effort* follows a relatively liberal line editorially and is often critical of the government. Within the last several years, a number of issues have been confiscated, including one in April 1962 which reported the death of twenty-five government prisoners in a train on its way to Yaoundé, a story the government very much wished suppressed. The issue in question was seized and its editor, a French priest by the name of Fertin, summarily deported. Two government papers in the East are more or less permanent: one is *L'Unité,* the official weekly organ of the Union Camerounaise, the government party; the other is *Le Bamiléké,* published under governmental auspices in the Bamiléké area.

In the West, the first newspapers appeared in 1960 in Victoria in the form of two weeklies which, until recently, appeared to publish without governmental interference. The *Kamerun Times* reflects KNDP views, while the other, the *Cameroons Champion,* reflected that of the CPNC and Dr. Endeley until it suspended publication in May 1962. There are indications that some official pressures were exerted to speed the collapse of the *Champion,* already tottering following the death of its founder, M. Peter Motomby-Woleta.

A number of other "newspapers" appear from time to time in the East Cameroun, most of them mirroring the views of opposition groups. The UPC currently has no official voice, but some of its militants publish various newssheets in printed or mimeographed form. These are devoted principally to violent denunciation of the government and its policies. The UPC sheets, under such titles as *Abolégé, L'Etoile, Le Crabe Noir, La Voix du Peuple,* and so on, are usually seized after a few issues but subsequently reappear under different mastheads. The Démocrates issue an irregular paper, *Le Démocrate,* which, however, is little read and appears so infrequently as to be of little importance.

Radio is wholly a government-controlled enterprise. The Radiodiffusion Camerounaise broadcasts from Yaoundé and Douala, with transmitters at Garoua, Ngaoundéré, and, recently, Bula. The West Cameroun had, until unification, a recording studio affiliated with the Nigerian Broadcasting Company, but this has since been closed down.

At the present stage of unification, little has been done to integrate the news and communications media except in the area of radio and telegraph services. The fact that newspapers must still serve two different language areas has maintained the geographical separation of the areas in which the principal newspapers are disseminated. It is, of course, possible to obtain copies of *La Presse du Cameroun* in Buea (brought over by air or boat from Douala), but it is local (and Nigerian and British) papers that still command most readers in the western state.

The Political Process

FORMAL STRUCTURE

The formal structure of the Cameroun Federal Republic is defined by the new constitution which became effective on October 1, 1961. This date also marked other events: the termination of the British Southern Cameroons trusteeship and the end of the Cameroun Republic born on January 1, 1960. It is of some interest to recall that the constitution of 1960 had created a republic that, with some minor adaptations to the local situation, was modeled on the Gaullist constitution of the Fifth Republic. It was a resemblance existing not only in the wording of the document but in the nature of the organs created by it, especially in the powers and prerogatives of the President. The 1961 constitution, however, owed very little to its predecessor. The document which emerged from the series of Cameroun-Cameroons conferences in the spring of 1961 was a curious mixture of presidential and parliamentary governmental forms, a mélange bearing the imprint of a series of political compromises between the respective positions of Ahidjo and Foncha. Essentially, the document appeared to have been drafted with three objectives in mind: (1) to create a set of federal institutions and delimit federal and state jurisdictions, (2) to preserve virtually intact the local autonomy hitherto enjoyed by the two states, and (3) to maintain as long as possible the political *status quo* in both Camerouns.[19]

Federal Divisions

Article 1, among other things, designates the former British Southern Cameroons and the Republic of Cameroun as the West and the East Cameroun, respectively. Until the United Nations ratified the results of the February 1961 plebiscite in the British Northern Cameroons, both Foncha and Ahidjo officially hoped that the Northern Cameroons would become the third component of the federation.

Federal Organs

Articles 4 through 37 of the constitution describe the organization and competence of the federal government and its various organs.

Federal authority, according to Article 4, is exercised by the President of the Federal Republic and the National Federal Assembly. The President, assisted by a Vice-President, is at once head of state and the chief of the federal government. Both President and Vice-President serve five-year terms following their election—from a single list—by direct, secret, and universal suffrage (Articles 8–10). A list of so-called "Transitional and Special Dispositions" (Articles 48–60), appended to the main body of the document, stipulate that until the tenure of the incumbent President of the Cameroun Republic expires, he and the incumbent Premier of the Southern Cameroons are to serve respectively as President and Vice-President of the Federal Republic. The effect of this dispensation was to guarantee Ahidjo and Foncha the top federal executive positions until May 5, 1965, when the former's presidential mandate under the 1960 constitution ends.

The Federal President selects the members of a federal government "from the inhabitants of each state." Although the constitution is silent on the subject of a division of ministries between the two states, it is nonetheless clear that both states will be represented in the federal cabinet. The federal cabinet named on October 20, 1961, included five West Camerounians, one as a full minister (S. Muna Tandeng,

---

[19] The circumstances surrounding the drafting of the 1961 constitution have been elsewhere discussed by the present writer: "The New Cameroon Federation," *Africa Report,* VI, no. 11 (Dec. 1961), 7, 8, 10, and "Unifying the Cameroons," *West Africa,* July 15, 1961, pp. 774–775. For a constitutional analysis of the federal constitution, see the two articles by P. F. Gonidec, "Les institutions politiques de la République Fédérale du Cameroun," *Civilisations,* XI, no. 4 (1961), 370–395, and XII, no. 1 (1962), 13–26.

Transport Mines, Posts, and Tele-communications), three as deputy
ministers (A. Jua Ngom, Public Health; E. Egbe Tabi, Justice; and
Nzo E. Kang, Foreign Affairs), and one Undersecretary of State
(Simon Nji, Production). There is no provision that federal ministers
be members of the Federal Assembly, and, in fact, at least three of
the eastern group of federal ministers were not parliamentarians (Jen-
Faustin Betayéné, Minister of Foreign Affairs; Charles Onana Awana,
Minister Delegate to the Presidency for Finance and the Plan; and
Dr. S. Tchoungui, Minister of Public Health).

In addition to the usual executive functions, powers, and prerogatives, the Federal President is given several other special powers by
the constitution. He appoints, after "consultation," the respective prime
ministers and cabinets of the states. He must be consulted by the
governments of the two states "before these Governments take measures which might affect (*susceptibles d'avoir des incidences*) the life
of the Federation" (Article 13). In practice, according to some authorities, this could give the President the power to intervene if either
state government does anything which might affect the nation as a
whole. Article 13 is reinforced by Article 14, which gives the President
the right to seek an advisory opinion from the Federal Court of Justice if state legislation appears to contravene the federal constitution
or a federal law. Further, in wording almost exactly like that employed by the celebrated Article 16 of the constitution of the Fifth
French Republic, the President may "in case of grave peril threatening the integrity of the territory, the life, independence, or institutions
of the nation" proclaim a state of emergency by decree and then
"take all measures he judges necessary." In so doing, he is limited
only by the necessity of "consulting" with the prime ministers of the
states and by the presence of the Federal Assembly, which may meet
for the duration of emergency.[20] In all, the constitution creates a
hybrid President who combines attributes of a British-style Governor-
General, a Fifth Republic President, and an American chief executive.
This new type of presidency does not appear to have parallels in
present or past constitutional practice.

Although there is no direct evidence to substantiate it, it has been
suggested that this new type of presidential regime was tailor-made
to suit the needs and demands of President Ahidjo. The legislative

---

[20] In French constitutional practice "consultation" does not necessarily imply
that advice tendered during such "consultation" need be heeded. All that is required is formal discussion.

committee of the Cameroun National Assembly which reported out the draft of the new constitution (see footnote 22 below) defended the portions of the document relating to the presidency by a reference to France and the virtues of what it termed "Presidential democracy," a concept to which Ahidjo is known to be attached:

The aim of the advocates of this constitutional revision was . . . to consolidate the authority of the State, avoiding the creation of a machinery of state that would be too complex or cumbersome, whose slowness could prevent it from responding to the increasingly urgent needs of modern life. . . .

The presidential regime is manifestly [that regime] which can best handle these imperatives and which most properly confers upon the executive [power] the qualities of performance that one can expect of it.

One may note, moreover, that the presidential system is on the increase throughout the world and that all the democracies use it more and more frequently. The change in the parliamentary system provided, for example, by the Fifth French Republic, is evidence of a vigorous—though incomplete —orientation toward presidential democracy.

There is little question, if it is assumed that constitutional forms have some influence on political events, that the definition of the powers of the Cameroun Federal President as noted above reinforced, rather than hindered, Ahidjo's attempt to create a one-party state.

The Federal Assembly is elected for five years by direct, secret, and universal suffrage in each state on the basis of one deputy for each 80,000 inhabitants (Article 16). The "Transitional Dispositions" (Articles 53, 54) postpone federal elections until at least April 1964; until that date the two legislatures select the members of the Federal Assembly from their numbers according to the 1:80,000 ratio fixed by Article 16. The "Transitional and Special Dispositions" do not specifically fix either the number of deputies in the Federal Assembly or the division of seats between the states; this is done indirectly by stating that for the purposes of the constitution at the time of its promulgation the East Cameroun has 3,200,000 and the West Cameroun has 800,000 inhabitants (Article 60). The first Federal Assembly selected in April 1961 comprised 40 deputies from the East and 10 from the West. The official population figures on which the distribution of seats is based do not, of course, correspond to any actual enumeration of population. They may, however, be modified by a federal law if a national census is taken.

The Federal Assembly meets annually in two sessions, one of which must be devoted to the budget and neither of which is to exceed 30 days' duration. Special sessions, called either by the President or two-thirds of the Assembly, may not exceed 15 days (Article 19). Voting is by simple majority of all deputies (Article 17) except in the case of the novel procedures described by Article 18 which provide for a curious system of regional checks on national action.

According to the terms of this article:

Before their promulgation, texts may be subject to a demand for a second reading by the President of the Federal Republic acting on his own initiative, or on the demand of one of the Prime Ministers of the federated States. In the second reading, the law is not adopted *unless the majority* defined by the preceding article *comprises the majority of the votes of the deputies from each of the federated States.* [Italics are added.]

This provision, in effect, creates a type of concurrent majority voting system whose use could prevent the passage of any federal legislation or constitutional amendment (Article 47) to which either state objected. Operationally the device could have even more serious consequences. If the current membership of the Federal Assembly is used as an example, the majority envisaged by Article 18 would have to include (by definition) 6 of the 10 West Cameroun deputies, plus 21 from the eastern state. Ultimately, any 20 easterners or (even more significantly) any 5 westerners could block any legislation. On the assumption of the West Cameroun government's support, the device amounts to giving 10 per cent of the members of the Federal Assembly a permanent veto over its deliberations. In view of the political circumstances surrounding the drafting of the constitution, one suspects that Article 18 was included as a means of guaranteeing Prime Minister Foncha a maximum of local autonomy coupled with a minimum of federal interference.[21]

The constitution completes the executive-legislative-judicial triad by creating two exclusively federal courts: one, the Federal Court of Justice (articles 33, 34), to cap the judicial system and the other, the High Court of Justice (Article 36), as a special court to try cases

[21] A preplebiscite communiqué defining the general "Constitutional Position of the Southern Cameroons in the Event of It Electing to Become a Part of the Republic of Cameroun," signed by both Foncha and Ahidjo on Oct. 13, 1960, presaged this article: "Certain federal laws will only be enacted in such a way that no measures contrary to the interest of one State will be imposed upon it by the majority (system of second reading with qualified majority)." See *The Two Alternatives,* Printed by Authority [of the Commissioner of the United Kingdom in the Southern Cameroons] (Buea, Dec. 1960), p. 14.

of high treason or conspiracy against the state or to judge instances of malfeasance by the President, the Vice-President, the federal ministers, the prime ministers, and the ministers of the states. The Federal Court of Justice is the final court of appeals for federal cases arising in the state courts, adjudicates disputes between the states or between a state and the federal government, has jurisdiction over cases involving abuse of administrative discretion by federal authorities, and decides on the constitutionality of state statutes and (upon application of Article 14, for example) of legislation pending before the Federal Assembly. In the latter cases, the size of the Court is doubled by adding to it from a panel of individuals annually selected by the President "by reason of their competence or experience" (Article 34).

Finally, the constitution creates a Federal Economic and Social Council and, by indirection, a Federal Judicial Council, plus a rather shadowy Federal Coordinating Committee. The Economic and Social Council, whose functions are not spelled out in the constitution, had not been created as of July 1962 but apparently is expected to be a consultative body incorporating representatives of industry, management, labor, agriculture, and so on. Its model is undoubtedly the East Cameroun's Economic and Social Council (which will remain in existence until the Federal Council is named), itself a vague and almost purely honorific body. The Judicial Council is not specifically created but according to Article 32 is to assist the President in the administration of the judicial system, particularly in the selection of judges and in matters of discipline. The Federal Coordinating Committee, mentioned in two articles (7 and 13), will probably be an *ad hoc* body created by the President to deal with possible conflicts of state-federal jurisdiction or authority in areas where, in the language of the constitution, the "states may temporarily intervene." These areas, as defined by Article 6, include all jurisdictions which fall within federal competence only after an undefined "transition period." The Coordinating Committee must also be consulted under the circumstances foreseen in Article 13.

Federal Jurisdictions

What is the scope of federal power? Superficially, it appears quite broad. Two lists are provided, one enumerating federal jurisdictions in which federal organs may operate "immediately" (Article 5) and the other listing areas which may become subject to federal authority after the "transition period" (Article 6). The first list includes such matters as nationality, national defense, foreign affairs, currency and money, federal administration, and the like. The second list, which includes secondary education, the "regime of public liberties," local judicial organization and administration, land law, and labor regulation, touches areas now under state control. The areas defined in Article 6 will, of course, eventually become federal concerns but, according to one official commentary, "There is less urgency about having them fall under federal competence, and besides, they pose extremely delicate problems of adaptation[;] . . . the Federated States may either legislate or direct appropriate administrative services in these areas until the Federal authorities step in." [22] It is interesting to note that this article refers to one of the two entrenched rights reserved to the West Cameroun, the maintenance of the customary law courts. The other entrenched right is mentioned in Article 38, which guarantees to the states—in addition to all rights not enumerated—the maintenance of the West Cameroun House of Chiefs.

The States and Federal-State Relations

The constitution has little to say about the relations between the states and the federal government, save to define the powers of the President in respect to the selection and termination of state governments and in relation to laws passed by the state assemblies. As to the former, the President designates each state's prime minister, who must, however, be invested by his state's legislature. Upon the nomination of the prime ministers, the President names and/or dismisses the members of the state governments. When and if a state government falls—when its legislature refuses confidence or votes a motion of censure—the prime minister concerned must submit his resignation to the President. If a state government and its legislature are "in persistent disaccord," the President may dissolve the legislature on his own initiative or on that of the prime minister involved and then call new elections after two months. The President promulgates all laws passed by the state legislatures; if he disapproves of a state law sent to him for signature, he may invoke Article 18 and call for a second reading or ask the Federal Court of Justice for an advisory opinion regarding the law's constitutionality (Articles 44, 45).

The states are each arrogated all powers not specifically given to

[22] Commission des Lois Constitutionelles, de la Justice, et de la Législation, de l'Administration Générale de la République, et des Forces Armées, "Rapport," cited in *La Presse du Cameroun* (Douala), Aug. 17, 1961, p. 4. The translation is the present author's.

the federal government, and all laws preexisting the constitution and not in conflict with it are permitted to remain in force (Article 46).

Each state has its own legislature; that in the West is composed of the House of Chiefs and the Legislative Assembly, that in the East of the unicameral Legislative Assembly. The constitution fixes five years as the life of the state legislatures and their membership at 37 for the West (excluding the House of Chiefs) and 100 for the East. One other stipulation is of interest: state elections are to be held under universal suffrage and representation is to be on the basis of "each administrative unit [represented] proportionally to the number of [its] population."

All in all, the constitution is rather nebulous regarding the states and their relations to the federal center; in any case the impression is inescapable that each state is to continue to maintain a considerable amount of local autonomy.

POLITICAL DYNAMICS

At this writing there had not emerged a "national" political picture in the sense that parties, leaders, and elections were important on the federal level. The constitution—Articles 53 and 54—effectively defers federal electoral activity until 1964. Its provisions embody, as it were, a guarantee that the two political systems go their respective ways relatively unhindered until living together in a federal system becomes part of the political consciousness of voters on both sides of the interstate border. This is not to say that a national political picture will not emerge before 1964; indeed, in June and July 1962, there was already evidence that both the KNDP and the UC had begun quiet proselytization in each other's constituencies. Furthermore, the constitutional stipulation regarding the popular election of the President and Vice-President—almost certainly one of Foncha's prices for federation—may help explain what appeared in the spring and summer of 1962 to be an attempt by Ahidjo and the UC to fashion a guaranteed electorate in the East by creating a single-party state. This trend represents but one of the contrasts between the two states and (like the rest) can best be understood in the context of principally local (here eastern) politics.

West Cameroun

The first general elections to the West Cameroun Legislative Assembly, which was enlarged to 37 seats by the federal constitution, were held on January 7, 1962. Prime Minister Foncha had chosen a

good time for the election; to no one's surprise the KNDP, still bask-
ing in the warm glow of reunification, won an absolute majority in
the Western Assembly. The final allocation of seats gave the KNDP
25; Dr. Endeley's CPNC took 10, the OK 1, and 1 went to an independent who (together with the OK member) immediately declared
he would support the government. Two aspects of the results deserve
mention. One is that, with the seating of the lone OK member, all
the major parties were represented, if only briefly, in the legislature
for the first time in the history of the Southern Cameroons–West
Cameroun. The other is that the distribution of seats reflected with
some accuracy the relative importance and electoral support of the
parties.

The situation had not been as clear following the elections of January 1959, when the KNDP narrowly won 14 seats to the 12 garnered by the KNC-KPP coalition. These 1959 results hardly reflected
the relative voting support of the two parties: 75,326 for the KNDP,
51,384 for the KNC-KPP, a ratio of 3:2, which, if translated into seats
in the House, would have given the KNDP at least a three-seat majority. Moreover, further to complicate matters, a KNDP member crossed
the floor during 1959 to the KNC-KPP side, producing a 13 to 13
House and acute embarrassment in government ranks. The KNDP
salvaged the situation only because it did not have to resign—not
having been defeated in the House—and because it appointed two
special members to bolster the government side.

The KNDP's present electoral base consists of the three divisions of
Bamenda, Wum, and Mamfe, an area in which slightly more than
half of the West Cameroun's inhabitants live. The key area of the
trio is Bamenda, the most populous (more than 270,000) of the West
Cameroun's administrative divisions. Foncha and Muna are both from
Bamenda, and they, with the help of Sam Moffor, W. S. Fonyonga,
and J. H. Nganje, successfully managed to organize the grassfields
into strong KNDP constituencies. Muna's defection from the KNC
in 1958 and his subsequent delivery of Bamenda West into the KNDP
camp probably marked the beginning of Foncha's rise to power. Since
then, increasing numbers of "grassfielders" have been voting KNDP,
many even—as in the February plebiscite—against the declared
wishes of their traditional chiefs. Other districts have, of course, strong
KNDP voting contigents, but the grassfields (excepting Nkambe) remain the pivot of KNDP power. There seems little likelihood that the
KNDP will lose its hold on the country in the immediate future, es-

pecially since the increase of seats in the Western Assembly gave the more populous grassfield divisions additional—and almost unavoidably KNDP—representation.

The KNDP has no identifiable ideology or philosophy. The beginnings of a leader-centered doctrine could be detected in the Cameroun *Times*'s attempt (April 2, 1962) to spell out a "Philosophy of Foncharism," but it is doubtful if it will have much currency beyond the ranks of the party faithful. In practice, the KNDP has never bothered to elaborate a philosophy; it has always identified itself with a set of programmatic goals and has been content to let support accrue to the party and its leadership on that basis. Its most notable success, the results of the February plebiscite, can be explained, at least in part, by the fact that the simple goals of reunification, separation from Nigeria, and independence (in unity with the Cameroun Republic) were at once broad and definite enough to be translatable into popular, local terms by the party's propagandists.

KNDP leadership is securely in the hands of Prime Minister John Foncha, whose small stature and quiet demeanor conceal a strong will and an ability to remain unruffled in the most trying situations.[23] His closest associates are Solomon Tandeng Muna, currently Federal Minister of Transport; Augustin Ngom Jua, West Cameroun secretary of state for finance; Moses Ngonja Ndoke, West Cameroun secretary of state to the prime minister; Peter M. Kemcha, West Cameroun secretary of state for labor, commerce, and industry; and Victor Mukete, chairman of the CDC. Muna is physically impressive, highly articulate, and undoubtedly the most influential politician in the West Cameroun after Foncha. Jua was one of the cofounders of the KNDP in 1955, and Ndoke and Mukete followed Muna out of the KNC to the KNDP. It is interesting to note that Foncha, Jua, Muna, and Ndoke all began their careers as schoolmasters.

The Cameroon People's National Convention (CPNC) was formed in May 1960 by the merger of two opposition parties, the Kamerun National Congress (KNC) and the Kamerun People's Party (KPP). The KNC, it will be recalled, was itself the result of the coalescence in 1951 of two earlier parties—the Cameroons National Federation

[23] This writer had the opportunity to watch Foncha in just such a situation in the days immediately preceding the 1961 plebiscite. Confronted by a group of deliberately hostile Nigerian newsmen and by questions that could only be termed provocative and even insulting, Foncha never once lost his aplomb or permitted his answers to be anything less than courteous and low-keyed. His performance was very impressive.

(originally organized by Endeley and Mbile in 1949) and the Kamerun United National Congress (created by Mbile following his split with Endeley in 1951). The CPNC currently holds ten of the West Cameroun Assembly's seats. Its principal electoral support lies in the Victoria and Nkambe divisions, with some strength in Kumba and in at least one district in Wum (Wum Central). In the Victoria area the CPNC has strong support from a number of the local ethnic groups, particularly the Bakweri. Endeley is himself a Bakweri and organized the first Southern Cameroonian cooperatives among Bakweri farmers and planters.

The CPNC, like the KNDP, has no defined ideology and has traded mainly (before the plebiscite) on a program of separation from Nigeria translated into anti-Ibo sentiment and fear of the disturbances over the Cameroun border. Originally, Endeley had sought separation from Nigeria and regional status for the Southern Cameroons and had promised to seek future unification with the French Cameroun. His abandonment of the goal of unification occurred in 1955, a change in orientation which cost him the support of John Foncha, who formed his own prounification party (KNDP), and thereafter the support of Muna, Ndoke, Mukete, and other party stalwarts. During the preplebiscite months, the CPNC conducted an oddly lackadaisical campaign, starting late and showing little of its former vigor. It sought to persuade the electorate to choose the Nigerian alternative for two principal reasons: (1) Nigeria had promised regional autonomy, a status that would effectively permit the Southern Cameroons to handle the "Ibo problem" (a new twist on the old anti-Ibo plank), and (2) unification with the Republic would expose Southern Cameroonians to the dangers of terrorism and police state methods and to the political uncertainty prevailing on the Republic side. Snapshots of mutilated bodies and severed heads, alleged to have been photographed across the border, were circulated by the CPNC during the campaign.[24] At one point in the preplebiscite campaign, the CPNC offered to support the KNDP if the government endorsed an alternative not involved in the plebiscite, that of independence. The proposition was rejected by the KNDP as "treacherous," a somewhat inappropriate label since Foncha had more than once sought an extention of the trusteeship and had discussed with the Colonial Office the

---

[24] The present writer was present at one CPNC rally at Tiko at which such pictures were passed hand to hand. Similar instances were recorded by other observers.

possibility of a period of independence.[25] Shortly after the plebiscite, Endeley and the CPNC declared a political truce and pledged support to the government so that transition to the new federal status could be achieved in unity and full accord. The truce ended with the beginning of the campaign for the December 1961 elections.

Dr. Endeley and N. N. Mbile lead the CPNC. Until his death in April 1962, Peter Motomby Woleta was the CPNC's secretary-general and the guiding spirit behind the opposition newspaper, the *Cameroons Champion,* which ceased publication shortly after Motomby's death. Mbile and Motomby were cofounders of the KPP (which later merged with the KNC to become the CPNC). Endeley, who began his career as a physician, is highly intelligent and an impressive speaker but since the decline of his political fortunes has become increasingly aloof in manner.

The One Kamerun Party (OK) was formed by Ndeh Ntumazah in 1957 following the expulsion of the UPC *comité directeur* from the Southern Cameroons. The OK, since its inception, has consistently campaigned for reunification; it even went so far as to enter into informal cooperation with the KNDP in some electoral districts during the plebiscite campaign. This *ad hoc* cooperation did not engender a *rapprochement* between the two parties, however, and the government and the OK continued to denounce each other once the plebiscite was over. The OK asserted that the results of the plebiscite were due to its influence, but there is nothing to substantiate the claim. Since 1957, the OK program has been patterned along UPC lines: reunification, independence from "colonial rule," opposition to "local imperialist stooges" (applied to Foncha and Endeley with an equal lack of discrimination), and revocation of the ban on the UPC in the West Cameroun. (Although the UPC was legally reinstated in the Republic in 1960, it has not been reinstated in the West Cameroun.)

Ndeh Ntumazah is the OK's leader and principal spokesman. He appeared to plead his party's cause before the United Nations in 1957, 1958, and 1959 and has, since the plebiscite, devoted himself to strengthening the party.

In addition to the main parties, several minor parties have emerged from time to time, none of which has had any noticeable impact on

---

[25] It was reported that Foncha had asked for a five-year period of independence to precede reunification. Foncha later denied that he had asked for five years but confirmed his request for independence. See *La Presse du Cameroun,* Nov. 17, 19, 1960.

the territory. During the 1961 plebiscite three such parties campaigned for a boycott of the plebiscite, and one for union with
Nigeria. P. M. Kalle, leader of the Kamerun United Party and one of
the founders of the KNC, became Speaker of the West Cameroun
Assembly when that body met for the first time following the elections in January 1962.

Both the KNDP and CPNC operate within what is essentially the
same organizational form. There are (1) local branches, under the
direction of a local secretary, which elect representatives to the (2)
National Convention, a body usually meeting once a year. The National Convention selects a (3) national executive consisting of a president, secretary-general, a number of secretaries, and, ex officis, all
parliamentary members of the party. The day-to-day affairs of the
party are handled by the party executive, whose decisions (in theory)
are subject to ratification by the National Convention.

Finally, the political picture in the West Cameroun is completed
by mention of the Kamerun Society—a group of West Cameroun intellectuals who seek to "inform" public leaders of the background and
content of issues before the country—and of the several Bakweri cooperatives which are represented, in effect, by Dr. Endeley and the
CPNC. It has been claimed that the main trade unions in the West
Cameroun have close links with the OK, but there is little evidence
to confirm this.

East Cameroun

Although it was still possible in October 1962 to describe the West
Cameroun as a multiparty system, with an active (though emascu-
lated) opposition, the East Cameroun appeared to have shifted from
the relatively flourishing multipartite system that had existed in the
territory since 1946 to a single-party system, in which the governmental party had driven virtually all its opponents from the field. The
change, while startling, was not wholly unexpected. The number of
one-party states has been on the increase, particularly among French-
speaking African countries. This fact, plus the advantages, for both
political and economic development, that one-party government confers upon leaders anxious to assert themselves nationally and internationally, was probably not lost upon Ahidjo and his colleagues. At
the end of 1962 the only unresolved questions of the new political
situation were the future of the dwindling opposition forces and
whether the West Cameroun would also go the way of its federal

partner. The first question could not then be answered. To the second,
only an incomplete answer was available: Foncha was in fact talking
of a merger of the KNDP with the UC and had begun to put additional pressure on the opposition to do likewise.

The trend toward a one-party system. In an open letter published
on June 23, 1962, four leaders of East Camerounian opposition parties
—Charles Okala, former Foreign Minister and secretary-general of
the Parti Socialiste Camerounais (PSC); Theodore Mayi-Matip, president of the parliamentary group of the Union des Populations du
Cameroun (UPC); André-Marie Mbida, president of the Démocrates
Camerounais (DC); and Dr. Marcel Beybey Eyidi, national secretary
of the Parti Travailliste Camerounais (PTC)—rejected the concept
of a *parti unifié* (unified party) proposed by President Ahidjo. They
said that such unity could be realized only by sabotaging their own
parties for the benefit of the ruling Union Camerounaise and would
ultimately culminate in a "fascist-type dictatorship." Although rejecting the Ahidjo formula, the four opposition leaders affirmed their
willingness to work toward the formation of a "united national front"
in which there would be "neither conquerors nor conquered and in
which the majority and minority would work together towards concrete solutions to national problems."

A subsequent communiqué issued by the President's office announced that "an impressive stock of weapons" had been found in
the homes of Okala and Mbida; all four leaders were arrested, tried,
and convicted on a charge of "inciting hatred against the Government and public authority, inciting conflict between ethnic and religious communities and disseminating news prejudicial to public
authorities."

The arrest and trial of the opposition leaders was the culmination
of a development that began in 1960 with the fusion of the Mouvement d'Action Nationale Camerounaise (MANC) and the Union
Camerounaise. This was followed in April 1961 by the disintegration
of the Front pour l'Unité et la Paix (FPUP), a parliamentary group
of Bamiléké which included a number of ex-UPC maquis that had
accepted collaboration with the government. In the succeeding three
months most of its members joined the UC. The group's nominal leader,
Minister of State Pierre Kamdem Ninyim, was the first to leave in
April. During the following month six more FPUP deputies joined the
UC, and by June the group had been absorbed by the UC. Besides
Kamdem Ninyim, the group had included Victor Kanga, ex-minister

of justice and present Federal Minister of National Economy, and Happi Louis Kemayou, president of the Eastern Assembly.

The parliamentary group of the Démocrates Camerounais similarly suffered severe attrition of its ranks during 1961 and 1962; by June 1962, the Démocrates, who had begun with eight seats in 1960, were down to four. In August 1961, the Union Camerounaise held a "leadership institute" in Yaoundé where a number of speakers, particularly Assalé, Awana, Kanga, and Kame, stressed the goal of creating a party that would unite all Camerounians and indirectly cast serious doubt about the ability of parties other than the Union Camerounaise to accomplish this end.[26]

The direction in which the party and the government were heading was confirmed by President Ahidjo in a press conference on November 11, 1962. Ahidjo pointed out that the imperatives of economic development, and of "alleviating misery," had made it necessary for many African states to adopt one-party systems. This system permitted the effective mobilization of "good will, if not the totality of [human] energies." The formation of such a "great unified national movement" would make possible the forging of national unity, hitherto nonexistent. Such a movement must not, of course, be either monolithic or totalitarian. For the Cameroun, the President went on,

I say that it is desirable that there be a great unified party. In any case, I personally hope for a great party, a great unified movement that will form itself upon an entente between existing parties; a great unified national party that Camerounians will enter only after having become convinced; a party within which democracy, freedom of expression, freedom of discussion would exist; a party within which many tendencies could exist, but with the understanding that the minority would follow the lead of the majority. I believe that it is possible to reconcile effectiveness with democracy and freedom of thought. I think, even though it be only in the beginning, that such a system is necessary in the Cameroun, in Africa.[27]

Finally, Ahidjo expressed the hope that "Camerounians, Camerounian political parties, Camerounian associations would examine each other's points of view and voluntarily settle on a common minimum program agreeable to all."

The first indication that the government intended to employ more forceful means to create national unity was the dissolution of the

[26] *Premier stage de formation des résponsables de l'Union Camerounaise* (Aug. 1–6, 1961; pamphlet issued by the *comité directeur* of the UC, Feb. 1962).

[27] *L'Effort Camerounais,* Nov. 26, 1961, p. 2 (translation by the present author).

UPC congress in Yaoundé on January 22, 1962, at bayonet point. The UPC's parliamentary group had already been reduced by the arrest and trial of Deputy Owono Mimbo Simon in 1961, by the expulsion of another UPC deputy, and by the elections (for these seats) at which UC candidates won. Incidentally, it has been claimed that the UPC candidates actually won these by-elections (in Dja et Lobo and Kribi) but that the UC candidates were declared elected.

In any case, the record showed that even though the UPC favored collaboration with the government, it rejected the *parti unifié*. The UPC's secretary-general, Emah Otu, offered to join the *parti unifié* in April, but indications are that he did not speak for Mayi or the majority of UPC members. At the PSC congress at Ntui in March, Okala characterized the *parti unifié* as a "play on words," the *parti unique* in a different guise. He indicated that he and the Socialists were prepared to support Ahidjo but implied that such support depended on a continuation of the "political dialogue."

On April 24 the Federal Assembly met for the first time. All fifty of its members represented the ruling parties in the East and West Cameroun, constituted into a single parliamentary group, the Group of National Unity. The absence of opposition members from the eastern and western legislatures occasioned some comment, but, according to H. L. Kemayou, president of the Eastern Assembly, the situation provided no cause for alarm since the Federal Assembly was "very representative." Significantly, both Mayi and Mbida had refused to participate in the selection of the forty eastern members to sit in the Federal Assembly.

By mid-May 1962, Okala, Mbida, Mayi, and Beybey Eyidi (whose Parti Travailliste Camerounais was only forty-five days old at the time) had made common cause in a United National Front, and on June 23, they issued the manifesto which ultimately led to their arrest. It may be added that the four opposition leaders were arrested under the provisions of an antisubversion law promulgated in March 1962. The new law provided stringent punishment—imprisonment of one to five years and/or a fine of between 200,000 and 2,000,000 CFA francs—for interference with public authority, incitement of hate against the federal or state governments, participation in "subversionary activity," and the starting or passing of false news, rumors, and reports (be they tendentious commentaries or exact news) injurious to public authorities. Repetition of the offense entails a compulsory jail sentence and, if the culprit is a member of the military services or a public official, he is debarred from ever holding any public office again.[28]

Whatever the truth or falsity of the government's charges against the opposition and however one interprets the refusal of the opposition parties to join in the *parti unifié*, there is no question that by July 1962 the East Cameroun had become, to all intents and purposes, a one-party state. Notwithstanding the continued presence of opposition deputies in the Eastern Assembly, the opposition in the East Cameroun had been so restricted that, at least insofar as its ability to challenge the government and the UC was concerned, its voice on the eastern political stage had become quite feeble. This does not mean that opposition to the regime or to the UC ceased to exist by mid-1962 but simply that organized opposition in the formal political arenas had been virtually nullified by that time. The question of the nature of what opposition still remained is another matter and can be better examined after a look at both the UC and the several opposition parties.

The Union Camerounaise. The founding of the Union Camerounaise as a political party took place in May 1958 at Garoua, where Ahidjo, formerly Vice-Premier under Mbida and newly installed as Premier (February 1958), convoked a meeting of 5 small local northern political groups. The parliamentary base of the new party consisted of the 29 northern deputies already constituted into the Groupe d'Union Camerounaise plus 5 others *apparentées* (electorally allied) to the UC group. The 29 UC deputies were Muslim Fulani from the northern regions (Adamawa, Benoué, Bamoun, Diamaré, Logone et Chari, and Margui-Wandala) and represented roughly 250,000 voters, about one-third of the total who cast their ballots in December 1956. The 1960 general elections gave the Union Camerounaise 50 seats in 8 departments, with the northern administrative units (now increased to 7) yielding about 600,000 votes or roughly 43 per cent of those cast. (The UC actually gained 45 per cent of the total vote.) The

[28] At their trial, Mbida, Mayi, Beybey, and Okala attempted to invoke their parliamentary immunity. The court refused to accept the plea, whereupon the four abandoned their defense. They were each fined $980 and sentenced to two and a half years in prison. The government, speaking through J. Bikanda, Commissioner-General for Information, maintained that the four had been plotting against the government and that "they did not hesitate to contact foreign embassies whose help they sought to support their criminal action" (*Afrique Nouvelle,* July 20–26, 1962, p. 6).

50 seats, it may be added, gave the UC half of those in the National Assembly. In short—even though the UC's seats had increased to 77 in April 1962 because of defections from the other parliamentary groups—its base of power remained (and remains) the northern constituencies.

Several factors in the northern Camerounian political situation help to explain the UC's hold in the seven northern departments. The northern electorate is mainly composed of Muslim Fulani; ethnic solidarity must be counted as a positive force tending to electoral conformity. The "Kirdi," who constitute the numerical majority in the north, are still largely unpoliticized, but the UC is already seeking out the more modern elements among them. Moreover, the northern traditional chiefs—lamidos, emirs, sultans, and so on—have aligned themselves behind Ahidjo, persuaded that continuing UC rule provides them with the best chances of survival in the face of the inevitable modernization of their areas. Their influence upon their traditional followers is still considerable, a fact attested to by the presence of several northern traditional chiefs in the Eastern and Federal assemblies. Finally, the UC, as the first political party in the north, was and still remains the principal avenue to the national political arena and its tangible rewards. The party has been and continues to be one of the most important modernizing forces in the north and one of the few channels available to young northerners seeking education, advancement, and a chance to participate in the development of the country.

Building upon its northern electoral base and on its control of the government, the UC has become a mass party incorporating not only its northern followers but the leadership and, presumably, the following of a number of erstwhile parties. Thus assimilated have been the Paysans Indépendants, the Action Paysanne, the Mouvement d'Action Nationale, the FPUP, and several so-called "traditional" ethnic-based organizations such as the Union Bamoun, the Kolo-Beti, and Charles Assalé's Efoula-Meyong. At the fourth party congress at Ebolowa in July 1962, the treasurer general claimed 300,000 dues-paying card-carrying members. Even if some exaggeration is granted, the figure still represents the largest number of adherents ever claimed for a political organization in the Cameroun. Not even the UPC in its preindependence heyday claimed more than 100,000 members.

In 1962 the party was organized according to a simple hierarchical pattern. The base was composed of a large number of cells grouped under base committees, operating at the village or *quartier* (a neighborhood whose residents are usually of the same ethnic background) level. The latter operated under the direction of subsections responsible to the sections, one of which heads the party organization in each of the East Cameroun's twenty-five departments. Once each year the sections send representatives to the party congress, the highest formal organ of the party. The congress elects the party's *comité directeur* (executive committee) and the *bureaux* (administrative boards) of the sections and subsections and is supposed to define the party's program and general policies. In practice, the *comité directeur* is the party's principal elaborator of program and principle; in recognition of this fact that the party's locus of power is in the *comité directeur,* the congress has been content to be a ratifying, rather than an initiating, body.

Until very recently, the Union Camerounaise could not be said to have had an official ideology; the simple goals of independence, reunification, and reconciliation, plus a more general evocation of the conventional African nationalist demons (colonialism, neocolonialism, imperialism, and so on), sufficed as the party's ideological and programmatic platforms. With the attainment of both independence and (partial) reunification and with the legal reappearance of the UPC on the national scene, the old goals had been attained. As the party in power, the Union Camerounaise began after October 1, 1961, to seek an official ideology suitable to its status and to a less revolutionary atmosphere.

During the course of Ahidjo's four-hour report to the fourth party congress at Ebolowa in July 1962, the President sought to define such an ideology by inventing a millennial Camerounian and then suggesting the means of his creation:

The sensitive man, the emotional man, the spiritual, religious man; in other words man arising of men, man in society, man strong and proud, even arrogant only because of the noble thoughts and ideas that he holds—in sum, the man whose spirit is imperishable constitutes the supreme aim of our entire enterprise. Thus have I tried to define our conception of life. . . .

To explain our ideology in twentieth-century terms, let us say that the theme of all our reflections, of all our political philosophy, both economic and social, is a socializing humanism or, in other terms, African socialism.

For us, Africans—as my friend Senghor has said—nothing that is material constitutes an end in itself. So it is that money, goods, technology in all its aspects have no value for us, Negro-Africans, except in the measure that they have a meaning in human and social utility.[29]

Ahidjo's report is interesting not only for what it contains but also in that it marks the appearance of the Camerounian President in a new role, that of chief party ideologist. Now a self-confident, vigorous individual, Ahidjo climbed the long ladder to political success without having had the benefits either of higher education (he completed secondary school in Yaoundé) or of a profession likely to lead him to politics (during World War II he was employed as a radio operator by the government). During his rise to power, he used his considerable political talents to fashion a highly effective political machine from the young, antitraditional elements of the Cameroun north. Articulate, highly intelligent, Ahidjo still occasionally displays an ingrained shyness and aversion to personal ostentation.

The fourth party congress, in addition to hearing Ahidjo's disquisition, elected the party *comité directeur*. The personalities for the top positions reflected with accuracy the relative importance of the UC's leaders both in the party and in the government:

Party		*Government*
President general	Ahmadou Ahidjo	Fed. President
Vice-president general	Arouna Njoya	Fed. Minister of State for Justice
Vice-president general	Charles Assalé	P.M., East Cameroun
Political secy.	Moussa Yaya	V.P., E. Cam. Assembly
Deputy political secy.	Mohaman Lamine	East secy. of state for interior
Deputy political secy.	Charles Onana Awana	Fed. Min. Delegate to Pres. for Territorial Admin. of Finances and the Plan
Administrative secy.	Victor Kanga	Fed. Min. of Natl. Economy
Deputy admin. secy.	V. Tchinaye	
Deputy admin. secy.	Joseph Abega	Deputy, E. Cam. Assembly
Secy. for press, inf. etc.	Eteki Mboumoua	Fed. Min. of Natl. Education
Deputy secy. for press, etc.	Henri Effa	Deputy Min. (Fed.) of Information
Deputy secy. for press, etc.	Bouba Bello	Deputy, E. Cam. Assembly

[29] *L'Effort Camerounaise,* July 15, 1962, p. 3 (translation by the present author). For keys to Ahidjo's thesis see Senghor's *African Socialism* (New York: American Society for African Culture, 1961).

Party		Government
Secy. for organization	Oumarou Sanda	Vice-premier, East Cameroun
Deputy secy. for orgn.	Sadou Daoudou	Fed. Min. of Armed Forces
Deputy secy. for orgn.	Silas Mbong-Bayem	Deputy, E. Cam. Assembly
Secy. for women's, labor union, and social affairs	Richard Manga Mado	E. Cam. secy. of state for labor
Deputy secy. for women, etc.	Julienne Keutcha	Deputy, E. Cam. Assembly
Deputy secy. for women, etc.	Wandji Nkuimy	E. Cam. secy. of state for finance

Ahidjo and Arouna Njoya are, so to speak, the party's founding fathers. In the party, as in the government, Ahidjo exercises full control; Njoya, as a cofounder of the party, is Ahidjo's second in command and probably exercises the next most influential voice in party affairs. Moussa Yaya, Mohaman Lamine, Oumarou Sanda, and Sadou Daoudou are all members of a small inner circle of the party faithful: they are all Ahidjo's men, they owe their present positions to him and have been schooled under his auspices in politics and in the uses of power. Of the group, probably the most important is Moussa Yaya, whose rise in the party corresponds with his own remarkable intellectual and social development. Assalé owes his position to the old MANC's presence in the governing coalition of 1960 and to the fact that he represents important cocoa growers' associations in the Abolowa area and also the powerful Association Bantoue Efoula-Meyong, which speaks for most Bulu-Beti-Eton south of Yaoundé. Assalé was instrumental in persuading MANC to merge into the UC. His position in the party, however, appears to be largely honorific, since he has never been considered to be close to Ahidjo and the inner circle of northern Muslim Fulani party leaders. Onana and Kanga are also Ahidjo's men, but in a special sense. Both are technicians—Onana a talented administrator and financial expert, Kanga an attorney and a vigorous public servant—with relatively little political skill. Onana never ran for office, and Kanga won his seat by the most narrow of margins. Both are dynamic and aggressive, however, and represent the young professional bureaucracy that Ahidjo is bringing into the government and the party. Effa, Mbong-Bayem, Keutcha, Manga Mado, and Wanji Nkuimy are members of the growing group of UC "notables" recruited from the opposition parties and associations. Their influence within the party is considered to be minimal, for the very good reason that although they are now needed to demonstrate the UC's national character, there is some suspicion that they are in the party as a temporary convenience and are not wholly dedicated to the party or its leadership.

The opposition. The dimensions of oppositional politics in the East Cameroun are difficult to define. There are, on the one hand, the formal parties of the opposition now temporarily banded together in the National Unity Front; on the other, there are a range of associations with explicit or implicit ties to the opposition parties, a variety of interest formations watching the government with growing uneasiness, the spectrum of maquis-guerrilla-terrorist groups still active in the west and southwest, and the "old exiles" in Conakry and Accra who claim to speak for the "true UPC" and who insist that they are directing the continuing violence in the East Cameroun. Finally, it is entirely possible that some of the new southern allies of the UC are allies of expediency, whose estimate of the situation seemed to point to the conclusion that the bandwagon is the safest place for them until the power of the UC has begun to wane. There is, it must be granted, little specific evidence to warrant the latter conclusion; yet an examination of the ranks of the newer UC converts does not reveal many southerners with long-standing affinity for either Ahidjo or his northern-based leadership elite. A word about each of the above elements will serve to highlight the nature of their opposition.

The Cameroun, as First Secretary Emah Otuh pointed out in his speech before the ill-fated January 1962 UPC party congress, was the only example in Africa where "the party which won the struggle for independence" was not represented in the government. Insofar, at least, as it was the UPC that first led Camerounian nationalism and as its techniques, slogans, and program later constituted the basis of action of other parties, Emah Otuh's contention has some justification in the facts. Whatever the case for a "neglected UPC," there is little question, however, that the present UPC lacks its former militancy, that its leadership is split, that its membership has fallen off, that its program flounders in vague negativisms, and that its mass appeal has dwindled a great deal. Some of these difficulties are exemplified in the split between the party's parliamentary leadership—which included Mayi-Matip, the "legal UPC's" titular chief—and the younger, more militant wing of which J. P. Sende is representative. The Mayi wing has sought to play the role of the responsible opposition; the younger wing has demanded more vigorous opposition and a return to the old revolutionary *élan* which characterized the party in preindependence days. The January congress, it should be noted, was convoked by a *provisional* national directorate and sought to heal the intraparty breaches which developed since independence. There are as yet no indications whether the forcible dissolution of the congress and Mayi's subsequent arrest have exacerbated or healed these divisions.

On one subject, at least, all members of the legal UPC appear to be in agreement, that is, in their condemnation of continued terrorism and of the Conakry exiles who have described Mayi and his colleagues as "imperialist stooges." Emah Otuh, in January, stated that the "outside UPC" was itself riven by dissension and that its members were "poorly informed of national realities." He also accused them of "deceiving international opinion and spreading the information that certain regions in the Cameroun were in the hands of the pseudo Army of National Liberation." [30] In April 1960, the UPC polled about 150,000 votes in the 11 departments where it ran candidates and won 8 seats in the National Assembly. Most of its strength has been concentrated in the departments of the southwest, particularly in Douala and other southern towns. In December 1960, it claimed 30,000 members, but that number has probably shrunk by two-thirds since then. The party appears to retain substantial support in the departments of Kribi, Dja et Lobo, Sanaga-Maritime, and Nyong et Kellé and was able to muster 800 delegates to the January 1962 congress.

The Démocrates, it will be recalled, reconstituted the elements of Louis Aujoulat's old Bloc Démocratique Camerounais and in 1957 formed the basis of André-Marie Mbida's short-lived control of the government. In its heyday, the party had been able to draw strong electoral support from the heavily Catholic Yaoundé area and enjoyed the support of the Catholic hierarchy throughout the country. Since Mbida's fall from power, the PDC has seen progressively leaner days. During Mbida's voluntary exile to Conakry, from which he returned early in 1960, the party fell apart organizationally and was held together only by its parliamentary members.[31] His return reinfused

---

[30] *Afrique Nouvelle* (Dakar) Jan. 24, 1962, p. 6.

[31] Mbida was implicated in a murder committed by some of his followers and left the Cameroun of his own will. In Conakry he consorted with the leaders of the exiled UPC—Moumié, Ouandié, Kingué—and even signed a declaration of common purposes with them. Unable to come to terms with them, however, and lured by the government's reconciliationist attitudes, he returned home in Jan. 1960.

some vitality into the party—he was even offered a ministry, which he declined—but his efforts did little to prevent the party from disintegrating still further. Members of the PDC parliamentary group were included in Ahidjo's first 1960 government, though they were soon expelled when their overt criticism became embarrassing to the government.

In 1961 and 1962 several of the PDC's parliamentary deputies defected to the UC, and Mbida developed a very strong antipathy toward the government and Ahidjo. In January 1962 the newly enthroned Archbishop of Yaoundé, Abbé Jean Zoa, was reported to have purged the Yaoundé hierarchy of pro-Mbida followers and thereby completed the Cameroun Church's dissociation from the Démocrates. The party garnered 63 per cent of the votes from Nyong et Sanaga (Yaoundé and its environs) in the April 1960 elections and in December of that year claimed 30,000 active members. There is little question that since then PDC membership has fallen sharply and that the party's electoral appeal has substantially diminished.

The Parti Socialiste Camerounais has never enjoyed much popular support in the Cameroun. Okala, the party's leader and one-time vice-president of the Mouvement Socialiste Africain, has been its principal representative in the various Camerounian assemblies and governments. Despite a claim of 2,000 members and 4,000 *sympathisants* in 1960, the party has been largely the organizational handmaiden of Okala. It provided him with a platform for his pronouncements, a staff of campaign workers, and the appearance of a mass following to echo his positions. There is, of course, nothing new in this sort of party in the Cameroun; many prominent Cameroun politicians have utilized the pseudo party, the personal organization, for their own political ends. André Fouda, the mayor of Yaoundé, Paul Soppo Priso, former president of the Legislative Assembly, Charles Assalé, Martin Abéga, Mathias Djoumessi, and Daniel Kemajou, among others, have availed themselves of this device to further their political careers. The most recent example—the fourth member of the National Unity Front—is the Parti Travailliste Camerounais, formed in March 1962 by Mbandja Malanga and Dr. Beybey-Eyidi. Mbandja is a former UPC activist. Beybey is a Douala physician with a long history as a political lone wolf supporting the UPC. He enjoys considerable popularity among the immigrants in Douala, particularly in New Bell, where his clinic is located.

Beyond the political parties of the opposition, the shape of most of the various groups and interests currently in opposition becomes increasingly blurred. Part of the difficulty lies in their low visibility, a function of their present unwillingness to be seen or heard in a situation in which being in opposition is not without its dangers. Under the circumstances, then, it is possible only to suggest the general social and economic areas in which they can be found; and even this is to do no more than make an educated guess of present attitudes in light of past positions. With these reservations, a few likely pockets of opposition can be discerned: (1) some labor unions, particularly those with former UPC ties; (2) ethnically linked commercial interests in the southwest, especially in the Douala, Kribi, Ebolowa, and Nkongsamba areas; (3) several traditional groups in the south and southwest who see the Ahidjo regime as a threat to their power; (4) a large percentage of Cameroun students studying abroad, since some of the most articulate pro-UPC, antigovernment criticism has come from Cameroun students in France, England, Nigeria, and elsewhere; (5) many discontented, highly politicized urban dwellers, found particularly among the unemployed and the immigrant Bulu, Ewondo, and Bamiléké groups; and (6) other discontented groups, in both rural and urban contexts, which are as yet unreconciled to the present regime or its leaders. In general, then, and despite the ostensible electoral and organizational strength of the UC, there probably remains considerable opposition to the regime, concentrated mainly in the southern departments. This opposition, as was suggested, has now largely submerged; how much longer it will remain so and whether the government can eventually win it over are questions which cannot now be answered.

More easily described than the "submerged" opposition is the visible extraparty opposition: the UPC exiles, who have steadfastly refused all offers of amnesty and reconciliation, and the bands of maquis and terrorists still operating at large. The "external UPC" is led by Ernest Ouandié and Abel Kingué, formerly vice-presidents of the national UPC. The death from thallium poisoning of Dr. Félix Moumié in Geneva on November 3, 1960, robbed them of their principal spokesman and leader. The external UPC leaders continue to insist nonetheless that they are the only true spokesmen of the UPC, that the Cameroun government is a puppet of France, and that the only hope for the Cameroun lies in the armed struggle being waged by the UPC maquis for the "liberation" of the country.

Despite the repeated avowals of the East Cameroun government that terrorism has definitely declined and indeed altogether disappeared in some sections of the country, reports continue to come from the Cameroun that guerrilla activity is still very much of a problem. The terrorists apparently continue to find their main support among disgruntled Bamiléké and within the *nouveaux arrivées* of the towns. Two sorts of maquis groups must be distinguished. One type includes the groups led by highly politicized UPC leaders, some of whom were trained abroad in guerrilla tactics. These groups often possess weapons apparently smuggled in from Guinea or Ghana.[32] The second type seems to consist of bands taking advantage of confusion and unrest to pillage, kill, and steal; they generally operate under *ad hoc* leadership and without specific political motivation.

Finally, mention must be made of the special position of the Catholic Church in the Cameroun. Since its dissociation from the PDC the Church has officially declared its neutrality vis-à-vis Camerounian political conflict and all partisan matters. That neutrality was difficult to maintain, however, in the face of political developments during 1961 and 1962, and during these two years the Church came into virtually open conflict with the government several times. Two related events illustrate the nature of the uneasy relationship between the government and the Church. Early in February 1962, 25 of 36 "political prisoners," including some women and children, who were being moved from Douala to Yaoundé suffocated in the railway freight car in which they were riding. The troop detail guarding them was instructed to bury the bodies in the forest secretly and without ceremony. One of the troopers, a Catholic, called for a priest to administer last rites. Word inevitably reached Archbishop Zoa, who published a pastoral letter in *L'Effort* calling for a requiem mass for the dead prisoners. The government, embarrassed, seized the issue of *L'Effort* and deported its editor, Father Fertin, a French priest. However, notwithstanding indications that it would do so, the government did not impede celebration of the mass, which hundreds attended despite the early hour.

[32] There does not now seem to be any question regarding either the foreign training of some maquis leaders or the presence of foreign weapons in their hands. A number of Czech 7.6 pistols have been found on captured terrorists, and even though Guinea and Ghana have categorically denied complicity in such matters, the weight of reliable official opinion places their origin there. It will be recalled that Guinea, Ghana, and Mali are the only sub-Saharan countries known to have received quantities of Czech small-caliber automatic weapons. One report (*Neues Afrika,* May 1962, p. 169) even claimed that some 300 Camerounians were being trained in guerrilla tactics in Communist China and Eastern bloc countries.

The government has claimed that the Church, through *L'Effort,* is in fact injecting itself into politics and contends that measures taken against the paper and its editor were fully justified. (In May, another issue of *L'Effort* was seized by governmental decree. This time an editorial entitled "What Are Our Liberties?" appeared to be the cause of the government's ire.) Whatever the justice of the government's complaint against the Church and *L'Effort,* the fact remains that the government looks upon the Church, and Archbishop Zoa, with some displeasure, possibly even to the point of considering it among its opponents.

ELECTIONS

The two Camerouns have maintained, with few modifications, the electoral systems they had prior to unification, even though under the terms of the constitution the franchise is to come under federal jurisdiction after the "transition period." The West Cameroun uses single-member districts, with elections decided by simple majorities in each district. The number of districts were increased from 26 to 37 during 1961; the usual rules of contiguity and approximately equal population were applied as they had been previously. Presently there are about 21,000 voters in each West Cameroun district. The East Cameroun continues to utilize the system introduced during the French administration. Basic to the system are the 25 main administrative divisions of the state, the departments. Each department has at least one deputy; thereafter a ratio of about 1:32,000 is followed. The Bamiléké department, for example, before its division into 5 departments in 1960, had 476,000 inhabitants by official count and was represented by 14 deputies. Benue, with 280,000, had 9. The system is thus founded upon the multiple-member constituency; voting involves choice between lists, without permitting ranking within the lists or the shifting names between lists but with the possibilty of *apparentage.*[33] In such a circumstance, the *apparentées* agree on a single list to place before the voters. Runoffs are unusual.

Suffrage qualifications in the two states are much alike. There are no restrictions as to sex; voters must be over twenty-one years of age, in full possession of their civil rights, and able to prove citizenship. Voting is secret in both states.

[33] A system in which parties join to present the same candidate or lists of candidates to the voters, used in France and in many French-speaking African states.

ADMINISTRATION

Both France and Great Britain left their respective Camerounian territories with well-organized and relatively well-functioning bureaucracies. In both Camerouns full-fledged administrative structures were created on both territorial and local levels long before independence became a fact; at the moment of French and British departure both Camerouns had the legal and physical impedimenta for a civil service operating along European lines. Independence, however, brought many unanticipated problems. Most of these derived from the fact that in both Camerouns the operating core of the bureaucracy had been composed of European expatriates and that with their inevitable departure in large numbers the two Cameroun governments had to recruit enough Camerounians to replace them and, possibly even more crucially, to try to operate the bureaucracies under rules and standards they inherited rather than created themselves.

Before the problems facing Cameroun administration are examined, a glance at the formal organization of the system is in order. Two levels of organization exist, corresponding to the constitutional divisions within the state: the federal, operating separately from the state systems but cooperating with the local ministries in areas of parallel or joint jurisdiction, and the two state systems, operating independently of one another but (theoretically) expected to maintain liaison through the appropriate federal ministries. The federal and state systems operate within the framework of functional ministries; exceptions include the independent commissions designated by the constitution and the several administrative agencies operating directly under the federal presidency or the states' prime ministers' offices. Following is a summary listing of the principal federal and state ministries and the names of their heads as of the dates given. In the East and the West Cameroun ministries the head is designated "secretary of state" except for the Public Works Ministry in the East Cameroun.

Of the two states, the West Cameroun has probably experienced the less painful administrative transition. Prior to unification, the public service was staffed by British expatriates, members of the Nigerian public service, and local Cameroonians. Official policy foresaw the steady replacement of nonindigenous personnel with qualified

Federal (February 1962)

Justice	Arouna Njoya, Minister of State
	Emmanuel Egbe Tabi, Deputy Minister
Finance, Plan, Federal Territorial Administration	Charles Onana Awana, Minister Delegate to Presidency
Foreign Affairs	Jean-Faustin Betayene, Minister
	Nzo Ekhah Nghaky, Deputy Minister
National Economy	Victor Kanga, Minister
Transport, Mines, Posts, and Telecommunications	Solomon Tandeng Muna, Minister
Armed Forces	Sadou Daoudou, Minister
National Education	Eteki Mboumoua, Minister
Public Health	Simon-Pierre Tchoungui, Minister
Without portfolio	Jean Akassou, Minister
Information	Vacant

East Cameroun (November 12, 1961)

Public Works	Sanra Oumarou, vice-premier
Interior	Mohaman Lamine
Rural Development	Jean Mabaya
Finance	Wandji Nkuimy
Stock Farming	Yadji Abdoulaye
Education	Josue Tatang
Labor	Richard Manga Mado
Public Service and Administration	Oumate Talba Malla

West Cameroun (January 1962)

Finance	Augustin Ngom Jua
Public Works and Transport	John Henry Ngange
Natural Resources	Lucas Nbo Ndmukong
Social Services	Willie Ndep Orok Effiom
Cooperatives and Community Development	John N. Bokwe
Labor, Commerce, and Industry	Peter M. Kemcha
Local Administration	Joseph Lafon

Cameroonians. In 1958 the Southern Cameroonian House of Assembly endorsed a goal of "100 per cent cameroonization of employment," but the goal is still a long way from realization. In March 1960, for example, 26 per cent (301) of the 1,160 officers then serving in the various departments of the Southern Cameroons were non-Cameroonians. The percentage was reduced after unification but at the cost of 250 Nigerians and some 80 British staff who have since returned to their respective home bases. About 50 British senior officials have remained in the West Cameroun, and a number of East Camerounian officials have arrived to take up some of the slack caused by the mass departure of the Nigerians. Sizable personnel gaps in the administrative structure remain, however, and it will probably be some time before sufficient West Camerounians return from schools abroad or are locally trained to take over both the vacant positions and those created since unification.

In the East Cameroun the problems of administrative transition have been similar in nature but vary considerably in scope and acuteness. First, "camerounization" acquired political overtones virtually absent in the West Cameroun. For East Camerounian politicians and officials, "camerounization"—actually pursued with vigor by Camerounian governments and the administering authorities during the latter years of the trusteeship—represented yet another method of eliminating the French colonial presence and asserting Camerounian independence. In the hands of Cameroun nationalists, it became a club with which to beat the French when the latter seemed reluctant to speed up withdrawal or a symbol which could be used to flout waning French authority. Overuse of "camerounization" as a political weapon was probably partially responsible, upon the attainment of independence on January 1, 1960, for the departure of a larger number of French officials than had been anticipated, indeed desired, by the Cameroun government. In 1960 and 1961, increasing numbers of Camerounians filled official posts; the last French departmental prefect left in 1961, and by the end of 1961 no more than fifty "technical advisers" from the civil service of overseas France (excluding the personnel of the sizable French military mission) were left in the eastern state.

In the East Cameroun also, recruitment problems largely absent in the West Cameroun developed during 1960, 1961, and 1962. Beginning in 1956 France pursued a plan whereby French officials in each department would be gradually replaced by Camerounian scholarship students who completed their studies in France. Accordingly, some 95 scholarship graduates were returned to the Cameroun in 1956, 71 in 1957, 42 in 1958, 51 in 1959, 14 in 1960, and 27 in 1961. A significant number of these returnees graduated from the two most important administrative training centers in France, the Institut des Hautes Etudes d'Outre-Mer and the Ecole Nationale d'Administration. Most of the rest were trained at various French universities. An unanticipated set of difficulties arose during 1960, 1961, and 1962 when it became obvious that many of the new returnees found their expectations shattered by the realities of bureaucratic life. As the trainees returned from France, the better positions at the top were quickly filled, and many young Camerounians who had anticipated placement at the higher ministerial or departmental levels found themselves relegated to lesser positions with lower pay, fewer prerogatives, and considerably less prestige. Under the circumstances, an increasing number of young graduates have been accepting official posts with reluctance or, if they are free to do so, seek other avenues to success. In some instances, the Cameroun government has even had to resort to severe measures to bring reluctant graduates home from France; in 1961 it terminated the financial support of a number of students.

Another factor which had considerable effect upon the recruitment program has been the high level of political activity among Camerounian students in France. A large percentage of them, at least in 1959 and 1960, were hostile to the Ahidjo regime and had aligned themselves with the UPC or with left-wing student groups or causes. In all, recruitment to administration has not been as satisfactory as the government might desire; not only do there remain many positions yet unfilled, but the ranks of the younger bureaucracy are becoming more and more restive. Undoubtedly many young officials feel that their ambitions have been thwarted and that the political leadership of the country has not recognized their talents properly. In addition, the government has recruited a large number of individuals who seem ill prepared for their tasks and more concerned with the status of their positions than the performance of their duties.

It is therefore not surprising that many Camerounians have been keenly disappointed in the performance of their officials. If President Ahidjo is to be believed, the East Cameroun civil service can be charged with nearly the entire catalogue of bureaucratic shortcomings. In March 1962, he excoriated East Cameroun officialdom in a well-publicized memorandum, parts of which deserve to be quoted at length:

A marked laxity among nearly the quasi totality of the civil servants is becoming more and more apparent. . . . In the majority of the administrative offices, even up to the central services and the different ministries, there reigns such carelessness and such anarchy that even the least informed and least aware are alarmed and sorely troubled over the future of our civil service. . . .

. . . among these failings are intemperance, dishonesty, and lack of courtesy; poorly done work, lateness and absenteeism, lack of disipline and insubordination, . . . inflated remunerations, and the simultaneous holding of several jobs. . . . Furthermore, civil servants should refrain from overt criticism of and insults to the Government or its policies.[34]

Even with allowance for rhetorical exaggeration, Ahidjo's broadside is remarkable for its frankness. Since independence, the East Cameroun government has been confronted with embarrassingly numerous instances of the very misconduct which Ahidjo condemned, a number of them involving high officials.[35] Yet, in all justice and in view of the monumental problems of recruitment, training, "camerounization," and indoctrination, most East Camerounian officials have served honestly and effectively even in the face of some flagrant abuses by many of their colleagues. The West Camerounian civil service, it may be added, still undermanned and largely inexperienced, has been largely free from scandal.

LOCAL GOVERNMENT

Under the terms of the federal constitution the states reserve jurisdiction over their respective local governmental systems. In the two states, local government follows patterns established under the trusteeships, patterns based upon English and French models and common throughout English- and French-speaking Africa.

[34] *Afrique Nouvelle,* April 4, 1962, p. 6. Translation by the author.

[35] Instances of mismanagement were conspicuous in the Ministries of Education, Finance, and Rural Development, for example. The chief customs officer of Douala was arrested, and the chief customs officer of Yaoundé absconded with over 2,000,-000 CFA francs in receipts, among them a customs payment from the present writer. Finance Minister Onana Awana instituted draconian measures to curb some of the worst examples of financial irresponsibility, but his fight has been only partially successful.

West Cameroun

The West Cameroun is divided into six administrative divisions: Victoria on the coast, Kumba and Mamfe in the forest hinterland, and Bamenda, Wum, and Nkambe in the grasslands. Each is in the charge of a district officer (now an African in each case) who is directly responsible to the West Cameroun government at Buea. Within each division, local administration and budgetary control are provided by a popularly elected divisional council functioning under the guidance and advice of the district officer and resident and visiting representatives of the specialized departments of the government. The divisional councils control the operations of subordinate district councils, also popularly elected, whose number varies from division to division. Where tribal authority systems remain strong, the district councils are ordinarily based upon the recognized traditional authority in the area concerned, usually a chief acting with or without a council. Where there are no customary authorities with power over a wider area than the village—as is often the case, for example, among the forest people —the representatives of extended families or groups have been formed into councils and given statutory powers as district councils.

To a large extent, then, local governmental units at the district level tend to be founded on existing traditional institutions. Thus, where tribal custom and loyalty are strong, the chiefs are capable of exerting considerable influence at local levels of government, and there is no doubt that some of them, notably the powerful grasslands chiefs (the Fons of Bali, Bafut, and Nsaw, for example), have done so in the past. With the growth of party organization, however, it appears that the influence of the traditional chiefs is somewhat on the wane. During the 1961 plebiscite the Fon of Nsaw openly advocated integration with Nigeria, but KNDP campaigners operating in the traditional Nsaw districts engineered a heavy majority for reunification. Finally, in addition to the area-based administrative structures, several of the larger towns such as Victoria, Buea, Kumba, Mamfe, and Bamenda have full-fledged municipal governments composed of elected municipal councils and officers.

East Cameroun

Local government in the eastern state rests upon a tripartite base composed of (1) the classic French prefectural organization, (2) a complex system of urban and rural communes, and (3) an array of minor and major chiefs.

Each of the twenty-five departments of the East Cameroun is headed by a prefect, who makes his headquarters in the departmental capital and supervises the local administration of central governmental services of the eastern state. These include education, telecommunications and posts, finances, public works, agriculture, health, and police. The departments are each subdivided into one or more *arrondissements*, and these, in instances where size or population require it, are sometimes divided into districts. *Arrondissements* and districts are under the authority of subprefects and district heads respectively, officers subordinate to the departmental prefects. Prefects, subprefects, and district heads are usually civil servants appointed upon the recommendation of the Minister of the Interior, under whose direct authority the entire prefectural system and its subdivisions operate.

Communes are of two main types, urban and rural. Urban communes are either *communes de plein exercice* (with full powers), *communes urbaines de moyen exercice* (with limited powers), or *communes mixtes urbaines de moyen exercice*. The two types of urban communes are created by governmental decree and represent the two stages of development toward the fullest municipal autonomy possible under the law. The communes with full powers are the older, established urban centers (such as Douala, Yaoundé, Nkongsamba, and so on) whose inhabitants already have considerable political and administrative sophistication. "Full powers" represents, in this context, complete control over municipal finances and services. The communes with restricted powers are those urban centers whose inhabitants are not deemed to have attained the maturity required for the status of communes with full powers. The technical difference between the two types consists in the manner in which the chief municipal executive is selected. In the former, the mayor is elected at large from the commune. In the latter, a mayor-administrator is nominated by the Minister of the Interior. Both types of communes have municipal councils elected from common rolls. The third variety of urban commune, the mixed urban commune with restricted powers, is in every way similar to the commune with restricted powers except that an ethnically mixed population may require special rules to determine the selection and composition of the municipal council. Ngaoundéré and Garoua, for example, have municipal councils in which two-thirds of the councilors are elected at large and the other third are "notables" (chiefs and so on) appointed by the Minister of the Interior upon the recommendation of the prefect in whose department the commune is located.

Mixed rural communes are a special form of local government, again created by governmental decree. They are usually coterminal in area with *arrondissements* but may be of any size fixed by law. They may also coexist with urban communes, in cases where the latter are physically located within rural communes. The mixed rural commune is headed by a mayor, who is appointed by the Minister of the Interior, and governed by an elected municipal council of 15 to 44 members, depending on the population in the commune.

In July 1960, the East Cameroun had 65 *arrondissements*, 18 districts, 11 *communes de plein exercice*, 6 *communes de moyen exercice* (mixed and unmixed), and 65 *communes mixtes rurales*.

Traditional chiefs continue to play an important role in local government in the East Cameroun, particularly in the seven northern departments where no *communes mixtes rurales* have been created. The northern chiefs (lamidos, emirs, laouanes), with their traditional councils or assemblies, enjoy considerable authority in local affairs and usually constitute the basis of local government in their areas of jurisdiction. In the southern departments, a variety of local chiefs (paramount chiefs, group chiefs, village chiefs, *chefs de quartiers*) either exercise local administrative authority as agents of the central government or participate in communal governments. All chiefs must be recognized by the central government and are financially compensated to the extent they perform governmental functions.

The entire system of local government is under the control of the Ministry of the Interior, locally through the officials of the prefectural organizations, and regionally (north and south) through *delegués du gouvernment* (inspectors general of administration) stationed in Douala and Garoua.

ROLE OF THE JUDICIARY

In neither of the Cameroun states has the judiciary shown any tendency toward involvement in the political scene. Two reasons probably account for this. One is that the tradition of judicial noninvolvement is very strong in both states; the other lies in the fact that both East and West Camerounian judicial systems contain numbers of nonindigenous judges, lawyers, and administrators. The East Cameroun Supreme Court and Courts of Appeal, for example, include several French judges sitting under the terms of the 1960 Franco-Cameroun Convention which provides for their presence until they can be replaced by Camerounians. Similarly, in the West Cameroun, British and English-speaking West Indian judicial personnel dominate the bench and judicial administration. Their very visibility has imposed considerable restraint upon them; they tend to perform the tasks required of them quietly and without publicity. This is not to say that their presence does not occasionally stimulate demands for their removal. In May 1962, the CPNC *Champion* attacked the West Cameroun attorney general and assistant attorney general and demanded their dismissal. Both are West Indians.

The judicial systems in the two states continue to function through their respective preunification courts and administrations. In the West Cameroun, a bifurcated system of courts—regular and customary—operate under the common law and statutes in use before 1961. Similarly, the unitary system introduced under the trusteeship continues to function in the East Cameroun; it is a system deriving its inspiration and tradition from French practice. The constitution envisages federal control of all judicial organs, a provision possibly reflecting the eventual synthesis of the two systems. It is more likely, however, that the eastern system will, in the long run, dominate the entire judicial structure.

Contemporary Issues

NATIONAL UNITY

In a statement issued following the constitutional talks held at Foumban in July 1961, Premier Foncha spoke of the "existence of two Cameroon cultures" and expressed the hope that by the "processes of evolution" the two cultures would eventually be replaced by an "indigenous one." Apart from whether two such "cultures" actually exist, it is nonetheless fair to say that a year and a half after unification Foncha's "indigenous" Pan-Camerounian culture had not as yet come into being. There is even some question whether in some respects the two Camerouns had not moved farther apart instead of closer together. It becomes relevant, then, to examine some of the main areas in which national unity—in the sense of unity between the two states—would have to be accomplished in order to make the federal union a reality. Such examination, in short, seeks the visible progress made toward the goal of which the federation is the ostensible symbol.

Three areas of immediate relevance are institutions, political activity, and economic life. All have already been treated at length, and it becomes possible now to suggest some of the conclusions which can be drawn from these discussions and indicate some additional problems in each area. Excluded from consideration will be the more intangible areas of popular culture, of language or even education (as instrumental in political socialization to the symbols of national unity). In any case, there is little question that the brevity of the federal experience and the restraints upon movement in the East have minimized contact between the citizenry of the states and discouraged the growth of anything more than the vaguest popular understanding about the content or consequences of the new union.

Institutions

Insofar as the constitution places a virtually unlimited federal legislative veto in the states, delays the election of a National Federal Assembly until 1964, certifies the respective chief executives of the states as federal chief executives until 1965, fails to make specific provision for the distribution of powers between the states and the federation, and neglects to delineate the nature of the relationship between the states and the federation, the Federal Republic has failed to achieve institutional unity. Federal institutions have an *ad hoc* character and from the evidence appear to have been primarily designed to become effective in an indefinite future rather than in the immediate present.

What is clear is, in short, that the federal leadership group, at least in the executive and legislative areas, is not national in character or identification and that its primary interests lie in the states rather than on the national level. This is not to say that a national executive and a national legislature with primary commitments to the federation will not emerge; it is simply to point out that at least for now those manning the federal institutions have not yet given them national character.

In another federal institutional area, however, considerable progress seems to have been made toward unity. The various federal ministries already operate on the national level, for example, foreign affairs, finance, economic planning, public health, and communications. Federal civil servants are to be found in both Yaoundé and Buea, and federal services now extend to both states despite the existence of complex problems raised by differing procedures.

Political Activity

A national political arena has yet to make its appearance; political activity remains primarily state political activity. It can be argued that political unity has become less likely with recent political changes in the eastern state. The continued—but apparently precarious— existence of a competitive party system in the West Cameroun and the crystallization of a single-party system in the East Cameroun do not augur well for the emergence of a national political activity that will precede the federal legislative elections in 1964 and the presidential elections in 1965. Not even the most farsighted can foretell what the effect on national politics would be if the two states' political systems continue to diverge.

Economic Unity

As Alan Warmington and others have pointed out, Camerounian unification has definite justification on economic grounds. The excellent communication facilities of the East provide advantageous routes of egress for the products of the West, particularly those of the grassfields area. Ethnic ties between the two states provide the basis of expanded and advantageous commercial intercourse. The problems of labor migration, both seasonal and permanent, have long complicated Cameroons-Cameroun relations; the central services of the federal government now become available to solve these problems and rationalize interstate labor exchanges. To all this must be added the fact that the Germans developed the West Cameroun–southwest East Cameroun area as a unit and planned roads, railways, and towns on that basis.

To point out the economic rationales for unification is not, however, to say that economic unity has been achieved. Crucial to the complex of economic problems raised by unification has been finances. *West Africa* summarized some of the difficulties:

The big issue of the financial status of the West Region within the Federation is not yet solved. Indeed, the problem goes beyond the mere difficulties of Federation: the fact is that West Cameroon has a chronically insolvent economy. Last financial year's deficit was £280,000 [$784,000], and this year's promises to be about £1m [$2,800,000] in the recurrent budget.

The West Cameroon financial year ended last March, whereas the Federation's year carried on until June 30. So in April supplementary estimates had to be made to tide over the extra period, enabling the two budgets to coincide. Last year's deficit was kept low because in the first half of it some items of expenditure were lower than anticipated, largely due to the lack of adequate staff. However, in the second portion of the year, lacking the British Colonial Development and Welfare Grants and Grants-in-Aid, and in spite of the U.K.'s parting gift of £575,000 [$1,590,000], the deficit was incurred.

In the present year, the loss of customs revenue incurred through the transfer of this source to the Federal Government will be some 1,159 m. francs CFA [$4,789,256] or two-thirds of the State's total resources. In compensations, the Federal Government will relieve Buea of such burdens as the medical services, the Attorney General's Office, the Ministry of Commerce, the Public Debt and agency services.

The Buea authorities firmly intend that this *ad hoc* arrangement for the current year shall be regarded as temporary, and that the Western State be given a form of financial autonomy, with a specific allocation of revenue, as in Nigeria.

In the [West Cameroun] capital budget, totalling some £480,000 [$1,-244,000] for the current year, there is envisaged a deficit of some £150,000 [$420,000], for which no visible source of income yet exists. Much now depends on current negotiations with the U.K. on the future of Colonial Development Corporation commitments. In theory, West Cameroon is eligible for French, Common Market, West German, and U.S. aid as well as British, but this comes through the Federal Government, which has earmarked £110,000 [$308,000] this year towards the West's development budget, a sum which is taken into account in calculating the £1,500,000 deficit.[36]

The $308,000 noted above as the 1962 contribution to the West Cameroun's development budget, it may be added, falls short of the added revenue that the state needs to keep up its capital development outlays. Kenneth Berrill estimated that the West Cameroun's recurrent outlays by 1961 would be at the rate of about $2.5 million per annum, and that another $1 million would be needed to maintain the development program.[37] Even if the costs were added of the various development projects now being undertaken through international agencies or under bilateral agreements, the total would still fall far short of Berrill's estimates.

In sum, the evidence seems to indicate that the two states' economies continue to operate autonomously of one another, with some

[36] *West Africa*, no. 2353 (July 7, 1962), p. 745.
[37] *The Economy of the Southern Cameroons*, p. 49.

central financial controls being exercised at the federal level. There are few indications that there has been increased traffic in goods or people between the states or that there has been a greater economic interplay between the states on any but the highest governmental or financial levels. Quite possibly the persistence of terrorist and guerrilla violence in the border areas and the strict control on travel in those areas have discouraged interstate movement. Probably wider economic cooperation can come about only after a period of adjustment. To expect that the two economies would already have meshed on all levels is to expect too much at this stage of the federation's development.

Thus, national unity is still rather far away. The complexity and magnitude of the problems facing the states, considered both individually and together, must temper even the most qualified optimism about the Camerounian future.

ECONOMIC DEVELOPMENT

A fundamental preoccupation of the Cameroun's leadership, as indeed of most Camerounians of modern persuasion, is the problem of the economic development of the country. To a large extent, the manifold problems of unification take on new meaning when seen within the context of the larger imperatives of national economic growth. The prevailing official mood, on the whole, is one of optimism that the federation can attain self-sustained growth; the plan elaborated in 1960 foresees a doubling of the average per capita income in twenty years, the product of a national growth rate approximating 4.6 per cent annum. The plan is based upon the fulfillment of certain key requirements, such as the full mobilization of human resources and major legislative and administrative innovations, and, of course, the attainment of a number of economic objectives—creation of a north-south communications axis, greater production and consumption of meat animals, refinement of distribution patterns and facilities, increase in the production of primary export products, a higher volume of savings, development of better credit facilities, and full development of the potential for the creation and operation of various types of cooperatives.

Before an examination is made of several of the 1960 plan's economic goals, the objectives of full mobilization of human resources deserves brief attention. One of the operations recommended to achieve this goal is the creation of what the plan calls "an obligatory

National Civic Service for stable [*sic*] young unemployed people 18
to 25 years old, and their distribution among . . . reclassification
centers." If the experience of such states as Ghana, Guinea, and the
Ivory Coast is of any consequence, the one-party state lends itself
admirably to the creation of just such a mobilization of surplus labor.

The cost of the program is also of interest at this point. For the
first five years, the plan estimates a total investment requirement of
approximately 45,000,000,000 to 50,000,000,000 CFA francs ($186,-
350,826 to $206,704,465), which when revised to include the require-
ments of the West Cameroun—the plan was drawn up prior to
unification—would amount to about $220,000,000 for that period. Al-
though the plan makes no projection for the full twenty years, utilization of its increment and investment percentages leads to an estimate
of its total cost by 1980 at over $1,100,000,000. Whether these figures
are realistic or not is a matter of opinion, but some doubts have
already been expressed privately that the plan is "utopian" in its
financing aspects, particularly since it specifically admits that between
40 and 45 per cent, at least for the first five years, will have to come
from outside sources. Since most of the Cameroun's development
funding has thus far been provided on the basis of bilateral agreements, the possibility arises that these sources, especially France,
either cannot or will not maintain their present rate of aid. The alternative is increased dependence upon multilateral and/or international
aid and investment, but, as Paul Marc Henry (speaking of the continent as a whole) has warned, "the net result of this reorganization
may well be a net decrease in the aggregate volume of aid received
by Africa and not the expected increase." [38]

If the 1960 plan has any key aspects, they undoubtedly lie in three
areas: agricultural reform and reorganization, the prospects for industrialization, and *le grand projet,* the north-south railway axis.

Agricultural Reform

The agricultural key envisages a reorganization of the rural economy (in the words of the plan) involving the creation of "a communal
structure of rural life, oriented toward cooperative development on
the human, social, and economic levels." Within each department,
there are to be instituted *communautés villageoises* (village communities) embracing 20,000 to 30,000 inhabitants—apparently on the

[38] Paul Marc Henry, "The United Nations and the Problem of African Development," *International Organization,* XVI, no. 2 (Spring 1962), 362.

models provided by similar projects on the Nile delta, in Iran, and in Chad—and organized to provide cooperative marketing and production facilities for output and to permit maximum coordination of governmental social and development services within the area. The operation of the various *communautés villageoises* would ultimately fall under the jurisdictional supervision and control of the Ministry of Rural Development, operating in cooperation with the national political agencies.

Some of the basis for this projected reorganization already exists. The extent and growth of production and marketing cooperatives have already been noted, particularly those involving major export crops such as cocoa, coffee, and the like. The East Cameroun has presently some 1,500 cooperatives, of which, however, about 1,300 are financial in nature. In addition to the cooperatives, five so-called Agricultural Modernization Centers (SEMCENTRES) were created by the government to coordinate development, research, and technical aid relating to the principal crops grown in the five geographical areas served by the Centers.

In conception, the rural reorganization plan is grandiose but certainly feasible. It must be pointed out, however, that implementation of this portion of the 1960 plan will involve solving some of the knottier social and political problems to which reference has already been made. For example, unless "the Bamiléké problem" is resolved and unless the violence which has already disrupted much of the economic life in the southwest can be stopped, little progress can be made toward agricultural reform in the very areas most critical to Camerounian agricultural production.

Prospects for Industrialization

Whatever else is said of the industrialization potential in the federation, two facts stand out at once: (1) that the greatest possibilities lie in the East Cameroun and (2) that major industrial projects designed to produce items for export are out of the question for the federation in the foreseeable future. The latter is one of the conclusions reached in a 1960 report prepared by a French firm assigned to study the possibilities for industrial development in the Cameroun.[39] Given the high cost of capital and construction, the poverty in the infrastructure, the limited natural resources of the federation, and

[39] Société d'Etudes pour le Développement Economique et Social, *Rapport sur les possibilités de développement industriel du Cameroun* (Paris: La Société, 1960), p. 2.

the difficulties involved in trying to compete in markets dominated by industrial nations, only limited industrial expansion can have any economic justification. The consequences of this conclusion are obvious. According to the report, Cameroun industrial development must be directed toward the creation of industry, most of it on a fairly small scale, designed to service local markets. Some dozen or so enterprises, including meat canning, flour milling and biscuit production, and the manufacture of matches, tennis shoes, soap, plywood, cement, and plastics would have utility within the range of the Cameroun's limited economic potential.

The Edéa aluminum plant, the single exception to the "no large industry" rule, was constructed, it will be recalled, to take advantage of the extremely cheap hydroelectric power available at the mouth of the Sanaga River. Its expansion seems to be economically unprofitable for the moment, principally because bauxite must still be brought to Edéa from outside sources and because the world market for aluminum is already quite inelastic. The report referred to does not discourage expansion of the already-existing facilities for the manufacture of aluminum utensils made from Edéa ingots. It stresses again, however, that economic reality must dictate that such production be directed to internal, rather than external, markets. Finally, a large area of uncertainty exists with regard to the exploitation of the extensive bauxite deposits at Martap near Tibati. The uncertainty is compounded by the fact that these ores will be available only when the Douala-Chad railway is extended more than 400 miles north from Yaoundé to reach the deposits and by the fact that this extension may not be completed for at least five to seven years. Further, the unpredictable state of the world aluminum market seven years hence and the extremely high initial costs of transportation on the railway pose still other problems.

The North-South Railway Axis

Since the German protectorate, extension of the Cameroun's railway system northward to the Chad Basin has been an object of great interest. In 1930, the French administration undertook a survey of the prolongation of the Douala-Yaoundé line north to Ngaoundéré and thence to the Chad territory itself. The project lay dormant, but not forgotten, until 1945, when interest was revived by the French, and in 1948 a series of studies were begun to determine the economic, political, and financial feasibility of a Douala-Chad railway. With independence, the

Cameroun Republic pushed the project even further, to the extent of adopting the studies made by a governmental agency charged with examining the project and seeking international financing for it. In 1962 the Cameroun government obtained a commitment of about $31,615,000 for the construction of the first 206 miles (Yaoundé to Goyom). Involved were France, the European Economic Community, and the United States, which pledged $11,033,000, $12,396,000, and $8,119,000 respectively. Work is to begin in 1963, with construction expected to be finished by 1965.

The plans, as of May 1962, called for extension of the railway to Ngaoundéré (438 miles from Yaoundé), then to Moundou in Chad (another 241 miles), making a total of about 780 miles. In April 1962, Ahidjo met with President Tombalbaye of Chad and discussed the possibility of a further extension to Fort Archambault (about 230 miles from Moundou). Fort Archambault is the southern terminal of the navigable portion of the Chari River which passes by Fort Lamy, the capital of Chad.

The political and economic ramifications of the project as a whole are far-reaching for the Cameroun and for the Chad–Central African Republic area of the Lake Chad Basin. (1) The Douala-Chad railway would provide a new and profitable means of access to the sea for an area of more than 193,000 square miles with over 2,700,000 inhabitants. The area in question has heretofore had only limited and difficult access to seaports. The north Cameroun–Fort Lamy areas have been served by the Benue from Garoua and by the Nigerian railway system's extension to Northern Nigeria and alternatively (for Chad) by the difficult connections overland and by river south to Brazzaville. The new rail line would shorten the distance to the sea, cut the time required to move goods in and out of the area, and eventually lower the cost of transportation from the region by over two-thirds. (2) The project constitutes one of the vital requirements for the realization of the Camerounian plan; without it, the development of the Cameroun north becomes almost impossible. (3) The railway opens the door to a closer integration of the Equatorial African group, which the Cameroun is definitely interested in joining.

Objections to the plan have already been voiced on both economic and political grounds. *West Africa* pointed out:

Although as the crow flies, Douala . . . is nearer to Fort Lamy than Lagos, the proposed railway has less logic in purely economic and geographical terms than if Chad had chosen Lagos as its main port.

For the Bornu railway is already in existence: the 170 mile Kuru Bauchi section is already open to traffic and the rest is already under construction[;] . . . the Bornu railway is scheduled to reach Maiduguri in 1964—which would bring it to within a hundred miles of the Chad border.[40]

It would appear, continued *West Africa,* that "politics has triumphed over economic considerations." "Not even within the proposed [Equatorial African] economic group," stated *Africa Digest,* "will the scheme be universally popular. It will encounter opposition in Brazzaville, since it would deprive the line from that city to Pointe Noire in Gabon of a considerable amount of goods traffic." [41]

Economically justified or not, the political implications of the project have given it great attraction for the Cameroun government. The prospect of making Douala the outlet for the whole of Central Africa could not but reflect great prestige upon any Camerounian government that achieved such a goal.

External Relations

WITH OTHER AFRICAN STATES

In general, the federation pursues its relations with other African states within the framework of its membership in the Organization of African and Malagasy States (OAMS, the so-called "Brazzaville twelve") and the broader grouping which emerged from the Conference of Independent African States held in Monrovia, Liberia, in April 1961. Camerounian commitment to the OAMS is undoubtedly grounded both in the members' common ties to France—and the European Common Market—and in the fact that the looseness of the organization permits each member state a wide latitude of individual freedom of action. The Cameroun's orientation to African affairs is frankly Pan-Africanist, but it is a Pan-Africanism tempered by the moderation of action and language characteristic of the Brazzaville group. In general, Camerounian foreign policy in the African arena has few specific objectives and has been directed to such vague goals as broader economic, social, and political cooperation between all African states, to increasing cooperation (as a part of the OAMS) with the European Economic Community, and to such indefinite policies as support of the United Nations' effort in the Congo, condem-

[40] *West Africa,* no. 2344 (May 5, 1962), p. 485.
[41] *Africa Digest,* IX, no. 6 (June 1962), 200.

nation of racism in South Africa and the Rhodesias, and the opposition to nuclear testing in the Sahara.

Ghana and Guinea constitute special problems for the Cameroun. Both Ghana and Guinea have played host to the exiled UPC leadership, and until very recently the Ahidjo government was an object of denunciation by leaders in both these countries. In January 1962, however, Ghana finally recognized the federation and has been seeking to establish diplomatic relations with Yaoundé. Guinea, on the other hand, continues to provide haven for the UPC exiles, and the federal government refuses to consider the possibility of relations with Sékou Touré's government until Guinea formally renounces its protection of the UPC revolutionaries. There are as yet no signs that Conakry has withdrawn its support of the UPC exiles, but it is doubtful if Guinea can continue to afford hospitality for long to a group whose cause now seems almost hopelessly lost. Even the United Arab Republic and Liberia, which once espoused the UPC cause at the United Nations, have made their peace with the Cameroun and opened embassies in Yaoundé.

WITH NON-AFRICAN STATES

By January 1963, some twenty-two foreign embassies had been established in the federal capital, sixteen being of countries outside Africa (Belgium, Canada, the Nationalist Republic of China, France, the German Federal Republic, Israel, Italy, Japan, Lebanon, the Netherlands, Pakistan, Spain, Switzerland, the United Kingdom, the United States of America, and Vietnam) and six from Africa (Ghana, Mali, the Central African Republic, Liberia, the United Arab Republic, and Nigeria). In addition, Denmark, Greece, Monaco, Norway, Sweden, and Chad had opened consulates. The Cameroun is an associate member of the Common Market, and all of its aid from abroad comes from Western sources. Consequently, almost all its foreign relations—as reflected in the countries represented in Yaoundé—have tended to be with Europe, North America, and nations conventionally associated with the non-Communist world. The first step to a wider series of contacts was taken in September 1962, when a good-will mission headed by Victor Kanga, Federal Minister of National Economy, visited Warsaw, Prague, and Moscow, as well as Stockholm and Copenhagen.

The presence of the Nationalist Chinese embassy in Yaoundé, it must be added, bears special witness to the Ahidjo regime's hostility to the government of mainland China, a hostility, periodically vented at the United Nations, stemming from the fact that the Chinese Communists have made no effort to conceal their financial and material support of the "external" UPC.

In all, the Federal Republic's contacts with non-African states have not been extensive, a fact due primarily to the high cost of spreading diplomatic posts to an increasingly large community of nations. Its primary contacts continue to be with the larger states of Europe, the United States, the United Nations, and its African neighbors.

WITH THE UNITED NATIONS

The Cameroun became a member of the United Nations in 1960 and maintains a permanent mission in New York. Within the General Assembly the Federal Republic's representatives orient themselves according to the postures developed by the "African caucus," and more particularly to the positions of the Brazzaville group at the UN. At least insofar as the Cameroun is concerned, the relationship with the Brazzaville group has been a salutary one. During the debates in the spring of 1961, the Brazzaville group supported en bloc the Cameroun's demand for a new plebiscite in the Northern British Cameroons.

The Federal Republic, on the whole, gives only qualified support to the United Nations, but it maintains its membership in various UN agencies such as the Economic Commission for Africa, the Commission for Technical Cooperation in Africa South of the Sahara, the World Health Organization, the International Labor Organization, the Food and Agriculture Organization, and the United Nations Educational, Scientific, and Cultural Organization.

BIBLIOGRAPHY

In general, the English-language literature on the Cameroun is extremely limited and concerns, with one notable exception, the British Cameroons. No full-scale studies of political developments in English have as yet been published, but two doctoral dissertations (by David Gardinier at Yale and by the present writer at the University of California, Los Angles) can be consulted on this subject. Among the works in English, only the most recent by the Ardeners and W. A. Warmington (*Plantation and Village in the Cameroons*), W. A. Warmington (*A West African Trade Union*), Phyllis Kaberry (*Women of the Grassfields*), McCullough *et al.* (*Peoples of the*

Central Cameroons), Edwin Ardener (*Coastal Bantu of the Cameroons*), and P. R. Kuczinski (*Cameroons and Togoland: A Demographic Study*) are generally found in college libraries. Harry Rubin's classic *Germans in the Cameroons* is out of print but can be found in the larger university libraries. It remains the only study of the German period in the Cameroun and one of the finest case studies of colonialism in print. Also usually available are the later (1955 to 1959) annual reports published by the Colonial Office, *Cameroons under United Kingdom Administration*. The 1959 report is the last in the series to be published; they are compact, informative, and basic for research projects. Finally, mention must be made of the several United Nations Visiting Mission reports. They are dated (the last mission visited the Camerouns late in 1958) insofar as much of the statistical data they contain is concerned but are invaluable for their discussions of political issues important at the time of the missions' visits. Except for the few articles noted below, there are as yet no studies in English dealing with the Federal Republic.

The literature on the French Cameroun is considerably more extensive but, save for a few articles in English, is almost entirely in French. Interestingly enough, most of these materials deal with nonpolitical matters; the few "political" works are either doctoral theses by Camerounian students at French universities (most of them, by the way, betray a srtong pro-UPC bias), formal studies of administrative institutions, or recent articles in periodicals. In any case, Cameroun materials in French are even harder to find than those in English. Only the libraries of universities offering extensive study of African culture and politics are likely to have more than an unrepresentative sampling. The best of the French-language material is undoubtedly that dealing with Camerounian anthropology and ethnography. In this connection, one of the few recent French works on the Cameroun should be mentioned: Claude Tardits' *Les Bamiléké de l'ouest Cameroun* (1960) is probably the best statement of the sociodemographic roots of *le probleme Bamiléké*. The French government, under the terms of the trusteeship agreement, also published annual volumes on the administration of their portion of the Cameroun. These volumes, however, go only up to 1957 and are as unwieldy as they are uninformative. Very few copies can be found in the United States.

A surprisingly extensive German-language literature on the Cameroun was published in Germany, not only during the period of their protectorate but during the interwar years when Nazi Germany launched a massive propaganda campaign for the return of the former imperial colonies. Much of this material reflects the political purposes for which it was published but within it can be found valuable accounts of settler life in the Kamerun, explorations, and economic and social conditions both during and after the protectorate. Again, unfortunately, these works are generally not available.

Probably the largest and best collection in the United States of German works on the Kamerun can be found in the New York City Public Library. Currently, only one fairly reliable account of Cameroun politics exists in German; Franz Ansprenger in his *Politik im Schwarzen Afrika* (1961) devotes Chapters XI and XXV to the "Kamerun's" political development.

OFFICIAL PUBLICATIONS

Cameroun, Etat du, Ministère des Affaires Economiques, Service de la Statistique Générale. *Résultats du recensement de la ville de Douala (1955–1956)*: *Population autochtone*. (Fascicule 2, Résultats d'ensemble.) Yaoundé: Imprimerie du Government, 1957. 86 pp.

Cameroun Republic, Chambre de Commerce et d'Industrie [by Gilbert Rathery]. *Cameroun, terre d'Avenir*. Douala, 1960. 86 pp.

——, Ministry of Finance. *Budget de l'exercice 1960–61*. Yaoundé: Imprimerie du Gouvernement, 1961. 533 pp.

——, Ministry of the Plan. *Cameroun: Plan de développement économique et social, travaux preparatoires*. (Prepared by Société Générale d'Etudes et de Planification, Paris—SOGEP.) 3 vols. Yaoundé, 1960.

——, Société d'Etudes pour le Développement Economique et Social, for the Ministry of the Plan. *Rapport sur les possibilités de développement industriel du Cameroun*. Paris, 1960. 224 pp.

——, Société d'Etudes du Chemin de Fer Douala-Tchad. *Avant-projet*. 4 vols. Yaoundé, 1959. Maps, charts, etc.

France, Ministry of Overseas France (or Foreign Ministry). *Rapport annuel du Gouvernement Français à l'Assemblée Générale des Nations Unies sur l'administration du Cameroun placé sous la tutelle de la France*. Paris, 1959. 247 pp. (Last year covered, 1957.)

Great Britain, Colonial Office. *Cameroons under United Kingdom Administration, Report for 1958*. London: H.M.S.O., 1960. xvi, 383 pp., map, and CDC Report, 1958.

——, ——, ——, *Report for 1959*. London: H.M.S.O., 1961. xiv, 209 pp., map, and CDC Report, 1959.

Nigeria, Federal Information Service, for the Government of the Southern Cameroons. *Introducing the Southern Cameroons*. Lagos: Federal Government Printer, 1958. 97 pp.

[Union Camerounaise Party, Comité Directeur.] *Premier stage de formation des résponsables de l'Union Camerounaise*. [Yaoundé, 1962.] 138 pp.

United Nations, General Assembly, Official Records. *Report of the United Nations Plebiscite Commissioner for the Cameroons under United Kingdom Administration, Plebiscites in the southern and northern parts of the Territory, on 11 and 12 February 1961*. (UN Doc. A/4727.) New York, 1961. 86 pp. and 2 maps.

——, ——, United Nations Visiting Missions to Trust Territories in West Africa, 1958. *Report on the Trust Territory of the Cameroons under British Administration.* (UN Doc. T/1426 and T/1426/Add. 1.) New York, Jan. 20, 1959. 173 pp.

——, ——, ——. *Report on the Trust Territory of the Cameroons under French Administration.* (UN Doc. T/1441.) New York, Jan. 23, 1959. 63 pp.

United States, Department of Commerce, Bureau of International Commerce, World Trade Information Service. "Basic Data on the Economy of the Federal Republic of the Cameroon," *Economic Reports,* pt. 1, nos. 61–68. Washington, D.C., Oct. 1961. 13 pp.

NEWSPAPERS AND PERIODICALS

Cameroons Champion. Victoria, 1960–1962.

L'Effort Camerounais. Yaoundé, weekly.

Kamerun Times. Victoria, weekly.

La Presse du Cameroun. Douala, daily.

Africa Digest. London, bimonthly.

Africa Report. Washington, D.C., African-American Institute, monthly.

Afrika. Hamburg, monthly.

Afrique Nouvelle. Dakar, weekly.

Etudes Camerounaises. Yaoundé, Institut des Recherches Camerounaises, quarterly.

Europe France Outremer. Paris, monthly.

Marchés Tropicaux du Monde. Paris, monthly.

West Africa. London, weekly.

BOOKS

Ansprenger, Franz. *Politik im Schwarzen Afrika.* Cologne and Opladen: Westdeutschen Verlag for the Deutsche Afrika-Gesellschaft e.v. Bonn, 1961. 516 pp. See headnote.

Ardener, Edwin. *Coastal Bantu of the Cameroons.* London: International African Institute, 1956. 116 pp. Ardener served as government anthropologist in West Cameroun from 1952 to 1961. The book embodies the essentials of existing literature (in English, French, and Douala) and of thorough field research conducted by the author and his wife.

Ardener, Edwin and Shirley, and Alan Warmington. *Plantation and Village in the Cameroons.* London: Oxford University Press for the Nigerian Institute of Social and Economic Research, 1960. xxi, 435 pp. A socio-economic ecology of the Southern Cameroons, with particular emphasis on labor problems of the Cameroons Development Corporation.

Bouchaud, Joseph. *La côte du Cameroun dans l'histoire et la cartographie dès origines à l'annexion allemande.* (Mémoires de l'IFAN Centre du Cameroun, no. 5.) Yaoundé: IFAN Centre du Cameroun, 1952. 212 pp. Precolonial history of the Cameroun coast, pieced together from a remarkable variety of sources.

Buell, Raymond Leslie. *The Native Problem in Africa.* Vol. II. New York: Macmillan, 1928. 1049 pp. Part IV details the writer's eyewitness findings in the Cameroun mandate. Buell, an American professor, caused a great deal of stir with the two-volume work.

Dugast, I[delette]. *Inventaire ethnique du Sud-Cameroun.* (Mémoires de l'IFAN Centre du Cameron, Série: Populations, no. 1.) Yaoundé: IFAN Centre du Cameroun, 1949. 139 pp. The only comprehensive work on the ethnic composition of the southern part of the East Cameroun. It is dated but still extremely valuable.

Gardinier, David E. "French Policy in the Cameroons, 1945–1959." Unpublished Ph.D thesis, Yale University, 1960.

Kaberry, Phyllis M. *Women of the Grassfields.* (Colonial Research no. 14.) London: H.M.S.O., 1952. xii, 220 pp. Although it focuses on the position of women in Bamenda, this excellent study offers a readable presentation of social and political organization among the grasslands tribes.

Kuczinski, P. R. *The Cameroons and Togoland: a Demographic Study.* London: Oxford University Press, 1939. xviii, 579 pp.

Lembezat, Bertrand. *Kirdi, les populations paiennes du nord-Cameroun.* (Mémoires de l'IFAN Centre du Cameroun, Série: Populations, no. 3.) Yaoundé: IFAN Centre du Cameroun, 1950. 101 pp. Still the standard work on the animist tribes of the Cameroun north, it complements the work of Jean-Paul Lebeuf in Chad.

Le Vine, Victor T. "The Cameroun: From Mandate to Independence." Unpublished Ph.D. thesis, University of California, Los Angeles, 1961. 492 pp.

McCullough, Merran, Margaret Littlewood, and I[delette] Dugast. *Peoples of the Central Cameroons.* London: International African Institute, 1954. 174 pp. Describes the Bamun, Bamiléké, Tikar, and other Cameroun highland groups. The chapter on the Bamiléké is based on the excellent work of Delarozière and is the only full statement in English of the Bamiléké social system.

Meek, C. K. *Land Tenure and Land Administration in Nigeria and the Cameroons.* London: H.M.S.O., 1957. vi, 420 pp.

Murdock, George Peter. *Africa: Its People and Their Culture History.* New York: McGraw-Hill, 1959. xiii, 456 pp. Probably the best full-scale treatment of African demography. The many Cameroun ethnic groups can be seen within their wider ethnographic context.

Mviena, P., and J. Criaud. *Géographie du Cameroun.* Yaoundé: Imprimerie de St. Paul, 1960. 111 pp. Designed for elementary schools, this little book provides a concise résumé of Cameroun geography.

Njoya, I. A., ed. *Histoires et coûtumes des Bamoun.* Trans. by Henry Martin. (Mémoires de l'IFAN Centre du Cameroun, Série: Populations, no. 5.) Yaoundé: IFAN Centre du Cameroun, 1950, 232 pp. Njoya, Sultan of Bamun (1884–1933), created a unique alphabet in which his scribes wrote this history of the Bamun people.

Rudin, Harry R. *Germans in the Cameroons, 1884–1914.* London: Jonathan Cape, 1938. 456 pp. See headnote.

Victoria Centenary Committee. *Victoria Southern Cameroons, 1858–1958.* Victoria: Basel Mission Book Depot, 1958. xii, 103 pp. A short but well-conceived social, economic, and political history of the Southern Cameroons.

Warmington, W. Alan. *A West African Trade Union.* London: Oxford University Press for the Nigerian Institute of Social and Economic Research, 1960. ix, 150 pp. Designed to complement the Ardener, Ardener, and Warmington volume (see above), this short work deals with the growth, activities, and structure of the Cameroons Development Corporations Workers' Union.

ARTICLES

Ardener, Edwin. "Cautious Optimism in West Cameroon," *West Africa,* no. 2313 (Sept. 30, 1961), p. 1071.

——. "The Kamerun Idea," *West Africa,* no. 2139 (June 7, 1958), p. 533; *ibid.,* no. 2142 (June 24, 1958), p. 559.

——. "The Political History of Cameroon," *World Today,* XVIII, no. 8 (Aug. 1962), 341–350.

"Assembly Charts Course for Cameroons," *United Nations Review,* April 1959, p. 15.

Brutsch, Jean-René. "Fernando Po et le Cameroun," *Etudes Camerounaises,* no. 43–44 (March–June 1954), pp. 67–78.

Chaffard, George. "Cameroun à la veille de l'indépendance," *Europe France Outremer,* no. 355 (June 1959), pp. 65–78.

Chilver, E. M., and P. Kaberry. "From Tribute to Tax in a Tikar Chiefdom," *Africa,* XXX, no. 1 (Jan. 1960), 1–19.

"Compromise in Cameroon," *West Africa,* no. 2353 (July 7, 1962), p. 742.

Delarozière, R. "Cameroun: Inventaire éthnique et linguistique du Cameroun sous mandat français," *Le Journal de la Société des Africanistes,* IV, no. 2 (1934), 203–208.

Devernois, Guy. "Cameroons 1958–59 from Trusteeship to Independence," *Civilisations,* IX, no. 2 (1959), 229–234.

Ducat, Marc. "Cameroun, du mandat à l'indépendance," *Marchés Tropicaux du Monde,* Nov. 21, 1959, pp. 2547–2554.

Gaudemet, Paul-Marie. "L'autonomie camerounaise," *Revue Française de Science Politique,* VIII, no. 1 (March 1958), 42–72.

Gonidec, P. F. "Les institutions politiques de la République Fédérale du Cameroun," *Civilisations,* XI, no. 4 (1961), 370–395; XII, no. 1 (1962), 13–26.

Hodgkin, Thomas. "The French Cameroons," a series in *West Africa* beginning Dec. 18, 1954, and running through Jan. 8, 1955 (four issues).

Horner, George R. "Togo and the Cameroons," *Current History,* XXXIV, no. 198 (Feb. 1958), 84–90.

"Independence Foreshadowed for French Cameroons," *United Nations Review,* Dec. 1958, p. 30.

Kaberry, Phyllis M. "Traditional Politics in Nsaw," *Africa,* XXIX, no. 4 (Oct. 1959), 366–383.

Kitchen, Helen. "Cameroun Faces Troubled Future," *Africa Special Report,* III, no. 1 (Jan. 1960), 14–15.

Le Vine, Victor T. "Calm before the Storm in Cameroun," *Africa Report,* VI, no. 5 (May 1961), 3–4.

——. "The New Cameroun Federation," *Africa Report,* VI, no. 11 (Dec. 1961), 7–8, 10.

——. "The Other Cameroons," *Africa Report,* VI, no. 2 (Feb. 1961), 5–6, 12.

——, and Henri M'Ballah. "[Education in the] Federal Republic of Cameroun," in Helen Kitchen, ed. *The Educated African.* New York: Praeger, 1962. Pp. 519–532.

Migeod, Frederick. "The British Cameroons: It's Tribes and Natural Features," *Journal of the African Society,* XXIII, no. 91 (April 1934), 176–187.

"Mission's Report on the Two Territories: End of Trusteeship Proposed for the French Cameroons," *United Nations Review,* March 1959, p. 31.

"Moskau's Taktik im Schwarzen Erdteil," *Ostprobleme,* 12th Year, no. 4 (Feb. 19, 1960), pp. 112–115.

Vandercook, John W. "The French Mandate of Cameroun," *National Geographic Magazine,* LIX, no. 2 (Feb. 1931), 225–260.

Warmington, W. Alan. "Prospects for the Cameroun Federation," *West Africa,* no. 2313 (Sept. 30, 1961), p. 1073.

——. "Savings and Indebtedness among Cameroons Plantation Workers," *Africa,* XXVIII, no. 4 (Oct. 1958), 329–343.

V

THE RHODESIAS
AND NYASALAND

By HERBERT J. SPIRO

Amherst College

Historical Background

The Federation of Rhodesia and Nyasaland, as it was founded in
1953, lasted for a decade. Its founding was opposed by an overwhelming majority of Africans, whose political consciousness and organization was stimulated and accelerated by the creation of this common
focus for their hostility. Since 1953, with only insignificant exceptions,
African political leaders and movements have been demanding the
breakup of the Federation. In 1963, the British government met this
demand, and the Federation, as constituted in 1953, was dismantled.
The inclusion of Southern Rhodesia, Northern Rhodesia, and Nyasaland in one section of this book may therefore seem to call for some
justification. After all, this book contains no separate section on the
short-lived Federation of Mali. And even if the Central African Federation lasted a good deal longer, the present section could hardly be
justified unless links between its three territories go farther back into
the past than 1953 and are likely to survive farther into the future than
1963. The antiquity (by historical standards of Africa) of past links

is a fact. The likelihood of some kind of future association is a presumption upon which this study is based.[1]

THE PRECOLONIAL PERIOD

The two Rhodesias are the only countries in Africa (and among very few in the world) named after a historical figure alive at the time of their christening. Memories of the overpowering personality of Cecil John Rhodes still pervade the politics of these two countries that bear his name. As in the Gold Coast and the French Soudan, the Rhodesian independence movements have advocated changing the names of their countries to something precolonial and authentically African.

For Southern Rhodesia, the new name suggested is Zimbabwe. Knowledge of the precolonial history of British Central Africa, as of preliterate societies generally, comes from three main sources: their own orally transmitted traditions; reports of literate travelers who penetrated their territories, in this instance beginning with Portuguese accounts of the sixteenth century; and archaeological evidence. The stone ruins at Great Zimbabwe and elsewhere in Southern Rhodesia and Mozambique indicate the existence, between the eleventh and fifteenth centuries, of a fairly elaborate political system, ruled from Zimbabwe by the Monomatapas dynasty. At the time of Portuguese penetration, this dynasty of the Vakaranga, a branch of the Mashona who are still one of the two major tribes in Southern Rhodesia today, had moved their capital toward the north and "ruled the Zambezi valley for about seven hundred miles of its length, from the Kariba gorge to the sea." [2] To the southwest of the Monomatapas, the Changamire dynasty held sway and built new stone structures at Zimbabwe and elsewhere.

[1] This chapter is the product of field work conducted in the Rhodesias and Nyasaland since 1959, most recently during the summer of 1962. The last trip was financed in part by the Social Science Research Council and the Non-Western Studies Program of Amherst College, Smith College, Mount Holyoke College, and the University of Massachusetts. For earlier fellowships, I am indebted to the John Simon Guggenheim Memorial Foundation, the Rockefeller Foundation, and the United States Educational Commission in the United Kingdom. For their careful reading and criticism of this manuscript, I am grateful to P. A. C. Laundy, librarian of the Southern Rhodesian Legislative Assembly, Lewis A. Gann, editor of the National Archives, and Theodore Bull, publisher of the *Central African Examiner*, all of Salisbury.

[2] Roland Oliver and J. D. Fage, *A Short History of Africa* (Baltimore: Penguin Books, 1962), p. 132.

Map 4. The Rhodesias and Nyasaland.

Similar political systems controlling large areas also existed in what was later to become Northern Rhodesia (which the Africans plan to rename Zambia). For example, in the eighteenth century, the Kazembe, a branch of the Lunda people, set up a kingdom based upon the Luapula River that was later to become a boundary between British and Belgian possessions in Central Africa. Another relatively sophisticated political system has survived to this day in Barotseland, a province of Northern Rhodesia, under the special protection of the British Colonial Office.

The Barotse kingdom was conquered for a short time in the mid-nineteenth century by a branch of the Sotho, who had in turn been displaced from their lands, in what is now Natal in South Africa, by the conquering Zulu under Shaka and his successors. The Zulu, who were reacting to pressure from Boers trekking north and east from Cape Colony, set off a whole series of migrations. In their course, most tribes located themselves in those areas where the imposition of European colonial rule was eventually to fix them permanently. For example, one group of Zulu, the Ngoni, raided all the way north to the shores of Lake Nyasa, where they finally settled. Another, the Matabele, established themselves in Southern Rhodesia at the expense of the weakened Mashona, whom they dominated until the defeat of the Matabele King Lobengula at the hands of the colonists of Rhodes's British South Africa Company, in 1893.

COLONIAL RULE

Before the administrative scope of the Chartered Company (so called because it had been established by Royal Charter) was extended to most of the area of the two Rhodesias in the early 1890's, Christian missionaries had been the forerunners if not first agents of colonization. The most famous of them was Dr. David Livingstone, who concentrated his activities especially in Nyasaland and Northern Rhodesia. The extent of his explorations and the impact of his mission are shown by two locations still bearing his name today: the town of Livingstone near Victoria Falls, which he discovered, and Livingstonia, site of an influential Church of Scotland mission school, whose founding he inspired. Its campus may soon be used for the planned University of Malawi, the name substituted for Nyasaland by the leadership of its independence movement.

The London Missionary Society sponsored Livingstone's explorations between 1851 and 1873. It had also set up a mission, in 1859, in Zambesia, as Southern Rhodesia was then called. But these were by no means the only early links between the two Rhodesias and Nyasaland. Dr. Livingstone at one point commended Africa to the attention of his British public for the sake of "commerce and Christianity." This combination may strike us as blasphemous or, at the least, in bad taste. But it should be remembered that Livingstone recognized the need to find a substitute for the slave trade. Moreover,

This was the age of *laissez-faire,* and it was generally assumed that the Christian gospel, combined with the natural propensity of man to traffic and exchange, would provide a sufficient stimulus. Missionaries would teach the Africans both to cover their nakedness and to obey the moral law. Traders would supply the means to satisfy the first requirement in the shape of bales from the mills of Lancashire, which would be exchanged for the primary produce grown by industrious, thrifty, Christian, African peasants. Tribes would combine into federations for the better advancement of commerce, and so the nations of the future of Africa would be born.[3]

Only when this automatic mechanism failed to operate as expected did European governments, as distinguished from missionary societies and chartered commercial companies, begin to participate directly in the "scramble for Africa." This happened in Nyasaland starting about 1883 as a result of threats from Portuguese (and therefore Roman Catholic) East Africa to the British and Protestant traders and missionaries on the shores of Lake Nyasa. Even after it became a British protectorate the British administration of Nyasaland received for several years an annual subsidy of £10,000 from Cecil Rhodes. In other words, in the earliest colonization of or contact with the three territories that were, sixty years later, to be joined in the Federation of Rhodesia and Nyasaland, there was brought into being a network of links between them. Moreover, this was superimposed upon the older network of ties among their peoples, based upon tribal relationships of common descent, alliance, or hostility.

Until 1923, both Southern and Northern Rhodesia were governed by the British South Africa Company, whose main aim was to pay good dividends to its stockholders in the United Kingdom. It did not in fact pay dividends until 1924, and it became truly profitable only after the later exploitation of the Northern Rhodesian copper deposits. The interests of the European settlers in the Rhodesias sometimes conflicted with those of the company's administrators. (In 1921, there were 33,620 Europeans in Southern Rhodesia and 3,634 in Northern

[3] *Ibid.,* pp. 144–145.

Rhodesia.) In response to petitions from the settlers, Winston Church-
ill as Colonial Secretary appointed the Buxton Commission, which
recommended that Northern Rhodesia become a protectorate under
the Colonial Office, a status already enjoyed by Nyasaland since
May 14, 1891. The electorate of Southern Rhodesia was given the
choice, in a referendum, of joining the Union of South Africa as a
fifth province or of being granted "responsible government" as a
British colony. The voters chose responsible government by 8,744
votes to 5,989, a ratio of about 60:40. This ratio was approximately
repeated in the Southern Rhodesian referenda of 1953 and 1962, on
the issues, respectively, of joining the Federation and of approving
a new territorial constitution.

The grant of responsible government to Southern Rhodesia—in
effect to its enfranchised population, which included very few non-
Europeans—can be looked upon as a major historical road fork for
British Central Africa. From then on, the Southern Rhodesian government was responsible and responsive to its almost exclusively European electorate. The one major limit on this local responsiveness was
a constitutional veto retained by the British government over legislation which it considered discriminatory against the native population. Although this veto was never used directly, it apparently served
to inhibit the Southern Rhodesian government from proposing grossly
discriminatory acts.

The Southern Rhodesian civil service was taken over intact from
the Chartered Company. It was locally based, and the powerful Native
Affairs Department, in charge of all aspects of African life, was for
practical purposes free of control by the British government. This
happened despite a provision in the constitution forbidding removal
of the Chief Native Commissioner without British assent. This provision was included in anticipation of conflicts between a progressive
Chief of the Native Affairs Department and the Southern Rhodesian
government. As things turned out, the Chief Native Commissioners
always lagged behind the government.

In Northern Rhodesia and Nyasaland, by contrast, all phases of
administration were in the hands of the British Colonial Service, controlled directly by the Colonial Office in Whitehall. Its top officers
usually rotated from one colony to another, so that they would not
develop strong ties to the local settler community. Moreover, they
were prohibited from acquiring local real estate, whereas no such
prohibition was imposed upon Native Affairs officers in the South.

These differences in "native policy" were crystallized by the so-called Passfield *Memorandum on Native Policy*,[4] issued in 1930 by the Labour government's Colonial Secretary, Lord Passfield, the socialist theoretician who is better known as Sydney Webb. This document proclaimed what came to be known as the doctrine of native paramountcy: "His Majesty's Government think it necessary definitely to record their considered opinion that the interests of African Natives must be paramount, and that if and when those interests and those of the immigrant races should conflict, the former should prevail."

Although no official document ever stated that, in case of such a conflict in Southern Rhodesia, the interests of the white immigrant race should prevail, such a statement would in fact have put in a nutshell the assumptions underlying Southern Rhodesian policies. This major difference between Southern Rhodesia on the one hand and Northern Rhodesia and Nyasaland on the other was to continue until the beginning of the Federation and, it seems fair to say, even until its end.

The difference did not necessarily operate to the economic disadvantage of Africans in Southern Rhodesia. The "white settlers," farmers, miners, and businessmen, found it in their interest, for example, to take public health measures in order to prevent the outbreak of epidemics among the Africans, since disease knows no color bar. Other forces of nature, like those leading to erosion of the land, also operate in this nondiscriminatory manner, and the Southern Rhodesian government consequently promoted conservation schemes on African reserves as in the European areas. Again, the government spent more money on African primary education than did the Colonial Office in its territories, mainly because it was in the interest of European employers to have available some at least minimally literate African workers. Politically and socially, however, Southern Rhodesia's Africans were generally worse off than those in Northern Rhodesia. This was given as the main difference in native policy in 1941 by Lord Hailey, who was then the outstanding authority in the field.[5]

The Southern Rhodesian Legislative Assembly, whose forerunner, the Legislative Council, had operated under Chartered Company administration since 1898, became wholly elective in 1923. It had thirty members, all of them white. The government consisted of a

[4] *Memorandum on Native Policy in East Africa*, Cmd. 3573, H.M.S.O., June 1930.
[5] Lord Hailey, *Note on the Bearing of Native Policy on the Proposed Amalgamation of the Rhodesias and Nyasaland* (confidential; London: H.M.S.O., 1941).

Prime Minister and his cabinet, all members of the Legislative Assembly, on the pattern of "responsible government" in other British colonies beginning with Canada in the 1840's. This meant that the Governor, as the official representative of the Monarch, was bound to take the advice of the Prime Minister; that the official post of Leader of the Opposition in Parliament was created; and that party politics on the British pattern began to develop.

In Northern Rhodesia, the Legislative Council, established in 1924, initially consisted of the British-appointed Governor, as its presiding officer, his Chief Secretary, the Attorney General, the Financial Secretary, and the Secretary for Native Affairs, all of whom, including the Governor, were civil servants of the Colonial Office; of four other members nominated by the Governor; and of five members elected by the local European community. This proportion was gradually changed in favor of Unofficials over Officials and of elected over nominated members. In 1948 for the first time a European elected member was placed in charge of one of the administrative departments; in later years more European elected members of the Legislative Council became members of the Governor's Executive Council. Eventually, after federation, a few Africans became members first of the Legislative Council and then, after the Federation began to function, of the Executive Council as ministers. Throughout this process, the doctrine of native paramountcy was repeatedly reasserted, though not always in unequivocal terms, by the British government and by its colonial officials on the spot, who retained control of the key offices in the Executive Council and of the territorial, provincial, and district administration.

There were further differences between Northern and Southern Rhodesian policies toward the African populations. For example, in 1936, a European member of the Northern Rhodesian Legislative Council, Sir Stewart Gore-Brown, who had been leader of the Unofficials, was designated as "Nominated Member representing African interests," a position for which there was never a parallel in Southern Rhodesia. In 1946, Northern Rhodesia set up an African Representative Council, whose members were indirectly elected by African Provincial Councils. In Southern Rhodesia, there were no African representative organs at provincial or higher levels. In all these respects, Nyasaland followed the Northern Rhodesian pattern, but with a time lag of several years, until it jumped ahead of its neighboring protectorate with implementation of the constitution of 1960. Under this constitution the leaders of the majority party among the African elected members of the Legislative Council became ministers in the Executive Council.

The Federation that was established in 1953 had no immediate effects of lasting consequence upon the most important difference between the two northern territories and Southern Rhodesia, that is, upon African policy. Nyasaland and Northern Rhodesia continued as protectorates and Southern Rhodesia as a self-governing colony. But the new Federal Assembly was to contain African members (until 1958, 6 out of 35; after 1958, 12 out of 59). Despite mounting opposition to federation from the independence movements, enough Africans to fill these seats—by election or nomination—presented themselves in the three federal elections, of 1953, 1958, and 1962.

Southern Rhodesia's native policy was at first barely affected by federation, but soon contradictions between this policy and the Federation's constitutional dedication to multiracial partnership and cooperation became too obvious to be overlooked. Discrepancies between Northern and Southern native policies had been one of the main reasons given by the Bledisloe Commission investigating closer association among the three territories when it reported, in March 1939, against early "amalgamation." These discrepancies in fact turned out to be the strongest basis for African opposition to federation, both before and after it actually came into existence—Africans in the northern territories feared that federation would extend Southern Rhodesia's discriminatory practices northward.

This fear was especially strong regarding the Southern Rhodesian Land Apportionment Act of 1931, which reserved less than half the colony's land for Africans and declared a roughly equal area open to European settlement. In terms of access to markets, the European area was much better provided for than the African reserves, since the Africans were still subsistence farmers and it was not anticipated that they would soon want to market their crops. Defenders of Southern Rhodesia's native policy often maintained that the Land Apportionment Act protected the Africans' land by prohibiting purchase of real estate in the reserves by Europeans or Asians. Africans in the northern territories, however, understood the Land Apportionment Act and its possible extension to them as a design to take away their land from them.

In any event, neither this nor other Southern Rhodesian discriminatory legislation was extended to the North. On the contrary, the reverse occurred, though at no great speed. Still, in 1962, the Southern Rhodesian government declared its firm intention to abolish all non-political racially discriminatory legislation on its statute books, took important steps in that direction, and even set about the virtual disestablishment of the Native Affairs Department, which was to be left with severely curtailed functions of a purely administrative nature. Moreover, under a new constitution that came into effect in December 1962, the Southern Rhodesian Legislative Assembly, hitherto made up of 30 European members, consisted of 65 members, 15 of them elected on a lower roll whose voters, as expected, elected Africans.

What lasting effects are these differences between British colonial administration and white settler rule likely to have upon the future politics of these three countries? The question can best be answered by comparing the rise of independence movements in the three territories. But first we should caution against exaggeration of the differences and rather stress those common elements of both British colonial government and local government by British people over an indigenous population.

These common elements contrast with the rule of Continental European colonial powers, in Africa and elsewhere. The Portuguese and the Belgians, whose African colonies bordered on the Federation, gave their African subjects virtually no political training, concentrating instead on their cultural assimilation or economic advancement. By contrast, the British made no effort toward cultural assimilation and, even on the Northern Rhodesian Copperbelt, lagged far behind the Belgians in Katanga with respect to African economic advancement. But they did provide valuable political experience, not only in the various councils already mentioned but also in many other, much more informal ways, such as Native Authorities (local government bodies) that adapted British parliamentary procedures or agricultural cooperatives and religious congregations that also learned to operate with British political forms. This has been true even in Southern Rhodesia although, unlike the northern territories, it never wholeheartedly introduced indirect rule and although, because of the pervasive and paternalistic role of the Native Affairs Department, it offered fewer opportunities for experience with local or associational self-government. One apparent effect of this aspect of British rule is a greater capacity for political organization on the part of British-trained Africans. In consequence, even in the unlikely event of the outbreak of violence on a large scale in Southern Rhodesia, the kind of disorder prevailing in the Congo after the Belgians' precipitate departure seems improbable.

One other distinctive quality of British rule deserves mention in this context—its (at least relatively) firm resoluteness. The Belgian administration in the Congo panicked after comparatively minor outbreaks of violence, and Belgian residents fled at the slightest provocation. In fact, many Belgians from Elisabethville sought refuge in the Rhodesias in 1960 and again in 1961. White settlers in Southern Rhodesia related as typical the story of a young Belgian bachelor who, upon hearing two shots fired in the distance, immediately left his house without even turning off the lights and drove alone in his car all the way to Salisbury—never stopping to give a ride to Belgian women and children who might also have wanted to flee. Rhodesians told stories about the flight of individual Belgians with such obvious disapproval that one may conclude most of them would react much more calmly in a similar situation. And the governments of all three territories, when they believed themselves threatened (however wrongly) by nationalist violence, acted with firm resolution, at least to the extent that the nationalists were given clear indications that the government would not respond to violence with political concessions. Nor, on the other hand, did any of the governments in the Federation ever take reprisals on such a massive, brutal, and uncalled-for scale as did the Portuguese government against the rebellion in Angola.

Without, at this point, condoning or condemning the actions of either nationalists or governments in the Federation between 1959 and 1963, in which more than a hundred Africans were killed by security forces in a series of incidents, the point should be made that African participants in these clashes could usually know just what to expect, because the government had given them due notice. In this sense, therefore, while Belgian and Portuguese reactions were erratic or brutal, British reactions were deliberate and limited. Moreover, even when the Southern Rhodesian Parliament passed its Unlawful Organizations and Preventive Detention Acts, in 1959, and the Law and Order Maintenance Act, in 1960, and amendments to them in 1962, all this legislation was widely denounced by, among others, church leaders and the bar as deviations from British traditions of the rule of law and due process. And it was significant that the government felt compelled to go to all the trouble of asking for this legislation and spelling out its extraordinary powers of repression. This at least clearly defined the rules of the game for the nationalists who, quite naturally, rejected the rules as iniquitous. But they had the advantage over their fellows in non-British colonies of knowing precisely how to become political prisoners, the traditional route of advancement for leaders of independence movements in British territories, whether in the Americas (Dr. Jagan), Cyprus (Archbishop Makarios), India (Mr. Nehru), Nyasaland (Dr. Banda), Northern Rhodesia (Mr. Kaunda), or Southern Rhodesia. Joshua Nkomo, president of the Southern Rhodesian independence movement, returned home voluntarily after his party was banned in September 1962, in the knowledge that he would be restricted to his native village. He had never before been arrested.

When future comparisons are made between members of the Federation and their ex-Belgian and ex-Portuguese neighbors, among the most enduring effects of British rule are likely to be found the use of British political procedures, a firmer commitment to the rule of law, and governments less likely to panic and generally more purposeful than those in the former possessions of Continental European states.

RISE AND CHARACTER OF NATIONALIST MOVEMENT

Each of the independence movements of the three territories has its own history and leadership. In fact, the lack of coordination between them could be considered remarkable in view of their shared demand for dismantling of the Federation, opposition to which gave to each movement its greatest impetus. Their separateness must be attributed to the different native policies of the three territorial governments, as well as to differences in geography, economy, and social structure.

Northern Rhodesia was the first to produce an effective African National Congress (as the independence movements of all three territories were called in their first stage lasting until 1959). The main reason it was ahead was economic—the phenomenal growth of the mining industry on the Copperbelt, particularly during World War II. Even before the war, in the early 1930's, educated Africans resident in the major towns on the Copperbelt and in Broken Hill (also a mining town) and Lusaka (the capital) had organized African Welfare Organizations. Their membership transcended tribal lines. They met regularly for discussions and occasionally submitted proposals to District Commissioners or the Secretary for Native Affairs. Another forerunner upon which the African National Congress was able to build was the African Mineworkers Union, founded in 1949 as an amalgamation of unions set up the previous year on the various mines. The main stimulus to formation of the unions came from industrial unrest on the Copperbelt and, particularly, from the stiff resistance to African economic advancement from the European Mineworkers Union. By 1959, the ANC, under the leadership of Harry Nkumbula, had organized itself on a territory-wide basis and had become the uncontested organ for the expression of African political opinion in Northern Rhodesia. By contrast with Southern Rhodesia, both the African United Trade Union Congress and the African National Congress in Northern Rhodesia were given some government encouragement in their organizational efforts during this stage. Among other factors, the nomination of European members to represent African interests in the Legislative Council, mentioned above, tended to stimulate African political consciousness and organization. So did the establishment, in 1946, of the African Representative Council.

As a result of this organizational head start, Africans in Northern Rhodesia were better prepared than their neighbors in the other two territories to mount a campaign against the Federation in the years before 1953. In early 1952, for instance, the Congress appointed a "Supreme Action Council" to coordinate anti-Federation activity. The council had nine members, five of them from the African United Trade Union Congress. The establishment of the Federation, despite this campaign and threats of strikes, resulted in increases in members and activities for the ANC. For example, in 1956, it organized a boycott against discrimination in (federal) post offices, butcheries, and other retail establishments. It also got involved in electoral politics for seats for Africans in the Legislative Council (indirectly elected between 1954 and 1959, directly thereafter).

Former leaders of the Congress also became members of the Federal Assembly, but at the cost of expulsion from the ANC. Here a common pattern was followed, in that the original leadership, upon becoming too cooperative with the government (or, in the case of the trade unions, with the employers), was either supplanted by more "radical" leaders, or the latter led a splinter movement from the parent organization. For the Northern Rhodesian African National Congress, this split was made just before the Emergency of 1959, when a majority under the leadership of Kenneth Kaunda split off to form the Zambia African National Congress. It was outlawed by the territorial government, and its leaders were either jailed or "rusticated." that is, restricted to remote rural areas. Upon their release, in the course of the next year, they reorganized as the United National Independence Party (UNIP), which subsequently became the majority African movement (in competition with the minority ANC under Nkumbula's continued presidency) and was recognized as such by the British government during the negotiations on constitutional advancement leading to the constitution of 1962 and the Legislative Council elections of October of that year.

Nyasaland lacked the equivalents of both the Copperbelt and Northern Rhodesia's substantial European population. (In 1951, there were 4,073 Europeans in Nyasaland, compared with 37,221 in Northern Rhodesia.) In consequence, it had neither the industrial focus for African political organization nor the fully developed Legislative Council brought into being in response to settlers' demands, in which the call for African representation could serve as one rallying cry for the nationalists. In fact, a large proportion of the territory's able-bodied males was usually away at work in the Rhodesias (or as far away as South Africa), where they and their descendants provided some of those countries' nationalist leaders. A Nyasaland African National Congress came into being after World War II, most of its members being government employees. Its organization received government encouragement, because the administration welcomed creation of this outlet for opinions of "advanced" Africans.

When two Africans were for the first time added to the Nyasaland Legislative Council, they were selected, however, by the Governor from a list submitted by the Protectorate Council, an indirectly elected equivalent of the Northern Rhodesian African Representative Council. A similar procedure was used to select Nyasaland's two African members of the Federal Assembly, in office from 1954 to 1959. These two African M.P.'s originally had the support of the ANC but suffered the same fate as the first group of leaders in Northern Rhodesia. The ANC asked them to resign from the Federal Parliament and, when they refused to do so, expelled them and subsequently labeled them "stooges." In 1956, when non-Africans on the Legislative Council (which was to serve until 1961) were elected directly for the first time, the 5 African members were elected by the three Provincial Councils, acting as an electoral college consisting of a total of 76 Africans.

Throughout this period, during which active industrial and electoral politics were being conducted in Northern Rhodesia, opposition to the Federation provided virtually the only focus for independence activities in Nyasaland. This was particularly evident during the year immediately preceding the founding of the Federation, when several demonstrations against it took place, involving many sectors of the African population and including respected old tribal chiefs. Several of these chiefs even journeyed to London in order to present a humble petition to the Queen, to whose presence they were, however, not admitted.

Nyasaland's independence movement did not really "get off the ground" until the return of Dr. Hastings Kamuzu Banda to the home he had left forty years earlier. Dr. Banda had received his college and medical education in the United States and Scotland. He had been in private practice in London until 1953, when he moved to the Gold Coast. Having kept up a correspondence and acquaintance with chiefs and other leaders in Nyasaland throughout his absence, he was invited, in 1958, to return as president of the Nyasaland African National Congress by some of its younger leaders. He succeeded at once in rallying the politically conscious population and, as it turned out, in frightening the government, in collaboration with the federal government, into declaring the Emergency of 1959. The ANC was outlawed, Dr. Banda and several hundred other officers and members were jailed, and sixty Africans were killed by security forces during the round up.

The dominant role played by Dr. Banda distinguishes his independence movement from those of the two Rhodesias, which lacked a parallel figure whose leadership remained uncontested. In Nyasaland, even those African members of Legislative Council who left the ANC when it was outlawed, as well as other ANC officers who founded competing organizations while Dr. Banda was in jail, failed to win away from his movement as much support as Harry Nkumbula's Northern Rhodesian ANC had when its fortunes were at their lowest ebb. As a result, once Dr. Banda was released from jail in April 1960, he was in a clearer, stronger negotiating position vis-à-vis the British government.

Dr. Banda's movement had meanwhile been renamed the Malawi Congress Party. The main planks in its platform were immediate secession from the Federation and "one-man one-vote." Although the British government granted neither demand, the constitution of 1960 was sufficiently advanced to satisfy both Dr. Banda and his followers and, in 1961, to sweep them into overwhelming majority control of the reconstituted Legislative Council and into ministerial offices. After this demonstration of Malawi's popularity in an orderly election and after the new African ministers had shown their drive, determination, and ability for a year, the British government, in December 1962, admitted that Nyasaland could secede from the Federation. Dr. Banda was, therefore, in the enviable position of having moved the farthest in the shortest time. He did not use this position, however, in order to try to assume leadership over the Rhodesian independence movement. Although the Malawi Congress Party maintained contacts with its brother organizations—for example, its Salisbury branch office was next door to the headquarters of the Zimbabwe African People's Union—it concentrated on its own immediate goals of achieving full responsible government free from both federal and British controls.

The Southern Rhodesian independence movement, also originally called the ANC, seemed at times to be held in contempt by its more successful counterparts in the other two territories. In the eyes of the Northerners, Southern Rhodesian Africans had suffered most under white rule and continued to do so in the early 1960's. After all, it was because of their knowledge of discriminatory legislation in effect in Southern Rhodesia—gained by many Nyasas from personal experience during employment there—that Africans of the northern territories opposed the Federation from the time it was first proposed. And yet the Southern Rhodesian African National Congress had appeared less militant than the two northern congresses. The same was true of the ANC's successor, the National Democratic Party, founded in January 1960. This, in turn, was banned in December 1961, only to be reorganized under the new name of Zimbabwe African People's Union (ZAPU). ZAPU, finally, was outlawed in September 1962, after passage of amendments to the Law and Order Maintenance Act designed to make impossible simple reorganization through adoption of another name.

The main cause for this relative mildness of Southern Rhodesia's African nationalists must be sought in local settler control of the country's government and its native policy since 1923. Africans were allowed to participate in European politics only if they satisfied initially high and steadily raised economic qualifications, and they were discouraged from organizing politics of their own. As already mentioned, there were neither African district nor provincial councils and, of course, no Africans in the Legislative Assembly before the election of December 1962. Although Southern Rhodesia's industrial development, while not as massive and concentrated as mining ac-

tivities on the Copperbelt, would have given opportunities for building an African labor organization, this was regarded as illegal until
1959. Strikes by Africans were often suppressed by force. Finally,
even opposition to the Federation could not be used as effectively
as a rallying cry for political organization as in the North because
Africans in Southern Rhodesia could reasonably expect an improvement in their lot as the result of the colony's joining the Federation.

Federation in 1953 not only committed Southern Rhodesia's government officially to a policy of partnership and cooperation between
the races but for the first time brought two Africans from Southern
Rhodesia into Parliament, through election from the common voters'
roll to the Federal Assembly. (Under the constitutional amendments
of 1957, four Africans were elected to the Federal Parliament from
Southern Rhodesia.) In fact, it was easier in Southern Rhodesia than
in the North to find Africans who were willing to serve the Federation in various capacities and to support the dominant United Federal
Party (UFP), led by Sir Roy Welensky after he succeeded Lord
Malvern as Federal Prime Minister.

This absence of the triple stimuli of territorial electoral politics,
industrial organization, and opposition to the Federation meant that
the Southern Rhodesian ANC did not catch up organizationally with
that of Northern Rhodesia until most of the hopes initially engendered
by federation had, in the eyes of African politicians, been disappointed. This point was reached in 1958, after a double disillusionment resulting from the approval by the British government of amendments to the federal constitution that changed the composition of
the Federal Parliament by enlarging its membership to 59, of whom
12 were to be Africans, and from the removal by his own caucus of
the Southern Rhodesian Prime Minister, Garfield Todd, because he
had made some minor concessions to Africans that his followers condemned as "too liberal." The Africans were particularly upset by
British approval of the amendment of the federal constitution, because the African Affairs Board of the Federal Parliament had reserved the amending bill as discriminatory against Africans. When
the British government rejected this interpretation, many Africans
felt that the African Affairs Board was not in fact functioning as
guardian of their interests and, beyond this, that written constitutional guarantees against discrimination were practically worthless.

Still, the ANC did not become a true mass movement until the
Emergency of 1959, when most of its leaders were arrested, a few of

the most important ones to be kept in detention for more than three years. Subsequent passage of the Unlawful Organizations and Preventive Detention Acts (1959) and the riots of 1960, in the course of which a number of Africans were killed by security forces, had the result of further increasing nationalist support. The Law and Order Maintenance Act of 1960 had similar effects.

The latter statute also helped Joshua Nkomo, the president of ZAPU, to plead a case for support from the United Nations, when he appeared before its Special Committee of Seventeen on Colonialism, in early 1962. The United States, in view of its professed commitment to due process of law, found it more difficult than usual to support the United Kingdom on this issue, because of this restrictive Southern Rhodesian legislation. In June 1962, the General Assembly passed a resolution urging the United Kingdom to suspend the new Southern Rhodesian constitution, to broaden the franchise before permitting new elections to be held, and to reassert its control over the white government of the colony. Armed with this declaration of support from an overwhelming majority of United Nations members, Joshua Nkomo returned to Zimbabwe, as ZAPU members called Southern Rhodesia, declared that he would negotiate only with the British, not the Southern Rhodesian government, and asserted that the elections then scheduled for the spring of 1963 would not take place or would not be democratic if they were held. He was immediately answered by Sir Edgar Whitehead, Prime Minister of Southern Rhodesia, who just as firmly reasserted his determination to maintain the new constitution until the election and declared that anyone who sought to interfere with electoral processes by unconstitutional means would be dealt with by the security forces. After sporadic outbreaks of violence, most of it intra-African, Whitehead fulfilled his promise by outlawing ZAPU in September 1962 and arresting or restricting more than a thousand of its leaders and members and then by advancing the date of the election to December 14, 1962.

Whatever the outcome in Southern Rhodesia, the African independence movements in the three territories constituting the Federation had succeeded by 1962 in setting off the slow "evaporation," as it were, of the Federation. The six Malawi ministers and two parliamentary secretaries in the Nyasaland Executive Council refused to have dealings with the federal government, and the British government ordered a study of the least painful method for extricating the territory from its constitutional links with the Rhodesias. Before the end of 1962, R. A. Butler, the British Deputy Prime Minister, announced that Nyasaland would be allowed to withdraw from the Federation and that Dr. Banda would become Prime Minister within two months. In Northern Rhodesia, where the much higher proportion of European residents and closer economic links with the southern colony made this problem more difficult for Great Britain, the Legislative Council elections of October 1962, and run-offs of December, failed to produce a UNIP parliamentary majority, leading instead to a UNIP-ANC coalition government under the Governor. But the election showed that African voters were as committed as their Malawi neighbors to sever their country's constitutional ties to Southern Rhodesia. On March 29, 1963, this brought the expected result, when R. A. Butler announced on behalf of the British government that Northern Rhodesia's right to secede would also be recognized.

Sir Edgar Whitehead had been talking of the virtual certainty of getting an African majority in the Southern Rhodesian electorate in twelve years' time by processes of natural growth, not amendment of the franchise. The Southern Rhodesian electorate and government had been pushed by Great Britain into making concessions to African demands which most observers would have regarded as most improbable a very short time before they were in fact made. And then, later in 1962, ZAPU succeeded in getting the United Nations to try to prod the unresponsive British government into acknowledging its continuing responsibilities for Southern Rhodesia as a "non-self governing territory" and to speed it toward government based on the consent of the African majority. But when the new Legislative Assembly was elected, on December 14, 1962, the opposition Rhodesian Front, much more reluctant than the UFP to grant African political advancement, gained a victory. Winston Field replaced Sir Edgar Whitehead as Prime Minister of Southern Rhodesia, and the new Southern Rhodesian government seemed no more enthusiastic about continuing the Federation than was the new Northern Rhodesian government. One result of these developments was the increasing isolation of the federal government and its Prime Minister, Sir Roy Welensky, and the possibility that, with the complete dismantling of the Federation, Welensky would try to form a coalition with the Rhodesian Front government of Southern Rhodesia in order to press the British government into granting that colony full independence in return for some broadening of the franchise. In any case, it was between its 220,000 Europeans and 3,600,000 Africans that the last

act of the Central African drama of the conflict between African independence movements and white settlers would be played.

PROSPECTS

What made the Rhodesian situation such a dilemma is the fact that
the Rhodesias have had not only black but also white nationalists or
independence movements. After Southern Rhodesia was granted responsible government in 1923, the major motive of advocates of amalgamation with Northern Rhodesia was the desire of white settlers in
the North to escape Colonial Office control, especially of native policy.
The federal constitution did not satisfy this wish. That was one reason
why the federal government and its United Federal Party had hoped
to obtain "full Dominion status" (that is, independence from Great
Britain such as possessed by Canada or Australia) as a result of the
review of the federal constitution that began in 1960. Southern Rhodesia, too, sought to eliminate the powers of reservation over discriminatory legislation that the British government retained under the constitution of 1923. It succeeded in this respect during the negotiations
that yielded Southern Rhodesia's new constitution, though at the cost of
concessions to Africans, on whose behalf ZAPU for a short time seemed
to accept the constitution. The concessions included a constitutional
Declaration of Rights, promises to abolish discrimination including the
Land Apportionment Act, and expansion of the Legislative Assembly
to a membership of 65, of whom the 15 elected from the lower roll
were expected to be Africans.

When the British government proved reluctant to relinquish its
controls over native policy in Northern Rhodesia and moved far ahead
of European opinion with respect to constitutional advance in both
northern territories, some European politicians, including Sir Roy
Welensky, occasionally threatened "to go it alone" and even to use
force if necessary. It seems, however, that only in Southern Rhodesia
will they be given the chance to act on such threats, and even there
the likelihood of anti-British—as distinguished from anti-African—
violence seemed slim, if the pattern of past actions is projected into
the future. In the past, the federal government, however reluctantly,
has always given in to British demands when these were stated with
sufficient firmness. And Southern Rhodesia's European electorate thrice
approved constitutional policies favored by British governments. It
therefore seemed likely, in 1963, that the dismantling of the Federation
would proceed without violence under British guidance.

The admission of Africans to full participation in the government and politics of Southern Rhodesia was expected to be a more troublesome process, probably to be accompanied by sabotage and occasional clashes between security forces and African demonstrators. But even in Southern Rhodesia, African government was likely to come long before the end of the twelve years of Whitehead's timetable for an African electoral majority. When this happens, the three members of the short-lived Federation are likely to get back together in some form of association, which may well include other adjacent African states.

Beginning in 1958, leaders of the Central African independence movements participated in the Pan-African Freedom Movement for East, Central, and Southern Africa (PAFMECSA). In 1962, Kenneth Kaunda, president general of UNIP, was elected to the top position, the chairmanship, in PAFMECSA. All these movements were more or less strongly committed to Pan-Africanism. Most of their members also agreed with Simon Kapwepwe, the treasurer general of UNIP, that "we must first win freedom in each of the artificial cages into which colonialism has put us." But after this goal of territorial independence has been achieved, the African leaders of Zimbabwe, Zambia, and Malawi are very likely to draw the political consequences of their precolonial and colonial history of cultural, economic, and constitutional links, to which may well be added the need of pooling military resources against the Republic of South Africa.

The Contemporary Setting

GEOGRAPHY

The geography of central Africa cannot be said to have created any "natural" unity between the three members of the Federation. The concept and fact of territorial boundaries was introduced into Africa by the colonial powers. But if frontiers had to be drawn within British Central Africa, they could hardly have been drawn better than they were. This applies especially to the River Zambezi, which comes as close as possible to forming a "natural frontier," in the nineteenth-century sense, between Southern and Northern Rhodesia (though in the twentieth century the damming of the Zambezi at Kariba Gorge required cooperation between them, forged a literal concrete link between the Rhodesias, and benefited the populations of both). The area west of Lake Nyasa that was incorporated in Nyasaland, rather than becoming a part of Northern Rhodesia, is separated from the latter by a watershed.

However, there may be one respect in which the two Rhodesias and Nyasaland will soon form a geographical unity—strategy. At present, the Federation is a kind of buffer state between the independent countries of Black Africa on the one hand and Portuguese Africa and the Republic of South Africa on the other. Moreover, at least one Rhodesian politician, Sir Edgar Whitehead, has taken the position, which seems to have no historical precedents anywhere, of seeking to play and relishing this role of the buffer—a role that elsewhere has usually been forced upon a reluctant small country by its more powerful neighbors who preferred to keep at buffer length from one another. Both Nyasaland and Southern Rhodesia border on Mozambique. Southern Rhodesia has a common boundary with the Republic of South Africa and with Bechuanaland, a British High Commission Territory moving toward responsible government but exposed to possible South African aggression (as are the other two British protectorates in South Africa, Swaziland and Basutoland). Northern Rhodesia also has a common boundary with Bechuanaland and, along the Caprivi Strip, with South-West Africa, the League of Nations mandate, whose administration by South Africa has been contested in the United Nations and before the World Court. The remainder of Northern Rhodesia's external boundaries are with Angola, the Congo, and Tanganyika; Nyasaland also shares a boundary with Tanganyika, more than half of it on the northern and eastern shores of Lake Nyasa. This may possibly make for strategic unity between the three members of the present Federation, for instance, in case the United Nations and/or a Pan-African grouping of states should try to take military measures against Portugal's two large colonies in East and West Africa or in case similar hostilities should arise with the Republic of South Africa, either directly or over South-West Africa or Bechuanaland. This strategic kind of consideration is likely to play a role in fashioning whatever new associations are brought into being after Southern Rhodesia's internal constitutional problems have been solved.

Most of the land in the Federation is higher than 2,000 feet, with much of it over 4,000 feet; for example, the altitude of Salisbury is 4,830 feet. This factor contributed to the influx of European settlers, because it makes for a remarkably mild year-around climate, except in the river valleys and on the shores of Lake Nyasa. The mean annual temperature in Salisbury and on the Copperbelt is between 65 and

70 degrees Fahrenheit. On the other hand, the Central African plateau, with the exceptions just mentioned, is relatively arid, with an average annual rainfall in Salisbury of 33 inches, in Ndola of 46 inches, and in Zomba of 54 inches, concentrated in a rainy season of about four months. This restricts the agricultural uses to which land can be put unless it is artificially irrigated. However, much of the area is suited for grazing, where this is not inhibited by tse-tse fly, which still infests two-fifths of Northern Rhodesia and some parts of Southern Rhodesia.

THE ECONOMY

Resources

Cecil Rhodes organized the settlement of Southern Rhodesia and the administrative take-over of Northern Rhodesia and Nyasaland for a mixture of political and economic motives that were typical of him. He wanted to paint red a route from the Cape to Cairo and, therefore, considered strategically vital British control of territory north of the Boer republics and of Nyasaland with its exposure to Portuguese threats. But Rhodes and the first settlers of the country named after him were also attracted by reports of its riches of gold and other precious metals. Although their excessive expectations were disappointed, Southern Rhodesia's gold mines continue to this day to produce sizable quantities of gold (in 1961, £7,164,000 worth). Other minerals are also found in substantial amounts, including especially asbestos (£8,400,000 worth in the same year), chrome ore (£3,-010,000), some of the rarer "jet age" minerals like tantalum, niobium, and lithium, and coal (£3,259,000).

For Northern Rhodesia, the British South Africa Company retained the mineral rights after it turned over administrative control to the Colonial Office. While Roy Welensky was in the Northern Rhodesian Legislative Council as leader of the Unofficials, he conducted protracted and occasionally acrimonious negotiations with the company over the revenues from these mineral rights. As a result, the company yielded the revenues to Northern Rhodesia in return for annual royalty payments of 80 per cent which will be terminated in 1986. Until the discovery of the Copperbelt in 1925, Northern Rhodesia produced mainly lead, zinc, and vanadium. Since then, copper has been its main source of income and, indeed, the single most important source of revenue for the Federation (in 1961, the value of copper exported was £111,900,000; of zinc, £1,874,000; and of lead, £728,000). As a result of needs created during the Korean War and with financial support from the United States government, the production of cobalt was also begun on the Copperbelt, and in 1961, £684,000 worth was exported.

There has been no significant mineral production in Nyasaland, though Dr. Banda believes that previous geological surveys had underestimated the country's resources, which might yield substantial income after an independent government seriously set about their exploitation. There are deposits of rich bauxite ore in the Southern Province and of coal near the Livingstonia School, but lack of transport facilities have so far prevented their exploitation.

Organization

The economy of British Central Africa has been used for "a case study of economic development in a dualistic society." [6] The dualism is that between the indigenous economy, which is mainly a subsistence economy, and the money economy, of which Africans are usually only part-time members. In view of the short life of the Federation and the incomplete merger which it was capable of bringing about, it makes sense to think not of two but of five more or less separate economies in British Central Africa, since the economy of Nyasaland is wholly agricultural and not as segregated as those of the Rhodesias, in each of which one can more clearly distinguish the money from the indigenous subsistence economy.

In Nyasaland, Africans have produced an increasing share, up to half, of two important cash crops, tobacco and peanuts, while the third and most valuable, tea, has been produced on European-owned plantations (1961 exports of tea were worth £4,412,000). But those Africans who produce peanuts, tobacco, or minor cash crops (for the market), like cotton, corn, and rice, are not necessarily full-fledged members of the money economy, since they often harvest just enough to pay their taxes and to buy other items that they cannot produce for themselves. At least this was true before Dr. Banda came into office, perhaps because the necessary incentives were lacking. In 1961, however, after he and his ministers had launched a major agricultural education campaign, record crops were marketed by African farmers.

The greatest participation of Nyasas in money economies happened outside the protectorate itself, through the export of migratory labor,

---

[6] William J. Barber's *The Economy of British Central Africa* (London: Oxford University Press, 1961) is thus subtitled.

especially to Southern Rhodesia and the Copperbelt. At the beginning
of the colonial period, Africans were deliberately encouraged—almost
forced—to work for wages on farms and mines, in their own or neighboring territories, through a tax imposed upon either huts or adult
males by the administration. The tax was payable only in money,
and money could be earned only by wage labor in this period before
Africans produced marketable crops. Since Nyasaland still lacks industry on the Rhodesian scale and also has much more limited local
employment opportunities, a high proportion of its able-bodied males
continues to migrate out of the territory for temporary work elsewhere. Southern Rhodesia in particular used to welcome Nyasa, as
well as Mozambique, workers, because its own Africans did not take
as readily to employment and were regarded as poorer workers. However, as population pressure on African land increased, the performance of Southern Rhodesian workers in European agriculture and industry also improved. At the same time, Sir Edgar Whitehead's
Southern Rhodesian government threatened to prohibit the immigration of "foreign" labor in reprisal for Nyasaland's threatened secession
from the Federation. European farmers, however, who are influential
in the electorate, resented this threat. They continued to prefer Nyasa
labor and expected to be able to apply enough pressure on the government to prevent its flow into the colony from being cut off. Shortly
after his election, Prime Minister Field flew to Nyasaland to confer
with Dr. Banda, and farm labor must have been an important topic
of discussion between them.

The Northern Rhodesian economy is dominated by mining. Of
Africans working for wages, only half as many have been on European farms as on the mines. Mineworkers used to be migratory, in the
the sense that they would return to their villages after they had been
at work for a year or two. More recently, since the 1950's, they have
become a stable labor force permanently resident with their families
in the company townships. Although a large majority of Africans in
Northern Rhodesia is still engaged in indigenous agriculture, the urbanized workers and their "intellectuals" have produced most of the
political leadership.

Southern Rhodesia has the most diversified economy and the best-
developed "infrastructure." Its mineral production has already been
described. Its European agriculture yields even greater export income, tobacco being the major export crop (£42,000,000 in 1961).
Corn and cattle are raised for both domestic consumption and export.

In addition, secondary manufacturing industries, including government-initiated steel and textile mills, have been growing, particularly since World War II. In recent years, there have been such additions as automobile assembly plants.

Salisbury, as the federal (and Southern Rhodesian) capital, experienced a great boom during the 1950's, after federation, when it became the financial and commercial center for all three countries; for example, the two great copper companies, Anglo-American and Rhodesian Selection Trust, transferred their headquarters from London to Salisbury, where the latter built itself a twenty-story skyscraper, appropriately named Livingstone House. Southern Rhodesia employed more than twice as many Africans as Northern Rhodesia in the money economy and was beginning to make provisions for encouraging a stable urban labor force comparable to that on the Copperbelt. But its problems of African urbanization seemed more troublesome. The high proportion of nonindigenous Africans employed—more than half—and the whole complex of legislation built around the Land Apportionment Act accounted for this difference. Moreover, whereas Northern Rhodesia normally employed about double the number of Africans in mining as in European agriculture, this ratio was almost the reverse in the South.

The overwhelming majority of Africans in all three countries remained full-time members of the indigenous economy, and even many African members of the money economy could and did return periodically to the subsistence base of their home villages, especially migratory workers from Nyasaland. But the expansion of the money economy and the parallel contraction of the subsistence economy could be expected to accelerate at the time of the dismantling of the Federation. In Nyasaland, this process was being encouraged by an active development program designed, among other things, to disprove once and for all United Federal Party claims about the economic benefits of federation to this least developed of the three territories. Northern Rhodesia's nationalists expected that the use of Copperbelt revenues for their country's exclusive development—instead of devoting the benefits to all three and particularly to Southern Rhodesia—would bring about a more balanced pattern of economic growth. And although Southern Rhodesians had most cause to fear the economic consequences of severance of links with the North, there, too, the shift of population from subsistence agriculture to the money economy and from rural life to permanent urbanization was bound to speed up.

Lines of Trade

Some of the recent growth of secondary industry in Southern Rhodesia has been due to federation, which enabled the federal government, in 1957, to pull Nyasaland and parts of Northern Rhodesia out of the Congo Basin Treaty of 1888, under which the Congo Basin area was kept a free trade area. Tariffs were then placed on many items manufactured in Southern Rhodesia which could previously be imported freely from cheaper sources. As late as August 1962, the federal government raised tariffs on many goods manufactured in Southern Rhodesia, to the dismay of the northern territories, whose governments were not even consulted ahead of the announcement.

In general, however, the main lines of trade, transport, and communications, both within British Central Africa and between it and the outside world, were not affected significantly by federation. It is true that the main highway between the two Rhodesias was improved, but surface transport between Nyasaland and the Rhodesias was not. Nyasaland's main link to the outside is by railway to the port of Beira in Portuguese East Africa, and its main link to Southern Rhodesia consists of a poor road, most of it also in Mozambique, where one crosses the wide Zambezi by ferry. Only the commercial aviation network, provided by the (federal) Central African Airways was expanded considerably, but even it provided only two weekly flights between Nyasaland and Northern Rhodesia.

Because the Rhodesias are landlocked, the problem of surface transport to the sea had to be solved early after colonization. On the initiative of Cecil Rhodes, railways were built from Beira and South Africa (through Bechuanaland) into Southern Rhodesia and across the Zambezi at Victoria Falls into Northern Rhodesia, to link up with the Congolese line in Katanga by 1909. Later, additional outlets were constructed, one to Lobito Bay in Angola, the other, quite recently, to Lourenço Marques, in Mozambique. The relative use given these outlets is shown by copper railings for 1960: Lourenço Marques, 294,023 short tons; Beira, 250,675; Lobito Bay, 66,601; and South Africa, 12,667.

More than half of this copper and about 47 per cent of the total exports of the Federation go to the United Kingdom; 37 per cent of its imports come from the United Kingdom, and 34 per cent from South Africa, which took 6 per cent of federal exports. In terms of both trade and communications, the Rhodesias were linked most closely with Great Britain, but some of the trade and most of the communications moved through South Africa. For example, the major Rhodesian newspapers belonged to a South African chain, and the only news agency serving them was the South African Press Association.

This pattern of communications was likely to change as Nyasaland and Northern Rhodesia got African governments which, already as independence movements, were oriented toward their East African neighbors. However, even with these probable changes, the pattern of trade could be expected to remain fairly constant, at least on the side of exports. African states, for example, are not likely to become more important customers for Rhodesian copper than are the main present ones—in order, the United Kingdom, West Germany, India, Italy, Sweden, the Netherlands, France, the United States, and Belgium. The same applies to the other mineral exports and to tobacco, of which the United Kingdom is again the main purchaser, followed at a great distance by Australia, West Germany, the Netherlands, Belgium, and South Africa.

Outside Economic Aid

Only Nyasaland can with certainty be considered dependent upon outside economic aid for its development, since it is the only one of the three territories with a wholly agricultural economy and with an overpopulation problem in its Southern Province. Even before the Malawi Congress Party achieved responsible government, Dr. Banda had secured some economic assistance and promises of more from the British and United States governments and private sources. Nyasaland received its first Peace Corps team in 1963, a project negotiated directly with its government without passing through federal channels.

Northern Rhodesia would need outside technical assistance, but more than that it would remain dependent upon the world price of copper for its own internal development, once it secured control over its economy. The two big copper companies could be expected to continue their development aid, more than half of which had gone to Northern Rhodesia even during federation. While Southern Rhodesia was also dependent upon world prices for its export commodities, its more diversified economy suggested that it might be able to promote its own development with relatively less outside assistance by furthering the integration of its African population into its money economy. But during the period of federation, Southern Rhodesia received loans from Great Britain, the United States, and the World Bank and other United Nations sources, mainly for purposes of the Native Development Fund and native education.

The federal government itself was the major recipient of such loans, chiefly in connection with the construction of Kariba Dam, for which the World Bank advanced the largest loan for a single project it had made until that time, $80,000,000. The dam produces hydroelectric power, some of which continues to be imported to the Copperbelt from the Belgian Congo, while the rest was formerly produced by coal, from the Southern Rhodesian field at Wankie or imported via Lobito Bay. The Kariba project won out over a competing one, Kafue Dam, which would have provided both power and irrigation but in Northern Rhodesia alone. Neither this project nor a similar one proposed for the Shire Valley in Nyasaland could have been financed internally. Both would presumably bring great benefits to the African population over a period of time by increasing food production (including fish) and thereby improving the Africans' diet, which is in most cases inadequate and unbalanced. Attempts to improve the diet from existing resources required European initiative and assistance during the period of European rule. For example, it proved difficult to persuade people living some distance away from lakes to eat refrigerated fish instead of the dried fish to which some had been accustomed or to get cattle-keeping tribes to breed their stock for slaughter and consumption by themselves. Ultimately, innovations of this kind that run counter to deeply ingrained customs can probably be brought about only on the initiative and under the leadership of popular African governments. These governments would draw upon outside aid, including one another's, but the direction and speed of change would be determined by themselves.

SOCIAL STRUCTURE

Racial Groups

The single most important fact about the Federation as a whole, and about Southern Rhodesia in particular, is the division of its population into Europeans and Africans. In 1961, Southern Rhodesia was estimated to have 3,200,000 Africans (most estimates of African populations have subsequently proved to be too low) and 221,000 Europeans; Northern Rhodesia, 2,510,000 Africans and 75,000 Europeans; and Nyasaland 2,920,000 Africans and 8,900 Europeans. There were also about 40,000 people in the Federation classified as "other races," that is, mainly Coloreds and Asians. Virtually all political issues in the two Rhodesias and in the Federation derive from this fact of racial composition, regardless of whether they appear to be social or constitutional issues, economic or power questions.

To give only one illustration of this fact, we can cite from the national income figures for the Federation for 1959. Personal income, from wages, salaries, and unincorporated enterprise, was listed as follows (in millions of pounds):

European	£166
Asian and Colored	9
African (including subsistence income, 85)	172

In other words, 312,000 Europeans had roughly the same income as 8,080,000 Africans. In 1961, Europeans had an average annual income of £1,266, Africans of £100.

Tribal Divisions

Although it is customary to think only of native populations as divided into tribes, it is important not to overlook the fact that the Europeans have their equivalent of tribal divisions and loyalties, particularly in British territories. The British themselves, of course, are divided into the great historic tribes of the English, Scots, Welsh, and Irish. British people in the Rhodesias are usually keenly conscious of their tribal origin and affiliation, and on occasion suspicion is expressed even between Lowland and Highland Scots or Lancashiremen and Yorkshiremen. In addition to people of British origin or descent, a good proportion of whom migrated to the Rhodesias from South Africa, there are other ethnic minority groups among the Europeans, especially Afrikaners, Jews (who could be subdivided into Sephardic and Ashkenazim), Greeks, Hollanders (mostly of Indonesian colonial background), Italians, Portuguese, and a variety of smaller communities.

The white population of the Federation almost trebled between 1951 and 1961 (from 117,000 to 345,000), and this, too, has made for noticeable social divisions. In fact, the majority of adult white Rhodesians came to Central Africa after World War II, and they have been a comparatively unsettled "settler" population. While immigration was high, so was white reemigration—for 1957, it was estimated as 39 per cent for the Federation as a whole.[7] In 1958, Northern Rhodesia actually lost 3,300 more emigrants than it gained immigrants. In 1961, the Federation suffered a net loss of 1,241 whites. Such facts have sociological and political import, because they indicate a constant turnover of Europeans and the consequent entry to the Rhodesias of whites many of whom are unfamiliar with African customs and multiracial living patterns. For example, according to the country of origin and the motives for leaving it, newcomers may not know how to deal with African domestic servants or, for that matter, with any domestic servants, in an environment in which even "poor whites" and the unemployed normally have at least one "houseboy." These figures also suggest that the Europeans' commitment to retaining full control over the countries of the Federation is less strong than if a majority of them were descendants of generations of native-born settlers, as the Afrikaners in the Republic of South Africa.[8] In fact, of the resident white adult population (aged twenty or over) in Southern Rhodesia, only 14.5 per cent had been born there, according to the census of 1956.[9]

Each of the three territories has of course its own distinctive tribal composition. Although all the African peoples of the Federation belong to the Bantu-speaking groups, the tribes are scattered as a result of the great migrations that had preceded the fixing of colonial boundaries. The distinctive feature, in this respect, is the virtual "duopoly" held in Southern Rhodesia by two large tribes, the Mashona and the Matabele. In both northern territories, the tribal composition is much more diversified. Among the larger Northern Rhodesian tribes are the Bemba, Ngoni, Chewa, and Bisa, in the northeast; the Lozi, Tonga, Luvale, Lenje, and Ila in the northwest; and the Senga, Lala, and Lunda, in both the west and the east. Among those of Nyasaland are the Ngoni, Nyanga, Yao, and Chewa.

Matabele-Mashona predominance in Southern Rhodesia means that this single tribal cleavage may play a role as a political issue. The concentration of members of these two tribes in different regions of

[7] Lewis H. Gann and Peter Duignan, *White Settlers in Tropical Africa* (Baltimore: Penguin Books, 1962), p. 96.

[8] For a discussion of the Europeans' commitment, see Herbert J. Spiro, *Politics in Africa: Prospects South of the Sahara* (Englewood Cliffs: Prentice-Hall, 1962), pp. 84–88.

[9] Cyril A. Rogers and C. Frantz, *Racial Themes in Southern Rhodesia* (New Haven: Yale University Press, 1962), p. 61.

the country—Mashonaland around Salisbury and Matabeleland around Bulawayo—and their different languages further contribute to this possibility. The issue has so far been raised only in relatively unimportant contexts. Thus, the president of ZAPU, Joshua Nkomo, belongs to the Matabele, but this was counterbalanced by the choice as chairman of the Reverend Ndabaningi Sithole, a Mashona. In any case, the predictions of intertribal violence as a consequence of African self-government, which are frequently made by its European opponents, may come true, if at all, only as self-fulfilling prophecies, that is, as a result of European incitement. Native Commissioners, in particular, were prone to a kind of tribal favoritism, which occasionally lent itself to aggravating tribal antagonisms that had long been dormant. Some Native Commissioners, for example, referred—in private—to the Mashona as "curs," who had always been inferior to the allegedly more martial and sportsmanlike Matabele.

Similar predictions had been made for Nyasaland before the Malawi Congress Party's great electoral victory of 1961. Indeed, the much greater diversity of tribes there, complicated by religious differences (the Yao, for example, are Muslim), led some to expect even greater disunity than in Southern Rhodesia. Tribalism did not become a significant political phenomenon, however, either during or after the election campaign. This may be due to one advantage Nyasaland had, in that about two-thirds of its people speak Nyanja and most of the remainder Timbuku. Moreover, English has been in general use among Nyasaland politicians, even when they normally spoke the same African language. This, in turn, may be because of Dr. Banda's influence, since he uses English, even to the point where he prefers to have his public speeches translated by an interpreter.

The diversity of tribes as well as the effects of the policy of indirect rule have contributed to making tribal identification fairly strong in Northern Rhodesia. For about twenty years, this was true even in the Copperbelt townships, where the mining companies appointed "elders" from the various tribes to adjudicate disputes among their respective members and to represent them vis-à-vis management. This system worked fairly well between 1931 and 1953, but it was better for domestic than for industrial disputes. By 1953, trade union organizations had completely replaced the tribal elders. In the unions, as in African political movements, different tribal groups are usually represented in the leadership as a "balanced ticket." In recent years, however, UNIP and ANC have made charges of tribalism against each other, and the elections of 1962 showed that support for the ANC was geographically concentrated in two districts in particular, in the Ila-populated area southwest of Lusaka. The most significant aspect about these accusations, however, is the outraged way in which they have always been rejected and turned against the accuser, with proof provided in the form of one's own balanced ticket and the alleged predominance of one or two tribes in the opposing group's leadership.

The potential problem of tribalism in Northern Rhodesia was further emphasized by the special status of Barotseland as a protectorate within the protectorate of Northern Rhodesia. This status was based on a "treaty" concluded directly between the Paramount Chief of Barotseland and the British Crown. Although several UNIP leaders came from Barotseland, direct political activity in this relatively underdeveloped province was not allowed before 1962, mainly to meet the desire of its governing class to maintain their special relationship with Great Britain in order to escape control by an elected African government in Northern Rhodesia. The constitution of 1962 apparently solved this problem by providing that Northern Rhodesian legislation specially affecting Barotseland could not come into effect without the assent of the government of Barotseland. Moreover, UNIP candidates won in Barotseland in the election of 1962.

Urbanization

Urbanization is the strongest counterforce to tribalism. This is not to say that urbanization and "detribalization" are one and the same thing. As already mentioned, most African workers in urban areas still retain strong links with their rural homes, where they may indeed be said to retire, in a very real sense. Moreover, all but a small proportion of "urbanized" Africans are in fact only transients in the towns, especially in Southern Rhodesia. "For example, in Salisbury 47 per cent of the men over the age of 15 were between the ages of 20 and 29. . . . In a normal rural community one would expect to find only 33 per cent in this age group." [10] Most of these "urbanized" men are bachelors or married men who have their families at home. In Salisbury, and to a lesser degree in Bulawayo, a large proportion of such men live in dormitorylike buildings. But even though most must still be classified as migrant labor and retain their tribal homes

[10] J. Clyde Mitchell, *An Outline of the Sociological Background to African Labour* (Salisbury: Ensign Publishers, 1961), p. 81.

and other ties, their urban exposure generally tends to weaken the political relevance of tribal bonds by broadening their horizons and giving them opportunities to participate in such activities as further schooling, labor organization, and various types of politics, which of necessity transcend tribal lines. Moreover, even in Southern Rhodesia the proportion of permanently urban Africans has been rising and will continue to do so, partly as a result of an amendment to the Land Apportionment Act that enables Africans to acquire freehold title to residential real estate. In Northern Rhodesia, as already indicated, the copper companies have encouraged the permanent urbanization of their workers in order to ensure a stable work force for themselves. More than 80 per cent of the African employees of most mines live in company townships with their families, and their average length of service is longer than that of European employees.

Urban townships to some extent perform the functions of a tribal melting pot. There is a good deal of tribal intermarriage, though again the extent should not be exaggerated. "In a sample of 183 marriages contracted on the Copperbelt, for example, 59 per cent were found to be between spouses of different tribes. But the proportion which would have arisen if there had been no tribal selection would have been 83 per cent." [11]

Regardless of the degree of detribalization produced by urbanization, the important aspect of this phenomenon is that the top leadership of all independence movements in the three territories has come from the most urbanized and most educated Africans: teachers, ministers, company welfare officers, journalists, and the very few lawyers and doctors available before 1963. What distinguishes these people is their relative mastery of spoken and written English and their familiarity with the modern world, gained in many instances through study and travel abroad. They did not achieve positions of leadership primarily as a result of tribal affiliations. This means that the general trend in the African societies of the Rhodesias and Nyasaland is away from the tribal-traditional and toward the urban-modern.

This trend should not be understood, however, to imply a necessary conflict between traditional and modernizing elements in African life, though European opponents of African advancement often emphasize such a conflict. Most chiefs in the northern territories opposed federation, and this fact made for an initial harmony between these traditional authorities and the African National Congresses. In many cases,

[11] *Ibid.*, p. 91.

this relationship continued, often because of the inept handling of the Federation issue by the federal and territorial governments. One should also remember that many of the best-educated Africans are relatives of chiefs; as such they were given preferred treatment in admission to government or mission schools, which have limited vacancies especially in the upper grades. Furthermore, traditional authorities were better able than commoners to pay for the education of their children. For example, two of the top officers of UNIP, the brothers Wina, are sons of a former "Prime Minister" of the Barotse government.

Social Organization

Among Africans in the three countries, classes in the conventional meaning of the term have not yet emerged. One reason for this is their very limited ownership of private property. Land is usually owned communally by a tribe, the chief holding it in trust. In Nyasaland, some effort is being made to change from communal to cooperative agriculture, without an intermediate stage of outright private ownership. In Southern Rhodesia, the government has been trying to bring into being a class of "peasant-farmers," who are allotted small acreages as "master farmers," a title bestowed after completion of an agricultural training course. But only a limited amount of land has been made available thus far for projects of this kind, so that relatively few Africans have profited from the program.

In the Rhodesias can be seen the beginnings of what, in Europe, might be called an African industrial proletariat, as well as the much more minute beginnings of an intelligentsia. There is also a small number of African businessmen in all three countries, but the development of this group has been inhibited by several factors, among them the lack until recently of credit facilities for Africans and the control of most branches of retailing by Asians, especially in the two northern territories. In Southern Rhodesia, the Land Apportionment Act probably operated in favor of the Africans in this respect because it kept both European and Asian traders off the African reserves, thereby effectively "reserving" retail trade there for Africans.

However much class consciousness might have been generated in a more placid political atmosphere, their common opposition to federation and/or discrimination in Southern Rhodesia has led most Africans, whatever their "objective" social or economic position, to submerge their conflicting interests in the independence movements. It is true that there have always been a few Africans, often businessmen, who have collaborated with the United Federal Party which, though clearly European-dominated, has always tried to maintain its multiracial composition. Some Africans have even collaborated with the Dominion Party, the official Opposition in the Southern Rhodesian and Federal parliaments until 1962. In the second Federal Assembly, which served from 1958 to 1962, an African M.P., who had been elected by the overwhelming European electorate in one of the four "African" constituencies of Southern Rhodesia, was even a member of the Dominion Party caucus. Other Africans have founded parties for the purpose of challenging such independence movements as Dr. Banda's Malawi Congress Party in Nyasaland. But the parliamentary collaborators have usually been branded as "stooges" who are interested only in the M.P.'s salary and other perquisites, while the dissident party organizers have failed dismally at the polls, despite financial support that they allegedly received from the UFP or its backers. In other words, the strength of feelings invested in the struggle against federation has led the vast majority of Africans to identify their own interests with those of the independence movements and to neglect whatever class interests they might otherwise have become aware of.

This kind of attitude makes good sense for anyone who looks upon society in the two Rhodesias as a two-class society, in which class position is determined by color. Ownership or control of the means of production—land, mines, manufacturing plants, basic transport and communications—has been almost exclusively European. At least in Southern Rhodesia, both the Chartered Company, when it controlled the means of coercion, and the state since then were used as instruments to perpetuate that control. To an orthodox Marxist in Rhodesia, colonial capitalism must have seemed to operate exactly the way Karl Marx claimed all capitalist systems were run, but more obviously so than in Europe, because all the class conflicts were made doubly graphic in their irreconcilability by the color difference between the exploiting bourgeoisie and the unenfranchised peasants and workers. On the European side of the color bar, too, this feeling of identity of interests in opposition to the Africans is evident among people who, in Europe, would regard themselves as members of different classes with conflicting interests. Among Europeans, economic strata run along the usual spread, from big capitalists in banking, mining, manufacturing, commerce, and large-scale agriculture, through the professional and other middle classes, to artisans, foremen, and lower-level employees—but it stops short of a true working class, which is supplied by Africans. Because the color line is the one really important social and economic division, Southern Rhodesia's white politics has usually been concerned with relatively minor issues. Whenever a serious issue involving African advancement has been brought up, the Europeans have usually rallied together.[12]

In Northern Rhodesia, social consciousness on the part of Europeans has been somewhat more complicated. The state played a more neutral role as arbiter between the races, and the servants of the state, officers of the British Colonial Service, kept themselves aloof from local interests or, failing that, at least set the tone for whatever white "society" there was. On the Copperbelt, real conflicts took place, not only between the European and African Mineworkers Unions but also between European labor and the employing companies. However, the Legislative Council system, discussed above, usually led to unity among the elected European members in opposition to the nominated Officials. But since the administration would not let itself be used against the Africans, the European residents in the end sought to promote their own "anti-African" interests by inviting help from the self-governing white settler community of Southern Rhodesia. Such motives led Roy Welensky, who had come to politics from the Railway Workers Union and was then leader of the Unofficials in the Legislative Council, to ally himself with Sir Godfrey Huggins (later Lord Malvern), the Prime Minister of Southern Rhodesia, in advocating "amalgamation" of the two Rhodesias. The British government opposed amalgamation, insisted on the inclusion of Nyasaland in the deal, and successfully pushed toward federal union instead. But Huggins, then allied with and subsequently succeeded by Welensky as Federal Prime Minister, had himself earlier faced a Labour Opposition in the Southern Rhodesian Parliament. In any case, with the achievement of federation, social consensus among Europeans of the two Rhodesias probably reached its greatest height.

European society in Rhodesia has a substitute for the kind of horizontal class consciousness which remains so evident in the "Mother Country," Great Britain. The substitute consists of a great variety of vertical social and economic organizations, which tend to lend a corporatist aspect to society. Not only do the European groups that were

[12] See Colin Leys, *European Politics in Southern Rhodesia* (Oxford: Clarendon Press, 1959).

mentioned earlier have their formal organizations, but so do the various religious denominations, ethnic minority groups, industries, branches of agriculture (like the influential Rhodesian Tobacco Association), and a great many private noneconomic associations. In Nyasaland, as in other British colonies all over the globe at a similar stage of constitutional development,

> shortly before the second world war a number of bodies representative of non-African interest-groups combined to form a Convention of Associations, which met about five times a year and agreed on communications to Government on matters raised by its members. This and the Chamber of Commerce were regarded as the appropriate bodies to submit names to the Governor for nomination [of Unofficial members of the Legislative Council].[13]

In other words, corporatism was institutionalized for purposes of political representation. The important point that emerges from this is that in Nyasaland, as in the other two territories, formal social differentiation among Europeans was more marked along vertical than along horizontal lines.[14] When really divisive political issues arose, the Europeans were easily united on their side of the horizontal line that divided them from the Africans below.

In recent years, whenever a European differed so seriously with the rest of his racial community as to go all the way over to the African side, he was denounced as a traitor to both his race and his class, though he might still retain his position in the vertical social hierarchy. Sir Stewart Gore-Brown and Garfield Todd are cases in point. Gore-Brown first came to Northern Rhodesia in 1911 with an Anglo-Belgian boundary surveying team. He later became leader of the Unofficial members of the Legislative Council and then the first and long-time member to represent African interests. In 1961, he actually joined UNIP and testified on its behalf before the Special Committee on Colonialism of the General Assembly of the United Nations. But he retained his "social" position sufficiently to have the Governor-General of the Federation (the nonpolitical representative of the Queen) spend some time on his estate, just before UNIP nominated him as a candidate—unsuccessful, as it turned out—in the Legislative Council elections of October 1962. Garfield Todd, who came to Southern Rhodesia

[13] Lucy Mair, *The Nyasaland Elections of 1961* (London: Athlone Press, 1962), p. 7.

[14] For a graphic illustration of the difference, see Herbert J. Spiro, *Government by Constitution* (New York: Random House, 1959), p. 329.

from New Zealand as a missionary, operated a mission school, became a farmer, and was Prime Minister of Southern Rhodesia until his removal by his own party in 1958. He similarly testified on behalf of ZAPU before the United Nations Committee of Seventeen, though he did not actually join ZAPU, continuing instead with his efforts to prepare European opinion in Southern Rhodesia for African government and himself for a possible transition role. He, too, was not completely ostracized from the vertical organizations to which he belonged. It seemed doubtful, however, whether either of these politicians could subsequently expect much European voting support from the settler community.

Trade Unions and Cooperatives

The quasi-corporatism of European society is mirrored in African social organizations of the modern as of the tribal type. Thus European trade unions were copied by Africans (whose admission to the European unions was, of course, never seriously considered in pre-Federation years). On the Copperbelt, as mentioned above, Welfare Organizations served as forerunners for industrial organizations designed to represent African miners in collective bargaining. After the African Mineworkers Union (AMU) had been set up, an African Staff Association was recognized by the Chamber of Mines, in 1955, as representing salaried employees, against the opposition, including strikes, of the AMU. The African Staff Association was the black counterpart of a white model, the Mine Officials, Salaried and Staff Association. For Northern Rhodesia as a whole, there is an African United Trades Union Congress.

In Southern Rhodesia, African labor organization was discouraged, although a number of industrial strikes occurred, particularly on the railways which were operated jointly for both territories from the beginning. In 1959, a new Industrial Conciliation Act was passed by the Southern Rhodesian Parliament and was meant to make unions "nonracial." However, the effect of the act, where it was implemented, was to put control of the integrated unions in the hands of their European members by use of constitutional devices that were reminiscent of the Southern Rhodesian franchise designed "to keep Government in the hands of civilized and responsible persons."

It made little sense to combine two groups of workers in one organization when the Europeans earned on the average about ten times as much as the Africans. Their economic interests, meant to be represented by trade unions, were obviously not the same. Therefore, despite legislation to the contrary, African unions in Southern Rhodesia increased their membership after 1959, as part of the generally raised level of political awareness. However, beginning in 1961, internal cleavages arose within the (African) Southern Rhodesian Trades Union Congress (SRTUC). These were outcroppings of a split between those African unions—elsewhere on the continent, including Kenya and Tanganyika—that favored affiliation with the International Confederation of Free Trade Unions (ICFTU), a Western organization supported by the AFL-CIO and the British Trades Union Congress, and other unions, led in the first instance from Ghana, that preferred an All-African Trade Union Federation, aligned with neither the ICFTU nor its Communist-controlled opponent, the World Federation of Trade Unions, based in Prague. The original SRTUC had received help from the ICFTU and was denounced for this and other reasons by Terry Maluleke, one of the original ANC detainees, soon after his release from detention in 1962. Most of the membership of SRTUC went over to the new African Trades Union Congress (ATUC) founded by Maluleke. SRTUC's original leadership, headed by Reuben Jamela, was actually expelled from ZAPU. The split was made more complicated by the fact that Jamela, as a ZAPU member, had initially opposed acceptance of the new Southern Rhodesian constitution at a time when ZAPU's president, Joshua Nkomo, had apparently agreed not to oppose it. The position of the ICFTU was also made so difficult by these intra-African quarrels and by the unprogressive policies of the European unions in the Federation that the ICFTU was considering whether to expel the Europeans. Meanwhile, ZAPU charged that Jamela was receiving money from UFP sources to help him found a new African party which would be willing to participate in the Southern Rhodesian elections, under the new constitution, then scheduled for the spring of 1963. Still, the intra-African breach did not seem irreparable, at least before the outbreak of some violence between ZAPU and SRTUC supporters. These events again illustrate the incontestable primacy of the politics of independence over industrial relations or indeed any other type of economic or social activity in British Central Africa during the preindependence period.

In 1962, this same primacy was also demonstrated on the Copperbelt, where the African Mineworkers Union struck for higher wages. Thereupon the Morison Commission was appointed by the Governor to report upon problems of industrial relations. Subsequently, the

companies made an offer based in part on the commission's recommendations. This offer was rejected by the AMU, which proceeded
to call another strike. However, the leadership of UNIP—between
whose membership and that of the AMU there was an almost complete overlap on the Copperbelt—denounced the strike call and was
backed by the territorial African United Trades Union Congress. The
AMU's leadership gave in to UNIP, though reluctantly, and except for
a few days' strike at one of the mines, work was not interrupted.
Shortly thereafter, the AMU accepted an improved employers' offer
and agreed to an eighteen months' moratorium on strikes. Once more,
the reasons for all this maneuvering were political. UNIP was preparing for the Legislative Council elections of October 30, 1962, and felt
that it could afford neither the unrest that the strike was likely to
bring nor the friction among Africans by which it might be accompanied. The eighteen months' moratorium was probably intended to
give the hoped-for UNIP government a period of industrial peace
during which it could initiate other programs and to give the AMU
protection against possible postelection pressure from UNIP for a
"political" strike.

This pattern of trade union activity suggests that, at least until
African governments come into office, industrial organization among
Africans will continue subservient to the independence movements.
Nor does such subservience go counter to the interests of the union
membership, since it is their primary goal to narrow the wide gap
between their pay and that of European workers, and this they are
likely to achieve only through political action.

African trade unions are not limited, however, in the ultimate effects
of their operations to substantive economic and political matters of
the kind just discussed. Along with agricultural cooperative societies
and many other types of associations, they afford their members valuable experience with the procedures of self-government, at a level
where everyone can participate and understand what is going on. Both
trade unions and cooperatives have to be registered with appropriate
government agencies, which often provide organizational assistance
and regularly audit their accounts. The membership thereby learns
how to elect officers, how to speak in a public meeting, how to keep
their officers accountable, and how to do all this according to the best
rules of procedure in the world, namely, British procedures. This
makes the conduct of "real" politics much easier and smoother.

Cooperatives also make a substantive contribution to the welfare of their members and to the economic development of the country. New crops can be introduced by means of founding cooperative societies. This was done, for example, with rice in the Kota Kota district of Nyasaland and with coffee in parts of Northern Rhodesia. (In Northern Rhodesia in 1961, 228 cooperative societies had 36,413 members.) But it may well be that, once the transition to independence has been completed, retrospective analysis—especially by comparison with neighboring non-British ex-colonies—will show that trade unions, cooperatives, and similar organizations made a major contribution to the relative smoothness of the process not so much by raising the standard of living of their members as by giving them experience, usually unavailable elsewhere, with those procedures of compromise that must serve as the framework for democratic politics.

Religion

Some religious organizations have begun in recent years to make similar contributions by turning their administration over to local people. For example, the Church of Scotland did this in Nyasaland (where it is known as the Church of Central Africa Presbyterian), and a number of mission stations have steadily increased the amount of participation by Africans in running their affairs. But most of the European denominations find this kind of devolution of authority to their African communicants difficult, for a variety of reasons. The Roman Catholic Church, for example, cannot deviate from its hierarchical principles of organization and can bring Africans into active participation only on the basis of the same principles. It has done this: there is now one African bishop in Nyasaland, and in neighboring Tanganyika an African cardinal serves as primate. The Roman Catholic Church has also been more strongly in favor of African advancement and the elimination of discrimination than most of its Christian sisters. Roman Catholics showed the most liberal attitudes on issues of race relations in an attitude survey conducted in Southern Rhodesia in 1959.[15]

But there are differences in this respect among both laity and hierarchy, even when all the bishops sign pastoral letters on such subjects. Many members of the Roman Catholic clergy, as of others, have served in Central Africa for a great many years, and they therefore find it difficult to adjust themselves to the new footing of political equality with Africans which the nationalists are intent upon bringing

---

[15] Rogers and Frantz, *Racial Themes in Southern Rhodesia*, pp. 306–309.

about. Here lies the basic reason why most of the Christian churches are having trouble adjusting to the great changes that are taking place: their mission—whether purely spiritual or educational or medical—is of necessity a paternalistic one. The missionaries "teach," and the teacher's attitude toward his pupils is modeled upon that of the father toward his children. But it is precisely against paternalism in all its forms—of the administrator toward his charges, the employer toward his workers, the European representative for African interests toward his constituents—that the nationalists are fighting. At least a cooling off was bound to occur, therefore, even between African ministers of religion and their European colleagues or superiors. This was true also because the pay and perquisites of African ministers and mission teachers were, until quite recently, always considerably lower than those of their European peers. Nevertheless, some remarkable adjustments have been made by missions, including those of the Dutch Reformed Church, whose Mother Church in South Africa endorses the principles of apartheid.

In British Central Africa, as elsewhere in Black Africa, a number of Zionist or Ethiopian churches has come into being, one or two fairly successful ones appearing in the 1950's. An early founder of this phenomenon was John Chilembwe from Nyasaland, who had spent some time at Negro colleges in the United States at the turn of the century. After his return home he set up his own church near Blantyre. In 1915, he staged a brief uprising, in the course of which a few Europeans were killed and he, too, met his death. Some Nyasalanders today regard Chilembwe as an early nationalist hero, and his case suggests that the teachings of the Christian churches can lend themselves to conversion into nationalist dogma. It also indicates that one should take with a measure of skepticism statistics of their African membership supplied by the various Christian denominations. Whatever motives may have led to the original conversions, Christian doctrines and practices were often so alien to the Africans' understanding and experience that their commitment turned out to be even less than skin-deep. The motives themselves often contributed to this impermanence of the conversion. At the same time, the missions provided, and still provide, in many areas the only available schooling or medical care. And there was a time when being a Christian was just as much a badge of modernity as possession of a membership card of an independence party is nowadays. Even at that, only about 15 per cent of Africans in Southern Rhodesia are claimed as Christians.

Among Europeans in Southern Rhodesia, the major denominations, in order of numerical strength, are the Church of England (40.8 per cent), Presbyterian (12.4), Roman Catholic (11.8), Dutch Reformed (11.0), Methodist (8.8), and other Christians (7.2).[16] The membership of the Dutch Reformed Church more or less coincides with the Afrikaner population. There is also an unusually large number of minor sects, some originating in the United States, which are operating large-scale mission programs. Among these are the Seventh-Day Adventists, Jehovah's Witnesses, and Church of the Brethren. There are also several Jewish congregations (3.2 per cent), Sephardic, orthodox, and reformed. It has already been mentioned that one Nyasaland tribe, the Yao, consists of Muslims, and Islam has been fairly successful in making converts among other tribes.

With a few exceptions, the churches have not interfered directly in politics. The Roman Catholic Archbishop of Nyasaland was accused by Dr. Banda of having committed one of the exceptions, when Chester Katsonga formed the Christian Democratic Party in October 1960. This party subsequently merged with T. D. T. Banda's (unrelated to Dr. Banda) Congress Liberation Party into the Christian Liberation Party. The Archbishop denied the link, and the party failed utterly at the polls. Moreover, at the same time in another diocese in Nyasaland, some priests were giving substantial support to Malawi and had been doing so even while its leaders were still in jail.

Rather than indirect participation in politics, the influence of the churches should be sought in the activities of some of their most prominent members. For example, Dr. Banda occasionally mentioned his status as an elder of the Church of Central Africa Presbyterian. The chairman of ZAPU, the Reverend Mr. Sithole, is a Protestant minister. Kenneth Kaunda's father was a mission teacher. Garfield Todd, Prime Minister of Southern Rhodesia from 1953 to 1958, is an ordained minister who started his Southern Rhodesian career as a missionary. The European M.P. nominated by the Governor of Nyasaland to represent African interests in the Federal Parliament, between 1959 and 1962, was a missionary of the Dutch Reformed Church, and his predecessor was a Presbyterian minister. Many similar examples could be cited. In this indirect way, the churches have continued to play the role which was set by Livingstone, Moffat, and the other great missionaries of the first generation of Europeans that opened up

[16] *Ibid.*, p. 67.

Central Africa to both the blessings and the evils of what is known as "Christian civilization."

Education

The most important initial contribution that the missions made in the three countries was education. In 1961, in the two Colonial Office protectorates, although there remained a majority of mission schools, an important part of schooling was performed by government schools. In Northern Rhodesia, in 1961, out of a total of 2,117 primary and secondary schools, 642 were operated by the government or local authorities, and all but 68 of the rest, that is, mainly mission schools, were government subsidized. Of the total enrollment in primary schools, almost 40 per cent was in schools administered by local education authorities, which also accounted for 45 per cent of the secondary school enrollment. These school boards, incidentally, provided opportunities for Africans to gain experience with political procedures in the course of administering substantial amounts of money for the education of their own children, that is, for purposes so close to home that anyone could understand them. In Nyasaland, in the same year, there were 23 government schools, 1,162 schools receiving government aid, and 2,008 unsubsidized schools, most of them operated by missions.

In Southern Rhodesia, in 1961, only 80 out of 3,082 schools for Africans were operated by the government, but the nongovernment schools received substantial and indispensable subsidies. In the budget estimates for 1962–1963, £5,155,000 out of total expenditures of £25,960,000 was set aside for native education. (In Northern Rhodesia, the figures were £3,197,000 out of £19,775,000; in Nyasaland, £1,132,000 out of £8,190,000.)

Under the federal constitution, African education was a territorial function, while European education came under federal control. The white constitution makers wanted to keep the two segregated in fact and in constitutional theory and even had enough foresight to ensure that no "separate but equal" doctrine could be used in the courts in order to thwart their intentions. As a result, educational issues were of major importance in the nationalists' fight for the breakup of the Federation. But even without this constitutional peg on which to hang discussion of this issue, the chances are that the tremendous African hunger for education and the inadequacies of available finance and teachers would still have played an important role in Central African politics.

Successive Southern Rhodesian governments have claimed that their record of providing primary education for African children was better than that of any other African country north of the Limpopo River. In terms of the proportion of children in school, this may have been true, as it was by comparison with the two northern territories. However, the quality of schooling provided was in most cases very poor, though probably no poorer than in Northern Rhodesia and Nyasaland. Teachers were often inadequately trained, because of the shortage of secondary schools and of teacher training schools. (In 1961, only 5,096 Africans were attending secondary schools in Southern Rhodesia.) Most teachers were poorly paid and, as a result, many of those qualified preferred employment of other types. Some of the best teachers naturally wanted to play prominent parts in nationalist politics, but they were inhibited by their civil service status. In 1962, the director of native education suggested that further restrictions should be placed upon teachers' political activities, allegedly for their own protection. This would cut off the most obvious source of trained political manpower for ZAPU and similar movements. The teachers may not be well educated, but they are better educated than most other Africans. African teachers were complaining at the same time that the Southern Rhodesian government was putting pressure on them to register as voters, since they were known to have the necessary educational and income qualifications, and forcing them to act as registrars of voters. They considered this a kind of intimidation, especially if, as ZAPU sympathizers, they wanted to boycott both registration and election.

The number of schools has been increasing in all three territories, and in Nyasaland Dr. Banda's government launched an ambitious school expansion program in 1962. In Southern Rhodesia, several incidents occurred when women and children demonstrated on behalf of school expansion in front of the offices of the Native Education Department. Subsequently, a community school for more than a thousand pupils was started in one of the African townships outside Salisbury. It was both initiated and operated by Africans. But this was a makeshift measure, and it appeared in 1962 that no government would be able to meet the African demand for more and better schools unless that government contained African members and was responsive to African voters. Even if a non-African government had the required funds and were willing to apply them to African education, it would probably fail to succeed with a program of school expansion because the Africans would withhold their cooperation.

Two examples tend to back up this last suggestion. First, there were a number of strikes and riots among students in African secondary schools, in both Rhodesias and, until Dr. Banda's return from jail, in Nyasaland. The governments concerned usually condemned these strikes as politically inspired and resulting from intimidation. The first of these claims was undoubtedly correct, even when the strikes were directed against unpalatable food in the school dining hall. In a sense, the small secondary school population in Central Africa acted as the equivalent of university students in Latin America or the Middle East. These Africans had the highest political consciousness, were the most frustrated, and, worst of all, still came under the control of European teachers or headmasters. Moreover, there was no African university population, except for the few African students at the (federal) University College of Rhodesia and Nyasaland, in Salisbury.

The University College provides the second example. It was founded in 1957, against opposition from Europeans who opposed the policy of racial partnership. Its supporters presented it as a genuine token of their good intentions, and the Southern Rhodesian Parliament had to amend the Land Apportionment Act to make possible its location inside a European suburb of Salisbury. Since it was going to maintain "European standards"—its degrees are awarded by the University of London—it would also educate Africans to a sufficient degree of "civilization and responsibility" to participate in multiracial politics on equal terms. In fact, however, African nationalists thought the standards, in education as for the franchise, were being used as obstacles to their admission. Even by 1962, only about a third of the 400-odd students were Africans. According to one estimate, entrance requirements were so high that, unless they were lowered, by 1965 only 60 Southern Rhodesian, 30 Northern Rhodesian, and 36 Nyasaland Africans would be able to pass the admission requirements. (For example, a foreign language is one such requirement; African languages are not recognized for this purpose, and the entrance examination must be passed before admission, that is, it cannot be made up after the first or second year, as at most American colleges.)

In 1962, Dr. Banda declared that degrees from the University College would not be recognized in Malawi and successfully urged most students from Nyasaland who were in Salisbury to withdraw and transfer to politically more acceptable institutions, like Makarere in

Uganda or British universities. Malawi intended to build its own university, based on the campus of the Church of Scotland school at Livingstonia. The United States promised funds for the construction of a polytechnic institute as well. Meanwhile, UNIP was thinking ahead to similar projects for Northern Rhodesia. All of this suggests that, in education as in other fields like agriculture, goals will have to be set by popular African leaders—though they may have to be implemented with the advice and assistance of non-African experts— before such projects are given the kind of enthusiastic support that they need to succeed. Anything that smacks of European paternalism or condescension is likely to fail.

The schools provided for European children by the federal government are much better than the African schools. The buildings are modern and spacious, and parents pay no tuition. Even in government boarding schools, provided mainly for European farmers who live far away from the towns, the anual fee is less than £100. Africans, on the other hand, usually have to pay tuition. This state of affairs, incidentally, was criticized in the Federal Parliament by African M.P.'s beylonging to the governing UFP, which illustrates the kind of service that Africans could perform in Parliament, even though they were denounced as stooges by the independence movements. But European M.P.'s of the same UFP made this point even more strongly in the Southern Rhodesian Legislative Assembly. One of them told the house that the federal government annually spent £110 on the education of each white child, while the government of Southern Rhodesia spent only £9 on each African child. The ratio is roughly the same as that prevailing between the pay received by Europeans and Africans for similar work. Yet the population ratio between the two races is roughly its inverse in Southern Rhodesia, which has the largest white population. It seems unlikely that the present problems of Southern Rhodesia and, therefore, of the Federation as constituted in 1953 will be solved until these relations and especially the franchise reach at least a 50:50 ratio.

PRESS, RADIO, AND TELEVISION

The major newspapers of the Rhodesias belong to the Argus chain, which is South African controlled. During the first few years of federation, these papers backed the ruling United Federal Party, but their enthusiasm varied from one editor to the next, under a policy of relative editorial discretion. Beginning about 1959, support for the

UFP weakened, though the papers still strongly favored the retention of federation in some form. The dependence of these newspapers upon the South African wire service has already been mentioned. This has meant a rather heavy concentration upon South African news and a rather South African perspective on foreign news, whether Asian, European, American, or from the United Nations. In terms of the background and outlook of most of the European population, this focus makes good sense. More than one-third came to Rhodesia from South Africa, some seeking refuge from the Afrikaner extremism of the Nationalist government. And the Republic continues to be a favorite vacation site for the white settlers. Moreover, a large majority of Rhodesians who received any higher education abroad (in 1962, there were 1,200 studying at foreign universities) did so in South Africa.

In 1962, the African newspapers of Southern Rhodesia were bought by the Thomson Group, a British concern. Previously, they had been controlled by a consortium of Rhodesian corporations, including the British South Africa Company, Rhodesian Selection Trust, and Imperial Tobacco Company. Editorial policy before the take-over was pro-Federation and antinationalist. Afterward, the African editors were given somewhat wider leeway to follow whatever editorial policy they deemed to be in the interest of their own community. But there still remained dissatisfaction between the African senior editor, Nathan Shamuyarira, and the European managing editor, P. G. Paver, over both editorial and personnel policies, and this led to Shamuyarira's resignation in September 1962.

Previous incumbents of the senior editorship followed rather similar subsequent careers. Jasper Z. Savanhu became a UFP member of Parliament and parliamentary secretary in the Ministry of Home Affairs, until his resignation from the party in August 1962 on the ground of the UFP's failure to live up to its multiracial ideals. Lawrence Vambe became a press officer in the office of the Federation's High Commissioner in London, until his dissatisfaction with the federal government led to his resignation in favor of an important public relations position with the Anglo-American Corporation in Rhodesia. Each of these former senior editors might play roles in Southern Rhodesian politics if their earlier support of profederal policies were forgiven.

The Central African *Daily News* is the main publication of the African newspapers, which also put out weekly and monthly maga-

zines. Their coverage of African and other international news seems
wider and is less South African slanted than that of the Argus papers.
They use the wire services of United Press International. One index
of the deliberate de-emphasis of tribalism that has been taking place
among Africans was the omission, after the change in ownership, of
a page or two in the Mashona or Matabele languages, carried, respectively, in the daily editions published in Salisbury and Bulawayo.

In Lusaka, the independent *African Mail* is published with a weekly
circulation of 20,000. Nyasaland had an independently operated daily
of low circulation, which also came under control of the Thomson
Group, although its editorial policy at first retained its anti-Malawi
orientation. In 1962, the Malawi Congress Party acquired a newspaper
press. Previously, MCP published a mimeographed newssheet, a practice also followed by UNIP in Lusaka until it acquired a press. With
the press, MCP turned out the *Malawi News,* at first on a weekly basis.

Before they got their own presses, all three independence movements had to contend not only with the generally antinationalist European papers but also with various publications of the government
information services, territorial and federal. These came out both in
English and in several African languages. The territorial information
services also wanted to use radio and television for their purposes,
but since telecommunications was a federal function under the constitution, they were not allowed to do so. Radio broadcasting was in
the hands of the Federal Broadcasting Corporation. Programs had
relatively little political content but included three daily newscasts
from the BBC in London. Several stations regularly carried programs
in African languages. Some of the African announcers acquired great
popularity among their listeners, and one of the most popular resigned
from the FBC in the summer of 1962 in order to work for UNIP.

In 1962, the Nyasaland budget provided for the establishing of a
territorial radio service, and the Southern Rhodesian government also
insisted upon the need for a similar service. The federal government
reasserted its constitutional prerogatives in the field, but it seemed that
the territorial governments would have their way as part of the gradual
dismantling of the Federation.

A television network began operating in Salisbury and Bulawayo
and on the Copperbelt in 1960–1961. It is operated by an independent
board, on which Argus and Thomson interests are strongly represented, under charter from the federal government. Rhodesian Television is financed by both commercials and license fees paid by set

owners. (Radio-set owners also pay fees, in keeping with British practice.) The programs are free of political content, except for news and discussion programs; the latter tend to support the Federation and oppose the alleged radicalism of the independence movements. But most of the five hours' daily telecasting time was taken up by American programs.

Newspapers have not had to contend with government censorship, but the Southern Rhodesia Law and Order Maintenance Act envisages the possibility. On the other hand, until the African movements acquired their own presses, it was financially very difficult for their sympathizers to publish weekly or monthly magazines supporting them editorially, because commercial advertising was virtually unobtainable, though circulation, for example, of *Tsopano,* could be quite high. The *Central African Examiner* was originally founded to support the Federation, with financial backing from Rhodesian Selection Trust. Published fortnightly, it was linked to the *Economist* of London. When the original backers' enthusiasm for the UFP's concept of federation began to wane, it was taken over by a group headed by Theodore Bull, who wanted to help smooth the transition to majority government. Bull is a descendant of Sir Alfred Beit, one of Rhodes's partners, who set up a philanthropic foundation for Central (and other parts of) Africa. The format of the *Examiner* was progressively narrowed down, and publication was placed on a monthly basis. *Tsopano* was published as a pro-Malawi monthly during 1960–1961, printed in Salisbury and then shipped to Blantyre, where no one willing to print it could be found. Like the *Examiner,* its purpose was to provide an outlet for otherwise unpublished opinions during a period of transition. Unlike the *Examiner,* its contents were designed to appeal to African readers alone, and it was fully committed to immediate African majority government. Both magazines filled a gap for a time, but neither had any *raison d'être* after the appearance of the African managed and controlled publications. In journalism as in education and agriculture, Africans had to set the policies and implement them in order to appeal to the African public.

The Political Process

FORMAL STRUCTURE

In 1963, the formal structure of government in British Central Africa still had at its apex the British constitution. The federal constitution had been proclaimed in 1953, as a British order in council, which was laid before and debated in Parliament at Westminster. Northern Rhodesia and Nyasaland were administered by governors and civil servants who were members of the British Colonial Service and appointed by the Colonial Office. In each of these territories, the Governor was the effective chief executive who presided over his Executive Council. The Governor of Nyasaland relied more upon his elected Malawi ministers than the Governor of Northern Rhodesia upon the nonnationalist elected ministers he had until December 1962. While the Colonial Office retained responsibility for the two northern territories, the Commonwealth Relations Office was in charge of relations between the British government and both the Southern Rhodesian and federal governments. Until negotiation of the new Southern Rhodesian constitution, the Secretary of State for Commonwealth Relations retained a veto over Southern Rhodesian legislation deemed discriminatory against natives. This same British minister, Duncan Sandys at that time, also convened and presided over the conference which negotiated the new constitution. As under the old Southern Rhodesian constitution, so under the federal constitution any bill declared to differentiate against Africans by the African Affairs Board, a standing committee of the Federal Assembly, required the assent of, or could be vetoed by, the Secretary for Commonwealth Relations.

The federal constitution provided for its own review, at least seven and at most ten years after it had come into operation, by a conference of representatives of the British government and the four governments in Central Africa. The review was to be held with an eye to advancing the Federation toward full Dominion status within the Commonwealth. On Sir Roy Welensky's insistence, it was convened at almost the earliest possible time, in December 1960, but soon recessed pending further constitutional advances in the member territories. The British government, a year before, had appointed the Monckton Commission to advise it on constitutional problems. The Labour Opposition in Parliament refused to nominate its candidates for the Monckton Commission, because it wanted the commission's terms of reference to mention explicitly the possibility of dismantling the Federation. However, despite the absence of Labour-nominated commissioners, the Monckton Commission, on which the four Central African governments were represented, did in fact recommend that the two northern territories should be given the opportunity to decide the question of secession, after their electorates had become more broadly representative. The commission included this proposal despite the fact that its hearings in Africa were boycotted by the independence movements.

All of this—and much more could be adduced to the same point— shows that, as of 1963, the most important issues of the politics of the Rhodesias and Nyasaland were still being formulated and resolved as part and parcel of the British political process. This was true before federation, as already brought out, but British political interest in Central Africa was increased as a result of federation which, from the beginning, was a contentious issue between the Conservative and Labour parties in the United Kingdom. On the whole, the Labour governments that were in office between 1945 and 1951 were unsympathetic to European demands for amalgamation of the two Rhodesias, whereas the Conservative governments in office since 1951 were rather more enthusiastic about the possibilities of creating genuine multiracial partnership through federation of the three territories. A Conservative government presided over the establishment of the Federation. However—and this suggests that there were splits on the question within party ranks—a Conservative government also presided over its liquidation.

When the latter process was initiated during Iain Macleod's tenure as Secretary of State for the Colonies, in 1959–1960, feelings within the Conservative parliamentary party ran so strong that the Marquess of Salisbury in the House of Lords accused Macleod of being "too clever by half," in an allusion to the fact that the Colonial Secretary had been one of Britain's bridge champions. It was also in the House of Lords, during debates on Central African issues, that important speeches were made by Rhodesian peers, such as Lord Malvern, the first Federal Prime Minister and previously, as Sir Godfrey Huggins, perennial Prime Minister of Southern Rhodesia; Lord Robins, head of the British South Africa Company; and Lord Graham, Duke of Montrose, a farmer in Southern Rhodesia who was also a federal M.P. of the Opposition Dominion Party until 1962 and became Minister of Agriculture in Winston Field's Southern Rhodesian cabinet at the end of that year.

Just how difficult the handling of the Federation issue had become for Prime Minister Harold Macmillan's Conservative government was shown by a series of cabinet changes between 1960 and 1962. Partly as a reward for his handling of the constitutional problems of Nyasaland and other colonies, Macleod was promoted to become leader of the House of Commons and chairman of the Conservative Party (with the formal portfolio of Chancellor of the Duchy of Lancaster). Lord Home, who had been Commonwealth Relations Secretary, became Foreign Minister. The two ministers were replaced, respectively, by Reginald Maudling and Duncan Sandys. Sandys presided over the Southern Rhodesian constitutional conference. Then it became apparent that the division of responsibility between the Colonial and Commonwealth Relations Offices was unwieldy and enabled the federal government to try to play one against the other. In 1957, the federal government had suggested that the Central African business of both offices be combined at the civil service level. This suggestion was taken up by the British government, but at cabinet level, by concentrating all responsibility for the Federation and its member territories in a newly created Central African Office, headed by R. A. Butler, senior member of the Macmillan cabinet, who was then Home Secretary and was subsequently promoted to First Secretary of State and Deputy Prime Minister. Sandys and Maudling also received promotions in the same cabinet reorganization of 1962, the former by having the Colonial Office added to the Commonwealth Relations Office, the latter by becoming Chancellor of the Exchequer. Ministerial performance with respect to Central African affairs was evidently regarded as important by the Prime Minister, and the speedy disposal of the problems of the Federation as sufficiently crucial for him to entrust them to his own Deputy.

After Butler's appointment as Secretary of State for Central African Affairs, the governors of the two northern territories became responsible to him and he negotiated with the Southern Rhodesian government. The British High Commissioner to the federal government, Lord Alport, formerly a prominent Tory politician, who was in charge of liaison between the British and federal governments, also reported directly to Butler.

The main task confronting the British government at each of these four levels was constitutional reform. The Nyasaland constitution negotiated under Macleod in 1960 had been fully implemented after the election of 1961 and was functioning very well in the judgment of the British government, of colonial officers on the spot, and of most observers, including previously critical ones. But Dr. Banda, as Minister of Local Government and Natural Resources and as life president of the MCP, successfully pressed for full responsible government, under which he would become Prime Minister, and for secession from the Federation. The Northern Rhodesian constitution, negotiated in stages under the chairmanship of both Macleod and Maudling and with participation by both Sandys and Macmillan himself, came into effect with the elections of October and December 1962 and immediately generated pressures for further constitutional advance from UNIP— and continuing demands for Northern Rhodesia's secession from the Federation.

Southern Rhodesia's new constitution, of which the probable provision of no more than 15 African M.P.'s out of a total of 65 was the most contentious issue, was disavowed by ZAPU, which threatened to boycott the election scheduled for early 1963. It was this new constitution that led to the resolution of the General Assembly of the United Nations urging the British government to increase African representation in the Legislative Assembly and to broaden the franchise before holding the election. The British government, while officially denying that it had the power to alter the constitution without Southern Rhodesian concurrence, apparently tried privately to persuade Sir Edgar Whitehead to make some changes in the direction demanded by the UN. But Whitehead, having just won his constitutional referendum from the European electorate of the colony, rejected the possibility of altering the constitution in any way, particularly under ZAPU's threat of a boycott, before the first election had been held under it. At the same time, both he and Butler hinted that broadening of African representation and the franchise might be undertaken soon after the election.

After Whitehead outlawed ZAPU in September 1962, the General Assembly of the UN again took up the question of Southern Rhodesia. In October, after hearing the testimony of officers of ZAPU and supporters of Sir Edgar Whitehead and listening to a defense of his policies from Sir Edgar himself (occupying the seat of the British delegate for this purpose), the General Assembly passed a resolution calling on the Acting Secretary General to "lend his good offices to promote conciliation among the various sections of the population of Southern Rhodesia by initiating prompt discussions" for, among other purposes, reform of the new Southern Rhodesian constitution and cancellation of the election scheduled for December 14, 1962. The resolution had been proposed by 50 Afro-Asian members and was carried by 81 to 2 votes, with 19 abstentions, 7 members absent, and the United Kingdom not participating. Only Portugal and South Africa voted against the resolution.

This vote occurred after an event which showed that deep divisions on this issue had come into being within the British cabinet and civil service. Sir Hugh Foot, who was the United Kingdom representative at the United Nations for colonial and related matters and who had just made the best of what was necessarily a rather weak case for his government during the Southern Rhodesian debate, resigned from his post over disagreement with this government. Sir Hugh had previously helped as Governor to smooth the transition to independence for Cyprus, and before that in Jamaica and Nigeria, as a high colonial officer. He enjoyed the confidence of most of the newer members of the United Nations, and his resignation tended to strengthen their stand against British policy in Southern Rhodesia.

The timing of the various constitutional reforms, conferences, and elections was of importance, because events on one level affected those that followed on another. This was especially true of the federal constitution and the Federal Assembly. The Federal Constitutional Review Conference of December 1960 was attended both by government representatives and by leaders of the African independence movements, including Dr. Banda, Kenneth Kaunda, and Joshua Nkomo. The British government took the recommendations of the Monckton Commission as its guidelines for the review. These recommendations included, in addition to the secession option already mentioned, return to the territories of certain "bread and butter" functions such as European agriculture in each of the Rhodesias (a federal function, by contrast with all agriculture in Nyasaland), European education, and medical services and change of the ratio of Africans to Europeans in the Federal Assembly from 12:47 to equality, that is, 50:50. The federal government's attitude toward these proposals was, on the whole, negative. In any case, reform of the federal constitution had to be postponed until after it was clear who was going to be running the territorial governments. The Review Conference was therefore recessed.

The Nyasaland election showed the direction in which Northern Rhodesia would go if given a similar constitution. When the first version of the "Macleod constitution" for Northern Rhodesia seemed to favor UNIP, the federal government and its Tory friends in Great Britain secured a temporary change in the make-up of the Legislative Council, but this was subsequently amended once more by Maudling, in response to pressure from UNIP and its friends in both the major British parties. The last change occurred after the new Southern Rhodesian constitution had been approved by referendum. Thereupon

Sir Roy Welensky made a precipitate trip to London, in the course of which he accused the British government of breaking faith with Southern Rhodesia's electorate and made allusions to "going it alone" and the possible use of force. When he got no satisfaction on the Northern Rhodesian issue from the British cabinet, he returned to Salisbury and asked the Governor-General for dissolution of the Federal Assembly, a request which under British practice the Monarch or her representative cannot deny the Prime Minister. In the election which followed, on April 27, 1962, only 15 elective seats out of 53 were contested and all but one of the elected members returned were members of the United Federal Party, because both the African independence movements and the Dominion Party, formerly the Opposition, boycotted the election. Welensky now claimed to have a "mandate" to back him up against the British government. He did indeed have such a mandate from his electorate, but this was so minutely small—because of the franchise, boycotts, uncontested seats, and apathy—that his bargaining position appeared weaker than before the election.

Welensky's position was further undermined by the defeat of his UFP in both Northern and Southern Rhodesia. Announcement of the formation of a coalition government by UNIP and the ANC in Northern Rhodesia the day before the Southern Rhodesian election of December 14, 1962, may have contributed to the victory of the Rhodesian Front there. Less than a week after Welensky's lack of electoral support in the two territories had been demonstrated in this fashion, R. A. Butler announced in the House of Commons: "H.M. Government accept in principle that Nyasaland shall be allowed to withdraw from the Federation. I should explain that such a withdrawal does not mean that the constitutional relationship between Northern and Southern Rhodesia is thereby broken." In reply to questions about assurances said to have been given by the British government that Nyasaland would not be allowed to secede without the consent of the federal government, Butler said, "It has been clearly established that H.M. Government have the inalienable right to take action on these matters."

Sir Roy Welensky's reaction at this point broke several precedents and can best be described as furious. In a speech to the Federal Assembly, on December 19, 1962, he charged:

By their action today the British Government have ratted on us. They have gone back on the most solemn understandings and intentions. They have wrecked the foundation upon which they themselves built the Federation and on which they were determined at that time to construct a lasting edifice. They have been guilty of an act of treachery. . . .

I am bound to say that the course of action the British Government have chosen to follow is typical of the change in morality towards public life that has taken place in the last decade in the United Kingdom, where expediency and not principle has become the guiding factor. . . .

The Federal Government have taken note of the biased platitudes that have again surrounded the British Government's announcement of its intentions. We are not impressed with these, and the history of our dealings with the present British Government now makes the Federal Government believe that there is little, if any, honour left in dealings with the British Government. I say that Britain has lost the will to govern in Africa, and that Britain is utterly reckless of the fate of the inhabitants of the present Federation.

Together with this bitter outburst, Welensky released transcripts of the highly confidential conferences at which the constitutional shape of the Federation had originally been negotiated. The British government regarded this publication as a grave breach of confidence, even though Lord Malvern, the Marquess of Salisbury, and several former Colonial Secretaries subsequently raised to the peerage supported Welensky's interpretation of British promises in the debate in the House of Lords. None of this, however, deterred R. A. Butler from supporting Nyasaland's secession or, during a subsequent trip to Central Africa, from achieving a better rapport with territorial politicians, both black and white, than with Sir Roy and his federal cabinet, which seemed to be taking on the characteristics of a lame duck administration. Butler finally administered the *coup de grâce* to them by recognizing, on March 29, 1963, Northern Rhodesia's right to secede, as a prerequisite for any negotiations on future relations among the three territories.

In any event, the main issues in the three territories and for the Federation as a whole were constitutional issues. Any further discussion of "formal structure" seems, therefore, useless. The formal structures have changed so frequently and are going to be transformed again before jelling, both internally and in their relations among themselves, that their past and present can best be discussed as "contemporary issues." The only feature that has remained stable so far is the use of British parliamentary procedure, down to the last detail of Mr. Speaker's wig and mace.

POLITICAL DYNAMICS

Political Parties

In politics as in economics, one can speak of a dual system in Central Africa. The condition of structural flux through which politics have been passing means that the African political organizations are better described as movements than as parties. Their purpose is to move their populations toward full control of government and, except for brief interludes when the structure of the British-type parliaments in which they may be functioning forces them to do so, they do not behave like conventional political parties. On the other hand, the European organizations—some of which claimed to be multiracial, though Europeans overwhelmingly outnumbered Africans in all but the Central African Party—conducted themselves as political parties on the British model. This was true not only because most of their personnel was in fact of British background but also because the procedure used in the legislative councils and assemblies made this unavoidable.

The European parties that existed in the three territories and the Federation were organized along standard British lines: annual congress, executive, chairman, leader, and parliamentary caucus. They raised money less through membership dues than from contributions of individuals and business firms; for example, the copper companies made substantial contributions to the UFP in its early years, and even some of the top organizers of the UFP were subsidized by one of these companies. The leader of the party was usually the Prime Minister or the leader of the Opposition. The European parties by themselves, that is, apart from the African National Congresses and their successors, formed a separate party system. In Southern Rhodesia, from before the grant of responsible government, the forerunners of the United Federal Party, under different labels, were in office for most of the pre-Federation period and under the Federation. Sir Godfrey Huggins was their territorial leader, until he became Federal Prime Minister in 1953. The supporters of the party were agreed on its program, which was the highest common denominator of European opinion on native policy, in the sense that Huggins favored as much African advancement as a majority of his electorate would tolerate. The several oppositions to the UFP and its forerunners were supported by voters who were more opposed to African advancement. These

Europeans were generally drawn from the lower economic strata—
among them artisans and relatively unskilled workers who felt themselves threatened by African educational advancement (hence one of
the Opposition parties called itself the Rhodesia Labour Party)—and
from farmers, especially of Afrikaner background. The Opposition also
normally contained a few genuinely racist white supremacists. Until
1962, the Dominion Party played the role of official parliamentary
opposition in both the Southern Rhodesian and Federal parliaments.
At that time, it reorganized as the Rhodesian Front, for which the old
Dominion Party provided the organizational core. The Rhodesian
Front opposed the new Southern Rhodesian constitution, boycotted
the federal election of 1962, and won the Southern Rhodesian election
of December 1962.

Changes in party make-up of this kind frequently occurred in European politics. Often when an obviously important issue of policy toward Africans was central to politics, the erstwhile opposition would
merge back into the UFP, from which its leaders had split off originally because of disagreement on some less important intra-European
issue. In 1963, it seemed possible that the Rhodesian Front and the
UFP would join forces. It is for this reason that Colin Leys refers to
European politics in Southern Rhodesia as a "one-party system." [17]
However, in applying this label, one should be careful to remember
that in the crucial constitutional referenda of 1923, 1953, and 1962,
roughly a third of the voters made up the losing minority.

To the extent that Northern Rhodesia had a party system at all,
it was both more complicated and more fluid than that of Southern
Rhodesia. Until federation, the elected Unofficials were usually united
in their opposition to the administration consisting of Officials. It was
only under the constitution of 1959, which provided for a complicated
system of constituencies, some of them with both European and African voters, that the UFP, the ANC, and the Central African Party
(later renamed Liberal Party after severance of connections with its
Southern Rhodesian parent) placed members in the Legislative Council. At this time, the Federal Assembly still contained M.P.'s of the
Northern Rhodesian Dominion Party, so that European political opinion was then represented by the middle-of-the-road (in European
terms) UFP, the right-wing DP, and the left-wing CAP. The CAP
had been founded by Garfield Todd after failure of his bid to return
to the Southern Rhodesian premiership upon his expulsion by his own

[17] Leys, *European Politics in Southern Rhodesia*, p. 173.

UFP. Its Northern Rhodesian branch was led by Sir John Moffat and Harry Franklin, both former officers of the Colonial Service. These two men replaced UFP ministers in the Governor's Executive Council, when the UFP protested against the Macleod constitution by going into opposition. By this time, the Liberal Party had disaffiliated from the Southern Rhodesian CAP, which virtually went out of existence.

This breakup of a party of federal (or two-territorial) scope followed a fairly common pattern. It was brought out earlier how and why the Northern Rhodesian Unofficials under Welensky's leadership joined forces with Huggins' governing party. The maintaining of close organizational links between the territorial and federal branches of the UFP proved difficult. Friction between the two led to the loss of M.P.'s by the UFP and contributed to the founding first of the Dominion Party and later of the Rhodesian Front. If the federal organization of the UFP had not had a virtual monopoly of access to major sources of campaign contributions, its discipline over the two Rhodesian territorial organizations might have been weaker than it was. (In Nyasaland, the handful of Europeans had only the UFP to look to in their vain attempts to prevent the coming of African government, and Nyasaland really had no party system before the election of 1961.)

In 1962, when an African government in Northern Rhodesia and the breakup of the Federation seemed imminent, there was some expectation that Sir Roy Welensky himself might try to replace Sir Edgar Whitehead as leader of the territorial UFP and, possibly, Prime Minister of Southern Rhodesia. Rumors to this effect were spread after Whitehead stated that he thought Welensky's dissolution of the Federal Parliament was untimely. It was also believed that Whitehead would have moved faster than he did with African advancement if Welensky had not applied a brake to him and that this brake consisted of federal control of campaign purse strings, when the Southern Rhodesian UFP planned to go to the polls in early 1963, a date then advanced to December 14, 1962. On the other hand, it was conceivable that the party's financial contributors would "ditch" Welensky after the election in the North and the defeat of the UFP in Southern Rhodesia.

The personalities and support of these two UFP leaders were quite different. Welensky was a self-made man, born in Salisbury of a Polish Jewish father and an Afrikaner mother, a former Northern Rhodesian Labour leader (and before that a boxer), who was very popular with the European voters because of his outspoken bluntness on their behalf. Whitehead, on the other hand, was born in the British Embassy in Berlin, the son of a British diplomat (a fact he seemed to forget when he spoke of his and his followers' "birthright" as Rhodesians). A university man, he was a member of what the British call the Establishment, who came to Rhodesia to farm in 1928. His economic expertise led to his service as Finance Minister under Huggins in Southern Rhodesia between 1946 and 1953; and he subsequently served as the Federation's first minister to Washington. He was recalled to take over the prime ministership after the ouster of Garfield Todd but, on his first attempt to qualify for this office by winning a parliamentary by-election, he was defeated. Thereupon, a general election was called, in which Whitehead won a relatively "safe" seat. As a confirmed bachelor of somewhat aloof disposition, he did not enjoy nearly as great popularity with the rank-and-file electorate as Welensky. On the other hand, he did move with unexpected resolution, simultaneously in both the repression of potential nationalist violence and the elimination of nonpolitical discriminatory legislation. At times it seemed as though he were using "Malvern tactics," since Lord Malvern had often "talked tough" against African political movements, while simultaneously (and almost surreptitiously) doing something to remove restrictions on the Africans.

Winston Field, who became Prime Minister of Southern Rhodesia in the upset election of December 1962, had previously been leader of the Opposition Dominion Party in the Federal Parliament. Born in England, he settled in Southern Rhodesia as a young man and became a successful tobacco farmer. He moved into politics through the Rhodesian Tobacco Association, but did so almost reluctantly. European opponents of federation and the Welensky government sometimes accused Field of being too gentlemanly as leader of the federal Opposition. On the other hand, Dr. Banda was known to hold Winston Field in higher personal regard than any other European politician in Central Africa, probably because Field was one of the few—if not the only one—who treated Banda as another political leader, that is, as an equal. Prime Minister Field's visit to Dr. Banda in Zomba shortly after he came into office did more than symbolize the good will prevailing between these two leaders. It also demonstrated that African nationalists prefer Europeans whom they can describe as "sincere" conservatives or reactionaries on issues of race relations to self-styled liberals whose professions of multiracial partnership the Africans regard as hypocritical and find more difficult to fight.

In this case, Field and Banda also had in common their opposition to continuation of the Federation in its current shape.

The political philosophies of the three chief European leaders probably differed less than their personalities. Welensky seemed to follow in Lord Malvern's footsteps in his public commitment to the policy of partnership between the races. The partnership was occasionally defined as one between the senior European and the junior African partners or, allegedly by Malvern, as one modeled on the relations between a rider and his horse. The Europeans were considered the senior partners, because they were said to have brought all the civilization that there is in Central Africa. It would take the Africans a long time to be raised (not to raise themselves) to the Europeans' level. Because European standards must not be lowered, "Government must be kept in the hands of civilized and responsible persons," an attitude reflected above all in franchise legislation, discussed below. In effect, this meant that Welensky and his UFP were willing to admit highly educated Africans to political participation—an African M.P. was named parliamentary secretary to a federal ministry in 1958 and to a second one in 1962. But the earlier appointee, Jasper Z. Savanhu, resigned later in 1962, giving as his reason the failure of the policy of partnership, especially in the appointment of Africans to higher levels of the federal civil service. The UFP in fact held out little hope of political advancement for the vast majority of Africans for one or more generations.

Adherents of this philosophy professed to witness demonstrations of its correctness every time they received reports of violence, corruption, dictatorship, or chaos from the independent African states in Black Africa. Their purpose was prevention of either a Mau Mau or a Congo-type situation in the Rhodesias. They frequently made analogies between nationalist leaders in the three territories—Banda, Kaunda, Nkomo, and others—and figures like Patrice Lumumba or Jomo Kenyatta. On the basis of such analogies, usually quite fallacious, they justified the repressive measures taken during the Emergencies of 1959 or under the Law and Order Maintenance Act of 1960 and its tightened and extended version of 1962. The UFP held African politicians responsible for whatever violence was perpetrated by any other Africans and rejected arguments based on the nationalists' lack of means for disciplining their people. Every time a wave of violence erupted in Southern Rhodesia, where until September 1962 arson, intimidation, beatings, and the like were always directed against other

Africans, not Europeans, the UFP responded by arresting African leaders and tightening security legislation. It was undeterred in this policy even when violence usually increased after the arrests, though this might have suggested to them that someone other than the arrested leaders had been responsible.

Supporters of the Dominion Party and its successor, the Rhodesian Front, shared most of these attitudes. But they openly rejected the policy of racial partnership and opposed federation as the instrument for the furtherance of this policy. They voted against the abolition of discriminatory legislation initiated by Whitehead's government in the last months of its incumbency. Some of them occasionally spoke of the concept of separate development, but in a rather vague and unideological manner. While in opposition, the Rhodesian Front was rather critical of the UFP's security legislation, for two mutually contradictory reasons: it was inadequate to the task of suppressing African violence and it violated due process. The latter criticism was made either on grounds of principle, or because the critics feared that the UFP government would use repressive measures against themselves. However, soon after coming into office, Prime Minister Field permitted the release of not only such recently restricted ZAPU leaders as Joshua Nkomo but also the so-called "hard core" ANC leaders who had been in detention since the Emergency of 1959. Nkomo and others were subsequently detained again. Field was generally regarded as the most liberal member of his cabinet, and some observers doubted whether he would be able to retain control over his followers. His government introduced further amendments to the Law and Order Maintenance Act (discussed below), designed to deter nationalist violence. At the same time, it gave notice of its intention to use the courts more regularly than the previous government, which had often arrested African politicians without even preferring charges against them.

The European leaders, with few exceptions, were unwilling to admit, at least in public, that some of their African counterparts might be reasonable human beings with whom they could bargain and reach an understanding based on compromise. This unwillingness was due to the leaders' estimate of the views of their European electorate which made them afraid of getting too far ahead of the voters, for fear of losing to a more reactionary group. Many of the voters, in turn, were chiefly afraid of losing their property—homes, farms, businesses, local investments—once the country had majority government. Constitutional guarantees designed to prevent such possibilities did not impress them as "safe."

The African independence movements present a great contrast with the European parties and, as already indicated, they also differ from one territory to the next. (There has never been an African party of Federation-wide scope.) The initial reason for this difference was that none of the African National Congresses started as an electoral organization. None of them was founded by parliamentarians in search of popular electoral support, because the franchise laws made this impossible. All of them either started or gained importance as protest movements. They boycotted most elections until they got an acceptable franchise, and they always won a franchise far short of universal suffrage. Even when this point was reached, which converted them into part-time electoral organizations, they continued to operate mainly as protest movements wanting to mobilize the political consciousness of the African masses. For example, during the Southern Rhodesian referendum on the new constitution, in July 1961, which ZAPU boycotted, ZAPU also ran its own unofficial mock referendum, in which it claimed the constitution was rejected by more than 400,000 votes against a couple of hundred. The drives for members periodically launched by all the movements achieved the same purpose and were also a major source of finance. The Malawi Congress Party charged an entrance fee of two shillings and an annual subscription of the same amount. On the other hand, for those Africans who join, possession of their membership card—which some of them cannot read— is a symbol of their membership in the modern world. In Nyasaland, parents frequently enroll newly born babies in the Malawi Youth League to show their solidarity with the movement.

The formal organization of the independence movements, as laid down in their constitutions, is quite similar to that of the European parties. The MCP, for example, elects its president for a three-year term at an annual delegates' conference, though Dr. Banda was subsequently elected life president. The president selects members of the Central Executive Committee from slates of candidates submitted by provincial committees. A National Committee, consisting of representatives, one from each district, meets half-yearly. Outside observers attending these meetings or the annual conference would probably be impressed by the orderly "British" way in which they are conducted, an indirect result of the procedural experience with which many Africans were provided under British colonial administration. But they would also notice the lack of intraparty opposition, and perhaps be upset by it. One reason for this phenomenon is the fact that all three movements—MCP, UNIP, and ZAPU—received their greatest impetus from the Emergencies of 1959, during which most of their top leaders were arrested. This dramatized much better than their own propaganda the simplicity of their mission, namely, the achievement of independence. Until that is reached, they feel that they cannot afford internal rifts. Hence also there is the tendency for internal dissidents to split off and attempt to organize their own parties.

Justification of nonoppositional one-party government for the post-independence period is somewhat more complicated, but again all three movements have taken this position, which they share with such otherwise different African leaders as Kwame Nkrumah and Julius Nyerere. In the Rhodesias and Nyasaland, they do so in part, because they model themselves on Nkrumah's successful Convention People's Party, not as a result of having received financial support from Ghana, but because they consider their problems similar to those of the Gold Coast. They feel that they cannot afford the luxury of an opposition on the Westminster model, especially if it would mean the exclusion of Opposition supporters from contributing to their country's development. This seems understandable for countries that have only a handful of trained or experienced persons available who are capable of making such contributions in leading positions. Finally, they also assert that there will be plenty of discussion within the councils of the single party before policy is arrived at and that this procedure is in keeping with African traditions of government by prolonged discussion and consent.

After Dr. Banda was released, on Macleod's initiative, from thirteen months in a Southern Rhodesian jail, he told the crowds he addressed in Nyasaland to be "peaceful and harm no one." Shortly afterward, he visited the United States. After a talk he gave to the National Press Club in Washington, he was asked whether he planned to keep Nyasaland in the Commonwealth once it got self-government and secession from the Federation. His answer was that he certainly would stay in the Commonwealth, to which the American chairman responded by saying, "That's the best advertisement for a clink that I've ever heard!" Perhaps even more remarkable is the relative absence of conspiratorial politics from all three territories, despite the incentive which their undeserved detention might have given to the African politicians. This may be attributed in part to the firmness combined with fairness that characterized the treatment they received in prison. But the personalities of the leaders must also be given some credit, since these were obviously formed before the experience of the Emergencies.

Dr. Banda's career has already been sketched. Europeans often painted an extremely evil picture of him, accusing him of everything from medical malpractice to wizardry and communism. When he demanded immediate secession and one-man one-vote upon his release, some observers predicted that he would not be satisfied with less from the British government or, conversely, if he were given less, that he would lose control of Malawi to his more radical younger lieutenants. In fact he was given considerably less than he had asked for, accepted it, and retained full control over his MCP while his popularity increased and his lieutenants cooperated wholeheartedly with him. At the time and in retrospect, he attributed the occasional anti-European violence and antigovernment demonstrations occurring in his country prior to his return from jail to white people's arrogance, government repression, and opposition to federation for which there was no legitimate outlet, for example, in Parliament. As proof he claimed that "not a single stone has been thrown at any European" since his release. Moreover, the cooperation of the African population with the government did improve markedly, especially after Malawi ministers came into office. Since that time, Dr. Banda's main concern, in addition to his older constitutional goals, has been the democratization of government within the country and its economic development. This outlook was revealed also by the ministries which he took over in 1961: Local Government and Natural Resources.

Banda maintains good relations with African leaders elsewhere, including President Nkrumah of Ghana, whom he came to know well during his five years' residence in that country from 1953 to 1958. This was the period straddling the Gold Coast's achievement of independence in 1957, and Dr. Banda must have learned something from Nkrumah's political tactics. There is at least one parallel between these two men, in that both of them may be described as charismatic leaders in their relations with their African followers. But while Nkrumah usually tried to emphasize African characteristics, for example, in his dress, Dr. Banda has not done this so far. His personal trademark, in contrast to a togalike garment, consists of a black Homburg hat, dark glasses, and a walking stick sometimes replaced by an African chief's fly whisk, with which he punctuates his speeches.

His forty years' residence in America and Britain may explain this difference, as well as the lack of an indigenous equivalent in Nyasaland of Ghana's "national" dress.

By 1962, Northern Rhodesia still had two independence movements, the senior ANC and junior but more widely supported UNIP, which had split off from the ANC in 1959. Harry Nkumbula, the leader of the ANC, was elected to the Legislative Council in 1959, while Kenneth Kaunda, the leader of UNIP (then Zambia), was in jail partly because of Zambia's boycott of the election, which was also the reason for the split in the ANC. Nkumbula too was to spend a year in jail, to his misfortune not for political reasons but for hit-and-run driving. While he was in prison, the ANC was led by Lawrence Katilungu, who was subsequently killed in an automobile accident. Katilungu had been head of the African Mineworkers Union, but made enemies among the nationalists when he accepted appointment to the Monckton Commission, which was boycotted not only by the British Labour Party but also by the major independence movement in each territory. The election of October 30, 1962, and the run-offs held in December, confirmed previous estimates of the relative strength of the two African movements. The figures show that 92,255 Africans and 37,330 Europeans went to the polls. UNIP received approximately 65,000 votes, ANC 17,000, and the UFP 22,000. But because of the complex requirements of the electoral law (see below), the final composition of the Legislative Council was UFP, 16; UNIP, 14; ANC, 7. Despite their apparent previous hostility, Kaunda and Nkumbula formed a coalition cabinet in which Kaunda became Minister of Local Government and Social Welfare, while Nkumbula was appointed Minister of African Education. The UFP continued in its previous role as official opposition, while the Liberal Party, which failed to return a single candidate, dissolved itself. Kenneth Kaunda took the inconclusive parliamentary reflection of the popular vote as his main argument in favor of demanding speedy reform of the constitution from the British government.

UNIP's leadership was younger and probably better educated than that of the ANC. Several of its leaders received part of their higher education in India, and this may account for their vegetarianism and public adherence to a policy of passive resistance. Kenneth Kaunda is said to be ascetic and highly principled. He can also be quite emotional, as he demonstrated by bursting into tears while testifying before the Special Committee on Colonialism of the United Nations

General Assembly in New York. Kaunda differs from Dr. Banda in that he openly invited criticism of himself and his policies at public meetings of the party. Also by contrast with his counterparts in the other territories, he directly appealed for European support, for example, by addressing large European meetings on the Copperbelt. Of course in Nyasaland there were not enough Europeans to make it worth while for the MCP to seek their votes, except in a few upper-roll constituencies. The peculiar make-up of the Legislative Assembly of Northern Rhodesia, on the other hand, made it necessary for UNIP to get some European electoral support if it was to gain a parliamentary majority and to put up European candidates on its ticket. In the election of October 1962, UNIP actually ran five European candidates, none of whom was elected because of opposition of white voters. Beyond this, Kaunda may have been genuinely less racial in his approach to politics than the others.

Those ANC leaders considered most radical by the Southern Rhodesian government that arrested them in 1959 had not been released from detention by 1962, when another 1,600 were arrested or rearrested. After unrest in 1960, the ANC's successor, the National Democratic Party, was also proscribed, in December of that year. Thereupon, it reappeared under a third name, Zimbabwe African People's Union. Joshua Nkomo could become its president, because he happened to be abroad at the time of the first wave of arrests in 1959. He stayed in self-imposed exile, until the government permitted him to return in time to participate in the constitutional negotiations of 1960. The movement profited not only from the original Emergency, as described above, but from subsequent repressive measures taken by the Southern Rhodesian government. For instance, under the Law and Order Maintenance Act, political meetings on Native Reserves were prohibited for a long time. As a result ZAPU had to send its organizers directly into the homes of potential members and was able to round up a greater number, with stronger personal commitment, than probably would have been the case if membership recruitment had taken place only at huge public rallies. However, arrests and detention orders took a heavy toll among the top leadership after 1959, and this makes it difficult to appraise their characteristics. For example, it is conceivable that those of them who had spent three and a half years in detention by the time they were released by Field's government may have turned bitter and violent and that they will try to overthrow other more moderate leaders.

For these and related reasons, the personality of Joshua Nkomo seemed less important, in 1962, for the future politics of ZAPU than those of Kaunda and Banda for UNIP and MCP. He was less firmly established as leader,* although his success at the United Nations had added somewhat to his popularity. However, even this and the repeated and prolonged trips abroad that he made in connection with his UN efforts earned him intraparty criticism for absenting himself so much from Southern Rhodesia where, it was felt, the main work toward independence would have to be done. Just before ZAPU was outlawed in September 1962, he reportedly transferred its funds to Dar es Salaam, preparatory to setting up a government in exile there. When he slipped across the border after ZAPU was outlawed, the other independence leaders denounced him for his cowardice, and he subsequently flew back to Salisbury, to be restricted to his native village.

The danger of splits also seemed greater for ZAPU than for either UNIP or MCP, at least until the arrests of 1962. One split had already happened when a few ZAPU figures founded the Zimbabwe National Party, which professed to be more determined than ZAPU to accept nothing short of majority government and also to have socialist goals. Both groups, however, opposed the new constitution, boycotted the election, and seemed close enough in other respects to have the possibility of a reconciliation with ZAPU.

Pressure Groups

For the preindependence period, African social organizations with political interests were unlikely to assert a role separate from that of the independence movements themselves. On the other hand, it seemed likely that, after the installation of African governments, a richly articulated system of interest organizations will come into operation. These groupings already exist, as noted earlier, and although they identified their special interests with the more general interest of the entire African community pressing toward independence, once that goal has been achieved they will presumably become more aware of differences among themselves and begin to apply political pressure toward their special goals. Indeed, the Malawi Congress Party had already made provisions for harnessing pressure

* On July 9, 1963, while this book was going through the press, the National Executive of ZAPU removed Joshua Nkomo as its leader for "inconsiderate, unconstitutional, blunderous, irresponsible and undemocratic" actions.

groups to its own wagon. For example, one of the seven major "aims and objects" stated in the preamble to its constitution was "to work with and in the interest of the Trade Union Movement, and other kindred organizations, whose aims and objects are in harmony with this Constitution." There was also a provision for organizations to become affiliated members of the MCP by accepting "the programme, principles and policy of the Party" and paying an affiliation fee of two pounds a year. If the MCP and its brother movements succeed in integrating pressure groups, then they may have one further argument in favor of a single-party political system, since different interests would be represented within the one party and could, therefore, contribute to the political process in a nonoppositional way.

Of European pressure groups there was a great variety, as one would expect from the earlier description of the corporatist structure of European society. Chambers of Commerce and of Mines, the churches (which have political interests partly as school proprietors), the Tobacco Association, European trade unions, the Association of Rhodesia and Nyasaland Industries, and others have already been mentioned. All are accustomed to having their representations listened to by the several governments, in keeping with the practice of colonial governors during the earlier stages of the constitutional evolution of their territories. Beyond that, and growing out of these practices, European parties customarily went to the polls, especially in Southern Rhodesia, with tickets that were well balanced in a corporatist sense. The career patterns of Southern Rhodesian and federal M.P.'s show many to have moved into politics by way of high office in agricultural, industrial, professional, or ethnic minority organizations.

One type of European pressure group deserves special mention in this context, the civil services. Colonial officials in the northern territories voted in elections, and their votes may have been decisive where, for example, an upper-roll constituency in Nyasaland had 203 voters, of whom only 73 voted for the UFP.[18] The remainder were probably Colonial Service voters, between whom and the federal government there was usually little love lost. In Southern Rhodesia, the voting impact of its locally based civil service has been in the other direction but was not so important because its members made up only an insignificant part of the total European electorate in any one district. On the other hand, branches of the civil service, especially the Native Affairs Department, exerted considerable pressure

[18] Mair, *The Nyasaland Elections of 1961*, p. 81.

on policy and public opinion. For example, the Secretary for Native Affairs and Chief Native Commissioner, in his annual *Report* in 1962 (publication of which followed the recommendations of the Robinson Commission to take away all nonadministrative functions from the Native Affairs Department) criticized aspects of government policy, especially amendments to the Land Apportionment Act. He was commended for this by Opposition M.P.'s in the Legislative Assembly and by other public figures. But neither the Colonial Service nor the Native Affairs Department is going to be able for much longer to operate as a pressure group in this fashion as they will disappear from the scene.

Elections

The franchise and representation were always treated as the most crucial issues in Rhodesian and federal politics, because European settlers were afraid that a broadened franchise would lead to their being "swamped" by the Africans who have always outnumbered them. In order to prevent this from happening, a fairly elaborate rationalization was worked out for the retention of high qualifications for the franchise. Its most concise statement was contained in the *Report of the Franchise Commission* of 1957, also known as the "Tredgold Report," after Sir Robert Tredgold, chairman of the commission, who was then Federal Chief Justice. The main task of the commission was "to consider and report on a system for the just representation of the people of the Colony in its Legislative Assembly, under which the Government is placed, and remains in the hands of civilized and responsible persons." [19] The central assumption of the *Report* was that there is a direct correlation between qualifications of voters and the "hands" to which government is entrusted. This is a dubious assumption, because no British-type government is in the hands of the electorate but in those of the Crown and its ministers. It would, therefore, have made better sense to place high qualifications upon candidates for parliamentary and ministerial office. However, this basic assumption was never questioned, not even by African nationalists. The *Report* also favored a common voters' roll, that is, a system under which voters of different qualifications would vote for the same candidates, so that no candidates could afford entirely to ignore the wishes of voters with the lower set of qualifications. But the commission denied that the qualifications were dependent

[19] *Report of the Franchise Commission* (Salisbury, 1957), p. 1.

upon race or color, since they were defined in terms of income, property, and education. In view of the virtual identity between the race cleavage and the class cleavage in Rhodesian society, this denial was given no credence by most Africans, including those who passed the higher set of qualifications. At any rate, the *Report* frankly admitted "the fact that for many years to come the voters qualifying on the ordinary qualification would be principally European, and those qualifying on the special principally African."

The most important qualifications for the ordinary or upper roll in Southern Rhodesia, before the election of 1963, were as follows: (1) adequate knowledge of English and the ability to complete the registration form in handwriting and (2) an annual income of at least £720 during the two previous years or possession of real estate worth at least £1,500, or income of £480 or real estate worth £1,000 plus completion of primary education, or income of £300 or real estate worth £500 plus four years' secondary education. Wives qualified through their husbands, unless married under a system permitting polygamy. Qualifications for the special or lower roll, whose effects on an election could not exceed 20 per cent of the total number of voters registered in the colony (a ratio never even approximated), were as follows: (1) the same language requirement and (2) an income of at least £240 during each of the two previous years, or an income of £120 during each of the two previous years plus completion of not less than two years' secondary education. In the election of the Legislative Assembly of June 5, 1958, the means qualification was either £240, toward which one could figure the value of food, housing, and clothing provided in kind, or occupation of property worth at least £500. At the time of that election, 55,158 voters were registered, 1,696 of them African—and the Parliament produced by this election, like all its predecessors, was all white.

The Southern Rhodesian elections of 1958 and 1962 were run with provisions for preferential voting. In the 1958 election, there were many three-cornered contests due to Garfield Todd's virtual expulsion from the UFP and his founding of another party, the United Rhodesia Party. The Opposition Dominion Party won the largest number of first preference votes, and the UFP gained its parliamentary majority only as a result of the transfer to it of second preference votes whose first choice had been a defeated URP candidate. In 1962, this provision had no effect on the outcome of the election.

According to the Federal Electoral Act of 1958, under which the federal elections of 1958 and 1962 were held, qualifications for general voters were the same as under the Southern Rhodesian act, with the additions that chiefs and certain ministers of religion were deemed qualified ex officio. Qualifications for special voters were as follows: (1) the usual English-language requirement and (2) income of at least £150 during each of the two preceding years or possession of real estate worth at least £500, or income of at least £120 during each of the two preceding years plus completion of two years' secondary schooling. One irony of these provisions, which could hardly have escaped interested Africans, was that those with two years of secondary education were very unlikely to be earning the lower income.

The real complication under the federal electoral system came from the composition of the Federal Assembly. It contained 44 ordinary members (24 from Southern Rhodesia, 14 from Northern Rhodesia, and 6 from Nyasaland), 8 directly elected African members (4 from Southern Rhodesia and 2 each from the two northern territories, all elected by general and special voters voting together), 4 indirectly elected African members (2 from each of the northern territories), and 3 Europeans representing African interests (1 elected by all the general voters of Southern Rhodesia voting together and 1 each nominated by the governors of Northern Rhodesia and Nyasaland), for a total of 59. The independence movements boycotted registration and the elections held under this law. As a result, the voters' rolls in the three territories, at the time of the federal elections of November 12, 1958, were composed as follows.

	Est. pop.	Roll	European	African	Other	Total
S. Rhodesia	2,640,000	general	no breakdown available			65,092
		special	125	635		
N. Rhodesia	2,300,000	general	not av.	39	not av.	20,249
		special	4	53	6	63
Nyasaland	2,710,000	general	2,112	5	389	2,506
		special	1	11	1	13

With respect to African participation, these figures speak for themselves.

The next small step on the road to a broader franchise was taken in Northern Rhodesia, for its election of March 20, 1959. Qualifications for ordinary voters were almost the same as under the federal act. For special voters, in addition to the provisions of the federal act, hereditary councilors and certain classes of village headmen were also admitted. This Legislative Council was composed as follows: 4 ex officio members, 2 nominated Officials, 2 nominated Unofficials, 12 ordinary members (from urban constituencies in which special voters were allowed to exert up to one-third influence), 6 specially elected Africans (from rural constituencies, in which ordinary and special voters counted equally), 2 reserved European seats (from two composite constituencies, covering the area of the ordinary urban constituencies, in which ordinary and special votes were counted equally), and 2 reserved African seats (from two composite constituencies covering the area of the ordinary urban constituencies, in which ordinary and special votes counted equally), for a total of 30. This time 23,358 ordinary and 6,846 special voters registered; 769 of the ordinary voters were Africans. The ANC had supported registration, while Zambia boycotted it. The boycott must have been the more effective policy, because it had been estimated that almost 25,000 Africans could have qualified for the special franchise. The returns were as follows: ordinary constituencies, 11 UFP, 1 Dominion Party; special constituencies, 2 CAP, 1 ANC, 1 independent, 2 not filled; [20] reserved for Europeans, 2 CAP; reserved for Africans, 2 UFP.

The first real breakthrough to an electoral system facilitating African government came with the Nyasaland constitution of 1960. It was negotiated with the leadership of the MCP, which therefore supported the registration drive and subsequently achieved a remarkable victory in an orderly and completely honest election. The country was divided into 28 constituencies, 20 for lower-roll and 8 for upper-roll voters. Combinations of qualifications for the lower roll were as follows: (1) literacy in English, an income of at least £120 a year or real estate worth £250, and a minimum age of twenty-one or (2) literacy in any language used in Nyasaland and payment of (or exemption from) taxes for ten years. Chiefs, headmen, members of Native Authorities (local government bodies), past or present members of district councils, master farmers, pensioners, and veterans automatically qualified for the lower roll. The taxation requirement was intended to disqualify younger and therefore presumably less responsible voters, because tax liability begins at eighteen. For the

[20] For nomination in a special constituency, candidates needed the approval of two-thirds of the chiefs in the district. This provision, proposed by the Governor, had been opposed by the UFP because of transportation difficulties in the rural areas. In the two unrepresented districts, no candidate had been able to secure the required number of chiefs' approvals.

upper roll, university graduates qualified automatically. For others, qualifications were as follows: (1) income of £300 or property worth £500 and secondary education, or (2) income of £480 or property worth £1,000 and primary education, or (3) income of £720 or property worth £1,500 and ability to complete the registration form in English.

About 106,000 voters registered on the lower roll, and 4,401 on the upper. Malawi Congress Party won all 20 lower-roll seats. All its opponents lost their deposits, a designated sum forfeited if the number of votes received is less than a set proportion. Only one of them, in fact, received more than 100 votes. Voting participation was everywhere higher than 90 per cent. On the upper roll, the UFP won five seats, the MCP won two, and one independent sympathetic to Malawi was also elected, who subsequently became Minister of Roads.

In the course of the campaign, UFP leaders, including Sir Roy Welensky, charged that Dr. Banda's followers were using intimidation, an accusation that was constantly made against African nationalists by their opponents and, as will be seen below, that led to specific anti-intimidation legislation in the other two territories. In Northern Rhodesia, a bill was passed before the campaign of 1962 making it an offense to ask people to show their party membership cards on any occasions other than political meetings. The UFP unsuccessfully tried to use its charges of intimidation to get the Nyasaland election postponed by the Governor. At one point of the campaign, nine houses in a small area were burned down, but the police denied that political arson was involved. Dr. Banda called upon his supporters to maintain peace and calm "before, during, and after the election." It later turned out that UFP followers had been responsible for several cases of arson. In the words of a careful observer:

After the election a number of UFP supporters who had accused Malawi Youth members of burning houses were charged with making wrongful accusations and convicted, and were required to pay compensation to Malawi members who had been wrongfully imprisoned. Some were also convicted of setting fire to their own houses.[21]

These facts are not meant to deny that the independence movements also employed certain forms of intimidation, though these did not always necessarily involve threats or the use of violence. In the relatively undifferentiated African communities, particularly rural

---

[21] Mair, *The Nyasaland Elections of 1961*, note 3, pp. 77 f.

ones, there is naturally a high degree of consensus. It also seems nearly impossible for people living in such communities to keep "secret" either their political sympathies or their votes. Indeed, such Africans probably have no equivalent of our notions of secrecy or even privacy. But by considering as fraudulent or farcical elections held in these circumstances—and in Nyasaland under the careful supervision of the British Colonial Service—one misses almost everything important about the functions performed by these polls. They quite literally "move" the territory across the major hurdle between colonialism and independence. And they also move the participating Africans across the major hurdle between political backwardness and political modernity. In the eyes of these first-time voters, they are not so much choosing between competing candidates for parliamentary office as they are expressing their "belonging" to the movement toward independence and their support of its leader.

After Nyasaland, Southern Rhodesia was next to change its franchise (since the Northern Rhodesian system of representation was not put into its final shape until after the Southern Rhodesian constitutional referendum). The old common roll was given up to the extent that the 15 M.P.'s, probably Africans, representing that many "electoral districts," were to be elected primarily by lower-roll voters, with up to 25 per cent influence exerted by upper-roll voters in these districts; while 50 M.P.'s, presumably Europeans, were to be elected from that many "constituencies" by both upper- and lower-roll voters, with the influence of the lower roll this time not permitted to exceed 25 per cent of the total votes cast by the upper roll. Qualifications for the upper roll were kept as before, except that chiefs and headmen qualified ex officio. Qualifications for the lower roll were changed as follows: (1) annual income of £240 during the previous six months or real estate worth £450 or (2) annual income of £120 during the previous six months or real estate worth £250, the educational requirements for these two classes remaining unchanged; or (3) a minimum age of thirty, knowledge of English, and annual income of £180 during the previous six months or real estate worth £350; or (4) a minimum age of thirty, knowledge of English, completion of primary education, and income of £120 during the previous six months or real estate worth £250. Ministers of religion automatically qualified for the lower roll, as did heads of kraals with a following of twenty or more heads of families and an adequate knowledge of English.

One thing emerges from all the franchise legislation: the outcome of an election is determined less by the actual poll than by the framing of the electoral system and the delimitation of voting districts. For example, the British government made it quite clear by negotiating the Nyasaland constitution of 1960 that it intended to have legislative and executive councils dominated by Dr. Banda's party. Similarly, the Southern Rhodesian government made it clear that it was willing to have an African Opposition of at least 15 in the enlarged Legislative Assembly. And it must have been evident to ZAPU that it could hardly elect more than 17 of its candidates (the number above 15 depending on the delimitation of constituencies). Hence it decided to boycott both registration and election. This and other boycotts were, moreover, easy to "sell" to the potential African electorate because of the very complexity of the franchise laws. Everyone can understand the principle of one-man one-vote and commit himself to it, even though he may be willing to compromise for a good deal less. But even the political scientist may be forgiven for not understanding fully (and not being able to describe clearly and in a simplified form) the electoral systems of British Central Africa.

That the franchise, systems of representation, and the delimitation of constituencies were believed to determine the outcome of elections was demonstrated by the haggling that went on for two years over the Northern Rhodesian constitution of 1962 and by its final acceptance, in its third form, by UNIP, which would have boycotted an election held under the second form.

The provisions under which the October 30, 1962, election was held were as follows. There were to be 45 members of the Legislative Council, 15 elected on a higher franchise, 15 on a lower franchise, 14 in pairs from seven "national constituencies"—in each constituency one member on the higher, the other on the lower franchise—and 1 from a "special national constituency" for Asian voters. In four of the seven national constituencies, the candidates on the higher and lower franchise had to be Europeans and Africans, respectively. In the national constituencies, the winning candidate on each franchise needed at least 10 per cent of the voters on the other franchise and 20 per cent of either race to be elected. Failure to achieve this meant that runoffs were to be held. Only two reserved national constituencies were filled in the election of October 30, 1962, leaving ten seats in the five remaining national constituencies to be contested in the runoff held on December 10. Even then, only two seats in different constituencies were filled. In one of these (to give an illustration of the complexity of the requirements), Luapula, an ANC-supported European, received 21.9 per cent of the upper-franchise votes cast, 12.6 of the lower-franchise ballots cast, 13.4 per cent of the African votes, and 26.9 per cent of the Europeans' vote. In Zambezi constituency, an African ANC candidate received 36.8 per cent of the upper- and 60.6 of the lower-franchise votes, 57.9 of the African and 34.7 per cent of the European votes.

Qualifications for the higher franchise were substantially the same as in Nyasaland, with the additional automatic qualification of such positions as chief, tribal councilor, member of Native Authorities or of native courts, holder of decorations, and government pensioner and of any persons with an annual income of £300 who had been in the same employment for the preceding ten years. For the lower franchise, applicants had to be able to fill in the registration form in Bemba, Nyanja, Lozi, Tonga, Lunda, Lovale, Gujerati, or Urdu, as well as to have an income of £120 or real estate worth £250, or to hold any of the positions just listed which also qualified for the higher franchise (thus such individuals had an option of which roll to get on), or to be headmen, veterans, or "improved farmers" of two years' standing. The income was figured for the preceding twelve months, and it included housing and rations. One wife could register on her husband's qualifications on either roll.

Administration

There are four administrations in British Central Africa: the federal one and those of the three territories. In none had africanization made any significant headway at the upper levels by 1963. However, some efforts were being made in the two Colonial Office protectorates to prepare the ground for the speedy africanization that would have to take place after the grant of responsible government. Until that time and—if one judges by the experience of other former British colonies—presumably for a few years afterward, some major administrative posts would continue to be manned by officers of the Colonial Service. The presumption about their postindependence retention could reasonably be made on the basis of good cooperation in Nyasaland between Malawi ministers and their civil servants, in some instances men who had been in charge of aspects of the Emergency operation against the very same nationalist politicians in 1959. In both Nyasaland and Northern Rhodesia, the Colonial Service had, on the whole, earned the respect of the African population. If anything, this respect was enhanced by federation, which was not welcomed enthusiastically by the colonial officers and was more or less actively opposed by some of them. The Emergency itself may also have raised Nyasalanders' appreciation of their Colonial Service administrators by giving them an opportunity to compare them with federal security personnel brought into their country.

The Colonial Office civil servants deserved the relatively high regard in which they were held. Even in the 1950's, the Colonial Service was still able to attract top-notch university graduates as cadets, among them "Firsts" and "Seconds" from Cambridge, Oxford, and Trinity College, Dublin. The new cadet, after a year's postgraduate work in England, normally was assigned as assistant district commissioner or district officer to a district, whose commissioner, the "DC," with a European staff of perhaps half a dozen (including a police officer, representatives of the agriculture and public works departments, and the attached federal medical officer), would be in charge of a population of more than 100,000 Africans. And the DC was fully in charge as head administrator and magistrate, to whom civil cases from Native Authority courts could be appealed. (Criminal cases were heard by itinerant full-time magistrates on circuit.) The traditions of this service have deep roots in British imperial history, including that of India, where DC's of the Indian Civil Service might be in charge of more than 1,000,000 people. In Central Africa as in India, these officers were given a maximum of discretion by their superiors, the provincial commissioners and the secretariat in the capital, headed by the Chief Secretary, who was second in command after the Governor himself.

Often officers who were not expected to rise to the top levels of the service would spend their entire career in one and the same territory, with more or less regular transfers from district to district or the secretariat. Those whose prospects looked more promising were, however, transferred from one colony to another, for example, from Tanganyika to Palestine, to British Honduras, to Aden, and from there first as Chief Secretary and finally as Governor to Northern Rhodesia (the career of Sir Evelyn Hone). Such men were expert administrators rather than specialists in the problems of one particular colony. They could be expected to be even more impartial than the others in dealing with disputes between various groups within their territory. Corruption, incidentally, was unheard of in the Colonial

Service. Another remarkable aspect of the British administrations in the two northern territories was the low level of security forces at their disposal and the utter confidence with which DC's and assistant DC's lived and moved, unarmed and unguarded, among the Africans —even, with a few exceptions, after the Emergencies of 1959. At that point, the security forces in Nyasaland were temporarily reinforced with federal forces and Northern Rhodesia police. The police forces of both territories started a recruiting drive for new European members, from the Rhodesias, South Africa, and the United Kingdom. But even with that move, the level of security forces remained relatively low and, in contrast with Southern Rhodesia, their presence was not very noticeable.

In Southern Rhodesia, the ratio of police to population has been higher and was increased more than in the North. In 1961, there was one policeman for every 636 inhabitants. The force is still called the British South Africa Police, although it no longer serves the British South Africa Company and has nothing to do with South Africa. The BSA Police had proud traditions, since Southern Rhodesia was originally "occupied" by a column of its officers and men, who had been specially recruited for this task by Cecil Rhodes himself. Between the Matabele Rebellion of 1893 and 1960, the Police had never had recourse to the use of firearms in line of duty, much less killed a man. Unfortunately, this record ended with the riots of the latter year. In 1962, parts of a report (the Packard Report) by a retired British general were published, in which he made certain recommendations concerning reforms of the BSA Police. He objected to the wearing of distinctive uniforms by African constables and to the fact that all African members of the force, regardless of their rank, were considered subordinate to any European member, regardless of his seniority or lack of it. He also recommended general increases in salaries and improved housing and other fringe benefits for Africans.

The BSA Police, because of its efficiency and size, was believed capable of handling any disturbance likely to arise in Southern Rhodesia. Despite this, however, the Southern Rhodesian and/or federal governments repeatedly mobilized the police reserves and army reserves (called territorials) to assist the regular police in maintaining order, for example, after strike threats. These European reserves lacked the experience to enable them to match the calmness of the regulars, which included a high proportion of African constables. In 1961, the BSA Police consisted of 1,741 European and 4,002 African regulars and 19,053 European and 5,464 African reserves. In the 1962–1963 budget, £4,467,000 was allocated to it—roughly one-sixth of the total expenditures (£25,960,000) or approximately the same proportion as in Northern Rhodesia (£3,763,000 out of £21,061,000), though more than in Nyasaland for that year (£1,030,000 out of £8,190,000). In 1960, the Northern Rhodesia police consisted of 5,632 regulars, including 843 Europeans. There were 1,673 European and 771 African reserves. Nyasaland, in 1961, had a force of 2,614 Africans (including 79 inspectors) and 215 Europeans.

Southern Rhodesia's civil service has been mentioned several times, especially the Native Affairs Department. What was said of it generally applies to the entire service. It was in the main recruited locally, with specialists brought in when needed from the United Kingdom, South Africa, and elsewhere. This eliminated the need for frequent rotation at the higher levels, as in the Colonial Service. Its members were in the service of a government virtually committed to the opposite of the policy of paramountcy of native interests. The attitude of native commissioners, and of other civil servants as well, was at best one of paternalism toward their African charges, at worst one of contempt. Toward the African National Congress and its successors they displayed nothing but hostility. The Native Affairs Department was in turn thoroughly disliked by the African politicians. Its commissioners had both civil and criminal jurisdiction on the Native Reserves but, because of their local background, were not as well qualified by education or outlook for these tasks. The fact that many native commissioners received in South Africa whatever university education they had did not help matters. And yet the position of the department and its chief was especially protected and entrenched by the Southern Rhodesian constitution of 1923, originally because it was recognized as protector of native interests. By 1962, it was still so powerful that, as already mentioned, its chief publicly disagreed with government policy. Nevertheless, the government proceeded with the removal of all but its administrative functions. At the same time, it planned to use many of the native commissioners, whose jobs would become redundant, as magistrates, that is, lower-level judges, although their qualifications were not of the highest order. Some optimistic African nationalists facetiously looked forward to the day when Southern Rhodesia would have an African government with a Chief Commissioner for European Affairs.

Southern Rhodesia lost parts of its civil service, more than the

other two territories, as a result of federation, when formerly territorial services—such as postal and medical services—were federalized.
By 1962, the federal public service consisted of more than 37,000
posts, of which 20,000 were held by Africans; 12,000 of these Africans
were in Branch IV, mostly as messengers and orderlies. Their minimum monthly wages were £6.12.0 in Southern Rhodesia, £8.1.0 in
Northern Rhodesia, and £4.6.0 in Nyasaland—pegged to territorial
wage scales. Branch III contained more than 5,100 Africans, including assistants in post and telegraph, audit, customs, engineering,
laboratories, health, and dispensary and medical fields, midwives,
telephonists, postmen, tailors, and storemen. Their annual salaries
varied between £117 and £576. Branch I contained nearly 13,000
Europeans, 199 Asians and Coloreds, and only 106 Africans. Of these,
according to Jasper Savanhu, when he resigned as parliamentary
secretary in the Welensky government over this issue, only nine had
top administrative rank. Salaries in Branch I ranged from £387 to
£2,203.

This low proportion of Africans in the upper reaches of the federal civil service (in Southern Rhodesia, non-Europeans could be only
employees, not civil servants, under the Civil Service Act) was often
given as an argument against speedier constitutional advancement
for Africans in Southern Rhodesia. Those who expected the Federation to break up, after both northern territories had African governments, also anticipated the reversion of the federalized sectors to the
territories. Southern Rhodesia would then have to rely on a civil
service composed mainly of white settlers, and these could not be
expected—according to this pessimistic argument—to work without
friction and disloyalty for African ministers. In fact, many of them
might be expected to leave the country, whereupon public services
might break down and chaos ensue on the Congo model.

In a similar vein, questions were sometimes raised about the ultimate loyalties of the Federal Army of Rhodesia and Nyasaland and
the Royal Rhodesian Air Force. External relations and defense were
federal functions under the constitution of 1953. As a result, military
units in all three territories came under a command based on Southern
Rhodesia and officered by Europeans whose primary loyalties should
be to the Federation—although, like all government officials and
registered voters, they swear an oath of allegiance to the Queen. The
federal government spent considerable amounts for defense in its post-
Emergency budgets. Since external threats to the Federation could not

then be considered very serious, the assumption was that maintenance of internal security, including possibly the forcible maintenance of the Federation, was a major purpose of the federal defense establishment. And when both federal authorities and African nationalists made reference to the use of force, "going it alone," and (quite misplaced) parallels with Algeria, these questions of the loyalty of the military were usually not far at the backs of people's minds. In 1961, the Federal Army consisted of 13,188 officers and men, of whom 5,171 were regular army, the remainder being territorials (the reserve). Of this figure, 3,293 were African "other ranks" (enlisted men), all the territorials being Europeans. The Royal Rhodesian Air Force numbered 850 members. In the 1962–1963 budget estimates, £4,316,-000 of a total expenditure of £70,937,000 was earmarked for the army and £3,835,000 for the Royal Rhodesian Air Force. In March 1963, it was announced that the two battalions of the King's African Rifles stationed in Nyasaland would be transferred from federal to Nyasaland control. Prime Minister Banda said that he would be glad to keep British officers, but officers from Southern Rhodesia or South Africa would have to go. Similar arrangements were expected to be made in Northern Rhodesia.

LOCAL GOVERNMENT

In Southern Rhodesia, under the Land Apportionment Act of 1931, there was "local government" in European areas and "administration" by Europeans of the Native Affairs Department on the Native Reserves or of municipal African affairs departments in African townships. The two Southern Rhodesian cities, Salisbury and Bulawayo, had elected town councils which, in turn, elected a mayor from among their midst. But until 1963, the African townships on the outskirts of these cities were not represented on the city councils. They were administered, and the European administrators were advised, by African advisory councils elected by ratepayers. (These elections, incidentally, were generally marked by apathy.) However, there was some sentiment toward integrating the African townships with regular city government, in step with amendment of the Land Apportionment Act and consequent opportunities for Africans to acquire freehold title to urban land.

On the Native Reserves, elected councils began to operate in 1958. They were in charge of such concrete matters as road maintenance, operation of mills, certain schools, and the like. At the end of 1960, only 61 councils were functioning on the reserves, their total tax collection amounting to £32,000. Because of the late start of these organs of local African government in Southern Rhodesia, they were still far behind their northern models in the contribution they could make in providing experience in political procedures to their members and to the population in general. Native commissioners continued as presiding officers of the councils. Even at that, however, members seemed to be learning very quickly and chief-council conflicts—of which the Native Affairs Department made a great deal— might not present a major problem. Chiefs were both agents of the government that appointed them and tribal heads and, therefore, subject to tensions. The government tried to give them a sense of solidarity as chiefs by, among other measures, convening provincial assemblies of chiefs and, eventually, having the latter elect representative chiefs to a National Council of Chiefs. This contrasted with earlier practice in the two northern territories, where Provincial Councils and the African Representative Council of Northern Rhodesia contained both chiefs and commoners. The contrast is the more remarkable, because tribal systems in the North rarely if ever became as disorganized as in Southern Rhodesia after its "Conquest." Chiefs and paramount chiefs in the North had usually played a more important role than in Southern Rhodesia, partly because the Colonial Office was more consistent in applying the policy of indirect rule. In the North, African local government was organized in levels of Native Authorities, each consisting of both elected and appointed members and initially presided over by the District Commissioner. Some Native Authorities operated with sizable budgets, and the Colonial Office during recent years made it possible for some of their administrative officers to take courses in local government at British universities.

Shortly after he came into office as Minister of Local Government in 1961, Dr. Banda reorganized and revitalized the district councils of Nyasaland by putting them on a wholly elective basis and broadening their responsibilities in such fields as education and agriculture. He also had all judicial functions taken away from the District Commissioners and, with the help of a Nigerian legal expert, organized a locally based system of courts, whose members were given short courses at a school established for this purpose. As a result, the tasks of the DC's were incidentally also made easier, which would facilitate their africanization. The changes in local government generated a great deal of enthusiasm and apparently liberated much hitherto dormant energy. The local people, instead of always turning to their DC and the territorial government, discovered that they had it within their own power to make improvements in their communities. During the first year of these reforms, there were few indications of friction between chiefs and elected councils. Indeed, the MCP's constitution states that its very first "aim and object" is "to work relentlessly to achieve self-government and ultimate independence for the people of Nyasaland and their Chiefs," adding, a little later in the same preamble, its desire "to secure and at all time maintain the unity of all the people and chiefs of Nyasaland."

THE JUDICIARY

In their legal systems and the judiciary, great differences are again found between Southern Rhodesia and the two Colonial Office protectorates. Southern Rhodesia like South Africa, from which it was settled, uses Roman Dutch law. This is a combination of English common law and the legal system brought by the original Dutch settlers to the Cape in the seventeenth century, that is, before Napoleon's codification systematized Roman law on the Continent. Northern Rhodesia and Nyasaland use wholly British legal systems based on English common law and, in the case of the criminal code, on the (British) Indian penal code. Legal training differed in that prospective lawyers for Southern Rhodesia had to study Roman Dutch law, and this could best be done in South Africa, though some British universities also offered courses in the subject. Until the Federal Supreme Court began to function, appeals from Southern Rhodesia lay to the South African Court of Appeals at Bloemfontein, and decisions of South African courts are still being cited as precedents in the Federal Supreme Court today. Judges in the two northern territories were members of the Colonial Legal Service and transferable from one colony to another. Judges in Southern Rhodesia were appointed by the Governor on nomination of the Prime Minister. Some of the High Court judges in Southern Rhodesia previously had political careers. Others have been invited to come from South Africa, for instance, Mr. Justice Abraham Maisel, who had previously gained fame as defense counsel in the treason trial in South Africa (he resigned from the Southern Rhodesian High Court in 1963, "for personal reasons").

The only federal tribunal is the Federal Supreme Court, consisting of three federal justices and the territorial chief justices, who occasionally sit with them on individual cases. There has been no important litigation on issues of federalism before either the Supreme or High Courts. The federal constitution did not encourage such litigation. Moreover, as of 1961, there was only one African lawyer in each of the three territories, with little prospect of an early significant increase in their number. In 1962, a proposal was made for setting up a law school at the University College in Salisbury, but the chances were that its first graduates would come too late to make a contribution to constitutional litigation as a means of smoothing the transition from European rule. In the same year, Herbert Chitepo, the first African advocate (barrister) in the Federation, left Salisbury to accept the position of chief of public prosecutions in Tanganyika. He did so with the approval of the leadership of ZAPU, which wanted him to gain experience which would be valuable after the achievement of African government.

In at least one instance in the life of the Federation, the judiciary in the person of the Federal Chief Justice, Sir Robert Tredgold, played a political role. Sir Robert resigned in protest against the Southern Rhodesian Law and Order Maintenance Act of 1960. A former Minister of Defense and Justice in Southern Rhodesia, he had earlier disagreed—though not in public—with the Southern Rhodesian government over its Preventive Detention Act and with the federal government over his powers as Acting Governor-General (a role played by British colonial chief justices in the absence of their governors) with respect to the reservation of federal legislation deemed discriminatory by the African Affairs Board of the Federal Assembly. Tredgold's subsequent attempt to launch a multiracial party failed, partly because African politicians still resented the *Report* of the Southern Rhodesian Franchise Commission, of which he had been chairman. His protest may have had in fact a greater impact upon public opinion outside than inside Rhodesia, because it dramatized for the outsiders Southern Rhodesia's apparent departure from the British tradition of due process of law.

Contemporary Issues

NATIONAL UNITY

Until 1962, the major problem of the Federation was its continued existence. Of the original backers of the federal scheme, very few were still committed to it in the tenth year of its life. The Africans, who were opposed to federation from the outset, demanded its breakup with increasing vehemence. The British government found the Federation a great liability in its relations with the colored members of the Commonwealth and at the United Nations. By 1963, it had already approved the withdrawal of Nyasaland and Northern Rhodesia from the Federation, and thereby acknowledged failure of this experiment in constitution building.

In Nyasaland itself, there was no serious problem of national unity. The small number of Europeans would either throw in their lot with Malawi or get out. The Asians made public professions of their support for Dr. Banda. Among the Africans themselves, even his very few opponents never questioned the unity of Nyasaland. Tribalism played no important political role.

In Northern Rhodesia, tribalism still had stronger political relevance, and UNIP was competing with the ANC, though the two were able to form a coalition government. The larger European population could not be left out of account as easily as in Nyasaland. The reason for this was the desirability of European electoral support of "national" candidates under the election law. Economic considerations were not given much thought in this respect, because at least one of the copper companies, Rhodesian Selection Trust, had let it be understood that it was quite ready to cooperate with a UNIP government and in fact preferred the change to African government to be made quickly. Kenneth Kaunda, too, had given assurances that the management of the mines would be left in European hands, so long as efforts were made to train Africans for industrial advancement.

But even here no one questioned the political unity of Northern Rhodesia—except for the ruling class of Barotseland, which wanted to retain its status as a separate protectorate of the Crown. But Barotseland would never be able to play the role of a Katanga because of its backwardness. Moreover, even majority opinion among Europeans had no objection to at least a major revamping of federal relations with Southern Rhodesia, especially in the fiscal field. For example, the mayor of Lusaka, capital city of Northern Rhodesia, complained in 1962 that 70 per cent of federal revenues for development purposes was spent in Southern Rhodesia. This figure might be hard to corroborate, and the mayor was a supporter of the Liberal Party, but the fact that a person who was elected to that position would make such an allegation shows the climate of opinion among

Europeans. The election of October 1962 also showed that much more unity existed among Africans in Northern Rhodesia than had been expected.

Only Southern Rhodesia could be described with the words of Lord Durham, applied by him to the Canada of 1840: "Two nations are warring in the bosom of a single state." Indeed, the Southern Rhodesian government felt the necessity, though too belatedly, of sponsoring a "Campaign to Build a Nation." The Africans were becoming more conscious daily of their common nationhood, although tribal divisions existed between Mashona and Matabele and although few of them might actually think of themselves as "Zimbabwians." Meanwhile, the Europeans gave signs of becoming more nationalist as Rhodesians, especially when they felt themselves not only threatened by African nationalism to the north but also let down—or even "sold down the river"—by the British government and the United Nations. At the same time, the more influential UFP politicians, led by Sir Edgar Whitehead, and even Winston Field, the new Prime Minister, seemed sufficiently realistic to recognize that they would have to move even faster toward greater African participation in politics and government. If they failed to do so, even though they might be able to keep down African nationalist aspirations by means of force for some time Southern Rhodesia would lose most (because it had most to lose) from a complete breakup of federation. It might then even have to apply for protection and subsidies from, and eventually union with, the Republic of South Africa—and few Europeans of British descent or origin relished that prospect. Shortly after he became Prime Minister, Winston Field stated: "There is an impression in Britain that if the Federation collapses we would look towards South Africa. I want to say categorically that that is absolutely out of the question." [22] Moreover, Dr. Verwoerd stated in 1962 that Southern Rhodesia would not be acceptable to the Republic so long as it maintained its policy of racial partnership.[23] And the measures that had already been taken on the basis of this policy, insufficient though they seemed to the Africans, were not reversible.

The only way to save what could be saved of the Federation was by remedying those aspects of Southern Rhodesia's politics which from the outset were the cause of northern Africans' opposition to

[22] *East Africa and Rhodesia*, XXXIX, no. 1997 (Jan. 17, 1963), 429; quoted from an interview in the *Sunday Telegraph* (London).

[23] *Rhodesia Herald*, Sept. 4, 1962, p. 1.

the federal scheme. The new constitution went some way in that direction. Its provisions for civil rights, as well as the elimination of racially discriminatory statutes, were regarded as impossible by most observers as recently as 1960. By 1961, however, most Africans considered these measures too little and too late, the more so because of the restrictive legislation and the banning of ZAPU, by which they were accompanied. The big question was whether the tempo of African demands could be sufficiently synchronized with the tempo of European concessions to avert even greater friction than had produced the sporadic violence of the period from 1960 to 1962. After the electoral victory of the Rhodesian Front, this seemed unlikely.

CIVIL RIGHTS AND MINORITIES

Most Southern Rhodesian discrimination against Africans, the vast majority of the population, was based upon explicit legislation. Much of this, according to its authors and enforcers, was intended to protect the African against exploitation by unscrupulous Europeans or Asians. This claim has already been discussed in connection with the Land Apportionment Act, under which members of neither race could acquire land in reserves of the other. Africans were not permitted to reside in European towns and, until 1961, needed to have passes from their white employers to move from one part of town to another, for example, on their day off. This led to such anomalous situations as one in which the author, a foreigner in Southern Rhodesia, had to write out a pass for his domestic servant, a native-born Rhodesian, permitting him to go to a shopping center two blocks from his home, since, without such a pass, the police could have thrown the Rhodesian in jail. By 1963, most legal discrimination of this kind had been eliminated. Earlier, in 1959, an act was passed permitting Africans to purchase European beer and allowing educated Africans, who had to apply for a special registration card, to purchase and consume hard liquor. Both had been prohibited previously.

The earlier Northern Rhodesian boycott against discrimination in retail trade has already been mentioned. In 1960, the Northern Rhodesian government had a bill passed that provided for fines for racial discrimination by operators of movie theaters, cafés, public bars, and similar public establishments requiring a license. If the proprietor could prove monetary losses as a result of integration, he could claim damages from the government. This legislation achieved the intended results. Race relations committees set up in all districts heard complaints and usually settled them through conciliation. The Race Relations Board entertained claims for damages. In 1961, it rejected two such claims and accepted twenty-two, awarding a total of £21,260. Thereafter, fewer claims were presented.

The federal government also began in earnest, about 1958, to eliminate discrimination in post offices and, among other installations, customs and immigration offices. Travelers from South Africa to the Federation can notice, for example, that south of the Limpopo River "Whites" and "Non-Whites" have to go to separate counters, whereas no such distinction is made north of this river. And shortly after Jasper Savanhu's resignation, a large number of Africans were promoted to Grade I of the federal public service.

The controversial new Southern Rhodesian constitution contained two long chapters devoted to problems of civil rights and the protection of minorities. First, there is "The Declaration of Rights," which consists of sixteen sections. Among other matters, it deals with protection of the right to life and to personal liberty, of freedom of expression and of assembly and association, and from discriminatory written laws and discriminatory action. All these rights are qualified in immense legalistic detail, and they can all be suspended during "any period of public emergency." On the basis of their experience with the Law and Order Maintenance Act, most Africans were not satisfied with the Declaration of Rights. However, after the enactment of bills, their constitutionality could be challenged in the courts and finally appealed to the Judicial Committee of the Privy Council in London. And even before the new constitution came into effect, Asians and Africans had won judgments from the Southern Rhodesian High Court and the Federal Supreme Court which held as *ultra vires* regulations excluding them from public swimming pools.

The Constitutional Council provided for by the new constitution was designed in part to protect the real minorities in Southern Rhodesia, that is, the non-Africans. It was to consist of a chairman and eleven elected members, including at least two Europeans, two Africans, one Asian, one person belonging to the Colored community, and "two persons each of whom shall be a lawyer of the High Court of Southern Rhodesia of not less than ten years' standing." (This meant that Southern Rhodesia's first African lawyer would not qualify for another two years, and his next colleague not for another eight years.) The main function of the council was to consider whether bills passed by the Legislative Assembly were consistent with the

Declaration of Rights. In case of an adverse finding, the bill would have to be repassed by a two-thirds vote of the membership of the Legislative Assembly before it could become law. (Under the intended composition of the Legislative Assembly, Europeans were expected to have better than a three-fourths majority, approximately 50:15.) This procedure seemed to reduce the likelihood of attacks on discriminatory legislation by way of constitutional litigation of which, as has been shown, there is little tradition in Southern Rhodesia.

But it seemed doubtful whether these provisions of the new constitution had sufficient appeal to be retained by an African Parliament and government. One of the main reasons for this doubt was the experience of Southern Rhodesian Africans with extraordinary legislation restricting their civil rights. Only one case need be cited. The Law and Order Maintenance Act of 1960, which specified a number of new criminal offenses, made minimum sentences mandatory upon judges for some of these and put the burden of proof upon the defendant. For example, under Section 24 of the act, "any person who in any manner whatsoever, without lawful excuse the proof whereof lies on him, intimidates or attempts to intimidate any other person or persons generally or any class or description of persons shall be guilty of an offence and liable to imprisonment for a period not exceeding ten years." Where the intimidation had political grounds, "the court shall impose a sentence of imprisonment for a period of not less than three years." Boycotting called for a maximum sentence of seven years, and political boycotts for a minimum sentence of two years. The use of opprobrious epithets in relation to employment called for a maximum fine of £100 and one year's imprisonment.

A novel provision, in Section 38 is that "whoever employs or solicits any other person to advise him or any other person by any non-natural means whatsoever, whether any law of the Colony or of the Federation should be resisted, either actively or passively, shall be guilty of an offence and liable to imprisonment for a period not exceeding ten years." This definition of witchcraft as a criminal offense was used, by proponents of the bill, to explain the need for legislation out of keeping with British traditions of ordinary due process. They claimed that the Africans were so primitive that they could be swayed to subvert law and order by various forms of intimidation, including witchcraft, and that ordinary Western legal concepts and procedures could not deal with that danger.

They went further by making authors of a long list of subversive statements guilty of an offense and liable to imprisonment for a maximum of five years. Among statements defined as subversive were ones likely "to engender or promote feelings of hostility between one or more sections of the community on the one hand, and any other section or sections of the community on the other hand, or to engender or promote feelings of hostility to or contempt of any class of the inhabitants of the Colony on account of race or colour." Subsequently in the same Section 39, provision was made "that a person shall not be convicted of an offence . . . if he satisfies the court that the statement alleged to be subversive was made in good faith . . . and fairly, temperately, with decency and respect and without imputing any corrupt or improper motive." Under Section 40, a minimum sentence of five years is provided for throwing rocks or other articles at motor vehicles.

Perhaps this Law and Order Maintenance Act, earlier ones like it, and amendments passed in 1962, designed to close loopholes, would not have aroused so much African resentment if they had been administered in a less one-sided fashion, as were similar powers exercised by the Governor of Northern Rhodesia. In the eighteen months starting in January 1961, under this act 1,212 Africans were charged, and 974 convicted. During the same period, two Europeans were charged, and one convicted under it. Perhaps Europeans are unlikely to use witchcraft for political purposes, but they do use intimidation, though it may be more subtle than that employed by Africans. However, Europeans have often made statements designed to promote feelings of hostility for Africans without being prosecuted. One European extremist organization, the Rhodesian Republic Army, was outlawed under the Unlawful Organizations Act, but the RRA was generally considered comic-opera stuff.

The African politicians, practically all of whom have at one time or another been charged under the various security acts, have little respect for the constitutional machinery used in other English-speaking countries to protect civil rights, although they still respected the judiciary (as distinguished from the lower-level magistrates) and may have realized that most of the judges were administering the law impartially and with high professional standards but were handicapped by the substance of the law. This African attitude, created by European politicians, may return to haunt the Europeans once they are relegated to the minority status which, in terms of numbers, they deserve. Perhaps their best hope then will lie in a better legal integration of Southern Rhodesia with the former Colonial Office protectorates to the north of it, combined with the emergence of more African lawyers able to educate their people in the respect for due process that has distinguished all the English-speaking peoples who are heirs to the traditions of English common law. In Nyasaland, the possibility was raised, in 1962, of bringing in lawyers and judges from independent African states (Nigeria has about 900, Ghana about 300) while local talent was being trained.

If the fears of the European minority of Southern Rhodesia should actually be removed by some such means, after "refederation" may have been made possible by African advancement there, then a task that was badly neglected by the federal government will have been attacked by its successors—the task of the legal integration of the three territories. The different legal systems of South and North made this difficult, to be sure, but other federal systems have overcome similar difficulties, as in Canada, where the Province of Quebec uses a version of the French Civil Code. The Federation did not even allow the free movement of citizens between its member territories; for example, African politicians from the northern territories were branded "prohibited immigrants" by the Southern Rhodesian government. The same label was also applied to an African Federal M.P. from Northern Rhodesia but was ignored in order to allow him to attend meetings of the Federal Parliament. Along with the failure to integrate Nyasaland into the surface transport network of the Rhodesias, the failure of legal integration may have been a reflection of lack of determination, even on the part of protagonists of federation, to create lasting ties with respect to anything but those matters of immediate interest to the white settlers in the two Rhodesias.

ECONOMIC ISSUES

Economic problems, too, have been discussed as constitutional issues. In Southern Rhodesia, both the Land Apportionment Act and the Native Land Husbandry Act of 1951 were regarded by Africans, but not by them alone, as basic to many of their economic grievances. The latter law was intended as a land conservation and development measure, and the territorial government spent millions of pounds in its implementation. Under it, only Africans trained and certified as "master farmers" were allowed to acquire title to their own, as distinguished from tribal, land. They were to be given assistance and encouragement in production and marketing (but normally not through cooperative societies, as in the North). On the other hand, those Africans who would be driven off the land over the years as a result of this legislation and of natural population increase were to have housing and other facilities provided for them in the urban areas. Many Africans, because of their deep attachment to the land, which is not only the economic but also in a sense the religious foundation of their existence, feared that the real intent of the white man's government was to take their land away from them. The independence movements cleverly played on these fears. The new constitution contained an entire chapter devoted to land, but it seemed unlikely that African fears for their land could be assuaged before there was a government in which Africans had confidence.

In Northern Rhodesia, agricultural development schemes on a smaller scale had been started, in some cases as pilot projects and with financial help from the great mining companies. Since the territory had relatively few European farmers and no equivalent of the Land Apportionment Act, rural Africans had fewer fears, but these were effectively mobilized against federation, which was pictured as a vehicle for the advent of Southern Rhodesian land policies to Northern Rhodesia. As elsewhere in Africa, the inoculation of cattle against sleeping sickness was misrepresented as a campaign to kill off tribal cattle. The independence movements similarly at times resisted inoculations of human beings against various diseases like polio. However, during a drive to provide oral antipolio vaccine in 1962, shortly before the election, UNIP cooperated.

In Nyasaland, as mentioned above, a variety of agricultural development schemes was initiated by Dr. Banda's first ministry. Even in cases where these virtually copied attempts made earlier by Colonial Service administrators, the people now responded enthusiastically, where they had resisted innovation before. And MCP organizers openly admitted that they were advocating measures which they had opposed before, because now it was their government, led by the "Great Kamuzu" (Dr. Banda's middle name). The year 1961 in fact yielded record crops from Nyasaland's African farmers, not because of good weather but because many of them now harvested most of their crops whereas in the past they had often harvested only enough to earn the cash they absolutely needed.

During his first period in office, Dr. Banda faced the dilemma of wanting improvements in medical services and electric power capacity but of being unwilling to accept these from the federal government which, under the constitution of 1953, controlled the relevant functions. For example, in 1962 the federal government canceled a hydroelectric scheme that had previously been under consideration, in retaliation for the Nyasaland government's lack of cooperation in this and other spheres. But there were many indications that Malawi would be able to raise the needed funds from the United Kingdom, other foreign governments, and international lending agencies.

Mention has already been made of opposition to the building of Kariba Dam as an excessive and unnecessary concentration of the Federation's borrowing capacity, whose benefits would be less widespread than those of a series of smaller projects. Beyond this, there was persistent dissatisfaction especially from Northern Rhodesia and Nyasaland, over the division of revenues among the three members, allegedly in favor of Southern Rhodesia. Northern Rhodesians would find out how justified these complaints had been after they achieved independence and the breakup of the Federation. Once it came into the exclusive enjoyment of its copper revenues, Northern Rhodesia would be the richest country in Black Africa, in terms of annual income per capita.

Finally, Africans everywhere felt that they were being exploited by Europeans, whose ten times higher standard of living was being more or less ostentatiously paraded in front of them. The original reasons for this difference in living standards were more complicated than their manifestations in the period of the Federation. For example, in order to attract skilled labor to the Copperbelt, disproportionately high wages had to be offered to recruits from Britain and South Africa. Similarly, the Colonial Service paid higher salaries to attract as much as possible the best talent of the better British universities. Even if Africans could attain the high standards of these civil servants, and few of them could, there would be no justification for paying them equally high salaries for serving in their own countries instead of 5,000 miles away from their home. Moreover, as more functions will be taken away from the administration to be given to organs of local African government, the need for broad-gauged men of the very highest integrity will be correspondingly reduced.

However, even if these original causes of the differences in standards of living are taken into account, it still appears to Africans that there is much in legislation and practice designed to keep the level of income even of highly skilled or educated Africans below that of their European counterparts. Examples noted earlier were the Industrial Conciliation Act of Southern Rhodesia, the lack of credit facilities for African businessmen, the admission standards of the University College in Salisbury, and inadequate educational opportunities, and many other instances could be added. Most Africans believe that only African governments could eliminate these economic discriminations, and it seems to them that, even if African governments fail to remove them completely, they will create a general atmosphere in which it will be easier for the economically underprivileged to accept their position and to harbor hopes for its improvement.

ADMINISTRATION

ZAPU and its successors can be expected to be unwilling to cooperate with civil servants who had anything to do with the Native Affairs Department. UNIP issued complaints against "a few misguided district commissioners" who interfered with its election campaign in 1962 by arresting local UNIP leaders for alleged violations of law. But otherwise Kaunda and his lieutenants proclaimed their willingness to cooperate with the Colonial Office after winning at the polls. Such cooperation was already taking place in Nyasaland. There, as in the other two territories, the real problem was the training of large numbers of Africans who could take over from the European administrators. In Nyasaland, the problem was taken in hand by expansion of an Institute of Public Administration. Among other courses, it offered one for the training of African members of courts. Meanwhile, African civil servants of some experience, as well as African students just out of school, were sent abroad for training in various aspects of public administration.

EDUCATION

Grants from foreign governments, such as the United States, for African scholarships abroad did not always suffice, because the Rhodesian governments occasionally refused to permit African recipients to leave. The governments were reluctant to expose their Africans to the American atmosphere for too long a time, because they felt that they usually returned home more "radical" than they had left. Educational problems, too, were converted into constitutional issues. This was most noticeable with regard to the division of functions in the field, European education being a federal, and African education a territorial, responsibility. But it seemed that even after integration

of the two school systems, it would be some time before the hunger
of the Africans for education could be satisfied. On the other hand,
the resentment generated by this hunger was likely to diminish as
African governments began to address themselves to solution of the
problem. Occasionally, peripheral issues were raised in this area, one
being that Europeans in mission schools in Nyasaland and Southern
Rhodesia had spread antinationalist propaganda or were uncoopera-
tive with the Malawi government.

There was also northern hostility to the University College at Salisbury, as well as the desire of Nyasaland and Northern Rhodesia to
build their own universities—perhaps as one of the most useful symbols of full independence. The institution in Salisbury continued to
award University of London degrees, and its curriculum was modeled
on that of the British universities. To some Americans, this seemed
about as useful as a Harvard education would have been to a young
Texan fifty or a hundred years ago. Such an education would undoubtedly have been useful to a few Texans of those periods, but most of
them and Texas would have benefited (and did) more from attending
the Agricultural and Mechanical College at College Station. At least
as important, the administration of Texas A. & M. would not have
dreamed of granting Harvard degrees or of trying to preserve Harvard standards of civilization and responsibility in the Great and
Sovereign State. It developed its own standards in response to its own
needs. The independent states in Central Africa may be expected to
do the same. Indeed, they are unlikely to feel truly independent until
they have done this and have joined the United Nations. These two
steps seem of almost equal importance to them.

External Relations

The federal government maintained good relations with the Republic of South Africa, with Moise Tshombe's regime in Katanga, and
on the surface at least with the Federation of Nigeria. Its officials,
especially the military, exchanged cordial visits with the Portuguese
administrations in Mozambique and Angola. But Dr. Banda also called
upon the Portuguese government in Lisbon, presumably because he
depended upon the port of Beira for his imports and might be able
to ensure continued access to it by restraining anti-Portuguese Africans in Nyasaland, of whom there are very many. There was talk of
a possible military alliance between Southern Rhodesia, once it stood
alone, and South Africa and the Portuguese. The federal government

under the constitution controlled its external relations except insofar as the United Kingdom continued to represent it because of its lack of full Dominion status and sovereignty.

When South Africa left the Commonwealth, both it and the federal government had to enact new legislation to cope with the removal of common citizenship. Speculation about the possibility of a union between Southern Rhodesia and South Africa continued but seemed as unfounded as ever since 1923, when the Southern Rhodesian electorate rejected it by referendum. For one thing, the Republic would probably want neither so large an addition of English-speaking people to its electorate nor another 3,500,000 Africans in its population. For another, the dominant British element in Southern Rhodesia were too British and too anti-Afrikaner—many of them had deliberately left South Africa—to favor this means of solving their problems.

Sir Roy Welensky's good relations with Tshombe, with whose province Northern Rhodesia has a long common boundary, were only strengthened by the attacks on the Federation from the General Assembly of the United Nations. This in turn strengthened the opposition of the independence movements, with the exception of the Northern Rhodesian ANC, to Welensky. UNIP in particular regarded Tshombe as an enemy of Pan-Africanism, to which it was committed. Moreover, Kaunda accused the ANC of receiving subsidies, and some of its members of receiving military training, from and in Katanga. When Welensky urged Africans who were unwilling to support the UFP in the Northern Rhodesian election to support the ANC rather than UNIP, the latter's suspicions of Tshombe were merely enhanced. But this did not prevent Kaunda either from calling upon Tshombe in Elisabethville to discuss his opposition to the policies of the Pan-African Freedom Movement for East, Central, and Southern Africa (PAFMECSA) or from forming a coalition with the ANC. Kaunda was the chairman of PAFMECSA, which had been founded in 1958 by East and Central Africans independence leaders, before any of their countries had achieved self-government. In this capacity, Kaunda chaired a meeting held in Léopoldville before the collapse of Tshombe's secession, at which PAFMECSA proclaimed its support for reunification of the Congo.

UNIP, the MCP, and ZAPU have received considerable financial help from Accra, Cairo, Tunis, Monrovia, and later Dar es Salaam and maintain representatives in some of these capitals. They also received other types of assistance from these sources; for example, the Tanganyika radio broadcast programs on behalf of Dr. Banda's election campaign in 1961 and on behalf of UNIP in 1962. President Nkrumah sent a message to the annual congress of UNIP in 1962, in which he expressed his solidarity with UNIP in its fight against the "slave Federation." The federal government resented this slap from another member of the Commonwealth, but this and similar criticism did not keep Welensky from meeting with Nkrumah and other Commonwealth prime ministers or their deputies at their conferences in London.

The heaviest volume of federal external relations was with the United Kingdom, and it was represented in London by a High Commissioner. In Washington, the Federation was represented by a Minister for Rhodesia and Nyasaland Affairs in the British Embassy, but his office was located in a separate building. The independence movements also maintained representatives in London and often dispatched leading figures to the United States, mainly to appear before or lobby at the United Nations. The federal government has often been critical of United States policies toward Africa in general and itself in particular, sometimes because it failed to make distinctions between government policies and the activities of private organizations, such as the American Committee for Africa. Welensky, in such contexts, usually stressed the menace of communism in Central Africa. Even when the United States voted with the United Kingdom against putting the Southern Rhodesian item on the agenda of the resumed session of the General Assembly and subsequently abstained on the resolution itself and again on the resolution of October 1962, urging that the ban of ZAPU be lifted, the federal government regarded this as merely lukewarm support.

On the other hand, leaders of the independence movements resented the same United States votes as hostile to themselves. Some of them concluded that the United States could not be relied upon to stand up against the colonial powers, when this involved opposing its NATO allies. The only truly reliable supporters of their cause appeared to be the Afro-Asian states and, for their own reasons, the members of the Soviet bloc. By 1962, this had not led the nationalists to become Soviet sympathizers in world politics or Communists in their domestic programs. Although a few of them had made trips behind the Iron Curtain, Soviet influence in British Central Africa was very low indeed. The independence movements were rather cultivating contacts with such countries as West Germany, Israel, and India, from whose economic resources or development experience they could hope to benefit.

The Federation would have been affected by Great Britain's links with the European Common Market, had the latter been allowed to join. The Common Market countries in turn were more hesitant about accommodating the special needs of the Federation than those of Britain's former East African dependencies, because of the political opprobrium that would have attached to identification with an unreformed Federation whose dissolution was demanded by African majorities. In fact, in August 1962, Kenneth Kaunda explicitly stated that in case Sir Roy Welensky should reach agreement with the Common Market, UNIP would not consider itself bound by this agreement after independence. This statement raised the possibility that both the British government and the business community in the Rhodesias might have applied new pressures to the federal and Southern Rhodesian governments to make political concessions to the nationalists out of sheer economic self-interest.

The loudest outside pressure, however, would continue to come from the United Nations which—partly for lack of anything more important left on its anticolonialist agenda—was increasingly concerning itself with Southern Africa. Less than two months after the General Assembly passed its first Southern Rhodesian resolution of June 1962, its Committee on Colonialism recommended strong action against the Republic of South Africa on the issue of South-West Africa and against Portugal on the issue of Angola. African independence movements from all three areas shifted their activities to the United Nations as a direct function of restrictions placed upon their activities at home. When these restrictions were increased in Southern Rhodesia and ZAPU was banned, ZAPU's reliance upon and expectations of the United Nations were increasing in direct ratio. Its representatives testified, no longer before the Special Committee on Colonialism but the Fourth Committee of the General Assembly, and the Assembly passed its second resolution on Southern Rhodesia, condemning the banning of ZAPU. Conversely, as Southern Rhodesia found itself in South Africa's and Portugal's company on the receiving end of United Nations attacks, Sir Edgar Whitehead's government was sliding into bedfellowship with regimes that had been pursuing very different policies during the decade of Southern Rhodesia's membership in the Federation.

That Whitehead, Welensky, the UFP, and the concept of building a multiracial federation had lost whatever support they might have enjoyed until then was shown by the Southern Rhodesian election of December 14, 1962. Only 9,814 Africans had registered as voters, although more than 60,000 probably could have qualified. But of this figure only 2,923 actually voted. Of the 90,389 Europeans who were registered voters, 69.5 per cent went to the polls. On the upper roll, the Rhodesian Front received 38,382 votes against the UFP's 30,943 (almost 44 per cent). The new Legislative Assembly contained 35 M.P.'s of the Rhodesian Front, 29 of the UFP, and one Independent, Dr. Ahrn Palley, a European associate of Garfield Todd, who was elected in a lower-roll constituency by a majority of 4 in a total poll of 108. The other 14 lower-roll M.P.'s were African candidates of the UFP, which also returned one colored upper-roll candidate. Even though ZAPU regarded the 15 nonwhite M.P.'s of the new Legislative Assembly as stooges, they (together with Dr. Palley) could be expected to give some representation to the overwhelming racial majority of the country for the first time in its history.

The Rhodesian Front, like its predecessor, the Dominion Party, counted among its supporters the original opponents of Lord Malvern and his concept of federation. As soon as he became Southern Rhodesia's new Prime Minister, Winston Field indicated that his government would do nothing to slow down the process of federal disintegration, even though it planned no initiatives to speed up the process. At the same time, Field also visited Dr. Banda in Nyasaland after the British government had recognized its right to withdraw from the Federation. Soon after this, in February 1963, Kenneth Kaunda and Harry Nkumbula, as ministers in the Northern Rhodesian coalition Government, introduced resolutions in their Legislative Council calling upon Great Britain to grant Northern Rhodesia the same right of secession coupled with universal suffrage. Kaunda stated that he would have no objection to the establishment of joint Southern-Northern Rhodesian boards to operate such common enterprises as Kariba and the railways. And R. A. Butler during his visit to the Federation in late January 1963 apparently sought to promote common services among the three countries in these and similar fields. Most of the leaders seemed to recognize that the dismantling of the Federation would be a complicated and time-consuming process. Those in the two northern territories were, at least at first, more willing to deal with the Rhodesian Front government in Southern Rhodesia than either with its UFP predecessor or with Welensky's federal government, and the British government acted on recognition of this fact, when R. A. Butler granted Northern Rhodesia the right to secede from the Federation, because it would not be possible to carry on fruitful negotiations on future relations between the territories without putting an end to federation.

The African leaders, both in Southern Rhodesia and the North, were not only giving assistance to one another but also looking beyond the boundaries of the Federation in planning for the future. The new Southern Rhodesian government anticipated one kind of assistance to the outlawed ZAPU from Northern Rhodesia, when it introduced a bill prohibiting the introduction of dangerous weapons into their territory from the outside and authorizing search without warrant of persons entering the colony from the North. Whether or not this measure, and an amendment to the Law and Order Maintenance Act calling for the death penalty or life imprisonment for arson, would have the desired results, there was nothing the European minority of Southern Rhodesia could do to keep independent or near-independent African governments from giving political and moral assistance to ZAPU and its successors. The sources of this assistance, especially as organized in PAFMECSA, gave a hint of the links that would be constructed in the future.

In the precolonial past, territorial boundaries had been unknown in this region of Africa, partly because there was no need for them. Possibly, in the postcolonial future, there will occur a downgrading of the importance of the geographical frontier as the principal manifestation of sovereignty. Overlapping public authorities may be created, to serve a variety of functions, economic, cultural, military, and other. During the period of federation, when African political consciousness expanded more than ever before, African politicians were forced to operate within institutions alien to them and their background. This made their task even more difficult than that of leaders of earlier independence movements in other British territories in West and East Africa, because the mixed motives of the founders and supporters of the Federation brought into being unusually artificial and complicated constitutional machinery. This fact and the Africans' preoccupation with demolishing the Federation inhibited whatever constitutional creativity they might have displayed in different circumstances.

The end of the Federation and the achievement of self-government would remove these inhibitions. A period of experimentation could then begin for the construction of internal institutions and for the

forging of new associations among the countries of Central, East, and
Southern Africa.

BIBLIOGRAPHY

A great many books have been written about the Federation. The high
point in the volume of publications apparently coincided with the inquiry of
the Monckton Commission in 1960, and some of this literature was designed
to influence the commission's recommendations. Even though this material
therefore bears the marks of political pamphleteering, some of it may turn
out to be of more enduring interest. The *Report* of the Monckton Commission itself, especially the five volumes of evidence, bears monumental
witness to the great care with which the British government sought to ascertain the opinions of all parties to the Federation controversy. The Hansards of the three territories, the Federal Assembly, and the British Parliament are the most useful official source for the period of the Federation.
Where these are not available, *East Africa and Rhodesia,* a weekly edited
by F. L. Joelson in London, can be consulted, because it carries extracts of
the relevant debates.

The publications of the Rhodes-Livingstone Institute at Lusaka provide
some of the best historical, sociological, and anthropological background for
contemporary politics in British Central Africa. The National Archives of
Rhodesia and Nyasaland, located in Salisbury in a supermodern building
that cost the federal government £250,000, are facilitating further historical
research, including a federally commissioned multivolume history written by
their chief editor, L. H. Gann.

OFFICIAL PUBLICATIONS

Federation of Rhodesia and Nyasaland, Central African Statistical Office.
   Monthly Digest of Statistics. Salisbury.
——, Federal Assembly. *Parliamentary Debates.* Salisbury: Parliamentary
   Printers.
——, Minister of Law. *The Constitution of the Federation of Rhodesia and
   Nyasaland.* Salisbury: Government Printer, 1959. 97 pp.
Great Britain
   Colonial Office. *Northern Rhodesia—Proposals for Constitutional Change.*
      Cmnd. 1423. London: H.M.S.O., June 1961. 12 pp.
      ——. *Report of the Nysaland Commission of Inquiry* (Devlin Commis-
      sion). Cmnd. 814. London: H.M.S.O., July 1959. 146 pp.
   Hailey, Lord. *Note on the Bearing of Native Policy on the Proposed
      Amalgamation of the Rhodesias and Nyasaland.* (Confidential.) Lon-
      don: H.M.S.O., 1941. 16 pp.
   Report of the Advisory Commission on the Review of the Constitution of

Rhodesia and Nyasaland (Moncktown Commission). Cmnd. 1148. London: H.M.S.O., Oct. 1960. 175 pp.

——, *Appendix VI, Survey of Developments since 1953,* Report by a Committee of Officials. Cmnd. 1149. 513 pp.

——, *Appendix VII, Possible Constitutional Changes,* Report by a Committee of Officials. Cmnd. 1150. 87 pp.

——, *Appendix VIII, Evidence, Volume I—Northern Rhodesia.* Cmnd. 1151. 310 pp.

——, ——, *Evidence, Volume II—Northern Rhodesia.* Cmnd. 1151–1. 264 pp.

——, ——, *Evidence, Volume III—Nyasaland.* Cmnd. 1151–2. 152 pp.

——, ——, *Evidence, Volume IV—Southern Rhodesia.* Cmnd. 1151–3. 444 pp.

——, ——, *Evidence, Volume V—Southern Rhodesia and United Kingdom.* Cmnd. 1151–4. 236 pp.

Report of the Conference on Closer Association in Central Africa. Cmd. 8233. London: H.M.S.O., March 1951. 43 pp.

——, *Comparative Survey of Native Policy in Southern Rhodesia, Northern Rhodesia and Nyasaland.* Cmnd. 8235. 91 pp.

Secretary of State for Commonwealth Relations and Secretary of State for the Colonies. *Southern Rhodesia, Northern Rhodesia and Nyasaland—Draft Federal Scheme Prepared by a Conference Held in London in April and May, 1952.* Cmnd. 8573. London: H.M.S.O., June 1952. v, 38 pp.

Statutory Instruments 1953 No. 1199, Rhodesia and Nyasaland Federation, The Federation of Rhodesia and Nyasaland (Constitution) Order in Council, 1953. London, Aug. 1, 1953. 55 pp.

Northern Rhodesia. *Official Verbatim Report of the Legislative Council.* Lusaka: Government Printer.

Nyasaland Protectorate. *Legislative Council Proceedings.* Zomba: Government Printer.

Southern Rhodesia, Legislative Assembly. *Debates.* Salisbury: Parliamentary Printers.

——. *Report of the Survey of the British South Africa Police* (Packard Report). C.S.R. 29 of 1962. Salisbury: Government Printer, 1962.

NEWSPAPERS AND PERIODICALS

Central African Daily News. Salisbury.
Central African Examiner. Salisbury, monthly.
Rhodes-Livingstone Journal: Human Problems in British Central Africa. Lusaka, half-yearly.
Rhodesia and East Africa. Ed. by F. S. Joelson. London, weekly.
Rhodesia Herald. Salisbury, daily.

BOOKS

Barber, William J. *The Economy of British Central Africa: A Case Study of Economic Development in a Dualistic Society.* London: Oxford University Press, 1961. xii, 271 pp. An interesting application of a new theory of economic development.

Barnes, J. A. *Politics in a Changing Society: A Political History of the Fort Jameson Ngoni.* London: Oxford University Press for the Rhodes-Livingstone Institute, 954. x, 220 pp. An anthropological case study.

Berelsford, W. V. *The Tribes of Northern Rhodesia.* Lusaka: Government Printer, 1956. A good survey of the tribal composition of the population.

Clegg, Edward. *Race and Politics: Partnership in the Federation of Rhodesia and Nyasaland.* London: Oxford University Press, 1960. x, 280 pp. An excellent analysis focused on Northern Rhodesia.

Clements, Frank. *Kariba: The Struggle with the River God.* London: Methuen, 1959. 223 pp. A popular account of the dam project by a Southern Rhodesian journalist.

Clutton-Brock, Guy. *Dawn in Nyasaland.* London: Hudder and Stoughton, 1959. 192 pp. Written by the expelled head of a mission cooperative farm in Southern Rhodesia, this book suffers from misplaced analogies between Nyasaland and Denmark.

Colson, Elizabeth. *Marriage and the Family among the Plateau Tonga of Northern Rhodesia.* Manchester: Manchester University Press with the Rhodes-Livingstone Institute, 1958. xvi, 379 pp. This and the following work are thorough studies by an American anthropologist, the second dealing with a tribe relocated to make way for Lake Kariba.

———. *The Social Organization of the Gwembe Tonga.* Manchester: Manchester University Press with the Rhodes-Livingstone Institute, 1960. xxii, 234 pp.

——— and Max Gluckman, eds. *Seven Tribes of British Central Africa.* Manchester: Manchester University Press with the Rhodes-Livingstone Institute, 1959. xx, 409 pp. Anthropological studies of the Lozi, Tonga, Bemba, Ngoni, Yao, and Shona tribes.

Creighton, T. R. M. *The Anatomy of Partnership: Southern Rhodesia and the Central African Federation.* London: Faber and Faber, 1960. 258 pp. Timed for the Monckton Commission.

Cunnison, Ian. *The Luapula Peoples of Northern Rhodesia: Custom and History in Tribal Politics.* Manchester: Manchester University Press with the Rhodes-Livingstone Institute, 1959. xiii, 258 pp.

Davidson, J. W. *The Northern Rhodesian Legislative Council.* London: Faber and Faber, 1947. 150 pp. A very useful account of the evolution of parliamentary practice.

Epstein, A. L. *Politics in an Urban African Community.* Manchester: Manchester University Press with the Rhodes-Livingstone Institute, 1958. xiv, 254 pp. An interesting study of Africans in Luanshya, a Copperbelt town.

Fraenkel, Peter. *Wayaleshi*. London: Weidenfeld and Nicolson, 1959. 224 pp. A popular account of the author's experience on the Northern Rhodesian African "wireless" (of which the title is a vernacular rendering).

Franck, Thomas M. *Race and Nationalism: The Struggle for Power in Rhodesia-Nyasaland*. New York: Fordham University Press, 1960. 369 pp. A lawyer's study, which is best in its chapters on restrictions of civil rights.

Gann, L. H. *The Birth of a Plural Society: The Development of Northern Rhodesia under the British South African Company, 1894–1914*. Manchester: Manchester University Press with the Rhodes-Livingstone Institute, 1958. xxi, 230 pp. A thorough historical account by the chief editor of the National Archives, who is also the author of forthcoming histories of the other territories and the Federation and coauthor, with Dr. Gelfand, of the forthcoming official biography of Lord Malvern.

—— and Peter Duignan. *White Settlers in Tropical Africa*. Baltimore, Penguin Books, 1962. 170 pp. After a very good historical introduction, the authors attempt to present "the White Man's Case." The book is based on a false analogy between the breakup of the Austro-Hungarian Empire and the departure of colonial powers from Africa.

Gelfand, Michael. *Northern Rhodesia in the Days of the Charter: A Medical and Social Study, 1878–1924*. Oxford: Basil Blackwell, 1961. xviii, 291. An interesting study by a Rhodesian physician who became a professor at the Medical School of the University College in Salisbury.

Gibbs, Peter. *Avalanche in Central Africa*. London: Arthur Baker, Ltd., 1961. 169 pp. A popular account of race relations in everyday life.

Gluckman, Max. *The Judicial Process among the Barotse of Northern Rhodesia*. Manchester: Manchester University Press with the Rhodes-Livingstone Institute, 1955. xxiii, 386 pp. A classical study of political procedure among the relatively ancient and stable Barotse kingdom.

Gray, Richard. *The Two Nations: Aspects of the Development of Race Relations in the Rhodesias and Nyasaland*. London: Oxford University Press with the Institute of Race Relations, 1960. xviii, 373 pp. This sequel to Philip Mason's *Birth of a Dilemma* deals with the period from the end of World War I to 1953.

Hanna, A. J. *The Beginnings of Nyasaland and North-eastern Rhodesia, 1859–95*. Oxford: Clarendon Press, 1956. viii, 281 pp. A historical account based on archival research.

——. *The Story of the Rhodesias and Nyasaland*. London: Faber and Faber, 1960. 288 pp. A short history.

Hazlewood, Arthur, and P. D. Henderson. *Nyasaland: The Economics of Federation*. Oxford: Basil Blackwell, 1960. 91 pp. Published in time for the Monckton Commission, this is an attack on the thesis that Nyasaland benefited economically from federation.

Holleman, J. F. *African Interlude*. Cape Town: Nasionale Boekhandel, 1958. 269 pp. The professional anthropologist's account in the entry below was followed in this work by the human being's perceptions of life among one of the two major tribes of Southern Rhodesia.

———. *Shona Customary Law—With Reference to Kinship, Marriage, the Family and the Estate*. London: Oxford University Press, 1952. xix, 401 pp.

Kaunda, Kenneth, *Zambia Shall Be Free*. London: Heinemann, 1962. 102 pp. The program of UNIP's leader, published before the election.

———, and Colin Morris. *Black Government?* Lusaka: United Society for Christian Literature, 1960. A discussion between the leader of UNIP and a sympathetic clergyman of the justice of nationalist demands.

King, Paul S., comp. *Missions in Southern Rhodesia*. Inyati: Inyati Centenary Trust, Southern Rhodesia, 1959. 80 pp. Shows the scope and variety of missionary activity.

Leys, Colin. *European Politics in Southern Rhodesia*. Oxford: Clarendon Press, 1959. xi, 323. An exemplary study of the subject, perhaps more thorough than it deserved, which concludes that Southern Rhodesia had a one-party system despite the existence of more than one party.

——— and Cranford Pratt, eds. *A New Deal in Central Africa*. London: Heinemann, 1960. xiv, 219 pp. A collection of contemporary essays designed to influence the Mockton Commission.

Loveday, Arthur F., O.B.E. *Three Stages of History in Rhodesia*. Cape Town: A. A. Balkemay, n.d. 109 pp. Interesting essays on such topics as Zimbabwe.

Mair, Lucy. *The Nyasaland Elections of 1961*. London: University of London, Athlone Press, 1962. 87 pp. A succinct account of Dr. Banda's victory.

Mason, Philip. *The Birth of a Dilemma: The Conquest and Settlement of Rhodesia*. London: Oxford University Press with the Institute of Race Relations, 1958. xi, 366 pp. A beautifully written sociological history by the director of the Institute of Race Relations and author of *The Guardians*, a history of the Indian Civil Service.

———. *Year of Decision: Rhodesia and Nyasaland 1960*. London: Oxford University Press with the Institute of Race Relations, 1960. x, 282 pp. Sequel to the previous item and Gray's *The Two Nations*, written to influence the Monckton Commission.

Mitchell, J. Clyde. *An Outline of the Sociological Background to African Labour*. Salisbury: Ensign Publishers, 1961. 95 pp. A concise presentation of tribal and urban life among African workers by the professor of African Studies at the University College in Salisbury.

———. *The Yao Village: A Study in the Social Structure of a Nyasaland Tribe.*

Manchester: Manchester University Press with the Rhodes-Livingstone Institute, 1956. xviii, 235 pp.

Morris, Colin. *The Hour after Midnight: A Missionary's Experiences of the Racial and Political Struggle in Northern Rhodesia*. London: Longmans, 1961. viii, 168 pp. By a controversial European minister sympathetic to UNIP.

Parker, Franklin. *African Development and Education in Southern Rhodesia*. Columbus: Ohio State University Press, 1960. xiii, 164. A very useful study by an American educationist of Southern Rhodesia's African school system and its problems.

Paver, B. G. *His Own Oppressor*. London: Peter Davies, 1958. 235 pp. By the white founder and managing editor of Southern Rhodesia's African newspapers, useful only because it reveals the intellectual poverty of paternalistic Europeans who consider themselves friends of the Africans.

Powdermaker, Hortense. *Coppertown: Changing Africa—The Human Situation on the Rhodesian Copperbelt*. New York: Harper & Row, 1962. xiii, 391 pp. A superb study, excellently written; the best anthropological work on the process of modernization in Central Africa.

Rayner, William. *The Tribe and Its Successors: An Account of African Traditional Life and of European Settlement in Southern Rhodesia*. London: Faber and Faber, 1962. 239 pp.

Rogers, Cyril A., and C. Frantz. *Racial Themes in Southern Rhodesia: The Attitudes and Behavior of the White Population*. New Haven: Yale University Press, 1962. xviii, 427 pp. A study, like Leys's perhaps more thorough than the subject deserved, of opinions rather than behavior of the white residents. By the time of publication, much of their behavior had become the reverse of their recorded opinions, e.g., acceptance of court decisions to discontinue segregation in municipal swimming pools.

Sanger, Clyde. *Central African Emergency*. London: Heinemann, 1960. 343 pp. A well-written account of the events of 1959 by a journalist who had been editor of the *Central African Examiner*.

Shepperson, George, and Thomas Price. *Independent African: John Chilembwe and the Origins, Setting and Significance of the Nyasaland Native Rising of 1915*. Edinburgh: The University Press, 1958. x, 564 pp. The story of the African clergyman who, after spending some time in the United States, founded his own church in Nyasaland.

Sithole, Ndabaningi. *African Nationalism*. London: Oxford University Press, 1959. 174 pp. An appealing autobiographical account by an African clergyman who later became national chairman of ZAPU.

Taylor, Don. *The Rhodesian: The Life of Sir Roy Welensky*. London: Museum Press, 1955. xi, 191 pp. A popular biography.

Tow, Leonard. *The Manufacturing Economy of Southern Rhodesia: Problems and Prospects*. Washington, D.C.: National Academy of Sciences—

National Research Council, 1960. xi, 141 pp. A study of secondary industry in the most advanced of the three territories.

Weinberg, S. *An Outline of the Constitutional Law of the Federation of Rhodesia and Nyasaland*. Salisbury: Federal Government, 1959. vi, 150 pp. An outline intended for civil servants by a lawyer in the Federal Attorney General's Department.

Wood, Anthony St. John. *Northern Rhodesia: The Human Background*. London: Pall Mall Press, 1961. ix, 164 pp. The author served in India, Nigeria, and Northern Rhodesia as an officer of the Colonial Service.

VI

SOUTH AFRICA

By THOMAS KARIS
The City College of New York

Historical Background

The trend toward the polarization of white and black politics in
South Africa since the end of World War II invites oversimplification
and analogies to Greek tragedy. Yet South Africa has not ceased to
be complex. Within its modern economy the several racial groups
continue to become more interdependent. Behind the reality of white
racial oligarchy and police-state control of nonwhites and their white
allies is also the reality of social and economic change that is beyond
the control of a virtually impregnable political leadership. The wide
variety of historical influences actively at work and the continued
plurality of groups make the possession of political power in South
Africa more vulnerable than appears on the surface. Although a review of the main developments since 1870 appears to confirm the
most pessimistic predictions of eventual racial violence, there is as
yet no obvious timetable for the future. The period of predictable
stability, however, is fast shortening.

For an understanding of the contemporary scene, four interacting
but also conflicting developments in South African history are especially important: the spread of racial integration in the economy, the
failure of liberalism, the rise of Afrikaner nationalism, and the emergence of uncompromising African nationalism. A historical watershed
marks each development: 1870, the opening of the diamond mines and

the beginning of South Africa's industrial revolution; 1936, the nadir of South African liberalism, when African voters in Cape Province were removed from the common voting roll; 1948, the coming to power of the first all-Afrikaner government; and 1960, following the shootings at Sharpeville, the driving underground of African leaders who had been committed to multiracialism and nonviolence. Touches of finality have been added to the polarization reflected in these developments by the proclamation of the Republic of South Africa in 1961 and the antithetical predictions by African political exiles that South Africa will come under African control in 1963.

Before these four historical developments are surveyed, it will be useful to sketch the major stages in the peopling of South Africa and the major shifts that have occurred in that country in political control and constitutional status.

THE PEOPLING OF SOUTH AFRICA

The 4 to 1 ratio of nonwhites to whites in the world's population is mirrored in South Africa. Among 15,841,000 people in 1960 (in the Union, excluding South-West Africa), there were 12,773,000 nonwhites and 3,068,000 whites. Of the nonwhites, 10,808,000 were Africans, 1,488,000 were Coloreds, and 477,000 were Asians. The substantial white minority of nearly 20 per cent dwindles to 2.5 per cent, however, when one looks at the population of sub-Saharan Africa. North of the South African Republic live some 130,000,000 Africans. The largest group of whites in middle Africa is in Southern Rhodesia, but it is smaller than the white population of Cape Town (about 279,000 in 1960).

Africans and whites can each claim longer residence than the other in some part of South Africa. Bantu tribes, probably migrating southward from central and east Africa, were in the area that is now the Transvaal and Natal at least by 1500 and perhaps centuries earlier.[1] But these tribes did not confront whites, the frontiersmen who were trekking east and north from the Cape, until the 1770's, when they met in the area between present-day Port Elizabeth and East London. By that time, whites had been settled at the Cape for over a century. When the Dutch East India Company established a halfway or re-

---

[1] Monica Wilson in "The Early History of the Transkei and Ciskei," *African Studies,* vol. XVIII, no. 4 (1959), reviews the evidence of Bantu occupation of the southeastern coastal districts in the sixteenth century.

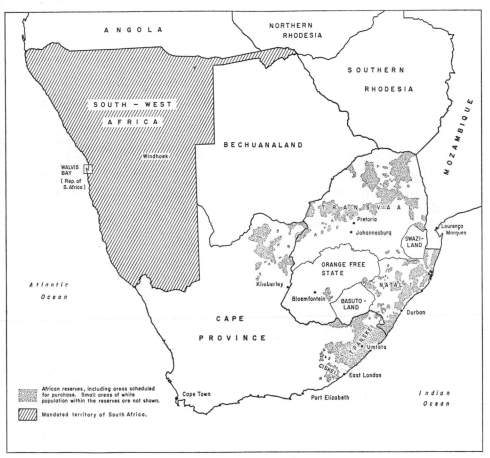

Map 5. The Republic of South Africa, including the African reserves.

freshment station at the Cape in 1652, only the short, yellowish Bushmen and Hottentots were there and in the hinterland.

During the period before contact with the Bantu, miscegenation among whites, slaves, Hottentots, and others had already produced a Colored population. The slaves had come mainly from Madagascar and the East Indies. Miscegenation with the Bantu beginning late in the nineteenth century added, though only slightly, to the Colored group.

Between Afrikaans- and English-speaking whites there are no competing claims to historical precedence. The three-fifths of the white population known as Afrikaners (whose home language today is Afrikaans, a distinctive language derived from Dutch) trace their ancestry to the small group of whites who settled at the tip of South Africa in the latter part of the seventeenth century. By 1707 about 1,700 whites were there, mainly to serve company ships en route to the East Indies. A slight majority were Dutch, and the others German and Huguenot French. Assistance to immigration virtually ended after 1707, and the Cape, which seemed remote and poor, did not attract settlers. By 1800 the white population, which had grown mainly through natural increase, numbered only about 16,000 within the borders of the settlement. In addition, there were about 17,000 slaves and possibly 20,000 Hottentots, Bushmen, and half-breeds. Beyond the company's effective control were a small number of cattle farmers, a group which had been moving eastward for more than a century.

After the British occupied the Cape during the Napoleonic Wars, small numbers of English-speaking persons came and stayed in that area. But not until 1820, when the British government assisted emigration because of unemployment in postwar Britain, did a substantial number of English-speaking people—about 5,000—settle in South Africa. During the next forty years they were followed by about 35,000 more immigrants, mainly English-speaking but including some Germans.

Indians began to arrive in the 1860's. They were brought to Natal as indentured labor to work on the sugar plantations, and many remained after serving their indentures. Free immigration was prohibited after 1911, but by then an Indian community of over 133,000 was already established with half a century of history as South Africans.

POLITICAL HISTORY

The rule of the Dutch East India Company lasted until 1795, when the British temporarily occupied the Cape at the beginning of the Napoleonic Wars. A second British occupation in 1806 became permanent. The withdrawal north and east from the Cape of some 10,000 Boers, or farmers, during the decade after 1836 in what is known as the Great Trek led to the establishment of Boer republics, north and south of the Vaal River, whose independence was recognized by the British in the 1850's. British policy in the second and third quarters of the nineteenth century responded in a vacillating manner to conflicting domestic pressures of evangelicalism, liberalism, and economy. But with the beginning of diamond mining in the 1870's in the disputed area of Kimberley and gold mining in the 1880's on the Witwatersrand in the southern Transvaal, the economic motivations behind British imperialism increased in southern Africa. Tensions grew sharp between *uitlanders* (outsiders) and Boers and between Whitehall and Pretoria. The result in 1899 was the Anglo-Boer War.

The Transvaal and Orange Free State republics were defeated in 1902, became crown colonies, and within five years were granted responsible government. Cape Colony had already been granted representative government in 1853 and responsible government in 1872; and Natal, which had been annexed by the British in 1843, had completed this constitutional development by 1893.

Economic and political pressures for closer union among the four colonies and a common anxiety about the need for a united front in governing the African population culminated in the formation of the Union of South Africa on May 31, 1910. On that date, a constitution drafted by a National Convention in South Africa and embodied in a British imperial statute came into effect. The Union's independence as a member of the British Commonwealth was recognized in the Imperial Conference of 1926 and given formal, legal effect by British and South African statutes in 1931 and 1934. South Africa continued to be a member of the Commonwealth until on May 31, 1961, the fifty-first anniversary of the Union's formation, the Republic of South Africa was proclaimed, outside the Commonwealth.

THE INDUSTRIAL REVOLUTION

The South African industrial revolution has been complicated by its racial setting: in particular, its color-blind implications have conflicted with white attitudes of superiority, self-interest, and fear. By 1870, these attitudes had been over two centuries in the making. The relationship of white master and nonwhite servant began with the importation of slaves in 1657. In 1717, reliance upon slave labor was confirmed by a company decision to bring in more slaves rather than European artisans. When Britain began its permanent occupation in 1806, the colony had 30,000 slaves, about 5,000 more than the number of whites. Some 20,000 other persons, many of them laborers on white farms or domestic servants, were mainly Hottentots and Cape Coloreds. Slavery continued until its abolition in 1834.

Bantu tribesmen, who were to provide the main reservoir for cheap labor in the future, entered the employ of white farmers and mineowners not as slaves or former slaves or, like the Hottentots, as members of weak and easily dispersed clans—they entered to a large extent as members of cohesive tribes defeated in battle. During the century before the mineral discoveries, white trekking farmers and Africans, both seeking land for their cattle, had engaged in a series of skirmishes and wars on the unsettled frontier. Pressed into small land areas, which were to become known as Native Reserves, and subject to taxation, many Africans became labor tenants on white land. Their way of life remained largely unchanged, and their relations to their employers were often similar to medieval relationships. Nevertheless, the process of change and collapse of the tribal structure was under way before 1870 as Africans progressed "from barbarism to pauperism." [2]

The revolutionary transformation of South Africa's economy that began with the mining of diamonds and, in 1886, of gold produced a new division within South Africa, the division between a white ruling class and an urban class of wage-earning Africans. Mining attracted capital and immigrants; railroads were built from distant ports; and cheap African labor became an essential element in the economy. But until World War I the economy remained predominantly rural, except for mining centers where unskilled Africans were employed on short-term contracts.

The full force of the industrial revolution was not felt until after the war. The rapid extension of industry and commerce in the 1920's stimulated economic and social mobility and attracted a heavy influx of Africans and Afrikaners to the towns. A government-sponsored

[2] C. W. de Kiewiet, *A History of South Africa, Social and Economic* (London: Oxford University Press, 1941), pp. 83–87.

iron and steel industry was built. Economic expansion and the growth of secondary industry were greatly accelerated after the depression of 1932–1933 and during World War II and the early postwar period. In 1951, Dr. H. J. van Eck, mentor of the South African industrial revolution, compared the changes with those in England from the 1780's to the 1840's. Describing South Africa's starting point in 1870 as one in which conditions for both the Afrikaner pioneers and African tribesmen were more primitive than peasant conditions a century earlier in England, he concluded that the changes in South Africa were "even more revolutionary." [3]

South Africa's late and rapid industrialization profoundly affected the relations of Afrikaners with Africans and, to a lesser extent, with the English-speaking group. The latter, having dominated finance and commerce during the nineteenth century, were the major promoters of economic expansion. The immigration of skilled miners and other skilled labor from Britain added to English-speaking predominance in the urban economy. Rural Afrikaners, unskilled and poorly educated, were in an inferior and resentful position when they migrated into the towns after the Anglo-Boer War and during the 1920's and 1930's. As whites, however, they were the beneficiaries of white trade union pressures, apprenticeship regulations, and customary and legislative color bars.

More disturbing to the new townsmen was the discovery that unskilled and even some semiskilled jobs were held by Africans. This new confrontation of Afrikaner and African was a bitter one for Afrikaners, who had been forced by poverty to move from unproductive farms. The "poor white" problem had originated late in the nineteenth century, with the gradual closing of the frontier. In the 1920's, nearly three-fifths of the Afrikaner population was in or close to a status of economic degradation. The scarring effect of this experience on the Afrikaner people is difficult to exaggerate. Governmental aid, preferential employment in public and protected enterprises, and the country's rising prosperity largely eliminated poor-whiteism. But fear has not disappeared that some working-class whites may fall below working-class Africans in the economic scale, a fear notably reflected in the racial "job reservation" legislation enacted in 1956.

Four-fifths of the white population has become concentrated in

[3] Dr. H. J. van Eck, *Some Aspects of the South African Industrial Revolution* (Hoernle Memorial Lecture, 1951; 2d and rev. ed., Johannesburg: S.A. Institute of Race Relations, 1953), p. 4.

urban areas. Meanwhile, the dependence of the South African economy on African labor has increased. As the African population grew
and pressures on the Native reserves became more intense, landless
Africans sought work in industry or on white farms or squatted on
vacant white land. By 1921, there were 500,000 Africans resident in
urban areas; by 1936, 1,000,000; by 1951, over 2,300,000. More than
half the African population by mid-century was in the urban and
rural working force of the white economy. Africans who remained in
the Native Reserves, which cover about 12.9 per cent of South Africa's
territory, depended on remittances from relatives to maintain a subsistence level.

Prime Minister Verwoerd has said that the Bantu influx into urban
areas must be expected to continue until 1978. Professor de Kiewiet's
explanation for the "failure" of South Africa to attract as many immigrants as Canada or Australia is still valid for the present day. "The
truth is," he said, "that she did receive a very considerable immigration. It was an immigration from within. Her immigrants were black." [4]

The continuation of industrialization and the development of an
integrated and country-wide economy are essential to many of the
government's aims: greater economic self-sufficiency, strengthened
national defense, full employment for whites, especially Afrikaners,
and the amassing of capital for the development of Bantu areas. Additional incentives are the fact that gold is a wasting asset (although
production continues to set new records), that Afrikaners have become
accustomed to economic prosperity, and that rising standards of living
subdue as well as incite nonwhite disaffection. A potentially enormous,
internal nonwhite market is ready, furthermore, to contribute both to
white and nonwhite prosperity, and a potentially skilled nonwhite
labor force is available for training and use. Nevertheless, the government has designed doctrinaire and long-range schemes of separate
development to reduce the proportion of Africans in the so-called
white areas. Because of these and more repressive policies, racial
tensions are unabated and foreign investment, important for South
Africa's continued economic growth, uncertain and mainly short range.
White political dominance is threatened, therefore, not only by the
long-range political and social implications of the industrial revolution
but also by any serious disruption of the economy that would result
in mass unemployment and the giving of job preference to whites.

[4] *A History of South Africa*, p. 87.

THE FAILURE OF LIBERALISM

The beginning of a new and indigenous liberalism among whites after World War II was partly the consequence of the maturing of the industrial revolution. The nineteenth-century Cape liberal tradition, that is, the tradition of racial tolerance and color blindness, had for over a century inspired only a small number of whites, although a larger number of whites in the Cape had become accustomed to it. Somewhat wider acceptance of nonracialism became possible with the growth of a permanently urbanized and Western-oriented class of Africans. In 1953, some supporters of the United Party, the major opposition party, formed the Liberal Party. Others hived off in 1959 to form the Progressive Party, which agreed with the Liberals on the goal of a universal franchise but proposed gradualism, high though nonracial qualifications, and rigid constitutional safeguards. In the 1961 general election, the Progressives won nearly 70,000 white votes. Even the remaining leadership of the conservative and white supremacist United Party had liberal potentialities in the South African sense (that is, nonracial) because of its pragmatic readiness to accept a racially integrated economy.

Despite their vigor and ability to recruit younger white members, the new generation of white liberals arose too late, however, to be able to sustain the hopes of African leaders for a progressive share in political power. The year 1936, when African voters were removed from the common roll in Cape Province, marked the nadir in the decline of the liberal tradition. It marked also a low point in the process of African disillusionment with the promise of liberalism. The hopes of some African leaders for effective consultation if not participation were temporarily sustained in 1936 by the establishment of an advisory Natives' Representative Council. But the council failed during the following decade to evolve into an effective body or to win the respect of Africans, including its own members. Its virtual demise came in 1946, when it suspended its sittings because of the absence of consultation and in protest against the violence with which the United Party government led by General Jan Christiaan Smuts had broken a strike of African gold miners.

The Cape's liberal tradition had failed to grow, partly because of its initial weakness in the early nineteenth century when it was transplanted to the colony from the outside despite the absence of any substantial demand by whites. Evangelicalism and movements of humanitarian and social reform in England that were pressed by missionaries and others recently arrived at the Cape were responsible for reforms introduced in the colony after 1806. In 1828 legal color bars were removed in principle, and the pass system for Hottentots (imposed earlier by British authority) was abolished. Slavery was abolished in 1834. The departure of about one-fourth of the Dutch-speaking population in the Great Trek facilitated the establishment of British political institutions in Cape Colony. In 1853 the franchise for elections to the Cape Parliament was made nonracial, and at the insistence of the British Colonial Office economic qualifications were made lower than the level desired by representatives of the colonists.

"Bantu political liberalism" arose in the 1880's under the leadership of John Tengo Jabavu, and Cape Colony, now largely autonomous in domestic matters, began the process of curbing the political expansion of the Bantu electorate.[5] Some 30,000 Africans, who had registered on the basis of their share in tribal lands, were eliminated from the voters' roll in 1887, and a further 3,300 in 1892. By raising franchise qualifications, the Cape Parliament avoided the imposition of a political color bar.

Political parties were fairly evenly balanced from 1896 to 1910, and the African voter held the balance of power in seven Cape constituencies. His vote, for which white candidates asked, was instrumental in preventing the adoption of discriminatory legislation like that being adopted elsewhere.[6] But his influence was steadily to be diminished.

Opposing the Cape tradition was the so-called northern or Boer republican tradition of racial inequality. It is true that, like the northerners, the large majority of Dutch-speaking and English-speaking whites in the Cape insisted on white supremacy. The overwhelming numbers of the Bantu and the gulf between their primitive culture and that of Europe or, in the eyes of South African whites, between barbarism and civilization, made the necessity of white supremacy seem self-evident. Boer attitudes, however, had deeper roots. Although open miscegenation had been accepted for a short while after 1652, attitudes of racial superiority, supported by the Calvinist doctrine of predestination, became entrenched during the 150 years before the

[5] See Edward Roux, *Time Longer than Rope: A History of the Black Man's Struggle for Freedom in South Africa* (London: Gollancz, 1948), ch. vii.

[6] Arthur Keppel-Jones, *South Africa: A Short History* (3d ed.; London: Hutchinson University Library, 1961), p. 174.

arrival of the British. Newcomers at the beginning of the nineteenth century found in the Dutch-speaking farmers a seventeenth-century people, accustomed to slavery, attached to an authoritarian church, and virtually untouched by the eighteenth century. During later years, the trekkers' perilous experiences of bloody conflict with the Bantu intensified their conviction that uncompromising white supremacy was necessary for survival and also strengthened their Old Testament sense of being a chosen people.

By trekking into the interior to escape British rule and color-blind practices, the Boers were once again insulated from the challenge of new and alien ideas. Among nineteenth-century Afrikaners, Professor de Kiewiet has said, there was no group "with roots in humanitarianism or the philosophic optimism of the eighteenth century." Nor did the simple pastoral society of the republics produce any "patrician element or privileged economic group" that would promote reform in race relations.[7] The policy of the republics was uncompromising: "The people desire to permit no equality between coloured people and the white inhabitants, either in church or state," said the republican constitution in the Transvaal.

The characteristic optimism of liberals that their liberalism would eventually prevail was evident in 1910 despite the fact that the Act of Union marked a further stage in its decline. The defeated ex-republics had retained their exclusive white franchise and, at the national convention, their representatives considered any change intolerable. Nor would they tolerate the presence of nonwhites in the Union Parliament, although nonwhites had been eligible for election (none had been elected) to the Cape Parliament. The franchise issue was resolved by leaving the matter to each province, and the Cape franchise was entrenched by the provision that it could be altered only by a two-thirds majority of all members (whether present or not) in a joint session of Parliament. But membership in the Union Parliament was restricted to whites. "Thus the Cape liberal tradition," wrote two exponents of apartheid in 1960, Professors Rhoodie and Venter, "suffered a blow from which it has not yet recovered." [8]

Of the racially discriminatory legislation enacted in the following two decades, the Natives Land Act of 1913 was a source of ex-

[7] C. W. de Kiewiet, *The Anatomy of South African Misery* (London: Oxford University Press, 1956), pp. 22–23.

[8] N. J. Rhoodie and H. J. Venter, *Apartheid: A Socio-historical Exposition of the Origin and Development of the Apartheid Idea* (Cape Town: H.A.U.M., 1960), p. 116.

ceptional grievance to Africans. It prohibited the acquisition of land except in the reserves (or, according to judicial decision, in Cape Province). A more sensitive test of liberalism continued to be the franchise. In 1924 the Nationalist Party came to power in coalition with the Labor Party, which represented the interests of white labor. Two years later, Prime Minister Hertzog introduced a bill to eliminate the African franchise but failed to win the two-thirds vote required by the Act of Union. In 1929, the Nationalist Party won an absolute majority in the House of Assembly. "This election was the first to be decided almost exclusively on the issue of the Black Danger," in the judgment of Professors Rhoodie and Venter. In 1930 the universal enfranchisement of adult white women and in 1931 the removal of voting qualifications for white men altered the racial balance of the Cape electorate.

Finally in 1936, over the outspoken opposition of African political organizations and white liberals, the newly fused United Party under Generals Hertzog and Smuts enacted the bill that had been pending in various forms for a decade. The number of Africans on the common roll had reached 16,481 in 1929; in 1935, it was down to 10,628. With only eleven members of the two houses of Parliament voting in opposition, African voters were removed to a separate or communal roll. Henceforth, qualified Africans in the Cape elected three whites to the House of Assembly, and Africans throughout the Union voted indirectly for four white senators. Concurrent legislation providing for enlargement of the reserves also extended the color bar to all purchase of land outside the reserves. "The Liberals were therefore defeated decisively in 1936," according to Rhoodie and Venter, "while the northern point of view achieved its greatest victory."

The 1936 "settlement," as it was called, endured until 1959, when the African communal roll and the parliamentary seats of the seven whites elected by Africans were abolished. In the interim, in 1956, Colored voters in the Cape were dealt with as African voters had been in 1936. (About 47,800 Colored voters were registered in 1949, some 5,300 less than in 1945, partly because of more onerous registration procedures required by the National Party government.)

The removal of the Coloreds from the common to a separate roll stirred up bitter controversy among whites during a period of six years. The Cape Colored franchise was a century old. Traditionally the Coloreds, who were described by whites (not invidiously) as an "appendage" of the white community, had received relatively favorable treatment. The controversy, although it basically concerned the deprivation of political rights, was fought mainly on the constitutional issue of the propriety of attempting to change the nonwhite Cape franchise by ordinary majority procedures. After judicial reversals, the government packed the Senate and with its newly acquired two-thirds majority removed the Colored voters from the common to a communal roll and also abolished the requirement of a two-thirds vote for future alterations of the Colored or African franchise. After 1960, only the Cape Coloreds (including Asians in Cape Province) among nonwhites retained a vestige of representation, by whites, in the South African Parliament. Despite the new liberalism that had begun to appear after World War II, whites and Coloreds who subscribed to the nineteenth-century Cape tradition had little confidence that the leaders of the National Party would allow this vestige to endure.

THE VICTORY OF AFRIKANER NATIONALISM

The roots of Afrikaner nationalism, like those of the northern tradition, are in the mid-seventeenth century, but Afrikaner nationalism as a self-conscious force is no older than the industrial revolution. Indirectly, the industrial revolution contributed to the generation of nationalism since it led to further political intrusions by the British and to an economic intrusion by the Bantu; these intrusions appeared to threaten the cultural survival of the Afrikaner people and the racial survival of the whites. In responding to this dual challenge Afrikaner nationalism had a dual appeal, but its appeal was directed exclusively to Afrikaners.

During the eighteenth century, the small numbers of whites in the isolated Cape began to coalesce into a distinctive people with common religious and social values. Nearly 200 French Huguenots had arrived in 1688 and soon afterward, but they completely lost their identity as a French-speaking group. By the end of the eighteenth century, a vernacular that was eventually to be known as Afrikaans was in common use. During the nineteenth century, a sense of identity grew in reaction to British policy—in 1828, for example, English became the only official language in the Cape—and as a result of the perilous and bloody experiences on the frontier and a pervasive fear of submergence by the Bantu. But not until the first annexation of the Transvaal in 1877 was Afrikaner sentiment fully aroused in both the north and the south. Victory over the British at Majuba Hill four years later gave a boost to self-conscious nationalism. Meanwhile, a half-century struggle in behalf of Afrikaans was under way. A movement had begun in 1875 in Cape Colony to develop Afrikaans as a written language and to encourage the speaking and writing of it.

Both democratic and authoritarian elements and divergent constitutional traditions developed in Afrikaner history during the nineteenth century. The republican institutions of the Orange Free State and, north of the Vaal River, of the South African Republic gave institutional expression to the authoritarian racial and religious attitudes described above. For whites, who were social equals in a simple pastoral society, the two constitutions were based upon political equality and were "highly democratic." [9] Strong leadership was also important, especially in the north and in circumstances of danger; but leadership was not always unified since individualistic trekkers often gave their political allegiance to individuals. Religious belief helped to eliminate any conflict between strong leadership and popular rule. "In the voice of the people," said President Paul Kruger in the Transvaal, "I heard the voice of God." Each republic had a popularly elected president, but the dominant institution was the Volksraad, the legislative assembly.

There were distinct differences, on the other hand, between the constitutional history of the Orange Free State and the South African Republic.[10] In the former, "the written Constitution was rigid, the judiciary was in fact completely free and independent, and the legislature did not in fact exceed its proper powers." Constitutional amendment required a three-fourths majority of the Volksraad in two successive sessions (as the leader of the Opposition reminded the Prime Minister during the debate on the republican constitution in 1961). In the South African Republic, "the written Constitution was often ignored, the judiciary became the creature of the government of the day, and the legislature passed laws on any subject, including constitutional amendment in the simplest possible way." Modern Afrikaans writers tend to ignore the former tradition and to write with enthusiasm of the latter.

Out of the bitterness of defeat in the Anglo-Boer War, Afrikaner nationalism came of age, and soon after the formation of the Union the successful battle began to redress defeat by political means.

[9] See James Bryce, "Two South African Constitutions," in his *Studies in History and Jurisprudence* (New York: Oxford University Press, 1901), pp. 359–390.

[10] This paragraph is based on L. M. Thompson, "Constitutionalism in the South African Republics," *Butterworths South African Law Review*, 1954, pp. 49–72, especially p. 72. See also *House of Assembly Debates*, Jan. 30, 1961, col. 353.

Afrikaners organized the first government, headed by General Louis Botha and supported by many English-speaking South Africans. Because of its policy of reconciliation and continued membership in the Commonwealth, the government failed to retain the allegiance of General J. B. M. Hertzog. Hertzog believed that unity of the two white sections and true South Africanism were possible only after development along "two streams" had rehabilitated the Afrikaners and enabled them to achieve full cultural equality with the English-speaking section. He left the cabinet in 1912 and formed the National Party. Hertzog's Nationalists opposed participation in World War I but remained apart from a small number of irreconcilables who engaged in an abortive military rebellion.

Reconciliation continued to be the policy of Jan Christiaan Smuts, a third Boer general who succeeded Botha as Prime Minister in 1919. Smuts brought about a political alignment in 1921 that was to characterize white politics for more than three decades: moderate Afrikaners and most English-speaking whites aligned against an exclusive party of militant Afrikaner nationalists. Following a postwar depression, the latter were able to come to power in 1924 when Hertzog entered into a kind of farmer-labor coalition with the urban and predominantly English-speaking Labor Party. The parties were bound together by opposition to capitalism and to any lowering of the industrial color bar and also by opposition to Smuts, who was described as the servant of the British Empire and the Chamber of Mines.

Hertzog's nationalism largely ran its course by the mid-1930's. Following a severe economic depression, his party entered a coalition with that of Smuts in 1933, and the following year the United Party was formed through fusion of the two parties. Afrikaans had been recognized as an official language in 1925, and dual flags and anthems had been adopted. Legislation had embodied "civilized labor" policies, entrenching the dominant position of white labor, particularly in the gold mines. Although there was still a great disparity in the economic strength of the Afrikaans- and English-speaking sections, most Afrikaner nationalists were at least formally satisfied by 1934 that their "nation" had achieved equal status domestically and that South Africa had achieved independence internationally. Republicanism became a distant goal. Hertzog had included two English-speaking members of the Labor Party in his cabinet after the 1929 election although the Nationalists had won a majority of seats. In 1933, with the formation of the Hertzog-Smuts coalition (with Hertzog continuing as Prime Minister), the proportion of English-speaking members of the cabinet increased.

Like Hertzog in 1912, Dr. Daniel F. Malan, who had been a member of the precoalition cabinet, was not satisfied with reconciliation. In 1934 he led a small and militant wing of Afrikaner nationalists into the "Purified National Party," which aimed at Afrikaner predominance and the establishment of a Christian National Republic. Renewed efforts were made to promote Afrikaner separatism in the social, economic, and educational life of the country. Nationalist fervor reached its highest emotional peak in 1938 during the centennial celebrations of the Great Trek. The split in the United Party the following year, when South Africa entered World War II by the narrow parliamentary vote of 80 to 67, gave new hope for Afrikaner reunification. About one-third of the United Party's members in Parliament followed Hertzog into opposition, but a substantial number of moderate Afrikaners continued to support Smuts, the new Prime Minister. In 1940, Hertzog merged with Malan in the "Reunited National Party."

The years of opposition during World War II revealed the complexity of the pressures and tendencies within political Afrikanerdom. The period displayed not only the splits, realignments, and attachment to individual leaders that often characterize Afrikaner nationalist politics but also the political strength of parliamentarians like Malan and the Nazi-minded extremism to which some authoritarian Nationalists were susceptible. Attitudes varied widely: Hertzog, essentially neutralist in the war and insistent on equality between Afrikaner and English-speaking South African; Malan, sympathetic to Germany and aiming at predominance for Christian National Afrikaner ideals; militantly authoritarian groups like the Ossewa Brandwag (OB or ox-wagon guard) and Oswald Pirow's New Order, which admired the Nazis; and a few men whose intransigence led them to commit treason or sabotage. (B. J. Vorster, who became Minister of Justice in 1961, was a general in the OB and was interned during the war.)

In June 1941, at the height of Nazi victories, supporters of Malan, of the OB, and others drafted an authoritarian constitution for a future republic. Hertzog and his followers had already split from Malan. The OB became increasingly militaristic, organizing storm troopers and scorning parliamentary institutions. Because of its growing threat to the role of the National Party as the political embodiment of the Afrikaner nation, Malan forbade membership in it.

Malan took a more moderate approach in the 1943 election than was desired by Nationalist leaders in the Transvaal and the Orange Free State and offered full guarantees to the English-speaking section. Nevertheless, his electoral appeal continued to be directed almost exclusively to Afrikaners. The OB did not participate in the election, but many of its members opposed Malan by supporting the pro-Hertzog Afrikaner Party. Neither this party nor the New Order won any seats, while the National Party reduced from about 40 to 32 per cent the proportion of Afrikaner voters who supported Smuts.

In 1948 the Nationalists voiced economic grievances and, under the banner of "apartheid" (racial separateness), exploited white racial fears in inflammatory attacks on vaguely liberal pronouncements by the United Party. The United Party won the support of 20 to 25 per cent of the Afrikaans-speaking population and of every predominantly English-speaking district (excluding a few districts won by the Labor Party). The opposition also included the Labor members and the three Natives' representatives. Nevertheless, the Nationalists, in coalition with the small Afrikaner Party, won an unexpected victory by winning practically every district that was predominantly Afrikaans-speaking, including a number of marginal districts. With a minority of popular votes, they had a slim majority of five seats in a lower house of 153. For the first time in the Union's history, the cabinet was entirely Afrikaans-speaking.

Afrikaner nationalism's political victory, which vindicated the tactics of its parliamentary leaders, was consolidated during the next dozen years. In 1950 the Nationalists absorbed the Afrikaner Party after winning all of the six new parliamentary seats that had been given to South-West Africa. The party's leadership shifted from the Cape to the more extreme Transvaal in 1954, when Johannes Strijdom, a blunt exponent of *baasskap* (boss-ship), became Prime Minister. His stern response to nonwhite protest enhanced the government's political appeal. In 1958 the succession of Dr. Hendrik Verwoerd, the present Prime Minister and the foremost ideologist of positive apartheid or separate development, invigorated the party's doctrine. Nationalist defectors failed to attract support. Although profound doubts and even dissent about aspects of the government's racial policy became evident among some influential supporters, rumors of insurgency proved to be little more than wishful thinking.

The party won a steadily increasing proportion of popular votes and parliamentary seats in general elections in 1953, 1958, and 1961 and strengthened its position in interim elections to the provincial councils. Although its parliamentary majority in 1953, like that in 1948, was won by a minority vote, the Nationalists received roughly 50 per cent of the vote in 1958. In 1961 they won a small popular majority and nearly two-thirds of the lower house of Parliament.

Meanwhile, Liberals and Progressives had split off from the United Party, in 1953 and 1959 respectively. The Federal Party, formed after the 1953 election, failed to gather strength, and the old Labor Party lost its small parliamentary representation in 1958 and disappeared. With the removal of the Natives' representatives in 1960, Liberal representation came to an end, and in 1961 only one of the eleven Progressive members of Parliament was returned to the House of Assembly. Although relatively strengthened in Parliament, the United Party won its seats in 1961 with reduced majorities.

The purified Afrikaner nationalism of the 1930's had not run its course by 1961. Despite the steady rise of Afrikaners in public and private spheres and the attainment of a republic, the new republic was seen as still far from embodying Boer and "Christian National" ideals. Republican political institutions still largely followed the English pattern; Afrikaners were still junior partners in the economy; and much of education, the press, and popular culture was cosmopolitan.

The greater priority of importance given to racial issues after Dr. Verwoerd became Prime Minister and the growing urgency of appeals for white unity after the events of 1960, described below, have muffled the militant and exclusive spirit of Afrikanerdom. The Nationalist leadership has sought to widen its appeal. Late in 1961, for example, two English-speaking members, the first since 1948, were added to the cabinet. Meanwhile, the steady enlargement of arbitrary state power to meet threats to white rule tends to make more difficult the position of whites opposed to Afrikaner nationalist rule.

THE FRUSTRATION OF AFRICAN NATIONALISM

The course of South African liberalism and its submergence by Afrikaner nationalism have profoundly affected the outlook of politically conscious Africans. The African opposition has moved from the "Bantu political liberalism" of the 1880's, when Africans were eligible for election to the Cape Parliament, to an extraparliamentary position (or pseudoparliamentary, since some Africans voted for whites in Parliament) during the half century of Union and since 1960 to activity underground. In particular, the African National Congress (ANC), the historic and national organ for the expression of African aspirations, has reacted to white official policy with six distinct attitudes, marking as many periods. Successively, the ANC retained liberal expectations, became more militant, attempted passive resistance, entered a multiracial popular front, was overtaken by impatient black nationalism, and moved underground.

During the years before 1936, many African leaders continued to hope that cooperation with liberally inclined whites would bring about a reduction in racial discrimination and a progressive share in political power. African aspirations had been encouraged in the nineteenth century by the Cape Colony's liberal tradition. In order to protest violations of this tradition and to promote a sense of national identity among Africans, members of a small class of educated and conservative Africans organized the ANC in 1912 in cooperation with tribal chiefs. With some notable exceptions, leadership remained through the 1930's in the hands of professional men and church leaders whose nationalism was coupled with respect for tribal authority. Agitation flared up occasionally after World War I, beginning with a demonstration in 1919 against the carrying of passes. In 1930–1931 attempts, inspired by Communists, were made to organize pass-burning demonstrations and boycotts of beer halls. Meanwhile, in 1927, the first conference of African, Colored, and Indian organizations was held, but no common front was formed.

The South African Communist Party, formed by whites in 1921, fully accepted African equality, though during the 1922 strike of white miners Communists supplied the slogan: "Workers of the World fight and unite for a White South Africa." The party recruited and trained some able Africans but was weakened by its adherence to directions from Moscow and made little headway among African intellectuals.[11]

The loosely organized Industrial and Commercial Workers' Union, on the other hand, overshadowed the ANC during the late 1920's. Its flamboyant leadership attracted more than 200,000 African members, but after squabbles over the leadership and the ousting of Communists, the ICU disintegrated.

The second period, 1936–1949, was marked by the failure of the Natives' Representative Council and the coming of age of a new and militant urban generation. Dr. A. B. Xuma, an American-educated physician who was president of the ANC from 1940 to 1949, concen-

[11] See Roux, *Time Longer than Rope*, p. 156 and chs. xvii–xxii.

trated on building an economically well-established urban movement
that could act independently of whites and Indians. The wartime
idealism of the Atlantic Charter was given African expression in a
1945 statement of "African Claims," which called for "the abandonment of any policy and all practices that discriminate against the
African in any way whatsoever." [12] These claims were expressed in
manifestoes, boycotts, and strikes. White, Indian, and African radicals
organized multiracial demonstrations, and nonwhite trade unions
claimed 50,000 members. Greater militancy culminated in 1946 in a
strike and peaceful demonstration by 70,000 African gold miners.
One consequence of the strike was the virtual demise of the Natives'
Representative Council. During the same year, Dr. Xuma himself
joined with Indian leaders to protest against discriminatory legislation aimed at Indians. Nevertheless, in 1949 the ANC Youth League,
which had been organized during the war, brought about Dr. Xuma's
displacement and the adoption of a "Program of Action." This called
for an end to cooperation with governmental institutions and for boycotts, strikes, and civil disobedience. The main inspiration of the
Youth League was militant African nationalism, not communism.

During the third period, 1949–1952, the ANC moved toward closer
multiracial cooperation and, with growing acceptance of Indian and
Communist support, waged a "defiance" campaign of passive resistance to "unjust laws." The new Nationalist government's racial
legislation affected all nonwhites and widened the common ground
upon which could be built a combined opposition of Africans,
Coloreds, Indians, and allied whites. The Suppression of Communism
Act of 1950, in particular, was so loosely defined that it appeared as a
common threat and strengthened the tendency of the younger ANC
leaders to cooperate more closely with Communists of various races.
(The Communist Party, which ostensibly dissolved itself, had approximately 2,500 members. Nearly half of them were Africans, but the
most influential members were whites and Indians.) Leaders of the
ANC and the South African Indian Congress cooperated in sponsoring
a one-day strike on May Day in 1950, which resulted in the killing of
18 persons and the wounding of 30. The deaths were commemorated
on June 26, which has become a sacred day in the calendar of protest.
Joint planning for mass action continued, and on June 26, 1952, the
defiance campaign began.

[12] The text is in Gwendolen M. Carter, *The Politics of Inequality: South Africa since 1948* (New York: Praeger, 1958), pp. 484–485.

By deliberately violating restrictions on African movement and minor apartheid regulations, the demonstrators sought to protest against four Nationalist laws in addition to the older pass laws and (as a protest against lack of land) measures aimed at culling cattle to reduce overgrazing. The four laws were those designed to confine each racial group to its own "group area," to reestablish tribal authority, to remove Coloreds from the common roll, and the Suppression of Communism Act. The ANC's membership of around 15,000 to 20,000 grew to 100,000; and about 8,500 volunteers, mostly Africans but including Indians and Coloreds, went to jail. Before the campaign died down by the end of the year, rioting and violence occurred, and about three dozen nonwhites and several whites were killed.

The fourth period, 1953–1956, began with the enactment of punitive legislation that seriously increased the personal risk, including whipping, to be run in any future campaign of protest and ended with widespread arrests on charges of high treason.[13] The challenge to authority became less direct as tactics shifted from disobedience to demonstration, but a climax was reached in the formation of a multiracial popular front. On June 25–26, 1955, the ANC, the South African Indian Congress, the newly organized Congress of Democrats (a few hundred whites, including some members of the banned Communist Party), and the Colored People's Organization joined in holding a so-called Congress of the People outside Johannesburg. Nearly 3,000 delegates endorsed a Freedom Charter, which demanded equal rights and opportunities for all. The Charter also, for the first time in the history of ANC demands, called for public ownership of mineral wealth, banks, and monopoly industry.

Leading Communists (of all races) deserve special credit for the skillful staging of the Congress of the People, but their ideological influence was limited. The Charter itself was clearly not a Communist document. Nor did the Communists, who had worked closely with Africans inspired by nationalism and Indians inspired by Gandhi, control either the omnibus ANC or the Indian Congress. Ex-Chief Albert Luthuli, a liberal and president from 1952 on, accepted support from all quarters in working for equality.

African leaders were divided during this period by the persistent

[13] The Criminal Law Amendment Act of 1953 provided that any person who committed an offense "by way of protest or in support of any campaign against any law" could be sentenced to a whipping of ten strokes, a £300 fine, three years in jail, or a combination of any two of these penalties.

question of whether or not to collaborate with radical whites, Coloreds, and Indians, whom anti-Communist leaders like Dr. Xuma especially distrusted. Nevertheless, nearly all African leaders were in basic agreement on the unacceptability of a white policy that promised neither political integration nor fully independent African states in the foreseeable future. Late in 1956, both Xuma and Luthuli took part in the most widely representative African conference to be held since 1935. The conference, called by a federation of African Christian ministers, found virtually no hope for racial harmony in officially sponsored proposals for separate development and appealed for further discussion with whites.

The major officials of the Congress alliance, including Luthuli, were among the 156 persons arrested in December 1956 on the charge of high treason, based essentially on documents like the Freedom Charter. Dr. Xuma was listed later among alleged co-conspirators. (The trial ended with acquittal in March 1961.) The arrests were the culmination of increasingly severe administrative restrictions on the activities and movements of nonwhite and radical opponents. Wide discretion for the imposition of such restrictions had been exercised since 1930. During the period after the defiance campaign, protest meetings and publications generally were not forbidden, but police surveillance and raids amounted to harassment and intimidation.

During the fifth period, from 1957 to the shootings at Sharpeville in March 1960 that are described below, younger and in some cases less disciplined African leaders urged greater militancy, racial assertiveness, and identification with Pan-Africanism. The readiness of Africans who share an economic grievance to cooperate effectively and almost spontaneously in local protests was notably evident in the successful boycott of Johannesburg buses by more than 50,000 Africans during three months early in 1957. (The boycott was settled only after private meetings between nongovernmental whites and Africans, including some of the treason-accused.) The trial blurred the distinction between long-standing aspirations and Communist aims. It also partly immobilized the ANC leadership and diverted it from effective or large-scale campaigns of protest and from activity against African nationalist rivals. Immediately prior to the general election of April 1958, the Congress alliance sponsored a three-day stay-at-home demonstration. Because of confused leadership, African dissension, and effective countermeasures by the government, the demonstration was a fiasco. In April 1959, African nationalists who opposed the alliance and were outspokenly anti-Communist formally established the Pan-Africanist Congress (PAC).

Following the 1958 election, progovernment Afrikaner intellectuals began holding a series of private meetings with Africans, including ANC leaders on trial for treason and PAC leaders. Similar meetings were held beginning in 1959 by the "Progressive" members of Parliament who had resigned from the United Party. Although their premises varied widely, these whites based their hope for eventual African consent on the preliminary step of African consultation. Meanwhile, late in 1957, the most widely representative multiracial conference in South Africa's history, held at Witwatersrand University, had endorsed the goal of nonracial, universal suffrage.

On March 21, 1960, at Sharpeville, south of Johannesburg, the sixth and current period began. On that day the police killed 72 Africans and wounded about 186 in a crowd that was demonstrating its support for a new defiance campaign against the carrying of passes and, according to the police, was threatening to overrun them. The campaign that occasioned these and later disturbances was initiated by the PAC and had been opposed by the ANC on the ground that it was "sensational" and might not succeed. After the shooting, however, Luthuli called for a stay-at-home Day of Mourning and made the defiant gesture of burning his pass.

The government, seeking a showdown, exercised for the first time the power granted to it by legislation enacted after the passive resistance campaign of 1952 and proclaimed an emergency, thus freeing itself from the restrictions of habeas corpus. By enacting legislation that resulted in the outlawing of both the ANC and the PAC, the government took one of the major actions that probably would have followed a successful prosecution of the treason trial. By arresting and indefinitely detaining 1,900 persons seized in early morning raids, it cracked down on political suspects whose names were apparently on a standing list, including pre-1950 members of the Communist Party who had not been arrested in December 1956. (More than 17,000 African "idlers" also were detained.) By jailing leaders of the anti-Communist Liberal Party without explanation and for the first time, the government acted in a manner predicted by critics who had seen danger to all opponents of official policy in the breadth of the prosecution's treason trial argument. By convicting the PAC leaders during the first six weeks after Sharpeville for incitement and by imposing penalties ranging from whipping to three years in jail, the government demonstrated again its ability to act effectively in cutting down African leadership.

Following the end of the emergency on August 31, 1960, the surface of South Africa's life resumed the appearance of normality, including the resumption of extraparliamentary activity by the ANC's allied organizations in the Congress movement. Leading whites, including supporters of the government and representatives of commerce and industry, made the most urgent appeals in 1960 for "consultation" with Africans that were ever heard in South Africa. In reply to suggestions that ANC and PAC leaders should be among these Africans, the Minister of Justice said that these organizations had a combined membership of "only about 70,000" and constituted "a small coterie of terrorists" who want "our country." [14] The ban on both organizations was renewed in 1961, 1962, and 1963. Nonetheless, despite these stringent restrictions, African nationalism continues to spread within South Africa even though its organizations are both banned and divided.

The Contemporary Setting

LAND AND PEOPLE

Because of its position at the southern end of the continent, between the Atlantic and the Indian oceans, South Africa has been of strategic importance in world politics since the Napoleonic Wars. The Cape route has been Britain's valued alternative to the Mediterranean and Suez. In safeguarding this route, the British navy has kept the sea lanes open for South African trade. British power in the past—in Africa, in the Indian Ocean, and in the Middle East—has also shielded South Africa from the north and the east. Although not directly threatened, South Africa followed Great Britain, its most important ally, into both world wars.

Since the end of World War II, however, South Africa's command of the Cape has become of questionable importance in world military strategy, and for the first time South Africa's own security is potentially threatened. The new African states are united in their hostility to South Africa's racial policy. But in 1963 South Africa was still from 700 to 1,000 miles south of the southernmost borders of the closest African independent states, the Republic of the Congo and

[14] *House of Assembly Debates*, March 29, 1960, cols. 4302–4303.

Tanganyika. To the north and northeast lay the British protectorates of Bechuanaland and Swaziland, the Rhodesias and Nyasaland, and Portuguese East Africa. To the north of South Africa's mandated territory of South-West Africa lay Portuguese Angola.

This northern tier of buffer states, in which whites are probably little more than 2 per cent of the population, does little, however, to reduce the feeling of most South African whites that they are racially isolated. This isolation has been confirmed by the country's diplomatic isolation in Africa. Since the United Arab Republic's closing of its Pretoria legation in 1961, South Africa has had no diplomatic relations with any independent African state. In these circumstances, the air routes to Europe and North America (only twenty-two hours by jet to New York) are particularly significant as bridges to hoped-for allies.[15]

Economically, South Africa dominates the great plateau of southern Africa, and dominant within South Africa itself is the gold-mining and industrial area of the Witwatersrand, whose financial and managerial heart is Johannesburg. (The Witwatersrand, literally ridge of the white waters, is the gold-bearing reef running roughly east and west in the southern Transvaal.) Industrial development in South Africa came in response to the markets created by gold mining and the towns on the Witwatersrand. A large explosives factory, for example, was built at Modderfontein, near Johannesburg, before the end of the century. Towns attracted industry, unlike the usual pattern of growth in the United States and Europe, where industrial development led to the growth of towns.[16] In order to meet the needs of the mines and of the town dwellers, some secondary industries developed, with governmental protection, although they depended upon imported raw materials. Local coal and power and the existence of a transport network centered on Johannesburg also stimulated the growth of the

[15] "Separated from other economically developed countries by vast stretches of ocean, jungle and desert, with the hub of economic activities in the interior, with mining and industrial enterprises which, for financial and technological reasons must maintain close contact with associated or parent concerns in Europe and North America, and with valuable commodities such as diamonds, gold, radioactive isotopes, karakul pelts, etc., to be carried, air transport between South Africa and overseas countries is of great and increasing importance" (Monica M. Cole, *South Africa* [London: Methuen, 1961], p. 494). The Belgian Congo, for example, benefited from South African air freight, receiving fresh eggs, fish, and fruits (p. 495).
[16] *Ibid.*, pp. 396–397.

southern Transvaal. Thus, an area far removed from seaports and originally pastoral became the major industrial region in southern Africa.

Mozambique, the Rhodesias and Nyasaland, and the British territories of Bechuanaland, Basutoland, and Swaziland are all sources of labor for the gold mines and industry. (In 1960, about 650,000 "foreign native" adult males were in South Africa, nearly half of them working in the mines, where they made up about two-thirds of the African working force.) Bechuanaland and Swaziland, both adjacent to South Africa, and Basutoland, an enclave within it, have often been described as being, in effect, native reserves of the Republic. These areas —Britain's High Commission Territories—also depend on South Africa for many services of administration, transportation, and communication.

Politically, South Africa has aspired to dominate southern Africa, but the vague sense of historical and national destiny that has encouraged aspirations for expansion has become less important in recent years than presumed needs of military security. The vision of South African policy makers has seen a greater South Africa that would include the High Commission Territories (whose transfer was foreseen in 1910), South-West Africa, and Southern Rhodesia. South-West Africa, of minor economic value to the Republic, is of strategic importance as a buffer. Although transfer of the High Commission Territories would also contribute little to South Africa's economy, it would more than triple the proportion of land reserved for Africans.[17]

Internally, there are elements of both strength and weakness for the regime in the fact that whites and Africans are heavily concentrated in a small number of urban and industrial centers. About four-fifths of the whites live in urban areas, and nearly one-third of these urban dwellers live on the Witwatersrand. About 27 per cent of the Africans —2,623,000 in 1957—live in urban areas, and more than two-fifths of this number live on the Witwatersrand. From 1951 to 1960, the white population on the Witwatersrand grew from 639,000 to 735,000; the African population, from 966,000 to 1,241,000. A large proportion of the remaining urban population is concentrated in the Cape Town area, Durban-Pinetown, and Port Elizabeth–Uitenhage. There, too, nonwhites far outnumber whites.

[17] Further consideration of the relations with these territories and with Portuguese authorities is in the section on external relations (see pp. 595–598 and 604).

The concentration of population and the distances between urban centers accentuate the problems of transport, supply (particularly of water), and internal security. South Africa is about three times the size of California, and its white population is less than the population of Chicago. Johannesburg is separated from Durban by over 400 miles by road, from Port Elizabeth by nearly 700 miles, and from Cape Town by 900 miles. Rail haulage has been heavily strained at times, particularly during and after World War II, and water transport is possible only between ocean ports because of the absence of navigable inland waterways. The road network is extensive; but because of the expense of imported materials (especially before the domestic production of oil from coal) and the priority given to the railroads, only the main roads outside the cities have an all-weather surface.

Within urban areas, the physical pattern of segregation strengthens control over Africans. Nearly all urban Africans live in townships outside the white areas. Resettlement projects during the past decade have moved large groups of Africans still farther away, sometimes more than 10 miles. Main roads enter the townships only at a few key points. White officials control not only nearly all transportation but also power and supplies. The importance of such control was demonstrated after the Sharpeville shootings in 1960, when one of the measures used to break the work boycott in Langa township, outside Cape Town, was the cutting off of the water supply.

Control over other nonwhites is similarly made more effective by the "group areas" policy. This long-range policy aims at unscrambling the residents of racially mixed areas and moving them to separate areas where only one racial group or sometimes subgroup may live and own property, including property used for business purposes.

The distribution of South Africa's people is marked not only by urban concentration and large areas of sparse population but also by sharp regional differences. Nearly four-fifths of the Coloreds live in Cape Province, and nearly one-fourth live in Cape Town and its immediate vicinity, the area of their origin. Over four-fifths of the Indians live in Natal, especially in and near Durban and Pietermaritzburg. Few Coloreds live in Natal or the Orange Free State. Small concentrations of Indians live on the Witwatersrand, in small Transvaal towns, and in Cape Town and Port Elizabeth, but virtually none in the Orange Free State.

Africans (like whites) are more widely distributed, although large numbers remain concentrated in areas of early settlement. Africans moving south along the Indian Ocean and white trekkers moving east and northward up the coast in the latter half of the eighteenth century were both seeking areas of satisfactory rainfall as well as vacant land. The westerly rain-bearing winds from the Indian Ocean make a pattern of rainfall that is heaviest—30 to 50 inches a year—along the eastern coast (and in a few southern areas of Cape Province), decreasing steadily as one moves to the desert areas of the west. The area in the general vicinity of East London, where Africans and whites met in the 1770's, is still known as the Border. The African reserves of the Ciskei, in the region of East London, and the Transkei, farther to the east, are heavily populated rural areas. Despite favorable rainfall, these reserves are "vast rural slums," in Leo Marquard's phrase; the land is eroded and overstocked, and productivity is low.[18] At any time, half or more of the adult males may be away working in white areas.

About 38 per cent of the African population—3,652,000—lived in tribal reserves or "Bantu areas" in 1957. These areas included about 12.9 per cent of the land of South Africa. An almost equally large number of Africans—about 3,261,000 or 35 per cent of the African population—lived in "white rural areas" (in official language), where many work on white-owned farms. African farm workers are widely scattered, but not many have reached the western area of Cape Province.

Like westerners in the United States, neither whites nor Africans appear to be dismayed by distance. Vacation trips from the Witwatersrand to the Natal coast or even to the southern Cape coast (if not the other way around) are not uncommon. The most regular white travelers are senior officials of the government who migrate each South African summer from Pretoria, the administrative capital (via Bloemfontein, the judicial capital, or Kimberley, the most direct surface route), to Cape Town, the legislative capital, where Parliament is in session during the pleasant summer months of January through April as well as May or June.

The most inveterate travelers are the Africans, although their movement is subject to a complex pattern of administrative regulations designed to control the flow of labor. Among those traveling regularly are workers who have short-term contracts in the mines and others

[18] *The Peoples and Policies of South Africa* (3d ed.; Cape Town: Oxford University Press, 1962), p. 39.

who migrate without their families from the Transkei and Ciskei, for example, to western Cape Province.

For one racial group, the Indians, South Africa is a compartmentalized country. Indians are forbidden to move between provinces except with special permit. Late in 1962, the Nationalist government made a relatively liberal innovation: when a family plans a trip, instead of each member obtaining a permit, the family's head may now obtain one permit for the whole group.

ECONOMIC STRENGTH AND VULNERABILITY

South Africa's economy has sources of strength and resilience, but it is highly vulnerable to internal and external circumstances over which it has only partial control. The economy is fairly mature and well-balanced (although white and nonwhite earnings are grossly disproportionate), rich in gold and other minerals, and highly industrialized. It has a well-developed structure of transportation and power and a highly trained class of managers and technicians. On the other hand, the relative prosperity of the country generally and of manufacturing in particular depends to a large extent upon the continued profitability of gold. The avoidance of economic stagnation and the continuation of a high rate of economic growth depend also upon foreign capital investment and expanded foreign trade. The economy's basic dependence, however, is upon poorly paid nonwhite labor and the maintenance of racial order. The intensification of hostile pressures at home or abroad would increase existing uncertainty and discourage further investment. And any serious or prolonged racial disturbance could lead to economic collapse.

South African politics and racial tensions have resulted in slowdowns in the flow of foreign capital, but thus far South Africa's economic attractions have repeatedly overcome these setbacks. During the decade after World War II, economic expansion was rapid, especially because of new gold fields in the "Far West Rand" and the Orange Free State. Foreign investment slowed down but later resumed following the National Party's electoral victories in 1948 and 1953. With the coming of a period of consolidation in the mid-1950's, the rate of advance became sluggish, although the economy continued to grow. Sharpeville greatly aggravated the apprehension of foreign investors. On the single day of March 30, 1960, when a state of emergency was declared, the aggregate value of shares on the Johannesburg stock exchange fell by £70,000,000 ($196,000,000), gold shares losing 5 per cent of their market value.[19] A large volume of capital left the country during the year, and the outsurge was renewed in March 1961, when Dr. Verwoerd withdrew his request for continued membership in the Commonwealth. Meanwhile, the government had imposed stringent exchange control measures and import restrictions. In mid-1961, despite earlier assurances, the government restricted the repatriation of certain categories of foreign capital for the first time in South Africa's history.

During the Republic's first year, South Africa's balance of payments position recovered rapidly because of these measures, the setting of new records in gold production (from 11,500,000 fine ounces in 1951 to about 21,400,000 in 1960), the growth in the size and diversity of the export trade, and the appearance of political stability. In August 1962, the country's gold and foreign exchange reserves reached a fourteen-year high. Dr. T. E. Donges, the Minister of Finance, was able to speak with confidence on October 2, 1962, when he described in Washington, D.C., the Republic's "capacity to withstand economic shocks and weather financial storms." [20]

South Africa was the West's "most reliable ally" in Africa, said Dr. Donges, and it contributed strategic materials to the free world. It produced two-thirds of the world's gold output (excluding the Soviet Union, whose output was estimated at not more than two-thirds of South Africa's). In 1960, he said, South Africa had the world's highest production of chrome ore, platinum, and gem diamonds, the second highest of asbestos and antimony ore, and the third highest of manganese ore, vanadium ore, industrial diamonds, and uranium, and it was among the first ten producers of a number of other materials. South Africa was among the countries from which the United States bought critical materials in its post-World War II stock-piling program. Professor Vernon McKay has warned, however, against "the tendency to exaggerate the vital need of the United States for these raw materials." [21] As a supplier of these materials, South Africa is probably expendable.

South Africa's production of base metals, most of them mined for export, has been strongly affected by world politics. Production of

[19] Peter Calvocoressi, *South Africa and World Opinion* (London: Oxford University Press, 1961), p. 26.

[20] *South Africa and the Free World*, address by Dr. T. E. Donges, issued by Information Service of South Africa.

[21] Vernon McKay, *Africa in World Politics* (New York: Harper & Row, 1963), p. 277.

certain metals fell during the 1930's, especially when the Soviet Union dumped large quantities on the world market, and rose to high levels during World War II and the later period of stock piling.

On the other hand, South Africa's search for self-sufficiency since World War I has been aided greatly by vast resources of coal, the most cheaply mined in the world. Fortunately located near the gold and diamond fields, coal provides cheap power in the virtual absence of hydroelectricity. (Uranium plus reactor technology makes possible the development of atomic power.) Coal is also important for the government-sponsored iron and steel industry. By 1952, South Africa met nearly two-thirds of its own steel needs; in 1959 it exported steel.

In seeking self-sufficiency, the government is continuing its traditionally active role in the economy. The colonial governments before 1910 supplied capital for the building of the railways. Beginning in the 1920's, Afrikaner nationalist governments sponsored industrial development, in part for motives of political independence, in part to provide jobs and economic opportunities for Afrikaans labor and management. During and since World War II, the government sought self-sufficiency for purposes of defense; more recently an important motive has been internal white security. By increasing the amount of public investment, especially since 1960, the government has also sought to stimulate more rapid economic growth and thus to offset sluggishness in the private sector. South Africa was able from its own internal capital formation, Dr. Donges said in October 1962, to achieve an annual increase in real income of about 2 per cent per capita. But for a higher rate of growth, he said, South Africa needed foreign investment.

The state largely owns and controls not only the railways and the iron and steel industry but also the airways, major irrigation works, radio broadcasting, electricity enterprises, and factories that produce oil from coal, insecticides, and fertilizers. Since acquiring ammunition factories in 1956, the Defense Department has claimed self-sufficiency in the production of rifles, machine guns, antitank rockets, and three-inch aircraft rockets. A ten-year plan announced in 1960 envisaged a total investment of more than $1,400,000,000 for further expansion of the public sector. For example, the government's thirty-year Orange River Project of hydroelectricity and irrigation, on which preliminary work is to begin in 1963, is expected to cost $119,000,000 in its first phase, scheduled for completion by 1968. One of the dams to be built will become the world's largest.

The dynamic expansion of South Africa's economy since World War
II has been most evident in the growth of manufacturing, which has
surpassed both mining and agriculture in contributing to the country's
income. Manufacturing has expanded mainly in response to the demand of local consumers, and now nearly everything needed in
modern society can be produced in South Africa. However, exports
of manufactured products as a group are still not sufficient to pay for
the importation of the materials and machinery that are essential to
South African manufacturing. The seriousness of the imbalance resulting from the dependence of manufacturing industry on credit
balances earned abroad by other products is a subject of continuing
controversy. New foreign markets—in Africa, if possible—could end
the imbalance. Meanwhile, one competent observer, pointing out that
the percentage of the credit balance derived from the precious-
mineral industries increased from 60 per cent in 1955 to about 70 per
cent in 1960, has concluded that "a serious set-back" in gold mining
"could result in a virtual collapse of the economy of South Africa." [22]

Inevitably, gold will be exhausted in time, and the consequences for
South Africa will be profound. If new gold fields are discovered or if
the price of gold is raised (an unlikely event), prosperity will be
prolonged; otherwise, gold mining may face a serious decline in the
next fifteen to twenty years.[23] Meanwhile, South Africa has been
sheltered from depression abroad by the virtual assurance that the
United States will buy its entire production at a price of at least $35
per ounce. Gold mining is vulnerable, however, to a number of possible developments (in addition to the extremely unlikely and disastrous event of a lowered price of gold): steadily rising production
costs, the serious decline in a few years in the price of uranium (a
by-product of gold mining), the gradually declining importance of
gold in international monetary affairs, and competitive pressures for
higher African wage levels.

Mining and industrialization are particularly important, and the
drive toward expanded industrialization is especially pressing, in part
because of the general poverty of agriculture. Only about 6 per cent
of the whole country is cultivated, and an estimated 85 per cent is not
even arable. Agricultural productivity is low, the soil is generally
poor, erosion (before World War II the most severe in the world) is

[22] F. P. Spooner, *South African Predicament* (London: Jonathan Cape, 1960),
p. 188.
[23] *Ibid.*, p. 197.

a major problem, rainfall is irregular, and droughts occur periodically. Agriculture remains an important enterprise, actively employing about 1,800,000 persons (of whom three-quarters are Africans) outside the African reserves. Thus, it employs more than twice the number engaged in manufacturing and three times the number in mining. However, it accounts for only about 12 per cent of the national income. Moreover, its major portion derives from pastoral or livestock production, particularly wool. Wool is South Africa's second most valuable export. Among agricultural products, fruit and wine follow it in value.

Since World War II there has been some expansion in agriculture. South Africa has become nearly self-sufficient in wheat (some has been imported from the United States in the last few years) as well as in corn, which provides the African's staple diet in the form of ground corn or mealie meal. White leaders and professional experts frequently deplore the long-continuing exodus of whites from rural areas and stress the need for improving agricultural productivity. There is little likelihood, however, that South Africa can develop large-scale or intensive farming.

Industrialization is especially needed for dealing with the badly overcrowded condition of the eroded and impoverished African reserves. Most of the inhabitants of these areas live at a subsistence level, relying on primitive agriculture, on their livestock, and also on cash earned by migrant labor. There is general agreement that the reserves must be rehabilitated and that industry must be developed either within or near them to attract surplus population (perhaps about half of their total population) from the land. In 1955, after five years of study, the Tomlinson Commission on the Socio-Economic Development of the Bantu Areas recommended vigorous action without delay: it recommended that $28,000,000 should be spent annually for ten years in order to promote industrialization within the reserves, that whites should be allowed to invest private capital in the reserves, and that progress should be made toward consolidating the 264 scattered reserves around 7 Bantu "heartlands," where separate political development could take place. Even if maximum progress were made, the commission concluded, there would still be some 6,400,000 Africans in the white sector at the end of the century.

Critics described the recommended expenditure as far from adequate. The government, on the other hand, rejected it as far too large and also rejected the recommendation regarding white investment. It declared that the official policy was to assist Africans to establish industries within the reserves and to encourage white industrialists to develop industries outside the borders of the reserves.

The government has moved slowly in making detailed investigations and plans, and industrial activity near the reserves has been minor and scattered. Most of the reserves are distant from the main industrial and urban centers and largely bypassed by lines of water supply and electric power and by railways and main roads.[24] Notable exceptions are the reserves in the Tugela River Basin, about 150 miles from Durban but near the main facilities that link Durban and Johannesburg. Africans lack the capital resources needed for industrial development and must depend upon the government's Bantu Development Corporation. (The corporation's assistance thus far has gone mainly to retail stores.) Industries already established by Africans are limited largely to the simpler crafts of basketmaking, weaving, woodworking, and furniture manufacture. A number of new factories that have been built near the reserves are devoted mainly to processing agricultural products or local natural resources, though large textile and clothing factories have been established at King William's Town, near the Transkei, and in the Tugela River Basin.

The mainly English-speaking business community criticizes the policy of so-called separate development as fundamentally unrealistic and potentially destructive. Harry Oppenheimer, chairman of the Anglo American Corporation, has described as "self-defeating" the policies of the government "which aim at social and racial solutions at the cost of economic development." He has pointed to the example of Europe, where "belligerent nationalisms . . . have given way to the cooperation of the Common Market," and urged South Africa's economic expansion as a single unit.[25] Among other economic critics are some white trade unions, particularly unions of garmentworkers, who have protested against the competition of cheap labor.

South African prosperity generally and, indirectly, the development of the African reserves—whether proceeding upon the government's or Oppenheimer's premises—depend largely upon South Africa's external trading and financial relations. Relations with Great Britain continue to be the most important and have been virtually unaffected by the

[24] For this and other data in the text, see T. J. D. Fair and L. P. Green, "Development of the 'Bantu Homelands,'" in *Optima*, Sept. 1961, pp. 7–19.

[25] Annual statement to the Anglo American Corporation. The full text is in the *Star*, June 7, 1962. The corporation is the largest mining finance house in southern Africa. Its title has been a misnomer since 1917, when the original American participation was largely bought out.

Commonwealth break. "Our economies are now largely interdepend-ent," Prime Minister Macmillan told the South African Parliament on February 3, 1960. "You export to us raw materials and food—and, of course, gold—and we in return send you consumer goods and capital equipment. We take a third of all your exports and we supply a third of all your imports." [26]

Approximately another third of South Africa's exports went to the following countries early in 1962: the European Common Market countries (mainly raw materials), the Federation of Rhodesia and Nyasaland (a major buyer of manufactured goods), and the United States. Excluding gold, the United States took about 12 per cent of South Africa's exports: uranium oxide (bought jointly with the United Kingdom under an agreement expiring in 1970) and, of lesser impor-tance, wool, diamonds, copper, and lobster tails. Under legislation enacted in the United States in 1962, South Africa was expected to receive a basic quota of 20,000 short tons of sugar a year.

After Great Britain, the United States is South Africa's most impor-tant supplier. In 1961 it provided about 16 per cent of total imports, including machinery, metal parts, chemicals, and automobiles. It is also an increasingly important source of capital, although still far less important than the British source. Much of South Africa's ma-terial progress had been financed by British capital, Macmillan said in February 1960, pointing out that at the end of 1956 nearly two-thirds of foreign capital investment was British. From then until the end of 1960, the proportion declined from 62 to 58.5 per cent. Mean-while, the American-owned share rose from 12.3 to 13.7 per cent. Over the longer period of 1950–1961, American investment rose from about $140,000,000 to about $600,000,000. This amount represents about three-fifths of all American capital investment that has been made on the African continent.

Trade with countries that have endorsed economic sanctions against South Africa or imposed boycotts on trade has been of minor impor-tance; with African states (other than the Federation of Rhodesia and Nyasaland), it has been almost negligible. But boycotts may be damaging if, by spreading, they spoil the climate of profitable invest-ment and South Africa's current standing as a good credit risk (at least for fairly short-term loans). Official boycotts of South African goods had been imposed by the following countries, according to the Minis-

[26] The text of the speech is in Calvocoressi, *South Africa and World Opinion*, pp. 45–56.

ter of Economic Affairs in the House of Assembly on January 23, 1962: the Soviet Union, Communist China, India, Malaya (excluding Singapore), Antigua, Barbados, Jamaica, British Guiana, Surinam, and (in Africa) Ethiopia, Ghana, Liberia, Nigeria, Sierra Leone, and Sudan. During 1962, Tanganyika and the Somali Republic imposed boycotts. Exports to the countries named by the minister were valued at about $24,900,400 in January–September 1960; they declined to less than $4,000,000 in January–September 1961. Of the African countries mentioned, the most substantial decline occurred in the case of Ghana, whose purchases from South Africa were about $3,150,000 in January–September 1960 and about $42,500 in January–September 1961. (The *South African Digest* has carried a report that "two African countries who led the fight for sanctions" have bought South African mining machinery via England.) Outside the Western countries that are South Africa's major trading partners, the area of special economic importance is the Middle East, in particular Iran, which supplies South Africa with much of its crude oil.

The effect on South Africa of external competition or sanctions may become aggravated by the fact that the most vulnerable occupations have the highest proportion of nonwhite employees. For each white, mining employs 7.5 nonwhites; agriculture, 6 nonwhites; and manufacturing, 2.5 nonwhites.[27] Wide unemployment in these sectors would be more likely to aggravate racial tensions than unemployment in transport and the public services (1 nonwhite to 1 white) and commerce (0.65 nonwhites to 1 white). Whites employed in the latter occupations, which are relatively sheltered from outside pressures, would be among the last to be affected by economic recession.

South Africa, in short, is vulnerable to foreign opinion, although more so to opinion that results in a drying up of capital than to opinion resulting in consumer boycotts. Further deterioration of race relations, or worse, would lead to such consequences. It is not an exaggeration to conclude that South Africa's economy is crucially dependent upon the continued quiescence of the urban African worker.

AFRICAN SOCIAL TRENDS: DIVERSITY AND UNITY

Contradictory trends both toward greater diversity and toward unity characterize South Africa's extraordinarily complex and rapidly changing social structure. The economic transformation of the country in the past half century has steadily increased the interdependence of

[27] Spooner, *South African Predicament,* p. 203.

whites and Africans and has resulted in the spread among Africans of Western material aspirations and cultural values. Economic change has also occasioned social disruption, which has been aggravated by racial discrimination and great cultural differences. On the other hand, the government, denying that Africans have permanent interests in so-called white areas, has sought to strengthen tribal diversity and traditional resistance to modern trends in order to prevent the growth of class consciousness or African nationalism. Under both foreign and domestic pressures, however, it also seeks to improve the living standards and public amenities of African workers and to promote industrial development in and near the African reserves.

If the dynamic development of a country-wide economy is assumed, the continued urbanization of Africans is "inevitable" (whether or not the country is multiracial or racially segmented), and the process of Westernization is "inexorable." [28] Diversity will inevitably continue to characterize an unpartitioned South Africa. What is uncertain is the effectiveness of diversity in delaying movement toward further consolidation of a common culture. Equally uncertain is the character of African leadership that will emerge under conditions of imposed racial separation.

Africans, unless their sense of identity is primarily Pan-African, African nationalist, or, in some instances, Communist, may identify themselves with one of hundreds of tribal groups. For its own purposes, the government under legislation enacted in 1959 for the "promotion of Bantu self-government" recognizes eight "national units" with which all Africans will be identified, regardless of whether they live inside or outside the reserves. Of these Africans (who are part of the wider group of some 70,000,000 Bantu who live in southern Africa), nearly nine-tenths fall within two major language groups, comprising six "national units." Within the Nguni language group are about three-fifths of the 10,808,000 Africans (1960) comprising three "national units": 3,423,000 Xhosa, 2,959,000 Zulu, and 301,000 Swazi.[29] Their reserves spread along the eastern coast: the Xhosa in the Ciskei

---

[28] D. H. Reader, *The Black Man's Portion* (Cape Town: Oxford University Press, 1961), p. 148; Ellen Hellmann, "The Application of the Concept of Separate Development to Urban Areas in the Union of South Africa," in Kenneth Kirkwood, ed., *African Affairs, Number One* (St. Antony's Papers, no. 10; London: Chatto & Windus, 1961), p. 146.

[29] Exact population figures for ethnic groups will not be available until 1964. The figures in the text are estimates (*House of Assembly Debates*, May 5, 1961, col. 5958, and Feb. 23, 1962, col. 1476).

and Transkei, the Zulu scattered throughout Natal, and the Swazi alongside Swaziland. The Sotho language group, the second largest, comprises over one-fourth of all Africans. It is grouped in three "national units": 1,089,000 South Sotho, 1,122,000 North Sotho, and 863,000 Tswana. Their reserves are, respectively, near Basutoland, centered in Sekhukhuneland in the northern Transvaal, and alongside Bechuanaland. The remaining 13 per cent include two language groups, each one a "national unit": Tsonga (366,000) and Venda (195,000), whose reserves are in the northernmost Transvaal. Other Africans are the Ndebele (209,000) in the southern Transvaal and about 280,000 who are not classified.

The values and institutions loosely described as tribal continue to have some importance, and the speed or slowness of their inevitable decline is difficult to forecast. The perpetuation of the migratory labor system helps to maintain ties between the African reserves and urban areas. Newer or unschooled townsmen, especially those in urban areas close to their homes of origin, often preserve "a 'tribal' type of moral conformism" and resist assimilation into urban society, although no ethnic or linguistic barriers stand in the way.[30] Governmental policies—for example, maximum use of vernaculars as instructional media, ethnic grouping in urban townships, the location of new housing at a long distance from urban centers, and increased powers for chiefs— may aid in preserving ethnic diversity and delay the acceptance of urban ways. Most educated Africans distrust these official policies, but many find themselves, in the words of ex-Chief Albert Luthuli, "in a real dilemma—our impulse is to be loyal to our chiefs, but we know full well that the Nationalists are turning more and more of them into their puppets."

Luthuli and many other Africans have desired "to preserve what is valuable in our heritage." Thus, Luthuli led in founding the Zulu Language and Cultural Society in the early 1930's; he has blamed collaboration with the government for its decline and eventual collapse.[31] In recent years, younger political leaders, influenced by the rise of independent African states, have more vigorously asserted the claims of African culture and tradition. On Africa Day 1958, ANC leaders appeared in tribal dress, though significantly in the dress of tribes other than their own.

[30] Philip Mayer, *Townsmen or Tribesmen: Conservatism and the Process of Urbanization in a South African City* (Cape Town: Oxford University Press, 1961), pp. 292–293.

[31] See Albert Luthuli, *Let My People Go: An Autobiography* (Johannesburg: Collins, 1962), pp. 37–38, 74 (including quotation in preceding paragraph).

Tribal culture, rooted in the land, has been declining in importance for more than half a century as African labor has flowed to white farms and the mines and as industrialization and growth of population have brought into being a landless African proletariat. Overcrowding on reserves that amount to less than 13 per cent of the land, the pressure of taxation, and the attraction of economic opportunity have helped to fill the demand for cheap and unskilled labor. From its side, the administration uses the pass laws and administrative controls to regulate the flow.

Poorly paid laborers and their families who live or squat on white farms have only tenuous ties to the tribal areas, and their opportunities for entering the urban labor market are severely restricted. Migrant laborers, universally used in mining but also relied upon for other employment, maintain family ties in the reserves but are exposed to the attractions of urban society and often seek to qualify for permanent residence. On the other hand, African migrants are often concentrated in bachelor quarters, where they tend to be isolated from the life of the urban African community. In Langa outside Cape Town, for example, 18,311 African men, of whom 12,390 were married, were housed in bachelor quarters in January 1963. There is some evidence that extremist underground groups have been particularly active in this concentration.

Of Africans working in urban areas, the Tomlinson Commission estimated that about two-thirds (or about 1,500,000) were "permanently" urbanized. This proportion appears to have been growing. Meanwhile, marriages have been taking place between persons from different tribal backgrounds. More stringent influx control policies may be proving somewhat successful, however, in "freezing" the number of Africans permanently resident in urban areas.[32]

The legal inability of Africans to acquire land outside the reserves and their inability to accumulate much capital have given rise to a position that Professor Gwendolen Carter has described as classically Marxist, with the white group controlling both the government and the instruments of production and a landless proletariat providing the bulk of the labor power.[33] The classical position is aggravated by racial discrimination. Virtually all African labor is confined to unskilled and semiskilled jobs, and the gap between skilled and unskilled wage

[32] Hellmann, "The Application of the Concept of Separate Development," pp. 130–131.

[33] Gwendolen M. Carter, "Multi-racialism in Africa," *International Affairs*, Oct. 1960.

rates (in most trades, four to five times higher for skilled than un-skilled workers; in mining, eight to ten times higher) is much greater than in countries having a more homogeneous labor force.

Within the white group, there are contradictory attitudes regarding economic opportunities for the proletarian group and the desirability of a growing African middle class. One observer has noted that the "curious phenomenon" of the division of economic and political power between the English and the Afrikaners is "explicable by the satisfaction that the giant mineowners feel with a government that guarantees them a supply of cheap, migrant black labor."[34] Nevertheless, certain mining enterprises attempted experimentally, until stopped by the Nationalist government in 1952, to provide married quarters for up to 10 per cent of their African workers on the new Orange Free State gold mines. Manufacturing industries, more strongly than mining, have favored the growth of a stabilized labor force and better utilization of African skills. Some half-million African industrial workers receive higher wages than do miners. Probably well over half of these industrial workers are semiskilled (especially in newer industries which are not inhibited by customary labor practices), and a small proportion are skilled, though not so graded.

A small African middle class began to appear in urban areas during the 1930's and continued to grow slowly in size and affluence after 1948. No reliable estimate can be made of its size. Education is one guide since it is the prime determinant of upward mobility and middle-class status. The review below of data on education and on occupations dependent at least partly upon educational qualifications indicates the size of various groups having social status outside the tribal structure and also the size of particular groups to whom either African organizations or the government may make special appeals. Another guide to middle-class status is home ownership. Vast housing projects have been built partly by the Nationalist government and still more by municipal authorities. Although existing freehold rights to land have been ended, in some developments Africans may build their own homes or purchase homes by installments over thirty years, acquiring a statutory title similar to a long lease.

South Africa's Africans are often described as better educated than

---

[34] Julius Lewin, *Politics and Law in South Africa: Essays on Race Relations* (London: Merlin Press, 1963), p. 16. Of course, a fuller explanation of the division of economic and political power, which both sides have sought to overcome, lies in historical circumstances.

any other African group on the continent, though this generalization is now less accurate than in the past. Marquard has estimated that probably about half the adult African population has a very elementary understanding of either English or Afrikaans or both. In 1955, according to the Tomlinson Commission, about 540,000 Africans in African areas and 1,260,000 in white areas were literate in one or another of these languages. From 1946 to 1959, official estimates of the percentage of the African population that was literate rose from 21.2 to 35. By 1962, the following numbers of Africans had met formal standards of achievement (according to statements made in Parliament on March 2 and April 27): 295,600 had passed Standard VI (equivalent to the eighth grade); 75,000 had passed Standard VIII; 15,200 had obtained a matriculation certificate or its equivalent (comparable to graduation from high school); and about 2,000 had university degrees. The government schools employed 25,800 African teachers in May 1959. As the statistics above suggest, the formal qualifications of the average teacher were low.

Other African groups whose size indicated "progress and development" were listed by the Minister of Bantu Administration in May 1959: 7,000 businessmen who had their own shops and trading licenses, 7,000 nurses, 12,000 policemen, 70 postmasters, and 1,265 other "public servants," presumably clerks and other white-collar workers.[35] About 50 Africans are lawyers. Estimates of the number of medical doctors range from 70 to 100. At the time of the Tomlinson Commission report, there were no African dentists. Publications of the South African Information Service provide much detail about "a new, privileged Bantu middle class" in the urban areas, where rising incomes make possible purchases of an increasing amount of quality goods in a growing number of Bantu-owned stores.

Official policy has aided new African entrepreneurs by giving them exclusive rights to business opportunities in urban African areas, but official policy is tending to limit the activities of these entrepreneurs in order to divert African capital to the reserves. Paul Mosaka, who has developed a funeral insurance company near Johannesburg, a dry-cleaning business, and a garage and who wished to establish branches of his insurance company in other cities, was told in 1962 that Africans in the future would be allowed to establish only one business and only in the area where they lived. "It is not the intention,"

[35] South African Information Service, *The Progress of the Bantu Peoples toward Nationhood*, no. 1 (n.d.), p. 18; see also no. 3, pp. 3–4.

Mosaka was informed, "to create capitalistic enterprises in White areas." [36]

Bantu or separatist church leaders, who are often looked upon with condescension or contempt by educated Africans, make up a group of leaders whose influence may be growing, especially in the absence of other outlets available to persons with a talent for leadership and ambition for prestige and power. The number of Bantu churches, found in both rural and urban areas, increased from about 30 in 1913 to 800 in 1948 and to about 2,000 in 1960. Dr. Bengt Sundkler has described the pre-World War II period as one of protest against white domination but the postwar period as one tending toward accommodation. After the war, some enterprising church leaders attained business success, enhancing their status among educated Africans. Education itself has become more acceptable to this group, partly because the Bantu Education Act removed fears of missionary influence.

The 1950's saw "a marked rapprochement" in some areas between local chief and local prophet and a readiness on the part of the latter to take over the authority lost by some weakened chiefs.[37] Separatist leaders generally shun politics and support apartheid, but their influence tends to be antiwhite and strongly nationalist. The number of their followers is uncertain—only ten Bantu churches were officially recognized in 1960—but is less than the number of African adherents of other recognized churches. Some 4,000,000 Africans are still pagan, however, and among them the influence of the Bantu churches is potentially great, particularly those branches which are "developing steadily in the direction of a synthesis with the pagan religion of African tribalism." [38]

THE PRESS AND OTHER MEDIA

For most Afrikaners and Africans, the press serves distinctive and contrasting functions. Probably three-fifths or more of the Afrikaners read only the Afrikaans press, which for the most part has been an instrument of nationalism, enhancing the cohesiveness of the Afrikaner community and largely insulating its readers from the liberal, cosmo-

[36] Muriel Horrell, *A Survey of Race Relations in South Africa: 1962* (Johannesburg: South African Institute of Race Relations, 1963), p. 167.

[37] Bengt G. M. Sundkler, *Bantu Prophets in South Africa* (2d ed.; London: Oxford University Press, 1961), pp. 296–297, 307–308, 310, 312.

[38] Quoted from an article by the Anglican Bishop of Johannesburg in the *Star*, Aug. 30, 1962.

politan, and antigovernment attitudes to be found in the English press. To a degree hardly equaled by the press in any other Western country, all five Afrikaans daily newspapers, beginning with the publication of *Die Burger* in Cape Town in 1915, are closely allied to political party leadership. For Africans, in contrast, the press has been largely an influence for the overriding of tribal differences and the promotion of both African nationalism and Westernization. Newspapers intended mainly for Africans have been published in the vernacular or in English or in both since the appearance of *Imvo Zabantsundu* (*Native Opinion*) in Xhosa and English in eastern Cape Province in 1884. In the past decades, English has become the prevailing medium in the so-called Bantu press, and African readers of this press and of newspapers that are directed mainly at English-speaking whites have grown steadily in number.

It is difficult to exaggerate the degree to which leading Nationalists see the influence of the English press at home and abroad as baleful. All thirteen English daily newspapers are critical of the government, although some have also been severely critical of the United Party. The English press, which has powerful financial support, notably from mining finance companies, easily surpasses the Afrikaans press in competition for readers. Its daily circulation in 1959 was 680,000; that of the Afrikaans press was only 168,000. The proportion of Afrikaners who read the English press may become smaller as a result of the lowering of standards of English comprehension among the increasing number of children being educated in Afrikaans-medium schools. Meanwhile, the government has sought indirectly to curb the English press through a variety of pressures that have amounted, in the opinion of that press, to attempts at intimidation. Pressures have ranged from the inquiries of a Press Commission, which was established in 1950 and published its first report in 1962, to ominous threats of future governmental control. The organized publishers made an effort early in 1962 to ward off such control by adopting a "Code of Conduct" embodying accepted standards of journalism enforced by a Board of Reference. Press coverage has been limited also by legislation prohibiting the reproduction of statements by banned persons (see p. 552) and by the official exclusion of the press from certain African areas.

Although historically more concerned about the influence of the English press on Afrikaners than on Africans, the government has become increasingly concerned about the latter. By the end of World

War II, 150,000 to 400,000 Africans had the newspaper habit, according to an estimate, made by Edward Roux, that may have been conservative. Because of interest in continental African developments and the growing political consciousness of women as well as advancement in literacy, the number of African newspaper readers probably has tripled.

Africans have founded and owned as well as edited a small number of newspapers, but often these papers have failed to survive (the organ of the ANC, for example, appeared from 1912 to about 1935) or have been taken over by white enterprise and management. *Imvo* and *Ilanga lase Natal* (The Natal Sun), the latter founded in 1904, were among the newspapers purchased by a nonprofit and white-financed company established in 1931 and known as the Bantu Press. These papers had a weekly circulation in 1959 of 14,000 and 42,000, respectively. (Recently, an Afrikaans press group bought *Imvo*.) The Bantu Press itself began the publication in 1932 of the *Bantu World,* a semiweekly written in English and the vernacular under African editorship. Because of growing demand in the Witwatersrand area and the wider use of English, the renamed *World* became a daily newspaper in January 1962, the first daily for Africans, and began appearing entirely in English. Taken over by an English press group, which hopes eventually to make a profit, it has been selling 50,000 copies daily. Two other widely circulated publications aimed at nonwhites are the weekly *Post* (Johannesburg)—about 81,000 in 1959—and the monthly *Drum*, both under white editors and ownership but staffed almost entirely by nonwhites. *Drum* sold about 82,000 copies within South Africa in 1959. An impartial readership survey reported in 1963 that about 13 Africans read each copy of *Post* and *Drum*.

The appeal of the publications above has been partly due, in the past, to their voicing of African grievances. The *Post* and *Drum*, for example, have published exposés of oppressive activity; but *Drum*, and to a lesser extent the *Post*, have largely given up campaigns featuring such stories. The hardest hitting publication, however, has been the Communist-line *New Age*. When it was banned in 1962 (see below, p. 553), it claimed a circulation of about 20,000, with 90 per cent of it among nonwhites. *Contact,* a fortnightly that supports the Liberal Party, has been equally hard-hitting but less widely circulated.

White-financed publications for nonwhites, other than *New Age* and *Contact* and several smaller antigovernment periodicals, have been accused since Sharpeville of becoming hesitant and fearful of offending the government. Greater caution is due in part to uncertainties and restraints introduced by recent legislation. On the other hand, some English newspapers read mainly by whites, notably the *Rand Daily Mail* and the Port Elizabeth *Evening Post,* not only have continued to attack the government with eloquence under brilliant and courageous editors but also have made notable efforts to improve their coverage of nonwhite opinion. An indication of changing attitudes (or, as some Africans have said, increasing appreciation of African purchasing power) has been the fact that most English newspapers have followed the example of the *Rand Daily Mail* in changing their usage from "Native" to "African." In doing this in April 1962, the *Star* of Johannesburg, which comes closest to being South Africa's *New York Times,* departed from its usage of seventy-five years.

The government's policy of emphasizing instruction through the vernacular may conceivably reduce future demand for English publications. Meanwhile, Afrikaans capital has established a number of ostensibly neutral (in effect, progovernment) periodicals that compete for African readers by appealing to urban tastes. The monthlies *Bona,* issued separately in Xhosa, Sotho, and Zulu, and *Zonk,* for example, had circulations of 91,000 and 58,000, respectively, in 1959. Their use in schools appears to be officially encouraged, and circulation there is allegedly subsidized.

The appeals that a publication is inclined to make in competing for urban African readers are to be seen in *Elethu,* a Zulu newspaper begun in 1962 largely with Afrikaans capital, including the financial support of leading Nationalists and members of the cabinet. The paper has used pictures of Luthuli and reported the award of the Nobel Peace Prize to him. In February 1963, changing its name to *Elethu Mirror,* it began to appear in English and was criticized in the Afrikaans press as "generously provided with half-clad Bantu women— and with criticism of the Government." The changes were defended as necessary solely to meet competition.[39]

Radio, said the Tomlinson Commission, is a medium of many possibilities for the diffusion of information to the Bantu and also a medium of unpredictable dangers. Traditionally, radiobroadcasting, a state monopoly conducted by the South African Broadcasting Corporation, has been careful to avoid political controversy, and it has

[39] *Press Digest,* Feb. 28, 1963, p. 83.

not been used for the indoctrination of Africans. Although the SABC broadcast political speeches during the 1953 election campaign and speeches by the Prime Minister and the leader of the Opposition before the 1960 referendum, it did not do so in 1958 or 1961. Since 1961, outside observers as well as antigovernment critics have found much evidence, both in staff changes and in programing, that the SABC is being transformed into a propaganda organ.[40]

The number of African listeners has undoubtedly grown since 1955, when the Tomlinson Commission estimated that Africans probably owned no more than 3,000 radios. The commission also reported that a rediffusion service established in 1952 in part of the Johannesburg area, providing a loudspeaker tuned to the SABC, had gained 9,800 subscribers within two years. In 1961 the SABC began an expensive five-year program to add to its two noncommercial stations (one in English and one in Afrikaans) and its bilingual commercial station, full-time stations in seven African languages directed to separate areas. A longer-range program is under way to establish a country-wide network of FM, or frequency-modulation, stations, thus avoiding interference from stations outside South Africa and also enabling the government to make special broadcasts to local tribal groups. A United Party critic has charged that the government's aim is to supply to Africans radios that can receive programs only within an area of about 50 miles. In 1962, Radio Tanganyika, which could be heard clearly in Cape Town, began broadcasting daily news bulletins, including statements by South African opposition leaders both inside and outside the Republic. Of particular concern to the government is the likely establishment of radio stations in the High Commission Territories and, as the Afrikaans press has suggested, the possible necessity of jamming.

One of the many media through which American popular culture continuously influences South Africa is the cinema, which is subject to fairly strict censorship. White South Africans probably spend substantially more time at the movies than do Americans. There are few cinemas for nonwhites, however, although in 1955 one company

---

[40] In Oct. 1962, in order to give "correct and authoritative information," the SABC began a series of programs on communism and liberalism, using some of the evidence in the earlier treason trial and the government's expert witness on communism in that trial. In these programs, said the *Star*, the SABC had become "a crude mouthpiece of the extreme Right" (*Star*, Oct. 24, 26, and editorial on Oct. 30, 1962).

operated thirteen in African urban areas. The criteria for censorship are many and wide. Films may be banned or cut or, if released, placed in categories that prohibit their exhibition to Africans or Coloreds or to other persons under a prescribed age between 12 and 18. For example, in 1962 *Gone with the Wind* could be shown to whites of any age or to Coloreds but not to any Africans; and *West Side Story* could be shown to whites over 12 years of age but not to Africans or Coloreds.[41]

Considerations similar to those underlying the censorship of films underlie the censorship of imported books and periodicals (extended in 1963 to domestically produced reading matter other than newspapers) and the government's refusal to permit the introduction of television. A less significant but sometimes cited reason for the government's opposition to television is that programing would be complicated by the necessity of providing service in two languages, if not more.

The Political Process

FORMAL STRUCTURE

South Africa's political institutions enable a strong and disciplined political party like the National Party to exercise virtually unlimited political power. Executive authority is concentrated in the political leader of the lower house of Parliament. He becomes Prime Minister, selects the members of the cabinet (the government), and has power to dissolve the lower house, to which he and the cabinet are technically responsible. Like the British Parliament, the South African Parliament—composed of the State President, who is the titular head of state, the House of Assembly, and the Senate—is legally sovereign. But unlike majorities in the British Parliament, the Nationalist majority is undeterred by constitutional convention. Nor is national power, which extends to all levels of a unitary system, restrained by federal limitations.

Only one element in the constitution is entrenched and presumably beyond the majority's reach—the official equality of the Afrikaans and English languages. To alter this equality, a two-thirds majority of both houses in joint session would be necessary. But recent constitutional

[41] For the full 1962 list, see *House of Assembly Debates,* Feb. 5, 1963, cols. 767–770.

history (described below) has demonstrated that the limitation is one of expediency and exists at the sufferance of the parliamentary majority.

The Republic has retained the political institutions of the Union. These institutions, in existence for fifty-one years, followed the British model and grew directly from the experience of nearly sixty years of representative government in Cape Colony. The basic constitutional document of the Union was the South Africa Act of 1909. Although drafted by a South African constitutional convention, it was enacted by the British Parliament and was never reenacted in South Africa and never given an Afrikaans version. The Republic of South Africa Constitution Act of 1961 was based on the 1909 Act. In introducing the bill, Prime Minister Verwoerd said that Nationalists had hoped "to create a constitution built on the lines of the republican constitutions of the past." [42] That they would base the new constitution on the South Africa Act "almost seemed impossible" until about a year earlier, he said, but he was prepared to make concessions for the sake of white unity and the welding of both language sections into one nation. A major "sacrifice" was the provision for a President whose position would be the same as that of the Queen rather than a President like Paul Kruger or Marthinus Steyn of the old Boer republics, who combined the roles of head of state and head of government. Existing constitutional conventions would continue, said Dr. Verwoerd, although much of Parliament's ceremony and procedure was not "characteristic or inherent" in republicanism.

The Republic's parliamentary institutions closely resemble those of Great Britain but differ in some minor respects. Major similarities, based on statute or convention, are the President's appointment of the Prime Minister and of ministers as noted above, the limitation of the President to acting only on the advice of the cabinet,[43] the necessity for each minister to be a member (within three months) of one or the other house of Parliament, the collective responsibility of the cabinet, its retention of office only so long as it has the confidence of the lower house, the cabinet's exclusive power to initiate taxation and appropriation measures, the President's summoning of Parliament at least once

[42] For Dr. Verwoerd's explanation of the bill, see *House of Assembly Debates,* Jan. 30, 1961, col. 323–351.

[43] The President, like his predecessor, the Governor-General, acts on the advice of the Executive Council. As in Great Britain, the council, which is in practice the cabinet, in theory included all past ministers. This anomaly was eliminated by the Republic of South Africa Constitution Act.

a year, and the power of the Prime Minister to bring about a dissolution before the statutory period of five years has expired. Within the lower house, the cabinet fully controls the legislative timetable, bills follow the British procedure in which discussion of principle during the "second reading" debate precedes the committee stage, the questioning of ministers occurs regularly, the Speaker's role is supposedly nonpartisan, and the leader of the Opposition is recognized as an alternative Prime Minister.

In recent years members of the Opposition have criticized the frequency with which ministers in replying to questions, particularly regarding bannings and the refusal of passports and entrance visas, have said that "it is not considered to be in the public interest to furnish reasons." Opposition members as well as neutral observers have also felt that Speakers since 1948 have not always met South Africa's traditionally high standards of impartiality. In 1958, in a break with tradition made once before during the wartime election, the Speaker was opposed in his constituency and actively campaigned there and elsewhere.

Unlike the practice in Britain, ministers may speak in either house; all ministers are members of the cabinet; and its size is prescribed by statute. Cabinet unanimity has not always prevailed over strong personalities, and on two occasions (in 1912 and 1927) the Prime Minister has resigned and then reconstituted his cabinet in order to get rid of a recalcitrant minister. Since 1948, however, no member of a Nationalist cabinet has publicly disagreed with a cabinet decision.

The main divergence from British practice is in the unparliamentary spirit that often characterizes Parliament. Many Nationalist leaders are lifelong parliamentarians, and some have been imbued with respect for parliamentary tradition. Nevertheless, the government's doctrinaire self-righteousness, backed by a phalanx of supporters who are inclined to equate dissent with treason, produces an atmosphere intolerant of criticism. Members of the Opposition, who may not openly express any sense of outrage, often feel a deep sense of suspicion and distrust of a government which uses parliamentary institutions to attain its own rather than public ends and which is determined never to be displaced from power. Informal consultation with leaders of the Opposition has been far less since 1948 than before. The Opposition itself, because of the nature of pending legislation or the speed with which bills are processed, has used obstructionist tactics, has broken off "pairing" arrangements on occasion, and has even boycotted the committee stage of a bill.

The bitterness expressed in the House of Assembly is the more remarkable because it emanates from a legislative body whose white
members would close ranks in the face of any imminent threat of racial
disorder. The Assembly's 160 members, all of whom are white, form a
fairly small group who meet in a congenial setting and generally enter
into the camaraderie of the lobbies. Even invective takes on a certain
warmth of familiarity. Yet Nationalist backbenchers have sometimes
exceeded the bounds of parliamentary interjection in their harassment
of critics, some of whom have replied in kind. During the second-
reading debate on the "Sabotage Bill" in May 1962, Nationalists not
only described one or more members of the Opposition as "stupid,"
"sick," and "half-mad" and as "liars," "clowns," "monkeys," and "political ducktails" but also as "saboteurs" and "traitors." [44] (Perhaps the
most unparliamentary comment was made by the Minister of Justice,
who replied to a speaker's question by saying, "Frankly I am not even
trying to follow your argument. . . . The plain fact is that you bore
me.") United Party members referred to individual Nationalists as
"stupid," "drunk," and "bullying," and one was recorded as saying,
"Shut up, you rat." Nearly all these interjections were challenged and
withdrawn at the insistence of the Speaker, but statements that leading Nationalists had been sympathetic to the Nazis went unchallenged.
Although tempers get hot, disorder like that which occurs in the
French National Assembly does not take place, however, in the House
of Assembly.

The debate on the "Sabotage Bill" was less heated than some debates
in previous years, but the substantive level of debate appears to have
declined. The House of Assembly has lost not only Sam Kahn, a
Communist whose repartee had enlivened proceedings and who was
expelled along with another Communist in 1952, but also the substantial contributions of five Labor Party members in 1958, the three
Natives' representatives in 1960, and ten of the eleven Progressives in
1961. The Progressives not returned to the House included Harry
Lawrence, one of the most experienced parliamentary debaters, and
also some of its ablest younger members.

The so-called constitutional crisis of 1951–1956 (see above, pp. 482–
483) illustrates the Nationalist government's persistence in moving
toward legislative goals without compromise but within a framework
of legal correctness. It argued that Parliament, having become sovereign with the passage of the Statute of Westminster in 1931, was no

[44] The debate is reported in the *House of Assembly Debates,* May 21–28, 1962.

longer bound by the entrenched-clause procedure of a two-thirds vote of all members of Parliament in joint session. (This procedure protected both nonwhite voting rights in the Cape and the equality of English and Afrikaans.) The Opposition replied that leading Nationalists had recognized the moral force of the guarantee in 1931, that the entrenched-clause procedure had been followed in removing Africans from the common roll in 1936, and that both legally and morally the guarantee was still in effect. In reply to accusations of constitutional immorality, the government insisted that it was merely following British practice and exercising parliamentary sovereignty in accordance with principles of majority rule. It also pointed to the 1937 Ndlwana case in which its view appeared to have been upheld.

During a period of emotional recrimination and mass protest, the following sequence of events occurred. In 1951 an ordinary act provided for the removal of the Colored voters from the common roll to a communal roll. The highest court unanimously held the act void because it did not follow the procedure for changing an entrenched clause. In 1952 an ordinary act provided that judgments of the highest court could be set aside by the "High Court of Parliament," that is, Parliament constituting itself as the highest tribunal. The highest court unanimously held this act void. In 1953 the government sought to validate the 1951 Act in a joint session but failed to win a two-thirds vote. Twice again it called joint sessions with no more success. In 1955 an ordinary act enlarged the highest court to eleven for the hearing of constitutional cases. Another ordinary act enlarged the Senate and changed the method of election, with the result that the government acquired a sufficient majority in that body to gain a two-thirds majority in a joint session. In 1956 this majority, meeting in joint session, validated the 1951 Act, removed the entrenchment of nonwhite voting rights in the Cape, and reentrenched language equality. Finally, the court—enlarged but with only one judge dissenting—upheld both the validated 1951 Act and the Senate Act.

The 1956 enlargement having served its purpose, the Senate was reconstituted in 1960. Its size, which had been increased from 48 to 89, was reduced to 54. The Senate continues, as it has since 1910, to be composed of a majority of members elected indirectly (in electoral colleges in each province composed of members of the House of Assembly and of the provincial council) and a minority appointed by the government. Under the general ticket or majority vote system introduced by the 1955 Act, the Opposition had won only the 8 elective seats allotted to Natal and the government had won 59 seats. The restoration of proportional representation in 1961 resulted in the Opposition's winning 15 elective seats to the government's 28. However, equality in the number of elective seats for each province, which had prevailed from 1910 to 1955, was not restored. Natal and the Orange Free State now have the minimum number of 8 seats each, Cape Province has 11, the Transvaal has 14, and South-West Africa has 2. In addition, two senators are appointed from each province and from South-West Africa (one from each province being appointed on the ground of his thorough acquaintance with "the interests of the coloured population," a category excluding Africans and Indians). One other senator is appointed (under the legislation by which Coloreds were removed from the common roll) to represent the reasonable wants and wishes of Coloreds in the Cape. The new Senate is notable also for the absence of the four senators who, in accordance with the 1936 settlement, had been elected indirectly by African electoral colleges throughout the Union.

Like the American House of Representatives, the South African House of Assembly is composed of members elected by direct popular vote in single-member constituencies. The total membership is 160, all of whom must be white. White voters in the four provinces elect 150 members, and in South-West Africa 6. The remaining 4 members are elected on a special day by Colored men in Cape Province who can meet educational and economic qualifications and register on the communal roll.

Legislative power and prestige are concentrated in the House of Assembly. The Senate usually suggests only minor changes in bills, and its power to delay the action of the House is slight. Before 1955, deadlock was resolved by majority vote in a joint sitting. In the case of taxing or appropriation bills, the joint sitting was convened during the same session; and in the case of other bills, in a second successive session. Only three joint sittings for this purpose have been necessary, all during 1926–1928, when the government was opposed by a majority in the Senate. Nevertheless, to prevent any future deadlock, the joint-sitting procedure was eliminated by the Senate Act of 1955. Taxing and appropriation bills now become law in the same session, and other bills in the second successive session even should the Senate reject them or propose amendments that are not acceptable to the House.

The members of Parliament, excluding the four representatives of the Coloreds, elect the President to a seven-year term. The reason for using this form of indirect election, Dr. Verwoerd has said, is that the President is not the chief executive as well as the head of state; the Opposition, in contrast, feels it is to ensure the Nationalist candidate. Since the President is expected normally to be an elderly man, he will probably serve only one term. But Nationalist republicans are not apprehensive that reelection would shift the balance of power. The President's function, in Dr. Verwoerd's words, is "to be the focal point around which the love and desire for unity of the people must be united." [45]

POLITICAL DYNAMICS

The Constitutional Arena

The major contest for political power in South Africa—that between Afrikaner nationalism and African nationalism—is taking place in the area outside the constitutional or parliamentary arena. But it is in the latter arena that the structure of law and the use of legalized force are determined. Within that arena, the National Party, the political agent of Afrikaner nationalism, has achieved a nearly impregnable position.

The National Party's strength lies in its nature as the organ of a community whose sense of national identity arises from still vivid historical memories and exclusive bonds of language, religion, culture, and economic cooperation. The party has achieved political success by appealing to the Afrikaans-speaking three-fifths of the white one-fifth of the population. In addition, especially since the emergency of 1960 and the establishment of the Republic, the party has stressed the need for white unity and thus has sought to appeal to English-speaking whites. At the same time, it seeks to counteract any loosening of Afrikaner nationalist ties that may result from the achievement of political goals and from urbanism and material prosperity.

The Afrikaans-speaking section of the white population has tended to grow in numbers and to become more solid in support of the National Party. The birth rate has commonly been higher among Afrikaans-speaking whites than English-speaking whites, although urbanization has tended to depress it. During 1951–1960 the proportion of whites whose home language is Afrikaans grew from about 54 to 58 per

[45] *House of Assembly Debates,* Jan. 30, 1961, col. 343.

cent.[46] (At the same time, over 70 per cent of the whites are "bilingual," a great increase from about 50 per cent in 1921.) Meanwhile, the proportion of Afrikaans-speaking whites voting for the National Party has grown steadily over two decades. The proportion is estimated at 60 per cent in 1938, 68 per cent in 1943, 75 to 80 per cent in 1948, 80 to 85 per cent in 1953, and 85 per cent in 1958. In the 1960 referendum and the 1961 election the proportion was probably higher.[47]

Many of the Afrikaners who have traditionally supported the United Party are older voters, particularly in rural areas, and are slowly dying out. Some have swung to support of the government. Meanwhile, provincial educational policies, except in Natal, have tended to isolate Afrikaans-speaking children from English-speaking children. Among younger voters, the National Party has had a stronger appeal than the United Party and undoubtedly benefited from the enlargement of the white electorate in 1958 to include eighteen-year-olds. "Two-thirds of them will vote Nationalist," said a member of the cabinet early in 1958.[48] This group voted in a general election for the first time in 1961.

The National Party steadily increased its popular vote and parliamentary representation during 1938–1961. Not until the 1960 republican referendum, however, did it win a clear majority of the vote—52.04 per cent. This majority probably included a small number of English-speaking persons. In the following year, the party won a clear majority of the estimated popular vote for the first time in a

[46] *Press Digest* (Johannesburg), Sept. 6, 1962, p. 353, referring to a special census report issued in Aug. 1962 (*Population Census 1960 Sample Tabulation No. 1—Industry Divisions, Age Groups, Home Languages, Whites*). A useful compilation of census data is Bureau of Census and Statistics, Union of South Africa, *Union Statistics for Fifty Years, 1910–1960,* Jubilee Issue (Pretoria: Government Printer, 1960).

[47] Election data are taken mainly from the following sources. For the period through 1953, see Carter, *The Politics of Inequality.* For the 1958 election, see R. R. Farquharson, "South Africa 1958," in D. E. Butler, ed., *Elections Abroad* (London: Macmillan, 1959), pp. 229–275; Edwin S. Munger, "Self-Confidence and Self-Criticism in South Africa," *Foreign Affairs,* July 1958, pp. 659–668; and Edgar H. Brookes, "The Union of South Africa: The General Election of 1958 and After," in Kirkwood, ed., *African Affairs, Number One,* pp. 147–162. For the 1960 referendum, see Ellison Kahn in *Annual Survey of South African Law,* 1960, pp. 1–6. For the 1961 election, see Newell M. Stultz and Jeffrey Butler, "The South African General Election of 1961," *Political Science Quarterly,* March 1963, pp. 86–110.

[48] Quoted by Brookes, "The Union of South Africa," p. 148.

general election. Its increase in popular and parliamentary strength is shown in Table 23. The table also shows the disparity between seats and votes won by the National Party in the last six general elections. In 1948 it won (with the Afrikaner Party) a slim majority in the House of Assembly with an estimated 40 per cent of the popular vote. In 1958, with barely a majority of the popular vote, the National Party won two-thirds of the seats. The percentage of seats shown in the table is based upon 150 seats in the first three elections

Table 23. National Party strength, 1938–1961

	Number of seats	Per cent of seats	Estimated per cent of popular vote
1938	27	18.0	29.6
1943	43	28.7	33.7
1948	79	52.7	40.0
1953	94	60.3	45.5
1958	103	66.0	49.0
1961	105	67.3	53.5

and, after the addition of 6 seats for South-West African whites, 156 in the last three elections. The table excludes Natives' representatives and representatives of the Coloreds. The popular vote is estimated because some seats were uncontested.[49]

The National Party's disproportionate strength in seats is largely due to the geographical distribution of its support although it is also aided by the overrepresentation of rural areas and some gerrymandering. Delimitation, commonly undertaken between each election, is carried out by commissions of three judges, appointed by the government. Commissions almost always give overrepresentation to rural voters and underrepresentation to urban voters; this has been possible because the commission may define districts whose electorate diverges as much as 15 per cent less or 15 per cent more than numerically equal representation. Recently they have also stressed "community of interest" in drawing some electoral boundaries. In any case, the

[49] The estimate of the popular vote through 1953 is taken from Carter, whose formula for uncontested seats is to give 85 per cent of 85 per cent of the enrolled voters to the winning party. The percentages for 1958 and 1961 are from Stultz and Butler. Taking the 1960 referendum as a base, since voting occurred in all constituencies, and comparing the referendum vote to that in selected constituencies that had been contested in 1958 and 1961, Stultz and Butler arrive at an estimate of the popular vote in the country as a whole in 1958 and 1961.

United Party wins overwhelming majorities or is unopposed by Nationalists in many urban districts; in effect, many of its votes are wasted. The National Party, on the other hand, has won marginal seats in urban and peri-urban areas with small majorities. In 1948, it won 31 of the 45 seats that were won by less than a 15 per cent majority; in 1953, 36 out of 40. In 1958, it won 9 of the 11 seats won by less than a 10 per cent majority; and in 1961, 1 of the 2 such seats.

The National Party's strength in some marginal districts was bolstered by favorable redistricting before the 1953 and 1958 elections. Of more basic importance, however, has been the steady migration of Afrikaners to cities and towns, especially on the Witwatersrand, where they have taken jobs in mining, industry, commerce, and the public service. The crucial areas in the 1948 and 1953 elections were the constituencies on the Witwatersrand, with their increasing number of working-class whites who thought of themselves primarily as Afrikaners. In 1926, some 60 per cent of the Afrikaners but less than 30 per cent of the English-speaking were rural. In 1951, over three-fourths of the white population were classified as urban. By 1960, Afrikaans-speaking whites had become a majority of the whites in the towns east and west of Johannesburg.

In consolidating and mobilizing nearly all of its potential support, the National Party appears to have neared the zenith of its strength. The number of marginal seats has declined, as shown above, and thereby the vulnerability of either major party to swings of opinion is lessened. A measure of the National Party's confidence in the stability of its support is the increase in the number of seats that it concedes to its opponents. In 1948 there were 12; in 1953, 18; in 1958, 31; and in 1961, 46. On the other hand, in 1961, for the first time, a large number of seats—50—were conceded to the Nationalists by the Opposition. Thus, the Nationalists contested only 60 seats, and only 8 of the 60 had been held by the Opposition. No Nationalist incumbent was unseated in 1961, and the party won 3 additional seats.

Party effort tends to concentrate upon the fairly small number of crucially important districts and the extremely small number of uncommitted or wavering voters or nonvoters. The turnout of voters is high in these districts. Party effort is also vigorous in safe districts, when they are contested, because of the importance to each party of a popular, country-wide mandate.[50] In 1953, 85 per cent of the elec-

[50] In the referendum campaign, the United Party faced a special problem in ten districts in getting voters to register (although registration is compulsory)

torate voted. In 1958, voting ranged from 89 to 91 per cent in each province except Natal, where it was 86 per cent. Such participation belies the common observation that most of the English-speaking population are politically too apathetic even to vote. In the 1960 referendum, 90.8 per cent of the white electorate voted. In 1961, when eighteen-year-olds voted in a general election for the first time, the turnout was only 77.9 per cent, but it was much higher in close contests. The highest voting average in the last two general elections was in Queenstown, eastern Cape Province: in 1958, a 96.2 per cent poll by 9,567 voters gave the United Party a majority of 13 votes; in 1961, a 96.5 per cent poll gave the National Party a majority of 379 votes.

The areas of solid support for the National Party—the platteland, or rural areas, and the villages, apart from those in Natal and eastern Cape Province—are virtually impregnable, barring a major disruption within the party. The fifty seats conceded to the National Party in 1961 were in these areas and in South-West Africa and also included four Afrikaans-speaking working-class districts in Pretoria. Among the provinces, the Orange Free State is heavily Nationalist, 77 per cent of its electorate voting yes in the republican referendum.

In Natal, where United Party support is greatest, 76 per cent voted no in the referendum. However, the Afrikaans-speaking workers in the coal-mining areas of northwestern Natal are increasing National Party strength in that province. The vote for the Republic was 56 per cent in the Transvaal, where the United Party has strongholds in and near Johannesburg, and only 50.2 per cent in Cape Province, where the United Party is strong in Cape Town and its environs and along the eastern coast. Support for the United Party is widely dispersed, but its scattered support in rural areas outside of Natal and the eastern Cape Province falls far short of a majority.

Differences of social and economic class exist between and within each major party, but within the National Party these differences are subordinated to the intense allegiance of Nationalists to the Afrikaans community. "So strong is this sentiment," in the judgment of Professor Carter, "that it may well be the most fervent nationalism existing in the African continent." [51] Ministers of the Dutch Reformed churches, teachers, and journalists perform distinctive roles in strengthening the

---

and to vote since these districts had never before been contested by the National Party (*Annual Survey of South African Law*, 1960, p. 4).

[51] Gwendolen M. Carter, "African Nationalist Movements in South Africa" (unpublished manuscript).

cohesion of the Afrikaans community that gives them a political importance far greater than that of their counterparts in the United Party. Nationalist supporters, nearly all of whom are Afrikaans-speaking, include other professional and academic groups, rich and not-so-rich farmers, a small but increasingly important class of financiers and men in commerce and industry, a skilled and semiskilled working class, and an overwhelming majority of the employees of the public services and governmental enterprises. Among the most fervent supporters of the National Party are the working-class whites who, but for jobs provided by or protected by the government, might sink to ordinary nonwhite levels. These would probably be among the last whites to be affected adversely by any external economic pressures on South Africa.

The exclusiveness of Afrikaner nationalism is illustrated by its attitudes toward Jews, an economically important and long-established group now numbering more than 108,000 persons, nearly half of whom live in or near Johannesburg. Although anti-Semitism is not deeply rooted among Afrikaners, Nationalist Party propaganda between the world wars attacked Jewish capitalism (symbolized by a cartoon character labeled "Hoggenheimer") as the power behind Botha and Smuts. During the 1930's, Nazi propaganda produced an outcropping of virulent anti-Semitism among Afrikaners who admired Hitler. Until 1951, the National Party in the Transvaal specifically excluded Jews from party membership.

Nationalist leaders have disclaimed anti-Semitism since 1948 and have praised Israel. Nevertheless, Jews remain apprehensive regarding their future in the Republic. Some Nationalists continue to link Jews with communism or pointedly to identify as Jewish the leaders of opposition groups that are distrusted, such as the Progressive Party, which is supported by Harry Oppenheimer, the most powerful figure in mining. The bitterness of official criticism of Israel in 1961 and 1962 when it voted in the United Nations for sanctions against South Africa aroused concern among South African Jews, especially among the many who are strong Zionists. Yet there are undoubtedly Jews among the small number of English-speaking persons who support the National Party.

Roman Catholics make up another small white group which is alienated by Afrikaner nationalism and, in particular, by the frequent warnings of Dutch Reformed Church leaders against the "Roman danger." Little more than 5 per cent of the white population is

Catholic, but, unlike the Jews, Catholics might be expected to increase in number through immigration. The Nationalist government has been cautious about admitting the followers of a church which has firmly opposed much of its racial policy and who would be likely to add to the strength of the Opposition. In September 1962, Dr. Verwoerd told a party congress that as South Africa is a Protestant country immigration would not be allowed to disturb the existing religious ratios.

Some observers have expected that the "detribalization" of Afrikaners who have moved to the cities would lead to an eventual party realignment based largely upon economic issues. But such a realignment, of which as yet there are no signs, would have to overcome the manifold and constant pressures of an exclusive community. The National Party has long acted effectively to diminish the influence of associations outside that community. Antigovernment and multiracial trade unions, which have enlisted Afrikaners, have been hampered or crippled through infiltration and divisive tactics and finally through legislation. The Labor Party (now defunct), though it appealed to the paramount interests of white labor, failed to withstand the counterappeals of nationalism and racism. Although from time to time economic issues have given rise to independent candidates or minor parties, their importance has declined. The Conservative Workers' Party, which was organized on the eve of the 1961 election, is an example of a rightist protest group based on an economic issue, unemployment. Supported mainly by Nationalists, it won only 6,229 votes in a few working-class constituencies, barely enough to serve as an irritant to the government before (in all probability) fading away.

The United Party is no electoral match for the National Party although it still has approximately as many popular votes, is more representative of the white population, has able leaders, and usually more money. In the elections of 1958 and 1961, its professional organizers were fully aware that victory was impossible. The distribution of United Party support, described above, is a key factor in explaining why. But Nationalist policies since 1948 have created further disadvantages through an immigration policy discouraging potentially anti-Nationalist immigrants, a citizenship policy delaying the time when British immigrants are eligible to vote (although lethargy may be as important a cause of delay in voting), an educational policy tending to isolate Afrikaans-speaking children from English-speaking children, the grant of disproportionate representation to South-West

African whites, the removal of Colored voters from the common roll, and the lowering of the voting age to eighteen.

The United Party's greatest political disadvantage, however, is its own nature as a middle-of-the-road and pragmatic coalition of diverse interests. That so many of these interests are business-minded, cosmopolitan, and traditional in approach makes the United Party constitutionally incapable of matching the National Party's stridency and doctrinaire certainty. Sir de Villiers Graaff, the party leader, and his key advisers personify the United Party's blending of conservative and liberal outlooks. United Party supporters represent most of the country's mining, commercial, and industrial interests and include wealthy farmers, professional people, and also small businessmen, clerks, and skilled workers. Virtually all of the English-speaking whites, excluding the supporters of minor, more liberal parties, and some 15 per cent or less of the Afrikaans-speaking whites support the United Party. Unlike the National Party, which is in effect allied with the Dutch Reformed churches and has few supporters who are not Protestants, the United Party also includes Jews, Catholics, and atheists.

The United Party is not unchallenged in its appeal to the country's business interests. Although Nationalist policies have been severely criticized for being doctrinaire and creating uncertainty, the Nationalist government has been cautious and pragmatic in implementing its racial policies in order not to disrupt business confidence or to discourage foreign investment. "The old nonsense about 'backveld Boers' is . . . obsolete," Professor Edgar Brookes has said. "Nationalists are no fools in the affairs of this world" but "men of penetrating minds and great ability."[52] The government's financial policy has been orthodox, and it has encouraged private enterprise. Pre-1948 demands for nationalization of mining are rarely repeated. Businessmen and investors retain grave doubts about the long-run effects of the government's racial policies and are likely to support the National Party only if they are Afrikaners, but the government's general soundness in practice in matters of particular interest to business encourages their political neutrality.

Since the National Party's victory in 1948, the United Party has acted as if it had realistic expectations of an imminent return to power. When pressed to move in a liberal direction on racial policy, it has been cautious for fear of moving ahead of white public opinion. At

[52] "The Union of South Africa," p. 155.

the same time, the party has moved slowly in a direction that is, for South Africa, relatively progressive. On changes in its policy regarding the parliamentary representation of Africans and Coloreds, see pp. 589 and 591.

As a party of white supremacy (or "leadership"), however, the United Party has sought to appeal to Nationalist supporters in marginal urban districts and even to Afrikaners in rural areas. Some United Party speakers, referring to the government's policies for African development, have accused the Nationalists of being "kafferboeties," or lovers of natives, a term of opprobrium usually directed at white liberals. Although these appeals have been ineffective, they have been defended as politically realistic if the United Party is to profit from any split in Nationalist ranks or to take the lead if circumstances arise in which a white fusion government becomes possible. With the acceleration of the government's plans for establishing self-governing areas that might eventually be independent, United Party leaders have warned of their danger to the whites. The time had come, Vause Raw, an M.P. of the party's extreme right, told its Natal congress in September 1962, for "this kafferboetie government" to do "something for the white people." [53]

Since 1953, the United Party's prospects of a return to power have become dimmer while questions of long-run racial policy have become more important. The United Party's parliamentary strength has been reduced in recent years by defections from both its left wing and its right wing. The steady decline in its strength dates from the mid-1930's, however, when the new Afrikaner nationalism began to rise. The decline in parliamentary strength was reversed only in 1961, when the United Party defeated a group of its own defectors. Thus, United Party strength in the House of Assembly after the five general elections of the period 1938–1958 was (out of 150 seats in the first three elections and 156 in the last two) 111, 89, 65, 57, and 53. Because 11 members had left to join the Progressive Party, the United Party had only 42 members on the eve of the 1961 election. With the defeat of 10 of the 11 Progressives, its strength rose to 49.

The importance of the stakes and also of principle have produced deep political splits among those who formerly supported the United Party. That success in white politics may come eventually to a group that is prepared to enter the political wilderness is illustrated by the

[53] English translation provided by *Dagbreek en Sondagnuus* (Johannesburg), Sept. 16, 1962, p. 4.

rise of General Hertzog's National Party, which was formed in 1912 and attained power a dozen years later, and Dr. Malan's "Purified Nationalists," who attained power after fifteen years of opposition. Instead of "trying to play the Nationalists at their own game," wrote Julius Lewin of Witwatersrand University in August 1952, the United Party should profit from the examples of Hertzog and Malan and adopt "a long-term strategy." It should undertake to lead public opinion (in his view, toward economic or nonracial liberalism and a welfare state) in order to build for victory in the future at the price of defeat in the short run.[54]

This reasoning has not been followed by the United Party, but it has by those members who split off in 1953 to form the Liberal Party and in 1959 to form the Progressive Party. Unlike the Hertzog and Malan splinter groups, however, these groups have no cohesive community to which they can make a deeply emotional and exclusive appeal. The relative strength of the National Party within the white political arena becomes still more apparent when one considers the response to and prospects of these parties.

The nonracial Liberal Party has sought to serve as a link between whites and nonwhites and has put up a few candidates in general, provincial, and local elections as a means of influencing white opinion.[55] Because of the party's special hostility to the Nationalists, it has not contested any district where it might jeopardize the election of a non-Nationalist. It has never won in a white constituency, and it has rarely saved its electoral deposit. (Africans on a separate roll elected Liberals to Parliament and to the Cape Provincial Council between 1953 and 1960.) In 1958 the Liberal Party broke new ground by using an African speaker in behalf of a white candidate, and in 1961 it used nonwhite canvassers for the first time.

Gradually and steadily, the Liberal Party has become more radical and shifted its main attention to the extraconstitutional area. The party's composition and orientation have changed as a consequence of its growing pessimism regarding the prospects of internal political change and its closer identification with the nonwhite opposition. Regarding the timing of universal suffrage, for example, the party moved by 1960 to endorsement of immediate action. By then, also, it sup-

[54] *Forum* (Johannesburg), Aug. 1952.

[55] In 1958, three Liberal candidates in safe United Party seats received a total of 2,934 votes. In the provincial elections of 1959, four received a total of 4,697 votes. In 1961, two Liberals received 2,461 votes between them while the United Party polled 13,218 votes in two upper-income, English-speaking districts.

ported external pressure on the government, for example, by foreign economic boycott. Some whites who opposed these policies have resigned, and some have joined the Progressive Party.

The early membership of the Liberal Party was predominantly white, except in Natal, but in recent years African members appear to have become a majority. Its members include distinguished writers (Alan Paton was national president in 1962), teachers, and professional men, a few of whom are Afrikaans-speaking. In 1958 the party had about 2,000 members and since then (although membership figures are not kept by race) has claimed that its African membership has grown in all sections of the country. At the 1961 congress, a majority of delegates and observers were Africans. The leading positions in 1962 were still held by whites, but one of the three vice-presidents (Jordan Ngubane) and the national treasurer were Africans.[56]

Whether white public opinion has grown stronger in support of the 1953 position of the Liberal Party—advocacy of a qualified but nonracial franchise and insistence on the need for consultation with African leaders—is difficult to assess. But the formation in November 1959 of the Progressive Party, which adopted that position, demonstrated that in six years organized liberalism had grown in respectability and won important allies. The party came into existence with the support of about one-fifth of the United Party's parliamentary strength. This group consisted of eleven of the twelve members whose increasing impatience with the United Party's conservatism finally resulted in resignation over a relatively minor issue, but one of principle, regarding the purchase of additional land for the Native Reserves. The new Progressives were among the abler and younger members of the United Party in Parliament, including Dr. Jan Steytler, an Afrikaner who became the party's leader, Dr. Zac de Beer, son-in-law of the former United Party leader, and Mrs. Helen Suzman. Harry Lawrence, veteran parliamentarian and a former Minister of Justice, became chairman. (Both Steytler and Lawrence were reelected to these positions in August 1962.) The most well-known Progressive was Harry Oppenheimer, South Africa's greatest financial magnate.

From the outset, the party has had political skill, energy, and conviction, practically unlimited money, and also outspoken support from a number of English-language newspapers, notably the *Rand Daily*

[56] Peter Brown, "The Liberal Party of South Africa," *Contemporary Review*, Nov. 1961; Randolph Vigne, "What's Happened to the Liberals?" *Forum*, Dec. 1961.

Mail. Party leaders also have systematically sought nonwhite cooperation. Even before their first congress in November 1959, they began
the practice of consultation by meeting over a hundred nonwhite
leaders, including Luthuli and progovernment chiefs. Later, nonwhites
who met the party's proposed franchise qualifications were invited to
become members, and a small number have joined.

The Progressive Party needed time if it were to convince the white
electorate to accept a policy that would theoretically lead to rule by a
black majority although with rigid constitutional safeguards. Presumably its parliamentary members had until 1963, when the next
general election was due, to win at least enough support to save the
seats which they had retained. Although welcoming the Progressives
as a foil, the Nationalists called a general election in 1961 which had
the effect of eliminating them with one exception from Parliament.
Nonetheless, Progressive candidates received 69,042 votes. Of this
total, 65,089 votes were cast in twenty districts in opposition to the
105,699 votes received by candidates supported by the United Party
and the National Union Party, a Nationalist splinter group with which
the United Party had an electoral pact and which later it absorbed.
Progressive Party strength was mainly in upper-middle-class, English-
speaking districts in and near Johannesburg and in Natal. Only one
seat was saved, the wealthy Johannesburg suburb represented by Mrs.
Suzman. But two seats were lost by less than 200 votes, and five others
by less than 1,000.

Since the 1961 general election, Progressive Party leaders have
worked diligently to establish branches throughout the country and
to organize campaigns in provincial and parliamentary by-elections
and in municipal elections. For a wide assortment of liberally inclined
persons who oppose Nationalist policies but find the Liberal Party
too radical, the Progressive Party has a distinct attraction. These persons include former supporters of the Torch Commando, an extraparty movement that attracted nearly a quarter-million members in
1952 during the constitutional crisis but was disbanded after the 1953
election; former members of the Federal Party; and well-to-do white
women in the Black Sash, a group organized in 1955 and now numbering about 2,000 who have staged silent demonstrations against
discriminatory or coercive legislation and have "haunted" cabinet
ministers. Progressive leaders publicly have expressed confidence that
white voters generally, as they come to face reality, will swing to the
Progressives; but privately they have become deeply discouraged.

Party membership is said to have doubled during the year after the election, to number about 15,000 members. Nevertheless, early in 1962 the Progressive Party generally lost ground in some half-dozen by-elections and failed to defeat a single one of the fifteen United Party candidates it opposed in the Johannesburg municipal elections.

In directing its main energies at the white electorate, the Progressive Party is impelled by a sense of urgency to demonstrate to African leaders and to the world outside that white attitudes are changing. Writing before the 1958 election, L. O. V. Gandar, the brilliant editor of the *Rand Daily Mail*, described the "calcification" of white political attitudes, the numbing effect of continual and long-drawn-out legislative battles, and the inability of people to maintain indefinitely a high state of moral indignation, as the Torch Commando and the Black Sash had discovered. But he also saw a ferment of ideas below the surface and some agonizing reappraisals in progress.[57] Evidence of this ferment, the Progressives believed, might help to repress the trend toward violence and allow more time for the ferment to continue. But if time ran out, said de Beer in 1962, and "if and when violence does break out—which God forfend—a party like ours will have an absolutely vital role to play in minimising it."[58]

The Extraconstitutional Area

Outside of the constitutional or parliamentary arena lies the area in which unenfranchised nonwhites seek to exert pressure on white policy makers. The area has both legal and illegal sectors, with boundaries that are indistinct. The weight of pressure has tended to swing from the legal to the illegal, from the illegal but nonviolent to the illegal and violent, from action above ground to action directed from the underground, and from a mainly domestic area to one in which external pressures are becoming increasingly important. The main catalyst of this trend has been the increasingly repressive policies of the government.

During the half century from 1910 to 1960, Africans opposed white supremacy in the main through extraconstitutional channels, usually in a legal manner and always professedly with nonviolence. Within the parliamentary framework, as noted earlier, Africans in Cape Province had a place before 1936 that was potentially important in principle though of negligible importance in practice. Token parliamentary

[57] Owen Vine (pseudonym of L. O. V. Gandar), *Election Viewpoint*, reprinted from the *Rand Daily Mail*, 1958, pp. 7–13.
[58] Zac de Beer, *Forum*, April 1962, p. 7.

representation of Africans (by whites) continued through the separate roll until 1960. Within urban localities, native advisory boards provided officially limited outlets for African opinion after 1923 and in form still do so today. Nationally between 1936 and 1951, the Natives' Representative Council was available to Africans as a government-provided mouthpiece.

Leaders of the African National Congress stood for the elected seats in the council and attended its meetings regularly until 1946. A small segment of African opinion, however, favored total boycott of all government-sponsored bodies and of the elections of natives' representatives. The ultimate ANC verdict on the Natives' Representative Council, as expressed by Luthuli, was that it was "pointless, wasteful and futile." [59] In 1946 its members, including the government-appointed chiefs, voted for an indefinite adjournment. The council was reconvened several times, but after the 1948 election, when Dr. Verwoerd, the Minister of Native Affairs, emphasized that it had no mandate to discuss matters of a political nature, the council again adjourned indefinitely. In 1951 it was abolished to make way for the elaborate scheme of government-controlled "Bantu authorities."

Meanwhile, the ANC and other nonwhite organizations asserted their claims by nonviolent tactics that were legal but sometimes bordered on illegality: meetings and demonstrations, resolutions and petitions, deputations, boycotts, and withdrawal of labor. African trade unions, for example, were not illegal but were not officially recognized, and their members faced severe penalties for striking, which was illegal. The South African Indian Congress (SAIC), whose orientation changed in 1946 from caution to militancy, undertook a two-year campaign of passive disobedience against legislation enacted that year which included residential segregation. Illegal but nonviolent action, in which volunteers courted arrest by entering facilities reserved for whites only, marked the defiance campaign of 1952, led by the ANC in close cooperation with the SAIC.

The nature and extent of permissible agitation by the unenfranchised opposition were at issue in the treason trial, although the critical issue was whether or not the ANC had adopted a policy to overthrow the state by violence. The indictment covered the period beginning on October 1, 1952, a few days before the first riots occurred during the passive resistance campaign, but demonstration rather than

[59] Luthuli, *Let My People Go,* p. 105. Luthuli accepted election to the council in a 1946 by-election. For his account of the council's last years, see pp. 102–105.

disobedience marked most of the period which ended on December 13, 1956. (The prosecution did not allege that violence had resulted from the activities of the ANC and its allied organizations in the passive resistance campaign or in later campaigns.) The prosecution affirmed that "legitimate and constitutional means" could be used to advocate changes "however radical and far-reaching." It also quoted with approval the dictum of a highly respected South African judge that "there is no intermediate course between constitutional action through the ballot box and treasonable action through illegal use of force." [60] Presumably speech by the unenfranchised was permissible as a means of influencing those who did have the vote, but "boycotts, strikes, civil disobedience, and stoppage of work" were referred to by the prosecution as "a long and flexible process" whose consummation was "revolution." In short, the area between ballot box and treason was murky and risky to enter, especially since the prosecution based its case on "hostile intent."

The three-judge special criminal court, which found the accused not guilty on March 29, 1961, did not define the limits of speech by the extraparliamentary opposition.[61] It did find that the ANC's 1949 Programme of Action "envisaged the use of illegal means" and that illegal action was taken during the 1952 campaign. Reviewing that campaign and also the 1954–1955 Western Areas Campaign directed at preventing the removal of Africans from Sophiatown and its environs in Johannesburg, the "Anti-Pass Campaign," the campaign against the Bantu Education Act, and the campaign for the Congress of the People, the court found that "some of the leaders of the African National Congress made themselves guilty of sporadic speeches of violence, which in our opinion amounted to an incitement to violence." But these speeches were "an insignificant part" of the total number of speeches made. In sum, the judgment was that

on all the evidence presented to this Court and on our findings of fact, it is impossible for this Court to come to the conclusion that the African National Congress had acquired or adopted a policy to overthrow the State by violence, i.e. in the sense that the masses had to be prepared or conditioned to commit direct acts of violence against the State.

[60] Justice O. D. Schreiner, p. 454 of the mimeographed trial record. The prosecution's opening speech of Aug. 10, 1959, begins on p. 453. A microfilm of the trial record following the arraignment in August 1959 is in the African collection of the Hoover Institution, Stanford University.

[61] The court's judgment is in Schedule 1 of the trial record. The quotations that follow are from pp. 11, 15–17.

During the 1950's, the ANC's opportunities to engage in legal protest were slowly constricted as a result of official restrictions and harassment, including bans on individual activity and meetings. Piecemeal banning of the ANC appeared to be in progress when the government, in exercising its power to declare an organization "detrimental to the peace, order, and good government" of Africans in areas falling under the jurisdiction of the Minister of Native Affairs, banned the ANC in March 1958 from Sekhukhuneland, the Zeerust area, and other rural areas of the Transvaal where violent disturbances had occurred. A more widespread limitation on ANC activity resulted from the ban on gatherings of more than ten Africans in all major urban centers beginning on April 12, 1958, a ban which had been in effect in some magisterial districts since 1954. The new ban, which went into effect shortly before the 1958 general election and a planned "stay-at-home" demonstration, was removed in piecemeal fashion in some but not all districts during a period of nearly five months.

Following the shootings at Sharpeville on March 21, 1960, the main organs of African protest moved underground when, on April 8, both the forty-eight-year-old ANC and the one-year-old PAC were declared illegal organizations for a year, their ban being renewed annually. Virtually all public channels of protest by the nonwhite opposition were closed during the state of emergency that was proclaimed on March 30 and lasted in some areas for five months. The resumption of apparent normality was marked by renewed activity on the part of the ANC's allies in the Congress alliance, the reappearance of the left-wing and pro-Congress weekly *New Age,* and the public activity of many persons who had been detained during the emergency. These persons included ANC and PAC members who were not themselves banned and also members of the Liberal Party.

Since the end of the national emergency, the imposition of stringent controls in rural districts, notably in the Transkei in eastern Cape Province near Natal, has amounted at times to a state of emergency. Additional powers granted to the Minister of Bantu Administration in 1960 included the power to prohibit movement into the Transkei and out of it. Discretionary powers were granted also to African chiefs to deal with Africans deemed subversive, and the chiefs were expected to turn over to the police persons described by the minister as "white Communist agitators." Violent opposition to Bantu authorities appeared out of control in East Pondoland in the Transkei late in 1960.

A state of emergency was declared on November 30, and thousands of troops moved into the area, a large number of them remaining until May 1961.

In other areas, the nonwhite opposition retained a measure of freedom to protest by the traditional means of public demonstration. But the obstacles and limits hedging that freedom were displayed during the period between the republican referendum on November 5, 1960, and the proclamation of the Republic on May 31, 1961. Chief Albert Luthuli, the President-General of the banned ANC, was restricted to his home district in Natal, and Robert Sobukwe, the National President of the banned PAC (who had been convicted on May 4, 1960, of incitement to support a campaign for the repeal of the pass laws), was serving a three-year sentence. But nonbanned members of both organizations in cooperation with prominent Africans of various points of view attempted to achieve a basis of unity that would lead to a widely representative and ambitiously labeled "All-in African Conference."

At the invitation of Luthuli, Z. K. Matthews (the country's most distinguished African professor), and three others, about forty African men and women met in a Consultative Conference on December 16–17, 1960, in Orlando, Johannesburg. They resolved that "because the African people were denied participation in the republican referendum they do not accept the result" and agreed on "the urgent need for African unity," the need for "effective use of non-violent pressures against apartheid," and "the calling of a national convention representing all the people of South Africa." [62]

The proposal of a new and multiracial national convention had been endorsed by leaders of both the Liberal and the Progressive parties. Hope for at least a multiracial conference was encouraged by the series of private discussions that had been taking place between whites, including big-business men and Afrikaans-speaking intellectuals, and leading nonwhites, especially since the general election of 1958. Writing in the March 1961 issue of *Fighting Talk*, the left-wing monthly, Professor Matthews, to whom has been ascribed the proposal that led to the Congress of the People rally in June 1955, observed that there was growing support "among groups with varying political views" for "a genuine, representative, all-in Convention to draw up a truly South African constitution." The call for such a convention was "not a cheap political debating point," he insisted, but the question

[62] The resolutions are in *Contact*, Dec. 31, 1960.

remained "whether the Whites of South Africa can rise to the occasion and refrain from spurning the hand of friendship while it remains outstretched." [63]

The undiscriminating nature of the government's later decision to arrest all members of the thirteen-member continuation committee is evident when one considers the composition of the committee and the split that destroyed its unity. The committee included not only Duma Nokwe, secretary-general of the banned ANC, Joseph Molefe, a PAC leader, and Govan Mbeki, who had been an active supporter of the Communist Party, but also the Reverend B. Rajuili, secretary of the Interdenominational African Ministers' Federation and a member of the Progressive Party, Paul Mosaka, the strongly anti-Communist president of the Johannesburg African Chamber of Commerce, and Jordan Ngubane, the equally anti-Communist national vice-chairman of the Liberal Party, who was chairman of the committee. The united front embodied in the committee was destroyed as a result of suspicions that former ANC members, guided by "the invisible hand" of Communists in the background, were distorting the mandate for unity and imparting to the future conference an ideological slant that served Communist ends.[64] Early in 1961 the PAC members resigned, and on March 4, when it was clear that the ANC element refused to postpone the conference until unity could be reestablished, Ngubane and Mosaka also resigned.

With former ANC members now predominant in the planning, the All-in Conference was held in Pietermaritzburg, Natal, on March 25–26, 1961. More than a thousand Africans from many parts of the country attended and observed the dramatic appearance of Nelson Mandela. Mandela, the son of a Tembu chief, a boxer, an attorney, one of the founders of the ANC Youth League, and former president of the ANC in the Transvaal, had been prevented by recurrent bans from attending gatherings. Now for the first time in nine years his ban

[63] *Contact*, July 13, 1961, p. 8, reported a notable private meeting that took place on July 1 in Johannesburg at the home of G. H. R. Edmunds, chairman of the board of the Standard Bank of South Africa and of the board of South African Associated Newspapers. About fifty persons were present, including eleven Africans, Afrikaans-speaking intellectuals, big-business men, church leaders, and representatives of the South African Indian Congress, the Liberal Party, and the Progressive Party. Among the Africans were a representative of Luthuli and other members of the banned ANC but no one from the PAC. No one from the left-wing Congress of Democrats was invited.

[64] Ngubane gives a one-sided account and makes assertions about "the invisible hand" in *An African Explains Apartheid* (New York: Praeger, 1963).

had expired and had not been renewed. He delivered a keynote address described by one observer as "magnetic." The conference issued an ultimatum to the government for the calling of a national convention before May 31, 1961, and, assuming it would be ignored, urged Africans to prepare for mass demonstrations.[65] Mandela was elected the leader of a National Action Council, which was to organize a three-day stay-at-home demonstration prior to the proclamation of the Republic. The identity of other members of the council was kept secret, and Mandela himself disappeared immediately into the underground.

Mandela's statements to the press describing the kind of demonstrations being planned and the thousands of leaflets distributed by the National Action Council had the familiar appearance of similar tactics in the past, but the secrecy of the council and the underground origin of the press statements reflected the new precariousness of nonwhite protest. From the earliest stages, the planning of the All-in Conference had encountered the usual harassment. The security branch of the police raided the Consultative Conference of December 1960 for documents, and the All-in Conference in March 1961 had to change its meeting place at the last moment because of reports that the scheduled hall had been wired by the police. The government also followed its practice of blanket arrests when, during the week before the March conference, all members of the continuation committee were arrested. Thus, Ngubane, Mosaka, and the PAC members who had resigned were also charged with furthering the aims of a banned organization, namely, the ANC.

The stay-at-home demonstration, which was openly opposed by members of the PAC, failed to mobilize mass support but succeeded in triggering a large-scale mobilization of white forces, thereby revealing the extent of white insecurity. The government's response was in many ways the same as the response to similar threats during the preceding decade. Prior to the 1958 general election, the government had banned gatherings, made a show of police strength, conducted raids and arrested leaders, attempted to persuade African workers that they would be protected while traveling to work, and made preparations to maintain essential services. Public and private employers also warned of dismissal if workers stayed away, and municipalities threatened to withdraw passes.

In 1961 the weight of coercive state power was so heavy and the

[65] The resolutions and a statement by Mandela are in *Fighting Talk*, April 1961, pp. 2–3.

development of new trends in state control was so marked that the stay-at-home of May 29–31 may be the last of its kind. The circumstances do not seem likely to recur in which any segment of the African opposition will be able or will wish to organize a mass public rally for the announcement of widespread demonstrations to be held many weeks later. During May, in early morning raids, the police arrested from 8,000 to 10,000 Africans, including many unemployed or delinquent youth—the so-called "tsotsi" element—who were suspected as intimidators. Many were detained in prison under newly enacted legislation described below. Beginning on May 19, virtually all meetings were banned for the period through June 26. The Liberal Party and the Black Sash were among organizations which requested and were refused permission to sponsor meetings. Military forces, which had stood by in 1958, were more closely coordinated with the police, and partial mobilization was ordered of military and civilian forces. Police loudspeakers broadcast attacks on the leaders, pointing out that they had absconded. Military planes flew low over African urban areas, and Saracen tanks were stationed at their gates.

Legislation enacted during the first half of 1961 furthered two trends in state control: closer coordination between the police and military forces and the bypassing of the courts. Increasingly (and to an intensified degree in 1962 and 1963), the government and its supporting newspapers warned of the danger of aggression by hostile states to the north, linked to a fifth column within. The broadened scope of military authority within the country was indicated in the amendment of the phrase "in time of war or internal disorder" to read "in time of war or during operations for the prevention or suppression of internal disorder" (in the Defence Amendment Act). A series of legislative amendments provided not only for the coordination of responsibilities for internal security but also for the establishment of a citizen's police reserve, more rifle commando units, more rapid domestic production of arms and ammunition, revival of a military but unarmed corps of Cape Colored, and other measures intended to put military forces at combat readiness.

The trend toward bypassing of the courts for short periods of time was furthered by the General Law Amendment Act of 1961: this empowered the Attorney General to prohibit a court for twelve days from releasing an arrested person if he considered detention "necessary in the interest of the safety of the public or the maintenance of public order." The police were still required, however, to bring the accused to court on a specific charge within forty-eight hours. Members of the Liberal Party were among persons arrested late in May and held for twelve days without bail. Some persons were then released on bail, but in many cases charges were withdrawn without explanation. The government was able in this manner to intimidate and temporarily immobilize large numbers of people it suspected. Thus, it could take action of an emergency nature without the embarrassment of declaring a state of emergency.

The proclamation of the Republic, festivities for which had been dampened by the preparations to counter the stay-at-home, inaugurated a period in which ANC leaders began publicly to accept violence as unavoidable. In a statement admitting that participation in the stay-at-home was disappointing, Nelson Mandela said, "If peaceful protests like these are to be put down by mobilization of the army and the police, then the people might be forced to use other methods of struggle." [66] Jordan Ngubane has observed that no ANC leader repudiated Mandela's statement. "He was merely making public a change in attitudes that had already taken place in the underground." [67]

No stay-at-home demonstration was organized for the eve of the October 18, 1961, general election. Instead, Freedom Charter slogans were painted on Afrikaans churches and public buildings, and power lines near Johannesburg were sabotaged. More sabotage (and the death of one African) occurred on December 16, Dingaan's Day, when Afrikaners commemorate the defeat of the Zulu at Blood River in 1838. Leaflets distributed on that day announced the formation of a new organization, "Umkonto We Sizwe" in Zulu, or "Spear of the Nation," which took responsibility for the sabotage. The new organization clearly shared the orientation of the Congress alliance.[68] In February 1962 in Addis Ababa, Mandela described the December sabotage as "only a small beginning." Umkonto We Sizwe, he said, "has certainly raised the morale of the people. . . . This organization can hit back in reprisal for attacks on innocent people by the Government." [69] A leaflet circulated by the ANC itself within South Africa during the following months announced "a radical change in outlook and methods." Oliver Tambo, the ANC's chief representative abroad, explained

[66] *New Age*, June 1, 1961, p. 1.   [67] *An African Explains Apartheid.*
[68] An abridged text of the leaflet is in Ronald Segal, *African Profiles* (Baltimore: Penguin Books, 1962), pp. 36–37.
[69] *Fighting Talk*, March 1962, p. 2.

in London, "From now on . . . we are calling on Africans to prepare for the worst." [70]

The scope and limits of extraconstitutional activity after the proclamation of the Republic were illustrated by the activities of Mandela. From May 31, 1961, when he returned to the underground (having left it, according to *New Age,* to lead the stay-at-home), until August 5, 1962, when he was arrested, he was an elusive figure, dubbed "the Black Pimpernel." Apparently with ease, he moved about the country, visiting both white and African leaders and issuing statements to the English-language press. In February 1961 he joined Oliver Tambo at a conference in Addis Ababa and, according to his testimony later, visited the prime ministers of Tanganyika, Senegal, and Algeria and, in London, Hugh Gaitskell and Jo Grimond. After his return to South Africa, he was apprehended, apparently as the result of inside information given to the police, and arrested on the charge of inciting certain classes of workers to act illegally by staying away from work and also on the charge of leaving the country without a valid permit. In order to prevent pro-Mandela rallies from being held, the Minister of Justice issued an order prohibiting "any gathering relating to Mandela in any place in the Republic of South Africa" during two days at the beginning of his trial. On October 20, all gatherings held to protest the arrest or trial of anyone for any offense were banned until April 30, 1963.[71]

During the five days in October 1962 when Mandela appeared in court and conducted his own defense and again while he was being sentenced on November 7, his dramatic conduct undoubtedly added to his almost legendary and possibly charismatic reputation. Front-page press coverage described the tribal dress affected by Mandela, his clenched fist and shouts of "Amandla" or "strength" (which were roared back by the crowd, when he entered and left), and the excited scenes of singing and dancing Africans both inside and outside the courtroom. In an hour-long address before pleading not guilty, Mandela denied that a white court could give a black man justice. He concluded by declaring that if unfair discrimination were not "remedied without delay we might well find that even plain talk before the country's courts is too timid a method to draw the attention of the country to our political demands." [72]

[70] *Observer* (London), April 15, 1962, p. 2.
[71] The text of the two orders are in the *Star,* Oct. 13 and 20, 1962.
[72] *New Age,* Oct. 25, 1962.

Shortly before the trial began, Mandela's name was added to a list of persons banned from gatherings; thereafter, under the Sabotage Act of 1962, described below, his statements could not be published. Reporting of judicial proceedings was permissible, however, "as long as it is not abused by creating a forum for such persons," to use the words of the minister.[73] Nevertheless, the press was inhibited. The *Star*'s lengthy report on the trial quoted only a few sentences from Mandela's address. *New Age*, on the other hand, quoted him in a front-page headline: "White Court Cannot Dispense Justice."

Described by the presiding judge as "the brain behind the entire organization" of the three-day stay-at-home, Mandela was sentenced to five years in prison. The government failed, however, in its effort to send to prison the thirteen members of the continuation committee. Once again, the protracted nature of legal proceedings and the independence of South African courts were illustrated. The accused, who were arrested in March 1961, were charged with publishing documents calling for the All-in African Conference, an act calculated to further the aims of the ANC. In October, twelve of the accused (Molefe of the PAC having fled the country) were found guilty and sentenced to a year in prison but were freed on bail pending appeal. Two judges of the Supreme Court upheld the appeal in April 1962. In seeking to promote the conference, they said, the accused conceivably could act in a manner that did not endanger public safety or order.[74] In October, the government announced that it was withdrawing its own appeal.

Coloreds who were in alliance with the ANC through the South African Colored People's Organization (SACPO), founded in 1953 and recently renamed the South African Colored People's Congress, faced official pressures after Sharpeville similar to those imposed upon the African opposition. SACPO, a left-wing group with probably only a few hundred active members, was not outlawed after Sharpeville, although its leaders had been among the accused in the treason trial and were detained during the 1960 emergency. Concurrently with the planning of the All-in African Conference, SACPO leaders had a minor role, in cooperation with a broad front of Coloreds who had not been politically active, or were active in other groups, such as the Liberal Party, in planning a Colored National Convention. The gathering was finally scheduled for July 7–10, 1961, but on the evening of July 6, the government banned the assembly of the convention or of

[73] *Star*, Oct. 23, 1962.   [74] *Race Relations News*, Oct. 1962, p. 8.

any of the Congress organizations in Cape Town and the surrounding area. Acting speedily and secretly, the leaders managed to bring together about 150 of some 300 delegates for an open-air meeting on a farm about thirty miles from Cape Town, outside the prohibited area. When asked in Parliament in January 1962 why the ban was issued, the Minister of Justice replied that to furnish grounds was "not considered to be in the public interest." [75]

During the period between the general elections of 1958 and 1961, SACPO abandoned its tactic of engaging in the electoral process. In doing so, it concurred with the policy of boycott that had been followed consistently by the small number of bitter Colored intellectuals who belonged to the Non-European Unity Movement (NEUM). The antecedents of the NEUM extended back to 1936, when the question of boycott of the Natives' Representative Council had split African opinion. The ANC withdrew at that time from the All-African Convention (AAC), which had been established by the national African conference of 1935 as a coordinating organization to oppose the pending African legislation. The AAC continued to exist and in 1943 joined with a federation of Colored organizations to establish the NEUM. The Colored organizations had come together to oppose with vehemence a new Colored Affairs Department and Advisory Council established by the wartime United Party government. The NEUM, whose leaders were inclined toward Trotskyism, categorically demanded full equality. It attacked all nationalisms, including African nationalism, and never overcame its preoccupation with vituperative attacks on all exponents of halfway measures.

Growing resentment of Nationalist policy and its effort to remove the Coloreds from the white political arena stimulated the growth of political consciousness among the usually apathetic Coloreds and support for a policy of noncollaboration. Registration among some 130,000 Colored (including Asian) males who were probably qualified to vote in Cape Province declined from 47,677 in 1953, in the middle of the constitutional crisis over their removal from the common roll, to 24,306 in 1959. During the preceding year, in April 1958, the first election was held for Coloreds voting on a separate roll. SACPO, despite dissension in its own ranks, supported two (white) candidates. Only 14,694 Coloreds voted, electing four unofficial United Party candidates. Each SACPO candidate received an average of only 454 votes, a low vote probably due in part to sentiment for boycott. In 1961, the Colored

[75] *House of Assembly Debates,* Jan. 26, 1962, col. 221.

National Convention endorsed a boycott of the second Colored election. In October, a fortnight before the general election, only 4,740 Colored voters went to the polls to elect four white representatives.

Deep disagreements among Nationalists regarding the future of the Coloreds have buoyed the hopes of those who continue to retain the traditional collaborationist aspiration for privileged treatment as whites. Such hopes were rekindled in 1960, when some Nationalists expressed gratitude for the "loyalty" of the Colored population during the disturbances after Sharpeville and urged a more rapid enhancement of Colored status. Intellectual leaders, mainly in Cape Province, suggested that Coloreds elect Coloreds to Parliament. Voices were also heard in support of total integration of Coloreds and whites.

Dr. Verwoerd replied categorically in December 1960 that the government would be as firm as "granite" in applying apartheid and under no circumstances would allow Coloreds in Parliament. Speaking one year later to the Union Council for Colored Affairs, which had been established in 1959 with fifteen appointed and twelve elected members, he envisaged self-governing Colored localities within five years and the development of the council into a Colored Parliament within ten years. Meanwhile, the Kleurlingvolksbond, a rural group which supports the government, and the Colored People's National Union, which consists of a small number of personal followers of George Golding, a school principal who cooperates with the council, took part in the election campaign of 1961. The council itself (whose chairman, Tom Swartz, was described by a United Party member in Parliament as "this servile, bowing and scraping man" [76]) called upon the government in 1962 to allow the election of Coloreds to Parliament.

With the establishment of a Department of Indian Affairs in September 1961, the government began to take tentative steps toward consultation with the racial group that was the farthest removed from the constitutional arena and from formal channels of access to white authority. No Indians in Natal were given a parliamentary franchise after 1896 or a municipal franchise after 1924.[77] The steady deterioration in Indian rights, especially in trading and property, was partly compensated for in 1946, the Smuts government thought, when provision was made for the communal representation of Indians by whites

[76] M. W. Holland in *House of Assembly Debates*, April 12, 1962, col. 3879.

[77] Anomalies persist. Indians who were on the municipal voters' roll in 1924 were not removed. In Oct. 1962, in Stanger, north of Durban, an electorate of 12 Indians and some 100 whites reelected an Indian businessman to the town board by a margin of nearly 5 to 1 (*Forum*, Nov. 1962, p. 14).

in Parliament (and by Indians or whites in the Natal Provincial Council). Because the new electoral legislation was coupled with provisions for residential segregation, the separate elections were boycotted and not held; and after 1948, the statutory provisions were repealed. Until 1961, Nationalist policy, endorsed by many English-speaking whites, was to treat Indians as unassimilable persons who should be repatriated if possible. The Department of Indian Affairs was established in that year, according to the Minister of Indian Affairs, because the government had "realized that the Indians are a permanent part of the population of this country." The government intended to follow a "pattern," he told Parliament in May 1962, that would be "more or less the same as that envisaged in respect of the Coloreds," but the steps would have to be worked on "in consultation with the Indians." [78]

Since Indian development was to be permanently separate, the government's policy offered no hope to Indians that they would ever be admitted to a share in white political power. The minister's own hope that Indians would organize representative "consultative committees," which he would recognize, and his promise of guidance toward an eventual "measure of self-government" could appeal only to a small minority of conservative Indians who had made no effort to win mass support. Even the conciliatory South African Indian Organization (SAIO), which had been formed in 1947 by conservative, largely Muslim businessmen after militant and left-wing Hindu leaders had won control of the historic South African Indian Congress, was initially opposed to the establishment of the Indian Affairs Department.

Resentment of the SAIO against the government appears to have been hardening. Despite a history of bitter recrimination between it and the SAIC, it cooperated with the SAIC in a joint statement condemning the policy of separate higher education and the exclusion of Indians from the University of Natal. Nevertheless, accustomed to exclusion from political power, believing that protest is futile, and anxious to protect its business position, the Indian Organization appears ready to use available channels for negotiation. On the other hand, the trend toward terrorism may discourage negotiation and possible collaboration. In December 1962, for example, the office of A. S. Kajee, a leading member of the SAIO and the only Natal Indian to at-

[78] For remarks by the Minister of Indian Affairs, see *House of Assembly Debates*, May 17, 1962, cols. 5814–5821.

tend the induction of the President in Pretoria in 1961, was damaged by a bomb.

The Indian Congress, on the other hand, occupies the precarious extraparliamentary position of an ally of the banned ANC. Its non-banned leaders continued to hold public meetings during 1962 and to stage demonstrations, for example, picketing the office of the Minister of Indian Affairs in Pretoria when he met with an invited group of Indians. Undoubtedly it cooperates also with the underground. Its members in exile, notably Dr. Y. M. Dadoo, who was president of the SAIC until he was banned in 1952, have participated in efforts to organize a united front abroad. The Transvaal Indian Youth Congress in August 1962 elected as honorary officers Dr. Dadoo and a non-Indian, Nelson Mandela.

Because of the importance for the government of successful collaboration with Coloreds, Indians, and especially Africans (African separate development is described under "African Administration"), the government saw an increasingly urgent need for repressing the radical opposition. Leaders of the government spoke with conviction of their belief that Communist agitators were responsible for disturbances at home and that their sympathizers, in particular the English-language press, were partly responsible for misunderstanding abroad. The opportunities for political expression that remained open to the extraparliamentary opposition when the new Republic came into existence were not looked on as safety valves in an explosive situation but as dangerous loopholes in the law that needed to be closed. The Republic began its life with long-standing and far-reaching powers for dealing with troublemakers (virtually unlimited power when an emergency was declared) and wide discretion for its ministers. With the advent, however, of Balthazar Johannes Vorster as Minister of Justice on August 2, 1961, and the promulgation on June 27, 1962, of the General Law Amendment Act, the so-called Sabotage Act, a new era of repression began.

The Sabotage Act consisted mainly of amendments to the Suppression of Communism Act of 1950, the Riotous Assemblies Act of 1956, and the Unlawful Organizations Act of 1960. It introduced no new principles but furthered the trend toward greater ministerial discretion not subject to challenge in the courts and increasingly severe punishment for widely defined offenses. Its provisions for silencing the radical opposition promised to be markedly more effective, however, than existing provisions that were available for nonemergency situations.

In the expansion of the statutory armory for dealing with trouble-makers, the first major developments had been the Native Administration Act of 1927 and the Riotous Assemblies Act of 1930. Under the former, anyone could be imprisoned for a year or fined £100 or given both penalties for words uttered or anything done "with intent to promote any feeling of hostility between Natives and Europeans." Under the latter, the Minister of Justice had administrative power to banish anyone from any area whenever he was satisfied that the person was promoting feelings of hostility between whites and nonwhites, including Coloreds and Indians. Proof of specific intent was not needed.

In 1950 the Suppression of Communism Act greatly enlarged ministerial power to ban an individual from an area, from membership in an organization, or from attendance at "gatherings." Such action could be taken, subject only to extremely limited judicial review, if the minister was satisfied that the person was encouraging or likely to encourage any act or omission to further "the achievement of any of the objects of communism." "Communism" in the act included any doctrine "which aims at bringing about any political, industrial, social or economic change within the Union by the promotion of disturbance or disorder, by unlawful acts or omissions or by the threat of such acts or omissions." This legislation and the earlier acts also gave certain ministers wide powers over assembly and publication if they expected that feelings of hostility would be aroused or the objects of "communism" furthered.

Nevertheless, in 1952 no available law or regulation was suitable for dealing with mass disobedience. Minor statutory offenses were punishable only by a short jail sentence with the option of a fine. Shortly before the 1953 general election, the Criminal Law Amendment Act, enacted with the support of the United Party, added whipping to the risks run by the radical opposition. The act provided that any person who committed an offense "by way of protest or in support of any campaign against any law" could be sentenced to a whipping of ten strokes, a £300 fine, three years in jail, or a combination of any two of these penalties. Upon a second conviction a fine could be imposed only in conjunction with whipping or imprisonment. For the person whose words or actions were calculated to cause another person to commit an offense as a means of protest, the maximum penalties above were increased by an additional £200 or two years.

Provisions of both the Act of 1950 and the Act of 1953 were incorporated in the Unlawful Organizations Act of 1960. This act empowered the government to outlaw the ANC and the PAC and any other organization which in its opinion was established to carry on their activities. The act extended to unlawful organizations the provisions of the 1950 Act that enabled the government to enforce the outlawry of the Communist Party and other organizations deemed to be Communist. The 1960 Act also applied the maximum penalties of the 1953 Act to legislation enacted in 1956, amending the Riotous Assemblies Act, which had provided maximum penalties of £50 fine or six months in prison or both for offenses such as intimidating persons to stay away from work or jeering at them for working. Thus, the penalty for such offenses was increased tenfold, to £500 or five years or ten strokes or a combination of two of these penalties.

The most far-reaching of all the government's statutory sources of authority is still today the Public Safety Act of 1953, which was enacted with bipartisan support. It empowers the President, that is, the cabinet, if public order is thought to be seriously threatened, to declare a state of emergency, during which time persons can be summarily arrested and detained. The government's only obligation is to submit their names to Parliament after thirty days. The emergency can last a year, subject to renewal; and while it is in effect, parliamentary and judicial functions can be suspended. The act has been invoked only once, during the period following Sharpeville.

The Sabotage Act of 1962, which went into immediate operation except for one provision noted below, blurred the distinction between times of emergency and nonemergency. Provision was made for applying certain emergency regulations in an area when an emergency had been declared elsewhere, thus avoiding the necessity (and embarrassment) of declaring an emergency in the first area. Another provision empowered the minister to close certain places to public meetings. On September 7, 1962, the Johannesburg City Hall steps, a traditional ground for the airing of dissent, were closed for one year to "any public gathering," excluding divine services. Presumably the Parade in Cape Town would be closed later. The likelihood that such a restriction would come to appear normal and would be renewed was suggested by the renewal of the twelve-day detention provision, described above. This had been enacted for one year in the face of the 1961 stay-at-home but was extended for an additional year on the ground that sabotage had taken place.

In creating a new criminal offense, "sabotage," the act made it possible, the minister admitted, for minor offenses to be treated as capital crimes.[79] Therefore, since the act is "worded widely" and the offense carries a minimum penalty of five years in prison and a maximum penalty of death, prosecution can begin only if personally certified by the Attorney General. A large and varied number of acts constitute sabotage if they are proved to be wrongful and willful and fall into certain broad categories, for example, endangering public health or safety or the maintenance of law and order. Once the prosecution proves the foregoing, the burden falls upon the accused to prove the absence of political motivation. He will be acquitted if he proves that his offense was neither intended nor likely to produce any one of ten general consequences, for example, encouraging the achievement of "any political aim, including the bringing about of any social or economic change in the Republic." Trespass and the illegal possession of weapons or explosives also constitute sabotage unless this burden of proof is discharged.

The act contains other major provisions, which the minister has begun to use. He is empowered, in his own words, to take steps ranging from a warning to cease "communistic agitation" to twenty-four-hour house arrest.[80] Magistrates have issued warnings, and during the month from mid-October to mid-November 1962, twelve house-arrest orders were issued. Nine of the twelve persons receiving orders were whites, and ten of the twelve were listed as having been active in the Communist Party. The orders were tailor-made, ranging from evening and weekend confinement to twenty-four-hour confinement. They can be challenged in a court only by proving that the minister acted mala fide. Though, in December 1962, a Transvaal Supreme Court judge held an order void on the ground that Parliament had not clearly indicated that "any place or area" could be defined as narrowly as a dwelling place, the minister's power was subsequently upheld by a full court. Loophole legislation can be expected, however, whenever the government feels it necessary.

A second provision met the problem of the person who was banned from attending gatherings but continued to speak through the press or whose speech was reproduced at gatherings (except at a particular gathering that he was prohibited from attending). No one without

[79] *House of Assembly Debates,* May 21, 1962, cols. 6075–6076.
[80] Quotations in the text regarding the bill are from the opening speeches of the minister and the leader of the Opposition in the second-reading debate; see *House of Assembly Debates,* May 21–23, 1962, cols. 6058–6092, 6108–6115.

permission may reproduce in South Africa any statement made anywhere at any time (including any time in the past) by a person who is banned from attending gatherings. An individual may also be prohibited from communicating with other persons or receiving visitors. On July 30, 1962, 102 persons, with others added later, were listed as having been banned from attending gatherings. The list included not only Luthuli, who was in effect exiled within South Africa, but also persons in exile abroad. *Die Vaderland* pointed out that Oliver Tambo could speak in Trafalgar Square, but now not a word could be reproduced in South Africa.[81]

Thirdly, new newspapers may be required to deposit up to the equivalent of $28,000, which is forfeited if the newspaper is later banned. (Furthermore, possession as well as the dissemination of a banned publication is now an offense. Six months were allowed to seek the minister's consent for retention or to dispose of such publications.) The left-wing *Guardian,* which began publication in 1937, had been banned in 1952 under the Suppression of Communism Act. It reappeared without a break as the *Clarion,* the *People's World,* and then *Advance* and was banned a second time in 1954, only to reappear the following week as *New Age.* Vorster, the Minister of Justice, was accurate in part when he described *New Age* as "the propaganda organ of the Communist party"; but Luthuli was also accurate, in the twenty-fifth birthday issue of March 22, 1962, in describing it as "the fighting mouthpiece of African aspirations" although he had "not always agreed with everything it says." *New Age* was undoubtedly a valuable source of information to the government and was not finally banned until November 30, 1962. According to its chief editor at that time, it had a circulation of about 20,000, about 90 per cent of this among nonwhites.[82] Since the publishers had taken the precaution to register another name before the deposit requirement came into effect, *New Age* reappeared the following week as *Spark.* No ban was placed on *Spark;* but, crippled by a series of bans on members of its staff, it announced in its issue of March 28, 1963, that it could appear no longer.

Meanwhile, restrictions on the leaders of the organizations allied to the ANC—the Congress of Democrats, the Indian and Colored congresses, the Congress of Trade Unions, and the Federation of South African Women—and surveillance and harassment of these organizations' activities were so extensive that there seemed to be little advan-

---

[81] *Press Digest,* Aug. 2, 1962, p. 290.   [82] *Star,* Nov. 30, 1962.

tage to the government in banning the organizations themselves and pressing them entirely into the underground. Nevertheless, the Congress of Democrats was outlawed on September 7, 1962, becoming the first organization other than the Communist Party to be outlawed under the Suppression of Communism Act.

The question of permissible extraconstitutional activity by the integrationist and unquestionably anti-Communist Liberal Party and other liberally oriented groups remained to be answered. Having no hope that the Nationalist government could be defeated in parliamentary elections, the Liberal Party has advocated the building of a nonracial opposition and tactics of nonviolent resistance. It also has invited external pressures. Following the Sharpeville emergency, when Liberals were detained for the first time, party activities became increasingly subject to surveillance and harassment.[83]

The Progressive Party was urged by Luthuli late in 1961 to "make common cause with the extra-parliamentary forces" in order to defeat the Nationalists.[84] But the party has continued to work within the white political arena and has opposed the tactics of stay-at-home, boycott, and external pressure. Meanwhile, in seeking to become a bridge between whites and nonwhites, an aim that originally inspired the Liberal Party, it has sought closer contacts with nonwhites and an increase in its own very small nonwhite membership. Vorster has frequently described the Progressive Party as "dangerous." Speaking more generally, he has condemned "liberalistic tendencies" in politics, the press, and universities as more dangerous than communism.[85]

As the Prime Minister's chief aide, and possible successor, Vorster occupies an important role in defining the permissible scope of activity for the Opposition. He was a "general" in the Ossewa Brandwag and was interned for about two years during World War II. B. J. Schoeman, a member of the cabinet, described him in 1948 as one "who believed in the authoritarian State principle and advocated the destruction of parties."[86] Vorster, who was forty-seven years old in December 1962, has vigorously denied that his policies endanger the rule of law

[83] In March 1961, the Suppression of Communism Act was used to ban Patrick Duncan, editor of *Contact*, the independent liberal fortnightly, from meetings for five years. In justifying the ban, *Die Burger* in Cape Town stated that Duncan's efforts to outbid the Communists among Africans were a form of "violent anti-communism" (*Contact*, May 31, 1962, p. 8).

[84] *New Age*, Nov. 2, 1961, p. 4.

[85] *House of Assembly Debates*, May 21, 1962, col. 6059; *Press Digest*, Oct. 18, 1962, p. 414.

[86] Quoted in the *Star*, Jan. 7, 1962.

or freedom of speech. "The security of the State," he said, during passage of the Sabotage Bill, is "an old well-known rule of law." "My problem," he told a party meeting on October 11, 1962, "is to marry the freedom of the individual to the freedom of the State." [87]

AFRICAN ADMINISTRATION

The Controlled Area and Its Political Dynamics

The Nationalist government since 1948 has not only tightened the control over African affairs that already existed but has also sought to undermine African nationalism through systematic alterations in the form of that control. Basing its policy on the premise that "the Bantu peoples . . . do not constitute a homogeneous people, but form separate national units on the basis of language and culture," [88] the government has bolstered the position of cooperative tribal chiefs and promoted ethnic separatism both in the African reserves and in urban areas. At the same time, the government has promised that there will be movement toward expanded self-government within the separate tribal "homelands" and "national evolution" toward eventual independence within a South African commonwealth of nations.[89]

In response to domestic and external pressures, the timing of such movement has recently been accelerated. Unquestionably, it is to proceed under authoritarian white control, whose withdrawal cannot be foreseen. But questions with far-reaching implications remain to be answered. Can white-sponsored tribal nationalism deflect or dissipate the impulses toward African nationalism and Pan-Africanism? What

---

[87] *Ibid.* [While this book was in press, the virtual abrogation of habeas corpus early in May 1963 marked a new and radical break from the rule of law in South Africa. The General Law Amendment Act, 1963, empowered any commissioned police officer to arrest a person on certain broadly political grounds of suspicion, without warrant, and to detain him for interrogation for repeated periods of ninety days. The police no longer need to charge such a person before a court, or to provide access to a lawyer or friends, or to accord the privilege against self-incrimination. Other provisions empowered the Minister of Justice to extend a term of imprisonment indefinitely. Sobukwe completed his three-year term on May 3 and was detained indefinitely. Whereas the Sabotage Act of 1962 had evoked public protests, the virtual end of habeas corpus occurred with relatively little public protest as well as the general concurrence of the United Party. On the past, see Sydney Kentridge, "*Habeas Corpus* Procedure in South Africa," *South African Law Journal*, Aug. 1962, pp. 283–298.]

[88] First clause of Promotion of Bantu Self-Government Bill of 1959.

[89] South African Information Service, *The Progress of the Bantu Peoples toward Nationhood*, no. 1 (n.d.), pp. 1–2; statement by Dr. Verwoerd, *Herald Tribune* (New York), Jan. 24, 1962.

pressures will be generated within it and how will they affect the relationship between Africans and whites?

Africans who accept the policy that political advancement can take place only within separate Bantu states also accept the government's demand that they withdraw all claims to representation in the national Parliament. Thus, they agree that Africans outside the Bantu areas may claim political rights only within those areas. By doing so they repudiate the aim of the educated Africans and tribal chiefs who founded the ANC in 1912 in order to promote a sense of national identity. Chief Kaiser Matanzima, slated to be the first prime minister of the Transkeian Bantustan, has said in a written statement, "White South Africa is 100 per cent agreed on the maintenance of White control of the White Parliament. Only their defeat on the battlefield will divest them of this resolution." [90] Accepting the exclusiveness of white political power, he accepts also the principle of including within the citizenry and electorate of the Xhosa-speaking Transkei all Xhosa-speaking Africans who live elsewhere in South Africa.

The official proclamation in 1963 of the Transkei, the rural African reserve south of Basutoland and Natal, as an African territory with modified powers of self-government is a major step in the Nationalist program to reverse the direction in which African administration had been drifting before 1948. The continuity of administrative institutions has not been broken since that date, nor have powers and functions changed greatly from those existing previously. Administrative control during the Nationalist period has had, however, a fundamentally different orientation from that in the earlier period. It is also confronting unprecedented problems.

The Department of Bantu Administration and Development, established in 1958, inherited the wide legislative and administrative powers over African affairs previously exercised by the Native Affairs Department. These powers had been vested in the Governor-General-in-Council in 1910 and were partly derived from the powers held by the colonial governors and their predecessors. In Natal, for example, the Governor had been declared Supreme Chief in 1850, with wide authority to appoint and control chiefs; and in the Transvaal, the President was declared Paramount Chief in 1885, with power to frame regulations. The authority of the Native Affairs Department depended also upon statute. The Native Administration Act of 1927, which clarified this authority, gave the government in effect "a practically un-

[90] *Star,* Nov. 26, 1962, p. 1.

fettered power of legislation in African matters by proclamation." [91] Legislation since 1948 has enlarged the supervisory role of the department over local authorities. More important is its new role in persuading (and indirectly coercing) Africans to accept a "Bantu authorities" policy that has been received by many with suspicion and hostility, resulting at times in violence.

The Nationalist policy for African self-government, enacted in the Bantu Authorities Act of 1951, greatly watered down the elective principle. Experience with partly elected or indirectly elected advisory councils and boards, meeting with white officials, had been part of the structure of African local government for some fifty years. This so-called Transkeian system began in 1894 in the African reserves of the Transkei and, south of it, the Ciskei. The system bypassed tribal institutions, which were considered barriers not only to the spread of civilization but also to the movement of African workers into a wage-earning economy.

The Transkeian district councils, a majority of whose members were elected, also sent representatives to a General Council, popularly known as the Bunga. The United Transkeian Territories General Council was formed in 1931 through federation with the General Council of Pondoland. Only a few chiefs attended the Bunga, in an ex officio capacity. Dr. Verwoerd, telling of his own observation of the Bunga, has described it adversely as "largely a body controlled by the Whites," with a white chairman and white officials sitting in the front benches while the Africans sat on the back benches.[92] More sympathetic observers, while agreeing that the Bunga was little more than an advisory body, have praised the quality and freedom of its debate on matters of general interest (direct representation in Parliament was demanded unanimously on several occasions) and the sense of responsibility which developed among its members.

The elective principle was somewhat extended and the nontribal interests of Africans gained somewhat greater recognition in the period between the world wars. The Governor-General was empowered in 1920 to establish local councils (whose members could be elected or appointed) in African reserves outside the Transkei and Ciskei. In the following three decades, nearly thirty councils were established. The Act of 1927 extended the system of councils; it also

---

[91] Lord Hailey, *An African Survey* (rev. 1956; London: Oxford University Press, 1957), p. 432.

[92] *House of Assembly Debates,* April 12, 1962, col. 3803.

provided for the appointment of chiefs and headmen and gave them some minor executive authority.

Local councils were not developed in urban areas, since Africans there were considered to be transitory residents. (The African "should depart therefrom when he ceases to minister to the needs of the White man," said a Transvaal official document in 1922.[93]) Municipalities began about this time, however, to create native advisory boards. Although never generally accepted by Africans, they linked the local African population to white municipal councils. The elective principle was also partly used in the formation of the Natives' Representative Council, a body which presupposed African interests that were national.

The various representative bodies that were in existence in 1936 were made use of when Africans in all provinces were given token representation for the first time in the Senate. The so-called natives' settlement of that year not only removed the Africans in Cape Province to a separate roll to elect three whites to the Assembly but also provided for the indirect election by Africans throughout the country of four white senators to represent their interests in Parliament. The four electoral units were the Transkeian Territories, the rest of Cape Province, Natal, and the Transvaal and Orange Free State combined. In the Transkei, the Bunga served as the electoral college. Elsewhere, the electoral college machinery was elaborate, various areas being represented by local councils, chiefs or headmen, native advisory boards, or electoral committees elected by resident taxpayers.

Reforms that would further reduce the role of traditional institutions appeared to be in prospect in 1948. The United Party government had under consideration proposals to give the Natives' Representative Council some authority over local African government and to allow local councils to become wholly elective bodies. It was widely expected that future policy would be influenced by the 1948 report of the important commission headed by Judge Henry Fagan. The commission recognized that the urban areas included not only migrant laborers but also "a settled, permanent Native population" and recommended that representative boards should be in close liaison with municipal councils.[94]

[93] Quoted by Hailey, *An African Survey*, p. 428.

[94] Lawrence Reyburn, *The Urban African in Local Government: A Study of the Advisory Board System and Its Operation* (Johannesburg: S.A. Institute of Race Relations, 1960), pp. 33–35.

In sharp contrast to these policies, the Nationalist government, during fifteen years in power, has systematically removed from the governmental structure institutions and practices that pointed "towards a single multi-racial community" and, at the same time, has provided elaborate machinery for the promotion of "Bantu self-government." [95] Major statutes have been the Bantu Authorities Act of 1951, the Bantu Education Act of 1953, the Promotion of Bantu Self-Government Act of 1959, and the Urban Bantu Councils Act of 1961. Respectively, these measures abolished the Natives' Representative Council and provided for replacing the other councils by tribal-based authorities; effectively transferred African education from mission and provincial control to the Department of Native Affairs; abolished African representation in the House of Assembly and the Senate; and provided for replacing the native advisory boards by councils linked to tribal authorities.

Regarding self-government, the 1951 Act provided for tribal authorities composed of a chief and his advisers, who were recognized or appointed by the government. (About 550 chiefs and 1,200 headmen were in the pay of the government at the end of 1959.) Based upon these "sound foundations of the Bantu's own essentially democratic system of selfgovernment," [96] a hierarchy of authorities was erected at the district (in the Transkei only), regional, and territorial levels. The 1953 Education Act provided for school committees and boards on which officially approved persons would represent local African communities. In time, these committees and boards were to be integrated into the Bantu regional authorities. The 1959 Act recognized eight "national units": North Sotho, South Sotho, Swazi, Tsonga, Tswana, Venda, Zulu, and—in the Transkei—Xhosa. It provided for white commissioners-general to serve as links between the government and these units and for tribal representatives (commonly described as ambassadors) to serve as links to members of the units who were working in urban areas. Finally, the 1961 Act provided, where possible, for councils in urban areas composed of Bantu who belonged to a certain national unit and for appointment to the councils of representatives of chiefs.

The government's policy for the reestablishment of traditional in-

---

[95] Union of South Africa, *Memorandum Explaining the Background and Objects of the Promotion of Bantu Selfgovernment Bill,* 1959, White Paper 3—1959, p. 5.

[96] *Ibid.*

stitutions has some anomalous features. Tribally based regional and
territorial authorities are innovations, which appear necessary for
efficient and comprehensive administration. Official policy also envisages establishing "ethnic authorities" instead of territorial authorities in the case of ethnic groups whose members are scattered. In
urban areas, furthermore, regional rather than ethnic councils may
be established where the Bantu "are intermingled and where one
cannot establish an exclusively ethnic council as yet." [97]

A second anomalous feature is essential to the maintenance of white
control—the official appointment of members of tribal authorities. An
exception exists in the Transkei, where a minority of the members at
this level are chosen by election. All membership, furthermore, is
subject to official cancellation. Since the membership of higher authorities is derived from the tribal authorities, official control at all
levels is assured.

Another apparent anomaly is the intention of the government gradually to reintroduce the elective principle and Western forms into the
Bantu authorities system.[98] Dr. Verwoerd has justified this policy as
part of the process of development. He apparently hopes also that
such a development will make the system more acceptable to foreign
observers. At least half the membership of the urban Bantu councils is
to be elected. More anomalous is the reintroduction of the elective
principle in the Transkei.

The all-African Transkeian Territorial Authority, which succeeded
the Bunga, as noted below, had eliminated the elective principle except for a minority of members at a lower level. (A majority of
members of the Bunga had been indirectly elected.) Early in 1962, however, a committee of the Territorial Authority drafted (presumably
with the help of white experts) a constitution providing for a cabinet-
parliamentary system in which 36 of 131 members of the future
Transkeian legislative assembly were to be elected. The remaining
95 were to be chiefs or nominees of chiefs. When consulted by the
committee in March 1962, Dr. Verwoerd recommended "a larger percentage of elected representatives as against chiefs." [99] The draft was
amended to provide that only 64 members in a body of 109 should

[97] *House of Assembly Debates,* June 15, 1961, col. 8146.
[98] *Ibid.,* April 11, 1961, col. 4315.
[99] *Ibid.,* April 12, 1962, col. 3804. For the first draft and the amended draft,
see *Fighting Talk,* March 1962, p. 3, and South African Information Service,
The Transkei: Major Steps on the Road to Self-Determination, Fact Paper 102,
Supplement to the *Digest of South African Affairs,* June 1962, p. 10.

be chiefs. Matanzima was later reported as saying that the committee had objected.[100] The objection, as he expressed it, was that "our chiefs are the traditional leaders who were appointed by God himself."

The extent of genuine support among Africans for cooperation with the government is exceedingly difficult to determine. "Most Africans," in the judgment of Leo Marquard, reject as "impracticable and undesirable" the policy of regarding the reserves as their only permanent homes.[101] Undoubtedly, however, many Africans in urban areas as well as on white-owned farms and in the reserves are poorly informed and apathetic. There has also been speculation, especially in recent years, that a sense of futility about opposition to the government is producing a political listlessness among some Africans. Among others, the conclusion has been drawn that realism calls for acceptance of any policy that might lead to partition.

Whatever may be the motives of the realists or the implied conditions of their support, the government is able to display a good deal of statistical evidence of African cooperation with the new bodies it has established. One may dismiss as extravagant the florid sociological jargon of ministerial or departmental pronouncements or the lyrical letters of gratitude published in *Bantu*. Official sources state, however, that by 1959, 30,000 African parents, whose "understanding of the new deal has . . . fired their imagination," served on 4,500 school committees; and 4,500 parents served on 500 school boards.[102] By October 1961 (the Minister of Bantu Administration and Development having been satisfied in each case that popular consent had been secured) there were in existence 381 of a possible 500 tribal authorities, 44 regional authorities, and 3 territorial authorities, Transkeian, Ciskeian, and Tswana. (The establishment of a Zulu territorial authority was expected in 1963.) The decision of the Bunga in 1955 to become a territorial authority was one of the government's most notable successes.

Despite these evidences of cooperation, the introduction of the Bantu authorities system has probably been met by more extreme hostility than any other Nationalist policy. That this has occurred in tribal areas justifies grave apprehension on the part of the government. The hostility has many causes, including dislike of government-

[100] *Press Digest*, Dec. 20, 1962, p. 515. The quotation that follows is from the *Star*, Oct. 5, 1962.

[101] *The Peoples and Policies of South Africa*, p. 120.

[102] White Paper 3—1959, p. 6; South African Information Service, *The Progress of the Bantu Peoples toward Nationhood*, no. 2 (1960), p. 27.

appointed chiefs and headmen, who are often autocratic and sometimes corrupt, the introduction of passes for African women, the unpopularity of various measures of agricultural reform, and opposition to influx and other racial controls experienced by tribesmen who have looked for work in the towns. The linking of "Bantu authorities" to the grievances felt by African townsmen has been partly inspired by urban political agitators, as the government has asserted; but what this proves, Marquard has observed, is that tribal Africans "are in closer contact with urban African opinion than was supposed, and are susceptible to influences coming from the urban areas." [103]

Government officials have been industrious in seeking consent while using a wide range of measures to deal with resistance.[104] The minister has urged Bantu affairs commissioners to treat Africans with tact and patience, and officials have toured the reserves with propaganda units equipped with loudspeakers. At important junctures the government has raised the salaries of chiefs and headmen. Tribal representatives have been warned that their groups would lose financial and social service benefits if they did not accept the Bantu authorities system. Opponents of the government, or agitators, have been exiled. Mass meetings, rioting, bloody clashes with the police, hut burning, and murder have resulted in mass arrests and mass trials and the sealing off of large areas. In some parts of the Transkei and in the Transvaal, especially during 1957–1960 and 1962–1963, opposition reached the stage of open revolt. Early in January 1961 it was disclosed that 4,769 Africans had been taken into custody in Pondoland, which had been occupied by thousands of troops, and that over 2,000 had already been brought to trial.

Soon after the worst violence in Pondoland had subsided, the Transkeian Territorial Authority set up a recess committee, in May 1961, to study the implications of self-government. Movement toward the replacement of all whites by Africans in the administration of the Transkei had been discussed since 1955, when the Bunga, both encouraged and pressed by the government, had voted unanimously to accept the principle of the Bantu Authorities Act. On November 10, 1961, Chief Tutor Ndamase, a member of the committee and the heir

[103] *The Peoples and Policies of South Africa*, p. 120.

[104] Chapter VI, "Maintaining Contact," of the *Report of the Department of Bantu Administration and Development for the Period 1st January, 1958 to 31st December, 1959*, describes its "daily contact with representatives of the Bantu from every level of society," including "even elements actively opposed to autogenous development," and its use of mass media "to inform the Bantu masses."

to Paramount Chief Victor Poto of West Pondoland, said publicly to the minister, "We want self-government for the Transkei by the end of 1963, and complete independence as soon as possible after that." [105] He did not make this statement, he said, because of letters from white agitators urging independence, as the minister suggested; the only letters he had seen were from Pondos threatening him with death if he continued to collaborate.

New defeats in the United Nations late in 1961 stimulated press speculation that a dramatic move was near. "Our hand is being forced, there is no doubt about that," V. M. P. Leibbrandt, the chief magistrate of the Transkei, told a reporter on January 9, 1962, "but the Transkei is just not ready for self-government." [106] On January 23, replying to the parliamentary opposition's no-confidence motion, Dr. Verwoerd made an announcement that disbelievers would find "dramatic," he said, and proof of "our earnestness": "the Government will . . . grant the Transkei self-government." [107]

The population destined for self-government consists of about 1,400,-000 Africans of various tribes but most of them Xhosa-speaking. Their area is significantly different from that of the other reserves, which are widely scattered; it is an almost unbroken black territory with few so-called "spots" of white residence and a long history of separate regional consciousness. About 250 university graduates live in the Transkei. Many of these graduates are among the 3,000 teachers, and a few are doctors and attorneys. In addition, there are some 600 African traders and numerous clerks. Also living there are 14,000 or more whites, many of them traders, and 11,000 or more Coloreds. Probably 1,500,000 or more Transkeian Africans live outside the Transkei.

One year after Dr. Verwoerd's announcement, the January 1963 issue of *South African Scope,* which is distributed in North America by the government's Information Service, announced on its front page: "Democratic Constitution Endorsed by Transkei Nation." "No Whites in the Transkei will be allowed any political rights," it said, "and conversely no Xhosa people will be allowed to vote on the affairs of the White South African nation." This distinctive feature of the future constitution, its ethnically exclusive base, was supported by a large

[105] Randolph Vigne, "Birth of Bantustan," *Forum,* March 1962, p. 10; *Fighting Talk,* March 1962, p. 3.
[106] Vigne, "Birth of Bantustan," p. 11.
[107] *House of Assembly Debates,* Jan. 23, 1962, cols. 74–75, 93.

majority of Transkeian chiefs during 1962. Presumably, the government believed that they represented the overwhelming majority of
Transkeian Africans. "I have confidence in the masses of our Bantu,"
Dr. Verwoerd had said in January, "with the exception of a small
group of agitators."

The government at the end of 1962 could point to a formal record
of harmony and near-unanimity among the Transkei's officially confirmed leaders. The 27-member recess committee had met with Dr.
Verwoerd in March "in such a harmonious spirit," according to the
Minister of Bantu Administration, that discussion was completed in
one day instead of two or three.[108] On March 30, the committee
unanimously accepted a draft constitution that extended political
rights to Africans only and provided for a legislative assembly of 64
chiefs and 45 elected members. The Territorial Authority approved
the committee's report on May 4. The proportion of chiefs in the
assembly had been challenged but had won acceptance by 70 votes
to 5.

When the Territorial Authority met in December 1962 to vote on
the draft constitution that was to be submitted to Parliament, a proposal that there should be an equal number of chiefs and elected
members was narrowly defeated by only 5 votes. On the fundamental
issue of a multiracial constitution, a small group broke from the
unanimity that had marked the May session. Only 10 votes, however,
were cast in support of multiracialism.

The majority in the Territorial Authority and the small group of
dissidents were led, respectively, by two young chiefs who are cousins:
Kaiser Matanzima, chairman of the Authority, and Sabata Dalindyebo,
Paramount Chief of the Tembu.[109] Matanzima is chief of the so-called
Emigrant Tembu, a group of about 80,000 who were settled separately,
for historical reasons, from the main group of about 420,000 Tembu.
He is a graduate of Fort Hare University College and has had legal
training. Matanzima is a strong personality and an astute politician, not
a stooge; some observers have described him as cold and ruthless. Al-
though junior to Sabata in tribal authority, he is slated to become the
Transkei's first prime minister.

[108] Fact Paper 102, p. 4.

[109] Much of the following discussion of Transkeian personalities and develop-
ments is based on reports in *Contact, New Age,* and the *Star* and articles by
Allister Sparks in the *Rand Daily Mail,* July 18–21, 1962; the *Eastern Province
Herald,* May 7, 1962; *Cape Times,* May 7, 1962; and Edwin S. Munger, "Transkei
Independence: Fact or Fantasy?" *Africa Report,* May 1962.

Sabata, whom Matanzima is said to dislike and to consider intellectually inferior, is described by sympathetic observers as a popular chief with a growing reputation. His formal education is limited to completion of Standard IX. Sabata has traveled privately outside the Transkei, and his experiences are said to have influenced his thinking in a liberal direction. He is closely related to Nelson Mandela, the ANC leader already described.

Sabata emerged in 1962 as the most prominent leader of the opposition to the government, but his role was contradictory and his position precarious, even as Matanzima's is, but for opposite reasons. He and other members of the opposition were members of the recess committee, and as "a Government man," in his own words, he voted for its report. But as a hereditary and traditional chief who expresses the consensus of his tribe, he issued a press statement, following the May meeting of the Territorial Authority, rejecting the proposed constitution. Sabata was undoubtedly under strong pressure from both sides. The government is reported to have exploited his naïveté and to have ordered him not to issue any further statements. In November it supplanted Sabata's personal advisory council with members of the Tembu regional authority. Many of Sabata's own councilors are said to have warned him of the consequences of opposition.

On the other hand, mass meetings of Tembu at Sabata's "Great Place" demonstrated their opposition to the government, and Sabata received much popular adulation (and praise from white liberals) as leader of the opposition. He defied government orders, complained of being misled and silenced at meetings of the Territorial Authority, and stated that advisers had been "forced" upon him. Following the December meeting, he virtually invited deposition when he made a radical statement to *Spark,* successor to the left-wing *New Age,* saying in part, "We have not given up the long struggle for equal rights and African freedom in our multiracial country. . . . We totally reject the concept of separate development, since we have now seen where it is leading—to a tiny black colony where we will be cut off from the Republic and from the outside world." [110]

The overwhelming majority of the small class of educated Africans in the Transkei undoubtedly agree with Sabata and oppose the establishment of an "apartheid" state. Prominent within this class are mem-

[110] *Spark,* Dec. 20, 1962. Compare Dr. Verwoerd's statement: "We are trying to establish well-disposed little Black neighboring states" (*House of Assembly Debates,* Jan. 23, 1962, col. 90).

bers of the Liberal Party, whose rural African support is strongest in the Transkei. The opposition includes teachers who have been dismissed and politicians who have no place within the Bantu authorities system. They and more radical Africans (and perhaps a few conservatives who agree generally with the Progressive Party) have called for a nonracial or multiracial constitution for the Transkei. This demand is primarily a challenge to the government's racial policy generally, but it is also a continuing irritant within the Transkei, a standing challenge to the limits imposed by the government on future semi-autonomy.

Restrictions on meetings and an atmosphere of intimidation have been partially effective in curbing organized opposition; the opposition now is underground. In December 1962, the Transkei began its third year under Proclamation 400, which provides that the police may arrest anyone suspected of an offense and hold him in prison without warrant until he answers questions fully and truthfully. (By January 1961, 360 Africans had been detained for questioning for periods from five to forty-three days.) It also prohibits meetings without a magistrate's permission, although apparently this restriction is not always enforced. The proclamation was in force "at the request of the Bantu leaders in the Transkeian territories," according to an official explanation, and would remain in force until they asked for its repeal.[111]

More pervasive has been the continuous threat of bans on activity, detention, exile, and—in the case of chiefs and headmen—deposition. The new practice of imposing house arrest was applied for the first time in the Transkei in December 1962, against a trader who had been active in the All-African Convention and had been dismissed as principal of a secondary school. An additional threat of removal or deportation has been added by the grant of power to certain senior chiefs, under Proclamation 400, to order persons to move to a prescribed area for an indefinite period of time.[112] Opponents of Matanzima who live far from the Transkei have reportedly been dealt with by the government. In November 1962, two Transkeian Africans who had lived in Cape Town for more than twenty years and had opposed a delegation sent by Matanzima to Cape Town were ordered under

[111] *House of Assembly Debates,* Feb. 2, 1962, col. 502.

[112] By May 1962, Matanzima had ordered the removal of five persons (*House of Assembly Debates,* May 4, 1962, col. 4956). The text of a later order by Matanzima is reproduced in *Contact,* Nov. 1, 1962, p. 4.

the Native Administration Act of 1927 to move permanently to restricted areas of the Transkei.

That political channels will be opened in the Transkei to allow full ventilation of African opinion and the free organization of political parties is inconceivable so long as official policy maintains that organizations such as the ANC and the PAC are subversive. Partisans of these organizations regard as too late any tactic of collaboration with government-sponsored institutions for the purpose of exploiting them. On the other hand, Africans whose political activities are still above ground, for example, those inspired by the Liberal Party, have considered the usefulness of contesting the 45 elected seats in the future Transkeian assembly. The members elected to these seats plus 10 chiefs would constitute a majority. Electioneering would take place not only in the Transkei but also, presumably, among the Transkeian citizens who live in urban areas. Many questions regarding the necessary conditions for effective political opposition remain to be answered, including the freedom of eligible voters to register, the freedom of organizers and campaigners to travel and hold meetings, and the freedom of the press to report such activities. Meanwhile, the Liberal Party, claiming a steady increase in membership, opened its first Transkeian office in Umtata in November 1962 and invited other groups to use it for nonracial meetings (necessarily restricted to no more than nine persons). In early 1963, however, leading white and African members of the Liberal Party were restricted by government order.

The opposition's hope for liberalization and the government's hope for harmony are being frustrated by the impossibility of isolating the Transkei from the rest of South Africa. Eastern Cape Province, of which the Transkei is a part, has been historically an area in which the ANC and also the AAC have been somewhat active; and among rural areas, the Transkei has been one of the more politically conscious. Both the fact of constant movement of labor between the Transkei and urban areas and the theory that Transkeian citizenship is held by Africans in urban areas make isolation impossible.

The underground activity, sporadic violence, and beginnings of organized terror in urban areas are evident also in the Transkei. Movement back and forth between the Transkei and western Cape Province, for example, is suggested by the arrest in Cape Town in November 1962 of nine Africans suspected of attempting to assassinate Matanzima during the preceding month. Poqo, an antiwhite terrorist group that has been linked to the PAC and to events in Paarl (near Cape Town) on November 22, 1962, resulting in the hacking to death of two whites, has been blamed by the police for an incursion into the Transkei and a bloody fight at Matanzima's home apparently timed to coincide with the December meeting of the Territorial Authority. While seeming to agree with this estimate, *Spark* has described the more extensive attacks on chiefs and headmen and the burning of their huts and kraals as the work of a local underground rather than outsiders. Since the government maintains that the mass of Africans in the Transkei favor cooperation, it is inclined to blame outsiders for trouble. At any rate, it does not treat agitation and underground activity there in isolation from similar activity nationally. Official resentment of the Liberal Party, for example, may become intensified because of the slaughter on February 5, 1963, of five whites (presumably the work of a terrorist group like Poqo) in the heart of Tembuland, where Liberal Party representatives have been active in urging resistance to the Bantustan policy.

Confronted by white liberals and black extremists, Matanzima is under pressure to back authoritarian counteraction and also to reassert his own brand of nationalism. He has attacked the African advocates of multiracialism as "nothing more than stooges" of hypocritical whites who seek to divide the Africans in order to prolong white control (a line of argument used by some African extremists) and also has called them "the protagonists of a revolution on Communistic lines." [113] Some observers have speculated that Matanzima may be a PAC man at heart who may evolve eventually from a parochial tribal nationalist into a Pan-African one. Meanwhile, Matanzima's claim to African nationalist legitimacy is evident in the constitutional provision that the Transkei's national anthem will be "Nkosi Sikelel' i-Afrika," "God Save Africa." Luthuli has described this song as "a sort of unofficial National Anthem of black South Africa, and the theme song of the African National Congress." [114]

In the immediate situation, Matanzima must make specific appeals outside the body of generally timid and ignorant chiefs and headmen in order to win support from the relatively small number of persons qualified to enter his cabinet and to move into administrative posts

[113] Written statement by Matanzima in the *Star*, Nov. 26, 1962, p. 1.
[114] *Let My People Go,* p. 81.

in "every department of the Transkei," whose full control by Africans he has asked for. Matanzima was "going all out to win some intellectuals to his side," *New Age* of November 29, 1962, reported, and had approached "attorneys, doctors, businessmen and MRA adherents." One supporter is George Matanzima, his brother, who is both a chief and an attorney and probably the future minister of justice. Another supporter is T. E. Tshunungwa, formerly secretary of the ANC in Cape Province and an accused in the treason trial, who has acted as an emissary to Tembu in Cape Town and Port Elizabeth. Matanzima's effort to win support is crippled by the absence of a political organization that is independent of official control and responsive to the energies of educated or politically ambitious Africans. Transkeian political allegiance depends largely upon personalities despite the substantial nature of current issues. Presumably these issues do not account for the report that several of Sabata's older half brothers are pro-Matanzima and that Matanzima's own son is pro-Sabata.

Matanzima and the few able men who surround him face the extraordinarily difficult task of appealing to the educated class without jeopardizing the dominant position of the conservative chiefs and of exerting pressure upon the government while remaining in its good graces. Many chiefs seem to have taken seriously the vision of "inkululekho"—self-government or, more accurately, freedom from bondage—and expect progressively larger autonomy to be granted to the Transkei. Some supporters of the Bantustan policy, including urban African politicians, envision the possibility of secession from the Republic. At the outset, the Parliament in Cape Town will retain power over external affairs, internal security, immigration, defense, the Transkeian constitution, and other matters; and the President of the Republic will have the power to veto all legislation. White guidance and ultimate control may need to continue for a century, leading officials have suggested. But Matanzima has been quoted by an official publication as saying, on the historic day of January 23, 1962, that "self-determination is assured within the next decade." [115]

There has been much speculation about the Transkeian state of the future and about such dramatic possibilities as representation in the United Nations. Of more crucial as well as immediate importance in demonstrating the government's good intentions and Matanzima's

[115] Fact Paper 102, pp. 3–4.

effectiveness are policies of language and social equality that can be implemented immediately. Matanzima may press for a speed-up in the timetable of independence, for greater economic aid, for an enlargement of territory, for a reversal of Dr. Verwoerd's position that Port St. Johns on the Transkeian coast will not belong to the Transkei, and for independent relations with adjacent Basutoland. More sensitive is the demand made over a number of years by the Territorial Authority and endorsed by Matanzima that the medium of instruction, excepting the earliest grades, should be one of the two official languages, Afrikaans or English, rather than Xhosa.[116] The general preference is for English. Even more sensitive is the demand for social equality between the races in the Transkei. Matanzima has been reported as saying that social apartheid will come to an end and that both Africans and whites will use the Transkei's few hotels.

Social equality is a touchstone that reveals attitudes that profoundly affect Transkeian developments: the desire of progovernment Africans for equal treatment within their own territories, the disapproval of even sympathetic foreign observers if such treatment is lacking, the unreadiness of most white officials and white residents in the Bantu territories to treat any Africans as social equals, and the fear of whites generally that such equality will have dangerous repercussions outside the territories. When William Buckley, Jr., encountered Matanzima on a hot afternoon in a small Transkeian town late in 1962 and suggested having a Coca-Cola while they talked, his guide said that this could not be done. "And so," Buckley has written, "I saw what is not so easily imagined: that even in the very heart of the area that is to be the headquarters of the new state, importunate American whites may not share a table with the Heir Apparent at a dirty little bar, miles from anywhere." [117] A sympathetic French journalist troubled by a similar experience was assured by Dr. W. M. Eiselen, a close associate of Dr. Verwoerd and commissioner-general to the North Sotho, that "social

---

[116] The report of the recess committee stated that Xhosa shall be the official language of the Transkei but that the Republic's two official languages and Sesotho shall be recognized for use wherever necessary. It is remarkable that the report goes on to say that the Transkeian government may provide for the exclusive use of any one of these languages for an official purpose (Fact Paper 102, p. 9). Constitutional challenge by the United Party to the language provisions proposed by the government led to an immediate use by the latter of the joint-session procedure for amending what is the one remaining entrenched clause of the constitution. Thus, Xhosa has been made an official language for the Transkei along with English and Afrikaans.

[117] *National Review*, Jan. 15, 1963, p. 22.

equality in the Reserves" was necessary and, furthermore, would encourage whites to leave.[118]

A separate and further question is often asked: should social restrictions be imposed on distinguished black visitors from new African states or on a Transkeian citizen when he is outside the Transkei? A farseeing Afrikaans journalist who expounds separate development has answered no. "On the other hand," he warns, "we dare not, with so many black people amongst us and with the ultimate political pattern not yet fixed, make social equality the wedge to destroy the whole principle of separate development." [119] Speedy resolution of this problem to the satisfaction of men like Matanzima requires rapid change of deeply ingrained white attitudes. Thus far, Afrikaner nationalist leaders appear to have failed in their personal relations with Africans to give the public lead that is necessary if such a change as this is even slowly to take place.

NATIONAL ADMINISTRATION

The Prime Minister and his cabinet, who bear ultimate responsibility to Parliament, provide over-all guidance to the administrative establishment. Ministers individually are responsible to Parliament for the actions of public servants in their departments. In administrative organization also, the British pattern is generally followed. Under the minister, departments are headed by permanent or career secretaries and undersecretaries. A large number of statutory bodies and public corporations exercise considerable autonomy outside the departmental structure. They submit annual reports to Parliament and are held accountable through the ministers.

The enlargement of the cabinet to meet the expanding scope of the national government, and also to respond to policies of racial separateness, undoubtedly increases the difficulties of coordination. The cabinet had 12 members in 1948, only 2 more than in 1910. The Prime Minister himself held the portfolio of External Affairs until 1955. Dr. Verwoerd, after becoming Prime Minister in September 1958, enlarged the cabinet from 14 to 16 members and had provision made, for the first time, for deputy ministers. Four were appointed. Dr. Verwoerd also introduced new terminology when the Department of Native

[118] Paul Giniewski, *Bantustans: A Trek towards the Future* (Cape Town: Human & Rousseau, 1961), pp. 226–230.

[119] Willem van Heerden, English translation provided by *Dagbreek en Sondagnuus*, Sept. 9, 1962.

Affairs was divided into the Department of Bantu Administration and Development and the Department of Bantu Education. Shortly before the end of 1961, the addition of 2 English-speaking ministers brought the number of ministers to 18, including the Prime Minister. Their titles referred to 27 of some 35 departments.

The Nationalist government, particularly under Dr. Verwoerd, has presumably clarified departmentalization by reshuffling responsibilities according to race rather than function. The process has not yet been completed. A major shift occurred with the transfer of African primary and secondary education from the provincial education departments to the Native Affairs Department in 1953 and subsequently to the Department of Bantu Education, to which African higher education was also transferred in 1959. A more recent transfer was that of African child welfare in 1961 from the Social Welfare Department to the Department of Bantu Administration and Development.

A similar process has been under way with regard to the Coloreds. Their separate administrative treatment may be traced to the wartime Smuts government, which set up a Colored Advisory Council. After 1948, a subdepartment for Colored affairs was organized which gradually collected a variety of functions. It became a department in 1958, and in August 1961 was placed under the first Minister of Colored Affairs. In June 1962 he announced that legislation would be introduced in 1963 for the gradual transfer from the provinces to the national government of all education for the Coloreds. The headquarters of the department is in Cape Province, where about 90 per cent of the Coloreds live, but the minister gave assurance that proper attention would be paid to the other 10 per cent through administrative decentralization.

Separate administrative treatment of the Indian population presents more difficulty because of its small size (about 477,400 in 1960). In September 1961, having decided to accept the Indian population as permanent, the government created a Department of Indian Affairs and assigned it to the Minister of Bantu Education. Presumably this development marked the beginning of a process of administrative consolidation similar to that affecting the Coloreds. One difficulty was the existence of administrative bodies that affect both Indians and Coloreds. In the month before the creation of the Indian Affairs Department, a Department of Community Development was created and given responsibility for the Group Areas Board and the development of local government by Coloreds and by Indians in their respective group areas. This new department was assigned to the minister who also holds the portfolio of Colored Affairs.

Racial clarity in administrative organization gave way to other priorities in November 1961 when the government created a Department of Information and placed it under one of the cabinet's new English-speaking members. Consolidated within it were the information services of the Bantu, Colored, and Indian departments and the State Information Service, formerly under the Department of Foreign Affairs. The Information Department's purpose is to coordinate and develop information services not only abroad but also between the state and nonwhite groups at home.

The burden of over-all coordination and control rests upon the Prime Minister and permanent officials, particularly the secretary for finance and the secretary to the treasury, both of whom are responsible to the Minister of Finance. Proposals have been made to enlarge and strengthen the Department of the Prime Minister, but little has been done to make it the effective center of administration. Within the broad outlines of policy he lays down, the budget is prepared in the office of the Minister of Finance after a process of informal consultation with the permanent heads of departments. Proposals for administrative reorganization and improved efficiency are made at this time by the secretaries and the Public Service Commission (described below). High officials in the Ministry of Finance have tended to think of the commission, perhaps unfairly, as a body whose proficiency does not extend to broad questions of administration.

The government's concern for coordination and consultation with members of the white community was reflected in the creation of an Economic Advisory Council in July 1960. The hope that this body will assist in long-range economic planning is similar to hopes once expressed about the Social and Economic Planning Council, which ceased to exist after the war. The latter body produced some valuable and detailed reports but never played an important role in the making of policy. The new council has over forty members: Afrikaans-speaking and English-speaking representatives of commercial, industrial, mining, farming, and labor organizations, professional and academic persons including several who are not partisans of the government, and a number of key officials. The council's chairman is an able and highly respected former secretary for finance. At the first meeting, held to discuss plans for the development of border industries near the African reserves, the Prime Minister made it clear that the government's fundamental program was not to be questioned but that advice on its economic implications was welcomed. The procedure of referring specific problems to the council and of review by officials appears to leave little opportunity for initiative. In July 1962 Dr. Verwoerd said the council's work was of great value.[120]

Effective executive control of administration is due to the vigor of most Nationalist ministers, their long experience in office, and the sympathetic cooperation of senior officials. Members of the Opposition, however, are dissatisfied with the effectiveness of legislative oversight of administration and the voluminous amount of delegated legislation. The Controller and Auditor-General, a civil servant appointed by the government and removable only at the request of both houses of Parliament, submits annual reports to the Select Committee on Public Accounts in the House of Assembly, and members of the committee may question heads of departments. But that this leads to effective control of public expenditure is, according to one observer, "very doubtful." [121] Rules and regulations, proclamations and notices, must be submitted to Parliament, where they may be criticized; but the Opposition is not staffed to review these adequately. In March 1962, a former Controller and Auditor-General criticized the failure of Parliament to design effective machinery to control "administrative justice," particularly as it affected the unenfranchised, and also the inadequacy of provision for appeal to the courts. Official arbitrariness, replied the Minister of Justice, could be "ripped wide open in Parliament" if the Opposition was wide awake,[122] but the latter is unconvinced.

With regard to the public service, or civil service, Parliament keeps informed through the annual reports submitted to it by the Public Service Commission. The nonpartisan tradition of the public service is entrusted to this body, whose three members are appointed by the cabinet for five years and are removable only at the request of both houses of Parliament. The commission recommends individual appointments, promotions, and transfers. Persons falling under the commission may be freely transferred between national and provincial levels. The cabinet may reject or alter a recommendation, but the commission must report such action fully to Parliament.

[120] *Star*, July 16, 1962.
[121] H. R. Hahlo and Ellison Kahn, *The Union of South Africa: The Development of Its Laws and Constitution* (London: Stevens, 1960), p. 185.
[122] *House of Assembly Debates*, March 23, 1962, cols. 3, 119–123, 142.

The expansion of state activity since 1910 and, since 1948, the enlargement of national responsibility and the statutory elaboration of public policy have placed a heavy burden on the public service. It has more than trebled in size since 1930, and today about one of six employable whites between 18 and 60 is regularly employed by the national or provincial governments. Thus, a high proportion of the electorate, as Marquard has pointed out, depends upon public employment. Its votes are sought after, but in accordance with the British tradition, it is excluded from public participation in politics.

References to the public service usually include the Department of Posts and Telegraphs, the police force, and the Permanent Defense Force but not the employees of the Railways and Harbors Administration (who are governed by a commission similar to the Public Service Commission), teachers, and employees of localities. In 1961, the public service and the railways had the following numbers of employees, respectively: whites, 109,600 and 110,385; Africans, 108,853 and 93,189; Coloreds, 10,892 and 10,187; and Asians, 717 and 696.[123]

The police force in April 1960 employed more nonwhites than whites (that is, 13,321 nonwhites, of whom 11,976 were Africans as against 12,850 whites). These numbers exclude the railways police force and municipal traffic police. In addition to their usual duties, the white police have considerable though routine administrative duties, acting as census enumerators and inspectors of licenses and at times as public prosecutors in rural areas.

Since 1910, the composition of the public service has altered radically from one that was overwhelmingly English-speaking to one that is overwhelmingly Afrikaans-speaking. In 1912 nearly 85 per cent of the public service was English-speaking, including Englishmen as well as English-speaking South Africans.[124] Young Afrikaners, many of them leaving the land, moved rapidly into the lower ranks of the public service, finding such entry easier than entry into business. Young English-speaking persons were more attracted to nongovernmental jobs. The police force, in particular, attracted recruits from the poorer sections of the Afrikaner population. Not until some years after 1948 did a majority of senior public service positions come to be occupied by Afrikaans-speaking persons. In part this shift was the normal re-

---

[123] Horrell, *A Survey of Race Relations in South Africa: 1962*, p. 168. The police statistics that follow are from the 1959–1960 *Survey*, p. 205.

[124] Sheila Patterson, *The Last Trek: A Study of the Boer People and the Afrikaner Nation* (London: Routledge & Kegan Paul, Ltd., 1957), p. 57.

sult of the growing proportion of Afrikaners in the lower ranks. To some extent, however, it was the result of vigorous implementation of the bilingual requirement which had been in existence since 1910. English-speaking officials who did not show proficiency in Afrikaans were passed over for promotion. Today, because a large proportion of entrants into the public service come from Afrikaans-medium schools, the main problem in the enforcement of bilingualism is raising the standard of proficiency in English. Some 4,400 persons have failed among 10,000 who have taken language tests in recent years, and a majority of these failures have been in English. "Strenuous attempts are being made," said the Minister of the Interior in May 1962, "not to teach English-speaking people Afrikaans, but to teach Afrikaans-speaking people English." [125]

The extent to which partisanship has determined promotion is difficult to establish. In the judgment of Marquard, a liberal but dispassionate observer, appointment and promotion occur "without regard to party political affiliations until a fundamental difference in policy manifests itself." [126] Nationalists were not promoted to key positions during World War II. After 1948 the government reversed several of the promotions, for example, that of the general manager of railways. It also overrode the recommendation of the Public Service Commission for the position of secretary for native affairs and appointed its own man. Allegations have been made but cannot be proved that key positions are being filled by members of the Broederbond, a secret Afrikaans society. (From 1944 to 1948 public servants were forbidden to belong to the Broederbond,[127] which was described by Smuts as "a dangerous, cunning, political Fascist organization.") The belief that English-speaking persons or non-Nationalists are at a competitive disadvantage has undoubtedly discouraged some of the ablest young persons from entering the public service. "Any English-speaking person who joins the Public Service," a member of the Opposition said recently on the floor of the House of Assembly, "is a fool." [128]

[125] *House of Assembly Debates*, May 7, 1962, col. 5099 and 5110.
[126] *The Peoples and Policies of South Africa*, p. 115.
[127] Carter, *The Politics of Inequality*, p. 252. D. G. Ross, a member of Parliament, said recently, "In the past we know too that these language tests were to keep the senior English-speaking Public Servants down and as an excuse for promoting Broederbonders over them. It seems to me as an English-speaking person that this process is now being completed" (*House of Assembly Debates*, May 7, 1962, cols. 5108–5109).
[128] *House of Assembly Debates*, May 7, 1962, col. 5109.

Low standards of English are said to have reduced the efficiency of the public service in its dealings with the English-speaking section. Bilingualism also imposes throughout the whole government the burden of maintaining all records in two languages. Another burden is language testing. Because of "the enormous turnover of personnel in the junior ranks," according to the minister, the Public Service Commission decided early in 1962 to suspend tests for persons in the junior ranks.[129] The level of efficiency has also been affected indirectly by other conditions: pay standards that are much lower than in commerce and industry (employers offer "fantastic salaries" to persons being trained on public service bursaries, the minister has complained [130]), unequal pay for women, and a five-and-a-half-day work week.

Since South Africa became a republic, Senator Johannes de Klerk, the Minister of the Interior, has defined the role of the public servant in a manner that has troubled the Opposition. South Africa faces the necessity, he has said, of deciding between "two directions": the French, in which officials are "the servants of the public" and, like politicians, are regarded with suspicion by the people, or the German, in which officials are "experts" and "co-rulers" and regarded with respect by the people. As republicans, according to de Klerk, public servants must be inspired by "the concept of the State" and "patriotism as the highest motive." [131] Since the government tends to identify patriotism with its policy, opponents regard these views as a threat to the traditional political neutrality of the public service.

PROVINCIAL AND LOCAL GOVERNMENT

The central government since 1910, and particularly since 1953, has tended to limit the scope of provincial government and to extend central control over the functions of local government. At the same time, local functions have become more extensive because of the use of local government as an instrument of national policy, especially with regard to nonwhites. The trend toward establishing a more comprehensive and uniform national policy has occurred through the exercise of parliamentary sovereignty in a unitary system, and no basic change has been made in the institutions of provincial government and intergovernmental relationships as established by the Act of Union.

The imperatives of white national interests, as seen by all govern-

[129] *Ibid.*, Feb. 20, 1962, col. 1353.   [130] *Ibid.*, May 7, 1962, col. 5122.
[131] *Ibid.*, cols. 5110–5112.

ments since 1910, have prevailed over weaker sentiment for increased provincial and local autonomy. The leading delegates at South Africa's constitutional convention, except those from Natal, agreed that strong centralized government was necessary to meet the needs of a vast and sparsely populated area and particularly its problems of drought, transport, and protection against African unrest and even insurrection. The police function, which is local in the United States, was assigned to the central government although municipalities have their own traffic police.

On the other hand, "education, other than higher education," also a local function in the United States, was assigned to the provinces for at least five years. The provinces were also given the power of direct taxation and power over hospitals, roads, local authorities, local public works, markets, and the preservation of fish and game.

Far from adding major powers to the provinces during the following half century, the central government acted a number of times to limit the scope of provincial taxation and also to enlarge its own functions. It took over mental institutions in 1910, sea-fish preservation in 1940, technical and vocational and other special education during 1945–1955, and African or Bantu education in 1953. It intends to take over Colored education in 1963 or afterward. Critics have suspected that passage of the National Advisory Education Council Act in 1962, giving the central government power to investigate particular schools, presages national control of education for whites.

The central government has called upon local government, however, to implement national policy that deals with the problems of urban areas: African influx, housing and slum clearance for whites and nonwhites, and public health. The heaviest burdens have been prescribed since 1923 by the Natives (Urban Areas) Act and its many amendments, under which local officials govern African locations (residential areas) and control urban entry and employment. Municipal bylaws affecting Africans need ministerial approval. In carrying out policy affecting nonwhites, local government has had less discretion, especially since 1948, than in providing the services that are usually thought of as local. In 1955, for example, national legislation prescribed the number of Africans who could work and reside in white buildings; in 1957 national authority over African hospitals, clubs, and similar institutions was enlarged.

When local governments have been slow or recalcitrant in dealing with problems of housing and relocation, the central government has exerted pressure or taken over responsibility. In 1954, by the passage of the Natives Resettlement Act, the central government bypassed the United Party–controlled Johannesburg City Council and provided for the removal of some 57,000 Africans from the so-called western areas of the city to Meadowlands, a national government-built township outside that city. Local councils have been called upon to propose racially separate areas under the Group Areas Acts, with the warning that the central government would take over this function if the legislation was not fully implemented. In Cape Province, where non-Nationalist city councils have resisted the imposition of stricter segregation, especially as it affects the Coloreds, the Nationalist-controlled Provincial Council has added to the growing restrictions on local autonomy.

The central government's predominance over the provinces has been evident since the early years of Union in restrictions on their taxing power and their dependence on annual parliamentary subsidies for at least half their revenue. (Only 5 to 6 per cent of the revenue of local government, on the other hand, comes from subsidies.) Varying formulas for provincial subsidy were provided by legislation in 1913, 1925, and 1945, but mutually satisfactory financial relations have never been achieved. The provincial taxing power has tended to diminish, and, indirectly through the national treasury, the wealthy Transvaal has contributed additional subsidies to Cape Province, the Orange Free State, and Natal. In 1957 an interim three-year subsidy scheme was adopted and later extended to the financial year that ends in 1963, when the latest commission on financial relations is expected to report. If its recommendations follow recent trends, the central government may tighten its control over provincial expenditure and, in other respects, reduce the status of the provinces.

The provincial system has been compared with federalism in some respects, but constitutionally and in practice the resemblance is false, now more than ever. The provinces originally had equal representation in the Senate, but this equality ended in 1955. Fairly extensive legislative powers were delegated to the provincial councils by the Act of Union, but Parliament may also deal with these matters. Furthermore, all provincial ordinances must be approved by the cabinet, and they have effect only insofar as they are not repugnant to an act of Parliament. A third apparent similarity to federal arrangements was the guarantee that Parliament may not alter provincial boundaries, abolish the provincial councils, or abridge their powers unless petitioned to do so by the councils concerned. But this guarantee, embodied in the Act of Union and reaffirmed by legislation in 1934, is not a legal restraint on Parliament, which has ignored it on the occasions when Parliament has abridged provincial power.

The subordination of provincial administration to the central government is illustrated by the position of the Administrator, the chief executive in each province, who is sometimes misleadingly compared to an American state governor. The Administrator is an officer of the central government with subcabinet rank; he is appointed by the cabinet for five years and is removable only by the cabinet. He is paid by the central treasury. Provincial appropriation ordinances require his recommendation, and money may be issued only with his warrant. He is the presiding member of the five-member Executive Committee, four of whose members are elected by the Provincial Council. The Executive Committee generally supervises provincial administration, and most of the Administrator's actions are in accordance with the decisions of its majority. But the Administrator also possesses a number of powers which he can exercise alone, for example, in town planning and over Africans, and he may be directed by the cabinet to act on matters over which the council has no power.

The central government has tended to concentrate power in the Administrator, who is usually but not always a partisan of the party in office although his position was traditionally regarded as nonpartisan. The Administrator has normally worked in harmony with the Provincial Council and the Executive Committee, but neither can hold him responsible. There have indeed been occasions of full or partial deadlock when he and a majority in the Provincial Council, which is elected for five years by the parliamentary electorate in each province, have represented different political parties. Administrators have continued in office regardless of this lack of confidence or even after the Administrator's party has lost control of Parliament. An Administrator opposed to participation in World War II resigned in 1940, but none has been removed from office.

The most recent friction has been evident in Natal, the only province in which the United Party controls the council and the Executive Committee. In 1958, after the resignation of the pro-United Party Administrator, whom the Nationalist government had retained in office, the government appointed a conservative English-speaking Administrator from outside Natal. This was the first appointment of an Administrator who was not a resident of the province. After he had joined the Nationalist cabinet in 1961, his successor was an Afrikaans-speaking Nationalist. In the interim, a notable disagreement occurred. The Public Service Commission, backed by the cabinet, recommended the appointment of an educational official who was not acceptable to the elected members of the Executive Committee. They resigned in protest, but the Administrator's judgment that he could not accept the advice of the committee but was bound to make such an appointment was upheld by the courts.

The provincial system, called by one observer "an unclassifiable monstrosity," [132] has been criticized as inefficient and irresponsible. Provincial boundaries are anachronistic, especially those of the over-extended Cape Province, and more natural regions are used in the administration of transport and other national services. The overlapping of national and provincial functions, especially in education and in health and welfare services, has been criticized as inefficient. An Inter-provincial Consultative Committee, composed of representatives of the central government and all provinces, meets infrequently and is a cumbersome device for dealing with this problem and for bringing about more uniform provincial policies. Nonetheless, public apathy and acceptance, as well as the resistance to change on the part of provincial politicians and officials, make any basic change unlikely.

Elections to the Provincial Council have always been along national party lines and have rarely generated wide interest in provincial affairs.[133] Council sessions usually last only a few days or, at most, weeks during the year. The Transvaal Provincial Council, for example, sat for 102 hours on twenty-two days in 1958, the year in which the allowance for councilors in each province was raised from £420 to £720 ($2,016) a year.

The Executive Committee, on the other hand, works nearly full time. Despite the expectation at the time of Union that it would be a nonpartisan body, it too has always been elected along party lines. The process is that the Provincial Council elects four members (almost always from its own membership) for five years by proportional representation. Executive committees, therefore, have usually been politically divided, unlike a responsible cabinet; and the Administra-

---

[132] Quoted by Hahlo and Kahn, *The Union of South Africa*, p. 178.

[133] Special interest was aroused in Cape Province as a result of the fact that Africans were eligible for election to the Provincial Council until 1936 and other nonwhites until 1956. Two Coloreds and one African have been elected. During 1936–1960, Africans voting on a separate roll elected two whites, and since 1956, Coloreds on a separate roll have also elected two whites.

tor has often held the balance of power. Like the Administrator, the elected members are not responsible to the council's majority, but unlike the Administrator they cannot be removed from office.

Support for reconstructing the governmental system along federal lines has been strong in Natal but nationally ineffective. A resolution passed by the Natal Provincial Council in October 1960 called not only for constitutionally guaranteed rights but also for entrenchment of the provincial council system, increased financial autonomy, and guaranteed provincial control of education, local matters, administrative officials, and a newly created provincial police force. Prime Minister Verwoerd made no concessions to the demand, replying, in part, that "the sovereignty of Parliament cannot be sacrificed." [134]

Local government has never attracted much interest; its autonomy is strictly limited, its functions are mainly routine, and its controversies have been traditionally nonpartisan. Since World War II, however, national partisan differences have spread into local affairs, most notably in Johannesburg. The appearance of a disciplined Nationalist Party caucus in some city and town councils that were formerly dominated by English-speaking businessmen and independents has brought to the fore issues such as the strict enforcement of bilingualism and closer cooperation with the policy of the government.

Hundreds of elected boards and councils in villages, towns, and cities (and in rural "divisional" areas in Cape Province) take part in local government, which is patterned on English local government. Councilors are elected by white voters in the Transvaal and by voters who are ratepayers in the other provinces. The municipal electorate includes nonwhites in Cape Province (though few Africans qualify) and Coloreds in Natal. Coloreds have served as councilors in Cape Town and Port Elizabeth; and in September 1960 two Coloreds were elected for the first time to the Kimberley City Council, defeating white candidates in racially mixed constituencies. These Coloreds will be ineligible to serve on existing councils, however, when the government implements its plan to establish Colored councils in separate areas. Councilors serve without pay but receive liberal expense allowances.[135] Opportunities for graft are fewer than in the United States;

[134] *Annual Survey of South African Law*, 1960, p. 7.

[135] The £50 monthly allowance of Johannesburg city councilors has been criticized by a former councilor as "gross overpayment" (A. J. Cutten, "Public Interest in Municipal Affairs Must Be Revived," *Forum*, Jan. 1961, pp. 7–9).

but, according to Marquard, "councillors have been known to become wealthy by buying land at the right time and place." [136]

In 1960 a Transvaal ordinance provided for the first major change in local government since 1903, when the principles of local government in Cape Province had been introduced into the Transvaal.[137] Generally following the recommendations of a commission of inquiry, the Provincial Council made the following changes: replaced the council's standing committees by one executive or management committee; strengthened the position of the "town clerk" as chief executive officer (retaining his traditional title) and made him generally responsible to the executive committee; and changed the tenure of municipal councilors from three to five years, with all councilors elected at one time rather than a third elected each year. Unlike the provincial Executive Committee, the municipal committee is elected by absolute majority vote instead of proportional representation, can be dismissed by the council, and can itself secure the dissolution of the council. The largely honorary office of mayor, filled by the council, was retained. Thus, authority has become more concentrated, but the institution of a powerful burgomaster, predicted by some anti-Nationalists, was not adopted. These reforms, which resemble cabinet-parliamentary government, may improve efficiency, clarify responsibility, and facilitate more effective control by a partisan majority.

THE JUDICIARY

The South African judiciary since Union has had an internationally recognized reputation for independence and ability. Dean Erwin Griswold of Harvard Law School, for example, has praised the highest court for providing "two great landmarks" by its decisions of 1951 and 1952 "which will strengthen constitutions and the traditions of the bench in many places." [138] Judges are appointed by the government, and until the age of seventy, when retirement is compulsory, their tenure is protected by traditional safeguards, as in Great Britain. Their remuneration may not be diminished, and they may be removed only at the request of both houses of Parliament for "misbehavior or incapacity." No judge has been dismissed.

The reputation of the South African bench remains high despite

[136] *The Peoples and Policies of South Africa*, p. 111.
[137] *Annual Survey of South African Law*, 1960, pp. 23–28.
[138] *Harvard Law Review*, LXVI (1953), p. 872. See above, p. 521.

appointments and promotions by the Nationalist government that have aroused apprehension. "It may be coincidental," it was observed in 1956, "that the majority of judges promoted since 1948 have been Nationalists, to the virtual exclusion of Jewish or liberally-minded candidates, and that the Nationalists appointed have usually had considerably fewer years of experience than non-Nationalists who were passed over." [139] Traditionally, judicial advancement is determined by seniority. In 1957 for the first time since Union a judge who was not the senior judge of appeal became Chief Justice. Two years later seniority was again ignored when Justice Steyn, the present Chief Justice, was appointed. In the same year Justice Rumpff, another ex-Nationalist, was promoted over senior judges to become the chief judge in the Transvaal and, a year later, a judge of appeal. Similar appointments have been made in Cape Province and the Orange Free State.[140] This has not necessarily meant, however, that the standards of the judiciary are declining. At one stage in the lengthy treason trial, for example, the defense maintained that Justice Rumpff showed bias, but in general the defense felt the trial was conducted fairly.

Appointments to the bench have almost invariably been made from senior advocates, that is, Q.C.'s (Queen's Counsel) or, in the Republic, S.C.'s (Senior Counsel), but the government has been criticized for failing to appoint the most experienced advocates.[141] One appointment in recent years came only a fortnight after the appointee had become a Q.C. In another case, appointment came four months later. Only rarely have members of the civil service been appointed to the bench. The appointment in 1951 of the senior government law adviser, now the Chief Justice, was protested by the Johannesburg bar, whose members refused to appear before him for three weeks.

In South Africa, unlike the United States, governments have made good use of their judges' reputation for fairness by assigning them fairly often to serve on official commissions of inquiry. They may inquire into the cause of a riot, for example, or investigate matters that are politically more sensitive. The redrawing of electoral district lines has been regularly performed since 1910 by judges who have held

[139] Patterson, *The Last Trek*, p. 91.

[140] Leslie Rubin, "Nationalist Contempt of Court," *Africa South*, Jan.–March 1960, p. 10.

[141] The legal profession is divided into some 400 practicing advocates, who make up the bar and plead cases in the higher courts, and some 3,000 practicing attorneys, who compose the side bar. The two groups correspond to barristers and solicitors in Britain (Hahlo and Kahn, *The Union of South Africa*, p. 281).

open hearings and issued detailed explanations. Especially since 1953, some of their decisions have been sharply criticized as partisan.

Some judges have been active in politics before going on the bench and after leaving it. Such activity has not made the courts a target for partisan attack in the past, but the recent activities of former judges may be undermining the courts' immunity. Most recently, Albert Centlivres, who had never been active in politics and who retired as Chief Justice in 1957, has called for a struggle against the rise of "totalitarianism" in South Africa.[142] Nationalists in Parliament, including the Minister of Justice, have spoken of him with contempt. Judge Henry Fagan, a liberally inclined ex-Nationalist who had supported Hertzog and headed an important inquiry on native policy for Prime Minister Smuts, succeeded Centlivres as Chief Justice. After retiring in 1959, he entered politics as an opponent of the government, but a more temperate one than Centlivres. He became leader of the National Union Party, a Nationalist splinter group, and in June 1962 led it into the United Party. It is notable that both Centlivres and Fagan were appointed to the chief justiceship by the Nationalist government.

Afrikaners, finding it difficult to advance in economic and financial life, have been attracted to the legal profession and have been among South Africa's most distinguished judges. Their disposition to uphold individual rights and opportunities for opposition to government may have been strengthened by the importance of such freedom for the rise of Afrikaner nationalism.[143] On the other hand, Nationalist political thought exalts the *volkswil* as a higher law and depreciates the judiciary as an independent force in a balanced constitution. Whenever the judiciary conflicts with the people's will, a striking precedent for its subordination is provided by President Paul Kruger's dismissal of the Transvaal's chief justice in 1898. During the constitutional controversy that began in 1951, Nationalist leaders made frequent attacks on members of the highest court, one cabinet member describing them disparagingly as "a bunch of liberals."

The role of the judiciary in determining the character of national life has been greatly limited in practice not only because of the virtual absence of judicial review as known in the United States but also more importantly because of voluminous legislation. Statutes have

[142] Albert van de Sandt Centlivres, "Rule of Law in the Republic," *Forum,* May 1962, pp. 12–16.
[143] Suggested by H. J. Simons in Ellen Hellmann, ed., *Handbook on Race Relations* (New York: Oxford University Press, 1949), p. 59.

almost entirely removed any discretionary area within which the judiciary can apply common-law principles of individual equality or insist on equal though racially separate conditions. The expansion of ministerial discretion, from which there is no provision for judicial appeal, has also narrowed the judge's role.

The South African judicial system is unified, its Supreme Court consisting of provincial and local divisions and the South-West Africa Division, whose judgments may be appealed to the Appellate Division in Bloemfontein. The judges apply a common law that is based on un-codified Roman-Dutch law, which has been influenced by English common law, especially in matters of procedure. Under the various divisions of the Supreme Court are magistrates' courts, where minor civil and criminal cases are tried. More serious criminal cases are tried by regional courts in which more experienced magistrates sit. Cases may also begin in provincial and local divisions of the Supreme Court.

Magistrates are hard-working and often able men, but as civil serv-ants who also perform administrative functions they do not have the independence of judges and are particularly subject to local white opinion. The academic qualifications of magistrates are generally low. Few have the LL.B. degree. Their conduct of cases involving Africans, unlike the conduct of judges in the superior courts, is often hasty; and the imposition of penalties, within prescribed limits, is often harsh.

The regular courts deal with members of all racial groups, but there are also special courts for Africans. These include chiefs' and head-men's courts, Bantu commissioners' courts, three Native Appeal Courts, and a Native Divorce Court. These special courts were established in order to give African litigants in civil disputes the advantage of lower costs, simplified procedure, and native law, if the Bantu commissioner decides to apply it instead of the common law. Native law is custom which is not contrary to "public policy and natural justice" and which will be enforced by courts in civil cases between Africans. (The Bantu commissioner's court also has the same criminal jurisdiction as a magistrate's court.) In practice, however, the expectations mentioned above have only partly been borne out. Since litigants usually do not conduct their own cases in the Bantu commissioner's court, costs have not been as low as expected. It is also doubtful whether the average Bantu commissioner has been well versed in native law and custom.[144]

---

[144] See Hahlo and Kahn, *The Union of South Africa,* pp. 327 ff., and Simons in Hellmann, ed., *Handbook,* ch. iv.

Contemporary Issues

What should be the white response to the African challenge to white domination? This central issue pervades all issues in South Africa. "The complete overthrow of White domination" is the aim of the Africanists, Robert Sobukwe has said; and in moving toward this end, the Africanists are "in step with the continent." [145] On this aim, the ANC agrees. The response of the Nationalist government has been uncompromising, although in theory it proposes a kind of compromise. "The present Government believes in the domination (baasskap) of the White man in his own area," Prime Minister Verwoerd said in January 1963, quoting a statement that he had made to the Natives' Representative Council in 1950; "but it equally believes in the domination (baasskap) of the Bantu in his area." The Bantu would move "step by step," he said later, from the tribal to a Western or parliamentary system "as and when he becomes ripe for it as a result of the experience we allow him to gain." [146]

The National Party and the United Party agree on the necessity of maintaining white domination (or, as the United Party puts it, "White leadership"), yet the Nationalists are correct in arguing that the two parties face in radically different directions. In the face of any African threat, the United Party closes ranks with the Nationalists, and the parties stand together. Their differences on many issues, furthermore, are relatively minor, for example, regarding the implementation of social and residential segregation. Since these are differences in degree, one may describe as "moderate" a change of Nationalist policy in the direction of less severity or thoroughness. Other differences, however, which may seem minor since they affect few Africans, reflect basically divergent assumptions and, because of their implications, have a symbolic importance. Examples are the issue of African freehold rights to land outside the reserves and eligibility for election to Parliament. The "moderation" of Nationalist policy for which some outsiders perennially hope means little of consequence to the African opposition if it is not concerned with the symbolic issues. And if it is, the change would not be moderate but radical.

The Nationalists characteristically pose two extreme and exclusive alternatives in defining the central issue. "The choice before us," said

[145] *Africanist* (mimeographed), Jan. 1959, pp. 8–9.
[146] *House of Assembly Debates,* Jan. 25, 1963, cols. 225–226.

a pamphlet before the 1948 election, "is one of these two divergent courses: either that of integration, which would in the long run amount to national suicide on the part of the Whites; or that of apartheid, which professes to preserve the identity and safeguard the future of every race.[147] Looking backward in 1963, Dr. Verwoerd said that at the crossroads of 1948, after following a road of segregation with elements of integration, the country had taken the right fork. Since then, it had progressed "step by step" on a road whose end was "total political separation." The time of arrival at the destination could not be known, but again Dr. Verwoerd predicted that "the influx of the Bantu to the cities, in spite of methods of control, would increase until about 1978. Thereafter we would be approaching the turning point as the result of the long-term policy of trying to obtain also further separation, human separation, and even territorial separation." [148]

Does Nationalist policy envision the possibility of granting sovereign independence to a Transkeian Bantustan and to other African areas that remain to be enlarged and consolidated, thus partitioning South Africa? Dr. Verwoerd's predecessors and high Nationalist officials have indicated that the Bantustans would be limited to self-government within a white-controlled association. Dr. Verwoerd, however, has compared the eventual relationship of the Bantustans and a white republic with the relationship of members in the Commonwealth of Nations. Presumably the "well-disposed little Black neighboring states" he envisions could become republics outside a South African commonwealth. Although not prepared early in 1963 to concede that the government might be unable "to control the timetable of the Transkei," he accepted the "possibility" that it might lose such control. Regarding such a development, Dr. Verwoerd has expressed a rhetorical conclusion, if not a prediction: if a choice were necessary between a smaller white state and a South Africa dominated by the blacks, "I choose division." [149]

The United Party, like parties and groups farther to the left, generally accepts as both irrevocable and desirable the fact that South Africa is "one integrated economic unit." [150] Accordingly, it accepts the class of urban Africans as permanent rather than transitory and

---

[147] D. W. Kruger, ed., *South African Parties and Policies, 1910–1960: A Select Source Book* (Cape Town: Human & Rousseau, 1960), p. 402.

[148] *House of Assembly Debates,* Jan. 25, 1963, col. 224.

[149] *Ibid.,* Jan. 23, 1962, cols. 89–90; Jan. 25, 1963, cols. 228, 239.

[150] Sir de Villiers Graaff, *ibid.,* Jan. 22, 1963, col. 37. For the paragraph, see *ibid.,* cols. 32, 40–41.

regards as impossible (except at the cost of economic disruption) the reversal of economic trends that are producing greater racial interdependence. Operating from these premises, United Party leaders talk of the unity of all the people as "South Africans." They advocate a gradually developing "race federation," a policy which vaguely promises the sharing of power through increasing representation in the South African Parliament for "each race . . . in accordance with the state of civilization it has reached." "For the foreseeable future," however, Sir de Villiers said early in 1963, a United Party government would maintain "White leadership and a firm refusal to permit political control to pass into the hands of an uncivilized proletariat."

Because the United Party faces in the direction of multiracial federation in one country and the National Party in the direction of a white-controlled association of racially separated countries, the two parties say yes and no, respectively, to the following policies regarding Africans: representation in Parliament, freehold rights to land outside the reserves, fostering "the emergence of a responsible Native middle class" in urban areas (in the words of Sir de Villiers), encouraging the growth of a stabilized labor force with provision for workers to bring their families from the reserves, and the right to organize trade unions (though initially under the "guardianship" of existing unions). The United Party's conservatism is indicated by the fact that Africans would vote on a separate rather than common roll for representatives in the House of Assembly and the representatives would be white. However, in 1959 the party endorsed not only the restoration of such representation for Africans in Cape Province but also its extension for the first time to the other provinces. Furthermore, the policy of race federation cannot consistently close the door to the eventual eligibility of Africans for election to Parliament. Africans cannot be deprived, according to Sir de Villiers, of "the right of being represented by their own people for all time to come." [151] To accept as a conceivable eventuality the entrance of one black man into Parliament is a radical divergence from Nationalist policy.

Many other issues that occupy much parliamentary attention do not necessarily imply a basically divergent orientation. Both major parties agree on the maintenance of social and residential segregation, control of the movement of African labor, the usefulness of migrant labor ("they fulfill a function," Sir de Villiers has said), and rehabilitation of the reserves. The United Party objects to the pinpricks and frictions

[151] *Ibid.*, Jan. 25, 1963, col. 277.

of "petty apartheid," "the increasing severity of the restrictive laws" regarding movement, "unjust" enforcement of the Group Areas Act, and "unscrambling schemes" like that for the removal of Africans from western Cape Province and generally opposes the practices of "more and more control and more and more State interference" if separate development is pursued.[152] It is satisfied that racial segregation would be sufficiently maintained if race relations were left in many areas to private arrangements, for example, those prescribed by autonomous universities, those made between management and trade unions, and those resulting from nominally nonracial principles such as "the rate for the job." It would reduce the weight of legal restrictions on non-whites (for example, abolishing legal reservation of jobs according to race) and give white business a freer hand (for example, allowing the investment of private capital in the reserves).

Within the theoretical framework that treats urban Africans as citizens of tribal homelands, Nationalist policy makers act pragmatically in order to meet long-run housing and community needs and to reduce racial tensions. Officials have urged the police to be courteous and tactful in dealing with Africans. Through such changes in policy as allowing Africans to buy liquor, beginning in August 1962, the government hopes to decrease the number of arrests. It also has claimed that racial friction will be lessened by legislation such as the Bantu Laws Amendment Bill of 1963, which consolidates laws affecting African movement and residence in urban areas (thus substituting one large ball in place of many small balls at the end of each African's chain, as seen in a *Contact* cartoon of February 21, 1963). However, since the bill also enlarges discretionary power, for example, over Africans born and long employed in an urban area, its doctrinaire application for the purpose of maximum reduction of the labor pool would undoubtedly intensify feelings of insecurity.

Within the accepted framework, there is disagreement among Nationalist intellectuals. For example, some Nationalists, who differ from the United Party since they believe the development of Bantustans is desirable, support private white investment and a policy of individual African ownership of land in the reserves, and thus they differ also from the government. Intellectual ferment among supporters of the government, often confined to private discussion, has ranged widely over other policies that have no Nationalist spokesman in Parliament.

[152] *Ibid.*, Jan. 23, 1962, col. 55; Jan. 22, 1963, cols. 34, 36, 38, 271.

One rather anomalous policy would support Bantustan development and partition, leaving a multiracial state in which the proportions of whites and nonwhites would make movement toward equal rights relatively safe for whites.

The specific issue of the status of the Coloreds has produced sharp division between the two parties and also within Nationalist ranks, thus indicating that the issue is largely separate from the central issue of white-African relations. Fear of the African majority, however, is an important element in policies toward the Coloreds. This factor is present, for example, in the attitude of a small number of National-ist intellectuals who seek to enlarge white strength by 50 per cent through full integration with the million and a half Coloreds. The United Party, though not going so far, endorsed in 1961 the policy of accepting the Coloreds legally and politically as part of the white population by supporting not only their restoration to the common voters' roll but also their eligibility for election to Parliament. On the other hand, the government has been challenged to deny that with the development of its separate "Colored Parliament" the whites who now represent the Coloreds would be removed from Parliament. Dr. Verwoerd has replied that they will remain but added: "Must I say for ever?" [153]

The orientation and end of policy, as already noted, divide the Nationalist government and its parliamentary opposition; a second major issue dividing them is the manner in which the government has proceeded in implementing its policies. "Invasions of the rights of individuals," Sir de Villiers Graaff has charged, "have been taken in a manner which denies entirely the rule of law in South Africa." [154] The United Party, though opposed to the Suppression of Communism Act of 1950, suggested during the debate on the measure that it was prepared to consider Communist activity high treason and punishable by death so long as the offense was defined by Parliament and judged by the courts. The party also opposed the Sabotage Act of 1962 and, in particular, its grant of "arbitrary and excessive powers never before vested in any Minister in time of peace." [155] On the other hand, the United Party supported in principle the more far-reaching emergency provisions included in the Public Safety Act of 1953, which was passed following the passive resistance campaign, and (despite talk about the

[153] *Ibid.*, Jan. 23, 1962, col. 95.   [154] *Ibid.*, May 21, 1962, col. 6089.
[155] *Ibid.*, June 12, 1962, col. 7631.

necessity for consultation with ANC leaders) voted for the legislation providing for the outlawing of the ANC and the PAC, following Sharpeville.

A related issue causing division is the government's powers of censorship, which are already extensive over imported books and films. In 1963 United Party leaders (and also some Nationalist intellectuals) criticized the bill on publications and entertainment, charging in part that it could result in censorship before publication within South Africa. The bill does not apply to newspapers published by members of the Newspaper Press Union, which have adopted a "code of conduct." Power already exists to ban publications under the Suppression of Communism Act, with authors and publishers having virtually no judicial recourse, and, under the Sabotage Act, to impose upon new publications what Sir de Villiers has called "a conditional fine in advance." [156] The banning of *New Age* only slightly stirred the parliamentary opposition. A potentially deeper issue, however, would be created by any proposals for less drastic yet pervasive restrictions that might inhibit the freedom of the English-language press. Some persons fear that such restrictions, not yet clearly defined, may be imposed following the next report of the Press Commission expected in 1963.

Authoritarianism has been historically a secondary issue in the relations among whites; during the past decade it has grown to be a major issue in the relations between whites and blacks. Authoritarianism has been traditionally evident in master-servant relations and in pressures, largely inspired by Calvinism, for state enforcement of public morality. It has challenged the liberal tradition, which is shared with a small proportion of Afrikaans-speaking whites, and the parliamentary tradition, which has been shared by Afrikaner Nationalist leaders like Hertzog and Malan. The growth of Afrikaner nationalism may have strengthened authoritarian elements in South African life; but despite some fears, Nationalist governments have not acted in an authoritarian way to subordinate the status of English-speaking whites. Many points of friction have arisen, however, as Nationalists have sought to equalize or strengthen the Afrikaner position by their policies, especially on immigration, education, and the electoral process, and by various preferential practices.

Issues regarding white-white relations have declined in relative importance, however, as white-black relations have become the central

[156] *Ibid.*, June 12, 1962, col. 7633.

issue. Distrust of "the Afrikaner nation" verging on disaffection undoubtedly still persists among many English-speaking whites. In Natal, sentiment is strong for federalism and a large degree of provincial autonomy. The republican issue, on the other hand, was argued for the last time during the 1960 referendum campaign, although the United Party has left open the possibility of the Republic's rejoining the Commonwealth. On election day in 1961, Dr. Verwoerd issued what he himself called a "clarion call" for "unity amongst the Whites"; and at the opening of the Parliament that followed, President Swart spoke of "the White nation." [157] Sir de Villiers agreed early in 1963 that "the old issues which divided us in the past have ceased to exist or to be of any importance in the political field." [158]

Nationalists have justified the growing authoritarianism of the past decade as necessary to meet the threat of African nationalism and, especially since the treason arrests of 1956, have insisted upon the Communist nature of that threat. Within Parliament, debate on this issue reflects diverse interpretations and estimates of the South African situation. Nationalists maintain that South Africa is, in effect, at war. They explain "much of the frustration, incitement, hatred, attacks and slogans, so rife in the world today," to use the words of President Swart, as due to "the communist factor," which "often shelters behind humanistic, liberal and moral propaganda." [159] Sir de Villiers, on the other hand, has blamed the government for the "frustrated and rootless" condition of the black population in the white areas and has maintained that "such a frustrated proletariat is the tilth on which the weed of Communism flourishes." [160]

The United Party is optimistic about the effect of "economic laws" and "concessions," is apparently willing to consult with ANC and PAC leaders as representative of one element of the African population, and is convinced that Bantustans and tribally based institutions such as universities are riskier than a policy of multiracial reconciliation. The National Party is pessimistically convinced of the "more than doubled fury" (in Dr. Verwoerd's words) that would follow Sir de Villiers' "policy of laissez-faire" and convinced also that the admitted risks involved in the Bantustan policy are less than those of a multiracial course, which they believe would lead inexorably to black domination.[161] They denounce ANC and PAC leaders as both unrep-

[157] *Ibid.*, Jan. 25, 1963, cols. 230–231; Jan. 19, 1962, col. 9.
[158] *Ibid.*, Jan. 22, 1963, col. 22.   [159] *Ibid.*, Jan. 19, 1962, col. 8.
[160] *Ibid.*, May 22, 1962, col. 6114.   [161] *Ibid.*, Jan. 23, 1962, col. 64.

resentative and dangerous and insist that the Bantustan policy is a recognition, in the long run, of nationalist demands for unqualified equality.

External Relations

South Africa's position in relation to Africa and the world has changed fundamentally since World War II because of "the rise to self-assertion of Asian and African peoples" and South Africa's determination to maintain white domination in the face of growing external pressures for its abandonment.[162] From being the continent's leading independent state with somewhat of a reputation personified by Smuts for enlightened leadership in the Commonwealth and the League of Nations, South Africa has come to be a target for the hostility of all independent African states and, according to the Nationalist *Die Burger*, "the skunk of the world."[163] A British government spokesman has described apartheid as "morally abominable, intellectually grotesque, and spiritually indefensible."[164] Although South Africa possesses elements of economic and military strength and at least temporarily the advantages of geographical isolation, it is not only the world's most isolated country ideologically but also vulnerable economically and easily penetrable by Africans coming in from the outside to reinforce the domestic underground.

In no other country do external affairs hinge as crucially as they do in South Africa upon a single though central element of domestic policy. Racial policy is the key to the change in South Africa's position after World War II, particularly in relation to the Commonwealth, defense, the High Commission Territories, other African states, and international organizations.[165]

THE WEST AND DEFENSE

The status of South Africa in relation to the United Kingdom and the Commonwealth, an issue in the domestic struggle between Afrikaner nationalism and its white opponents, was the central issue of

[162] Rupert Emerson, *From Empire to Nation: The Rise to Self-Assertion of Asian and African Peoples* (Cambridge: Harvard University Press, 1960).

[163] Quoted by McKay, *Africa in World Politics*, p. 85.

[164] Major Patrick Wall in the United Nations Trusteeship Committee (*New York Times*, Nov. 13, 1962).

[165] J. E. Spence, "Tradition and Change in South African Foreign Policy," *Journal of Commonwealth Political Studies*, May 1962, pp. 136–152.

external policy during the three decades before World War II. After the war, however, the beginning of Asian and African attacks in the United Nations made Commonwealth membership appear more important. Whereas Prime Minister Malan had aimed at republican status outside the Commonwealth, Dr. Verwoerd, before the 1960 republican referendum, declared that South Africa should remain within it. Meanwhile, representatives of the outlawed ANC and PAC (at that time cooperating abroad in a South African United Front) and their allies were lobbying in Commonwealth capitals for South Africa's expulsion. The issue was dramatized when Dr. Julius Nyerere of Tanganyika, which was not yet independent, wrote privately to the prime ministers who were assembling in March 1961 for a Commonwealth conference and at the same time wrote in the *Observer* (March 12, 1961) that "to vote for South Africa is to vote us [Tanganyika] out." In the conference, Dr. Verwoerd was directly challenged by an old and white Commonwealth member, Canada, when Prime Minister Diefenbaker proposed a joint declaration repudiating racial discrimination. Dr. Verwoerd withdrew his application, and on May 31, 1961, South Africa became a republic outside the Commonwealth. Thus, the old Boer tradition of republican isolation emerged victorious partly as a result of the hostile campaign for an intensification of external pressure.

Only in recent years has South Africa felt the necessity to build up a defense force capable of repelling invasion and maintaining internal order in the event of invasion. Before World War II, South Africa faced no threat from the north and felt assured of the protection of the British navy. Although South Africa and the United Kingdom have had a naval agreement since 1955 providing for the transfer to South Africa of the British base near Cape Town and the British use of South African bases, South Africa has no defensive alliance with the British, or at least no publicly acknowledged alliance. Nor is it a member of any regional defense pact. South African officials talked hopefully during the 1950's about the establishment of such a pact in southern and east Africa. By the 1960's, the prospect had faded away. Meanwhile, resistance to Portuguese authority in Angola poses a threat to South-West Africa, and resistance to white authority in Southern Rhodesia an eventual threat to South Africa itself. African states have alleged that South Africa has secret military agreements with Portugal and Southern Rhodesia. South Africa has denied that it is a party to any military agreement other than the naval agreement noted above, but consultation between South African and Portuguese authorities is becoming closer. Either Portugal or Southern Rhodesia may have occasion to request military assistance in the future, to be extended covertly or even openly, and circumstances might be such that South Africa would comply.[166] The political and military repercussions in Africa and the United Nations would be profound.

The extent of South Africa's growing defense preparations is a measure of its isolation and anxiety. Cabinet ministers have spoken of secret plans by unnamed African and Asian countries to invade South Africa, perhaps even in 1963. In 1962, the budget for military spending rose by about 67 percent more than the preceding year, to a level higher than that in World War II; and in 1963 the allotment was over 25 per cent higher than expenditures in 1962. Some 10,000 white men under twenty-five were being called up annually for military training. More than 250,000 men could be mobilized, if necessary, according to the Minister of Defense.

South Africa's hope for Western aid rests mainly upon its proclaimed anticommunism and its reliability as "the only sure and stable friend Western nations have in Africa." [167] The American ambassador to South Africa during 1959–1961, after noting that South Africa's racial policy was "deplored by most Americans," has written as a private citizen in praise of South Africa's anticommunism and stated that the purchase of jet fighters from France and the naval build-up "underline her desire to constitute a strong anti-Red base in Southern Africa." [168]

Despite such sentiment, both the American and British governments, in addition to deploring apartheid, have sought to avoid identification with South Africa's domestic policy, in part by limiting the sale of arms. The British spokesman whose description of apartheid was quoted above defended on November 12, 1962, the sale of thirty bombers to South Africa, stating that British policy was to sell "only those types of arms which would be unsuitable for measures of internal

---

[166] Dr. C. W. de Kiewiet wrote late in 1960, "I am confident that the white population of Southern Rhodesia—terribly shaken by the events in the Congo—will add their strength in some form to the white population of South Africa" (*Foreign Policy Bulletin,* Jan. 1, 1961, p. 62).

[167] Dr. Verwoerd, quoted in *Christian Science Monitor,* June 2, 1961.

[168] Philip Crowe, quoted in *Fortnightly Digest of South African Affairs,* Jan. 8, 1962, p. 9. In praising South Africa's willingness "to stand up and be counted in the ideological war," Crowe also noted that South Africa had "backed her convictions in two world wars."

repression." [169] American naval units have occasionally cooperated with South African forces in training exercises, and American military technicians have set up a deep-space tracking station near Johannesburg, activities pointed to by Nationalist leaders (and prominently publicized by the Information Service) as evidence of common interest underlying the surface rhetoric of politically inspired criticism. Nevertheless, the American representative in the United Nations Special Political Committee on Apartheid said on October 19, 1962, that "the United States has already adopted and is enforcing the policy of forbidding the sale to the South African Government of any arms, whether from governmental or commercial sources, which could be used by the government to enforce apartheid either in South Africa or in the administration of Southwest Africa." [170]

THE HIGH COMMISSION TERRITORIES

The needs of defense and of the Nationalist government's racial policy have made incorporation of the British High Commission Territories of Basutoland, Bechuanaland, and Swaziland a matter of special importance in recent years, but Dr. Verwoerd declared in September 1962 that incorporation was "no longer practical politics." [171] Incorporation was a traditional aim of South African policy after 1910 and was reaffirmed during the 1950's, when the Tomlinson Commission stated that it was essential if the proposed Bantustans were to occupy nearly half the land of a greater South Africa. On the other hand, fears that the territories would be used for political refuge and as bases for subversion of white authority were realized after Sharpeville. Deeper anxieties about the effect on African opinion within South Africa have also been aroused by the British policy of moving the territories toward self-government, although Dr. Verwoerd has contended that this policy was not different from his own. The Nationalist government moved in 1963 to tighten its control of movement between the Republic and the territories and to establish numerous control points on the borders. It also seeks to maintain cooperative relations with the

[169] *Star*, Nov. 13, 1962. Harold Wilson, leader of the British Labor Party, referring particularly to the sale of armored cars, has reiterated the party's policy to "stop this bloody traffic in weapons of oppression." He added, "We will, by international action, take steps to see that the South African Minister of Defence does not place those contracts anywhere else" (*Rand Daily Mail*, March 18, 1963).

[170] U.S. Delegation to the General Assembly, Press Release no. 4067.

[171] *Race Relations News*, Oct. 1962, p. 3; *House of Assembly Debates*, Jan. 25, 1963, col. 233.

British, although the continued use of the territories as bases for subversive activity within South Africa will undoubtedly strain these relations as pressures grow for economic or other retaliation.[172]

INDEPENDENT AFRICA

The ideological attack on South Africa has been spurred by Pan-Africanism, led at least initially by Ghana, which became independent in 1957. Traditionally, before World War II, South Africa provided a good deal of Africa's professional and technical leadership, and its universities provided training for some of the Africans who were to become prominent in the new states. Under Prime Minister Strijdom, Dr. Verwoerd's predecessor, South Africa sought to establish diplomatic relations with these states, and the press discussed future problems such as the identification and nondiscriminatory treatment of African diplomats within South Africa and the risk of their involvement with the nonwhite opposition. In December 1958, the first conference of political parties linked in the All-African Peoples' Organization met in Accra and responded to the ANC's pleas by calling for economic sanctions and boycott of South Africa. (States boycotting South African trade in 1962 are listed on p. 506.) At the time of Sharpeville, only the United Arab Republic among independent African states was represented in South Africa.

Eric Louw, Minister of Foreign Affairs, described in Parliament in April 1962 the treatment of South Africa after Sharpeville.[173] Dr. Nkrumah, he said, had invited him in 1959 to visit Ghana, but at the conference of Commonwealth prime ministers in 1960, Nkrumah had said "in the presence of the other Prime Ministers" that the invitation was canceled. Later Ghana imposed a trade boycott and allowed South Africans to pass through Ghana by air only if they declared their opposition to apartheid. Then, said Louw, the United Arab Republic broke off diplomatic relations "without any reason whatsoever." Somalia announced a number of restrictions, including refusal to permit South African planes to fly over the country. South Africa was warned that it would not be welcomed at the next conference of the

[172] South African officials in January 1962 allowed a Transkeian African, Anderson Ganyile, to return to Basutoland following an international incident over his arrest in Basutoland by South African police who, said the South Africans, had crossed the border unwittingly in a nighttime mist. The British Parliament's South Africa Act of 1962 prescribes that political fugitives shall not be returned to South Africa. British authorities are lenient with exiles so long as they do not interfere in local politics, but Rhodesian authorities repeatedly have turned *émigrés* over to the South African police.

[173] *House of Assembly Debates,* April 18, 1962, cols. 4169–4170.

CCTA (Commission for Technical Co-operation in Africa South of the Sahara), and South African delegates were refused visas to attend a number of other specialized conferences. "We have gone out of our way to co-operate with the African states," said Louw, "but we have had no response. We have had nothing but rebuffs." Even during 1962, he said later, South Africa requested the French government to ask the Malagasy Republic if it would be prepared to exchange diplomatic representatives and was informed that the Malagasy government, in Louw's words, "felt that the time was not opportune." [174]

Independent African states, especially since 1962, have been engaged in a campaign for the exclusion of South Africa from regional and world-wide bodies. South Africa itself resigned from UNESCO in 1955 because of that organization's attitudes regarding race. Therefore South Africa has been absent from meetings like that on African higher education held in Madagascar in September 1962. South African officials insist that they will not allow themselves to be excluded from any activity they have a right to participate in. Accordingly, they participated in the 1962 conference of the International Labor Organization, whose constitution does not provide for expulsion, although an overwhelming majority in the preceding year had asked South Africa to withdraw. After a similar resolution at a regional conference of the United Nations Food and Agriculture Organization late in 1962, South Africa's continued participation was met by a retaliatory walk-out by eighteen African states, which brought the conference to an early close. Despite continued "willingness to co-operate," Eric Louw told Parliament on January 24, 1963, "South Africa can no longer attend conferences on the Continent of Africa." Even aid to Africa through the CCTA, of which South Africa was a founding and proud member, was foreclosed. "At its last meeting," he said, "we were formally kicked out." [175] The major Pan-Africanist objective remains—exclusion from the United Nations, where South Africa itself has boycotted various sessions. In November 1962, as noted below, a two-thirds vote was finally won in the General Assembly on a resolution requesting the Security Council to consider South Africa's expulsion.

Driving the ANC and PAC underground in 1960 resulted for the first time in the formation of an exiled group of leaders whose energies are directed toward intensifying external pressures on South Africa. A few nonwhite leaders had left the country earlier. Others had traveled

[174] *Ibid.*, Jan. 24, 1963, col. 154. South Africans in transit through Ghana were later exempted from the requirement of a declaration.
[175] *Ibid.*

abroad, for example, touring capitals behind the Iron Curtain or attending conferences such as that at Bandung in 1955, but they had returned to South Africa. Immediately following Sharpeville, the National Executive Committee of the ANC decided to send Oliver Tambo, the vice-president, to London via Bechuanaland and Tanganyika to serve as its ambassador abroad. Representatives of the PAC also left, and late in 1960 both organizations (joined by the South African Indian Congress and the South-West African National Union) formed a South African United Front, with representatives in Accra, Dar es Salaam, Cairo, London, and New York. Largely because of the PAC's distrust of the ANC's non-African and Communist allies, however, and following a split within the PAC itself, the Front was dissolved in March 1962.

The ANC and the nationalist organizations based in South-West Africa and the High Commission Territories affiliated themselves with PAFMECA (Pan-African Freedom Movement of East and Central Africa), a regional unit of the All-African Peoples' Organization, at its meeting in Addis Ababa in February 1962. PAFMECA added "Southern" to its name (becoming PAFMECSA) and, apparently in response to a stirring speech at its conference by Nelson Mandela on the inadequacy of nonviolent tactics, adopted a new constitution that omitted references to nonviolence.[176] PAFMECSA's headquarters is in Dar es Salaam, which has become the most important center for exiled leaders and political refugees from southern Africa. The Tanganyika government and the Tanganyika African National Union extend equal hospitality to both the ANC and the PAC.

While much energy is absorbed in exile politics and lobbying, ANC and PAC representatives also face continuing problems in maintaining relations with the underground at home and allies outside. They must demonstrate that they hold a mandate from movements that are effectively organized and led and must contend with the occasional impatience of African leaders (for example, Dr. Hastings Banda) who have spoken critically of politicians cut off from the struggle.[177] Repre-

---

[176] A correspondent from India at the conference is reported to have said, "The calibre of the South Africans always seems so much higher—head and shoulders above most of the Africans from other countries who come to these conferences" (*Counter Attack*, Bulletin of S.A. Congress of Democrats, March 1962, p. 2).

According to one authoritative source, PAFMECA has not officially become PAFMECSA.

[177] *Fighting Talk*, Oct. 1962, p. 4. See also the *New African*, July 1962, pp. 12–13.

sentatives of ANC and PAC have ideological differences, which may easily be exaggerated, and differ over tactics (for example, the former appears to favor carefully planned sabotage and the latter, a mass uprising). There is ground for distrust, also, in rumors about sources of funds. A pro-ANC English clergyman has claimed that "increasing evidence" supports the belief that the PAC is "a brain-child of the U.S. State Department" and receives "unlimited funds" from it.[178] An official South African government report, on the other hand, has alleged that Poqo, the terrorist group, was synonymous with the PAC and had received $70,000 from Ghana.[179] Jordan Ngubane, a Liberal Party leader who is strongly anti-Communist, has observed that an "unexpected switch" in PAC tactics prior to Sharpeville was apparently due to Ghanaian influence and that ANC leaders in Basutoland were reportedly receiving ample funds from the Central Committee of the Communist Party of the Soviet Union.[180]

THE UNITED NATIONS

The new African states, now numerically strong in the United Nations (33 among 110 members in 1962), have made that organization increasingly important as the chief focus of opposition to South Africa. Unlike the League of Nations, which South Africa regarded as a protector of small nations and in which it firmly supported sanctions against Italy in 1936, the United Nations has been characterized by the moral fervor of underdeveloped countries seeking change rather than preservation of the *status quo.* On South African resolutions, independent African states have had no difficulty in securing the cooperation of Asian, Near Eastern, and Communist states in the face of arguments regarding domestic jurisdiction and the shortsightedness of punitive action. Of crucial importance, however, if moral exhortation is to lead to action that will seriously affect South African policy, are the policies of the United States and the United Kingdom.

The perennial and impassioned debates on South Africa have come to proclaim as their objective the imposition of sanctions and South Africa's expulsion from the United Nations. Debate has dealt with the treatment of Indians, initiated by India in 1946, with South-West

[178] Rev. Trevor Bush, *New Age,* Nov. 22, 1962, p. 2.

[179] *Rand Daily Mail,* March 22, 1963. Potlako Leballo, a PAC leader, in a press conference in Maseru, claimed that PAC and POQO are synonymous (*ibid.,* March 25, 1963).

[180] Ngubane, *An African Explains Apartheid.* Funds from Communist China have also been reported.

Africa, and, beginning in 1952, with the broader question of "the racial situation." On resolutions that were critical of South Africa, the United States abstained until 1958, when it voted with 69 others (against 5, including the United Kingdom) for a resolution expressing "regret and concern" that South Africa had not modified its policy. This action disturbed Afrikaner nationalist leaders more than all preceding actions of the United Nations and intensified existing anxiety about the course of American policy. Were South African whites, they asked privately, to be considered expendable?

Even more disturbing to a wider public was the State Department's speedy reaction to the shootings at Sharpeville: on the very next day (March 22, 1960), not even consulting with the American ambassador in Pretoria, the Department issued a statement deploring police violence.[181] When the Security Council took up the matter, the United States voted on April 1, 1960, for a resolution (9–0, with the United Kingdom and France abstaining) that blamed the South African government for the shootings and called upon it "to initiate measures aimed at bringing about racial harmony based on equality."

Shortly after Dr. Verwoerd withdrew his application to remain in the Commonwealth, the United Kingdom and Australia abandoned their policy of abstaining and voted for a resolution that South Africa's racial policies flagrantly violated the Charter and that all states should consider taking such separate and collective action as was open to them to bring about the abandonment of these policies. South Africa and two other members were absent; no one abstained; and only Portugal opposed the resolution.

Resolutions recommending specific sanctions failed to win a two-thirds vote in the General Assembly in 1960 and nearly succeeded in 1961. "It was a very nervous moment for us when the voting was taking place," said Louw later.[182] But on November 6, 1962, a sanctions resolution at last won the necessary two-thirds vote: 67 for and 16 (including the United States and the United Kingdom) opposed, with 23 abstaining and 4 absent. The resolution recommended that members should break off diplomatic relations, close their ports to South African ships and their facilities to South African airplanes, and boycott all trade. It called also for the appointment of a special committee to keep South African policies under review and asked the Security

---

[181] McKay, *Africa in World Politics,* pp. 299–300. The text of the Security Council resolution, quoted below, is in Calvocoressi, *South Africa and World Opinion,* pp. 58–59.

[182] *House of Assembly Debates,* April 18, 1962, col. 4163.

Council to consider expulsion (which can be ordered by the General Assembly on the recommendation of the Security Council). The sanctions agreed to by the General Assembly have been implemented by only a few states, but the pressures are increasing to put them into more general effect.

Critics of the South African government may be divided into two categories: those who are hopeful that it may "moderate" its policy and those who are not. In opposing sanctions, Ambassador Francis Plimpton expressed a hopeful estimate of that government's capacity to change. The "shocking" Sabotage Act of 1962, he said, had "not stilled the voice of protest." He called for a mobilization of "the influence of world opinion on South Africa" and pledged "our best efforts to encourage South Africa to abandon" its disastrous policies.[183] Pessimistic estimates of the government's responsiveness to pressures from the United Nations and world opinion, on the other hand, are supported by the intransigent spirit of Afrikaner nationalism. "The United Nations knows where it stands and what to expect from my people in this southern corner of Africa," the Minister of Bantu Administration and Development said in Pretoria's Church Square on election day in 1961. "We will die—each and every one of us, every son and daughter of South Africa—rather than give up our nationhood." [184]

The attitudes of South African officials to the United States are clearly ambivalent. The United States is embraced as the leading anti-Communist power, whose business and military interests are served by an expanding and stable South Africa. It is also distrusted as a country considered to be subject to liberal and Negro pressures at home. Some South Africans believe that it is ready, therefore, to sacrifice South Africa for nonwhite support in the cold war abroad. These ambivalent attitudes are fostered by the apparent inconsistency of American officials engaging in public condemnation but failing at high diplomatic and ambassadorial levels to match this with strongly expressed private representations. Thus, after Plimpton's attack on apartheid in 1961, Eric Louw maintained in Parliament that the speech could not have been cleared with Secretary of State Rusk since shortly before its delivery Rusk had talked with Louw at length in "a friendly and cordial spirit." [185]

[183] U.S. Delegation to the General Assembly, Press Release no. 4067, Oct. 19, 1962, pp. 2, 5.
[184] Quoted in the *Economist* (London), Oct. 28, 1961, p. 358.
[185] *House of Assembly Debates*, April 18, 1962, cols. 4158–4159.

SOUTH-WEST AFRICA

On at least one matter everyone, including South Africa, is agreed—
that South-West Africa has an "international character." [186] Virtually
everyone—apart from South Africa—also agrees that South Africa is
accountable to the United Nations to some extent for its administration
of South-West Africa. Thus, South-West Africa is often described as
South Africa's Achilles' heel; critics of apartheid feel they have their
best chance to attack that policy by seeking to terminate South Africa's
control of South-West Africa, where that policy extends.

The nature of South Africa's accountability has been discussed
periodically since 1946, often in a legal context. Critics have urged
political action to divest South Africa of its control, but they have
marked time since 1960, hoping that pending adjudication by the International Court of Justice will strengthen their position. South-West
Africa, "whose exact juridical status is a mystery" (according to Hahlo
and Kahn), was assigned to South Africa as a mandated territory in
1919, became virtually a fifth province in 1949 when its small white
population was given direct representation in the Parliament at Cape
Town, and was integrated more closely in 1954 when the administration of native affairs was transferred from Windhoek to Pretoria.
Meanwhile, the International Court, in an advisory opinion in 1950,
confirmed South Africa's contention that it was not legally obliged to
place South-West Africa under United Nations trusteeship. On the
other hand, South Africa has continued to dispute the Court's opinion
that the League of Nations mandate had not lapsed and that it was
obliged to submit reports to the United Nations.

In 1960, Liberia and Ethiopia, which had been members of the
League, asked the Court to declare that South Africa had violated the
mandate since it had "failed to promote to the utmost the material
and moral well-being and social progress of the inhabitants of the Territory." [187] More than two years later, on December 21, 1962, the
Court decided 8 to 7 that it had jurisdiction. South Africa did not
concede this point, Dr. Verwoerd said later, but it would go ahead

---

[186] Ronald B. Ballinger, *South-West Africa: The Case against the Union* (Johannesburg: South African Institute of Race Relations, 1961), p. 34. Walvis Bay, the
main port of South-West Africa, and about 400 square miles of the hinterland
'were annexed by the British in 1878 and are now an integral part of Cape
Province.

[187] The text of the mandate and extracts from the application instituting judicial
proceedings are in Ballinger, *South-West Africa*, pp. 48–53.

with its defense. The Court may make a ruling, as distinct from previous advisory opinions, in 1964. Enforcement (if necessary) by economic, military, or other sanctions would rest with the United Nations Security Council or, in the event of a veto, with a two-thirds majority of the General Assembly.

While adjudication was pending and shortly after the two-thirds vote in the General Assembly had called for sanctions, a group of African and Asian delegations sponsored a successful resolution in the Trusteeship Committee on November 19, 1962, that commanded the widest agreement ever recorded on a South African issue. Not even Portugal voted no—and only Portugal abstained—on a resolution approved by ninety-six members, which called upon the Secretary General "to take all necessary steps in order to establish an effective United Nations presence in South-West Africa as a first step to prepare the territory for independence." [188] South Africa was absent on the ground that the issue of South-West Africa was *sub judice,* and after the vote it rejected the proposal of a United Nations presence. Spokesmen for both the United States and the United Kingdom expressed reservations but described the resolution, which did not call for sanctions, as "constructive." The British delegate also stated that no action should be taken by the United Nations until after the Court's decision and that South Africa should be bound by that decision.

THE END OF WHITE DOMINATION

At some time between 1963, the PAC's proclaimed year of liberation, and the year 2000, which is a good round number and only thirty-seven years hence, existing trends suggest that white domination will come to an end. What is imponderable is when and how white power will crack and the consequences that will follow. Might white domination end with the realization of Dr. Verwoerd's vision of a South African commonwealth of one white and many black nations? Could white rule survive on the African continent even in a small state in which whites are a majority? Might partition occur as a result of externally aided insurrection and foreign intervention? On the other hand, the present unit of South Africa might remain unbroken; and, following widespread violence, white domination might be succeeded eventually by African control. Or might some form of multiracial government, dependent upon an African majority, emerge?

[188] Horrell, *A Survey of Race Relations in South Africa: 1962,* p. 237. The resolution was adopted later in the General Assembly without a roll-call vote.

The dynamics of South Africa's industrial growth and its vulnerability to external events make radical change inevitable. Underlying all developments is population growth: the proportion of Africans to whites will gradually increase, according to the government's Tomlinson Commission, and by 2000, South Africa will contain more than 21,000,000 Africans and about 4,588,000 whites. Coloreds and Indians will exceed 5,000,000. Given substantial and steady immigration, the whites might reach 6,000,000. Meanwhile, barring events that disrupt the economy, the country's multiracial labor force will become economically more integrated. The government's long-range policy of decentralizing industry to the borders of the African reserves will continue the process of economic interdependence rather than reverse it. Diverse pressures for enlarging the internal market of African consumers will be insistent, and the westernization of Africans will advance. Thus, common interests will spread, overriding the parochial interests of tribal leaders and broadening the base upon which powerful African nationalist or Pan-Africanist movements can arise.

Part of the fascination South Africa has for the outside observer is the fluidity and complexity as well as the inevitability of its change. South Africa may employ increasingly repressive police measures, but its racially exclusive oligarchy cannot rely for stability on the traditional sanctions of a cohesive and authoritarian society. It may attempt to insulate both whites and nonwhites from agitation and sedition, but the gulf separating whites from the African mass makes impossible the use of totalitarian means to win mass support. Change is characteristic of attitudes within all racial groups. A genuine intellectual ferment adverse to racial discrimination has been at work among a small but growing minority of both English-speaking and Afrikaans-speaking whites, and Afrikaans-speaking as well as English-speaking businessmen have shown increasing concern about the need to remove the grievances of urban Africans. These trends and the development of common economic interests, which have encouraged liberal hopes for racial reconciliation, require time. The government also, for differing motives, seeks time. One should not underestimate its power to crush large-scale disorder, its readiness to make changes that may lessen tension, and its capacity to make dramatic moves (regarding Bantustans, Coloreds, and South-West Africa, for example) that may defer Western sanctions.

Yet, because of the virtually total alienation of independent African leadership from white authority and the spread on both sides since

1960 of a fatalistic acceptance of violence, South Africa's immediate future is unpredictable. Beneath the deceptive surface of tight control, the lines of authority are tenuous, and the situation is chronically unstable. The decimation of African political leadership and the disorganization of mass movements make coordinated and disciplined resistance extraordinarily difficult. If protest flares beyond police control at any point, Africans themselves may be unable to control spontaneous repercussions. Meanwhile, a cell-based underground is being built, saboteurs are being trained, police and military forces are being strengthened, and foreign hostility and pressures are being mobilized. The forces of violence are moving at accelerating speeds, rapidly leaving behind all hope of racial reconciliation.

BIBLIOGRAPHY

One of the many features that distinguish South Africa from other African states is the wealth of material available for its study, yet equally remarkable is the amount of scholarly work that waits to be done. Only one comprehensive analysis of South African politics has been written by a political scientist: Gwendolen M. Carter, *The Politics of Inequality: South Africa since 1948* (New York: Praeger, 1958). The selected bibliography that follows is a supplement to Carter's bibliography. Other useful bibliographies are Phillips Talbot, ed., *A Select Bibliography: Asia, Africa, Eastern Europe, Latin America* (New York: American Universities Field Staff, 1960), and Reuben Musiker, comp., *Guide to South African Reference Books* (3d rev. ed.; Grahamstown: Rhodes University Library, 1963).

The best general introduction, recently brought up to date and published in paperback, is still Leo Marquard, *The Peoples and Policies of South Africa* (3d ed.; London: Oxford University Press, 1962). The standard history, Eric A. Walker, *A History of Southern Africa* (3d ed.; London: Longmans, Green, 1957), and a short account, Arthur Keppel-Jones, *South Africa: A Short History* (3d ed.; London: Hutchinson University Library, 1961), have both been revised. Two other works, not revised, are basic: C. W. de Kiewiet, *A History of South Africa: Social & Economic* (London: Oxford University Press, 1941), and Ellen Hellmann, ed., *Handbook on Race Relations in South Africa* (London: Oxford University Press, 1949).

OFFICIAL PUBLICATIONS

An indispensable source is the weekly *Government Gazette*. A list of official publications issued each month appears in the *Gazette* and is also obtainable gratis in mimeographed form from the Government Printer in Pretoria or Cape Town. The *House of Assembly Debates* (*Hansard*) and the *Senate Debates* are revealing sources, a fact recognized by the Minister of Foreign Affairs on April 18, 1962 (col. 4165), when he said, referring to critics at the United Nations, "They all get the Hansards; they know exactly what is going on."

Much useful data are available in annual departmental reports, although these reports are often slow in appearing. The latest *Report of the Department of Bantu Administration and Development,* which is particularly revealing of official attitudes, is for 1958/59 (U.G. 51/1960), but this can be supplemented by *Bantu,* the Department's informal monthly publication. The administration of Colored affairs is dealt with in *Report of the Department of Coloured Affairs for the Period 1st April 1955 to 31st December 1958* (U.G. 32/1960). Recent annual reports of interest are the report of the Commissioner of the South African Police for 1959 (U.G. 73/1959) and the following reports for 1961: Education, Arts and Science (R.P. 24/1961), Labour (R.P. 43/1962), Justice (R.P. ?), and the Public Service Commission (Fiftieth Annual Report, R.P. 26/1962). The latest edition of the *Official Year Book* is no. 30-1960. The Bureau of Census and Statistics usefully filled the gap in time between the issuance of this and the preceding yearbook (1956–1957) by preparing *Union Statistics for Fifty Years: Jubilee Issue 1910–1960.* Since 1960 a commercially published yearbook, heavily flavored with progovernment propaganda, has been available: *State of South Africa: Economic, Financial and Statistical Year-Book for the Republic of South Africa, 1962* (Johannesburg: Da Gama Publications, 1962).

Commissions of inquiry provide voluminous data. A basic report is that of the Tomlinson Commission (U.G. 61/1955). The reproduction and availability to the public of reports tabled in the House of Assembly may be delayed, sometimes for translation, usually from Afrikaans into English. A notable example of delay in publication is the first report of the Press Commission. Important and available is *Report of the Commission of Enquiry in Regard to Undesirable Publications* (U.G. 42/1957). Reports on Sharpeville and related events, tabled in the House of Assembly, have been summarized in *A Précis of the Reports of the Commissions Appointed to Enquire into the Events Occurring on March 21, 1960 at Sharpeville and Langa* (Fact Paper no. 10-1961; Johannesburg: S.A. Institute of Race Relations). Other disturbances are reviewed in *Report of the Commission of Inquiry into the Occurrences in the Windhoek Location on the Night of the 10th. to the 11th. December 1959 and into the Direct Causes which led to those Occurrences* (U.G. 23/1960).

Information on administration may be culled from the reports to the House of Assembly of the Select Committee on Public Accounts. Since 1955 and 1960, respectively, a series of interim reports have been issued by the Commission of Inquiry into the System of Local Government in the Transvaal and by the Committee of Enquiry into the Financial Relations between the Central Government, the Provinces, and Local Authorities. Much information is also available in the reports of the provinces and municipalities, particularly reports of the managers of municipal departments of nonwhite affairs.

The Department of Information produces much material, some of it valuable. The weekly *South African Digest* (before October 1962, the *Fortnightly Digest of South African Affairs*), issued from Pretoria, provides the fullest general coverage. It is supplemented by Fact Papers, numbering over 100 in 1962.

Regarding the United Nations, of special interest in recent years are reports of the Special Political Committee and *Report of the Special Committee for South Africa* (General Assembly Official Records, 17th Session, Supp. no. 12, A/5212, 1963). In April 1962, the South African government issued a White Paper, *Report on the Proceedings at the Sixteenth Session of the United Nations on Questions Affecting South Africa, September to December 1961.*

NEWSPAPERS AND PERIODICALS

The mimeographed weekly *Press Digest,* issued by the Jewish Board of Deputies (Johannesburg, P.O. Box 1180), continues to be the most comprehensive review of the English and Afrikaans press and covers some of the nonwhite press. The English reader may also follow the Afrikaans press in *Thought: A Journal of Afrikaans Thinking for the English-Speaking,* issued as a quarterly since 1957 by the South African Institute of Race Relations (Johannesburg). *Dagbreek en Sondagnuus* (Johannesburg) issues a weekly four-page English translation of its leading articles. Another periodic guide to Afrikaans thought is the monthly *D.R.C. Newsletter* (Johannesburg: Information Bureau, Dutch Reformed Church).

Newspapers and periodicals that may be loosely described as left-wing include *New Age* and *Spark,* whose termination dates are noted in the text; *Fighting Talk,* which has also ceased publication; *Counter Attack,* the organ of the South African Congress of Democrats, before the organization was banned; *The New African* (Cape Town, P.O. Box 2068), which began monthly publication in January 1962 and in 1963 went on a five-week schedule; *Contact* (Cape Town, P.O. Box 1979), a fortnightly close to the Liberal Party but not officially its organ; that party's monthly *Liberal Opinion,* available gratis (Wynberg, Cape, P.O. Box 66); and the monthly *Forward,* edited by Alex Hepple, former leader of the Labor Party (Johannesburg, P.O. Box 10476). The ANC in exile publishes *South Africa Freedom News* (Dar es Salaam, P.O. Box 2239). PAC literature issues from SSS, 62 Queen St., E.C.4, London, N.W.1. The outlawed South African Communist Party issues *The African Communist* occasionally but usually quarterly from London (52 Palmerston

Road, London, S.W. 14). At the other extreme is *The South African Observer: A Journal for Realists* (Pretoria, P.O. Box 2401), a monthly that reprints much material from publications of the John Birch Society and whose editor is reputedly close to some members of the cabinet.

BOOKS, PAMPHLETS, AND ARTICLES

An anthology useful for both high school and college students is Grant S. McClellan, ed., *South Africa* (The Reference Shelf; New York: H. W. Wilson, 1962), which has a bibliography of recent popular and scholarly articles. Comprehensive studies are the lectures by H. M. Robertson, a South African economist: *South Africa: Economic and Political Aspects* (Durham, N.C.: Duke University Press, 1957), which has a lengthy bibliography; Alexander Brady, *Democracy in the Dominions: A Comparative Study in Institutions* (3d ed.; Toronto: University of Toronto Press, 1958), which draws comparisons with Canada, Australia, and New Zealand; and Harm J. de Blij, *Africa South* (Evanston: Northwestern University Press, 1962), a readable interpretation by a geographer, whose book also deals with other areas in southern Africa. Many of the thoughtful and sprightly reports written by Edwin S. Munger as a member of the American Universities Field Staff have been reproduced in *African Field Reports, 1952–1961* (Cape Town: Struik, 1961). Other general analyses are Julius Lewin, *Politics and Law in South Africa: Essays on Race Relations* (London: Merlin Press, 1963), eight brilliantly suggestive essays written during 1955–1960; Gwendolen M. Carter, "Crisis in South Africa," *Independence for Africa* (New York: Praeger, 1960); Charles R. Nixon, "The Conflict of Nationalisms in South Africa," *World Politics* (Oct., 1958); and K. L. Roskam, *Apartheid and Discrimination: Some Remarks with Regard to the Relationships between the White and Respective Non-White Ethnic Groups in the Union of South Africa* (Leyden: A. W. Sythoff, 1960), a dogmatic and generally unreadable doctoral dissertation but one with some useful footnotes.

A major work of recent historical scholarship is L. M. Thompson, *The Unification of South Africa, 1902–1910* (London: Oxford University Press, 1960). A study of the South African frontier has been written by the leading authority on South Africa within the United States government: Waldemar B. Campbell, *The South African Frontier, 1865–1885: A Study in Expansion* (Pretoria: Office of the Chief Archivist, 1960). The period he covers has been examined from a different standpoint by a leading Afrikaans historian: F. A. van Jaarsveld, *The Awakening of Afrikaner Nationalism, 1868–1881* (Cape Town: Human & Rousseau, 1961). Another Afrikaans historian has written a political history of the Union prior to Dr. Malan's victory: D. W. Kruger, *The Age of the Generals: A Short Political History of the Union of South Africa, 1910–1948* (Johannesburg:

Dagbreek Book Store, 1958). Kruger has also edited *South African Parties and Policies, 1910–1960: A Select Source Book* (Cape Town: Human & Rousseau, 1960). For the significant wartime period, Michael Roberts and A. E. G. Trollip, *The South African Opposition, 1939–1945: An Essay in Contemporary History* (London: Longmans, Green, 1947) is still of basic importance; and Sheila Patterson, *The Last Trek: A Study of the Boer People and the Afrikaner Nation* (London: Routledge & Kegan Paul, 1957), is still the only book-length study of the subject in English.

Dr. D. F. Malan has written his memoirs: *Afrikaner Volkseenheid: En My Ervarings op die Pad Daarheen* (Cape Town, 1959). Oswald Pirow, an admirer of Hertzog, has written a biographical memoir, *James Barry Munnik Hertzog* (Cape Town: Howard Timmins, 1957); G. Heaton Nicholls, an admirer of Smuts and the first leader of the Union Federal Party, has written *South Africa in My Time* (London: Allen and Unwin, 1961); and Morris Kentridge, a Labor Party leader and veteran parliamentarian, *I Recall: Memoirs of Morris Kentridge* (Johannesburg: The Free Press, 1959). Theodore Gregory's careful study, *Ernest Oppenheimer and the Economic Development of Southern Africa* (London: Oxford University Press, 1962), is a wide-ranging history of the diamond industry and the Anglo American Corporation. A major work based on the Smuts Archive is Sir Keith Hancock, *Smuts: The Sanguine Years, 1870–1919* (New York: Cambridge University Press, 1963), the first of two volumes.

On politics, a valuable work whose bias is easily discerned and discounted is Ronald Segal, *Political Africa: A Who's Who of Personalities and Parties* (New York: Praeger, 1961), which has biographical sketches of 43 South African whites and 31 nonwhites and historical sketches of parliamentary and extraparliamentary parties. Similar information is provided for South-West Africa and the High Commission Territories. Analyses of the general elections of 1958 and 1961 are cited in the footnotes to the text. Basic documents of the Progressive Party and the Liberal Party are *Franchise Proposals and Constitutional Safeguards: A Report Prepared for the Progressive Party of South Africa by a Commission of Experts* (Molteno Report, vol. 1; Johannesburg: Progressive Party of South Africa, 1960); *The Constitution: Incorporating the Principles of the Party* (Johannesburg: The Progressive Party of South Africa, 1961); and *Non-racial Democracy: The Policies of the Liberal Party of South Africa* (Pietermaritzburg: Liberal Party, 1962).

On nonwhite politics, the indispensable background is in Edward Roux, *Time Longer than Rope: A History of the Black Man's Struggle for Freedom in South Africa* (London: Gollancz, 1948). The best brief history of the ANC before 1958 is the sympathetic and readable account by Anthony Sampson, *The Treason Cage: The Opposition on Trial in South Africa* (London: Heinemann, 1958). Mary Benson, a journalist who displays her commitment to the ANC but is fair to its African critics, has filled the need for a far more detailed history and also covered the period since 1958 in her *The African Patriots: The Story of the African National Congress of South Africa* (London: Faber and Faber, 1963). Edward Feit, *South Africa: The Dynamics of the African National Congress* (London: Oxford University Press, 1962), a brief study which tends to accept pro-Africanist interpretations of the struggle within the ANC, provides a useful analysis of ANC campaigns. A. J. Luthuli, *Let My People Go: An Autobiography* (Johannesburg: Collins, 1962), is vivid about policy but says little about the internal politics of the ANC. Edward Callan, *Albert John Luthuli and the South African Race Conflict* (Kalamazoo, Mich.: Western Michigan University Press, 1962), is an essay to which Luthuli's Nobel Peace Prize Address is appended. Jordan K. Ngubane, the leading African member of the Liberal Party, has written a brilliantly discursive book, which ascribes to the Communists an importance that is open to question: *An African Explains Apartheid* (New York: Praeger, 1963). Patrick Van Rensburg, *Guilty Land: The History of Apartheid* (London: Penguin Books, 1962), includes an interpretation of the extraparliamentary opposition as seen by a white liberal.

On the treason trial, see Sampson, noted above; Lionel Forman and E. S. Sachs, *The South African Treason Trial* (London: John Calder, 1957), an inside account of the opening phase; and Helen Joseph, one of the accused, *If This Be Treason* (London: André Deutsch, 1963). Alfred Hutchinson, another accused, describes his escape and travels in *Road to Ghana* (London: Gollancz, 1960). The trial itself is reviewed in Thomas Karis, "The South African Treason Trial," *Political Science Quarterly* (June, 1961).

Legal aspects of South African government are surveyed in H. R. Hahlo and Ellison Kahn, *The Union of South Africa: The Development of Its Laws and Constitution* (London: Stevens and Sons, 1960), which is generally more perceptive than H. J. May, *The South African Constitution* (3d ed.; Cape Town: Juta, 1955). Kahn has written a supplement, *The New Constitution* (1962), which includes the text of the Republic of South Africa Constitution Act. A detailed analysis of "Crime and Punishment, 1910–1960" by Kahn appears in *Acta Juridica 1960*. An excellent addition to the literature on the constitutional crisis of 1951–1956 is Geoffrey Marshall, *Parliamentary Sovereignty and the Commonwealth* (London: Oxford University Press, 1957). A bibliography of legal materials during this period has been compiled by A. M. F. Towert, *Constitutional Development in South Africa, 1946–1959* (Cape Town: University of Cape Town, 1959).

South Africa's external relations are placed within a wide context by Vernon McKay, *Africa in World Politics* (New York: Harper & Row, 1963). Peter Calvocoressi, *South Africa and World Opinion* (London: Oxford University Press, 1961), analyzes South Africa's position after Sharpeville. Perspective is supplied in an excellent article by J. E. Spence, "Tradition and Change in South African Foreign Policy," *Journal of Commonwealth Political Studies* (May, 1962). Regarding South-West Africa, a careful study is the booklet by Ronald B. Ballinger, *South-West Africa: The Case against the Union* (Johannesburg: S.A. Institute of Race Relations, 1961). Liberal attitudes are in Dr. Bernard Friedman and others, *Looking Outwards: Three South African Viewpoints* (Johannesburg: S.A. Institute of Race Relations, 1961), and the attitudes of progovernment intellectuals are in *South Africa in the African Continent* (Papers Read at the Tenth Annual Conference of the South African Bureau of Racial Affairs; Stellenbosch: S.A.B.R.A., 1961). The main unofficial statement of American liberal attitudes regarding South Africa is Collin Gonze and others, *South African Crisis and United States Policy* (New York: American Committee on Africa, 1962).

On the economics of apartheid, F. P. Spooner, a South African who has extensive governmental and industrial experience and is sympathetic to the Progressive Party, has written a critique: *South African Predicament* (London: Jonathan Cape, 1960). Heinz Hartmann, *Enterprise and Politics in South Africa* (Princeton: Industrial Relations Section, Princeton University, 1962), contributes to an understanding of the role of the Afrikaans businessman and problems of manpower. G. V. Doxey, *The Industrial Colour Bar in South Africa* (Cape Town: Oxford University Press, 1961), is a historical analysis of the development of the labor market. Monica Cole, *South Africa* (London: Methuen, 1961) has nearly 700 pages of information on South Africa's physical and economic geography, richly illustrated with photographs, maps, and diagrams. Two lengthy articles by well-known authorities have been issued as supplements to *Optima*, the quarterly review published by the Anglo American Corporation (Johannesburg): S. H. Frankel, *The Tyranny of Economic Paternalism in South Africa: A Study of Frontier Mentality, 1860–1960* (Dec., 1960), and Sheila T. van der Horst, *The Economic Implications of Political Democracy: The Road to Economic Progress* (June, 1960). Anglo American has also reprinted H. F. Oppenheimer's lecture, *The Conditions for Progress in Africa*. The best introduction to the economy is D. Hobart Houghton's forthcoming *The South African Economy* (Cape Town: Oxford University Press, 1963).

The history of trade unionism in South Africa is not yet written. Meanwhile Ivan L. Walker and Ben Weinbren, two trade union veterans, have performed a labor of love in collecting information for *2000 Casualties: A History of the Trade Unions and the Labour Movement in the Union of South Africa* (Johannesburg: S.A. Trade Union Council, 1961), which is concerned mainly with white labor. E. S. Sachs has written a firsthand account of the Garment Workers' Union, *Rebels Daughters* (London:

MacGibbon & Kee, 1957), a title referring to Afrikaans women, some of them descended from Boers who were rebels in 1914. A comprehensive survey concerned particularly with racial issues is Muriel Horrell, *South African Trade Unionism* (Johannesburg: S.A. Institute of Race Relations, 1961).

Important studies of rural and urban Africans have been completed by anthropologists and social scientists in recent years. Among recent volumes of the long-term Natal Regional Survey, begun at the University of Natal in 1945, are E. H. Brookes and N. Hurwitz, *The Native Reserves of Natal* (Cape Town: Oxford University Press, 1957), and H. R. Burrows and others, *Baumannville: A Study of an Urban African Community* (New York: Oxford University Press, 1960).

The Border Regional Survey, concerned with the area extending roughly from East London to Queenstown, has been in progress since 1955 under the direction of the Institute of Social and Economic Research at Rhodes University. The Institute has published a number of occasional papers and, under the editorship of D. Hobart Houghton, a distinguished economist, *Economic Development in a Plural Society: Studies in the Border Region* (Cape Town: Oxford University Press, 1960). Social anthropologists have completed the trilogy "Xhosa in Town, Studies of the Bantu-speaking Population of East London, Cape Province": D. H. Reader, *The Black Man's Portion: History, Demography and Living Conditions in the Native Locations of East London, Cape Province* (1961); Philip Mayer, with contributions by Iona Mayer, *Townsmen or Tribesmen: Conservatism and the Process of Urbanization in a South African City* (1961); and B. A. Pauw, *The Second Generation* (1963). All are published in Cape Town by Oxford University Press.

An African social anthropologist has made a study of the impact of western ideas on tribesmen near Durban: Absolom Vilakazi, *Zulu Transformations: A Study of the Dynamics of Social Change* (Pietermaritzburg: University of Natal Press, 1962). Notable is the reprinting of Monica Hunter's classic study, *Reaction to Conquest: Effects of Contact with Europeans on the Pondo of South Africa* (2d ed.; London: Oxford University Press, 1961), with a new introduction and Bengt G. M. Sundkler, *Bantu Prophets in South Africa* (2d ed.; London: Oxford University Press, 1961), with a new chapter.

Specialized studies of urban Africans are Laura Longmore, *The Dispossessed: A Study of the Sex-Life of Bantu Women in Urban Areas in and around Johannesburg* (London: Jonathan Cape, 1959), and J. C. de Ridder, *The Personality of the Urban African in South Africa: A Thematic Apperception Test Study* (London: Routledge & Kegan Paul, 1961). Monica Hunter Wilson and Archie Mafeje have observed the area on the periphery of Cape Town that was linked with Sharpeville—*Langa: A Study of Social Groups in an African Township* (Cape Town: Oxford University Press,

1963). The many useful publications of the South African Institute of Race Relations are listed in 76 mimeographed pages: *Classification of Publications Issued by the S. A. Institute of Race Relations* (Johannesburg, 1962).

On Indians, the major study is by Hilda Kuper, an anthropologist, *Indian People in Natal* (Pietermaritzburg: University of Natal Press, 1960). A valuable sociological study is Leo Kuper and others, *Durban: A Study in Racial Ecology* (London: Jonathan Cape, 1958).

Intellectual ferment among whites regarding race relations is reflected in much writing during recent years. Diverse attitudes are expressed in a collection of essays, most of them by whites, written before Sharpeville and compiled by Hildegarde Spottiswoode, *South Africa, The Road Ahead* (London: Bailey Bros. & Swinfen Ltd., 1960). One of the best statements in defense of the policy of separate development is by *Die Burger*'s foreign correspondent in S. Pienaar and Anthony Sampson, *South Africa: Two Views of Separate Development* (London: Oxford University Press, 1960). A ponderous academic treatise is N. J. Rhoodie and Prof. Dr. H. J. Venter, *Apartheid: A Socio-historical Exposition of the Origin and Development of the Apartheid Idea* (Cape Town: H.A.U.M., n.d.), whose bibliography includes many Afrikaans sources. Another ponderous and well-documented treatise, which takes issue with some of the Afrikaners referred to below, is by a theologian, Prof. Dr. A. B. Dupreez, *Inside the South African Crucible* (Cape Town: H.A.U.M., 1959). J. H. Grobler, an Afrikaans journalist and senator, argues for "SEPARATE CONSTITUTIONAL DEVELOPMENT" in Africa south of the Sahara in *Africa's Destiny* (2d ed.; Johannesburg: Book of the Month Club, 1958).

Eleven leading theologians of the three Dutch Reformed Churches denounced racial discrimination in November 1960 in a book that had many repercussions: A. S. Geyser and others, *Delayed Action!* (Pretoria: N. G. Kerkboekhandel, 1960). H. A. Fagan, leader of the former National Union Party and an ex-Chief Justice, has written a small book in Afrikaans, translated as *Our Responsibility: A Discussion of South Africa's Racial Problems* (Stellenbosch: Die Universiteits-Uitgewers en-Boekhandelaars, 1959?). P. V. Pistorius, an eloquent Afrikaans professor of Greek, argued for multiracial discussion in *No Further Trek* (Johannesburg: Central News Agency, 1957) and since then has moved leftward into the Progressive Party. That party's analysis of the South African situation is presented by a young Afrikaans physician, Dr. Zac de Beer, in a booklet, *Multi-racial South Africa: The Reconciliation of Forces* (London: Oxford University Press, 1961). More liberally inclined is a scholarly work, which finds inspiration in theories of natural law, by D. V. Cowen, then professor of comparative law at the University of Cape Town: *The Foundations of Freedom: With Special Reference to Southern Africa* (Cape Town: Oxford University Press,

1961). The inner turmoil of South African intellectuals is illustrated by Edgar H. Brookes, a distinguished political scientist, the author of a small but profound book, *The City of God and the Politics of Crisis* (London: Oxford University Press, 1960), who joined the Liberal Party in March 1962.

Many impressionistic and journalistic books deal in whole or in part with South Africa. Several, for example, were written following Sharpeville: *Shooting at Sharpeville: The Agony of South Africa,* which has thirty photographs and lengthy extracts from evidence at the official inquiry, by Ambrose Reeves, the Anglican bishop of Johannesburg; *South Africa—Yesterday and Tomorrow: A Challenge to Christians* (London: Gollancz, 1962), which is more general, also by Reeves; *Go Well, Stay Well: South Africa, August 1956 to May 1960* (London: Hodder & Stoughton, 1961) by Hannah Stanton, a worker at an Anglican Mission, who was detained and deported; *White Madam* (London: Gollancz, 1962) by Myrna Blumberg, a liberal newspaperwoman who was detained; and *The Tragedy of Apartheid: A Journalist's Experiences in the South African Riots* (New York: McKay, 1960) by Norman Phillips, a Canadian newspaperman.

Tom Hopkinson writes vividly, and with many insights, of his experiences as editor of *Drum: In the Fiery Continent* (London: Gollancz, 1962). Morris Broughton, a South African editor, is discursive in *The Press and Politics in South Africa* (Cape Town: Purnell, 1961). Two South African popular writers who are informative about personalities are Jan Burger, *The Gulf Between* (Cape Town: Howard Timmins, 1960), and Bernard Sachs, *The Road to Sharpeville* (Johannesburg: The Dial Press, 1961). Paul Giniewski, a French newspaperman, writes so sympathetically in *Bantustans: A Trek Towards the Future* (Cape Town: Human & Rousseau, 1961) that his book is distributed, reportedly, by the Department of Information. Allard K. Lowenstein, a liberal American lawyer, has written firsthand about South-West Africa: *Brutal Mandate: A Journey to South West Africa* (New York: Macmillan, 1962).

Novels and other fiction, not noted here, are important sources for understanding the South African scene. A critical introduction to some of this writing is in *The African Image* (New York: Praeger, 1962) by Ezekiel Mphahlele, a South African in exile.

INDEX

[*"Federation" in this Index refers to the Federation of Rhodesia and Nyasaland.*]